A Biography of the Australian Continent

Aboriginal Australia

A Student's Guide

M. H. Monroe

Copyright

A Biography of the Australian Continent: Aboriginal Australia

Copyright © Michael Monroe, 2017

First published July, 2017

All rights reserved. Without limiting the rights under copyright reserved above, no part of this publication may be reproduced, stored in or introduced into a database and retrieval system or transmitted in any form or by any means (electronic, mechanical, photocopying, recording or otherwise) without the prior written permission of the owner of copyright.

ISBN: 978-0-6480769-9-5; 14/07/2017 e-Book

ISBN: 978-0-6480769-8-8; 14/07/2017 Paperback

Published with the assistance of: www. loveofbooks.com.au

ACKNOWLEDGEMENTS 1
INTRODUCTION 3
CHAPTER 1 - ANTHROPOLOGICAL HISTORY 7

ORIGINS 7
THE SOUTHERN ROUTE: 7
WLH-50 AND THE COMPLETE REPLACEMENT BY OUT OF AFRICA THEORY 8
HOMO ERECTUS NEAR AUSTRALIA 8
AN EXIT INTO SOUTH WEST ASIA DURING THE LAST INTERGLACIAL 10
AN EXIT DURING MIS 5E – FOSSIL EVIDENCE IN EAST ASIA 11
ARGUMENTS AGAINST AN EXIT DURING MIS 5E THAT WAS SUCCESSFUL – SUMMARY
.... 13
AMH RECENT EXIT MODELS – SINGLE VERSES MULTIPLE 13
THE SOUTHERN RATHER THAN THE NORTHERN ROUTE – GENETIC EVIDENCE 15
DATING OF MIGRATIONS 15
THE ARRIVAL OF AMH IN INDIA AND EAST ASIA – DATING 15
INDIA AND TOBA 15
INDIAN GENETICS – TOBA 16
GENE FLOW TO AUSTRALIA FROM INDIA IN THE HOLOCENE SUBSTANTIATED BY
GENOME-WIDE DATA [26] 17
GENETIC RELATIONSHIPS BETWEEN POPULATIONS 18
ARCHAEOLOGY OF SUNDA IN THE PLEISTOCENE 20
ORIGINS - THE REGIONAL CONTINUITY HYPOTHESIS 21
OUT OF AFRICA VS REGIONAL CONTINUITY 24
MULTIREGIONAL VIEW VERSUS REGIONAL REPLACEMENT 24
LIMITED ARCHAIC INTERBREEDING OUTSIDE AFRICA 24
INTERBREEDING WITH NEANDERTHALS 25
INTERBREEDING WITH DENISOVANS – CHINA 26
HUMAN REMAINS FROM THE PLEISTOCENE-HOLOCENE 28
TRANSITION, SOUTH WEST CHINA, APPARENT COMPLEX EVOLUTIONARY HISTORY
FOR EAST ASIANS 28
NEUROCRANIUM: 34
MANDIBLE: 35
INTERBREEDING WITH DENISOVANS IN OCEANIA 37
DENISOVAN ADMIXTURE AND THE FIRST MODERN HUMAN DISPERSAL INTO
SOUTHEAST ASIA AND OCEANIA 43
DID THE DENISOVANS CROSS WALLACE'S LINE? 45
PLEISTOCENE SEAFARING - SAHUL 50

CHAPTER 2 - OCCUPATION OF SAHUL (GREATER AUSTRALIA) 52

- DEEP SEA FISHING - OLDEST KNOWN EVIDENCE 52
- THE FIRST BOAT PEOPLE 54
- PLEISTOCENE ARRIVAL OF HUMANS IN SAHUL AND NEAR OCEANIA – DATING 62
- ARCHAEOLOGY, RADIOCARBON AND LUMINESCENCE DATING 62
- GENETICS 62
- THE COLONISATION OF GREATER AUSTRALIA IN THE PLEISTOCENE - A RE-EXAMINATION 65
- GREATER AUSTRALIA AND SOUTH EAST ASIA - PLEISTOCENE GEOGRAPHY 66
- ARCHAEOLOGY OF SUNDA IN THE PLEISTOCENE 67
- FROM SUNDA TO SAHUL 68
- THE INITIAL SETTLEMENT OF SAHUL 70
- ACCEPTED DATES FOR THE INITIAL OCCUPATION OF SAHUL - THE CONVENTIONAL RADIOCARBON METHOD 71
- EARLIER DATES FOR THE OCCUPATION OF SAHUL 73
- PLEISTOCENE ARRIVAL OF PEOPLE IN AUSTRALIA 74
- THE DATING CONTROVERSY - EARLY AUSTRALIAN SITES 76
- DATING THE FIRST AUSTRALIANS 80
- THE ARCHAEOLOGY OF SAHUL OR GREATER AUSTRALIA 81
- THE ARCHAEOLOGY OF SAHUL OR GREATER AUSTRALIA - THE LOWLANDS OF MELANESIA 86
- ABORIGINAL OCCUPATION OF GREATER AUSTRALIA - THE PATTERN OF COLONISATION BEGINNING IN THE LATE PLEISTOCENE (SMITH[47]) 95
- DISPERSAL PATTERNS AND PROCESSES 96
- CONTINENTAL COLONISATION - ARCHAEOLOGICAL EVIDENCE 100
- HIGH LATITUDE REGIONS 100
- DESERTS 101
- THE FIRST SETTLERS IN AUSTRALIA 104
- THE RESTAURANT AT THE END OF THE UNIVERSE: 105
- THE LANDING SITE OF THE FIRST SETTLERS IN AUSTRALIA 105
- OCCUPATION OF SAHUL (GREATER AUSTRALIA) 109
- ABORIGINAL OCCUPATION OF AUSTRALIA - TIMELINE 109
- OCCUPATION OF SAHUL (GREATER AUSTRALIA) 114
- ABORIGINAL OCCUPATION - POPULATING THE CONTINENT - THE EVIDENCE 117
- ABORIGINAL OCCUPATION - POPULATING THE CONTINENT - DESERT 122
- AUSTRALIA'S DESERTS – THE 'DESERT TRANSFORMATION' CONCEPT 127
- ABORIGINAL OCCUPATION - THE WESTERN COAST - PILBARA 128
- SAND RIDGE DESERTS - BIOGEOGRAPHY, HUMAN ECOLOGY AND PREHISTORY ... 142
- SAND RIDGE DESERTS - A BIOGEOGRAPHIC UNIT 143

BARRIER DESERT THEORY 143
BARRIER DESERTS - DIFFERENCES 145
BARRIER DESERTS - NEW CHALLENGES? 146
FLORISTIC AFFINITIES - OTHER DESERT HABITATS 147
ABORIGINAL OCCUPATION – TEMPERATE AUSTRALIA 149
ABORIGINAL OCCUPATION - TASMANIA (FLOOD, 2004) 149
THE SOUTH WEST 152
ABORIGINAL OCCUPATION - POPULATING THE CONTINENT - FINAL PHASE - TASMANIA 153
ABORIGINAL OCCUPATION OF SOUTH CENTRAL TASMANIA IN THE PLEISTOCENE - PALAEOECOLOGY 156
ABORIGINAL OCCUPATION OF SOUTH CENTRAL TASMANIA IN THE PLEISTOCENE - A PALAEOECOLOGICAL MODEL (COSGROVE, ALLEN & MARSHALL, 1998) 159
ABORIGINAL OCCUPATION OF SOUTH CENTRAL TASMANIA IN THE PLEISTOCENE - ARCHAEOLOGICAL DEPOSITS - ARTEFACT DENSITY (COSGROVE, ALLEN & MARSHALL IN MURRAY, 1998) 164
ABORIGINAL OCCUPATION OF SOUTH CENTRAL TASMANIA IN THE PLEISTOCENE - FAUNA (COSGROVE, ALLEN & MARSHALL IN MURRAY, 1998) 166
ABORIGINAL OCCUPATION OF SOUTH CENTRAL TASMANIA IN THE PLEISTOCENE - STONE INDUSTRIES 172

CHAPTER 3 - THE SUBMERGENCE OF THE BASSIAN PLAIN – BASS STRAIT 176

RISING WATER, DISAPPEARING CONTINENTAL SHELF (CANE, SCOTT, 2013) 176

CHAPTER 4 - MATERIAL CULTURE 181

ABORIGINAL WEAPONS AND TOOLS 181
GROUND-EDGE AXE – OLDEST IN THE WORLD COINCIDES WITH HUMAN COLONISATION OF AUSTRALIA 181
CARPENTER'S GAP SHELTER 1 183
AXE PRODUCTION DEMONSTRATION 185
ARCHAEOLOGICAL COMPARISON 185
TECHNOLOGICAL NOVELTY AND THE COLONISATION OF AUSTRALIA 186
TECHNOLOGICAL DIVERSITY AND REGIONAL TRADITIONS 187
THE SPEAR AND SPEAR THROWER 189
DEATH SPEAR 190
SPEAR THROWER - WOOMERA OR ATLATL 190
POINTS 190
THROWING BOOMERANGS 192
BACKED BLADES 192

Cane 193
Wyrie Swamp tools 194
Adze Flakes 194
Australian Pleistocene Technology 194
Backed Artefacts in Southeast Australia - Changing Abundance Possibly Linked to Holocene Climate? 195
Artefacts 196
Arnhem Land Sites 196
Comparing earliest Australian stone tools with contemporary tool industries in Europe and Africa 197
Aboriginal Stone Tools 199
Morphology 207
Choppers 207
Flake Tools 209
Vertically oriented rocks Brian Hayden in Murray, Tim, ed., 1998 210
Wear patterns 211
Package of cultural Innovations (Hayden, 2008) 211
Bone tools 212
Darwin Glass 213
Stone Artefacts - Tasmania 214
Bone Artefacts-Tasmania 215
Kartan tool industry 216
Karta Culture on mainland Australia 218
Aboriginal Shelter 219
Stone structures 219
The roofing of the walls 224
Timber-framed domes western Victoria 225
Ngalawuru or High Cliffy Island 228
Georgina River 230
Stone walled game hides 231
Stone-walled bird hides 232
Covers protecting sacred objects 232
The evidence for stone structures 233
Whale bone house structures 234
Dugong bone grave site at Stewart River 236
Spinifex houses of the Western Desert 236
Aboriginal Stone Arrangements 238

CHAPTER 5 - ARCHAEOLOGY OF AUSTRALIA 240

Sahul 240

	244
TROPICAL AND ARID AUSTRALIA	244
CAPE YORK PENINSULA	246
ALLEN'S CAVE	246
BASS POINT	247
BIRRIGAI SHELTER	247
BONE CAVE	248
BURKES CAVE - FLAKED STONE ASSEMBLAGE VARIATION IN WESTERN NEW SOUTH WALES, AUSTRALIA	249
BURRILL LAKE ROCK SHELTER	250
CAPE RANGE AREA, WESTERN COAST ARID ZONE, WESTERN AUSTRALIA	250
CLOGGS CAVE	251
COLLESS CREEK ROCK SHELTER	251
CRANEBROOK TERRACE	251
THE DJADJILING ARCHAEOLOGICAL SITE	252
FERN CAVE	252
STONE WORKING TECHNIQUES	254
ASPECTS OF SITE USE	255
SIGNIFICANCE TESTING	255
INGALADDI ROCK SHELTER, NIMJI	257
JANSZ CAVE, CAPE RANGE PENINSULA, WESTERN AUSTRALIA	257
JAWOYN COUNTRY	258
JINMIUM ROCK SHELTER, NORTHERN TERRITORY1,	259
JINMIUM ROCK SHELTER, NORTHERN TERRITORY – EARLY OCCUPATION OF NORTHERN AUSTRALIA BY HUMANS[4]	260
THE STUDY AREA	260
THE ROCK SHELTER	261
JUUNKAN-1	264
JUUNKAN-2	266
KAKADU, OCCUPATION SITES, ALONG THE BASE OF THE CLIFFS	270
KENNIFF CAVE	271
KOOLAN SHELTER 2	273
KULPI MARA	273
OPTICAL DATING OF GRAVE-INFILL OF HUMAN BURIALS, LAKE MUNGO, AUSTRALIA	274
CONTINUITY AND ANTIQUITY (R.M. & C.H.BERNDT, 1964; FLOOD, 2004; HABGOOD & FRANKLIN, 2008)	274
LAKE MUNGO – EVIDENCE FOR SEED GRINDING IN THE PLEISTOCENE[27]	275
MALAKUNANJA II (MADJEDBEBE) SITE IN ARNHEM LAND ASSOCIATED WITH EARLY COLONISATION	279

ARCHAEOLOGY, CHRONOLOGY AND STRATIGRAPHY[4]	280
CONCLUSION OF CLARKSON ET AL.	284
BURIAL PRACTICES IN WESTERN ARNHEM LAND, AUSTRALIA – A GROUND PENETRATING RADAR STUDY	286
MADJEDBEBE SITE	288
CONCLUDING REMARKS	290
MAMMOTH CAVE	290
MANDU MANDU CREEK ROCK SHELTER	291
THE MIRIWUN ROCK SHELTER	292
MONTE BELLO ISLANDS	293
ABORIGINAL STORIES	293
MT CONNER, ESPECIALLY THE CAVES, IS A REFUGE TO SOME ROCK-DWELLING MARSUPIALS AND BATS.	294
MT NEWMAN ROCK SHELTER OREBODY XXIX	294
EARLIEST KNOWN DRAWING	295
NGARRABULLGAN CAVE	298
SITE AND STRATIGRAPHY	298
DATING	298
PAIRED AGE COMPARISON	299
THERMOLUMINESCENCE DATING OF FLINT FROM PALAEOLITHIC SITES - ADVANTAGES AND LIMITATIONS	300
CONCLUSIONS	300
PURITJARRA CAVE ROCK SHELTER	301
WALLEN WALLEN CREEK	303
WIDGINGARRI 1 & 2	304
WIDGINGARRI 2	304
WILLANDRA FOOTPRINTS	304
KEEP RIVER REGION, EASTERN KIMBERLEY, AUSTRALIA – COMPARATIVE OCCUPATION RECORDS	305
KEEP RIVER ARCHAEOLOGICAL RECORDS – REVIEW OF ARCHAEOLOGICAL EXCAVATIONS	307
COMPARISON OF SEQUENCES OF SAND SHEETS AND ROCK SHELTERS	309
EASTERN KIMBERLEY, WESTERN KIMBERLEY AND ARNHEM LAND – REPRESENTATIVE RECORDS OF OCCUPATION	310
INTENSIFICATION AND THE HOLOCENE RECORD	313
MINING AND QUARRYING -	316
THE NULLARBOR PLAIN	316
ARCHAEOLOGICAL SIGNIFICANCE	316
MINING & QUARRYING IN PREHISTORIC AUSTRALIA	317
ABORIGINAL FLINT MINING	318

- Ochre Mining 318
- Wilgie Mia (Wilgamia) 319
- Karrku Quarry 320
- Late Pleistocene 320
- Colonisation of the Arid Zone 322
- Temperate Australia 322
- Western Australia - Upper Swan River site 322
- Devil's Lair 323
- Tasmania - 324
- Cave Bay Cave 324
- The South West 326
- Kutikina Cave 326
- Karta: Island of the Dead - Kangaroo Island 329

CHAPTER 6 – HUMAN REMAINS IN AUSTRALIA 332

- Lake Nitchie Burial 334
- Lake Tandou Skull 335
- West Point Midden 335
- The Willandra Lakes Hominids 338
- Cossack Skull 342
- Keilor Skull 344
- King Island Skeleton 344
- Kow Swamp 346
- OSL ages for the Kow Swamp people 349
- Oldest Human Remains in Australia (Cane, 2013) 349

CHAPTER 7 - ABORIGINAL CULTURE 352

- Aboriginal Agriculture 360
- Abrupt Change in Vegetation in South East Australia Following Megafaunal Extinction in the Late Quaternary 367
- Bogong Moths 368
- Fire-Stick Farmers 369
- The Fire-Stick Farming Hypothesis 371
- Food Preparation – Poison 372
- Other foods 373
- Food Gathering - desert country 374
- Eel Farming 376
- Fish Traps at Brewarrina 378
- James Dawson - possible first hand description 379
- Alexander Ingram - early site description 380

GEORGE AUGUST ROBINSON	381
FISH TRAPS AT BREWARRINA	381
YAMS	382
NATIVE DOCTOR INITIATION	382
WURADJERI	382
DIERI	383
NGADJURI	383
BIRRUNDUDU	384
GUNWINGGU	385
ABORIGINAL MORTUARY RITES - DISPOSAL OF THE BODY	387
ABORIGINAL MORTUARY RITES - CANNIBALISM	390
ABORIGINAL MORTUARY RITES - CREMATION	392
ABORIGINAL MORTUARY RITES – DESICCATION	393
ABORIGINAL MORTUARY RITES - INTERMENT	395
ABORIGINAL MORTUARY RITES - PLATFORM AND TREE DISPOSAL	399
THE UPPER GEORGINA DISTRICT OF QUEENSLAND	399
ABORIGINAL TOTEMISM	400
INDIVIDUAL TOTEMISM	401
SEX TOTEMISM	401
MOIETY TOTEMISM	402
SECTION AND SUBSECTION TOTEMISM	403
CLAN TOTEMISM	403
LOCAL TOTEMISM	404
CONCEPTION TOTEMISM	404
BIRTH TOTEMISM	405
DREAM TOTEMISM	405
MULTIPLE TOTEMISMS	406
TOTEMISM - 2 MAJOR CATEGORIES	406
SOCIAL ORGANISATION AND STRUCTURE	408
CYCLE ABORIGINAL OF LIFE	408
ABORIGINAL KINSHIP SYSTEMS	409
THE INDIVIDUAL	414
LAW AND ORDER	415
CONFORMITY	416
DISCIPLINE FOR MINOR OFFENCES & CHILDREN	417
NEGATIVE SANCTIONS	418
RIDICULE	418
THE BROTHER-SISTER TABOO	418
THE THREAT OF PHYSICAL VIOLENCE	419
THE THREAT OF NOT ONLY BEING KILLED BUT BEING DENIED FUNERARY RITES	420

OFFENCES WITHIN THE TRIBE OR CLAN	420
SACRED LAW	420
OFFENCES AGAINST PROPERTY	422
MAINTENANCE OF ORDER	423
ABORIGINAL EMBRYONIC COURT	424
ABORIGINAL INQUEST	427
CAPITAL PUNISHMENT - RITUAL KILLING	434
ABORIGINAL TRADE	435
ABORIGINAL ART	437
ROCK ART	437
AGE OF PETROGLYPHS	438
ABORIGINAL ART - THE PILBARA ENGRAVED STONES	441
ARCHAIC FACES PANARAMITEE TRADITION	446
ELVINA TRACK ENGRAVING SITE	449
ABORIGINAL POLE STRUCTURES	449
ABORIGINAL ASTRONOMY	451
AUSTRALIAN ABORIGINAL ASTRONOMY – OVERVIEW	454
THE SUN, MOON AND PLANETS	455
ORIENTATION AND PREDICTION	457
ARCHAEOASTRONOMICAL SIGNIFICANCE	458
RECORDS OF SUPERNOVAE IN INDIGENOUS TRADITIONS?	459
ABORIGINAL ASTRONOMICAL TRADITIONS, OOLDEA, SOUTH AUSTRALIA, PART 2: ANIMALS IN THE OOLDEAN SKY	460
ANIMALS OF THE ABORIGINAL SKYWORLD	462
ANIMALS IN THE OOLDEAN SKY	463
TERRESTRIAL BEHAVIOUR OF OOLDEAN SKY ANIMALS	464
THE AUSTRALIAN BUSTARD – VEGA	464
ALTAIR, THE CROW MOTHER AND DELPHINUS, HER CHICKS	465
THE EMU (COALSACK NEBULA)	466
THE BLACK COCKATOO – ANTARES	467
THE OWLET NIGHTJAR (CANOPUS)	468
THE DINGO (ACHERNAR)	469
THE THORNY-DEVIL LIZARD (PLEIADES)	470
THE WEDGE-TAILED EAGLE (CRUX)	471
THE REDBACK SPIDER (ARCTURUS)	472
BORA CEREMONIAL GROUNDS, SOUTH EAST AUSTRALIA – ASTRONOMICAL ORIENTATIONS	472
NOTICE TO ABORIGINAL AND TORRES STRAIT ISLANDER READERS	473
BORA CEREMONIAL GROUND	474
ANTHROPOLOGICAL SUPPORT FOR AN ASTRONOMICAL CONNECTION	475

- Hypothesis testing 477
- Aboriginal Astronomy 481
- Stone Arrangements 481
- Wurdi Youang 482
- The Morieson Hypothesis 484
- Secular Changes in the Sky 485
- Newly Identified Alignments 486
- The climate in Aboriginal Australia 488
- Central Australia 495
- William Blandowski 496
- The Biggest Estate on Earth: 502
- The Dingo 511
- The Dingo - Domesticated Dogs 512

CHAPTER 8 - 514

THE BAIINI (BAJINI) AND MACASSANS 514

CHAPTER 9 - ABORIGINAL MYTHOLOGY 520

- Mythology 521
- Myth Content 523
- Myths connected with the sky and constellations 529
- Emu in the sky 529
- The Milky Way 530
- Wuriunpranilli, the Sun Woman 531
- Kangaroo Island Mythology 531
- Ngurunderi 531
- Baiame 532
- Baiame - How Swans Became Black 535
- Bunjil the Great Eagle Hawk 536
- The Djanggawul cycle 537
- Dhurramulan 539
- Great Ancestor Spirit - South Eastern Australia 539
- The Great Serpents - Rainbow Serpents 540
- Ngalyod 541
- Borlung 541
- Jeedara 542
- Giant Serpents - Eastern Australia 542
- The Wilpena Pound Serpents 544
- Tagai the Warrior 544
- Arkaroola, SA (the place of Arkaroo) 545

KIMBERLEY SNAKES - THE KIMBERLEY	546
MEGAFAUNA AND THE DREAMTIME	548
MEGAFAUNA DREAMTIME STORIES	555
GIANT EMU IN THE DREAMTIME	556
GIANT FROGS IN THE DREAMTIME	557
GIANT KANGAROOS IN THE DREAMTIME	557
DEPICTED IN ROCK ART	558
OCHRE MINE AT WILGIE MIA	559
THE YAMUTI	559
LAND OF THE DEAD	559
MEMORIES OF THE GREAT FLOOD - THE FLOODING OF THE CONTINENTAL SHELF	567
ABORIGINAL MYTHOLOGY OF LAKE EYRE	569
WIKUNDA HUNTING THE KANGAROO THAT BECAME LAKE EYRE	569
MYTHOLOGY OF THE NULLARBOR PLAIN	570
THE SUN MOTHER	570
MYTHOLOGY OF SOUTH EASTERN AUSTRALIA	571
ABORIGINAL BELIEFS CONNECTED WITH ULURU (AYER'S ROCK) KUNIA & LIRU	571
THE CARPET-SNAKES, KUNIA (KUNYIA), AND THE VENOMOUS SNAKES, LIRU	572
MYTHOLOGY OF THE SIMPSON DESERT	575
THE TWO BOYS	576
WURRU THE ANCESTRAL CRANE	576
ANCESTRAL RAIN HISTORIES	577
MYTHS THAT MAY BE ORAL HISTORY OF ACTUAL EVENTS	578
ABORIGINAL RELIGION	578
RANGES ON THE EAST COAST AND RELIGION	581
THE KUNAPIPI	581
ABORIGINAL DIVISION OF LABOUR IN RITUAL	583
INCREASE RITUAL	585
ARA, THE RED KANGAROO	590
ABORIGINAL FERTILITY CULTS	590
THE UBAR	590
DJANGGAWUL	591
WAWALAG SISTERS	594
THE FERTILITY MOTHER	595
LINKS	**597**
LIST ONE	597
LIST TWO	600
APPENDIX LIST	**602**

Appendix A - Archaeological Sites 602
Appendix B - Timelines 608
Appendix C - Some journal articles on Aboriginal Australia 627
Appendix D - Collapse of Prehistoric Aboriginal Society in North Western Australia triggered by an ENSO Mega-Drought 628
Appendix E - Australian Aboriginals' Adaptation to their Environment – Temperature-Responsive of Thyroxine 630
Appendix F - 630
Tulas - Are They Linked to ENSO in Australia? (Veth, Hiscock & Williams, 2011) 630
Appendix G - 640
Desert mammals and Fire 640
Appendix - H[26] 641
Australian-Indian Phylogenetic Link Reconstruction 641
Appendix I[4] - 645
Mungo and Willandra Lakes –Archaeology, Past and Future 645
Appendix J[3] - 647
Spear Technologies 647
Appendix K[42] 653
Stone Tool Manufacturing Methods 653
Appendix L - 658
Point Technology in the Kimberley – New Data[39] 658
Appendix M[20] - 661
The Eve theory 661
Appendix N [66] 663
Earliest Hominin Occupation in Sulawesi, Indonesia 663
Appendix O[21] - 668
Aboriginal Engravings analysis of the Kybra Site in Western Australia 668
Appendix P[30] - 673
Sahul - Explanations for patterning in the "Package of Traits" of Modern Human Behaviour 673
Taphonomy 673
Social and Symbolic 677
Bindjarran Rock shelter, Manilikarr Country – the archaeology 680
Birriwilk Rock shelter, Manilikarr Country, South west Arnhem Land, Northern Territory, a Mid- Late Holocene Site 683
Manilikarr Country 685
Keep River Region. North Western Australia, Comparison of Histories Inside and Outside Rock shelters 687
References 691

Acknowledgements

I thank Dr. Richard Robins, director/archaeologist at Heritage Consultants Pty Ltd, for his advice concerning the content and of this book. There are a number of his suggestions I am unable to carry out at this time which I hope to comply with later.

Introduction

Since the Aborigines were first seen by European explorers their origin has been the subject of debate. Aboriginal people have lived in Australia for at least 60,000 years, arriving by boat from south Asia by about that time. Very controversial dates from Jinmium in the Northern Territory place the early arrivals at the site by 116,000 ± 12,000 years ago. These dates have been strongly disputed, about 60,000 BP being the date generally accepted as the most likely time of the first arrival. The site has been re-dated using TL and the results suggest the site is actually no older than about 10,000 years.

Recent studies have found that ages of sites in the sand plain outside the rock shelters and between rock shelters are as much as 18,000 BP. From the results of the latest research it seems the rock shelters were probably not being occupied at the time of the first occupation of the Keep River region, where the Jinmium RockShelter is located.

It has been suggested that the first arrivals were coastal people, basing their economies on the sea and river mouths, originally spreading around the coast then up the rivers. If this is the case, the mouths of the rivers they would have been entering for the first time could have been hundreds of kilometres seawards of the present coastline, as the continental shelves would have been exposed due to lower sea levels than at the present. How long did they spend on the coast and river mouths before spreading to the earliest known sites on present-day dry land? The dates that have the first arrival in Australia around 60,000 years ago are from occupation sites on present day dry land. Presumably the first landing would have been on part of the continental shelf that is now submerged, an unknown number of years earlier than the known dated sites. The Berndts have suggested the first arrival may have been about 75,000 BP or even earlier (Berndt & Berndt, 1988).

If the ancestral Aborigines were indeed coastal dwellers, what was the incentive to expand inland? In South Western Tasmania the people lived almost exclusively on the coast for 30,000 years, based on the dating of the known sites, apparently rarely venturing into the thick rainforest. At the time of first European contact they were still living in a narrow coastal belt between the horizontal rainforest and the sea. While they lived well on the coast, with plentiful and easily available food, why would they want to move to a habitat that was more difficult and where food was less plentiful and required more time and energy to collect? When the continental shelf was exposed there would have been rivers, possibly with deltas, lakes and swamps, as well as the nearby sea, where they could get all the food they needed, and with very little effort.

The evidence of the possible occupation of the area around Lake George in New South Wales, a long way from the points of entry into Australia in the north, prior to 100,000 years ago has been rejected.

At the time of the arrival of Europeans in Australia it was declared an unoccupied land, as the Aborigines didn't practise agriculture, so the colonists could take over without even consulting the locals.

The Aborigines were believed by some of those Europeans to be at best, like children. Others regarded them as sub-human, so there was no problem treating them as though they were animals, especially when colonisation got under way and colonists wanted to take over their hunting territory for raising cattle and sheep, or farming. They were mostly tolerated as long as they didn't try to stop pastoralists taking their land, when they got in the way, they were often treated like animals that ate the colonists' crops or killed their cattle for food.

It has since been realised that they did indeed farm the land, even the parts that were unusable by the colonists, and for a very long time. It has been called fire-stick farming. During their long period of occupation they developed a system of burning off limited areas at certain times of the year, which encouraged the grass growth that supported the animals they hunted. So while they lived by hunting, over large parts of the continent it was in effect managed hunting. In fact, they were possibly the first farmers.

It has been said of the Aborigines that 'they are unchanging people in an unchanging land', implying that they didn't adapt. One of the world's best known, and highest regarded anthropologists, Claude Levi-Strauss, called them 'intellectual aristocrats' among early peoples. Once overlooked features of Aboriginal culture include sophisticated religion, art and social organisation, an egalitarian system of justice and decision-making and complex far-reaching trading networks. And they adapted to and survived in the some of the world's harshest environments for survival, which demonstrated that they did indeed adapt very well.

Another way the Aborigines, especially in the driest areas of the inland, adapted to the very arid conditions was by neighbouring groups often allowing each other to hunt in their territory when their neighbour's territory was more affected by drought, which occurs at unpredictable times and for varying lengths of time.

Archaeologists have also found that their stone tools have evolved over the time of their occupation. Like elsewhere in the world, the earliest known tools were heavy, simple tools, the later ones becoming progressively smaller and finer, and eventually to more complex composite tools, that are mounted or hafted to a shaft for better leverage. At the time of European colonisation most tools were of the composite, hafted type.

Archaeology has shown from digs in the Northern Territory that human history in Australia began sometime before 50,000 years ago. The Aborigines obviously could not have evolved in Australia, as the earliest human ancestors were present only in Africa, long after the 2 continents had split from Gondwana, so there was no land connection between the continents during the time of their evolution.

It is known that early people were present in Southeast Asia for more than a million years, so the only thing stopping some from crossing to Australia was the ocean barrier, so they needed to develop some sort of sea-going craft before they could begin the migration, probably by island-hopping as the Polynesians did many thousands of years later when they spread across the islands of the Pacific, probably from southern China. The closest Australia came to connecting to Asia by land was at the height of the Last Ice Age, but even then there was still a gap of about 90 km separating the 2 continents by the ocean.

Since the studies of Alfred Russel Wallace in the 19th century it has been known that there is a distinct, dramatic transition between the faunal types to the north of the zone called Wallacea, and that of the southern side. The oriental faunal region, to the north of Wallacea, the no man's (or no animal's) land, is separated from the Australian faunal region to the south of Wallacea. The boundaries of the oriental region coincide with the edge of the Asian continental shelf, and the Australian region coincides with the edge of the Australian continental shelf. It was precisely this gap between the faunal regions where the land between the 2 continents didn't join, even at the height of the Ice Age.

At the time of lowest sea level, - 60 m, at the height of the Ice Age, there would have been a chain of islands parallel to, and visible from, Timor, on the northern side of Wallacea, about 90 km from the Australian islands. Once they reached the first island they could have island-hopped to the Australian mainland, though they probably didn't realise they had reached another continent when they arrived.

There would also have been broken tongues of land jutting out from north-western Australia and from Joseph Bonaparte Gulf on the east. Between the outer islands and the tongues of land there were stopovers at Ashmore Reef, Cartier Islet and Maurice and Troubadour Shoals.

The only other non-flying animals to reach Australia from the oriental faunal region were dingoes, which came across with the Aborigines, and rats and mice. The latter 2 could have travelled by rafts of tree trunks, etc. from the Asian area.

Chapter 1 - Anthropological History

Origins
Out of Africa Replacement Hypothesis

The Regional Continuity Hypothesis

Package of Cultural Innovations

A Complete Skull, Dmanisi, Georgia and Early Homo Evolutionary Biology

Hominid Fossils from Dmanisi - Their Place Amongst Early Hominids

The Southern Route:
In order for the Southern route to become a viable option, several things needed to happen. The first was sea levels needed to drop. During an ice age, the sea level falls significantly, due to huge amounts of water being trapped in glaciers. The falling sea level allowed for humans from Africa to cross the mouth of the Red Sea, using rafts to island hop in some instances. Crossing from Africa, they could then move into India following the coastline. Continuing along the coast, early humans likely found their way down into Indonesia within 10,000 years. Low sea levels at this time allowed a dry walk from Aden to the tip of Java.

While recent archaeological finds have suggested human occupation dates as old as 62,000 years ago, sea levels between Timor and Australia were at their lowest some 3,000 years earlier. Thus it is more probable that the first humans crossed into Australia some 65,000 years ago. The original landing site would now be submerged beneath the sea, as it would have been on the continental shelf that was dry land about the time of the first arrivals.

WLH-50 and the complete replacement by out of Africa theory

The calvarium (the skullcap, upper portion of the Neurocranium which covers the neural cavity) of WLH-50 has been used in a study to test the recent African origin theory, which suggests the complete replacement of the archaic forms, known as ***Homo erectus***, so that ***H. erectus*** did not contribute to the ancestry of modern Australasians. They compared data for WLH-50 and 3 potential contributors to the ancestry of WLH-50 (Ngandong, Late Pleistocene Africans, Levant hominids from Skhūl and Qafzeh) concluding that the results unambiguously refute the complete replacement of these potential contributors to the ancestry of the Australasians, suggesting that the Ngandong hominids should be reclassified as ***Homo sapiens***, Hawks et al., (2000). (21)

Not all agree with Hawks et al. Brauer, Collard and Stringer criticise the methods of Hawks et al., not accepting that their study disproves the Out of Africa hypothesis that requires the complete replacement of earlier populations.

The 2 main theories of the evolution of modern humans are the Out of Africa Hypothesis (The Noah's Ark model) and the Regional Continuity Hypothesis (the candelabra model). Both agree that the migrants left from the Africa, they differ on when and whether the previous populations of Eurasia were replaced or interbreeding took place with existing populations of ***H. erectus***

Homo erectus near Australia

Evidence of occupation on the Indonesian island of Flores has been found indicating that ***H. erectus*** had reached the island by 800,000 years ago, (*Nature*, Vol.392, 12 March 1998, pp 173-176). Fission track dating was used to date the volcanic tuff above and beneath stone artefacts and associated remains of extinct animals.

It would have required a water crossing for ***H. erectus*** to have reached Flores from the nearest other land, about 19 km across the sea. Some form of sea-worthy water transport was required, both to reach Flores from the nearest island and travel from the Asian mainland which has never been connected to the islands, Flores being separated from the mainland by 3 deep-water channels.

The isolation of the island is confirmed by the impoverished nature of the fauna, the only animals being those that could have arrived by flying or other means such as drifting tree trunks from other islands.

Prior to the dating of the Flores material the oldest use of watercraft that evidence has been found for was the arrival of the Aborigines in Australia about 60,000 years ago. If *H. erectus* could make short sea crossings prior to 800,000 years ago, there would be no problem for the Aborigines travelling to Australia, also from one of the Indonesian Islands.

The recent find of the diminutive Hobbits on Flores has sparked research that suggests they may have descended from the Asian *H. erectus* population also on Flores.

Out of Africa – which route?

There are several clear implications of a single exit from Africa of anatomically modern humans (AMH) that is successful. The number of subsequent route options was decreased as there was only 1 exit route. A multiroute model also has to explain how the colonisation of both Europe and Asia could have taken place from the same single exit group, whichever was the initial route.

The southern rather than the northern exit – genetic evidence

There are 2 logical reasons for identifying the southern route that crosses the mouth of the Red Sea, based on genetic evidence.

Of only 2 branches of L3 mtDNA outside Africa (M and N), both are present in East Asia, including South Asia, where they have the most autochthonous lineages of M and N, though only N is present in West Asia.

There is less diversity in the N representatives in the Levantine and Europe, being more derived and younger than those from Arabia and South West Asia (for full discussion see Oppenheimer, 2003; Richards et al., 2006; Fernandes et al., 2012).

Archaeology of the exit route – climate

Whether the exit route from Africa was southern or northern an implication of a single genetic exit is that the establishment of a beachhead must have been very difficult as they moved from sub-Saharan Africa during the Upper Pleistocene (e.g. The Arabian Gulf; Oppenheimer, 2003: 88), which is assumed to have been as the result of the Saharan-Arabian arid zone barrier across their route out of sub-Saharan Africa. In times of interglacials are the only times when this barrier was freely permeable, though it may have been open between 80 and 75 ka during the early MIS 5a (see Rosenberg et al., 2011), a period that was characterised by a moist refugium, a 'Gulf Oasis' (Rose, 2010; Fleitmann et al., 2010; see also Petraglia et al., 2011).

An exit into South West Asia during the last interglacial

There have been 2 full interglacials over the past 150,000 years, the last of which, the Eemian Interglacial, occurred in MIS 5e, and the most recent during the Holocene. A diverse movement of fauna from the African savannah occurred from sub-Saharan Africa to the Levant and Arabia during each of these interglacials (Turner, 1999). Oppenheimer suggests that the skeletal evidence at Skhūl and Qafzeh is evidence that during MIS 5e AMH used the climatic window to exit by the northern route, though this dates to between 120 ka and 90 ka (Grün & Stringer, 1991). There is archaeogenetic consensus at the present that in populations of the present there are no descendants of this early exit (contra Petraglia et al., 2010). There is a long gap, archaeologically, of 40,000 years between Skhūl and Qafzeh AMH fossils and the reappearance of AMH, which was signalled by the Early Upper Palaeolithic in West Eurasia after 49 ka, this period being intercalated by the presence of Neanderthals in the Levant. See (Shea, 2008) for a recent perspective of dates and causes of these switches. In regard to genetics there are no mtDNA or Y lineages outside Africa that date even a possible exit near MIS 5e at 120 ka, or even 90 ka, the less relevant bracket, which evidence virtually excludes survival of this Levantine AMH colony, that was very real, into the ex-African gene pool of the present (Oppenheimer, 2003; Richards et al., 2006).

In regards to recent claims of AMH reaching Jebel Faya in southern Arabia between the beginning of MIS 5e and 90 ka, an identical issue applies (Petraglia et al., 2010; Armitage et al., 2011). In this case lithic evidence is all that is available, the tool kit showing affinities to the Late Middle Stone Age of North East Africa. The presence of AMH in the Arabian Peninsula at 2 different times was inferred based on this evidence: a phase of occupation during MIS 5e, 2 OSL dates, 123 ± 10 ka and 127 ± 16 ka, and another, later one, at 95 ka, 94.8 ± 13.0 ka; see (Armitage et *al*., 2011; Petraglia et *al*., 2010). The recent finding (Rose, et al., 2011) of a Middle Stone Age complex of Nubian typology in Dhofar, Oman dated to 106 ka (OSL), which also had no fossils.

The chronology and implications of these putative, limited appearances of AMH outside Africa during MIS 5e, with the exception of the absence of fossils, and its disappearance before 94 ka, are similar to Skhūl and Qafzeh, in that the colonies appear to have died out leaving no descendants. Oppenheimer suggests it would not be very surprising if the Skhūl and Qafzeh event, out of Africa by the northern route had been duplicated by the southern route as well, though it does not necessarily end with genetic survival of such a migration, given the low population densities of the period. As there is no skeletal record of humans from Arabia in the Pleistocene, the users of the Jebel Faya assemblage are unknown, and the possibility of these being Neanderthals cannot be ruled out. The African Middle Stone Age typology of the tools would not necessarily rule out this possibility, as stone tools are a poor guide to identifying the hominin that made them. Also, it provides a plausible scenario for Neanderthal admixture into an AMH population ancestral to West Eurasians, as well as to East Asians, as is predicted by the single southern exit hypothesis, if Neanderthals were known to be in Arabia.

An exit during MIS 5e – fossil evidence in East Asia
It has been claimed that the recent finding in Zhiren Cave, Zhirendong, South China, of an anterior mandible containing 2 molars is possible evidence for the expansion of AMH into East Asia during MIS 5e (Liu et *al*., 2010b). It is argued that the mandible dates to more than 100 ka (but see Kaifu & Fujita, 2012) and that it has modern human features that are derived, distinct from any known late archaic human, and they also place it close to humans from the later Pleistocene (contra Kaifu & Fujita, 2012). Dennell commented in *Nature* (2010, 513) agreeing with the dates of "100,000-113,000 years old, and possibly older", based on stratigraphy and faunal associations, though he questions the need to postulate interbreeding, at least in relation to the molars: "the latter are small, and would be

considered as modern in a Late Pleistocene Eurasian (post-Neanderthal) sample."

It has Also recently been suggested (Westaway et *al.*, 2007a) that the possibility of AMH in Java during MIS 5e, based on 1 tooth from Punung Cave, that has been reported (Storm et *al.*, 2005) that was classified to be small enough to be classified as ***Homo sapiens***. Until more evidence is available this claim is considered to be very tentative.

The Liujiang Skull, a cave specimen, also from South China, has also been claimed to be of a similar antiquity. This skull is clearly anatomically modern, and a date of 111-139 ka has been obtained from the breccias in which it was found (Shen et *al.*, 2002), possibly putting it in the same time frame as the fossils from Zhirendong and Punung Caves, though these dates are very controversial and younger dates obtained from the flowstone covering them, all of which are 67 ka, seem to Oppenheimer to be a much safer minimum.

Arguments against an exit during MIS 5e that was successful – Summary

For the out-of-Africa mtDNA branch L3 the recalibrated age estimates and confidence intervals (CI) of 71,600 years ago (CI: 57,100; 86,600 (Soares et *al*., 2009) comfortably exclude the range of dates implied by an Asian exit during MIS 5e, as also did previous age estimates of L3: Oppenheimer 2003; 2009). According to Oppenheimer the phylogenetic evidence suggests a single exit that was successful, the exit could have taken place either only during MIS 5e or later, i.e. during MIS 5a-4, but not both. A population leaving Africa during the last interglacial and surviving *substantially* into the gene pool of the present appears to be extremely unlikely. It is therefore necessary to presume that as with the exit of Skhūl and Qafzeh, any exit to Asia by AMH during the last interglacial must have been similarly evanescent. The archaeological record for the terminus of putative early Africa-Arabia exists in Oman, which is older than the range of L3 age estimates, is consistent with the view mentioned above.

AMH recent exit models – Single verses multiple

The worldwide mtDNA tree allows 2 more fundamental observations. Most of the 12 or more L branches of the tree that are present only in Africa are much older than L3, M or N. The genetic age of the deepest L branch point (192 ka; Soares et *al*., 2009) is consistent with recent fossils that have been dated in East Africa (164 ka: White et *al*., 2003; 195 ka: McDougal et *al*., 2005).

As mentioned previously, the most singular observation is that 'L3', which is the remaining African branch, as it encompasses all non-African branches that originate outside Africa, namely M and N (Oppenheimer, 2002, 2003; Metspalu et *al*., 2004) makes it unique. This means that, in effect, the remainder of the world has been colonised by 2 descendants of the ancestral haplotype for M and N (a subtype of L3 root holding a 195 nucleotide transition). According to the corrected molecular clock that latter now dates to 71,600 (CI: 57,100; 86,600) years ago (Soares et *al*., 2009). For L3 the overall estimate of age, which includes all the branches in Africa, is the same, which probably indicates an upper limit for the exit from Africa, with L3 possibly being older, though not younger than, the exit. It can be seen that on this estimate the confidence intervals straddling the YTE, which therefore prevents a genetic solution of the problem of whether AMH entered South Asia before or after the Toba eruption. Oppenheimer suggests the exit of a single mtDNA lineage is unambiguous evidence of a single exit from Africa of AMH, which is paralleled closely in the male-NRY tree, as well as being reflected clearly in the X chromosome and several autosomal loci (Oppenheimer, 2003; Hudjashov et al 2007; Richards et *al.*, 2006; Abu-Amero, 2009).

The fact that the same close African ancestor is shared by all non-African descendants from both the mtDNA and Y lines is in itself an indication of a period of drift in a small isolated founding group. It is suggested that there is negligible chance that 2 or more founding exit episodes that are separated in time and place gave rise to the same source African lineage by drift in all parts of the non-African world; the default that remains is single exit (Oppenheimer, 2009).

According to Oppenheimer any claims of earlier exits of AMH during MIS 5e that are based on fossil or lithic evidence should be taken seriously, as they are not necessarily implausible in practical terms. Based on the evidence of dating from Skhūl and Qafzeh, which variously approach and significantly exceed 100 ka (Stringer et *al.*, 1989) there was at least 1 abortive exit of AMH near MIS 5e means that other similar claims of an exit by the southern route may turn out to be demonstrated by the fossil record, though not in the NRY or mtDNA of moderns populations. If this is the case Oppenheimer suggests such dispersal events must be presumed to have been evanescent. Though autosomal evidence is much more sensitive than uniparental study, as it has many more loci and no drift, and can therefore show less than 5 % admixture of Archaic into AMH outside of Africa, it would be far less specific when comparing AMH with AMH, therefore would lose that advantage searching for AMH genetic survival from the last interglacial.

The southern rather than the northern route – genetic evidence

Dating of Migrations

The arrival of AMH in India and East Asia – dating

To date there has been little fossil evidence or genetic evidence in India or Southeast Asia dating to the period immediately before the eruption of Mt Toba, though there may be archaeological or physiological evidence, that is evanescent, of the presence of AMH in Arabia or southern China a short time after the close of the last interglacial. There is, instead, a congruence of proxy evidence to either just prior or just following this event, the pre-Toba being only cultural or the post-Toba now including several fossils and the recalibrated genetic dates in East Asia

India and Toba

A lot of archaeological work has been focused on India, where there are the most extensive deposits of younger Toba tuff (YTT) (Jones, 2007), given that it had been suggested previously (Oppenheimer, 2003) that AMH may have arrived in Southeast Asia prior to the super eruption of Mt Toba volcano 73 ka. Hominin fossils have not been found associated with the YTT despots, though stone artefacts from the Middle Palaeolithic have been found that were associated with several of the YTT deposits in India, both above and below the deposits, whilst *H. sapiens* may have made these assemblages, there is no evidence to rule out other possibilities.

In spite of these issues, there have been recent articles (Blinkhorn & Petraglia)[1], (Petraglia et al., 2007; Petraglia, 2010, 2011; Clarkson et *al.*, 2012), it has been argued, based on lithic evidence from both below and above the Toba ash in the Jureru Valley, Southern India, for the presence of AMH in India at the time of the YTT event, with survival afterward. Much of the argument supporting the claims that these tools, both before and after Toba, were made by AMH is based on their tight statistical typological associations with South African Middle Stone Age and Australian and Southeast Asian AMH Palaeolithic cultures, and the differences between them and the North African and Levantine cultures, archaic hominins and very early modern humans and later Aurignacian assemblages, were detailed and analysed (Clarkson et *al*., 2012) and (Clarkson)[1]. It is obvious this nuanced perspective is consistent with the dispersal of AMH by the southern route, as according to Clarkson: "There are no obvious differences between the Jureru assemblages and newly reported assemblages from Arabia dating to MIS 5a" (Clarkson et *al*., 2012, 178). When there are no hominin fossils associated with the recovered technology there are the usual problems of attempting to match a particular technology to a particular hominin. According to Oppenheimer when this work was presented at a 2010 meeting in Oxford, he was convinced by the visual and statistical associations, and several other archaeologists were also convinced, with the exception of Paul Mellars (reported in Balter, 2010). Pre- and post-Toba ash cultural dates for the first site (Petraglia, 2007) had previously both been close to the YTE at 74,000 BP or earlier, though the post-Toba dates were nearly all about 55,000 BP or younger (Balter, 2010), therefore raising a question as to their key claim of rapid human recovery in India post YTE.

Indian genetics – Toba

The 'catastrophic' interpretation of the conjunction of tools and ash in India predicts that a deep, wide and genetically sterile furrow would have split East Asia from West Asia, though Petraglia et *al*. are apparently not influenced by this prediction, following which India eventually recovered from this genetic bottleneck, either locally of by re-colonisation from argued for evidence of this furrow. The presence of M groups around the Bay of Bengal in eastern India is either side (Oppenheimer, 2009). The genetic map of Asia (Oppenheimer, 2003, 18-184) first also consistent with a possible local Indian bottleneck, though these M groups are numerous, they are notably much younger than at other places along the Indian Ocean trail (Oppenheimer, 2009; Sun et *al*., 2006; Soares et *al*., 2009). Dates for haplogroups N and R, which are, however, located further to the west in South Asia, where there was less ash fall, are relatively higher (Oppenheimer, 2009; Soares et *al*., 2009; Oppenheimer, 2003), which is consistent with the local drift near the east coast of India and an exit before the Toba eruption.

Gene Flow to Australia from India in the Holocene Substantiated by Genome-Wide Data [26]

It is commonly believed that following the initial occupation of Australia the continent remained relatively isolated until European first contact, though the genetic history of the Aboriginal People has not been explored in detail in regards to this issue. Pugach et *al.* carried out analysis of large-scale genotyping data of aboriginal Australians, New Guineans, Island Southeast Asians and Indians. Their work indicates an ancient association between Australia, New Guinea and the Mamanwa, a negrito group from the Philippines, and divergence times for these groups being 36,000 years ago, which supports the view that these populations are representatives of an early "southern route migration" out of Africa, with other populations in the region arriving by a separate dispersal. They also detected a signal that indicated substantial gene flow between the Indian populations and Australia long before European contact, which is contrary to the generally accepted view that there was no contact between Australia and the remainder of the world. The estimate arrived at by Pugach et *al.* is that the gene flow occurred during the Holocene, 4,230 years ago. They also point out that this is also the time when there were changes in tool technology, food processing and the arrival of the dingo, the evidence appearing in the archaeological record of Australia, which they suggest may be related to the migration from India.

It is suggested by genetic and archaeological evidence that anatomically modern humans (AMH) expanded from Africa (Ramachandran et al., 2005; Liu et al., 2006) to colonise all parts of the world, in the process replacing local archaic *Homo* populations, such as Neanderthals (Green et al., 2010) and Denisovans (Reich et al., 2010; Reich, 2011), with a limited degree of gene flow. Pugach et *al.* say it appears the anatomically modern humans proceeded by 2 routes: the northern route giving rise to the modern Asians 38,000-23,000 years ago (Gutenkunst et al., 2009; Rasmussen et al., 2011) and an earlier southern dispersal along the coast around the Arabian Peninsula and India to the Australian continent (Reich, 2011; Rasmussen et al., 2011). The ancestral Australian Aborigines and Papua New Guineans diverging from the ancestral Eurasian population 75-62 ka (Rasmussen et al., 2011) and, based on evidence from archaeology, reached Sahul (the combined land mass of Australia, Tasmania and New Guinea) by at least 45 ka (O'Connell & Allen,2004; Kayser, 2010; Summerhayes et al., 2010). Subsequent additional gene flow to coastal New Guinea, though not to the highlands, from Asia, that was associated with the expansion of Austronesians (Kayser, 2010), though the extent of isolation of the Australian Aboriginals after the initial colonisation remains a subject of debate. There are some mtDNA and y chromosomal studies suggesting there was some degree of gene flow from the Indian subcontinent to Australia during the Holocene (Redd & Stoneking, 1999; Redd et al. 2002; Kumar et al., 2009), though according to the prevailing view that prior to the first European contact in the 18th century there was little if any contact between Australia and the remainder of the world (Rasmussen et al., 2011; Hudjashov et al., 2007; McEvoy et al., 2010).

In this study Pugach et *al.* analysed genome-wide SNP data, finding that there was a significant signature of gene flow from India to Australia which they suggest was at about 4,320 years ago. Pugach et *al.* assembled genome-wide data from the across Northern Australia (AUA) (Reich et al., 2011; Redd & Stoneking, 1999), the highlands of Papua New Guinea (NGH) (Wollstein et al., 2010), 11 populations from island Southeast (SE) Asia (Reich et al., 2011), and 26 populations from India (Reich et al., 2009), which included Dravidian speakers from South India (Reich et al., 2011; Cordaux et al., 2003). They also included data from Yorubans from Ibadan; Nigeria (YRI); individuals of northern and western European ancestry that were living in Utah (CEU); Han Chinese individuals from Beijing (CHB); and Gujarati Indians from Houston, TX (GIH) (Altshuler et al., 2010). There were 344 individuals in the final dataset; and following data cleaning and integration there were 458,308 autosomal SNPs for use in the analysis.

Genetic relationships between populations
Discussion

An ancient ancestral association between Australia, New Guinea, and the Mamanwa (a negrito group in the Philippines), is suggested by the results of this study, with a divergence occurring at least 35 ka, which implies a common origin but early separation for these groups, and supports the view that these populations are representatives of the descendants of an early "southern migration route" (Reich et al., 2011; Rasmussen et al., 2011). Pugach et *al.* also found it striking that there was a signal of substantial gene flow between Indian and Australian populations prior to European contact. Pugach et *al.* estimated the data of this gene flow event to be 141 generations ago which suggests that the gene flow may be associated with the documented changes in the Australian archaeological record that occurred at about this time, which is around the time the dingo arrived in Australia.

Pugach et *al.* say the signal of Indian gene flow might not necessarily be from India directly; a scenario can be envisioned according to which the Indian ancestry comes indirectly to Australia, such as contact with island South East Asian populations. Some trade between the north east coast of Australia and Indonesia is believed to have taken place prior to European contact (Hiscock, 2008). There were 11 populations from island SE Asia included in this study, but the results showed no signal of recent gene flow from India into these populations or from those populations into Australia, which according to Pugach et *al.* renders the scenario of Indian ancestry by way of SE Asia unlikely.

It has been shown that there is patterning similar to those generated by admixture could be produced by ancient population structure (Eriksson & Manica, 2012). According to Pugach et *al.* even in the ancestral population of the AUA and the NGH, if this substructure existed, however, the suspicion that the gene flow detected in this study might be an artefact, that was attributable to this substructure, would require this ancestral age to be much older, old enough to predate the occupation of Sahul (Sankararaman et al., 2012). An argument against this possibility is the fact that the date obtained by this study is comparatively recent. Also the Australian Aboriginals shared approximately the same amount of Denisovan ancestry with Papua New Guineans that was shared between the Papua New Guineans and the Denisovans (Reich et al., 2011). As it is not expected that later mid-Holocene gene flow into Australia, though not into Papua New Guinea, should diminish the proportion of the Denisovan ancestry in the Australian Aborigines, though not in the ancestry of the Papua New Guineans, this might appear surprising.

Given that the total Denisovan contribution to the ancestor of these populations is about 3-5 % (Reich et al., 2011), and the amount of the contribution from Indians is estimated to about 11 %, it is expected that the impact of Indian genetic material would be to decrease the Denisovan ancestry in the Australian genome by about 0.3-0.5 %, which is below the detection threshold of the data generated by this study.

Though the samples that have been presented in this study were collected from a broad geographical area across northern Australia, they might not be representative of the Australian Aborigines as a whole. As has been pointed out by others (McEvoy et al., 2010), it would be very helpful to have comprehensive studies of the genetic variation in Australian Aboriginal people in order to further understand their history which is increasingly complex.

Archaeology of Sunda in the Pleistocene

Flaked stone artefacts are invariably vastly more common than fossils of hominins in East and Southeast Asia as is the case in Europe. In China and Southeast Asia, and even Australia, the few dated AMH fossils date from MIS 4-3, showing a much older age bracket, of 67-40 ka, than the oldest of such fossils in Europe ($\leq$ 35 ka: Trinkhaus, 2003), though none predates the Toba eruption, with the possible exception of the Punung tooth.

In East Asia the small number of dates for the early arrival of AMH are older than their equivalents in Europe (reviewed in Oppenheimer, 2012a, 2012b) and elsewhere[1] and need not be discussed here. The predominant use of radiocarbon-based dating with its low ceiling limits them, even when the cultural dates are secure the lack of diagnostic fossils, and the lack of secure direct dating even when the fossils are deemed to be securely AMH. For the newly recalibrated estimates of genetic ages of M, N and R haplogroups in East Asia, which now cluster around 60,000 BP or less, there is also a problem, (Soares et *al*., 2009), 5,000-15,000 years less than before (Oppenheimer, 2009), rather than the new archaeological estimates of up to 67,000 BP. For the new genetic dates for all haplogroups, confidence intervals are still wide enough to include 67,000 BP, and even Toba.

Origins - The Regional Continuity Hypothesis

There are 2 main theories for the origin of anatomically modern humans, the older proposed by Weidenreich, and later of Thorne and Wolpoff, is the regional continuity theory, the rapid replacement hypothesis, or out of Africa theory, is espoused by Stringer, and others.

According to the rapid replacement hypothesis of Stringer a single African origin of Homo sapiens occurred about 200 000 years ago. Since then the archaic people of areas outside Africa were replaced by successive waves of increasingly advanced peoples from Africa. The most recent wave of African migration, based on mitochondrial DNA analysis, proposes that a small group of modern humans left Africa about 70,000 BP, replacing all earlier populations throughout Eurasia and Australia, and eventually North and South America.

According to the regional continuity hypothesis, the already differentiated ancestral, archaic peoples had already spread from Africa, and further evolution occurred in several geographic regions. Australasia (Indonesia, New Guinea and Australia) is considered to be a key area for testing the latter because many physical anthropologists believe there is a link between *H. erectus* - Java Man - and both prehistoric and modern Australians. Proof of regional continuity in this area would show that **Homo sapiens sapiens** evolved in the region, not by replacement from Africa. The main problem with finding proof either way is that the skeletal remains from Asia of the required age are very scarce, and what there is comes mainly from Java and China.

Some biologists do favour a combination of the 2 theories, migrations from Africa together with genetic assimilation of the older, more archaic pre-existing populations. All the known early hominids of Java are *H. erectus*. Their brains were larger than their predecessors, and they made more sophisticated tools. The cranial capacity of the Sangiran *H. erectus* was 950 ml compared to the average modern human capacity of 1300 ml. Early humans had brain capacities less than half this.

Until 1994 it was believed that the Sangiran remains were about 1 million years old. In 1994 Swisher and Curtiss published a paper in *Science* showing that they securely dated 2 Java sites to 1.8 million years, the same age as the oldest *erectus* remains in African. They dated the volcanic pumice associated with the skull of a young child at Modjokerto to 1.81 million +/- 40 000 years, and cranial remains from Sangiran to 1.66 million +/- 40 000 years. So there were erectus populations in at least 2 different parts of the world, Africa and Asia, living at the same time about 1.8 million years ago, before ***H. sapiens*** had arisen. Did ***H. erectus*** move out of Africa about 2 million years ago, about 600,000 years before the advanced Acheulean tools characterised by hand axes, stone cleavers and other bifacially-worked stone implements?

The complete absence of hand axes from Java, as well as all other known ***H. erectus*** sites, has been a puzzle. Hand axes first appeared in Africa about 1.4 million years ago. If ***H. erectus*** moved out of Africa prior to 1.4 million years ago they wouldn't have stone axes, it is unlikely they would forget how to make such useful tools. It has been suggested that it was actually an earlier ancestor of *erectus* that moved out of Africa, possibly ***H. Habilis*** or even ***Australopithecus***, but no evidence has been uncovered of either of these species in Asia.

Some don't accept the dates of Swisher and Curtis, preferring the estimated age for Sangiran of 700,000-1,000,000 BP.

The 11 Ngandong crania from Java are the youngest remains of ***H. erectus***, previously called ***H. soloensis*** - Solo Man - found in a Late Pleistocene terrace on the Solo River. The skulls from Ngandong are large and broad, and have a capacity of 1150 ml. They were originally dated to 100 000 BP, but Swisher has since unconfirmed dates of 50,000 BP for them. Ngandong is generally classed as very early ***H. sapiens*** and is regarded by the proponents of the regional continuity theory as being the connection between the Javan ***Homo erectus*** and ***Homo sapiens***.

In 1992 Thorne claimed that early Australian skeletons show the Java complex of features, along with braincase expansion and other more advanced features. Several dozen well preserved Late Pleistocene and Early Holocene skulls demonstrate the same combination of features that distinguished those Indonesian people from their contemporaries also distinguish living Australian Aborigines from other living peoples. A comment was made in 1965 concerning the Australian fossil skulls that "the mark of ancient Java is on all of them."

According to Thorne, the Javan features are 'thick skull bones, with strong continuous brow ridges forming an almost straight bar of bone across their eye sockets and a second, well-developed shelf of bone at the back of the skull for attachment of the neck muscles. Above and behind the brows, the forehead is flat and retreating. These early Indonesians [the Sangiran *Homo erectus*] also have large projecting faces with massive rounded cheekbones. Their teeth are the largest known in archaic humans from that time.' Other features are 'a rolled ridge on the lower edge of the eye sockets, a distinctive ridge on the cheekbone and a nasal floor that blends smoothly into the face'.

This 'unique morphology' was stable for at least 700,000 years in Java, according to Thorne, and is reflected in the Ngandong series of skulls, though their brain cases have evolved into the modern range. After Ngandong there is a serious gap in the South East Asian fossil record.

Philip Habgood has rigorously evaluated the morphological links between the Indonesian and Australian hominids and concluded that 'there are a number of morphological features which, when found in combination, appear to document continuity between the early Indonesian material and some prehistoric and modern Australian crania'. He cautions that 'the present skeletal sample from Australasia is not adequate to allow a clear distinction between the two competing explanations as to the origins of modern humans in the region'.

The 'stamp of early China' has also been identified by Thorne on the 'gracile' fossil group. Keilor and WLH 1 are claimed to closely resemble the Linkiang skull from southern China, the Zhoukoudian upper cave people, Niah from Borneo and Tabon from the Philippines.

Recently, the Jinniushan skull from China, an early form of homo sapiens, has been dated to 200,000 years ago. The age - ESR and uranium series dating is considered reliable, making it almost as old as some of the latest Chinese *Homo erectus* fossils, such as Skull V from the upper stratum of Zhoukoudian. Chen Tiemel and colleagues in Beijing commented 'This raises the possibility of the coexistence of the 2 species in China. The morphology of the skull suggests a strong local component of evolution, consonant with the "multi-regional continuity" model of the evolution of *H. sapiens*'.

Thorne and Wolpoff stressed less parallels with China, less than with the Javanese affinities of the robust Australian hominids. Wolpoff wrote in 1980 'the resemblance of some specific characteristics to the morphology common in the Solo [Ngandong] sample that it is difficult to deny an evolutionary relationship in the Australasian region, a point suggested by Weidenreich several decades ago'.

The review of Sahul (Greater Australia) during the Pleistocene by Habgood & Franklin (2008) found no indication that the Package of cultural Innovations that had been suggested to have been taken from Africa with migrations that were suggested by the proponents of the 'Out of Africa' Hypothesis had reached Australia. The same applies to South East Asia, where there is no evidence of a 'package'.

See The Eve theory

Out of Africa vs Regional Continuity

Multiregional View versus Regional Replacement

According to Oppenheimer there are 2 contrasting models proposing how and when anatomically modern humans first appeared in Europe and Asia. The postulate of the Multiregional Hypothesis that populations of ***Homo sapiens*** that were differentiated geographically arose independently from a common ancestral population in different regions, speciation being avoided by some level of gene flow between neighbouring populations. As proposed here replacement models maintain that *H. sapiens* arose in Africa between 100 and 200 ka and later left Africa and effectively replaces (with acknowledgement of possibly some admixture [Oppenheimer, 2003, 49]) replaced populations in Europe and Asia.

Limited archaic interbreeding outside Africa

The replacement model, contrary to popular perception, doesn't depend on the assumption of a lack of interfertility, and therefore zero gene flow, and the different indigenous regional populations of humans. If the degree of replacement is ignored both regional and replacement models turn out to have a point, and it is necessary to clarify this point to be able to lay to rest the misassumption that is sometimes made by proponents of the multiregional model that the recent replacement model would necessarily be disproved by any evidence of any degree of admixture (i.e. reticulation) outside Africa, however small (Wolpoff et *al.*, 2000). Replacement is simply implied by degree, not necessarily 100 %, so would not be disproved by some degree of admixture.

Interbreeding with Neanderthals

The recent claims of an introgression of 1-4 % of the Neanderthal genome into Eurasians of "South East Asia" the present raise the issue of interbreeding (Green et *al.*, 2010). Oppenheimer accepts that there is at least a prima facie case, he says that if valid, this evidence is not at variance with the simple view involving complete replacement, or with the unambiguous lack of uniparental evidence pointing to Neanderthal introgression amongst the vast number of uniparental mtDNA/Y genomes already studied. He suggests that it needs to be remembered that the effective population of the haploid uniparental genome would be a quarter that of autosomes. Oppenheimer suggests that the finding of only single African lineages (L3 and M168) in non-African mtDNA and NRY (non-combining region of Y chromosome) respectively excludes the multiregional model at these loci as well as a severe founding drift event. According to Oppenheimer the extinction of minority lineages, such as less than 4 % maximum estimated initial introgression among putative uniparental genetic material acquired from pre-dispersal interbreeding, is likely to have been caused by this drift. Oppenheimer says it is debateable whether such hypothetical extinction of putative acquired uniparental Neanderthal lineages among AMH would have occurred after admixture outside Africa, which is Green's preferred option, but depends on what and how soon admixture occurred following exit and the population sizes involved.

It has been difficult to think of a way a geographic scenario involving the acquisition by East Asians could have acquired simultaneously the same dose of Neanderthal autosomal genes as Europeans acquired other than by the acquisition occurring between exit and before East - West divergence. As Oppenheimer claims, the authors acknowledge that for this to take place the gene flow from Neanderthals into ancestral non-Africans prior to the divergence of European groups from each other (Green et *al.*, 2010, 710) depends exclusively on the single exit hypothesis of AMH, in this case having been recruited to explain autosomal miscegenation.

Large lacunae are left in South Asia by the current distribution of Neanderthal remains in North West Eurasia. The possibility of Neanderthals living in this region as well as Arabia cannot be discounted because no fossil evidence of Neanderthals has been found in this region. If this is the case it may have been in this region that the admixture took place with immigrant AMH populations prior to the differentiation of Europeans from East Asians.

Interbreeding with Denisovans – China

An additional Denisova-related intrusion that was centred on East Asia (mainly China, though extending to 2 populations in South America, has been demonstrated (Skoglund & Jacobsson, 2011), who cast doubt on the 'exclusivity' of the Oceanic Denisovan admixture by adjusting for founding genetic drift that is coupled with ascertainment bias. This result adds to the support for similar references for East Asia that were published 4 months previously (Abi-Rached et *al.*, 2011).

Speculation about which hominin was intrusive and a search for morphological evidence of hybrids would be tempted by a discrete 3rd hominin (Denisova-like) admixture event in China. In that region there is a scarcity of unambiguously archaic candidates that date to less than 100,000 BP. Some large-brained archaic individuals have been found, Xujiayao, Maba and Dali, that were morphologically intermediate between ***H. erectus*** and AMH, though none of them date to earlier than the terminal part of the Middle Pleistocene (Brown, 1999; Kaifu & Fujita, 2012). With regard to a morphological change among AMH that is unexplained, the candidate displaying the change that was sought came surprisingly late, and followed the appearance of conventional AMH fossils from the Late Pleistocene such as those from Upper Cave 101, Zhoukoudian and Liujiang in China (Brown, 1999). The late, sudden appearance throughout East Asia and the New World of *Mongoloid* fossil skulls that were first clearly evidenced in the Asian Early

Holocene-Early Neolithic record, with skulls such as Baoji, appears to have been this change (Brown, 1999). It is possible these features were anticipated by distinctive 'broad-cheeked' older AMH fossils, such as the Minatogawa 1 skull (about 20 ka; Brown, 1999), and more recently Longlin 1, which dates to the transition from the Pleistocene to the Holocene (Curnoe et *al.*, 2012). Oppenheimer suggests that for morphological and age reasons "*Mongolanthropus*" also needs to be mentioned here. It has been suggested that it is possible that the onset of the Late Glacial and Early Holocene warming resulted in conditions that allowed populations to expand from the refugia where they had remained during the worst of the glacial period and interact with each other. It is also suggested that in the Far Eastern refugia of the LGM hybridisation could have already occurred (see elaboration of these 2 expansion-contraction hybridisation scenarios that have been attributed speculatively to Darwin, Hewett & Arnold in Stewart & Stringer, 2012).

Looking for locations of refugia, most known hominin archaeological sites from the LGM in China are north of the Yangtze in Sinodont, northern Mongoloid regions, that might fit dental clines (see figs. 6.3, 5.4, 5.3 in Oppenheimer, 2003), though ascertainment bias is possible. However, as mentioned in the case of Neanderthal intrusion, either model would still need to assume a subsequent bottleneck period of selection or drift, possibly during the Younger Dryas refuge period, which was followed by expansion. As in the case of the Neanderthal story, this would explain the lack of evidence of uniparental admixture, though also the more uniform gracile suites of cranial features that are present in southern and northern Mongoloid populations.

Genetic phylogeography can test several predictions of the recent replacement model, by the use of non-recombinant-DNA such as mtDNA and the NRY. If recent replacement took place outside Africa there should be older lineages within Africa and younger lineages outside Africa, which would depend on the degree of replacement. The first time this was shown unequivocally (Oppenheimer, 2003) was 16 years after the 'Mitochondrial Eve' paper (Cann et *al.*, 1987). This followed improvement of the knowledge concerning the variation of mtDNA that had been improved by a set of complete sequence data from 32 individuals that were distributed around the world (Ingman et al., 2000).

Oppenheimer dated the branches of the world mtDNA tree, that had been reconstructed from those first 52 complete sequences, which showed that there were 2 sister twigs that all non-Africans belonged to (M and N), both were aged at only 70,000 BP, and had arisen from L3, which was one of the youngest of more than 12 branches that originated in Africa. Tens of thousands of mtDNA sequences have since been analysed and this broad conclusion has not been subsequently falsified.

Human Remains from the Pleistocene-Holocene

Transition, South West China, Apparent Complex Evolutionary History for East Asians

Human evolution in the Late Pleistocene in East Asia is still poorly understood as a result of a scarcity of fossils that are well described, classified reliably and dated accurately. Genetic research has indicated that south west China is a hotspot of human diversity, containing lineages of ancient mtDNA and Y-DNA, as well as producing a number of human remains believed to derive from deposits of Pleistocene age. (Curnoe et al., 2012) say they have prepared, reconstructed, described and dated a new partial skull from the sediment block, that has been consolidated, that was collected in 1979 from Longlin Cave, Guangxi Province. New excavations at Maludong, Yunnan Province were undertaken by the authors[1] to clarify the stratigraphy and dating of a large sample of human remains from the site that are mostly undescribed.

A detailed comparison was undertaken by (Curnoe et al., 2012) of crania, including a virtual endocast from the Maludong calotte, mandibular remains from these 2 localities, both samples probably being derived from the same population, which exhibited an unusual combination of traits of modern humans, characters which are probably plesiomorphic for later *Homo*, as well as some unusual features. They dated charcoal by the AMS radiocarbon and speleothem method with the U-series technique, the results showing that both samples were from the Pleistocene-Holocene transition:~ 14.3-11.5 ka.

There are 2 plausible explanations that are suggested by this analysis of the morphology sampled at Longlin Cave and Maludong. The first explanation is that a late-surviving population may possibly parallel the situation of the Dar-es-Soltane and Tamara, North Africa, and maybe also in southern China and Zhirendong. An alternative possibility is that during the Pleistocene multiple waves may have colonised East Asia, with the morphology from Longlin and Maludong possibly reflecting deep population substructure in Africa prior to the dispersal of modern humans into Eurasia.

Europe, Africa and the Levantine corridor connecting them has historically been the focus of human evolution fossil research, resulting in the role of the vast continent of Asia being virtually unknown with regard to the fossil record of humans during this time of the evolution of modern humans. In South Asia the fossil record from the Upper Pleistocene of known human remains contains few human fossils; those that have been found are confined to 2 sites that date from possibly within the 33-25 ka range (Trinkhaus, E., 2005). Human fossils are more numerous in East Asia (Wu, X. & Poirier, 1995), though it has been difficult to assess the significance of these fossils because of the poor knowledge of their geological context and inadequate dating (Trinkhaus, E., 2005, 2-3). East Asia is considered to comprise the region that is bordered by the Ural Mountains in the west, in the south west by the Himalayan Plateau, Bering Strait in the north west, as well as extending into island south west Asia.

The Liujiang skeleton from southern China has been discussed widely as a candidate for the oldest human in East Asia (Wu, X & Poirier, F.E., 1995), though the geological age of this individual has been the subject of "an everlasting dispute since the discovery of the fossil in 1958" (Bräuer, G. & Mímisson, K., 2004, p. 62) because of lack of documentation regarding the exact stratigraphic position of the human remains.

Other similarly problematic specimens are the fossils from the Upper Cave, Zhoukoudian, that have been a major source of uncertainty since their discovery in the 1930s, estimates range from 33-10 ka (Wu, X & Poirier, F.E., 1995, Bräuer, G. & Mímisson, K., 2004). Also, the provenance of the child from Niah Cave in East Malaysia is uncertain (Barker et *al.*, 2007). A proposed age of 45-39 ka for the cranium has been suggested (Barker et *al.*, 2007) as the result of a recent field and lab program that was aimed at assessing the stratigraphy and dating of the deposits at this site.

There is also a problem with most other candidates for the earliest humans in East Asia. The only specimen that is taxonomically diagnostic among the human remains that were recovered from Tabon Cave, Philippines, is a frontal bone that has been assigned to *H. sapiens* (Dizon, E. et al., 2002), that has been dated to 16.5 ± 2 ka (Détroit et al., 2002). Also, the oldest specimen from the site that has been directly dated to 47+11/-10 ka (Détroit, F. et *al.*, 2004), could possibly be from an orang-utan (Dizon, E. et al., 2002). A hominin metatarsal recovered from Callao Cave, Luzon, has been directly dated to an estimated 66.7 ± 1 ka (Mijares A.M., et *al.*, 2010), though it has been difficult to classify this specimen reliably, which has made its assignment to *H. sapiens* uncertain (Mijares A.M., et *al.*, 2010). Recently an individual recovered from Tianyuan Cave, not far from Zhoukoudian town, north east China, has been estimated to be 42-36 ka (Shang, H. et al., 2007). The partial skeleton from Tianyuan is comprised of 34 pieces that appear to be from the same individual, the femur of which has been dated directly to 40,328 ± 816 cal. yr BP. The best candidate for the earliest modern human in East Asia appears to be provided by this specimen, though it is significantly younger (>20 kya) than estimates from genetic clocks for the colonisation of the region. Finally, in Zhirendong, southern China, a mandibular fragment has been recovered that has been dated to more than 100 ka based on stratigraphic grounds, though the specimen is fragmentary and is comprised of a mosaic of archaic and modern characters that make its taxonomic status unclear (Liu, W., et al., 2010; Dennell, R., 2010).

Palaeoanthropologists have needed to rely on genetic sequencing results of samples from living populations to attempt to reconstruct the origins of humans in East Asia because of the uncertainties concerning the human fossil record. It is suggested by genetic research that the earliest modern humans dispersed from Africa into Eurasia about 70-60 ka, after which they spread rapidly into Southeast Asia and Australia (Zhong, H., 2011; Kong, Q-P., 2011; Stoneking M. & Delfin, F., 2010; Rasmussen et al., 2011). Later migrations involved spreading within Eurasia after 40-30 ka adding the founding populations of modern North East Asians and

Europeans (Rasmussen, M. et *al*., 2004). Curnoe, et al. (2012) also suggest that there seem to have been several migrations later within the region, some of which were associated with the Neolithic (Zhong, H., 2011; Kong, Q-P., 2011; Stoneking M. & Delfin, F., 2010), and finally a hominin fossil from Denisova Cave, Central Asia, belonging with the Neanderthal lineage that shares features exclusively with Aboriginal Southeast Asians and Australasians (Reich, D. et *al*., 2010; Reich, D. et al., 2011; Abi-Rached, L., 2011). An interpretation of this has been as 1) evidence that interbreeding occurred between Denisovans and the earliest modern humans colonising the region; and 2) implying that this archaic population occupied Southeast Asia during the Upper Pleistocene (Reich, D. et *al*., 2010; Reich, D. et al., 2011).

A collaborative research project was begun in 2008 (Curnoe et al., 2012) aimed at age determination and to provide detailed comparisons of human remains in south west China that were possibly from the Pleistocene, as the fossils from East Asia are considered to be of central importance to the testing of the regional and global scenarios of the evolution of humans. In this paper (Curnoe et al., 2012) have focused on the human remains recovered from 2 localities: Longlin Cave (Longlin or LL) and Malu Cave (Maludong or MLDG).

In 1979 a petroleum geologist, Li Changqing, discovered the human remains opportunistically in a cave near De'e, Longlin County, Guangxi Zhuang Autonomous Region, Guangxi Province. A short time after the discovery a block of consolidated fine-grained sediment that contained the human remains was taken to Kunming in the neighbouring province of Yunnan. At the time it was taken to Kunming a partial mandible and some post-cranial bone were prepared from the block (Wu, X & Poirier, 1995), the remainder of the skull and more post-cranial bones were prepared from the sediment by Curnoe's team in 2010. A thin flowstone was found that was adhering to the surface of the vault of the partial LL 1 skeleton, and fragments of charcoal were recovered from the sediment within the endocrinal cavity. The association of the cranium, mandible and postcranial elements, all with similar preservation, in a small block of sediment, less than 1 m^3 in volume, suggests there was limited post-depositional disturbance. The cave has been closed to the public and the Curnoe team have not been able to carry out the research needed to clarify the stratigraphy and geological context of the human remains.

Located near the city of Mengzi, Honghe Prefecture, Hani and Yi Autonomous Region, to the southeast of Yunnan Province, Maludong is a cave that has been partially mined (Wu, X & Poirier, 1995; Zhang et al., 1991). A Chinese team that included 1 of the Curnoe's team, BZ, originally excavated the site in 1989, at which time most of the fossil and archaeological material were recovered (Zhang et al., 1991). A re-evaluation of the remaining stratigraphic section and the collection of a number of samples that were to be used for dating and archaeomagnetic analysis were allowed by excavations undertaken in 2008 by several of the present authors (DC, JX, AH, BK, BZ, ZY and LY). During the current study more human remains were recovered, both during the small-scale excavation by (Curnoe et *al*., 2012) 50x50x370 cm, for stratigraphic analysis, as well as from unstudied and unsorted fossils that were recovered during the 1989 field season.

Discussion

A range of individual features and a composite of characters that have not been seen among populations from the Pleistocene or recent *H. sapiens* populations are presented by the human skull recovered from Longlin Cave, and the human calotte, partial mandibles and teeth from Maludong. According to Curnoe et al. (2012) the remains share no particular affinity with either East Asians from the Pleistocene, such as Liujiang or Upper Cave 101, or recent East Asians. It is also suggested that these features belong to multiple developmental-functional complexes (Enlow, D.H. & Hans, M.G., 2008), which span the neurocranial vault, and include endocranium, cranial base, facial skeleton, mandible and dentition. Where they can be assessed, the metrical dimensions that are involved are mostly characterised by moderate to high heritability (Sjøvold T., 1984; Carson A.E., 2006; Sherwood R.J. et *al*., 2008; Townsend GC, Brown T., 1978). It seems likely that both samples are from the same population, given their morphological similarity, close geographical proximity, less than 300 km apart, and a geological age that is younger, Pleistocene-Holocene transition.

Multivariate analysis of the shape of the vault, a method which has been shown to track neutral genetic distances (Weaver, T.D., Roseman, C.C. & Stringer, C.B., 2007), indicates a picture that is somewhat mixed with respect to the phenetic affinities of LL 1 and MLDG 1704. The first principal component, which accounts for 45-46 % of the total variance, indicates that the dominant phenetic signal in these analyses shows that LL 1 and MLDG 1704 are at the edge of variation within *H. sapiens* from the Pleistocene, and in some analyses they are also shown to be on the edge of variability of *H. erectus*. Principal component 3 in particular, 12-14 % of total variance, shows them to exhibit a cranial shape that is unique among all hominins from the Pleistocene.

The conclusion, that these remains show affinities with *H. sapiens* is supported by a range of features:

Neurocranium:

Moderately projecting and laterally thin supraorbital part, which has the bipartite form in MLDG 1704; frontal bone with a moderate chord and arc length, but broad maximum width; and an endocast with long, broad and tall frontal lobes.

Viscerocranium:

Superior facial breadth is narrow; facial skeleton is vertically short (superior facial height and orbit height and nasal length; and nasal breadth relative to height is moderate.

Mandible:

Mental foramen is in mesial position; and a medial pterygoid tubercle is absent.

Dentition:

Anterior dental crowns are small (narrow).

The fossils from Longlin and Maludong also have many features that are either rare or missing from *H. sapiens* from either the Pleistocene or the present, many of which are plesiomorphies included among later *Homo*, including :

Neurocranium:

Endocranial volume is moderate; frontal squama high arched; parietal bones are short; short parietal lobes on endocast; postorbital region is narrow; and bipartite supraorbital morphology is lacking in LL 1.

Cranial base:

In LL 1 only there is a long mandibular fossa (A-P), broad (M – L) and deep (S – I).

Viscerocranium:

In LL 1 only: alveolar prognathism is strong; mid-face is flat at both the nasal root and zygomatic process of the maxilla; facial skeleton is broad (interorbital, bizygomatic and bimaxillary); nasal bones very narrow; piriform aperture is broad; canine fossa lacking and deep *sulcus maxillaris* is present; laterally flared zygomatic arch; strongly angled zygomatic to the extent that its inferior margin is well lateral to the superior part; small zygomatic tubercle that is lateral to a line projected from the orbital pillar (anterior aspect); attachment area of anterior masseter marked by broad deep sulcus;

lateral orbital pillar (lateral aspect) has strong transverse incurvation; anterior wall of the zygomaticoalveolar root placed anteriorly (above P^4/M^1).

Mandible:
Sagittal keel and distinct Lateral tubercles absent; chin small (MLDG 1706 Rank 3, LL 1 Rank ?3); mandibular foramen bridging (MLDG 1706); transverse tori thickened; mandibular notch asymmetrical (MLDG 1679); lateral positioning of retromolar space, crest of mandibular notch (MLDG 1679); and anterior symphyseal angle is low (MLDG 1706).

Dentition;

Post-canine crowns broad (BL diameters large); and molars are taurodont.

See Source 1 for a detailed description of features supporting the inclusion of these remains in *H. sapiens*.

It is unusual, especially in Eurasia to find human remains with such a combination of modern human (*H. sapiens*) and archaic (putative plesiomorphic) characters. There are several Pleistocene remains in Africa that also display a combination of modern features with plesiomorphies of putative later *Homo*; from Klasies River Mouth Cave (Smith F.H., 1992) and Hofmeyr (Crevecoeur, I. et al., 2009), South Africa, Iwo Eleru, Nigeria (Harvati, K. et *al.*, 2011), Nazlet Khater, Egypt, and Dar-es-Soltane and Témara, Morocco (Trinkhaus, E., 2005; Trinkhaus, E., 2007; Crevecoeur, I. et al., 2009). Though most of them are much older than Longlin and Maludong: Dar-es-Soltane and Témara are not dated, but they are associated with Aterian lithic assemblages dated recently to between 107 ± 3 ka and 96 ± 4 ka at another site in Morocco, La Grotte des Contrebandiers, (Jacob, Z., et al, 2011); the remains from Klasies River Mouth are from 2 units dating to more than 101 ka and more than 104-64 ka (Millard, A.R., 2008); Nazlet Khater 2 is possibly ≈ 42 ka (Millard, A.R., 2008); and Hofmeyr 36.2 ± 3.3 ka (Grine, F.E. et *al.*, 2007). The Iwo Eleru calvaria has, however, been dated to ~ 16.3-11.7 ka (Harvati, K. et al., 2011), and Curnoe et al. say it is clearly of similar age to the remains from China.

Outside of Africa there are various fossils from the Upper Pleistocene that have also been described as exhibiting an unusual mosaic or characters (e.g. Trinkhaus, E., 2007). Some of them, such as from Israel, Skhul and Qafzeh, and in Romania, Pestera cu Oase were included in the analyses carried out by the authors[1], and overall they appear to be metrically well within the range for *H. sapiens* from the Pleistocene. The former (Levantine) samples, however, exhibit some similarities, in univariate comparisons, to LL 1 and MLDG 1704.

The problem that needs to be answered is how to explain this unusual morphology that is present in the Pleistocene-Holocene transition in East Asia. It is suggested (Curnoe et al., 2012) the Longlin and Maludong remains could represent individuals that were very robust within an Epipalaeolithic population that was previously unknown in south west China. They also consider this explanation to be unsatisfactory because there are several features that are apparently unique that are present, which are combined with an unusual mix of modern and archaic features is seen in several specimens spanning multiple developmental-functional complexes, as mentioned above. Curnoe et al., (2012) suggest that this hypothesis could be invoked as an explanation for the morphology seen in the remains recovered from Klasies River Mouth Cave, Hofmeyr, Iwo Eleru, Nazlet Khater, Dar-es-Soltane, Témara and Zhirendong, though it has not been because many of their archaic features are rare or not present among *H. sapiens*. As is indicated strongly here, the same situation applies to the remains from Longlin and Maludong.

It has been suggested (Curnoe et *al.*, 2012) there are explanations that are more plausible, a possibility being that the remains from Longlin and Maludong represent an archaic population that were late surviving, possibly similar to that sampled at Dar-es-Soltane, Témara (Trinkhaus, E., 2005; Trinkhaus, E., 2007; Crevecoeur, I. & Trinkhaus, E., 2004) There is problem with this suggestion as the morphology of these remains from North Africa is not well known, and their affinities and taxonomy are uncertain (Trinkhaus, E., 2005; Trinkhaus, E., 2007; Crevecoeur, I. & Trinkhaus, E., 2004). In East Asia the Zhirendong mandibular fragment that has been described recently also has a mosaic of modern and plesiomorphic characters that causes problems with the taxonomy of the fossil (Kaifu, Y. & Fujita, M., 2012; Liu, W. et al., 2010; Dennell, R., 2010). Though it has been dated based on stratigraphy to more than 100 ka (Liu, W.

et *al.*, 2010), which is of a similar age to that of the Aterian assemblage from North Africa, but much older than Longlin and Maludong. The site at Salkhit, Mongolia, contains another specimen that has also been described recently has also been described as being of an archaic taxon that is unspecified (Coppens, Y. et al., 2008). A preliminary date of ~20 ka has apparently been reported, though dating is uncertain (Kaifu, Y. & Fujita, M., 2012). Also, there have been expressions of doubts about its archaic affinities (Kaifu, Y. & Fujita, M., 2012), and Curnoe et al. (2012) could not include this specimen in their analyses because they found errors in the measurements in this and other specimens in Table 1 of Coppens et *al.* Coppens, Y. et al., 2008).

It is also possible that the Longlin and Maludong remains retained a large number of ancestral polymorphisms in a population of *H. sapiens*. Where features of interest are also present in allopatric populations of the same taxon the concept of lineage sorting that is incomplete is often invoked as an explanation (Mavárez, J. & Linares, M., 2008). Related to this it has been suggested by recent morphological studies that *H. sapiens* were deeply geographically subdivided in the Pleistocene within Africa prior to its dispersal into Eurasia (Gunz, P. et al., 2009). The same explanation has also been invoked to explain the unusual morphology of the Iwo Eleru calvaria (Harvati, K. et al., 2009). At Longlin and Maludong the morphology that has been documented might be interpreted with this hypothesis, the remains from China possibly sampling a human population that was unknown previously (or a migration?) that may not have contributed genetically to recent East Asians. Attempts to extract DNA from a Maludong specimen has to date been unsuccessful, as there is a lack of recoverable genetic material.

Either way, the unusual morphology sampled at Longlin and at Maludong during the Pleistocene-Holocene transition indicates that in East Asia human history is more complex than has been suspected previously. It also highlights the need for more research in the region (Curnoe et *al.*, 2012).

Interbreeding with Denisovans in Oceania

There is an alternative scenario that Green et al. (2010) didn't consider for that publication, though as co-authors, they subsequently offered in the context of the hominin phalanx and molar tooth, Middle Palaeolithic/Upper Palaeolithic transitional context in Denisova Cave, Southern Siberia (Kraus et *al.*, 2010; Reich et *al.*, 2010) that were recently sequenced, is the possibility that AMH interbred with other non-Neanderthal populations, such as **H. Heidelbergensis**, or descendants of **H. erectus** that were moving from China to Central Asia.

In the first report of the Leipzig group (Krause et *al.*, 2010) argued from the complete mtDNA of the phalanx that the Denisovan lineage had long ago branched off (1.04 Ma, CI: 0.779-1.3 Ma, so that the Neanderthal and the modern human lineages are more closely related to each other (0.493 Ma, CI: 0.3744-0.6121 Ma) than either were to Denisova.

They reported in their second publication another complete mtDNA sequence, that was from the tooth, which proved to be very close, though not identical, to that of the phalanx that had been recovered from the same site, and this indicated the presence in the cave of 2 'Denisovan' individuals that were very similar to each other at the mitochondrial locus, and which confirmed the phylogenetic age estimates, with a slightly reduced error (0.982 Ma, CI: 0.7805-1.208 Ma. The Denisova tooth was shown to group tightly with early **Homo** specimens morphologically (**Australopithecines, H. habilis**, and African **H. erectus**) all of which had teeth that were significantly larger than a group that was more modern that contained Neanderthals, **H. heidelbergensis** and all other European humans, both ancient and modern, all AMH, and **H. erectus** from China. Specimens from **H. erectus** in Indonesia tended to be intermediate between the 2 groups. A massive, splayed lingual root is another non-metric feature that grouped the Denisovan tooth with the **erectus** types. For 2 other genetic comparisons, in offline material, the Leipzig group displayed Venn diagrams of autosomal segmental duplications that show that those held in common, first between a human of the present (NA18507), a Neanderthal, Denisova and a chimpanzee, then between Neanderthal, Denisova and a human from the present. The modern and Neanderthal in each case shared most segmental duplications with each other and least with Denisova (Reich et *al.*, 2010).

According to Oppenheimer these 4 comparisons, 3 of which were genetic and 2 morphological are all consistent with each other, first in making the Denisova the biological outgroup when it was compared with the European group that were related closely to each other (AMH, Neanderthals and *H. Heidelbergensis*), though further it could imply that Denisova could have descended from an earlier African population. Martinón-Torres (2010) has argued the case for a Eurasian origin for Denisova.

In the second Denisovan paper (Reich et *al.*, 2010) also reported extensive sequencing which they claimed shows that 4-6 % of provisional autosomal signatures obtained from the Denisovan finger bone were found in 3 Melanesians, 2 Papuans and a Bougainvillean, though not in any of the other groups of modern humans they tested, African: San, Yoruba and Mbuti; 5 "Eurasians": French, Han Chinese, Sardinian, Cambodian, and Mongolian; and South American: Karitiana. The inclusive or exclusive geographical scenario could be consistent with ancestral Oceanic AMH mixing, not with *H. erectus* from North China, but with *H. erectus* in the region of Indonesia of the present, given all the genetic and morphological observations summarised so far.

It has been suggested that 'Solo Man' was a version of *H. erectus* that was significantly larger brained than *H. erectus* from Ngandong and Sambungmacan in central Java, may have survived to only 27 ± 2 to 53.3 ± 4 ka (Swisher et *al.*, 1996), and as this was controversial the regional distinction is important. Some of the same researchers revisited the site because of the high degree of controversy about the dates obtained the first time, the results of this study were dates that were higher, but were conflicting, the youngest being an ESR/U-series date of 143 ka (+20/-17) (Indriati et *al.*, 2011; see Dennell Ch. 4). Oppenheimer suggests that whether or not the first dates were correct these evolved *H. erectus* descendants could be brought to the Upper Pleistocene.

It was argued for a closer descent relationship between Neanderthals and the Denisovan hominin, than either had with AMH (Reich et *al.*, 2010), though in view of the erectine links and the range of the genetic and morphological evidence, which Oppenheimer found surprising. The change in emphasis was based on another comparison, autosomal SNPs (single nucleotide polymorphisms) between Denisovans, chimpanzees, and Neanderthals, though based on the relative degree of sharing of SNPs that were distinctive to Neanderthals. According to Oppenheimer the results and implications of the latter were different when compared with the previously mentioned 4 genetic and morphological comparisons, and the simple explanation for this is that they didn't test for Neanderthal-Denisovan admixture.

He suggests the strength of the evidence their assertion is based on for more recent common descent for the 2 archaic groups was not as convincing as that for the simple intrusion of Neanderthal into AMH. According to Oppenheimer this is the result of not testing a more likely explanation for the autosomal SNP associations between Neanderthals and Denisovans in this more complicated 3-group interbreeding puzzle. Prior to the arrival of AMH, that would have been extended direct hybrid interbreeding between the 2 archaic human groups locally in Central Asia, as supported by their geographical, physical and temporal overlap, which is consistent with the presence of Neanderthal mtDNA in that part of Central Asia (as shown in Okladnikov Cave, not far from Denisova Cave; Krause et *al.*, 2007b). Oppenheimer suggests interbreeding would constitute only admixture, of course not recent descent, and could be the explanation for the extraordinary plesiomorphy as seen in the "*Mongolanthropus*" that was discovered recently at Salkhit in Mongolia. This skullcap fragment, that has marked superciliary arches "shows multiple similarities with Neanderthals, Chinese ***Homo erectus***, and west/Far East archaic ***Homo sapiens***" (Coppens et *al.*, 2008; but see also Kaifu & Fujita, 2012), who mention its dating of 20,000 BP and regard it as within the range of Late Pleistocene AMH.

The comparison of autosomal SNPs was in Denisovans with a variety of those from a number of different Eurasian populations in the paper by Reich et *al.*, (2010) was the result that Oppenheimer found to be most interesting which revealed that Denisova shared 4-6 % of its genetic material with Melanesians of the present in the Pacific, which are a quarter of the globe away from Denisova Cave, though not with any other population that was closer to the Cave. Other research (Rasmussen, 2011) has shown that there is the possibility of archaic admixture in Oceania was reinforced by the discovery of Denisovan admixture in an Aboriginal man [from the far south west of Western Australia who allowed a lock of his hair to be taken 100 years ago, before European colonisation reached his area] that was similar in degree to that found in Melanesians. It was also postulated (Rasmussen et *al*., 2011) that 2 dispersals of AMH populations that were African-derived, into Australia: the first occurring 72,000-62,000 years ago, and a later dispersal 38,000-25,000 years ago. Oppenheimer suggests their interpretations were influenced by selective use of autosomal-dating of demographic events, which had not been supported archaeologically. Oppenheimer suggests that their analysis and interpretation of the phylogeny of ancestral populations depends, as in the case of Green et *al*., (2010), on a statistical association test that is based on only 4 complete genomes, and not on any genetic phylogeny.

Oppenheimer suggests the results of (Rasmussen et *al*., 2011) still extend the 'Denisovan DNA' influence in Oceania more broadly into the Sahul region (as predicted, Oppenheimer, 2012b) and do not falsify the consensus of a single AMH exit model that is the preferred option in this book[1]. As Oppenheimer points out there is skeletal evidence that would reverse the morphological order of their "two Australian waves" as the earliest human crania known from Australia are gracile and more modern in appearance, though robust skulls at the Kow Swamp and Coobool Creek sites have an archaic appearance, and have a radiocarbon date of at most 14,300 years ago (Brown, 1992).

A more recent study (Reich et *al*., 2011) has extended this antipodean problem by reporting an extra 33 more locations in Asia, Southeast Asia and Oceania. The 15 populations tested on the eastern side of Huxley's line, which include 1 Negrito and 1 non-negrito group, in the southern Philippines, Near Oceania and Polynesia, show significant evidence of Denisovan intrusion, as high as, but no higher, than that found in Melanesians (i.e. near Oceanians), and now a similar level has been found in Australians. To the west of the Huxley Line 27 Asian and Southeast Asian (SEA) populations, that included 2 Negrito groups, none show any significant evidence of such intrusion, according to Reich's analysis. Therefore it appears all admixtures occurred offshore in Wallacea or Sahul, as the true eastern limit of the Asian mainland up to 10,000 years ago. It is possible more westerly admixture with later extinction is possible, though it is much less likely.

Oppenheimer suggests relevant questions about these findings are how many times, from where, and when? In the case of the Philippines the results of relative admixture are all consistent with a single proximate common source of Denisovan admixture: Wallacea, Australia or New Guinea along with subsequent fresh external diluting with AMH gene flow. In Wallacea, Oceania and the Philippines the non-Denisovan admixture analysis shows that New Guinea and Australia are tightly correlated, major alternative candidate sources of AMH gene flow for the Pacific Region, though Australia is consequently the richer one, overall by 40 %. If Near Oceania was the primary dispersal source, the apparent anomaly could still be compatible with it, though with the New Guinea highlands (Gosden, 2010; See Summerhayes & Ford)[1], having gone through founding event(s), isolation and subsequently drift, a scenario that is inferred from shared human leucocyte leukocyte antigen (HLA) markers (Serjeantson & Hill, 1989). Based on geographic considerations Wallacea (Nusa Tenggarah and/or Moluccas) still seems the most parsimonious Denisovan source. A plot of individuals' Denisovan admixture against Near Oceania (New Guinea) admixture has been constructed (Reich et al., 2011) which shows tight correlation and high values of Denisovan admixture (ranges from 30-100 % for Wallacea and Fiji, and this speculation is consistent with that plot. Polynesians, though they group together with the lower end of the distribution for Wallacea, with lower values of 20-30 %, and still correlating with admixtures as found in Near Oceania, have been shown to have consistently less Denisovan intrusion than they would be expected to have had from that admixture, which Oppenheimer suggests is a likely result of later South eastern Asia admixture and drift.

When compared with the other 13 sites the south Philippines are anomalous, as 3-4 times more Denisovan intrusion is shown than would be expected from their Near Oceanian (i.e. non-Denisovan) admixture values and no clear correlation with them. A separate admixture event and subsequent dispersal is probably indicated by this, though north Wallacia could still be the source region.

It is suggested in Melanesians and Australians, the similar, asymptotic Denisovan intrusion that the main admixture event occurred in a single source population before Sahul was colonised, and this probably occurred in Wallacea. The paucity of regional samples from Sahul, which could allow for subsequent migrations or even admixture events, is a caveat on the above fresh inferences.

Denisovan Admixture and the First Modern Human Dispersal into Southeast Asia and Oceania

Recent genetic research has shown that the ancestors of the native population of New Guinea and the people of Bougainville have inherited part of their genetic material from Denisovans. There has been only sparse sampling of Southeast Asian and Oceanian populations for analysis. In this paper Reich et *al*. quantify the admixture of Denisovan genetic material in 33 additional populations from Asia and Oceania. Genetic material from Denisovans has been inherited by Australian Aboriginals, Near Oceanians, Polynesians, Fijians, east Indonesians (west New Guineans), and Mamanwa (a "Negrito" group from the Philippines), though populations from mainland East Asia, western Indonesia, Jehai (a Negrito group from Malaysia), and Onge (a negrito group from the Andaman Islands), have not inherited Denisovan genetic material. It is indicated by these results that the flow of genes from Denisovans occurred into common ancestors of New Guineans, Australians, and Mamanwa, though not into the ancestors of the Jehai and Onge which also indicates that relatives of East Asians of the present were not in Southeast Asia when the genes from Denisovans entered the genomes of those who received the Denisovan genes. The findings of this study, the descendants of the earliest inhabitants of Southeast Asia do not all have the admixture of Denisovan genetic material is not consistent with a history in which the interbreeding with Denisovans took place in mainland Asia after which it spread over Southeast Asia, leading to all of the earliest modern human inhabitants of South East Asia having the admixture. Instead of this the most parsimonious interpretation of the data suggests the Denisovan gene flow actually occurred in Southeast Asia. According to this scenario archaic Denisovans must have occupied an extraordinary extensive territory stretching from Siberia to tropical Asia.

Discussion

It has been shown by this study that modern humans settled Southeast Asia in waves: The ancestors of the present-day Onge, Jehai, Mamanwa, New Guineans, and Australians, some of whom admixed with Denisovans, and a second wave that contributed much of the ancestry of the present East Asians and Indonesians. Reich et al. suggest that this scenario in which the human dispersals are broadly consistent with the archaeologically-motivated hypothesis that there was an early migration by the southern route that led to the colonisation of Southeast Asia (2) though it also clarifies this scenario. In particular, no evidence of multiple dispersals of modern humans out of Africa is provided by the data of Reich et al., as all non-Africans have amounts of Neanderthal DNA that are statistically indistinguishable (12,18). The data produced by this study are instead consistent with a single dispersal out of Africa (as has been proposed by some southern route hypotheses (1), from which there were then multiple dispersals to South and East Asia.

According to Reich et al. this study also provides a clue concerning the geographic location of the flow of Denisovan genes. It is difficult to use genetic data from populations of the present to infer the location of demographic events in the past with a high degree of confidence, given the high mobility of human populations. It has been found that Denisovan genetic material is present in eastern South East Asians and Oceanians, which includes Mamanwa, Australian Aboriginals and New Guineans, but not in west Asians, the Onge and Jehai, or from the north west, the Eurasian continent, which suggests that the location of the interbreeding may have been in South East Asia. The results from the study reported in this paper uncovered further evidence from locations in South East Asia of ancient gene flow from relatives of the Onge and Jehai into the common ancestors of Australian Aboriginals and New Guineans following the initial flow of genes from Denisovans; and it is suggested by this that the ancestors of both these groups, though not East Asiana, were present in the region at the time. Reich et al. suggest that an alternative history in which some genetic material of Denisovans was initially present throughout South East Asia – which was subsequently displaced by subsequent migrations of populations related to populations of present-day East Asians – though such a history cannot, according to Reich et *al.*, parsimoniously explain the absence of Denisovan genetic material in the Onge and Jehai. It is therefore suggested by the evidence from South East Asian locations for the Denisovan admixture, which has been presented in this paper, that the Denisovans were spread throughout a wider ecological and geographic region, stretching from the deciduous forests of Siberia to the tropics, than any hominin other than modern humans.

Reich et *al.* suggest this study is methodically important as it shows that there is much to learn about the relationships among modern humans by the analysis of patterns of genetic material that was contributed by archaic humans. Archaic genetic material is easily detected in the genomes of a modern human, even if only a small proportion of the ancestry is contributed, as the archaic genetic material is highly divergent; this makes possible the use of archaic genetic material to study the ancient gene flow in the same manner as dye material that has been injected into a medical patient allows the tracing of blood vessels. Reich et *al.* suggest a priority for future research should be to obtain direct dates for the gene flow from Neanderthals and Denisovans, as these will provide a better understanding of interactions among Neanderthals, Denisovans and ancestral populations of the modern human populations of the present.

Reich, D., N. Patterson, M. Kircher, F. Delfin, Madhusudan R. Nandineni, I. Pugach, Albert M.-S. Ko, Y.-C. Ko, Timothy A. Jinam, Maude E. Phipps, N. Saitou, A. Wollstein, M. Kayser, S. Pääbo and M. Stoneking "Denisova Admixture and the First Modern Human Dispersals into South East Asia and Oceania." The American Journal of Human Genetics **89**(4): 516-528.

Did the Denisovans Cross Wallace's Line?

Genetic evidence has been found of the hybridisation of Denisovans (Krause et *al.*, 2010; Reich et al., 2010) with populations of modern humans in Island Southeast Asia, Australia, and the Pacific (Reich et al., 2011), a situation that was completely unexpected. The Denisovan genome (Meyer et al., 2012) reference specimen, from a young girl's distal phalanx, was recovered from Denisova Cave that is geographically distant, in the Altai Mountains of Russia. 3 mitochondrial genomes from material in the cave, that was dated by associated faunas (Gibbons, 2011) that have been poorly dated to more than 50,000 BP. The Denisovan population had a larger overall size, in the long term, than the Neanderthals (Pääbo, 2013; Pennisi, 2013) which suggests the Denisovans were previously widespread across the East Asian mainland. Interbreeding with modern humans appears to have occurred only in Island South East Asia, and such a situation would require marine crossings, which would raise questions about the Denisovan distribution and fossil record in Island South East Asia.

The distribution of modern populations that contain detectable amounts of Denisovan DNA is unexpected as there are no known such populations in mainland Asia. Introgressed DNA referred to a small amount of DNA from a species that is found in the DNA from another species. Islands to the east of Wallace's Line are the only places where Denisovan DNA has been found. The isolated Aboriginal populations of New Guinea and Australia, with about 3-4 % (Meyer et al., 2012), are the populations of modern humans, though lower percentages have been found in a range of populations in Island South East Asia. Early South East Asian hunter-gatherers and later Neolithic farmers (Reich et al., 2012) are believed to be ancestral to groups in this area,

The border between ecosystems dominated by placental mammals to the west, Wallace's Line (Huxley, 1868), one of the biggest biogeographic disjunctions in the world, and Lydekker's Line, that is less well-known, the border that has the ecosystems dominated by marsupials to the east, with only 2 terrestrial mammals known to have crossed it, anatomically modern humans and rats. Wallacea is a zone of biological transition situated between Wallace's Line and Lydekker's Line, and an area that needs to be crossed by any animals migrating between Asia and Australia. A separate dispersal across Wallace's Line is indicated by the discovery in 2003 of the "Hobbit", ***Homo floresiensis*** (Morwood & Jungers, 2009), while a foot bone from Callao in the Philippines, from about 67,000 BP represents a small-bodied hominin, the taxonomic affiliation of which is unknown (Stewart & Stringer, 2010). It is suggested that other hominin species had the capacity to cross the powerful ocean currents that formed and maintain Wallace's Line, even at times of low sea level, though these taxa remain enigmatic.

The diverse ecological range of Denisovans appears to have covered mainland Asia and Island South East Asia. Cooper & Stringer (2013) suggest the large historical population size that is inferred is consistent with the use of extensive regions of savannah on the Sunda Shelf that was exposed as a refugium during glacial phases of the Pleistocene (Stewart & Stringer, 2012). During climatic cycles the exposed shelf would have allowed migration, northwards and southwards.

The Denisovan DNA gene flow into modern human populations somewhere on the Asian mainland might have been suggested by the location of the Denisovan reference specimens in the Altai Mountains, before it spread throughout the South East Asian region. Overwriting by the DNA of incoming East Asian populations in areas other than Island South East Asia is suggested by Cooper & Stringer (2013) to be possibly the easiest explanation of the lack of Denisovan introgression in current mainland populations. No evidence was found, however, by analysis of the indigenous negrito/hunter-gatherer populations of Malaysia and the Andaman Islands, which revealed there was no introgression of Denisovan DNA, in spite of the Andaman Islanders being isolated for a long period of time, show no admixture with other populations of East Asia (Reich et al., 2011). Genomic analysis of an ancient modern human from China, Tianyuan, about 40,000 BP, did not detect any Denisovan DNA (Fu et al., 2013), which Cooper & Stringer (2013)suggest argues against the existence of a prehistoric interbreeding signal that has been overwritten.

According to Cooper & Stringer (2013) these observations, together, argue for no introgression of Denisovan DNA on the Asian mainland. The source of Denisovan gene flow appears to have been to the east of Wallace's Line, with the missing Denisovan DNA in mainland populations being explained by the limitation of the reverse dispersal of introgressed populations by Wallace's Line. The Denisovan-introgressed populations outside of Australia and New Guinea appeared to have been diluted by subsequent movement of East Asian/Neolithic modern humans, and also carried the signal further throughout the area and across the Pacific (Reich at al.,

2011). ***Homo floresiensis*** is the only hominin that has been well characterised to have crossed Wallace's Line prior to modern humans, their affinities still remaining enigmatic, though it is suggested by morphological analyses of their remains that they derived from an early ***Homo erectus***, or possibly even more primitive species (Morwood & Jungers, 2009). An early presence is supported by a stone tool record on Flores that dated to more than 1 Ma (Morwood & Jungers, 2009). Trying to identify ***Homo floresiensis*** as a regional representative of Denisovans, in spite of its presence beyond Wallace's Line, is difficult to reconcile with the enlarged molars of the Denisovans, and the divergence date of modern human populations from Denisovans which has been estimated by using DNA at about 1 Ma, or 170,000-700,000 years ago with genomic data (Meyer et al., 2012).

According to recent reports the Denisovan genome contains large amounts of introgressed Neanderthal genomic DNA (Pääbo, 2013; Pennisi, 2013), which has been suggested to possibly relate to the considerable differences between these estimates of the divergence dates. Estimates of both phylogenetic relationships and genomic divergence dates between Neanderthals, Denisovans, and modern humans will be affected by this. An alternative suggestion is that the older mitochondrial divergence date of about 1 Ma may reflect the input of more Ancient Asian populations or possibly all the dates are overestimates that result from the temporal dependency of molecular rates, and the erroneous low rate that is produced by the distant chimp-human external calibration (Ho et al., 2011).

Cooper & Stringer (2013) have therefore inferred that ***Homo floresiensis*** was an endemic species with a lineage that originated at least 1 Ma, which was restricted to a small region of Wallacea, while the Denisovans probably arrived during the mid-Pleistocene, sometime after 600,000 years ago, and then spread more widely in the region. To the east of the line the Denisovans may be represented by the Callao specimen in the Philippines, or possibly have not yet been recognised. In Asia, other enigmatic hominin remains - from Narmada (India) and Dali, Jinniushan, Maba, and Xujiayao (China) - may represent the Denisovan population that was apparently previously more extensive, or possibly yet other species.

It has also been reported that the Denisovan genome also contains a small contribution from another archaic population that is unknown at the present (Pääbo, 2013; Pennisi, 2013). A question is whether the Denisovans interbred with a more ancient species, such as ***H. erectus***, ***H. antecessor***, or possibly a ***H. heidelbergensis*** in Asia (Stringer, 2012). The genomic divergence may be compatible with a recent model, given the uncertainties of the molecular dates, that suggests modern humans, Neanderthals and Denisovans are a trichotomy that originated from ***H. heidelbergensis***, a species that was widely dispersed in the Middle Pleistocene, possibly about 400,000 BP (Stringer, 2012). Tantalising glimpses of a diversity of hominin groups is all that can be obtained from the fragmentary and disparate fossil record of East Asia. Across Wallacea the apparently widespread distribution of early hominins, exemplified by the discoveries on Flores and in the Philippines, raises the possibility that they may have extended to the Sahul Shelf, as well as regions such as Australia and New Guinea. There is a question as to why the gene flow between Denisovans and modern human populations occur primarily mainly east of the Wallace Line and not the mainland of Asia. The first groups of modern humans to encounter the established Denisovan populations were likely to have been of very limited size, given that the intentional dispersal to Wallacea would require the use of watercraft. Either interbreeding may be more likely under these circumstances, or any interbreeding occurring is more likely to be preserved as a signal in descendants. Gene flow from the Denisovans is suggested by genomic evidence to have been largely male-mediated, providing some clues regarding the nature of the interactions (Meyer et al., 2012). Additionally, rapid dispersal of modern humans into Wallacea is likely to have subjected them to a wide range of pathogens they had previously not been exposed to, with the result that alleles for disease resistance that were obtained by hybridisation with native populations may have had selective advantages (Abi-Rached et al., 2011). The first group of modern humans to leave Africa, also probably of limited size, similarly appear to have interbred with the established Neanderthal populations they initially encountered in western Asia (Green et al., 2012). According to Cooper & Stringer (2013)an anticipated wealth of new genomic data are set to illuminate still more the nature of interactions between modern humans and Neanderthals and Denisovans, as well as the extent and the possible functionality of the DNA exchanged.

Pleistocene Seafaring - Sahul

Seafaring in prehistoric times, defined by the authors as the deliberate, place-to-place, open-ocean voyaging, is usually thought to have begun about 10,000 BP. Some have proposed that it must have begun much earlier, as archaeological evidence indicates that the first arrival of humans during the Pleistocene on the coast of Sahul, Greater Australia, comprised of Australia and New Guinea, occurred much earlier than 10,000 BP, possibly as early as 60,000 BP, though O'Connell, Allen & Hawkes (2008) suggest dates of 45,000-46,000 BP. O'Connell, Allen & Hawkes (2008) suggest that, despite the apparently solid evidence from archaeology, this is often ignored, at least in part because of unfamiliarity with the prehistory of Australia, but mostly because of a narrowly inductive approach to the archaeological record and a widespread reluctance to credit the innovative and adaptive capabilities of early modern humans, those ancestral to the Australian Aborigines in particular O'Connell, Allen & Hawkes (2008).

O'Connell, Allen & Hawkes (2008) have developed an argument for the early origin of seafaring, together with the underlying coastal and marine economies, emphasising the Sahul data, as well as reviewing the information relating to the initial settlement of Sahul (Greater Australia) and the identity of the first to arrive, that was current in 2008.

O'Connell, Allen & Hawkes (2008) divide the area into 4 parts (Fig.1). Sahul is at the centre, at present represented by Australia and its continental islands. Large areas of the continental shelf have been exposed repeatedly during the last several million years by glacio-eustatic fluctuations of the sea level, forming a single landmass from New Guinea to Tasmania at times when the sea was low enough to expose the continental shelf sufficiently.

The Sunda shelf, to the west of the Australian continent, comprises the Malay Peninsula and the western Indonesian islands. At times of low sea level there was a large sub-continental peninsula that extended from the present SE Asian mainland through Borneo and Java to the east.

The Wallacean Archipelago, 1,500 km wide, lies between Sunda and Sahul. Its overall extent has been reduced periodically as a result of falling sea levels, which increased the size of the islands, though it never connected Sunda to Sahul by dry land in the time period in question. It was much more than 1,000 km wide, west to east, even when the sea level was 120 m lower than that of the present. There are 2 main routes across it - in the north, Sulawesi through Halmahera or Ceram, and Lombok through Timor in the south. Island-hopping along either route would require 8-17 crossings (Birdsell, 1977). There is at least 1 crossing of more than 70 km and 3 of more than 30 km, whichever route is taken. As no large-bodied terrestrial mammal succeeded in crossing between Sahul and Sunda in either direction before the arrival of modern humans gives some indication of how significant the biogeographic barrier was. If any did make it across the gap there were not enough to establish a viable population (Van den Bergh *et al.*, 2001).

The islands of *Near Oceania* such as the Bismarck Archipelago and the Solomon Islands, lie to the north east of Sahul. There are water gaps between the Bismarck Archipelago and mainland New Guinea, and between the neighbouring islands of the Bismarck Archipelago and the Solomon Islands, that are generally in the range noted for Wallacea. There are exceptions, such as between New Ireland and Bougainville, 140-170 km, and Manus Island to New Hanover, 200-300 km, the distances at any particular time depending on the sea level. These straits mark important biogeographical divides, the biodiversity dropping sharply to the north and east of Sahul (Metcalfe *et al.*, 2001). See Archaeology of Sahul or Greater Australia - Melanesian Lowlands.

Chapter 2 - Occupation of Sahul (Greater Australia)

Deep Sea Fishing - oldest known evidence

According to a paper published in *Science* excavations in Jerimalai on the eastern end of East Timor uncovered the earliest known fish hooks. The earliest known boats come from France and the Netherlands and are 10,000 years old. The excavations at this cave by Sue O'Connor and her team from the ANU have uncovered evidence suggesting that deep sea fishing may have been taking place by 42,000 BP, the age of the earliest levels of the site that has been excavated. About 56 % of the fish remains found at the site are from pelagic, fast-swimming species that are found in deep water, indicating that some form of water craft capable of taking the fishermen some distance from the shore to reach the deep water was being used. Also found at the site are fish hooks made from mollusc shells, which at 23,000-16,000 BP are the oldest known fish hooks in the world.

There are those who disagree with the suggestion that the presence of pelagic fish among the remains indicates deep sea fishing, suggesting that as many of fish are smaller than the full adult size they could be juveniles that strayed close to shore. Some have pointed out that because of the steep topography of the seabed around such islands as Timor the deep sea is comparatively close to the shore in places. O'Connor has countered that because they are fast-moving fish they would be very difficult to spear while so near the shore.

The well-preserved bones from Jerimalai Cave, of animals and fish, were from a total of 38,000 fish bones from 2843 individual fish. As fish comprised more than half the bones at the site they must have been the staple diet of the inhabitants. Among the deep sea fish present are grouper, parrotfish, trigger fish and snapper. There were also the bones of marine turtles, sharks and many shellfish. A mystery that has also been seen in parts of Australia is that the proportion of deep sea fish in the diet declined over time until by 5,500 BP it was down to 24 %. The island lacked animals larger than snakes and bats, making the sea food an important part of the diet.

According to Prof. Nick Barton, Palaeolithic Archaeology at University of Oxford, "it provides some of the oldest tangible evidence of sea fishing using line anywhere in the world and offers growing support for an early southern route into the Sahul by seafaring modern humans. It also stokes the current controversy over ***Homo floresiensis***. Why did modern humans apparently not use Flores as a stepping stone island en route to Australia?"

Acceding to Graeme Barker, professor of archaeology at the University of Cambridge "the humble fish hook discovered by the ANU team is testimony to the extraordinary capacity of our direct ancestors to invent new technologies and develop new behaviours to deal with unfamiliar environments as they encountered them. This adaptive plasticity appears to have been the main reason why they were able to out-compete other hominin species, such as the Neanderthals of Europe and the 'hobbits' of Flores, so successfully."

Evidence has been provided by these discoveries that suggest the earliest people to colonise Australia had advanced skills with regard to working stone, bone and wood, as well as some form of watercraft capable of crossing stretches of ocean, such as the short distances between islands and between the nearest island and the mainland of Australia.

Evidence from Lake George

A core drilled into the sediments of Lake George found pollen and charcoal that were dated to more than 100,000 years ago. In the top 8.6 m, covering 350,000 years, the longest continuous record of fire and vegetation history in Australia was found. The core was drilled 72 m deep, the base of which was estimated to be from between 7 and 4.2 Ma. The sediment depth was estimated to be 134 m below the depth reached by the core, putting the estimated time for the formation of Lake George at about 20 Ma.

Pollen analysis (palynology) established the sort of plants in the vegetation growing in the environment around Lake George. In Zone F of the sediment there is a large increase in the amount of charcoal. It was suggested that the most likely explanation for this increase in charcoal is that it resulted from the arrival of humans in the area, with their fire-stick culture, for driving animals from cover and also as a method of encouraging fresh growth to support the populations of the animals they hunted, attracting their prey species to the area. The increase of fire led to the reduction of the number of fire intolerant species and the increase in the number of fire-tolerant species, and the first expansion of the area covered by the fire-tolerant Eucalyptus-dominated vegetation that has persisted to the present (Flood, 2004).

Gurdip Singh, who drilled the core, dated the sediment of zone F to 120,000 years ago, but Richard Wright has disputed this date, placing it closer to about 60, 000 years ago. This would also fit with dates from Kakadu.

In 1980 a number of small amorphous quartz flakes were found in a gully. The site would have been the lake shore during the Ice Age. They were found in aeolian sand subsequently dated to 26,000-22,000 BP. In 1983 more were found in a perched sand dune on top of Butmaroo Hill near the highest former eastern shore of the lake.

In the 1.5 m deep sand deposit they found stratified stone artefacts. In the upper 12-20 cm was a micro-blade industry dated to about 4,000 years ago. Based on 6 radiocarbon dates it is believed the base of the deposit dates to at least 10,000 years ago. The sand was on a large deposit of quartz and heavily metamorphosed volcanic rocks which were resting on bedrock. In this deposit there was a quartz core with negative flake scars - scars left when flakes had been removed by humans. Several large, heavily weathered artefacts of metamorphosed volcanics have been found on the lake floor and in the tailings from sand mining operations. These artefacts include large flakes with rough lateral retouch, flaked cobbles, and dome-shaped 'horsehoof' cores - or core tools. It is believed these date from the terminal Pleistocene or possibly earlier.

The First Boat People

The dreamtime stories of a number of Aboriginal tribes tell of canoe crossings made by their dreamtime ancestors from islands to the north of Australia, which agrees with the thoughts of scientists about the arrival in Australia of the first Aborigines, based on archaeological evidence.

The Riratjingu people of the east coast of Arnhem Land believe they are descended from Djankawa who crossed from the island of Baralku with his 2 sisters in a canoe, led by the morning star to the shore at Yelangbara, on the east coast of Arnhem Land. They followed the rain clouds across the country. When they needed water they plunged their sticks into the ground and water flowed out. They gave their descendants their laws and taught them the names of the animals.

The arrival of Aborigines in Australia was certainly before 50,000 and probably more than 60,000 years ago, the most widely accepted date for the peopling of Australia. At that time the sea level was much lower than present because a lot of water was locked up in glaciers during the Ica Age. Even with lower sea levels there was still about 70 km of ocean that needed to be crossed from Southeast Asian islands to the closest parts of the Australian continent, Arnhem Land, Kimberley, and Cape York. It would have been possible to walk from New Guinea across a wide plain, but they would still have to travel across the seas to get to New Guinea.

It is believed they probably arrived in canoes or maybe bamboo rafts, possibly from Indonesian islands such as Flores, possibly via Timor, either intentionally or by accident. If they drifted to one of the islands near the Australian mainland they probably wouldn't have been able to return because the currents and winds wouldn't take them in the right direction.

At the time of the low sea levels there would have been a chain of islands near the Australian mainland that ran parallel to some of the more easterly small Indonesian islands that would have been visible from the Indonesian islands. As long as they had some sort of craft that could have made the short crossings between islands they could have island hopped to the Australian mainland.

As if to back up the theories of the crossing to Australia, Dreamtime stories across to the top of Australia have various dreamtime ancestors travelling by canoe from the North West, the direction of Indonesia.

The oldest known occupation sites in Australia are found in Arnhem Land in the northern part of Western Australia. The 2 oldest known sites are Malakunanja II and Nauwalabila rock shelters. These sites have very similar cultural sequences that have been dated by radiocarbon and luminescence techniques to 53,000 and 60,000 BP.

Sites dating to more than 40,000 BP have also been found in the south east and far south west of the continent.

It has been suggested that the colonisation of the continent probably started by spreading along the coast and up river valleys, having an assured food supply in the form of fish and shellfish from the rivers, and small animals around the rivers. From there they spread out until they inhabited the entire continent.

During the lacustral phase, a time when the inland lakes like Lake Frome and Lake Mungo, etc., were filled, though they were surrounded by arid areas. By 60,000 BP they had reached the Willandra Lakes region. By 30,000 BP arid central Australia had been occupied. Evidence for this occupation comes from Puritjarra Rock Shelter, west of Alice Springs, and Allen's Cave and Koonalda Cave on the Nullarbor Plain. The area they populated extended from New Guinea to the glaciers of south-western Tasmania.

The first Australians were among the earliest *Homo sapiens*. No evidence has been found that *Homo erectus* had ever reached the Australian continent, including the continental shelf. The remains found at Lake Mungo in New South Wales are of a gracile people, with slender build. The site was dated to 60,000 BP (later redated to about 42,000 BP).

This is a problem; all younger remains are of a more robust type of human, appearing more archaic. It is not known if the Mungo people are a continuum of the same population or a distinct population. It seems unlikely that the robust people are descended from the more gracile population. But according to the dates, if one population is descended from the other, the robust type did indeed descend from the gracile type. Was it an adaptation to the much harsher conditions?

There are now in excess of 120 Pleistocene sites known in Australia. It is also known that these ancient hunter-gatherer people had all the hallmarks of advanced humans elsewhere. They used fire for hunting and managing their environment to maximise the food source for the animals they hunted, and used ground ochre for decoration, wore ornaments and honoured their dead. The earliest burial known from Australia dates to 60,000 BP [42,000 BP]. The corpse was covered with powdered ochre.

By 20,000 BP they were mining flint in underground mines like Koonalda Cave on the Nullarbor Plain. In north Queensland at that time they were hafting handles to ground-edge axes. The only rival for this level of sophistication of stone tool manufacture at this time was in Japan at a similar early time.

Industries in Australia were distinctive, having some special tools such as large waisted axes and the horsehoof core, a single-platform core, which was sometimes used as a chopping tool. They are similar to the Mousterian industries in Europe and the Middle East, and the Middle Stone Age in Africa. They also used the Levallois technique of flake production.

Once they arrived in Australia they were relatively isolated from the rest of the prehistoric world. They didn't undergo the 'creative explosion' that occurred in western Europe. It has been suggested that this 'creative explosion' occurred because of the necessity to adapt to the freezing conditions of the Ice Age. In Australia the Ice Age had the effect of increasing the dryness of the already arid continent even more. The Aborigines adapted to the increased aridity by moving to areas with more reliable water sources, then moving back when wetter times returned. The result of this reaction to the Ice Age in Australia meant that there was no urgent need to innovate to survive, so technology and art underwent a gradual development.

When Aborigines arrived in Australia the megafauna had not yet completely gone extinct. There has been some debate as to whether the arrival of humans was connected with the extinction of the megafauna. Now that a number of dating techniques have been developed and more archaeological and palaeontological sites have been discovered it is becoming apparent that as the humans moved into an area the megafauna went extinct in that area soon after. The debate is, at least partially, changing to whether it was caused by overhunting or the use of the fire-stick destroying the original environment, making it more suitable for their preferred prey. Their use of fire to change an environment was so successful that the present vegetation type over much of Australia has been referred to as an Aboriginal artefact. The debate is becoming was it by overkill, gradual attrition of populations, or by environment change.

They adapted so well to the arid conditions that they maintained healthy populations in some of the harshest environments on Earth.

Some of the European explorers died of starvation and thirst in the same areas in which the Aborigines flourished. And in parts of Australia European agriculture failed miserably where the firestick agriculture was a brilliant success. they ate a healthier diet than most of Europe, even today, and they were so successful at surviving that they had plenty of time for a spiritual, cultural life.. A corroboree for every occasion, and different ones for men and women, and some for everyone, men, women and children.. They actually had more time to devote to matters of the mind - art, dance, music, festivals and ceremonies, than most Europeans until recent times.

By about 35,000-25,000 years ago they had occupied all major environmental zones in Australia. Possible exceptions have been suggested to be the north Queensland rainforest, the dune field deserts and possibly small offshore islands.

Cane[1] suggests the first settlement of Australia occurred soon after about 75,000 BP following the Toba super volcanic eruption in Sumatra that had occurred at that time, the people travelling to Australia as it was as far as they could travel from their homeland that had proven to be so dangerous. He[1] points out that long before the settlement of Australia *Homo erectus* must have made sea crossings in sufficient numbers prior to 840,000 BP as by that time they were present on the island of Flores, Indonesia. Though it is not known how they made the crossings there were a number of options open to them as even after normal tropical storms there is plenty of floating vegetation and logs around the Indonesian islands, and there are also logs that they could have hollowed out, that in spite of their appearance are actually stable and can't sink.

Cane (2013) describes incidents in his travels in the more remote parts of Indonesia that demonstrated to him how surprisingly easy it was to travel by sea in logs that had been dug out, dugout canoes, often with bamboo stabilisers, even in rough weather, at least in the hands of a competent user of such watercraft. He said that these crossings could just as easily have occurred 75,000 years ago, though he points out that there would always have been hazards involved, the sea being a dangerous place. He suggests that even in normal times, when there has not been a super-eruption to add to the normal dangers of life, the dangers of a sea crossing would probably be no greater, especially to people who spend their lives travelling and fishing in the waters around their island home in various forms of primitive watercraft.

People had reached Bali from Lombok, the islands being close enough to each other that one can be seen from the other on a clear day, but the currents between them are much faster than is usual for currents in Indonesia, the diurnal current is strengthened by the prevailing wind, and it is among the strongest currents in the world reaching speeds of up to 6 knots, or 11 km/hr, and it is made much more dangerous by such phenomena as 'frightening overfalls, eddies and windborne turbulence'[1]. A current of 130 km/day was reported in 1909.

According to Cane (2013) before the super-eruption of Mt Toba there are no reasons known that could explain the push to colonise Australia, given the potential risks of the trip, but he suggests the aftermath of the Toba eruption could have been the reason people decided to look for another home. Around 75,000 BP the sea level was about 60 m, and possibly to 80 m, lower than the present level, which would have meant that Ashmore Reef would have been about 10 m above sea level, located on the tip of a long peninsula, as much of the continental shelf along northern Australia was exposed at that time. Ashmore Reef is 130 km from Timor, and closer to Timor another part of the continental shelf that formed a large plateau-like island, which was 25 km across, 18 km to the north east of Ashmore Peninsula, that is 90 km from Timor, that is 4 times the distance that had already been crossed in previous inter-island crossings. Cane (2013) suggests that it is unlikely the first arrivals knew how far Australia was from their departure point, given that the original travellers were competent, was only relevant in proportion to that competence. He suggests the critical elements were probably knowledge, including seamanship, craft, provisions and timing.

The primary consideration with regards to knowledge was an awareness that there was in fact another landmass to the south, likely to have been known because of the strong environmental indicators At the present the aridity of Australia, that is more than 500 km from Timor, can be sensed from Timor and the haze at the end of the dry season can be seen when standing on the south-western tip of Timor. The weather in Timor is influenced by the Australian continent, Timor is hotter than further north and there is a pastel orange haze in the sky. Even at a distance of 500 km the sense of a large, hot landmass to the south is implicit. The author[1] also suggests that when the distance to Australia was 90 km it must have been possible to smell Australia. At night the glow of bushfires must have been visible, as would large smoke-filled clouds in daylight, even at the present dust from the southeast trades makes visibility poor across the Timor Sea. Though Australia is too low to be seen, violent thunderstorms may have been sighted. A clear indication of land to the south would also have been provided by migratory birds.

It would have been helpful to know the best season to sail, and to know not to sail in the dry season when the winds and currents flowed away from Australia. Apart from the risk of storms, the wet season would have been a better choice, as it is the season when both winds and ocean currents would generally take any craft towards Australia, and there would have been rain to provide drinking water. Another advantage of travelling to Australia in the wet season would have been plenty of drinking water available when they arrived. In Timor and the southern Indonesian archipelago the climate was similar to that of northern Australia, dry in the dry season and wet in the wet season.

There has been speculation concerning the type of craft that may have been used for the journey. One suggestion is craft made from bamboo, though in the southern latitudes of Indonesia there is less bamboo of large size.

Fishermen and coastal foragers in remote parts of Indonesia use bamboo to carry sweetened rice and water in the natural compartments of bamboo stems. They can steam the mixture in the bamboo over fire, though the rice is often pre-cooked, and the author[1] suggests that in the past treated rhizomes, nuts and palm sugar may have also been carried in bamboo, as well as fresh shellfish such as giant clam. They could have also carried live turtles by leaving them upside down on the decks.

Cane (2013) suggests tree trunks, lashed together or singular, modified or not, could have been an alternative form of sea-faring craft, and possibly some form of propulsion such as paddles, and/or some form of sail such as bark, large tropical broad leaves, and single leaves on branches, bound or matted. According to Cane (2013) the windage of such materials, that are natural and unmodified, is surprisingly effective. Even at the present people living in the remote parts of Indonesia continue to use broad leaves and palm fronds for down-wind sailing in dugout canoes, and he adds that anyone who has paddled a stand-up paddleboard into the wind will understand how effective the windage of the human body is.

At the present the wind and sea conditions are mild in comparison to typical sea breezes around southern Australia, and at 75,000 BP the state of the sea was probably considerably calmer, the cooler climate having reduced the currents, wind and swell. Between the Moluccas and New Guinea the present-day current across the Banda Sea moves at about 20 km/day, this together with a favourable wind would carry people to land in 3-4 days. A distance of 40 km could be travelled in a day with a current of 1 knot, therefore the 90 km between Timor and Australia could have been crossed in 2-3 days by sailing downwind in the wet season. This becomes more possible as evidence has been recovered from south-eastern Timor that 42,000 BP coastal fishermen were using sophisticated fishing technology to catch open ocean fish such as tuna, which indicates that these ancient people were knowledgeable about the sea.

According to oral history 9 generations ago, about 200 years, a vessel with a cargo of palm sugar ran ahead of a storm for 5 days which brought them to the open sea, and not knowing where they were followed sea birds returning to land because they thought that would bring them to another country where they could get help. They eventually saw the green reflection on the clouds so sailed on eventually reaching the western end of Ashmore Reef. As they had no compass they used the Southern Cross as a back bearing to steer north and eventually reached their home.

There has been considerable debate about the route taken by the original settlers of the Australian continent. According to Cane (2013) the sea crossing to Ashmore Reef was possible. If they travelled about 50,000 BP the sea level was possibly 20 m higher and the Ashmore Peninsula as well as its neighbouring islands, would have been submerged, and the distance to Australia at this time was 200 km, making it more likely a more northerly route via the Moluccas from Sulawesi to New Guinea was followed. As the actual route(s) followed and the possible landfall(s) have been submerged for the last 15,000 years the debate must remain speculation. As it is not possible to know how, where or exactly when the first people arrived in Australia, Cane (2013) suggests is that what is known is that about 70,000 BP the conditions were conducive to setting out on such a voyage and the aftermath of the Toba super-eruption may have provided the incentive needed to leave.

Pleistocene arrival of humans in Sahul and Near Oceania – dating

Archaeology, radiocarbon and luminescence dating

The first archaeological evidence of occupation in Melanesia was found in the Ivane Valley, upland New Guinea, where radiocarbon dates were obtained ranging between 49,000 and 43,000 cal BP and to the east, on the Pacific island of New Ireland, 44,890 and 43,100 cal BP (Summerhayes et *al.*, 2010; Summerhayes & Ford[1]). For dating sites in Australia the carbon ceiling has been raised to about 48,000 years by use of the ABOX-SC method (Turney et *al.*, 2001a; Summerhayes et *al.* 2010). Substantially earlier occupation of Australia by 50-60 ka has been suggested by the use of non-carbon dating techniques to date cultural remains (Roberts et *al.*, 1994, 2001; Bird et *al.*, 2002, 2004). Oppenheimer suggests it is clear more non-radiocarbon work is required. According to Oppenheimer this review was intended to point out that the 'oldest non-carbon dates' are not inconsistent with the colonisation by 50-60 ka. Sea-level curves produced recently, that concentrated on troughs (Siddall et *al.*, 2003), have suggested that for such a long crossing over the Sahul shelf from Timor the best window of opportunity would have been about 65 ka, a time when sea levels would have been lower by about 100 m, occupations in the Northern Territory becoming visible on littorals of the present only from 60-50 ka onwards, as a result of higher sea levels of the present (Oppenheimer, 2004).

Genetics

Genetic phylogeography, as previously mentioned, is a tool that is more suited to elucidating tracks of migration than for dating. In regards to the Melanesians and Australian Aboriginals, resolution on their main descent from the single exit is clear. Oppenheimer (Oppenheimer, 2003) initially made the point that the mtDNA of the

Melanesians and Australians is all of the M and N lineages, which is consistent with a single exit, and complete sequencing and NRY work has since confirmed this on an expanded set of samples (Macaulay et *al.*, 2005; Hudjashov, et *al.*, 2007).

The previous genetic dates of arrival of the vanguard in the Sahul, estimated by Oppenheimer based on mtDNA, were consistent with a pause of about 10,000 years in Bali before making the final crossing to Australia (Oppenheimer, 2009). When the dates for colonisation of Australia by Roberts (Roberts et *al.*, 1994, 2001) with genetic ages that have been recalibrated, of M, N and R in East Asia would not allow time for a pause before their arrival in Australia 60-50 ka. A transit from Africa to Australia would have been inferred that was extremely rapid, of about 12,000 years, given the recalibrated genetic age of the out of Africa L3 lineage at 71,600 years. Colonisation at this speed is consistent, however, with the phylogenetic observation that the great dispersal arc was effected entirely by the haplotypes M, N and R, the 3 primary root haplotypes, each of which gave rise to multiple sets of daughter branches, that are regionally unique, in every sector around the Indian Ocean.

Conclusion

The archaeological evidence that has recently been found is consistent with a southern exit of AMH from Africa not long before the eruption of Mt Toba about 74,000 years ago; though no fossil hominins have been found. The African-type Middle Stone Age assemblages are assumed to have been made by AMH, though Neanderthals or other archaic types cannot be ruled out as the makers of these tools. Evidence of a prolonged recovery following the Mt Toba eruption is consistent with a local bottleneck in India, as suggested by the preliminary evidence of the dating of the cultural layers after the Toba eruption. A single exit from Africa, probably by the southern route, is suggested by the parallel phylogeography of both uniparental lineages (either only the female line or the only male line) mtDNA and male NRY.

Most previous genetically dated estimates have recently been recalibrated and corrected for non-linearity of the mtDNA molecular clock, which reduced most of these dates, based on L3 as an upper limit of this exit to about 72 ka (CI: 57-87 ka) with rapid migration around the coast of the Indian Ocean to Australia. The founding ancestor of the 2 primary non-African clades, M and N, at 72.15 ka (CI: 57.0; 86.4) could explain the lower limit of the estimate, or failing that the age of the clade that the most south westerly, N estimated in South Asia at 71.2 ka (CI: 55.8; 87.1), though elsewhere the ages of haplotypes M and N are younger than this date. The date of the Toba event is straddled by these confidence intervals so therefore are unable to resolve the issue of whether human dispersal took place before the Toba eruption, they do appear to exclude a significant (>5 %) survival of any AMH from any earlier exit during MIS 5e, as claimed from Jebel Faya, Zhirendong as well as a controversial older dating of the Liujiang skull.

There is a possibility that a less than 5 % contribution from any other human demic source could be missed by uniparental studies, because of their known problem of drift, and including that from an AMH exit during MIS 5, as is the case with the recent reference of Neanderthal and Denisovan admixture outside Africa. Oppenheimer suggests it is unlikely the autosomal genomic methods that have been used recently to infer archaic admixture would resolve this issue any time soon as they are statistical and relatively non-specific and don't have a method of dating.

Firmer methods of dating the definitive exit of AMH from Africa could potentially be provided by palaeoclimatology, palaeoanthropology and archaeology, though with no evidence older than the Toba eruption that is fully convincing. Diagnostic fossil evidence, which is dated contextually uncontroversial, from China and Southeast Asia goes back to only 50 ka. This asymptote is partly an artefact of method, which has been largely based on radiocarbon. A definitive AMH skull from Liujiang in southern China, as well as an accurate and textually conservative minimal date of 67-68 ka, and Australia has cultural evidence of between 50 and 60 ka. A strategic approach to dating sites in South and Southeast Asia, as well as an ongoing source of controversy in the absence of any relevant fossil evidence, is offered by the fallout of the Toba super-eruption. It would help to resolve this issue if any AMH fossils dating to a period from 74-90 ka were discovered.

The Colonisation of Greater Australia in the Pleistocene - A Re-examination

In this paper the problem with the initial peopling of Australasia is re-examined in light of recent evidence suggesting that settlement may have taken place earlier than the conventional view of 40,000-35,000 BP. The initial settlement of people in Australia earlier than the applicable limits of conventional analysis is suggested by dating methods including palaeoecological changes that are interpreted anthropogenically, and the application of luminescence dating techniques. At the Ngarrabullgan Cave (David et *al.*, 1997), Malakunanja II (Roberts et *al.*, 1994), Nauwalabila I (Roberts et *al.*, 1994) and Jinmium (Fullagar et *al.*, 1996) are suggested by Zazula (2000/2001) to indicate clearly that the initial phase of Australian prehistory needs to be re-examined and that the age determination of the initial settlement in Australia by the radiocarbon age determination may not be applicable in regards the earliest arrival of people on the Australian continent.

In the latter part of the 20th century radiocarbon dating became available for the archaeological sites in Australia that provided evidence that the ancestral Aboriginals arrived in Australia during the Pleistocene. The first settlers in Australia originated in the closest proximal landmass in Pleistocene South East Asia. These 2 land areas have not been connected at any time during the Quaternary; therefore watercraft must have been used to reach Australia from Asia. A temporal chronology for the initial occupation of Australia has been attempted by the past generation of research into the prehistory on the continent and the now adjacent islands of Tasmania and New Guinea. Much scholarly debate continues as to the peopling of Greater Australia, though a large amount of information has now been accumulated. In this paper Zazula (2000/2001) reviews the issue of the first Australians and the current state of the archaeological, palaeoenvironmental and palaeoanthropological evidence, as well as the major interpretations of the material discussed. The debate concerning the timing and species involved in the initial hominid occupation of Australia is focused on, and the related debate on the dating methods used for the Pleistocene material.

Greater Australia and South East Asia - Pleistocene Geography

The geography of Australia and South East Asia has changed over time (Lowe & Walker, 1997), with global water reserves being largely stored in continental glaciers in the Northern and Southern Hemispheres throughout much of the Pleistocene. The sea levels dropped 150 m lower than their present level as a result of the dramatic change in the hydrological regime of the Earth resulting in the exposures of the continental shelves of Australia and the South Pacific (Birdsell, 1977). This resulted in open plains connecting the present islands of Tasmania and New Guinea to the mainland of Australia, leading to the formation of the vast continent of Greater Australia, aka Sahul, during the Pleistocene. The present islands of Sumatra, Java, Bali and Borneo were connected by land bridges of exposed continental shelf to South East Asia to form the continent of Sunda, allowing the islands of Wallacea, comprised largely of Sulawesi and Timor, to become probable "stepping stones" connecting the 2 continents of the Pleistocene (Fagan, 1995). An important point is that between Sahul and Sunda there was never a land bridge connecting these 2 continents and the islands of Wallacea were never connected to either continent. At the lowest sea levels of the Pleistocene gaps of 30 km remained between Wallacea and Sunda and of about 90 km between Wallacea and Sahul. During this period these relatively short distances are considered to be key factors that allowed the probable colonisation by humans of Sahul (Birdsell, 1977).

Archaeology of Sunda in the Pleistocene

Zazula, (2000/2001) suggests an understanding of the inhabitants of Sunda is necessary as the earliest colonisers of Sahul originated on the Sunda landmass. At Sangiran in Java (Jones, 1989), a ***Homo erectus*** dated to 1.16 Ma was the first evidence to be found of the earliest hominid population in south eastern Sunda, though some still debate the antiquity of this find (Fagan, 1995), but there is firm evidence of ***H. erectus*** being in the region by 780,000 BP (Jones, 1989). ***Homo erectus soloensis***, with a more modern appearance, apparently a more advanced stage of evolution, has since been discovered and may have existed in Java from about 200,000 BP to 100,000-75,000 BP. It has been indicated (Jones, 1992) that a single lineage of ***erectus*** populations have been present on the shore of Sunda for almost 1 million years. Zazula (2000/2001) suggests there are potentially revolutionary implications for the multi-regional approach to the origins on a global scale, based on evidence of the presence of ***H. erectus*** populations with a more modern appearance in Java between 75,000-100,000 BP, as well as for the species of hominid populations that initially colonised Australia.

Though there is a long fossil record the archaeological evidence from the islands or the mainland of South East Asia is very scarce (Jones, 1992). No reliable evidence has been found in archaeological material associated with any of the ***H. erectus*** fossils known from Java in Sunda (Jones, 1989). Zazula (2000/2001) suggests the lack of cultural evidence from ***H. erectus*** sites may possibly be attributed to geomorphic conditions that hinder site formation in the beds bearing hominids. It may also be possible that the populations from Java did not use stone tools, relying instead on split bamboo as the material of choice for cutting purposes (Jones, 1989). Zazula (2000/2001) also suggests the hypothesised ability of ***H. erectus*** to make tools from wood and plants may suggest they may have had the technological capability to build rafts or boats. One of the hallmark cultural innovations is the use of fire, and evidence of its use may exist in the archaeological and palaeoecological record in the form of charcoal or charred food processing remains. It is likely ***H. erectus*** populations from Sunda left some record of their cultural activities that are yet to be discovered.

On the island of Flores in eastern Indonesia archaeological evidence suggesting the activity of *H. erectus* on the islands of Wallacea, which have been dated to 880,000 ± 70,000 BP have recently been discovered (Morwood et *al.*, 1998). Faunal material native only to continental Sunda, as well as stone tool assemblages that have been dated by the fission-track method (Morwood et *al.*, 1998). The faunal material must have crossed a water gap to get to get to Flores as the island, to the southeast of the biogeographic line of Wallace, was never part of Sunda. As the faunal components were found associated with the archaeological components suggested to the researchers that they must have been with the population when they crossed to Flores by some form of watercraft (Morwood et *al.*, 1998). This is the only known archaeological evidence that suggests *H. erectus* populations were present in Flores or the remainder of Sahul. It is clearly shown by the stone tool assemblages that *H. erectus* must have crossed an expanse of sea, so had the potential to colonise the Australian continent, provided the stone tool assemblage date is accepted.

From Sunda to Sahul

The routes and method of travel used in the crossing from Sunda to Sahul are matters of conjecture; though there is general agreement that human colonisation of Greater Australia from Sunda took place during the Pleistocene. According to the first hypothesised route it involved a set-off point from the Sunda Shelf for Sulawesi which passed through a series of islands and eventual reaching the northern tip of New Guinea, or the exposed shelf of Sahul between New Guinea and north eastern Australia. Such a route would include about 3 major optional sub-routes and a minimum of 8 water crossings and on each route there would have been 1 or more crossings of more than 65 km, based on an estimated eustatic sea level drop of 150 m during the period around 53,000 BP (Birdsell, 1977). The more southerly of the major routes would leave from Sunda near the present eastern shore of Java and pass through the island chain to Timor, with 2 sub-routes that arrived in the Sahul shelf of northern Australia. It was surmised (Birdsell, 1977) that the more southerly route would have been more attractive as its initial water crossings are considerably shorter than the northern routes.

Along this route the final water crossing would have been at least 90 km, though there were shorter island hops along the majority of the voyage. It is suggested by computer simulations that a drifting raft would have taken 7 days to reach the coast of Australia from Timor with the assistance of monsoon winds (Fagan, 1995).

There is also evidence that at about 13,500 BP there was a major expansion of global ice volume. The Blake Event apparently occurred at the same time as a climate cooling with a build-up of ice that followed immediately, and terminated the Eemian, the last interglacial stage. It has been found by studies of oxygen isotope ratios in deep-sea cores (Shackleton, 1976, 1977; Johnson, 1978) and sea level changes recorded in tropical reef terraces (Mathews, 1972) suggest that at about 115,000-110,000 BP the sea level dropped 60-70 m in less than 10,000 years (Andrews & Mahaffy, 1976). See Possible Global Ice Volume Changes and Geomagnetic Excursions and Earth Orbital Eccentricity

Intervisibility was a major factor for water crossings between Sunda, Wallacea and Sahul, and this proposal has been examined (Birdsell, 1977), according to which at least 3 of the northern sub-routes would have involved intervisibility along the entire island chain. There would have been at least partial intervisibility along the 2 remaining northern sub-routes, with the more southerly routes being completely blind along inter-island voyages, though these determinations are hypothetical models of possible conditions during the Pleistocene. It is believed (Lourandos, 1997) that intervisibility between islands was an important factor concerning international colonisation. Some islands may not have been intervisible along various water-crossing routes, it is suggested the extant *H. erectus* must have had some idea that other lands must have existed over the horizon, as they could have noticed the direction from which migratory birds flew.

Considerable debate continues over whether the earliest settlement of Greater Australia was intentional or accidental. The long sea trips taken on the route to Sahul is believed to "...[imply] that the settlement was both accidental and unlikely to have been much supplemented by later voyagers" (White & O'Connell,1982:46). It has been suggested, in contrast, that the colonisation of Greater Australia was a result of a "...constant if somewhat straggling trickle of small groups of human beings over all or most of the routes" (Birdsell, 1977:123), Birdsell also hypothesising that the groups probably consisted of small biological family units as the water craft that would likely be used would be too small to carry large groups. These people had the technology to build ocean-going watercraft capable of surviving long, treacherous crossings between islands, and when needed, up to 90 km of ocean suggests they had sufficient knowledge of sea-faring skills and navigation on the ocean to colonise Sahul. It has been suggested that with many short inter-island crossings experience was gained and it is likely the number of intentional voyages and the distances crossed by these voyages increased (Irwin, 1992:29). These populations probably inhabited a coastal environment so already had knowledge of nearby islands, and it has been surmised they would assume that travelling further away from land would likely result in the discovery of more islands. Zazula suggests that this worldview would have been largely a product of their environment, possibly leading to ocean exploration by coastal populations due to their familiarity with the marine cultural strategies. It has been suggested that to explain the expansion of the original population following the initial arrival in Sahul there were probably many later arrivals of several individuals, both men and women, needed to maintain a viable breeding gene pool. According to the author[1] the settlement of Australia could have occurred by accident in a number of isolated events that were unrelated, it is more likely the continued colonisation of Australia was an intentional act in order to expand their resource base, or even to satisfy human curiosity in exploring a new frontier.

The initial settlement of Sahul

The antiquity of the earliest evidence of human occupation in Sahul has been hotly debated, with much of the debate focusing on the reliability of the current dating methods, TL or radiocarbon, and how the archaeological material is dated by these methods. According to conventional views the earliest arrival in Australia was about 35,000-40,000 BP, essentially as this is the oldest date found for recovered archaeological materials (Allen & Holdaway, 1995). More recently there has been criticism of these conventional views, with the suggestion that the reasoning on which these 40,000 BP dates are based may simply reflect the limitations of the radiocarbon dating of these sites, not the actual age of occupation (Roberts et *al.*, 1994; Chapell et *al.*, 1996). According to the other view of the occupation of Australia, it suggests humans were present in Australia prior to 40,000 BP, based on more recent work in which TL dating was used and including palaeoenvironmental change evidence (Singh & Geissler, 1985; Kershaw, 1986). It has been suggested (Arnold, 1995) that radiocarbon dates must be reviewed, given the known limitations of the radiocarbon dating method, based on more recent evidence from TL dating (Roberts et *al.*, 1994; Hutt & Raukas, 1995; Chapell et *al*, 1996).

Accepted dates for the initial occupation of Sahul - the conventional radiocarbon method

The time range of 35,000-40,000 BP is the earliest dates for the initial occupation of Australia (Fagan, 1995). This date range has been found throughout the Australian continent, such as sites on the Swan River (Pearce & Barbetti, 1981), Devil's Lair and Lake Mungo (Lourandos, 1997). Throughout Greater Australia an age of 40,000 BP is the earliest date that has been found by radiocarbon dating of archaeological material (Allen & Holdaway, 1995). Near the coast of south western Australia the Swan River has provided the cultural evidence of human occupation which has been suggested to be demonstrably the oldest on the mainland (Lourandos, 1997). More than 200 retouched and un-retouched flakes have been recovered from this site, and 4 radiocarbon dates ranged from 35,000-39,500 BP for associated material. The excavators of this site regard these radiocarbon dates as too recent for this site as they are too close to the limit of radiocarbon dating (Pearce & Barbetti, 1981:177). As insufficient amounts of measurable radiocarbon remains in these samples, Zazula (2000/2001) suggests this site clearly portrays the limitations of dating by the radiocarbon method for material from the Pleistocene.

The Devils Lair site, situated in a coastal limestone cave in south western Australia is another archaeological site where dates have been reported within the period that is considered to represent the conventional view of the earliest occupation of Sahul, the upper layers displaying a clear record of human activity occurring throughout the stratigraphic profile of the site. A layer of charcoal was found in the lowest stratified layer, though stone tools are not present, is believed to be a cultural deposit, the charcoal giving a radiocarbon date of 38,000 BP (Jones, 1992).

Sites in the Willandra Lakes system, and Lake Mungo in south eastern Australia, have produced evidence of early cultural activity in the form of archaeological material and human remains that were buried intentionally. At Lake Mungo the finds consist of tools, hearths in which there are charred animal bones, and stratified shell middens (Bowler et *al.*, 1970). At Lake Mungo stone tools from the lowest level of the lunette dune were found associated with a sample of charcoal which gave a radiocarbon date that was indistinguishable from background, leading to the belief the archaeological site may be older than 40,000-45,000 BP (Jones, 1989). At Lake Arumpo, a nearby lake, other shell middens were dated by radiocarbon to 37,000 BP, though the reliability of the ages obtained from freshwater shell material must be questioned because of the common reservoir effect, according to which carbon accumulation is common in such specimens Taylor, 1987).

Earlier dates for the occupation of Sahul

It has been proposed that there are 2 lines of evidence placing the arrival of humans in Australia much earlier than 35,000-40,000 BP. One is based on palaeoecological data, while the other is based on thermoluminescence dating of contextual archaeological sediments. It appears to be suggested by both lines of evidence that the initial arrival of humans in Sahul may have taken place in the last interglacial at 125,000 BP. Zazula (2000/2001) suggests these reports can be revolutionary, both in terms of conventional views of the prehistory of Australia and cultural chronology on a global level.

Kershaw (1986) and Singh & Geissler (1985) proposed the line of evidence based on palaeoecological research. Pollen studies of the Lake George site, south eastern Australia, have shown there was a sudden change in vegetation according to the pollen present in sediments that are indicated to date to oxygen isotope sub-stage 5e. There was a decrease in fire-sensitive species of trees and ferns that was accompanied by a definite increase in fire-adapted eucalyptus and grasses of open savannah type. There was also a sudden increase in charcoal in the same deposits that occurred concurrently. The Lake George record of charcoal persisted from the last interglacial to the Upper Pleistocene, which included periods of treeless full glacial conditions. Such a change in vegetation history and the frequency of fire could not be explained on the basis of climate change, so they were considered to be the result of human fire use that began about 125,000 BP (Singh & Geissler, 1985). According to Zazula (2000/2001) it needs to be noted that correlation of marine sediment sequences with terrestrial records poses some problems (Lowe & Walker, 1997), and the age of the Lake George sediments that were proposed by Singh & Geissler (1985) may prove to be not completely accurate. Analysis of the Lake George cores was carried out (Wright, 1986) and the zone of change in question was correlated with the interstadial within a glacial period dating to 60,000 BP.

Pleistocene arrival of people in Australia

It has been suggested that the analysis by Wright is more consistent with the archaeological record (Jones, 1989), though the introduction of fire into the area around Lake George could have caused the changes seen in the core record from Lake George. Therefore the interpretation of the material from Lake George (Singh & Geissler, 1986), may yet prove to be valid evidence of the colonisation of Australia about 125,000 BP, when it is associated with more recent palaeoecological evidence that is discussed below, though more palaeoecological studies of this nature are needed to prove their hypothesis.

The other, more recent work, conducted at the Jinmium rock shelter site (Fullagar et *al*., 1996) is also potentially supporting evidence of the occupation of Sahul around the last interglacial. In the lowest stratigraphic unit (Unit 1) there were multi-platform quartzite cores, flakes, fragments, unifacially retouched flakes, and a quartzite pounding stone cobbles that retained attached starch residue. The fluvial sands present above the lowest artefacts in Unit 1 gave a TL date of 116,000 ± 12,000 BP (Fullagar et *al*., 1996). Evidence of artistic expression as early as 75,000 BP was also found (Fullagar, 1996), together with evidence of human activity very early in the Upper Pleistocene. Significant quantities of red ochre were found between the upper and lower TL dated sediments, 75,000 and 116,000 BP, have been interpreted as possibly being used for the drawing on cave walls. A weathered sandstone fragment that had circular depressions similar to the engraved depressions on the wall of the rock shelter that was excavated was associated with TL dated sediments from more than 58,000 BP. It is believed (Fullagar et *al*., 1996) this piece of sandstone was detached from rock engravings on the wall of the shelter and possibly represents the earliest direct evidence of rock art found in Australia.

According Zazula (2000/2001) Fullagar and colleagues (1996) are confident that this date is evidence of north western Australia being occupied by humans by at least 116,000 BP. They remain confident in the TL method, though possible problems of TL are examined, as "they draw primarily on internal consistency of TL and the archaeological context to evaluate the age determinations" (Fullagar et *al*., 1996:771). The possibilities of artefacts being moved downwards through the deposits, and possible insufficient resetting of the TL in the sands, have been ruled out by evidence that has been presented Zazula's (2000/2001) reason for supporting these early TL ages presented are: "the stratigraphic consistency of TL ages:...good correspondence of TL and ^{14}C dates in the younger parts of the deposit and archaeological integrity of the deposit, including trends in the density of the components" (Fullagar et al., 1996:771). Fullagar et al. remain critical, even with all the evidence that has been presented for the early occupation of Jinmium, having stated "...the ages cannot yet be accepted unequivocally; neither can they be easily dismissed."

According to Zazula (2000/2001) the only artefactual evidence to provide evidence that early humans occupied Greater Australia 116,000 BP is the work conducted at Jinmium Rock shelter. The existence of archaeological material dating to the Last Interglacial would support the suggestion by Singh & Geissler (1985) of anthropogenic fire causing the ecological change evidenced by the cores at Lake George, if the work of Fullagar and colleagues (1996) is accepted. The possibility of other Australian sites displaying similar ecological changes to those at Lake George is suggested by these combined lines of evidence. Zazula (2000/2001) suggests that further evidence of such palaeoecological changes, in turn, might also be correlated with cultural deposits from this age.

Evidence of a pre-40,000 BP occupation of Sahul has been suggested by the use of TL to date other sites in Australia and New Guinea. They tend to support the presence of humans in Sahul in the period which is clearly beyond the practical limit of radiocarbon dating, though these TL dates are nearly half the age of those from Jinmium. A TL age determination of 45,000 ± 9,000 BP has been determined from a sample of sediment overlying feature that contained stone artefacts and haematite from Malakunanja II site in the Northern Territory (Roberts et al., 1994). Deposits associated with the lowest artefact that has been recovered at the site gave TL ages of 61,000 ± 13,000 BP. Their results were checked (Roberts et al., 1994) by also investigating the Nauwalabila I site in northern Australia. The sand lens deposit that produced the earliest artefacts had an upper OSL date of 53,400 ± 5,400 BP and the lower OSL date was 60,300 ± 6,700 BP. A rubble layer in the stratigraphic profile ruled out post-depositional disturbance, according to the researchers, as it would have prevented artefact movement in or out of the sand lens.

According to the author[1] Roberts and colleagues are confident of the "stratigraphic integrity and chronological coherence of the Malakunanja II and Nauwalabila I sites", suggesting that at these 2 sites there is clear evidence of human occupation between 53,000-60,000 BP in northern Australia based on age determinations by a combination of the TL and OSL methods. At Malakunanja II there is accordance between luminescence and ^{14}C dates from associated charcoal samples at 3 points in the upper portion of the stratigraphy, though the earliest TL dates at both sites could not be cross checked with radiocarbon ages. Further support of these early dates of occupation of Australia is given by a statement by Chappell et al. (1996:551) "...the luminescence method has been well supported beyond the age range of the early Australian archaeological sites, with the same type of sample material, there is no good reason to doubt the TL or OSL dates reported by Roberts et al. (1994)." At these 2 sites the evidence provided implies that human occupation of Australia occurred at least 15,000-20,000 years earlier than is suggested by the conventional view of colonisation based on previous radiocarbon dates.

Further evidence that the OSL method for dating early Australian archaeological material is a reliable technique (David et al., 1997) came from their work at Ngarrabullgan Cave site in north Queensland. At this site the lowest stratigraphic layer was dated using both OSL and radiocarbon methods, given an OSL age for the sample of 34, 700? ± 2,000 BP, which is about 2,200 older than the average radiocarbon age for the stratum. It is believed by David and colleagues that these 2 dating techniques will produce ages that are broadly comparable for the period between 35,000-40,000 BP following proper calibration of the ^{14}C results, and they also suggest that their results support the TL and OSL ages reported by Roberts et al. (1994).

The dating controversy - early Australian sites

The considerable controversy regarding the reliability of the radiocarbon method for dating archaeological layers that were deposited before 40,000 BP is emphasised by evidence provided in support of the opposing views that have been outlined above relating to the age of the initial settlement of Australia. Investigations of the integrity of using radiocarbon dating of archaeological material from the Pleistocene have been taking place over a long period (e.g., Jones, 1989; Roberts et *al.*, 1994; Chappell et *al.*, 1996). The problem being that very little isotopic material remains to measure the decay; the counts required being too long, even with AMS, as disintegration is an extremely long process. The practical limit of radiocarbon measurements is reached at about 40,000 BP, given the half-life of ^{14}C, even when mass spectrometry is used.

An assumption that is made when using the radiocarbon method is that the sample had remained in a closed system from the time of formation to the time of measurement, with no carbon exchanges. The archaeological material being dated could have been contaminated by carbon migration within the sediments during burial. There is also the risk that modern carbon could come into contact with, and be mixed in with the sample, at the time of recovery, which would make the dates obtained from the sample incorrect. According to Zazula (2000/2001) it is difficult to test if the process of isolating the ^{14}C is the only tracer, though various methods are used in the lab to isolate the original ^{14}C in a sample, the problem being that there is only a very small amount of original carbon isotope remaining in very old samples that makes it difficult to measure the remaining isotope. If a sample that is actually 50,000 years old is contaminated with 0.5 % of modern carbon the age obtained from the sample will be about 35,000-40,000 BP (Allen, 1994). A time range of 35,000-40,000 BP for the initial occupation of Australia, when obtained by radiocarbon dating, was referred to as an "event horizon," (Chappell et *al.*, 1996). It has been suggested (Roberts et *al.*, 1994) that ages of 35,000-40,000 BP that are reported are actually older, and problems with contamination affect the early part of the ^{14}C chronology for the early human arrival in Australia. It has been concluded that"...our ability to measure low levels of ^{14}C often surpasses our ability to remove contamination by sample pre-treatment; at the very least all ^{14}C dates near 40,000 BP require close scrutiny." (Chappell et *al.*, 1996:551). It is suggested by the TL ages provided (Roberts et *al.*, 1994; Fullagar et *al.*, 1996) that radiocarbon dating no longer be trusted to represent the initial colonisation of the Australian continent.

Radiocarbon ages of 35,000-40,000 BP obtained for the initial settlement of Australia are still advocated by some workers to be valid. It has been claimed (Allen & Holdaway, 1995) that the supposed "event horizon" for radiocarbon ages exists for only Australian archaeological samples, and there is sufficient evidence for radiocarbon ages up to 54,000 BP, for geological contexts in Australia. They claim the reason for the no radiocarbon dates older than 40,000 BP (uncalibrated) being that humans did not arrive in Australia prior to 40,000 BP. It has been stressed (Allen, 1994) that it is unreasonable to assume that all ages of 35,000-40,000 BP obtained by radiocarbon dating result from contamination, the only way to determine which dates are accurate is to re-excavate and re-date the sites in question. He also suggests that when a proper calibration curve for radiocarbon dating becomes available the results may change (Allen, 1994).

Discussion

An alternative approach for dating the earliest archaeological sites in Australia has been provided by TL dating techniques. Luminescence is 1 of a number of techniques that can be used for samples older than the 40,000 BP limit of radiocarbon dating, and according to Zazula (2000/2001) has proved to be reliable in the upper stratigraphic sequences at some sites from the Pleistocene where it was possible to obtain radiocarbon dates for comparison. The earliest sites are too old to be dated by radiocarbon dating because of its limit of 40,000 years. TL and OSL dating techniques seem adequate methods having been employed successfully beyond the range of radiocarbon dating. Zazula (2000/2001) suggests it would be useful to re-date the sites that are believed to represent the earliest evidence of people in Australia by luminescence techniques instead of the radiocarbon method.

In the islands of South East Asia and Wallacea there is a long record of fossil hominids, which Cane [1] suggests poses many questions concerning the antiquity and species that first settled in Australia. It is suggested by fossil evidence from Java and archaeological evidence from Flores that there were populations of humans on the shores of Sunda and Wallacea for almost 1 million years. Zazula (2000/2001) suggests it probably seems unlikely to most archaeologists that a ***H. erectus*** population could have reached Sahul by watercraft, and he suggests this possibility should not be ignored, in spite of no material being found. Recent finds in Flores seem to indicate that by 880,000 BP ***H. erectus*** had the technology to allow a water crossing on craft that possibly also carried animals (Morwood et *al.*, 1998). If ***H. erectus*** had the technology to construct watercraft there is no reason to doubt they could have reached Australia, suggesting that Australian archaeologists and palaeoanthropologists can no longer ignore the likelihood and bear this in mind as they search for sites of early settlement which must be continued. It will only be known if ***H. erectus*** were the original settlers in Australia if their skeletal remains are found in Sahul.

The first modern humans, ***Homo sapiens sapiens***, in the world are estimated to have arisen between 200,000-100,000 BP (Wilson & Cann, 1992; Thorne & Wolpoff, 1992). However, there is a suggestion, based on the fossil evidence (Thorne & Wolpoff, 1992), of a regional continuity of hominid populations from ***H. erectus*** to modern ***H. sapiens sapiens*** in the Australasian region. Cane[1] suggests the fossils from Java of a modern-looking ***H. erectus soloensis*** population that is more evolved, that lived 100,000-75,000 BP, may also be the population that is ancestral to the occupants of northern Australia. As it seems a population of ***H. erectus*** could cross Wallace's line by watercraft at 880,000 BP, then it is very likely the same cultural ability to cross open water was retained by the more highly evolved ***H. erectus soloensis***. The Java and Flores discoveries suggest to Cane [1] a lineage of non-African, modern ***Homo sapiens*** that evolved locally, either in Australia, Wallacea or South East Asia. The possibility that the inhabitants may have been equally of a late ***H. erectus*** lineage, an archaic or transitional ***Homo sapiens***.

At the time of writing only fully modern skeletal material has been found in Australia, though there is a degree of variation that is evident in the skeletal morphology within the populations, it is not possible to determine the degree of modernity in the initial settler population from the current osteological material. It has been argued (Thorne & Wolpoff, 1992) in favour of regional continuity in the Australasian region during the Pleistocene, and link the population of Australia back to ***H. erectus*** populations in Java.

Conclusion

In world prehistory the age of the initial settlement of Australia is a highly debated topic. Providing a chronological date for the crossing of the Straits of Wallacea, which occurred at some point in the Pleistocene, has proven very difficult for archaeologists. TL and OSL dating at Malakunanja II, Nauwalabila I sites provided archaeometrical evidence that apparently suggests that the human occupation of Australia occurred much earlier than the conventional date of 35,000-40,000 BP. According to Zazula (2000/2001) confirmation that the radiocarbon ages between 35,000-40,000 BP should no longer be used as the only line of evidence of the initial settlement of the continent comes from the existence of TL and OSL dates from at least 3 archaeological sites in Australia, which challenges the conventional view of the prehistory of Australia. It is confirmed by luminescence dates that radiocarbon dates of the range 35,000-40,000 BP should be considered with a great degree of scepticism. Evidence has been provided that the OSL and TL methods cover a dating range with enough time depth to determine reliable ages of Australia's first people, by the work at Ngarrabullgan Cave (David et *al.*, 1997), Malakunanja II (Roberts et *al.*, 1994), Nauwalabila I (Roberts et *al.*, 1994), and Jinmium (Fullagar et *al.*, 1996). Early occupation sites in Australia should also be dated by a 3rd technique such as Electron Spin Resonance (ESR) (Blackwell, 1995) to confirm the ages obtained by the use of the luminescence method, and the building of a stronger chronological case for the occupation of the continent. It appears the conventional views of Australian prehistory, that were based on radiocarbon dating, are being overthrown by luminescence dating that is becoming a method that is more applicable for the provision of accurate ages for the early settlement of the continent.

Dating the First Australians

In this paper Zazula (2000/2001) reviews the dating of selected archaeological and megafaunal sites in the Australian region, with emphasis on some recent work on some of the oldest sites. Many of the results processed decades previously have been confirmed using improved chemical procedures with decreased analytical background for ^{14}C analysis, combined with new luminescence methods which have increased the maximum age of some other sites. In 4 different regions that were reliably dated by multi-method results the occupation horizons are in the range 42,000-48,000 calendar years, overlapping with the age range for undisturbed sites containing the youngest extinct megafauna, which were similarly well-dated. That some archaeology may be earlier, and some megafauna may have survived later than this period, is suggested by less secure evidence.

The Archaeology of Sahul or Greater Australia

In his book, *Archaeology of Aboriginal Australia*, Tim Murray says it is no longer possible to see either the continent of Australia or the first inhabitants to be static and unchanging. It is now known that during the time the Aborigines have been living in Australia the climate and the environment have undergone some very drastic changes. The first arrivals would have found familiar conditions and food at the places of their arrival on the margins of the continent, but the further they penetrated into the interior the more unfamiliar everything would become, with different plants, animals, climates and ways of finding water. According to Murray, they have proven to be exceptionally flexible and inventive.

Once they had adapted their behaviour to survive in the new and often harsh environment, they had to do it all over again as the climate changed, becoming even more extreme as the Last Glacial Maximum approached. At the time the first people arrived, most likely from outer islands of Indonesia, the climate of central Australia was much wetter that it became later?. When Aboriginal people were living around the margins of the then full Lake Mungo, arriving in the area some time before 40,000 years ago, possibly as much as 60,000 years ago, they were able to catch large fish in the lake, which is now a barren desert. Rivers of sand of the present? were at that time flowing and the region was much greener than? it became? as the glacial period intensified and the lake dried up about 17,000 years ago as the climate became much drier, the most extreme time lasting for about 5,000 years, at which time the continent was even drier than at the present. At this time the people as well as the animals of the area had to adapt or die. Their adaptability was again tested by the changing climate.

According to Murray, when referring to evidence that had been found suggesting behaviours of the people in deserts and glacial areas as the climate deteriorated in the Pleistocene, "... *the old image of unplanned, ad hoc responses to the trials of life simply does not match the clear evidence of purposive behaviours which are of the same order of those exhibited by the Aboriginal people thousands of years later during the Holocene. Instead of a featureless landscape of human beings struggling to come to grips with their world, we are now confronted by a richness and variety which only a decade ago was simply undreamed of.*"

According to Allen the Pleistocene records of Greater Australia have been thought to reflect groups of humans that are characterised by populations with low density with subsistence strategies that were undifferentiated and limited, and using uninventive technologies. It has been generally accepted, though without demonstration, that throughout Greater Australia the people must have been primitive and few in numbers for at least 30,000 years. There has been uncritical acceptance of the Australian Core Tool and Scraper Tradition, that is an undefined and continent-wide, fitting most lithic evidence into it, though its distribution is far from being across the entire continent.

The view of the people of the Greater Australia as being unchanging as a starting point for the suggestions of social and economic intensification in the Middle to Late Holocene has been criticised (Cosgrove *et al.*, 1990). Another consequence of the accidental discovery of sites dating from the Pleistocene, as opposed to finds resulting from directed searching, that were often followed by ad hoc explanations, is that the models that were developed for Greater Australia during the Pleistocene have been minimalist models, often dominated by the shortest sea routes and the lowest sea levels between Asia and Greater Australia, the smallest founding population sizes that are viable, the accidental and most frequent number of landings and the dispersal routes requiring the minimum number of adaptations. According to Allen, minimalist hypotheses based on few or no data require testing and revision that is continuous, the danger being that superficial support from fragmentary data will not be later questioned, the need for new alternative explanations often being obscured by just such support. In Australia and PNG more recent investigations of the Pleistocene record have reviewed the data and interpretations.

All Pleistocene sites that had been reported for Melanesia were in the New Guinea Highlands up until 1986, with 1 exception, Misisil Cave on the island of New Britain. Dating from the terminal Pleistocene at its base, this is an archaeologically limited site (Specht *et al.*, 1981). After carrying out a review of these sites in 1983 (in Hope *et al.*, 1983: 42-5) Golson concluded that it was not possible to say anything very specific about the nature of the occupation during the Pleistocene based in the available evidence, though some disparate archaeological facts did result from Golson's work.

The 2 oldest known Highland sites, Kosipe (White *et al.*, 1970), 2000 m above sea level, and Nombe (Mountain, 1983), 1720 m above sea level, were both occupied by 25,000 years ago, at least. Adjacent to a high altitude Pandanus swamp from which palynological evidence was recovered of the clearance of forest occurring at 30,000 years ago (Hope, 1982), that is thought to have possibly been carried out by humans, Kosipe is an open site that has been interpreted as a focus for the collection of Pandanus, at least seasonally. Evidence of the hunting of diverse animal species has been found in the Nombe Rock shelter. Humans appear to have shared the site with other predators at the time the earliest layers were being deposited. There were 2 species of **Protemnodon**, and extinct species of **Dendrolagus**, an unidentified diprotodontid and a thylacine in association with stone tools. In the succeeding level there are more large marsupials in association with stone tools. It seems from this evidence that if the humans were not hunting or scavenging these large marsupials, then at least they were familiar with them, and their predators. The evidence suggests that Kosipe and Nombe were both in or near mid-montane forest, at high altitude and 100 km or more from the coast, though otherwise they were quite different sites. The distinctive stone artefact usually called a waisted blade, though it has been described as a hafted axe (Groube, 1986: 172), has been found at both Kosipe and Nombe, about 400 km north east of Kosipe, dating to about 25,000 years ago, though he distinguishes between the waisted axe at Kosipe and the early stemmed axe from Nombe, conceding that in New Guinea the stemmed axes and the waisted axe are consistently associated, suggesting they are a significantly associated form (Groube, 1986: 169). Allen groups the 2 forms as waisted tools. In the Yuku Rock Shelter, 1,300 m above sea level, 150 km north west of Nombe, accepted to be of Pleistocene age, though it is undated, as well as other sites in Australia and Melanesia, waisted axes are also found.

According to Allen, there appears to be an increase in the density of archaeological evidence in the Highlands in the terminal Pleistocene, though he admits the apparent increase may by the result of the limited number of sites and sequences that have been found. Continuing through this period, there is a wide range of forest and forest-grassland ecotone prey animals in the Yuku site. It has been reported that at Nombe Stratum C, covering the period between 14,500 and 10,000 years ago, 'considerable' amounts of bone, that includes burnt bone, stone artefacts, as well as a wider range of species than occurs either side of this layer, have been found in this site. The presence of humans in a range of upland environments, carrying out a range of activities, such as claims for the construction of houses at Wañlek 15,000-12,000 years ago (Bulmer, 1977: 65) and at NFX, 18,000 years ago (Watson & Cole, 1978: 35-40), is indicated by occupation of other rock shelters such as Kafivana (White, 1972), Kiowa (Bulmer, 1975), and Manim (Christensen, 1975) and at open sites such as Wañlek (Bulmer, 1977: 65) and at NFX (Watson & Cole, 1978: 35-40).

Allen suggest it can generally be assumed, in spite of the fragmentary and non-complementary nature of the data, that people were quite familiar with a wide range of environments in the uplands and highlands in New Guinea well before 25,000 BP, and especially with the resources found in them. It has been suggested that many of the plants would have been familiar to the people first arriving in the area (Golson, 1971a), and it can be assumed that by the time they reached the area they would also have become familiar with the marsupial fauna they encountered at high altitudes and at temperatures that are low relative to the coastal areas.

Allen says that whether or not the familiarity with the plant species facilitated their movement into the upland forests, by this time a range of marsupials are found such as wallabies, tree kangaroos, phalangers, bandicoots and echidnas, as well as placentals such as bats and rats, are common at these sites, suggesting distinct adaptations to environments away from the coast.

Though it is suggested by Allen that such small amounts of evidence can be stretched too far, the lateral spread of the waisted axe, a specific artefact type, indicates either a common origin for the groups among which this implement was important, or there was a connection throughout the Pleistocene between the groups along the spine of New Guinea. It has been suggested that these tools were used for clearing forest, indicating that the widespread evidence of forest interference from the Pleistocene didn't result simply from hunting practices (Groube, 1998: 298-302), suggesting instead that the clearing was deliberately done to encourage the growth of the most useful and productive food plants that grow best in these small clearings, '*Restricted natural stands of food plants such as aerial yams, local bananas, swamp taro and such tree crops as sago and **Pandanus**, could be promoted by judicious trimming, canopy thinning and ring-barking, and perhaps with the aid of fire, some minor felling*' (1988: 299).

It has been suggested (Groube, 1988: 296-7) that soon after the arrival of people in Greater Australia, and following the initial exploration of the Highlands forests, that Groube believes are likely to have been events that were synchronous archaeologically, that occurred at least 40,000 years ago (1988: 302), maintaining that the forms, wear-marks on the waisting, damage to the edges and breakage patterns, are consistent with their use for the management of the forest for the production of food plants. This would have set the people on the path that led to fully developed, and apparently widespread, horticultural subsistence practices in the Highlands in the immediate post-Pleistocene (Golson, 1988).

There was apparently a good deal of human altitudinal movement, that occurred concomitantly, as indicated by the location of sites and the faunal suites, as reflected in the Early Holocene in the presence of marine shells at Kafiavana (White, 1972: 93). The small amount of evidence that has been gathered indicates a high degree of adaptation and patterning of human behaviour in the Highlands during the Pleistocene, as well as possibly interaction networks between distant areas of the Highlands and the lowlands of eastern New Guinea.

See Tasmania in the Pleistocene
See Stone Tools
See Source 1 for more information and illustrations.

The Archaeology of Sahul or Greater Australia - The lowlands of Melanesia

Near Fortification Point on the Huon Peninsula, on the northern coast of PNG, waisted axes were found *in situ* that were between layers of volcanic ash on the uplifted coral terraces, for which Groube obtained TL dates of about 40,000 BP (Groube *et al.*, 1986). There are several buried axes and many stone axes on the surface, broken and complete. Groube mainly based his functional analysis on the 70 stone axes that were found in this site. At Bobongara Point, the Peninsula is comprised of 7 raised coral terraces, the upper terrace being about 400 m above sea level at the present. The coral terraces, some up to hundreds of metres wide, were formed when glacio-eustatic sea level rises overtook land, which was also being uplifted by tectonic activity. The unnamed site that has been excavated adjacent to Jo's Creek, an ephemeral stream, that is surrounded by surface finds of flaked stone artefacts, and more than 100 waisted and grooved flaked axes, often more than 20 cm long, and often more than 1 kg, over a more extensive area (Allen & O'Connell, Source 3).

An archaeological focus has been provided for the Pleistocene by these artefacts that are relatively specialised, though one that remains enigmatic. In the Highlands of Melanesia they have been found dating from 40,000-6,000 BP, while in the lowlands and the islands they are surface finds that are undated, as in the Solomon Islands (Groube, 1986: 172). The finding of such artefacts near Mackay, north Queensland (McCarthy, 1949; Lampert, 1983) in rainforest/open forest locations has been suggested to possibly be accommodated as part of a single geographical distribution that includes the Melanesian tools in the north. Their inclusion in the Kartan Culture on Kangaroo Island, at the opposite end of the Greater Australia (Sahul) continent poses some obvious questions.

It has been suggested that waisting was an aid in hafting that might be a significant technological aspect of the archaeological record that occurred on both sides of the Wallace Line (Golson, 1971b: 131-5). Lampert later addressed the question of any relationship between waisted axes in Australia and New Guinea, seeking to extend the comparison to Australia (Lampert, 1983, 145). The results of his multivariate analysis comparing the 2 Australian sets with that from Kosipe indicated that the 3 sites were unrelated to each other, the only common trait being waisting. He suggested that, at least in Australia, the waisted axes resulted from independent invention, though his argument that waisting was a universal method of hafting as support for his argument for independent invention, appears at odd with his argument that waisting was found only at 2 sites about 2000 km from each other in a continent such as Australia that is relatively well known (Lampert, 1983: 151).

Groube came to a diametrically opposite conclusion to that of Lampert as a result of a similar comparison he carried out using the Huon waisted axes and tools of similar shape from Botel Tobago and late Jomon Japan, that are believed to be hoes (Groube, 1986: 169), using a different statistical approach. He concluded that the waisted axes from Australia and New Guinea are distinct from the set from north Asia that were included in the comparison, being part of a single population, and on this basis, suggested that the waisted axes were invented in Greater Australia, no Asian influence being present (Groube, 1986: 174).

Fragmentary evidence, which is often separated by large distances and often through time, and poor chronological resolution, are examples of the type of problems encountered that are highlighted by these 2 analyses. Allen suggests these analyses lack control over the variabilities within each data set, both of the analyses having been constructed to measure the similarities between the data sets, and not their variability. He asks a number of questions regarding the data sets used. Such as the time frames of the collections, the different physical properties of the different raw materials used to explain what differences there are between sets. Also the different collecting procedures have created what differences between the data sets (he says this point was raised by Groube, 1986: 170), and what variability of use of these implements may have occurred over space and time. Allen also suggests that though the functional explanation proposed by Groube for northern Greater Australia may be extended to cover the waisted axes from Mackay, it would appear to require a lateral shift, at least, of the use of these tools from opening patches in the canopy to allow enough sunlight to the surface to grow food plants, to a need for the clearing of forest for other purposes in the case of Kangaroo Island. The use of these tools for the clearance of forest could explain the distribution pattern that has been found, being supported by observations that waisting is widespread in New Guinea but not Australia (Lampert, 1983: 151). With regard to hafted tools in Australia see Stone Tools.

The marine transgression that occurred following the Last Glacial Maximum about 18,000 years ago, submerged most Melanesian coastal sites from the Pleistocene, though some have been preserved as a result of what Allen describes as "idiosyncratic geological events". Some archaeological sites were preserved from inundation by the coastal uplift of about 3 m/1000 years that occurred before and during the human occupation of the Huon Peninsula (Groube, 1986: 171, 1988, 295). Several sites on New Ireland have been found in caves in the limestone terraces that were exposed along much of the east coast by a similar process. It has been suggested that it may have been steep underwater coastal contours that kept the sites close to the coast during the Last Glacial Maximum, at which time the sea level dropped to about 130 m below the present level (Chappell & Shackleton, 1986), and possibly not resulting so much from the uplift. The Kilu Rock Shelter on Buka Island in the northern Solomon Islands is in the same category (Wickler & Spriggs, 1988: 704).

The number of sites known from the Pleistocene in Melanesia had increased by 7 between 1985 and 1998, when Allen's article in Source 2 was written. 2 m of cultural material continue down below a layer with a radiocarbon date of 12,000 BP in **Pamwak**, a limestone cave (Ambrose, pers. comm. to Allen). Among the animal remains reported from the site are an introduced bandicoot, 1 rat species, bats, reptiles and fish. ***Canarium*** nuts have been preserved as macroscopic charcoal in the Pamwak and Kilu sites, and at the Kilu site there were artefacts on which were residues suggesting they had been used in the processing of root vegetables (Wickler, 1990). Among the animal remains found at Kilu were lizards, fish and marine shellfish (Flannery & Wickler, 1990; Wickler,1990: 140-1), and bats, birds and 5 endemic species of rat (Spriggs, Source 2).

On the east coast side of New Ireland there are 5 limestone cave or rock shelter sites, covering about 200 km from Matenbek and Matenkupkum, the most southerly of the sites that are 70 m apart, to Panakiwuk, about 40 km from the northern end of the island, and between these sites at the opposite ends of New Ireland there are 2 other sites, Balof 2, about 50 km southeast of Panakiwuk, and Buang Merabak, 50 km further southeast of Balof 2. Of these sites, all but Buang Merabak have been reasonably reported, according to Allen (Allen *et al.*, 1988; Allen *et al.*, 1989; Marshall & Allen, 1991; Gosden & Robertson, 1991; White *et al.*, 1991). A basal date of 31,990 ± 830 BP (ANU-6614) has been obtained from Buang Merabak, and shell middens are present throughout the deposit (Balean, 1989: 7). Matenkupkum Cave also has shell middens throughout the deposit and basal dates cluster around 33,000-32,000 BP. These 2 sites were the oldest of the Melanesian island sites to be excavated, and Kilu being dated to 29,000 BP. On New Ireland, Matenbek has given 4 dates in the range of 20,000 - 18,000, and Panakiwuk and Balof 2, the 2 northern sites, appear to have been occupied for the first time 15,000-14,000 BP. Allen suggests 3 qualifications are necessary to understand the importance of these dates, accessibility, proximity and location.

Accessibility

There would have been no problem crossing the sea between New Guinea and New Ireland for people who had already crossed wider expanses of ocean to reach Greater Australia, as has been discussed (Irwin, 1991). The same would apply to the crossing from New Ireland to the Solomon Islands, New Ireland remaining in sight after Buka Island can be seen, with the result that the Solomon Islands were occupied soon after the arrival of people in Greater Australia. The crossing to Manus Island is different, in that crossing there is a gap of 60-90 km before Manus Island comes into view, Irwin suggesting it could have delayed the occupation of Manus. Radiocarbon dates taken from charcoal, shell and the seeds of *Celtis* are 12,000 BP (14,000 BP calibrated).

Proximity

Allen suggests that as Matenbek is only 70 km from Matenkupkum, in this respect they might be seen as 2 foci of 1 site. The dates from Matenbek come from the back of the cave, as a collapsed cave mouth has buried the front of the cave. Based on this, Allen suggests that Matenbek may have been used earlier than is implied by the available dates, as he believes that at Matenkupkum the materials are distributed more towards the front of the cave. He also suggests that Matenbek may have been a subsidiary site to Matenkupkum. A problem is posed by the 2 sites being taken in combination, as the occupation of Matenbek from the Pleistocene partially fills a gap that has been proposed in the sequence between 21,000 BP and 14,000 BP at Matenkupkum. Allen points out that this detracts from the suggested abandonment of the Matenkupkum Site at this time being a result of lowered sea levels. There is difficulty interpreting the relevant dated portion of the stratigraphy at this point as has been discussed (Gosden & Robertson, 1991).

Location

The 2 sites that are the most northerly are also further from the coast. At Balof 2 marine resources are present throughout the sequence. At Panakiwuk marine resources first appear in the sequence about 8,000 BP when the sea approached its present position. Based on Allen's previous discussion of the sites in the Highlands, the 'inlandness' of Panakiwuk and Balof 2, 4 km and 2 km respectively from the coast, can be seen as only a short distance. The faunal lists for sites such as Yuku and Nombe, as opposed to those from Pamwak and Kilu, indicated, according to Allen, further adaptation as people moved to the Melanesian islands. Green has noted that, excluding extinct animals that were present 40,000 years ago, in Papua New Guinea there are presently 2 species of anteaters (echidnas), 5 wallaby species, as well as a range of bandicoots and phalangers. On the far side of the Vitiaz Strait there is 1 bandicoot, 1 wallaby and 2 phalanger species. Of the species of bird, there are 225 in eastern

Papua New Guinea and on West New Britain there are 80. There is also a reduction of plant species across this divide (Spriggs, Source 1). Allen says it is not well known (in 1998 when Source 1 was written) how the colonisation of the Bismarck Archipelago was affected by the pauperisation, suggesting that they be seen as points of discussion based on the evidence from a small number of sites, insufficient evidence to construct a definitive prehistory.

A strong dependence on coastal resources in seen in the earliest levels of such sites as Matenkupkum, Matenbek, and Allen assumes, Buang Merabak at 32,000 BP. The marine fish bones that were present in the earliest levels ay Matenkupkum were claimed to be the oldest fish bones in an archaeological site in the world (in 1998), a few bones found not suggesting a specialised technology for catching fish, such as nets, lines, poisons or fish spears, not even deliberate pursuit. The few bones would be accounted for by the accidental or intentional trapping of fish on the outgoing tide on reefs, when the fish were opportunistically speared. The data available did not allow the dating of the beginnings of deliberate pursuit of fish. The site at Balof 2, a younger site from the Pleistocene, contained the best evidence for fishing, fish bones, which have been identified as 5 families of reef fish, being found throughout the deposit. The families found are Acanthuridae, Carangidae, Balistidae, Scaridae and Pomacanthidae. In Balof 2 there were 3 species of small shark, found only in the levels dating from the Holocene, strengthening the evidence for deliberate fishing as these sharks are most often found in the open sea, though they do enter lagoons (White *et al.*, 1991).

According to Allen, echinoderms and shellfish were the most common remains of food found in the earliest levels, suggesting that the search for food was centred on slow moving organisms on the reef. Allen suggests that the strandlooper strategy apparent in New Ireland may be an indication of the food gathering strategy adopted by the earliest colonists in Greater Australia, a strategy that would require the least change in behaviour from their previous home in South East Asia, though if this is the case it raises the question of whether Matenkupkum and Buang Merabak, that have similar earliest dates, are actually sites of earliest colonisation of New Ireland. This bears directly on the question of minimalist explanations. Allen suggests that such a coast, that has familiar climate and resources, could be expected to be colonised early in the colonisation, probably before mid-montane forests, assuming other things were equal. Allen asks the question, was the occupation of this coast significantly delayed by the comparatively depauperate nature of its terrestrial biota in comparison to the northern coastlines of Greater Australia further west?

Allen argues that the initial colonisation of central eastern New Ireland is represented by Matenkupkum, Matenbek and Buang Merabak based on the shell evidence in the earliest levels of the 3 sites (Balean, 1989:33-4), Spriggs strictures in Source 1 notwithstanding. Large individuals of a large species of ***Turbo*** were prominent for the 10,000 years of the record at Matenkupkum and Matenbek, dominating the earliest levels, indicating a long period of low-level human predation. At Matenkupkum there are clear changes in the subsequent exploitation of shell (Gosden & Robertson, 1991), especially in the period after the Last Glacial Maximum. Between 30,000 BP and 20,000 BP there is an apparent lack of change in the shellfish remains that allows for the possibility that the same low level of predation was occurring for 10,000 years prior to its commencement at Matenkupkum and Buang Merabak. Allen suggests, based on the coincidence in the dates of commencement at these sites strengthens the view that it did not occur earlier.

In the terminal Pleistocene these changes in shell use occur at the same time as other changes in the archaeological record, such as the presence of obsidian originating in the Talasea area of West New Britain that is found in small amounts, though continuously in levels at Matenbek from 20,000-18,000 BP. The earliest published age of the appearance of obsidian in the cave at Matenkupkum was about 12,000 BP (Allen *et al*., 1989: 554), though in 1998 this was being reviewed following further excavations there in 1988. Allen suggests that in light of the apparent gap in the record at Matenkupkum between about 21,000 BP and about 14,000 BP, the discrepancy between Matenkupkum and Matenbek appears to be of a stratigraphical nature, so likely to be resolved. Allen makes 3 points about Talasea obsidian distribution in the sites on New Ireland.

The transportation, at least 18,000 years ago, of a useful raw material across a straight line distance of about 350 km

The transportation involved a water crossing from New Britain to New Ireland, the earliest known demonstration of canoe transport in the region that was not accidental-illustrating patterning in another aspect of human behaviour.

Talasea obsidian has not been found in Balof 2 or Panakiwuk, the 2 northern sites, in the Pleistocene, though is present in levels from the Holocene, 8,000-7,000 BP in Balof 2, and probably at the same time in Panakiwuk, signalling a change of some sort.

Obsidian doesn't appear to have reached Manus Island or the Solomon Islands in the Pleistocene. Archaeologists found it easier to accept the transport of stone raw material at an early time than the transport of living animals across biogeographic boundaries. ***Rattus mordax***, found in the earliest levels of all sites, that is believed to be locally extinct, possibly replacing ***Rattus praetor***, a species found in levels from the Holocene in the sites at Panakiwuk and Balof 2, though it not found in Matenkupkum and Matenbek. Another species that appears to have been introduced is ***Phalanger orientalis***, which is found in the earliest layers at Matenbek but not in the sites of Matenkupkum, Panakiwuk or Balof 2. Allen suggests ***P. orientalis*** may have appeared earlier in southern than northern New Ireland. In the Holocene layers in the northern sites the thylogale makes its first appearance, ***Thylogale brunii***. Evidence from Balof 2 suggests this was separate from, and earlier than the first appearance of domestic animals such as the pig in New Ireland. In the Pamwak sequence on Manus Island the bandicoot is present.

Allen considers the evidence compelling for the implication that wild animals were transported by humans across water barriers in the terminal Pleistocene and Early Holocene, though conceding there are inconsistencies (Allen *et al.*, 1989: 556). He suggests that the establishment of breeding populations may not necessarily have been the intention of the humans, suggesting it is more probable that the introduction of the animals was a by-product of colonisation. The transportation of useful products over relatively long distances across water by the terminal Pleistocene, based on evidence from obsidian and fauna, increases the probability that useful elements, and possibly whole horticultural systems for producing food were occurring in New Ireland as early as they did in highlands of New Guinea. It has been observed (Groube, 1988: 298) that the manipulation of swamps for food production was occurring at Kuk (Golson, 1998) about 9,000 years ago, as soon as it was permitted by the improvement of the climate at the end of the Pleistocene suggests it may have been practised at lower altitudes during the Pleistocene. The small amount of evidence that he considers might support this view (Allen, 1989: 558), though criticised by Spriggs (Source 1). Allen disputes Spriggs' treatment of the data, suggesting Spriggs' explanations are not in any way more parsimonious or compelling.

The lithic assemblages from these sites that have been described (see Freslov, 1989; Allen *et al.*, 1989: 552-4; Marshall & Allen, 1991; White *et al.*, 1991) appear to vary considerably between sites suggesting different raw material resources rather than cultural continuities in regard to their manufacture and use. The record clearly indicates that changes took places that were quite distinctive during the last 20,000 years of the Pleistocene, though data from the islands of Melanesia are fragmentary.

According to Allen, it is possible to see in the data a progression from initial occupation that was of low density that was coastally oriented, to a more intensive, extensive use of the region. Archaeologically, Matenbek, which is 18,000 years old, appears different from Matenkupkum, that is 32,000 years old, and Balof 2 that is 8,000 years old, displays a different, more intensive usage than Panakiwuk that is 14,000 years old. There are also hints of even greater difference between the Papua New Guinea highlands and the islands of Melanesia that cannot easily be explained by differences in the environment. An increasing degree of divergence in human behaviours between the islands and the Highlands of Melanesia throughout the Pleistocene may have been dictated by human strategies predicated on sea travel rather than land travel, the result being a broad spectrum and extensive solutions to the problems of acquiring a subsistence living, as well as more specialised, intensive solutions.

Aboriginal Occupation of Greater Australia - the pattern of colonisation beginning in the Late Pleistocene (Smith[47])

The dynamics of the settlement of Australia by Aboriginal people, that took place prior to 30,000 BP, is not certain. Smith (Smith in Murray, 1998) gives several factors by which the direct reconstruction of the way in which colonisation took place has been constrained. The range and quantity of data derived from archaeology are insufficient to determine distribution prior to about 30,000 BP, about half way to the first arrival at about 60,000 BP. His second factor is lack of precision of dating methods in this time period (Allen, 1994; Allen & Holdaway, 1995; Roberts, Jones & Smith, 1994). Other sources of data are often used to interpret archaeological evidence regarding the colonisation of the continent.

Smith suggests the first arrival of people in Australia and New Guinea occurred at some time before 35,000 BP (Allen, 1989; Groube, *et al.*, 1986; Pearce & Barbetti, 1981), and probably between 50,000 and 60,000 BP (Roberts, Jones & Smith, 1990; Roberts *et al.*, 1994). He believes to reach Australia and New Guinea it would have required people to make a crossing of the ocean of a few days duration from the nearest islands of the Indo-Malaysian Archipelago, also suggesting that the migration was equally likely to have occurred as a steady trickle as a single discrete migration. The first arrivals would have presumably been familiar with island and tropical environments, and would have been using watercraft for some time before making the crossing (Irwin, 1992).

The first settlement of the coast, as well as estuarine and riverine environment, would have been assisted by their familiarity with the continuity of useful species of plant and marine environments across Wallacea in northern Australia and New Guinea, though the terrestrial fauna would have been different and unfamiliar. People would have migrated to the east, remaining in the tropics as they colonised the Bismarck Archipelago and the Solomonlands, both rich in marine resources, though their terrestrial environments were depauperate in both terrestrial plants and animals. When they moved to the east or the south they would have been confronted by an environment like nothing they had ever encountered before, such as the montane regions of the cordillera in New Guinea, arid central Australia and in Tasmania, the high latitude temperate environments.

By 30,000 BP they were thriving in all these disparate environments (Smith & Sharp, 1993).

For much of the time earlier than 30,000 BP, when colonisation was taking place, the sea level was between 60 and 80 m lower than at present (Chappell, 1994), and as the present islands of New Guinea and Tasmania were both part of the single landmass of greater Australia, the area of the continent was substantially larger than at present, especially as there were also large areas of the continental shelves around the margins, especially in the north-western (Sahul) part of the continent, exposed by the lower sea level. Whenever the sealevel dropped by 12 m or more dry land, or at least a shallow strait, connected New Guinea to the Australian continent. When the sea level was 55 m or more below the present level the island of Tasmania was connected to the southern margin of the main landmass of Australia by the Bassian Rise. Following the revision of estimates of sea levels (Chappell, 1994), it would have been possible for people to walk from southern Australia to Tasmania any time between 60,000 BP and 10,000 BP.

Dispersal patterns and processes

According to Smith, there are 2 broad categories of proposed scenarios, those that favour early dispersal across the continent that took place rapidly, and those favouring slower, patchier dispersal, with parts of the continent being occupied up to 10s of thousands of years after the first arrivals on the shores of Greater Australia.

Several assumptions are made as the basis for scenarios of rapid dispersal and occupation that include a very flexible response to environmental conditions encountered, and a high intrinsic population growth rate, that resulted in occupation of the continent that was rapid. Some propose that the dispersal across large areas of the interior followed the drainage systems (Birdsell, 1957; Mulvaney, 1961), such as those of the Murray-Darling Basin and the Lake Eyre Basin, that between them cover a vast area of central Australia. As they moved from the early arrival points in the north of the continent there would have been a gradient in the vegetation cover of the land towards the south, allowing the people to adjust gradually to changing plant foods, as they gained ecological knowledge that eventually allowed them to settle the arid interior

(Golson, 1971). Quantitative models have been constructed that show that it would be possible for the continent to have filled to saturation, with a population of about 300,000 people, (the estimated population current in 1957) in between 845 and 4134 years after initial arrival (Birdsell, 1957). The estimated pre-contact population has since been increased to about 750,000 (White and Mulvaney, 1987). Key components in these proposed dispersals include rapid demographic growth that drove dispersal, groups from the main population centres moving to new areas when carrying capacity is approached, a process in which social groups are replicated.

Others have questioned these assumptions. It has been suggested that the Aboriginal population may have grown slowly for the first few millennia after first arrival (White & O'Connell, 1982: 46-54). Suggestions have been made that stochastic fluctuations affect small founder populations (McArthur, Saunders & Tweedie, 1976). It has also been suggested that the population growth rate could have been reduced by the presence of endemic malaria in coastal lowlands in the northernmost third of the continent (Groube, 1993). It has also been suggested that if small groups continued arriving from Asia for several millennia after the first landing it may have offset these factors. The same results could have been achieved by the presence of several founder populations along the north coast and western New Guinea. Even when populations have growth rates that are almost stationary the population grows substantially over 5,000-10,000 years. Selective parameters appear to change when empty territory is available, rapid dispersal taking place (Kitching, 1986; Stodart & Parer, 1988; Rindos & Webb, 1992). Smith suggests small groups may have moved into new territory that had a rich terrestrial fauna before the carrying capacity of their original group was reached, possibly without replicating social formations. In the desert areas some desert groups have historically managed to maintain social and demographic units, even when the population density is as low as $1/200 \text{ km}^2$ (e.g. Long, 1971).

An alternative view was proposed according to which some habitats, coastal or riverine zones, were preferentially occupied, because of the lack of anything more than the barest capacity to adapt to ecological conditions they had not previously encountered (Bowdler, 1977) or (Hallam, 1987; Horton, 1981). According to

Smith, Bowdler proposed the most influential of these models, suggesting the focus would have been strongly on aquatic resources at the beginning of colonisation, resulting in the groups being tied to littoral, lacustral and riverine habitats, suggesting that it was not until 12,000-10,000 BP that montane and desert regions were occupied. One of the key parts of her suggestion is that after 15,000 BP lakes and rivers in semi-arid areas of south-eastern Australia failed, such as occurred in the Willandra region. According to this scenario (See Millet Harvesters), the drying up of lakes, such as the Willandra lakes, forced the people to rely on terrestrial food sources such as grass seeds and acacia seeds, both of which are present in the ethnography of central Australia, widespread settlement of inland arid areas becoming possible following the glacial period as a result of the shift to terrestrial food sources.

According to Smith the arid zone is singled out in a number of other models as a particularly problematic environment for occupation (Horton, 1981, Veth, 1989), and it has been suggested that woodland that was well watered would have been the preferred environment for settlement, over both aquatic and desert environments, as a result of a more flexible response towards the terrestrial environment than was allowed for in the model of Bowdler (Horton, 1981; Hallam, 1987). Potable water availability was seen as a key factor in early occupation, especially by Horton, who also suggests that the distribution of the large megafauna were a guide to woodland that was well-watered in the late Pleistocene, assuming at least some of the large herbivorous megafauna were extant at the time of the first arrivals in Australia. Rock art in the north west of the continent and elsewhere have been found that are believed to be of species of the megafauna. See Megafauna and the Dreamtime, ***Diprotodon optatum***, Giant Kangaroos of the Dreamtime ***(Sthenurus)***, ***Palorchestes azael*** Quinkana, Marsupial Lions. Smith says that the context in which all these models were proposed has been changed radically by archaeological work that has been carried out since 1977 (Allen *et al.*, 1988; Allen, 1989; Bowdler, 1990a; Kiernan *et al.*, 1983; Smith, 1987; Cosgrove 1989). Models for the occupation of the major continental dune fields that occurred late, about 5,000 BP, have been proposed that are somewhat similar (Veth, 1989, 1995). A common factor in these models is the special difficulties associated with these regions that have drainage that is uncoordinated, hummock grasslands and dune fields, the suggestion being made that before these dune fields could be occupied it was necessary to make adaptations, both technological and social, in adjacent regions.

Smith suggests the timeframe is a major problem for all these proposed models, as he believed it was unlikely the people took 10s of thousands of years to adapt to ecological conditions that were either difficult of unfamiliar, especially in the light of archaeological evidence indicating that habitats such as montane (Gillieson & Mountain, 1983; Mountain, 1993; White, Crook & Ruxton, 1970) and arid (Maynard, 1980; Smith, 1987, 1989) were exploited long before 14,000 BP, and it is now apparent that terrestrial-based economies were operating prior to this time in a number of places across Australia (e.g. Bowdler, 1990b; Cosgrove, 1989; Kiernan, Jones & Ranson, 1983).

Smith says these arguments risk confusing dispersal with optimisation strategies (see Rindos & Webb, 1992), suggesting that optimal adaptation to the local environment, and population densities that are comparable to ethnohistoric levels, need not occur at the time of the initial settlement. Smith believes the case for the initial occupation of these regions taking place in the Holocene because of the requirement for adaptations, economic and social, before they could be occupied, is overstated by Veth, (1989) (Smith, 1993). This model was later recast (Veth, 1995), shifting emphasis more on to areas where the drainage systems were uncoordinated, though according to Smith it is 'clearly at odds with archaeological evidence' here (Cane, 1995; Gould, 1977; Martin, 1973; Wright, 1971; Smith, 1987, 1989). According to Smith, the picture of the settlement of deserts has changed rapidly following the finding of clear evidence of the use of sandy deserts during the Pleistocene, indicating that the chronological framework at least needs to be recalibrated (Smith *et al.*, 1991; Veth *et al.*, 1990; Veth, 1995; Veth & O'Connor, 1996).

Major time lags between the coastal region occupation and that of the continental interior are believed by Smith to be unlikely (Source 1). It is difficult to model the growth of population because of the linear configuration of the coastal zone without concluding that some movement into the interior took place long before the populating of the coastal zone of the continent was complete (White & O'Connell, 1982, Fig. 3.7). Westward movement around the margin of the continent would be expected to have required adaptation at an early stage to arid conditions, as the continental western coast is arid, as well as less emphasis on littoral resources (Nicholson & Cane, 1994; White & O'Connell, 1982: 52). If a suggestion about the presence of malaria in northern and swamp regions is correct (Groube, 1993), groups moving inland would have been free to grow and disperse while those in the malaria infested areas would have been slowed down. It has also been suggested that larger territories would be needed, as a result of reduced carrying capacity in arid areas, higher dispersal rates also resulting in these areas (Birdsell, 1957). This has been confirmed by studies of rabbits, which have spread throughout arid and semi-arid regions at 100 km/y, those in coastal and forest habitats spreading at 10-15 km/y (Stodart & Pared, 1988).

Continental colonisation - archaeological evidence

Smith suggests that because of the remoteness of the time of first arrival there are problems with the archaeology and the chronological resolution of this event. These problems make it difficult to investigate the pattern and rate of settlement, only in the very broadest terms being possible. According to Smith, current data [1998] suggest that all parts of the continent had been occupied by 15,000-10,000 BP, though in places, such as south-western Tasmania, the New Guinea Highlands and parts of the arid interior did not have a record of continuous occupation at the time of writing, 1998.

High latitude regions

In Tasmania, the south west region that is densely forested, has produced a number of finds such as Beginners Luck Cave (Murray *et al.*, 1980), Kutikina Cave (Fraser Cave) (Kiernan *et al.*, 1983) and Nunamira Cave (Bluff Cave) (Cosgrove, 1989) that demonstrate that the region has one of the richest records in Australia of occupation during the Pleistocene that begins about 35,000 BP. The occupation sites were being used at a time when the region, on the extreme southern margin of the continent, was vegetated by exposed alpine grasslands. The oldest date of 35,000 BP was obtained from Warreen Cave in south-western Tasmania. These early dates for occupation in the Tasmanian south west indicated that humans were exploiting highland and extremely high-latitude regions much earlier than expected, causing problems for the previous models of the occupation of Australia. The archaeological evidence apparently shows that the region was occupied continuously throughout the last glacial period, when the largest Tasmanian ice sheet existed. These sites also provided evidence for a much richer fauna, dominated by small macropods, than had been expected, prompting Bowdler (1990a) to reassess her coastal colonisation model, conceding that the evidence showed that adaptation to the exploitation of terrestrial resources had occurred much earlier than she had believed.

The occupation sites of Tasmania, is one of only a few parts of Australia to provide an opportunity to test the proposals of speed of colonisation of the continent. At Parmerpar Meethaner a sterile layer is present that has been dated to about 40,000 BP, the earliest occupation layer having been dated to about 34,000 BP (Cosgrove, 1995). Cosgrove suggested that this has put the time of arrival of people in Tasmania at about 34,000 BP. If the excavator is correct it would suggest that there was a large time lag, of about 20,000 years between the time of the earliest arrival in northern Australia and the arrival of the first people in Tasmania. As it is not known how long the sterile layer took to accumulate it is not certain if this actually brackets the earliest arrival in the region, if it took a relatively short time to form it would suggest that the earliest time of arrival has not been effectively bracketed.

Deserts

Archaeological evidence for occupation of arid areas was interpreted as opportunistic use of the upper reaches of coastal catchments or the landward section of coastal territories, when the dates obtained were of Late Pleistocene age (Bowdler, 1977). This interpretation was based on evidence from such sites as the Newman Site in the Pilbara dated to 21,000 BP (Maynard, 1980), and on the Nullarbor Plain, Koonalda Cave, 22,000 BP, (Wright, 1971 and Allen's Cave (N145), more than 20,000 BP (Martin, 1973). Puritjarra Rock shelter (Smith, 1987, 1989; Smith *et al.*, in press in 1998) that has been dated to about 35,000 BP provided archaeological evidence of the early occupation of the arid central regions of the Australian continent. Later finds in the arid zone are such sites as the JSN site, 14,400 BP (Smith *et al.*, 1991) in the dune fields of the Strzelecki Desert (see Australian Archaeological Sites), Cuckadoo 1 Rock Shelter, 15,000 BP (Davidson *et al.*, 1993), Katumpul, about 22,000 BP (Veth, 1995: 36) in the Laverton region and at Serpent's Glen, about 24,000 BP (Veth & O'Connor, 1996). According to Smith the remaining evidence, though sparse, indicates that the arid interior of the continent was already being exploited over widespread areas in the Late Pleistocene, from at least 30,000 BP. The Little Sandy Desert (Veth & O'Connor, 1996) has provided more recent evidence, dates that the Pleistocene occupation pattern included some of the more arid areas of Australia that included the major continental dune fields . It has been suggested that this represents a form of opportunistic use of the arid zone (Bowdler, 1990a; Veth, 1995) and not a fully operating system (cf. Smith, 1989). As more recent evidence accumulates Smith says it has become more difficult to maintain the interpretation of the evidence as possibly indicating opportunistic use of the arid zone.

The initial occupation of these sites had been believed to be controlled by their adaptation to new plant resources, mainly grass seeds and acacia seeds. The archaeological evidence is not consistent with this being the case, seed-grinding implements that are identifiable not being found until about 4,000-3,000 BP, suggesting that these plant foods were not the first resources to be exploited in the arid regions (Smith, 1986). Though direct evidence of prehistoric subsistence is rare, the faunal assemblages at the Silver Dollar Site, 25,000 BP, in which macropods and emu egg shells predominate, suggest the early adjustments were to these resources (Bowdler, 1990b). Small macropods also dominate the rich faunal assemblage found in Allen's Cave (Cane, 1995) on the Nullarbor Plain where the occupation extends to about 39,000 BP. An early adaptation to very arid regions is demonstrated by the sites on the Nullarbor Plain, occupation at Allen's Cave apparently continuing throughout the last glacial maximum, at which time the site was on a vast arid inland plain, situated on a saltbush steppe.

Situated in the south-eastern sector of the arid zone, **Karolta** has been reported to have been dated to about 30,000 BP, based on cation ratio assays and AMS radiocarbon dating of charcoal that was embedded in rock varnish (Dorn *et al.*, 1988; Dorn & Nobbs, 1992). If these dates are confirmed it would strengthen the argument that fully operating regional systems were established early in the colonisation of the arid zone.

Islands See: Archaeology of Sahul or Greater Australia - Melanesian Lowlands

Conclusion

Smith's conclusion is that the initial settlement of the coastal and riverine environments of northern Sahul probably took a few thousand years, and included the movement of people to the large islands of northern Melanesia, possibly involving deliberate as opposed to accidental voyaging. He also concludes that the northern Australian savannahs and those of the Sahul Shelf were probably widely occupied before the colonisation of the coastal environments was complete. He suggests that settlement began slowly, becoming more rapid over time, the drier climates of the interior leading to better health of the people in those regions that allowed more rapid dispersal, and the larger territories that were necessary to support each of these groups in the interior. Smith suggests similar factors may have operated in the colonisation of the central Cordillera of New Guinea, the richest terrestrial fauna being found in the montane forests and alpine habitats, with the added benefit of relief from malaria in the cooler climates.

He suggests that the northern and eastern coastlines of Australia, with their rich coastal habitats, probably promoted rapid selective settlement. On the west and North West coasts the arid littoral zone probably promoted a move to exploitation of terrestrial resources at an early stage of colonisation, as part of a broad spectrum mixed economy. He suggests settlement of the arid zone may have taken place within a few thousand years of the first arrivals in Australia, though populations in the deserts have probably always been low and widely dispersed, and subject to the vagaries of the erratic climate of these regions. The last parts of the continent to be occupied may have been the major Australian deserts, both sand ridge and stony deserts, or at least the last places to have an established fully operating regional system, though he says it is uncertain if the colonisation of these arid areas lagged behind the colonisation of the northern savannahs by 10s of thousands of years.

In Tasmania, the high latitude temperate habitats were occupied at an early stage, based on the available archaeological evidence it appears that Tasmania was first occupied about 35,000 BP, though he considered the dates of 35,000 BP for both Tasmania and New Ireland to be difficult to reconcile with other archaeological evidence that indicates that Greater Australia was first occupied about 50,000-60,000 BP. He believes lags of 10s of thousands of years are unlikely to be correct.

See Stone Tools

The First Settlers in Australia

The founding population of Australia is suggested by genetics to have comprised around 1,000 people, a figure that the author[1] finds surprising and intriguing, as he suggests it is larger and more focused than he would have expected. According to this genetic conclusion it would seem colonisation was a simultaneous event, and not the sporadic, incremental event over a long period of time, with the founding population seeming to comprise a single migration comprised of a number of separate events that were closely spaced. There appears to have been 5-10 women, so about 10-20 individuals in each landing party. There must have been either quite large boats or a large number of boats, at least 50 if there were about 20 people in each. Questions posed include why did they come, and why did they all come at once? How many began the journey if some were presumably lost at sea? What were they thinking and what did they expect to find when they made landfall?

A link is provided by the genetic evidence, directly or indirectly, between the catastrophic events that occurred at Mt Toba and the colonisation of Australia. The estimated antiquity of common maternal genetic ancestors of all Aboriginal people living at the present is similar to the date of the Mt Toba explosion, though the temporal window is wide, with Australia being colonised between 45,000-75,000 BP based on the genetic research. The primigenial conclusion being that the most recent common female ancestor of the Australian Aboriginals lived more than 70,000 years ago. Were their ancestors already in Indonesia when the Toba catastrophe occurred? Or did they come later? Based on the available evidence either suggestion may be the correct one, though increasingly the indications are that they were already present in Indonesia. According to the author[1] there is already some evidence of modern humans being in India and south-eastern Asia more than 70,000 years ago, and genetic evidence of the first Australians being in Asia between 70,000-62,000 BP. If they were there and survived the eruption they may have migrated east, possibly continuing on to Australia. If they were not there, then others soon were.

The Restaurant at the End of the Universe:
Modelling the Colonising of Australia

O'Connell & Allen (2004) have previously developed a speculative model of the colonisation by humans of Sahul-Pleistocene Australia and New Guinea. In this paper the authors[1] elaborate that model by the use of behavioural ecology and Palaeoclimatology data, and ethnography of modern hunter-gathers. Their argument of colonisers is mainly focused on coastal ecotones during the Wallacea crossing, though in favourable habitats they spread more widely following the landing in Sahul. In terms of archaeology, movement was instantaneous, being primarily driven by serial depletion of high-ranged prey. O'Connell & Allen (2004) suggest that subsequently human populations remained much smaller than sometimes imagined, which was probably as a result of difficult climatic and environmental conditions and archaeological data are generally consistent with these expectations. O'Connell & Allen (2004) suggest these findings challenge the frequent assertions that only human colonisation led to significant changes in the ecology of Sahul, and may go some way in explaining the simplicity of the lithic technology in the Pleistocene.

The Landing Site of the First Settlers in Australia

At the time the first settlers arrived at the Australian coast it was on the exposed continental shelf, as the sea was about 70 m lower than the present level, which continued from the western Kimberley to the Torres Strait and then another 2,000 km from the Gulf of Papua to north Fraser Island. The continental shelf covered a total area of

1.6 million km² before it was flooded about 10,000 BP. The coastline along which the settlers would have advanced along was probably a diverse subtropical plain covered with pristine rainforest, grassland, woodland and savannah.

Between 70,000 and 60,000 BP global temperature was decreasing and the sea levels were dropping and the land was continuing to dry, then after about 60,000 BP the world began to warm and the sea level began rising. Over the next 10,000 years there were 2 cycles of global warming and cooling, the overall trend being to cool and increasing aridity. In spite of the cyclic ameliorations to this more general trend the climate was getting colder and drier. The climate was cool and dry again by 50,000 BP and the sea levels were 70-80 m lower than at the present. Over the next 10,000 years the climate continued to oscillate, going through 2 more cycles of warming and cooling, then after 45,000-40,000 BP the conditions were more arid. There were 2 environmental stages over this period of time, the first from 70,000-60,000 BP, when the conditions began the slide toward glacial conditions, with sea levels about 70 m below the present sea level. The second was from 60,000 BP to about 18,000 BP, when the world, including Greater Australia, endured long periods of increasing aridity and increasing cold. The overall pattern was gradual cooling and drying. Almost 120,000 BP was the last time the Australian climate and environment looked and felt as it does at the present.

Wherever the first arrivals landed it is likely they settled near water on a reasonably soft shoreline. Cane suggests it is reasonable for them to have been on a peninsula similar to the Coburg Peninsula of the present, though they could have landed anywhere along the coastal plain that is now submerged, possibly near a river mouth, blown up against a precarious rocky promontory, in a mangrove forest or on a broad, long open beach. Wherever they landed the coastal hinterland would have been not much different from what it is at the present, wide valleys that were sloping towards the sea, subdued plains and broad river systems. It would have been an environment that would allow them to survive long enough to become established.

They could possibly have landed in the far north, within the west-facing arm of the cordillera in New Guinea. They could have moved inland, along rivers and into the mountains, though Cane believes it is more likely it would have been a coastal route where they would be directed by the topography towards a broad land bridge that joined Cape York and Papua New Guinea. The sea is 12 m deep in Torres Strait; at the time when it was Torres Plain it would have been 40-50 m above sea level. Some channels cut through the land to depths of up to 120 m, which would have provided estuaries and sea channels where hunters and gatherers would have been able to find plenty of food. If they crossed to the south over the Torres Plain they could have arrived at a huge embayment that surrounds what is now the Coral Sea. At that time they could have walked to the margin of what is now the Great Barrier Reef, and foraged in the lace-like network of ridges and canyons that now anchors the reef.

An alternative could have been the western route to the Australian mainland via the open plains and many river systems into the lakes and lands of Carpentaria. The Gulf of Carpentaria was dry land with a vast lake in the middle between 70,000 and 50,000 years ago. Lake Carpentaria, the central lake, was fed by 37 ancestral rivers carrying a total of 12,700 gigalitres of fresh water into the lake system per year. For comparison Sydney Harbour holds 560 gigalitres. The lake was one of the largest ever lakes in the world, at 500 km long and 250 km wide, though it was shallow, being 15 m deep on its eastern side. The nature of the lake fluctuated along with the sea levels. The environment changes from a lake to an embayment as the sea level rose, as there was a channel connecting the lake to the Arafura Sea when the sea level was high enough. When the sea level was 75 m lower than that of the present it was a lake, though once the sea level had risen 15 m, to about 60 m below the level of the present, it became a brackish swamp. It became an embayment surrounded by many lakes when the sea rose another 15 m.

Cane suggests the lake must have been a perfect Eden-like environment, though an Eden with giant crocodiles, snakes and goannas. From the sea in the greater region any experienced sailors would have recognised the signs of a body of fresh water, by the travel directions of sea birds and migratory birds, and in the sea, the presence of flood-washed vegetation, driftwood, and discolouration of the sea as a result of freshwater discharge.

Settlement at this location would have been close to ideal, with plenty of fresh water, many rivers, tributaries and small lakes which they could live around, as well as hunt, gather shellfish, fish, dugongs and turtles, birds and terrestrial game. Pollen analysis of sediments deposited over the last 40,000 years has revealed the presence of black soil plains that were vegetated by eucalyptus, bottlebrush and *Callitris* pines and growing in the waterholes and lakes, water lilies, yams and bulrushes, which all sounds very similar to Kakadu of the present. The extensive systems that drain towards Lake Eyre Basin would have provided a corridor for the settlers to travel south. The continent was open to them, though the deserts were also in front of them, Cane suggesting expansion may have been sporadic, as allowed by the cyclical climatic ameliorations of regional weather patterns.

The Arnhem Land coast, with magnificent escarpments, is located to the west of the Lake Carpentaria. At that time the Alligator, Wildman, Mary and Adelaide rivers all eventually fused into a single river, to form the Arnhem Land River that was deeply incised. Between Coburg Range, that is now the Coburg Peninsula, and Melville Hill, that is now Melville Island, this river flowed through a gentle valley onto the extensive Arafura Plain, that is now the Arafura Sea, eventually joining the giant Arafura River, flowing south from Papua New Guinea and on to the Indian Ocean. The Arnhem Land Plateau, 200 km wide and 250 m above the alluvial plains was, and remains, a living environment that is remarkable, with small rivers incised, overhung with waterfalls, and skirted by fertile wetlands and savannahs. The total environment had abundant food, water and shelter.

If the settlers had landed at, or travelled west along the great northern coast, they would have arrived at the Ashmore Peninsula, now Ashmore Reef, beside a huge basin central to the Joseph Bonaparte Gulf of the present. There was a large lake in this basin with an area of 20,000 km^2 and with a large freshwater catchment that was 350,000 km^2, Lake Argyle, for comparison, is 1,000 km^2. A valley that was relatively deep-sided connected the lake to the ocean, the sub-oceanic Malita Valley. Tidal movements in this area are massive and dangerous at the present, as they may have been in the past. If this was the case in the past the out-pouring of water through the Malita Valley must have been spectacular.

Cane suggests it is likely the lake and associated embayments would have been rich living environments, with both marine resources near the coast and freshwater resources further inland, where monsoonal rains penetrated the great basin by great rivers. Something of the magnitude of these rivers in past times can be seen in the rivers of the present, though they are now smaller. Some of these rivers are the Mitchell River, 117 km long with a catchment of 2,970 km^2, the Drysdale River, 423 km long and a catchment of 8,400 km^2 and the King Edward River, 221 km long and a catchment area of 15,690 km^2. These were long and fertile avenues that could have been settled and from which they could expand their territory and lead the settlers to the rugged plateaus of the Kimberley, and from there other large freshwater rivers ran to the west and south, eventually reaching the sea, as well as leading people to the desert. An example is the Fitzroy which skirts the Kimberley for 640 km, which has an extensive catchment of 83,000 km^2. Following this river eventually leads to the Sturt Creek and dendritic channels of Tjurabalan (Milkwater), and to Paraku (Lake Gregory), a large seasonal lake that borders the Great Sandy Desert.

Occupation of Sahul (Greater Australia)
Aboriginal Occupation of Australia - Timeline (After Cane, 2013)

Cane has constructed a timeline of events in connection with the occupation of Australia by humans, beginning with a suggestion of why the first migrants travelled to Australia, the volcanic eruption of Mt Toba in Indonesia that occurred 74,000 BP.

74,000 BP

This is suggested as the time of the first crossing From Indonesia to Australia. Arriving by boat the first people to settle in Australia made the first ocean crossing in the history of the world.

There is a dramatic increase in the charcoal found at various locations throughout Australia between about 73,000-60.000 BP. Cane concedes that the increase of charcoal may have been a natural occurrence, though could also have resulted from the arrival of the first colonists on the Australian continents, and firestick farming has been practised in Australia for a very long time.

60,000 BP

The earliest signs of occupation by humans in northern Australia are found in archaeological sites beginning at this time.

51,000 BP

The settlement of south eastern Australia. Artefacts found at sites in the ancient Willandra Lakes system have been dated to between 52,000-45,000 BP.

50,000 BP

Humans penetrate the Australian desert, based on a single stone artefact that was found at Paraku (Lake Gregory) at the northern margin of the Great Sandy Desert.

47,000 BP

The whole of the continent was apparently occupied by this time, with people living at Devil's Lair in far south-western Australia.

46,000 BP

The first appearance of hafted axes. Starch traces have been found on some of the axes, some of which were found associated with charred nuts that may date to as much as 49,000 BP.

45,000 BP

The arid lands of central Australia were occupied about this time and the last of the megafauna become extinct, possibly as a combination of hunting, burning and a changing climate.

44,000 BP

By this time glacial Tasmania was occupied, with people living in caves and hunting wallabies around Parmerpar Meethaner, as well as many other cave sites in south-western Tasmania under subantarctic conditions.

42,000 BP

First known evidence of burial and cremation. The full skeleton of a man has been found, and the nature of his burial suggests belief in an afterlife. Cane suggests this could be the first of its kind in the world. The burnt remains of a small woman have also been found in the Willandra Lakes, which is suggested to possibly be the earliest known cremation in the world.

40,000 BP

The oldest known evidence of art in the world has been has been found in the form of ochre coating a slab of limestone at Carpenter's Gap in the Kimberley.

36,000 BP

In the New Guinea Highlands new technology, environmental management and the procurement of food suggests pre-agricultural activity at least 15,000 years before anywhere else in the world.

35,000 BP

Fragments of a ground edge axe have been found at Nawarla Gabarnmang in western Arnhem Land.

33,000 BP

Variable evidence has been found of seeds of grass and succulents being processed and consumed in the Willandra Lakes and the Kimberley 10,000 years before anywhere else in the world.

32,000 BP

Shell beads have been found at Carpenter's Gap and Riwi in the Kimberley and Mandu Mandu Rock Shelter on North West Cape that date from 30,000-32,000 BP, making them amongst the oldest jewellery in the world.

30,000 BP,

The Great Drought, the beginning of the glacial drought. At this time Australia entered a major ice age, with a dropping sea level cooling temperatures, and an extreme drought affected much of the continent for the next 10,000 years.

28,000 BP

A charcoal drawing has been found on a rock fragment at Nawarla Gabarnmang that dated to 28,000 BP.

25,000 BP

The earliest known depictions of human faces that are found throughout the arid areas of Australia, part of the Panaramitee artistic tradition that is believed to be between 10,000-25,000 years old.

22,000 BP

In the Willandra Lakes a group of 23 people left tracks as they walked and hunted.

21,000 BP

The colonists occupied the continental shelf as it was emerging as the sea level dropped. According to the author[1] they were living in areas such as the Bass Plain, the area that is now covered by Bass Strait between Tasmania and the mainland of Australia 22,000 BP and on the North West Shelf more than 30,000 BP.

20,000 BP

The first known appearance of the ancient Gwion and 'Dynamic' art in the Kimberley and Arnhem Land dated to between 16,000-23,000 BP, which displays elaborate personal decoration and technology.

18,000 BP

The Great Flood. As the ice age ended and the climate began to warm the sea levels rose which flooded the continental shelves around Australia, with the climate becoming wetter and windier, as well as more unpredictable.

13,000 BP

Conflict. It is suggested by artistic representations from across northern Australia that there was increasing territorial conflict at this time, that is suggested by the author[1] to possibly have resulted from the loss of territory as the continental shelf was flooded by the rising sea causing increasing competition for land and resources.

10,000 BP

At this time the sea flooded across what are now Bass Straight and the Gulf of Carpentaria, forming thousands of islands around the coast. Populations that remained on Flinders Island and Kangaroo Island eventually died out.

The oldest known boomerang was found in a swamp in south-eastern Australia.

9,000 BP

Around this time a range of tools that are more diverse and efficient developed, including 'backed' blades, spear throwers and composite spears.

6,000 BP

Burning and rainfall result in the production of large amounts of sediment that choke estuaries around Australia, eventually leading to the formation of enormous mangrove swamps, that grow into flood plains over the next 1,500 years.

5,000 BP

At about 4,500 BP the dingo arrives in Australia, which indicates there were new migrations to Australia. It is also believed there was another migration about 7,000 BP.

4,000 BP

The well-known x-ray art of Arnhem Land arises, that portrays human and animal anatomy.

3,000 BP

At this time there is evidence of territorial demarcation and conflict, believed to be a response to increasing population. There is intense use of coastal resources in south-eastern Australia, and economies specialise. The increase of sea level peaks and climate becomes increasingly unpredictable and drier.

2,000 BP

Across south-eastern Australia villages arise. Watercraft are used and aquaculture develops, and some evidence of gardening. Complex social and religious systems develop.

1,000 BP

The development of extensive trade routes across the continent for the distribution of precious resources, such as ochre and narcotics and tools, including boomerangs, grindstones and axes.

300 BP

Along the northern coast Indonesia fishermen arrive to trade. The coastline is explored by Dutch, Portuguese and British, and the British colonists arrive,

Occupation of Sahul (Greater Australia)
Aboriginal Occupation - Populating the Continent

Nearly everything required by hunter-gathers was provided for by the coastal environments of northern Australia - fresh water, shelter, fire and food - the available food being in a variety of forms, fruits, nuts, tubers, fish, shellfish, birds and their eggs, reptiles and marsupials, which made for a secure foundation. The numbers of marsupials, birds and reptiles were very high, which would have made it easy for the first settlers to live off the land in the vicinity of their first settlements until they worked out what could and could not be eaten in the vegetation away from the landing site, the composition of the vegetation becoming more different with distance from the coast and rivers. At the landing site they would also have to be wary of possible predators, but as they moved further inland they would have had to become familiar with the large megafauna predators that inhabited any new environments they encountered.

Once they had become familiar with the new predators they needed to find a defence against them, and the occasional cyclone, fire or flood they needed to learn how to deal with, life in general would probably have been relatively safe and free in their new homeland.

To colonise the new continent they needed, as would any animal colonising a new environment, access for the men to breeding females. It is shown by demographic simulations that in order to avoid extinction or in-breeding at least 2 groups of about 100 individuals each would be needed for the exchange of women to allow both groups to achieve a stable demographic state. It is indicated by genetic analysis that the people colonising Australia did so in a number of landings that took place close to simultaneously, in small groups that totalled about 1,000 individuals. As the entire continent was populated in what some suggest may have been a relatively short time, then it is obvious that there were enough breeding women, though in some cases in very small groups there may have been a degree of incest if women from other groups were not available.

An open social and environmental horizon confronted these first settlers to which they needed to adapt, breed and consolidate, and then they could expand into the rest of the continent. Cane suggests the first settlement and colonisation of the continent might have been quite fast, though he suggests northern Australia was such a fertile environment at the time of the first settlement that there might not have been much need for nomadism. He also suggests that the establishment of a relatively small area may have been encouraged by the country being foreign and fertile which may have been a significant disincentive to extreme nomadism.

On the other hand there were few constraints on territorial expansion once a social group was secure, as the population increased and the existing resources became less abundant. It is suggested to be possible that an ancient population that had steadily grown and expanded proportionately, that was never far from water and always within reach of its own geographic traditions, constantly sought new country to live more easily in. A sinuous colonisation process that eventually appears to have as Cane puts it, a surprising agility.

It is therefore possible to imagine a founding population growing, their country becoming increasingly larger along the coast, up rivers and across the savannah and on into escarpments and hills that were well watered. When the founding population first arrived the shores and hinterland where they settled, which is now under water, was a landmass that was greater in area than the present day Northern Territory and twice the size of New South Wales. It was a large area and would appear to have been a large area for the settlers and their descendants to colonise, though it may have taken less time than is at first believed possible. Assuming a population of 1,000 settlers, and that population was comprised of family groups each of about 20 people who had a territorial configuration similar to that of coastal Arnhem Land at the present, and a population growth of 1-2.5 %/year, the entire coastal plain, that is now submerged, could have been populated in 400-900 years.

If this is correct it would have been possible that a founding population arriving in Australia 70,000-50,000 BP could have settled the entire coastal plain, now submerged, in a period that was too short to be detected by even the best of the modern dating techniques, being in that sense instantaneous. But as people are social beings with a strong sense of place, to the extent that people are dependent on their society and their society is dependent on the country it is attached to, then these people are partially geographically contained. The necessity for territorial expansion is opposed to the need for a unified society, and such a tension is broken only under particular environmental conditions, such as drought, or changed conditions such as overpopulation that leads to decreased environmental opportunity. Therefore it is difficult to predict population growth as the ties of social adhesion bind it, and the environmental necessity stabilised, at some point, by the relationship between them in the context of indeterminate time elements, diversity of environments, the variability of the climate, and the evolution of the culture. The dynamic is active, the balance is variable and there are unpredictable demographic consequences. It is obvious that people did colonise the entire continent, but it is less obvious what the pattern and rate of colonisation was. Therefore it is not known if colonisation was as rapid as is suggested by demographic modelling, or as slow as it is supposed to be by intuition, being tentative at the start, of incremental form and in time comprehensive, always being contextualised by human capacity, constraints of the environment and the changing climate over the millennia of occupation.

Aboriginal Occupation - Populating the Continent - The Evidence

Cane suggests that coastal settlement taking place 70,000 BP, on the continental shelf that is now submerged, might have left some evidence further inland by 65,000 BP, even if it got off to a slow start, gradually gathering momentum, taking 5 times longer than is suggested by hypothetical modelling. And if they arrived 50,000 BP evidence could be expected to be present inland by 45,000 BP. It is hard to be confident in any predictions concerning the timing of landfall, and of the archaeological evidence that maybe related to it, as there are a vast number of demographic possibilities. There is also a problem with the many destructive variables making it hard to believe it is possible that any traces of lives lived so long ago, whether or not they are related to landfall, would still be present . A few sites have been found relating to that era, in spite of all the destructive possibilities they could have been exposed to.

At a location that Cane says is surprisingly small, has been found under the sheltered overhang of a sandstone outlier, Malakunanja, which has more recently been called Madjebebe. Overlooking the flood plain of the Magela River, a tributary of the East Alligator River in sub-tropical Arnhem Land, which would have been cooler and drier at that time. At the time of first landfall Malakunanja was 500 km from the coast but is now only 50 km inland. It is not known how long it took to reach this site from the coast. On the walls there are faded paintings from the distant past and the floor contains histories from that past, the sediments having been accumulating for 105,000 years. The first signs of human occupation begin abruptly, the first time humans were in the bush of inland Greater Australia.

About 100 artefacts have been recovered from the sediments at this location, the oldest of which was dated to 61,000 BP. Over the next 15,000 years, in the next 30 cm of the deposit in the shelter, 1,500 artefacts were left at the camp. An age of 52,000 BP has been retrieved from the middle of this horizon. At some time between 52,000 and 45,000 BP someone dug a small pit in the ground, a fragile feature that is 20 cm deep and about 40 cm wide, which is about the size of a typical oven that is used to roast goannas or bake tubers in earth pits at the present. What is amazing is that this feature has not been disturbed or displaced since it was dug, the sediment having been found to have last been exposed to light about 45,000 BP, which indicates a minimum age for the pit and associated artefacts that were still present within it.

These age determinations have a measure of statistical uncertainty, which is consistent with the ambivalence of time. There is a 1 in 3 chance that the actual date of the site could be either 10,000 years younger or 10,000 years older, the result of which is that the occupation of Malakunanja could be as much as 71,000 BP or 51,000 BP. The older date is consistent with the settlement of Australia resulting from the impact on human populations in Indonesia of the Mount Toba eruption, and the more recent date is consistent with the broader age of occupation that has been discovered in other locations in Australia.

Artefacts made of quartz and silcrete were left by people under the overhang, as well as a grind stone and pieces of igneous rock they had brought to the shelter. Ground haematite (a very high quality source of red ochre) crayons that were use-striated, were left at the camp, as well as other fragments of red and yellow ochre, pieces of mica and chlorite. Mica is sheeted silica that is perfectly laminated, which gives it a sparkling, crystalline quality that produces 'a magical sheen when rubbed into the skin' Cane (2013). Cane has observed mica being mixed with ochre and applied to the skin to give a dramatic effect in the most sacred ceremonies. Chlorite is soft enough to be scratched with a fingernail and also has a sparkling quality and the powder produced is green and feels oily. The purpose implied is either decoration or ceremony, either of which entails social awareness and consequential social consciousness. The coloured crayons, when conservatively interpreted, alludes to an ancient artistic expression that is expressed, at least as decoration, possibly on the peoples' skin or hair, or wooden artefacts and valued possessions, such as bags, string, dishes and adornments. According to the author[1] as there is a possible association between ochre and ritual activity is equally obvious, and requires that a sophisticated social and political system existed in the deep past. The presence of these materials implies creativity and aesthetic appreciation, as might be understood at the present, whatever the function implied for them, among ancient people very early in the ancestral Aboriginal occupation of Australia.

Antiquity and artistry seem to have been characteristic of the great past in Arnhem Land, and of the discoveries by archaeology. The Nauwalabila site, 70 km from Malakunanja, is another example. Early occupation at this site is also associated with ground haematite. This larger rock shelter, in Deaf Adder Gorge, was formed by a boulder toppling off the adjacent escarpment. An old man who had once camped in the rock shelter led archaeologists to it early in 1972, and their subsequent excavations found that the probable ancestors of his people had occupied the site continuously from the first time it was occupied. More than 30,000 artefacts were found in the deposit, of which 230 were within sand and interlocked gravel that has been dated to 60,000-53,000 BP, with a 1 in 3 chance of being from 67,000-48,000 BP.

Nawarla Gabarnmang Cave

In the archaic tradition of Australia the bedrock of Arnhem Land asserts itself in such a grand style. About the same time people were grinding ochre and making stone tools in Arnhem Land, ancient Australians were camping on the coast and occupying the highlands of New Guinea. At that time the climate was about 4°C cooler than at the present, and the tree line was lower, the deciduous forest and the savannah extending to the sea. The mountain valleys were covered by broad areas of dense rainforest, though trees didn't grow above 3,000 m, and above 4,200 m glaciers covered the mountains.

At Bobongara, the Huon Peninsula, on the north east coast of New Guinea, an ancient camp has been found, that at the time it was occupied was on a shore that was productive and hospitable, that was vegetated by mangroves and located among lagoons that overlooked fringing reefs, and there were forests in the hinterland. The camp and the old shore line have since been raised by continuing tectonic activity that powers orogenic activity so that the site of the camp is now located on a raised coral terrace about 40 m above the sea. A number of stone axes were recovered that were sealed beneath consolidated volcanic ash adjacent to a stream on the terrace, and hundreds more were present in the creek. These were flaked axes with a chipped groove to form a 'waisted' axe for attachment to a handle. These waisted axes are at least 44,500 years old and possibly as much as 61,000 years old, making them the oldest known hafted axes in the world.

The coastal people are indicated by the presence of these waisted axes to have been utilising the forest, clearing areas of the forest for occupation and food collection, and they were also used by nomads living in the mountains. At the time people were living in the forest there were also people living in the Ivane Valley 2,000 m above sea level which at that time, when the climate was in a cool phase, was vegetated by beech forests. In Greater Australia (Sahul) these ancient nomads had begun to tame the forest. The settlers had an established forest tradition, and the clearing of the forests for hunting, gathering and living was aided by the development of hafted axes (axes fixed to a handle). Cane suggests the hafted axes were used to penetrate and utilise the forest, possibly by clearing trees, splitting wood, ring-barking trunks, trimming branches, clearing roots and opening the canopy of the forest to allow sunlight to reach the forest floor for the production of food plants, various bush bananas, vegetables and beans and to improve the production of fruit on *Pandanus* palms.

Microscopic grains of starch were still attached to some of the artefacts that were recovered from this valley which indicated that *Dioscorea* yams were being harvested, processed and consumed. The identification of charred *Pandanus* nuts indicated that both yams and nuts were being consumed 49,000-44,000 years ago. *Pandanus* was growing abundantly in the local area at that time, but yams grew at lower altitudes, which indicated either the nomads occupied large territories, or that food exchange was being carried out with other groups of people who lived in different altitudinal environments.

Cane suggests it is not surprising that a colonising population felled trees, as they had come from tropical Southeast Asia which was forested and were probably familiar with the variety of potential foods, such as forest yams, taro, sago and *Pandanus* nuts. The ancient axe heads that still had organic remains adhering to them are testimony to the high degree of ingenuity, environmental adaptation and social organisation of the first settlers in Australia. It is demonstrated by the ancient sites in New Guinea that the penetration, management, exploitation and successful occupation of forest environments at high altitude occurred about 40,000-60,000 years ago.

Aboriginal Occupation - Populating the Continent - Desert

The Riwi Cave site is on the Fitzroy River that borders the desert, this river leading to the Sturt Creek (Tjurabalan) that fills Lake Gregory (Paraku) which is an extensive freshwater lake. Paraku is an unusual desert lake, in that it is usually a freshwater lake but after droughts it becomes saline and sometimes dries completely. This was a mega-lake 300,000 BP when it covered 6,000 km^2, though in the historic period its area has never exceeded 1,700 km^2. Over the last 60,000-40,000 years there have been oscillating wet and dry periods, including a period of increased fluvial activity and lake enlargement from 50,000-45,000 BP. At the time of occupation the temperature of the area was lower than at the present when the evaporation rate is more than 10 times the annual rainfall, the desert continuing to desiccate, though in the past as the desert was cooler, surface water tended to stay longer.

At the present Paraku is still an attractive living environment. After rain large numbers of birds, including sea birds, arrive at the lake to breed, nesting on the shores of the lake which contains mussels and small fish. Marsupials gather around its fringes, and there is rich vegetation along the creeks and floodplains, such as tubers, (***Vignia***) bush onions (***Cyperus***) and bush tomatoes (***Solanum centrale***).

Cane suggests it is not difficult to understand why nomads of the ancient past would come to Paraku and stay there, the problem has been finding evidence of their occupation there, but an ancient stone core flaked from an old river cobble has been found in the sediments of the lake that date from at least 45,000-50,000 BP. Though such a find is small it has great implications as it places people in the desert earlier than almost any other geographical location in Australia. People were therefore in the desert an extraordinarily long time ago, as indicated by the artefact, but it also indicates that the occupation of the continent that occurred on the northern Australian coast must be considerably older than the time suggested by the northern Australian sites that have been found.

According to Cane he knew people who had walked to Paraku in their youth prior to 1900, along a small number of traditional walking tracks that extend for 350 km from Wilkinkarra (Lake

Mackay) in the Great Sandy Desert. The tracks followed the desert ranges and escarpments, fertile plains and large salt lakes, that in ancient times were themselves lake and river systems. As previously mentioned, at 40,000 BP the climate was cooler and marginally wetter that at present, which would probably have made it easier for early settlers to access the deserts from secure environments in the north, such as Paraku, than it was for people who walked the tracks in the 1800s.

Following effective monsoonal rains these ancient river systems filled, this type of rainfall is irregular but impressive events at the present, and it is suggested by climatic implications that it would also have been so in earlier times. Following heavy rain the ancient drainage system becomes rivers and lakes, and following such an event in 2001 the area west of Wilkinkarra became an inland sea that remained for 3 years. As the great sand deserts have many soaks they are not the major impediment to occupation by expansion into the desert they appear at first sight to be, it is a deceptive landscape. They differ from almost every other environment in the world as the water is hidden underground, and it takes knowledge and skill to find it.

See Tjukurrpa

The skill of hunter-gatherers of the deserts appears to be boundless, an appreciation of which allows anyone unfamiliar with the landscape to understand how it might have been used. For those with the necessary skills food is abundant in the desert and, allowing for the season, is of high nutritional value and takes little labour to acquire sufficient to feed the whole family. Cane has observed people hunting goannas (***Varanus***) and collecting bush tomatoes, he noted that a person can collect enough goannas in an hour to feed himself for a day and picking bush tomatoes for an hour can feed a family for a day. Enough bush onions were collected in 20 minutes on one occasion to feed 12 adults with plenty left over. In the northern deserts wild sweet potatoes (***Ipomoea***) are very abundant, to such an extent that they appear domesticated, and to some extent they are, as parts of the tubers are often snapped off and reburied thus ensuring there is a crop for the next season. The Cane[1] suggests that as these tubers can be gathered in such numbers in a couple of hours enough can be acquired to feed an entire family; they could have been a drawcard for the early settlers.

According to Cane at the time he recorded the subsistence practices of the deserts they had been largely unoccupied for 30 years, and in this comparatively unexploited state he suggests it could be compared with the deserts at the time of first settlement, though with obvious caution, as this resource had previously been untapped. He notes that there were fields of grass seeds and hectares of tubers that had not been harvested, and the animals were unaware of human predation. In this state the relatively unexploited environment probably resembled the conditions at the time of first settlement. Some of the problems they could have encountered with desert living include bad seasons, good supplies of water and food are not always available in all parts of all deserts, but to the first settlers it could have been more attractive than it would seem in its present state of aridity to Europeans with their dependence of food obtained from a relatively small number of farmed food crops which require a constant water supply. An advantage of life in the desert is there would have been no giant crocodiles (***Pallimnarchus)*** and much less chance of encountering possum lions (marsupial lions) (***Thylacoleo***), in such dry, open conditions and very few trees. And there were probably few giant goannas (***Megalania***).

Once people appeared at Paraku it was not long before they occupied the desert. The walking distance between Paraku and Wilkinkarra is 350 km, or 250 km by direct travel. The central Australian ranges are a further 250 km. In the 1950s 2 men walked across the northern part of the treeless section of the Nullarbor Plain. Walking in winter, though across very harsh rocky, waterless terrain, they took 3 days to cross the 260 km, walking at night and in the cooler parts of the morning and afternoon. Several months later one of the men walked back. Just part of life for desert nomads. When considered from the perspective of a desert nomad it is easy to conceive of people settling, walking and occupying the country between Paraku and central Australia early in the occupation of Australia. Evidence of this has been found at Puritjarra Rock Shelter near the Cleland Hills that has been dated to 45,000 BP, in the form of several flakes, a core and pieces of red and purple ochre. The ochre had been obtained from an ochre quarry on Karrku ('ochre') located 125 km onto the sand plains north west and 150 km to the east of Wilkinkarra. According to Cane this source is renowned for its high quality and its lustrous rouge-like texture and appearance. Senior Aboriginal religious leaders treasured this ochre for its particular ceremonial value, with the result that it was traded extensively. The Puritjarra ochre has been described as having been for personal decoration and for paintings in the cave, though Cane suggests there may have been a deeper religious significance as well as other mystical activities that are secreted within the archaeological utilitarianism of painting and personal adornment. It seems the ochre had great value in the distant past, as it still has at the present, as in the past people walked 250 km to get it or traded commodities for it. This raises the possibility of a desert trading system 40,000 BP, and also indicating that mining, the extraction of ochre, was taking place at Karrku a very long time ago. At present the mine extends 80 m underground and is suggested by Cane to possibly be the oldest active mine site in the world.

It seems that among the earliest settlers there was a certain adaptive genius, and a focused, resourceful socio-economic system, as indicated by the presence of the ochre at Puritjarra and the geographic relationship between that site and Karrku. An evolutionary character might be assumed for the ancient strategies of occupation that enabled the settlement of the desert so long ago, and given the reliable food staples, strategies for hunting and gathering that were flexible and water availability, allowed desert occupation in the long-term. Extreme mobility must have been required to be sure of access to necessary resources, and an inclusive social and economic network operating over a vast area that was implicitly required to ensure survival. The Tjukurrpa articulates and maintains that network at the present.

In the desert the early settlement left a light footprint, though one with a large personality. With minor elaboration nomadic settlement and social cohesion would lead to people occupying all desert environments within the next 10,000 years, and which would continue defining society across the arid zone of greater Australia until the arrival of Europeans.

Cane suggests the Nullarbor Plain, the harshest and most unappealing of the Australian desert landscapes, is possibly the best environment to demonstrate the diversity and adaptability of human ecology in the desert through ancient occupation. The few trees are low, the ground is very porous and there is a limited nutritional base. It is dangerous to cross this limestone plain at night because of the nature of the surface that is so pitted with caves, tunnels, blowholes, and dolines. It has been suggested it is more similar to the surface of the Moon than an Australian desert, with thin soils and very rocky ground.

It is indicated by palaeoenvironmental conditions that 40,000 BP the regional climate was drier than at present, and that the cliffs near the Bight, that are up to 100 m high, were an escarpment at that time, though then they overlooked a huge flat coastal plain that was 70 km further seaward than at present. At that time people were visiting Allen's Cave on what was then the inland plain, with signs of occupation from 40,000 BP, and possibly up to 43,000 BP, being found in that rock shelter.

See Allen's Cave

At Dempsey's Lagoon near Port Augusta, South Australia, a similar antiquity is indicated by an old cooking hearth. This hearth has been dated to more than 40,000 BP. Port Augusta is a port that is now near the sea. With an annual rainfall of less than 250 mm/year it is dry, though it was even drier at the time of earliest known occupation, as well as being further inland. Port Augusta is located at the northern end of a broad, flat plain and is flanked by low cliffs. This plain was flat and dry 40,000 BP, and the coast was at least 400 km away.

A major story is told, according to Cane, of the adaptability and ingenuity of the first settlers, by such minimal archaeological evidence of the desert occupation. There is evidence for people having settled the north, centre and south of the Australian desert 40,000-50,000 BP, at Allen's Cave, 3 pieces of ancient flaked stone, 1 flaked cobble at Paraku, and at Puritjarra a handful of flakes and ochre. It is presumed the desert was settled from lands that were more fertile via the semi-arid margins, and the core deserts were eventually soon settled, as well as the arid ranges and barren plains.

Australia's Deserts – The 'Desert Transformation' Concept

One possibility that has been widely canvassed is that at the time of colonisation there may have been only modest aridity, in which case the first people to arrive would have encountered a more productive landscape with active rivers and large permanent lakes. *'Reliable rainfall extended across the heart of the continent. Active rivers drained into permanent lakes ... there was a spread of rain-forest flora over the centre of the continent ... [and] a diversified and predominantly herbivorous land fauna* (Mulvaney, 1961: 63). Following Bowler's work on the Willandra Lakes, it was suggested *'the Mungo Lacustrine Phase would have given major access to the reactivated river and lake systems which ringed the arid heart'* (Jones, 1979: 453). This was accepted by many researchers (White & O'Connell, 1982; Hiscock, 1988a; Ross, Donnelly & Wasson, 1992; Thorley, 1998a; Hiscock & Wallis, 2005: 43). It has been argued in the 'coastal colonisation hypothesis' (Bowdler, 1977) that in the Murray-Darling Basin early sites represented a 'transliterated coastal economy' that was centred on rivers and lakes. This idea was extended to central Australia when it was suggested (Thorley, 1998a) that more regular and abundant resources would have been provided by the Lake Amadeus and the Finke-Palmer River system at the time the first humans arrived than at the present. These ideas were brought together in the 'desert transformation' model (Hiscock & Wallis). They argued that prior to 45,000-40,000 years ago exploration and exploitation of these unique interior landscapes were facilitated by the presence of large permanent water bodies. In this scenario the Australian deserts of the present formed where the early settlers had been living rather than the people moving to the already established desert areas (2005, 41-3). In his book Smith endorses the alternative view according to which the first people in Australia found arid landscapes with xeric biota when they moved to the interior of the continent. The vital statistics of the desert into which they moved differed somewhat from the deserts of the present, though still an arid environment. This is a case in which chronology is critical to this question. The series of fluvial and lacustrine events in the interior has recently been unpicked by the use of luminescence and palaeomagnetic dating.

According to Smith these archaeological ideas risk creating an amalgam of landscapes with ages and potential that differ widely, conflating evidence from the last interglacial (MIS5.5, 132,000-115,000 years ago) with conditions in early MIS3 (60,000-45,000 years ago), as a more detailed history has emerged.

Aboriginal Occupation - The Western Coast - Pilbara

The desert extended to the west as far as the sea 40,000 years ago, and at that time the western desert was cooler than elsewhere and it is indicated by ancient pollen records from the Pilbara that it was colder between 42,000 and 39,000 BP than at any other time in the last 100,000 years. It appears the area was in a period of climatic transition from cooler wetter to cooler drier, having an average of 9 dry months per year, low rainfall and very little summer rain. It is still not known how the ancestral Aboriginals first colonised this part of the Australian continent, whether they moved from the arid interior or arrived on the coast. Both possibilities are suggested by the archaeological evidence. The author[1] suggests that both of the possible routes of settlement would have had difficulties, one of which was, and would also have been at the time of colonisation, the few rivers present along this part of the coast, as well as the desert extending to the coast.

An example is the old coastline that ran to the south from the Kimberley, a flat area about 300 km seaward of the present coast which comprised a vast fan of arid country that extended to the west from what is now the Great Sandy Desert, with no permanent rivers. The Murchison River, Gascoyne River and the Fortescue River are the largest rivers in the Pilbara, none of which are permanent rivers, though they are long. The Fortescue River flows more than 1,000 km from the desert to the sea. They take large quantities of water to the sea in the wet season, and are believed to have done so in the past. Following the heavy rains of the wet season at the present the Murchison River has an average flow of about 200 gigalitres, though on occasion it has carried more than 1,800 gigalitres in time of extreme flood. In the wet season there are raging torrents in the Pilbara Rivers and those of the Kimberley, leaving intermittent streams in the dry season in which freshwater pools are linked by underground sections of the rivers, which would have provided conduits for settlement between the desert and the sea and the sea.

Sites of great antiquity have been found on both sides of the Pilbara Block. Djadjiling on the Hamersley Plateau has been dated to 39,400-41,700 BP and Jansz Cave on the Cape Range Peninsula has been dated to 39,000-41,300 BP. See The Djadjiling Archaeological Site.

A unique aspect of the living environment of the Pilbara at the time of first settlement is that its shores are set against a steep continental shelf. As a result of this steep continental shelf the coastline of the present is similar to what the coastline was like about 40,000 BP, the difference between 40,000 years ago and the present coastline being 12 m. The author[1] suggests the Pilbara coast is probably the only coastline in Australia where the living conditions of the first settlers can be seen, at least to some extent. All other sites of coastal occupation have been submerged by rising sea levels since the close of the last ice age, though in the Pilbara not all ancient coastal sites were flooded. It is therefore possible to uncover evidence of early occupation of the coast, and such evidence has been found in Jansz Cave on the Cape Range Peninsula situated between Exmouth Gulf and the Indian Ocean. At this cave the occupants were exploiting both marine and terrestrial resources, hunting kangaroos, turtles and fish and collecting emu eggs and shellfish about 40,000 BP. The oldest evidence of marine subsistence in Australia has been found in a mixed economy at this site, as well as others such as Mandu Mandu Shelter that is a short distance to the south, which included bandicoots, bettongs, and possums. In the basal layers of these deposits there are also thylacine bones.

The country south of the Pilbara is also arid along the coast of Western Australia, and there are no permanent rivers for more than 1,200 km until the Swan River near Perth. The Swan River flowed further west across the coastal plain at 40,000 BP, beyond what was then Rottnest Hill, and is now Rottnest Island, until it entered a huge canyon. Now under water, this canyon begins at the 50 m contour, and by 160 km into the sea it reaches 2,000 m in depth. This canyon is longer and deeper than the Grand Canyon, and at the time of the first settlement it would have been an intriguing natural feature that would have been a source of plentiful food as the marine life emerged from the deep to feed on the abundant life in the oceanic upwelling near the coast. There is provisional and indirect evidence of human occupation about 50,000 years ago on Rottnest Island, which became an island about 6,500 years ago. While it was still a hill on a broad plain, about 50,000 years ago, it would have overlooked the oceanic canyon.

Artefacts have been found strewn on an old living floor further inland along the Swan River, the artefacts being believed to be at least 38,000 years old, and possibly up to 40,200-46,900 years old. Of these artefacts a small number were made from fossiliferous chalcedony obtained from a source on the coastal plain. This same material has also been found in other archaeological sites in southern Western Australia but is not found in the archaeological record after 4,600 years ago as by then the rising sea had submerged the quarry making the original source inaccessible. The people living inland along the Swan River are indicated to have moved between the river and the coast to acquire the material by its presence in their occupation site.

In Western Australia the most southerly part was dry 40,000 years ago, which is similar to the situation at the present, though at that time there was a belt of forest to the west of Bunbury and Albany, extending for 20 km past Naturaliste Hills (now islands) and Leeuwin Hills (now capes) to the west across a narrow coastal plain. This area was also settled a long time ago, based on evidence of human occupation in a limestone cave, Devil's Lair, 46,000-47,000 years ago, that has artefacts that are scattered at levels that the author[1] suggests are more likely to have an age of 50,000 years. The cave was 25 km from the archaic coastline when the first colonists arrived. The evidence of their presence is a bit sparse, 4 old fire places and 111 implements, suggesting a small number of people visited the site only infrequently. The occupants of this cave lived in semi-darkness, and included among the bones indicating what they ate were bones of possums, wallabies, snakes, lizards, frogs, bats, birds and emu eggs, the latter suggesting they lived at the site in winter. There were also megafauna bones, **Protemnodon**, **Sthenurus**, and possibly **Thylacoleo**. Among the implements were a surprisingly large number of bone tools, more than in the rest of the country, that are among the oldest bone tools known from

Australia. Some have been either split or ground to form awls, some of which are so small that it suggests they were used as needles to puncture and sew animal skins together. The cave probably provided some degree of warmth in winter, which was cold there at that time. The fur coats may have been used for hunting in winter.

Devil's Lair is about 3,000 km from Arnhem Land; therefore people who had occupied that site were living at the most southerly location. Cane (2013) suggests the great antiquity of Devil's Lair might be compared to that of Malakunanja in Arnhem Land to give some idea of the enormity and nature of settlement and adaptation across the continent. According Cane (2013) the *'timescale involved is immense, the terrain traversed is colossal, and the scale of human accomplishment is difficult to comprehend. Comprehension finds corroboration through archaeological interpretations and physical chronologies that tell a human story of great social, geographic and chronological magnitude'*. At Devil's Lair archaeological findings demonstrate that ancient people explored, established and expanded throughout the vast dry continent in a manner that absorbs and validates the oldest calibrated antiquities that have been asserted for human settlement. *'Colonisation at such a grand scale requires and gives proof to great uncontested antiquity, both documented and implied, through the establishment of regional societies of cohesion, order and engagement'* Cane (2013) . Settlement throughout Australia was based on sequential regional occupation, and required traditions of community and domesticity, creativity, self-awareness, and a resolute adaptability. *'It belongs to a greatness of time, by proof of the science that defines it, fundamentally beyond our intuitive grasp'* Cane (2013). Everywhere in palaeo-Australia there are landscapes of great antiquity that are embedded with innovation, artistry and adaptation. As Cane (2013) says *'It is a land of seafarers, woodsmen, fishers, hunters and gatherers, adventurers, explorers, artists constituting a super-nomadic continental tradition at the very edge of measureable time.'*

Aboriginal Occupation of the Simpson Desert

A number of Aboriginal tribes (more correctly, language groups) and branches of tribes occupied parts of the Simpson Desert. The western margins of the desert were occupied by the Lower Southern Aranda and Eastern Aranda. Along the eastern fringe of the desert there were the Wangkamadla and the Karanguru. The territory of the Wangkamadla also extended into the northern part of the desert, and that of the Wangkanguru extended to the central and southern central regions of the desert.

In the past it was believed the Aborigines never penetrated the central areas of the Simpson Desert. This belief was based, at least in part, on the writings of European explorers in the 19th century, such as Charles Winnecke, who wrote in 1883 that he was almost certain "this country has never been visited by natives." More than 50 years later Cecil Madigan stated that the Aborigines around the margins feared the desert and lacked knowledge of its interior. According to Madigan the area of the Simpson Desert and around Lake Eyre was under the malevolent influence of Kuddimukra (kadimakara) that were often associated with the bones of *Diprotodon* and other animals from the region. Madigan said the Aborigines of the region believed it to be "a djinn-like" spirit which may appear in the form of a giant snake with the head of a kangaroo, likely to do much harm to the unwary traveller." He claimed the Aborigines avoided the lake, saying that all who had gone into the desert have become victims of Kuddimukra (kadimakara). He believed Leichardt's remains were in the Simpson Desert, and the reason the Aborigines never found it was their taboo on the area.

Madigan and Winnecke later changed their minds about the Aborigines never travelling in the desert. It was claimed by others that the Aborigines only entered the desert after good rain, mainly because there was no water or food.

Archaeological excavations of the 'barrier deserts' and adjacent dune fields - Rudall Lake, Balgo region, Simpson Desert, Lake Eyre Basin, Coongie Lakes and Cooper Basin has found hundreds of sites from the last 5000 years. Pleistocene sites in these areas haven't been found yet (Flood, 2004).

In 1886 David Lindsay crossed the southern and central parts of the desert, taking a man from the Wangkangurru Wangkanguru people who knew where water could be found at 9 native wells (soaks). It was stated in Lindsay's Journal that the Wangkangurru? people were living in the desert on a permanent basis at the time of his expedition. Since 1980 all 9 wells mentioned in Lindsay's journal have been found. Detailed descriptions of places and life in the Simpson were given to Dr Luise Hercus who spent 20 years working with the Wangkangurru? people, including some who were last members of their tribe to be born in the Simpson Desert, and the story of how they left it (Hercus, 1985). Hercus visited the sites of the wells and was able to confirm the detailed description he had been given by story and song by Irinjili (Mick McLean), a tribal member born in the desert, being able to find direct evidence of habitation and lifestyle. She made accurate maps of the occupation sites surrounding the wells, as well as the 9 wells.

Based on Hercus' findings it is now known that the Wangkangurru? centred their life around the wells, or mikiri, the only known sources of permanent water in the desert that were essential to their existence in such an arid environment. The wells are now known to be at the sites of shallow freshwater soaks that formed on gypseous flats where depressions in the centre of swales allowed rainwater to collect. Rainwater infiltrated coarse sand around the depressions, percolating down to impervious layers of clay. The water accumulated until it came close enough to the surface to be reached by digging. Narrow shafts up to 7 m deep were dug to reach the water. Being so deep beneath the surface it was mostly protected from the extreme heat and dryness of the surface allowing it to remain for much longer than it would at the surface. Making the shafts narrow, whether intentional or not, would tend to reduce the evaporation rate. Though the soaks depended on rain to maintain them, they were apparently permanent enough to support the tribe for up to thousands of years. It is not known how the Wangkangurru? first found the soaks, as they had to dig to reach the water. Hercus suggests they may have followed the water as it flowed along the gypseous flats after rain.

Hercus has found a total of 18 mikiri, most being silted over by wind erosion since the people left the desert and no longer maintained them. The work of Hercus with the Wangkangurru? has found that a unique character and significance, as well as mythological significance, was associated with each mikiri, and its usefulness as regarded by the people. The mikiri that have been visited have been found to retain the same quality and taste as recorded by Lindsay in 1886.

According to Irinjili his tribe spent their entire lives around the wells. He spent his childhood around the mikiri, and playing on salt lakes or catching small birds. He said they didn't record the passing of time. Every day the men hunted and the women collected seeds in the dune fields, of which a favourite were the seeds of pigweed (*Aizoon quadrifidium*) from the edges of dunes and clay pans. The sporocarps (spore capsules) of nardoo (*Marsilea drummondii*) were collected by the women from nardoo meadows growing in shallow pools, especially on the eastern and northern parts of the desert that received more regular floods. The sporocarps were harvested when they dried as the pools evaporated. The flour made by crushing them on grindstones was mixed with water to make dough to be cooked in the manner of damper, on the ashes of a fire.

Archaeological evidence from the sites near the mikiri confirms that stone was a precious item in the desert, every stone implement being used until it was worn away too much to be useful. The Paltrhirri Pithi stone quarry on Anna Creek station near Sunny Creek, to the south west of the desert, was a favourite source of stone for grindstones. This required a long walk from their home in the desert, but the shortage of stone in the desert made it necessary.

The use of wood for the construction of mia mias (humpies or wiltjas) by the Wangkangurru made it a valuable commodity. Mia mias were mainly made from gidgee. In the dry environment of the desert wooden implements, digging sticks, waddies and bowls, are preserved well, as are the wooden frames of wiltjas that can still be seen 90 years after they were erected. Stone and wooden artefacts, still in good condition, can be found around the mikiri.

Archaeological evidence of the diet of the desert people can also be found at the occupation sites around the mikiri. The animal remains from these sites reveal that they ate a wide variety of animals such as bandicoots, bettongs, hare-wallabies, bilbies, desert rat-kangaroos, spinifex hopping mouse, rats, dingoes, carpet snakes, lizards, emus and a number of smaller birds (Shephards, 1992).

One of the animals the people of the Simpson Desert ate was the desert rat-kangaroo *Caloprymnus campestris*, described for the first time in 1843. According to most references in books it was found only on stony interdune flats and gibber plains in the north-eastern parts of South Australia, and in Queensland in the far south west. Its bones in the occupation sites of the central Simpson Desert indicate that it also lived in the sand ridges of the desert.

One of the food items spoken of by Irinjili was the carpet snake, which the men would go to great lengths to catch, tunnelling into the holes the snakes were in to dig them out, and because of the loose nature of the sand, risked the tunnel caving in and burying them. He said they always had enough meat to not worry much about food, as was found with other people in the Western Desert. In both localities there was enough time after gathering food to develop a rich cultural and spiritual life. In the area of the occupation sites there are many graves, the body being laid out in a simple shallow grave and branches placed upon it.

In good seasons, when rain had left water in sites away from the wells, such as irpi (claypans) and ikara (swamps), not the sort of places usually thought of being in the Simpson Desert, at times when the monsoon brought heavy rain to the north west of the continent a number of watercourses brought water to the edges of the Simpson Desert, even into the swales - the Macumba River, Todd River, Hale River, Plenty River, Hay River and Warburton River, and Eyre Creek, Kallakoopah Creek and Illogwa Creek. After rain these streams often had large waterholes that hold large amounts of freshwater.

It was at these times that the Wangkangurru? held their big totemic rituals and corroborees, and general celebrations, meeting the neighbours as they held all types of ceremonial activities. Also at these times initiations were carried out at sacred places, such as the ritual centre associated with the Two Men at the clay pan Mararu. These times when they were away from the mikiri could last for months and even years. As well as a time for ceremonies and a chance for an easier life for a while as they could collect more and different food, that could be obtained easier than during their normal life, it also allowed the plants and animals of the country around the mikiri to recover.

When Irinjili's uncle Imatuwa left the desert he was the last person out, the culture that had lasted for thousands of years was ended (Shephard, 1992)

Links with the Southern Aranda

The links between the Wangkangurru? and the Southern Aranda included marriage exchanges and joint ceremonies associated with Ancestral beings that crossed the country of both tribes.

In the Footsteps of Lindsay (Reproduced here with Denis Bartell's permission) Chapter 5 from the book Desert Walker, by Denis Bartell, in which he relates his finding of 9 abandoned wells (mikaris) (soaks) in the Simpson Desert that had been used and maintained by the Aboriginal tribe living in the Simpson Desert until they finally left the desert.

Aboriginal Settlement in the LGM at Brockman, Pilbara, Western Australia (Slack, Fillios & Fullagar, 2009)

Slack et *al.* say this paper describes the results and implications of recent excavations on the Hamersley Iron Brockman 4 tenement, close to Tom Price in Western Australia. The results were from 2 rock shelters in which evidence of Aboriginal occupation was found that began at least 32,000 BP, continuing throughout the Last Glacial Maximum (LGM). Slack et *al.* propose the nature of Aboriginal foraging patterns that are displayed, based on the records of flaked stone and faunal remains, for the Brockman region.

Since excavations began in the Pilbara about 30 years ago there are 2 research questions that are still to be answered the age and continuity of the occupation sites. In regards to the settlement of the continent the age of the sites continues to be important for determining the timing and the direction from which the settlement took place. At the time the first synthesis and review of the initial archaeological excavations for the Hamersley Plateau (Brown, 1987) the oldest date that had been determined for an archaeological site was 26,300 + 500 BP (SUA1510) that had been obtained for the Newman Rock Shelter (P2055.2) (Brown, 1987:22, Troilett, 1982). It is not until recently that the antiquity of this site has been surpassed by estimate of the age from excavations at Djadjiling, Hope Downs in the eastern Hamersley Range, in spite of intensive archaeological work over 20 years, that was mostly carried out by consulting projects that included more than 50 excavations and more than 100 radiocarbon dates (see Slack, 2008). The date from Djadjiling indicates that occupation dates from at least $35,159 \pm 537$ BP (Morse in the same issue of Archaeology in Oceania).

According to Slack et *al.* (2009) there is a question concerning whether following the occupation of the Pilbara by the Aboriginal people the occupation continued throughout period of increased aridity that occurred during the last glacial period during OIS2, between about 29,000-15,000 cal. yr. BP (see Burroughs, 2005: 30, 93), and the aridity of the LGM in particular, a time when the sea levels were at their lowest between 22,000-19,000 cal. yr. BP (Yokoyama et *al.*, 2000). Slack et *al.*, (2009) say that over the past few decades there has been a consistent focus of research on the occupation of the Pilbara throughout the LGM, with the Hamersley and Chichester Rages being proposed as likely to have been refuges (Hiscock, 1988; Smith, 1987, 1989; Veth, 1989, 1993). Over these same few decades it has been shown by research that the impact on climate of the LGM has been more severe, and to have occurred at an earlier time than had previously been believed (and peaking in the Greenland ice-core isotope stratigraphy at 21,200 cal. yr. BP see Turney et *al.*, 2006; Barrows & Juggins, 2005).

According to Slack et *al.*, (2009) the nature of regional patterns of occupation during the LGM that has been revised and extended has been summarised on the basis of 7 specific rock shelter sites in the Pilbara Uplands that have been argued to exhibit refuge occupation during the LGM (see O'Connor & Veth, 2006: 33-39). Yirra (Veitch et *al.*, 2005) and Milly's Cave (Marwick, 2002) have been said to be the only sites to exhibit persuasive evidence of occupation during the LGM. The suggestion that there is no unequivocal evidence of occupation during the LGM at the remaining 5 sites (Marwick, 2002) is agreed with by (O'Connor & Veth, 2006). According to the analysis by Marwick the first 2 of these sites, Newman Rock shelter (Troilett, 1982) and Newman Orebody XXIX Rock shelter (Maynard, 1980), have stratigraphic records and radiocarbon chronologies that suggest, though don't confirm, there is evidence of human occupation17,000-13,000 BP [i.e. 20,000-15,000 cal. yr. BP] (OxCal v4.0.5 was used in radiocarbon calibration in this article) (Marwick, 2002: 23; see also Comtesse, 2003). Similarly, evidence of human occupation at this period is regarded as ambiguous. Uncertainties have been a problem for the interpretation of artefacts and their relationship to carbon dates at Mesa J J24 (Hughes & Quartermaine, 1992), Malea Rock shelter (McDonald, Hale & Associate, 1997) and Manganese Gorge 8 (Veth, 1995:736).

The only sites in the interior of the Pilbara for which there is good evidence of occupation during the LGM are Yirra and Milly's Cave. It has been said that at Yirra and Milly's Cave artefacts are found between conventional radiocarbon ages of 19,270 ± 140 BP (Wk-8954) (23,440 – 22480 cal. yr. BP) and (16,950 ± 90 BP (Wk-9148) (20,300 – 19,889 cal. yr. BP) which are consistent with refuge occupation during the LGM (Veitch et al., 2005:58). It is, however, not certain whether Yirra was occupied more intensively at the height of the LGM of immediately following it, as there are acknowledged unresolved problems with bioturbation, with critical dates at the peak, and with little additional information about the frequency of artefacts, the site and climatic history of the locality of the site.

According to Marwick's 2002 paper the only clear indication of human occupation during the LGM has been found at the Milly's Cave site. Slack et al. (2009) agree but it is suggested by re-evaluation of the timing of the LGM (Yokoyama et al., 2000; Lambeck & Chappell, 2001) that the site may have been only sporadically occupied before the close of the LGM. More intense occupation immediately following the peak of the LGM is suggested by Slack et al. (2009), to plausibly be indicated by the lowest radiocarbon determinations and frequency of artefacts at Milly's Cave, and beneath this level, between about 21,000 and 30,000 cal. yr. BP, rates of discard are very low (see Marwick, 2002:25). Slack et al. (2009) have also noted that at this site the lower 2 radiocarbon dates of 14,150 ± 320 BP (18,024 – 16,022 cal. yr. BP) and 18,750 ± 460 BP (23,686-21,075 cal. ye. BP) are separated by as little as 5 cm of deposit. Slack et al. (2009) suggest that, as such, the data from Milly's Cave is more compelling evidence for increased occupation towards the end of the LGM, rather than an increased level of occupation throughout the LGM.

If it is accepted that the Hamersley Plateau was a refuge area for humans during periods when aridity was extreme, the question arises what was the nature of this occupation? Referring to Milly's Cave, Marwick suggests the ranges of territories were of reduced area. It is considered more generally by O'Connor and Veth that retraction to and within the ranges occurred, though it would be evident that there would be differences in reference to local catchments that range from being abandoned completely through to increased use (O'Connor & Veth, 2006:41).

The shortage of evidence for subsistence is a significant barrier to understanding the utilisation of refuge areas before, during and following the LGM. The main evidence that is needed is organic remains that are systematically analysed in conjunction with flaked stone. The move towards broad-spectrum diets at the terminal Pleistocene that has been discussed (Edwards & O'Connell, 1995), but a true understanding of the phenomenon has not yet been achieved, mainly as a result of the very few sites containing evidence of occupation that includes faunal and floral remains, and not just flaked stone.

Solid evidence has been found showing that the Pilbara region was occupied prior and during the LGM, though cultural remains have been found in a few sites that have been excavated and even fewer sites for which the work has been published. Sites such as Newman Rock shelter, Newman Orebody XXIX Shelter, Malea Rock shelter and Milly's Cave have contained little faunal material. Faunal remains were found at Malea (Edwards & Murphy, 2003), but mostly is still to be published, little more than a species list of fauna and the fact that it is highly fragmented had been published at this time this article was published (Edwards & Murphy, 2003:45). Faunal material was recovered at Malea in only some of the excavation units, being confined to the upper 16 units. It is argued by Edwards & Murphy that this distribution of faunal remains is likely due to preservation factors, not the actual absence of the remains. Further work has been carried out at Malea and the analysis is now in progress and it is hoped that it will supply information that is needed to increase understanding of the subsistence and settlement of the area. At Marillana A, faunal remains were preserved, though discussion is limited to a quantitative analysis of the density per stratigraphic unit (Marwick, 2005:1362-4).

In Newman Orebody XXIX faunal remains are limited to 1 macropod molar found in the top excavation unit (Maynard, 1980:5), and data is missing from Newman Rock shelter and Milly's Cave (Marwick, 2003). A significant problem is caused in the understanding of refuge areas by the absence of faunal data, as well as to knowledge of subsistence of early Aboriginal settlers as a whole.

In this paper (Slack et *al*. 2009) have reported new sites in the region that have the potential to provide subsistence data that is important and frameworks that are more robust concerning Aboriginal settlement on the Hamersley plateau during the LGM.

Brockman 4, Hamersley Plateau – Excavations

Excavations at 2 particular sites of a series of excavations in the Pilbara, about 60 km west of the of the town of Tom Price, Juunkan-1 and Juunkan-2 have provided further substantiation for the antiquity of the occupation in this region of more than 30,000 years. They have also provided compelling evidence that occupation continued even at the height of the LGM, 22,000-19,000 cal. yr. BP. As the location of Brockman 4 mining tenement, in which the sites are located, is well within the central Hamersley Plateau and is more than 75 km north of the nearest substantial watercourse, the Ashburton River, though it is ephemeral, and this location of the sites makes the finds interesting and to some extent unexpected.

Juunkan-1 and Juunkan-2 are both located within a small ironstone gorge not far from a small ephemeral watercourse, the Purlykunti Creek. There are 3 other Rock shelter sites in this gorge, though the occupation sequence at all 3 is very recent. There is also a very large scatter of artefacts on an extensive floodplain below the gorge. It is believed that all the dominant raw materials, ironstone, chert, quartz and siltstone, are available from the creek at and near to open scatter.

Discussion

Slack et *al*. say new information concerning the prehistory of the Pilbara is provided by the results of their excavations at Brockman. Early occupation of beyond 35,000 BP is further supported by the data they provided. A continual, though infrequent, occupation of the Brockman region during OIS 2, and even at the height of the LGM, is indicated by the cultural sequence at Juunkan-2.

Analysis of the data in terms of landscape use by hunter gatherers was limited by the size of the sample, though Slack et al. (2009) made a number of observations and suggested hypotheses. It is indicated by the evidence from these 2 rock shelters that people have been living in this area of the Hamersley during the LGM. The local population may have been more residentially mobile at times of more severe aridity than might be expected, given the dominant refuge models and their previous application to the Pilbara (see Veth, 2005: 101). According to Slack et *al*. (2009) it is clear that people were retreating into gorges on the margins of the ranges near main river courses, as well as making a more complex use of the landscape. It is also suggested that they were *'possibly following local weather patterns and allowing access to the less drained areas occurred*' (Slack et *al*. 2009). In this paper it is also considered likely residential mobility decreased following the LGM as rainfall increased. If this suggestion is correct it would explain the high discard rate at Brockman; the increase in faunal remains density at Juunkan-2 in the later phases of occupation, as well as those trends in the flaked stone that were observed at Milly's Cave (Marwick, 2002: 29). Slack et *al*. (2009) also suggest that though there was a decrease in residential mobility there was an increase in logistical mobility, at least on the local level. The greater range of the raw materials and the larger sizes of the flaked material over the last few thousand years of the Pleistocene, which continued to the Middle Holocene, is the basis for this suggestion. The intensity of the apparent reduction and frequency of artefact discard increased slightly in the Middle and Late Holocene. Behavioural implications that are suggested by the faunal remains provide additional support for the occupation increase that occurred in later periods, though it is also shown by the fauna that both Juunkan-1 and Juunkan-2 were occupied continuously in all periods. This trend is considered likely to be related to increased levels of population, as has been suggested (Marwick, 2002), given the results of other excavations within this area all dating to this period.

Conclusion

It is suggested that the results of this ongoing project further emphasise that the archaeology of the Pilbara region will continue to play an important role in developing an understanding of the timing of arid settlement, and the nature of hunter gatherer subsistence during periods of uncertainty such as the LGM.

Sand Ridge Deserts - Biogeography, Human Ecology and Prehistory

The first Europeans to see this extremely arid part of Australia were the members of Sturt's 1844-45 expedition, to be followed by a number of other expeditions such as Warburton in 1875, Lindsay in 1886, Giles in 1889 and Carnegie in 1898. The surgeon on Sturt's expedition, a Mr Browne, wondered if man had ever seen such a place. The later expeditions found that there were small, scattered groups of people occupying the dune fields who were apparently flourishing.

Until recently it was believed the arid interior had not been occupied until about 15,000-10,000 BP (cf. Bowdler, 1977; Horton, 1981). Since then evidence has been accumulating that the major desert uplands and river systems had been occupied by sometime in the Late Pleistocene (Brown, 1987; Lampert & Hughes, 1988; Maynard, 1988; Smith, 1987; Smith *et al.*, 1991). According Smith discussion has now moved to the question of the nature of the occupation (Hiscock, 1989; Smith, 1989) and the timing of occupation of different parts of the arid zone.

Attention has been drawn to the lack of evidence supporting the occupation of the major sand ridge deserts before about 5,000 BP (Veth, 1989b) in which it was argued that the mid-Holocene would have been the time when the arid sand ridge deserts were first occupied, proposing what has been called the 'barrier desert' theory by Smith. According to Smith, the barrier desert theory should be examined critically as it forms the cornerstone of a new model that has been explicitly proposed as a new framework for desert prehistory (Veth, 1989a, 1989b).

Smith's paper examines 4 aspects of the barrier desert theory:

Do the major sand ridge deserts, the Great Sandy Desert, the Great Victoria Desert and the Simpson Desert form a coherent biogeographic unit?

Are the 'barrier' deserts different from anything prospective colonists had seen previously in other parts of the arid zone?

What were the social and technological prerequisites for colonisation of these regions?

What is the archaeological evidence for this theory?

Sand ridge deserts - a biogeographic unit

According to Smith, the first point he takes issue with is whether or not the sand ridge deserts actually form a biogeographic unit, suggesting that Veth has implied that they do by lumping together the Great Sandy Desert, the Great Victoria Desert and the Simpson Desert, these deserts have many features in common, as well as strong contrasts with neighbouring regions. Smith says the case for this is not as strong as could be supposed, as can be seen by a cursory search of the biogeographic literature.

The continent of Australia has been divided into 3 biogeographic provinces by Baldwin Spencer, the Torresian Biogeographic Province, the Bassian Biogeographic Province and the Eyrean Biogeographic Province (Spencer, 1896). Since that time biogeographers have retained the basic divisions of Spencer (Archer & Fox, 1984; Burbidge, 1960; Heatwole, 1987; Horton, 1984; Johnson & Briggs, 1975; Tyler, 1990), though with disagreements over whether Cape York Peninsula and south west Western Australia should be regarded as separate provinces. Whichever scheme is supported, the continental interior of Australia is still recognised as a single biogeographic province, though with different names given by different authors, Eyrean, Eremean or Sturtian. There has been a proposal for a preliminary subdivision of the Eremean flora into northern and southern elements (Diels, 1906, cited in Carolin, 1982) and (Tate, 1896), and similar suggestions have been made more recently (e.g. Nix, 1982). The significant fact is that biogeographers do not suggest the sand ridge deserts are a distinct unit different from the remainder of the arid zone. Those biogeographic divisions that are recognised within the arid zone divide the arid zone into northern and southern zones crosscutting any grouping of the 3 sand ridge deserts as a single unit.

Barrier desert theory

In a larger model, 'Islands of the Interior', of which the 'barrier desert' theory forms a part, Veth has argued for a post glacial re-colonisation of the arid zone from refuge areas occupied by humans during the Last Glacial Maximum (Veth, 1989b, following Smith 1988: 5-57, 293-343). Unlike earlier formulations it singles out the major sand ridge deserts, suggesting they were regions where colonisation was independent of these palaeoenvironmental changes. He proposes that various socioeconomic changes in neighbouring areas of the arid zone during the mid-Holocene led to the occupation of these regions.

It has been argued that the sand ridge deserts, as well as lowland desert habitats, would probably have been initially occupied in pre-Glacial times, then abandoned at the Glacial Maximum, then recolonised by the expanding population following the end of the Glacial period (Smith, 1988), Veth argues that the colonisation in the mid-Holocene was the first time these regions have been occupied.

Veth uses the biogeographic terms *barrier, refugia* and *corridor* to emphasise the distinction between different habitats (cf Heatwole, 1987). Under the scheme proposed by Veth:

Barriers are the major sand ridge deserts, the Great Sandy Desert, the Great Victoria Desert and the Simpson Desert.

Refugia are the Pilbara, the Kimberley, Flinders Ranges and the Central Australian Ranges.

Corridors are the intervening areas, the Tanami Desert, the Strzelecki Desert, the Gibson Desert and the Tirari Desert, The Nullarbor Plain and the Barkly Tableland.

A major problem for people trying to colonise the 'barrier' deserts would have been the association of dune fields with hummock grassland and drainage that was uncoordinated, according to the theory. The people would have been unfamiliar with the hummock grassland environment, and poor in plant food species if they lacked the technology or ecological knowledge required to harvest and process large quantities of grass seeds. Another problem would have been the spatial patterning of water sources that were shallow enough to reach without the technical knowledge needed to construct and maintain wells. According to this theory a range of developments, technological, economic and social, were necessary before they would be capable of occupying the barrier deserts on a permanent basis. The following list has been proposed (Veth, 1989b: 83):

Instruments needed to be developed for the working of desert hardwoods and wild seed processing;

detailed distribution knowledge and the methods for processing useful seed-bearing species in the hummock grasslands;

the technical ability necessary for the construction and maintenance of wells deep enough to tap the groundwater; and

the development of extended social networks.

Veth suggests these were probably developed in adjacent regions, adaptations to the local conditions under increased population pressure. According to Veth, the result was 'the emergence of regionally specific settlement and subsistence systems' (Veth, 1989b: 83). Smith suggests likening the process outlined by Veth to one of *exaptation* where new niches for exploitation were opened as a result of these changes, in this case, the sand ridge deserts that were adjacent.

The chronological framework of the theory is based on 2 lines of argument. The first is evidence that in the Late Pleistocene groups were unable to cope with arid conditions, that is suggested by Veth to support this, citing evidence from Colless Creek Cave where it has been found that at the time of full glacial aridity stone from outside the river and gorge system was not used (cf. Hiscock, 1989). He says that as the initial occupation took place at a time before the interior became as arid as it is at the present, the first occupants of the now arid areas may not have been fully pre-adapted to a desert environment. His second line of argument is that the social, economic and technological changes that are prerequisite for a long-term move into a desert did not take place before 5,000 BP, though according to Smith he is not explicit as to the reason these are necessarily part of the package of changes. Smith suggests Veth clearly sees a need for a long adjustment period to local conditions in the *corridors* that are adjacent, that were re-occupied following the Last Glacial Maximum.

Barrier deserts - differences

Extensive dune fields, uncoordinated drainage systems and a hummock grassland understorey are features that are common to all 3 of the major sand ridge deserts, though they also have sufficient differences to suggest different opportunities in the form of plant resources, landforms and hydrology, for any humans wishing to occupy them. The dominant vegetation in the Great Sandy Desert is hummock grassland, either ***Triodia*** or ***Plectrachne***, with ***Eucalyptus*** forming an open tree or shrub layer in the northern part, and in the south, mixed desert Acacias. There are extensive tracts of mulga (***Acacia aneura***) woodland, mallee (***Eucalyptus gongylocarpa***) and ***Casuarina cristata*** woodland in the Great Victoria Desert. In the Simpson Desert the sandhill canegrass (***Zygochloea***) is the dominant dune vegetation in the south eastern third of the Simpson Desert, not ***Triodia*** and ***Plectrachne*** (Atlas of Australian Resources, 1990). Smith suggests differences in the distribution of important plant food species could be expected because of the differences in light, thermal and moisture regimes that result from the wide latitudinal differences between the 3 deserts, 19° S-29° S. In the arid zone, 2 broad plant groups have been recognised that have characteristic temperature response patterns, one in the north and the other in the south, and in the coastal part of the region, a wide overlap zone (Nix, 1982: 64).

According to Smith, among the 3 deserts there are significant differences in landforms and landscapes. Of the 'barrier' deserts, the Simpson Desert forms a much smaller region than the other 2, and differs from them in some important characteristics (Graetz *et al.*, 1982). 8 rivers that originally formed part of the Lake Eyre catchment, having been severed by the dune field formation, the Todd, Hale, Illogwa, Plenty, Hay, Field, Mulligan and Kallakoopah, that flow deeply into the dune field. Rivers that flood out into the Simpson Desert at the present occasionally channel large amounts of floodwater into the dune field (Kotwicki, 1986). The dunes in the south eastern part of the Simpson Desert are formed of pale pelletal clay (Wasson, 1983) instead of the red siliceous sand comprising the bulk of the dunes in the 3 regions. There is also an extensive belt of closely spaced playas in this sector of the dunes.

Barrier deserts - new challenges?
The premise that the 'barrier' deserts represented a habitat that was fundamentally different from anything the people had ever encountered before, either in the *corridors* or the glacial *refugia* is the basis of the theory. Smith suggests this does not stand up to

detailed scrutiny, especially when comparing 'barrier' deserts to the adjoining *corridors* or *refugia*.

The move to the 'barrier' deserts would, at least in many cases, have been to a poorer environment than that of the environment from which they had moved, though in terms of structure and composition it would have been basically familiar. As there are large areas of hummock grassland, dune fields and drainage that were uncoordinated in areas outside the 'barrier' deserts, the combination of these features would not have been new to the colonists. It has been suggested that before moving into the 'barrier' deserts the people would most likely have visited them opportunistically, especially after good rain (Veth, 1989a: 229;1989b: 81), permitting the people to accumulate specific local knowledge regarding water supplies and other resources, possibly over several generations after occupying the adjacent *corridors* and *refugia*. Smith suggests that any barrier posed by the sand ridge deserts to colonisation would have been associated with their aridity, not with their biogeographic characteristics; the difference found in the sand ridge country would have been more in degree than kind.

Floristic affinities - other desert habitats

Biogeographers believe that the flora and fauna of the 'barrier' deserts are strongly linked to those of the *refugia* and *corridors* that are adjacent, and are not areas of ancient endemic flora and fauna (Greenslade & Halladay, 1982; Schodde, 1982). The basis of this belief is the floristic gradients that have been found from north to south across the Great Sandy Desert (Burbidge & McKenzie, 1983: 82-3) and in the Simpson Desert, from west to east (Fatchen & Barker, 1979). In the Great Sandy Desert, the northern sector has many species of vertebrate and plant in common with the Kimberley region, that is adjacent to it, leading to the suggestion it could be considered to be a formal interzone between the Torresian/tropical biogeographic province in the north and the Eyrean/Eremean biogeographic province to the south.

The endemic genera of hummock grasses (aka spinifex) ***Triodia*** and ***Plechtrachne***, are also widespread, so not restricted to the sand ridge deserts, an understorey of hummock grasses covering 26.9 % of the Australian continent (*Atlas of Australian Resources*, 1990, Vol. 6,

Table 1) though pure hummock grasslands are not common. Both formations are present in regions that have been classified as *corridors* or *refugia* and in 'barrier' deserts (Veth, 1989b: Fig. 1). In places such as the Pilbara and the Great Sandy Desert, species inhabit both upland and sand ridge desert habitats (Jacobs, 1982: 288). In prolonged droughts **Triodia** and **Plechtrachne** both die (cf Beard, 1969). It has been suggested, based on a study of speciation in these 2 genera, that during the Last Glacial Maximum hummock grasses were probably confined to *refugia* outside sand ridge deserts, recolonising the sand ridge deserts after the close of the LGM (Jacobs, 1982: 290), leading to the suggestion that humans would have been familiar with these taxa in areas that Veth identifies as glacial *refugia*, long before they colonised the sand ridge deserts.

The acacias comprising an open shrub layer in the 'barrier' deserts also display this pattern. There are a number of species that are highly variable, such as **Acacia ligulata** and **A. aneura**, across the arid zone. A high proportion of species of *Acacia* in the Great Sandy Desert have been found to also be present in neighbouring regions, especially the Tanami Desert (50-64 %) and 41 % with the Central Australian Ranges (Maslin & Hopper, 1982). A similar pattern has been found for the Great Victoria Desert, 54 % of *Acacia* species present there are also present in the Central Australian Ranges. It has been pointed out that there is a pattern in the distribution of groups of species that are closely related in which 1 taxon in a related pair is present on the periphery of the sandy deserts and the other member of the pair in present within the desert (Maslin & Hopper, 1982: 311). Data have been provided showing that within the arid zone there is widespread distribution of species comprising the sand ridge flora of central Australia (Buckley, 1982).

Smith suggests that it seems highly unlikely that the flora of the sand ridge deserts was unfamiliar to the people who were trying to colonise them, having to learn to cope with them. It has been pointed out that before people moved into the arid zone they would have had the opportunity to acquire at least part of the ecological knowledge that would be essential for successfully settling in central Australia while they were still in northern Australia (Golson, 1971). Any people colonising the 'barrier' deserts from *refugia* or *corridors* would have had the same opportunity. Comparing the species of plant being exploited for seed by the people of the Great Sandy Desert with those exploited in central Australia provides a demonstration of this. Of the plant species used for seeds in the Great Sandy Desert (Veth & Walsh, 1988: Appendix 1) 56 % (23 species) are also used for seeds in central Australia (Latz, 1982: Table 4; O'Connell *et al.*, 1983). There were also 3 plant species used for seed in central Australia but in the Great Sandy Desert they were used for other purposes.

Aboriginal Occupation – Temperate Australia

It was surprising to find early sites in the far southeast and south west of Australia, but the dates for the more southern sites fit with a spread over the continent beginning about 60,000 BP. South west Western Australia has 2 known sites dating between 40,000 & 30,000 BP. In the south east sites of similar age have been found at the Willandra Lakes and a more controversial early date near Sydney.

Some archaeologists doubt the early dates from Kakadu, this would make for a very unusual spread, from south to north, that seems barely believable, where the colonists could have come from to the south of Australia, and the alternative seems not much less likely, colonists travelling down the coast to land along the southern part of Australia.

Aboriginal Occupation - Tasmania (Flood, 2004)

Darwin glass

Artefacts-Stone

Artefacts-Bone

Food

Whale bone huts

The Tasmanian Aborigines are the only surviving human population who are known to have been isolated so completely by a natural barrier from the rest of the world for about 10,500 years. Once the land bridge joining Tasmania to the mainland had been flooded by the rising sea the difficult nature of the 250 km wide Bass Strait, with frequent storms and strong currents, as well as many submerged rocks that made any sea crossing in primitive craft such as canoes, sea-going or not, extremely dangerous and not likely to be attempted without good reason.

It is still recognised as a rough passage, it is the connection between the Indian and Pacific Oceans, with contributions from the Southern Ocean, the conditions made worse by its depth, only about 50 m. The huge volumes of water pushing through such a shallow section make for strong currents and rough seas. All this is made even worse by powerful winds. In the days of sail many ships were lost in it, often with no trace being found. It has been said to be twice as wide and twice as rough as the English Channel.

As a result of this isolation new technology or ideas couldn't be brought from the mainland, and as the dingo arrived and spread across the mainland after the drowning of the land bridge, it never reached Tasmania.

It has been estimated on ethnographic data that the population of Tasmania was about 3,000 - 5,000 at the time of the first European contact. This has been disputed on biological grounds, suggesting that such a small population inhabiting an island about 67,870 km^2, about the size of Ireland would have undergone genetic drift over a period of 10,000 years resulting in biological divergence. An alternative suggestion is that the initial population at the time Tasmania was first occupied, about 35,000 years ago, had risen to a much higher level by natural increase by the time of isolation, declining subsequently to the comparatively low level at the time of European contact.

Excavation of a number of occupation sites has shown that the tool kit at the time of separation from the mainland was very similar to that on the mainland.

Tasmania is the most southerly part of the world inhabited during the Ice Age. Glaciers were present on Tasmania's mountains and icebergs would have drifted past its coasts from the Antarctic, 1000 km further south. When sea level dropped as a result of glaciations, a broad land bridge was exposed from early in the Ice Age. It is thought the land connection would have been available from about 60,000 BP, early in the Ice age, so was present when the first Aborigines arrived in northern Australia. It lasted until about 10,500 BP.

So far the earliest occupation site in Tasmania dates to a bit more than 35,000 BP. At least 4 other sites, Nunamira, ORS 7, Palewardia Walana Lanala, and Bone Cave, all have dates of 30,000 BP or more. No doubt there would have been occupation sites on the now-submerged land bridge that could be even older.

A feature of the Tasmanian cave occupation sites is that at the start of occupation there is light, intermittent use of the caves, especially during the period of the glacial maximum. Another constant feature of these sites throughout the Pleistocene is the constant exploitation of the red-necked wallaby and marrow extraction. They appear to have been red-necked wallaby specialists.

It has now been shown that by 35,000 BP Aborigines had developed a way of life that allowed them to live in the alpine environment of upland Tasmania. At the glacial maximum, about 18,000 BP, annual average temperatures were about 6° C lower then present, and glaciers in Tasmania extended to 800 m above sea level. The treeline was at least 235 m lower. The glacial Tasmanian climate has been equated with that of the Australian Alps at Mt Hotham, at 1862 m, of the present, but with shorter summers.

In the times prior to, and at the height of, the last glaciation the climate here was periglacial, sub Antarctic, but the river valleys were free of big trees which made movement through them much easier than when the rainforest became established by the end of the Pleistocene. It had previously been suggested that the intermittent nature of occupation in the highland caves of Tasmania was because they were used during summer hunting expeditions. If they were actually winter campsites, the occupants would be able to escape the worst of the freezing conditions prevailing in the area in winter, and could explain why the vast majority of prey seemed to come from a single species, the red-necked rock wallaby, which would have been easily available to the hunters.

In some cave deposits emu eggshells have been found. These are available only in spring and early summer, so they could have varied their diet with the eggs while the weather was still cold, before the conditions warmed up enough to move out for the summer. It is possible they might have remained in the caves all year, but that would require them to be comparatively sedentary and mean they hunted only rock wallabies all the year.

The inhabitants of south west Tasmania had a more highly structured economy than any other part of Australia during the Ice Age. The Pleistocene Tasmanian industry differs from that of other Australian sites of this time. Darwin glass was transported over 100 km, indicating a probable trading network. There were also differences between the east and west of Tasmania during Pleistocene times, showing the adaptability of these people to changing environments. Changes in technology and economy also occurred over time. In the lowest layers there is neither Darwin glass nor thumbnail scrapers, and there is possibly an increase in mobility, and land use patterns changed during and after the glacial maximum.

The finds from Pleistocene sites in marginal climatic regions in Tasmania show a highly complex society. Pigmented art shows the possibility of religious activity in the deep caves of Tasmania. There are further indications of complex societies, with their own distinctive archaeological signatures prior to the mid-Holocene when changes were thought to have occurred.

During the Pleistocene there was a wide variability between the assemblages in the south west and the south east of Tasmania. There were also cultural differences between the 2 areas. In the west, temperate rainforest covered the fold structure of the south west, with its impenetrable horizontal forest. In the east there were dry sclerophyll forests on the fault-structured geology. This pattern differs from the concept of an Australia-wide Pleistocene culture and technology that was uniform, simple and unchanging.

By the end of the glaciation the link with the mainland had been cut by rising sea levels. The inhabitants of south west Tasmania thrived though 20,000 years, the last 10,500 years in isolation.

The South West

The south west of Tasmania has one of the last remaining temperate wildernesses in the world and in it is some of the densest rainforest in the world. At the time of European contact the population of Tasmania was largely restricted to a narrow coastal belt only a few hundred metres wide that they kept open with fire. Their main food source was from the sea. They tended to travel along the coast rather than inland, and only a couple of tracks through the rainforest are known, as from Port Davey to the south coast. Little, if any, occupation is known of in the wilderness of the south west. The horizontal scrub and the fast-flowing rivers would have been a significant disincentive to try to penetrate inland, especially as they lived so well on the coast. The rivers are still a problem for anyone wanting to travel upstream in a boat; jet boats are required to overcome the powerful flow.

The first evidence of Aborigines in the rainforest was found by accident, stone tools being found on the bank of the Gordon River around the base of a fallen *Nothofagus*. The tree roots had exposed the stone tools as they pulled out of the ground. There was a quartz pebble core with the flakes that had been chipped from it scattered around it. The flakes fitted exactly with the scars on the core, and they were still extremely sharp. 12 tools were found, including a quartz hammerstone. Associated charcoal at this site gave a disappointingly recent date of 300 ± 150 years. The Aborigines had at least traversed the area in recent times.

The next find, only 3 weeks later, was at Kutikina Cave.

Aboriginal Occupation - Populating the Continent - Final Phase - Tasmania

At the time the Willandra Lakes area was first occupied the climate of the temperate landscapes of south-eastern Australia was cooler, becoming colder with increased latitude and altitude in the southern parts of temperate Australia, and with large areas of the Snowy Mountains and the southern ranges being glaciated. This was the time when much of the Earth was being affected by a great ice age, a time when sea levels were substantially lower as a result of the water being locked up in vast ice sheets. Tasmania had become part of Greater Australia, or Sahul, by 43,000 BP as a result of lower sea levels.

As a result of the lower sea level Tasmania was a southern cape of Australia connected to mainland Australia by a land bridge, the Bassian Ridge, at present submerged beneath Bass Strait, that was part of a very large continental plain that covered an area of about 1.1 million km^2 that stretched from Kangaroo Island to Cape Howe on the southern coast of New South Wales. The Bassian Ridge was 3 times the size of Tasmania being 215,000 km^2 in area. This ridge, that is now submerged, was just above sea level at the time humans were camped at the Willandra_Lakes, and it was part of a broad, undulating plain stretching south towards Mount Flinders, now Flinders Island, which attained a height of 760 m above it. Pollen records from central Tasmania indicate that it was vegetated by grasses and daisies, small evergreen conifers and pockets of casuarinas and eucalyptus. On this open plain the ranges over 400 m high were covered by alpine vegetation. It was occupied by emus and kangaroos, as well as some of the megafauna species such as ***Zygomaturus***, ***Palorchestes***, ***Protemnodon*** and ***Thylacoleo***. According to Cane (2013) the plain would have been a cold, bitter place windswept by westerlies, though the climate was a little warmer than it had been in previous millennia. On this plain there was an extensive freshwater lake, 400 km long by 120 km wide, formed by surrounding ranges that are now islands, Furneaux Range (now Furneaux Islands), Mount King (now King Island) that reached 400 m above it. As the wind blew across this lake it would have sharpened the chill of the westerlies. At times, when the sea level was higher, the lake would become a large embayment, eventually being inundated about 14,000 BP as the sea level rose for the last time. Prior to its inundation it would have been a fertile environmental keystone along the migration route of humans to Tasmania from the mainland. At the time of the migration across the land bridge to Tasmania the island of the present was more similar to the subantarctic Macquarie Island of the present than the Tasmania of the present.

According to Fane (2013) at the time the colonisers were moving across the land bridge to the shore of ancient Tasmania they passed to the east of the Bassian Lake along the Bassian Ridge, past Mount Flinders. It is suggested they are likely to have occupied the hinterland, settling along rivers, then moved further into the foothills, exploiting the mountains in central and south-western Tasmania. The mountains were shrouded with ice caps with glaciers extending from the mountains into the upper Derwent Valley in the south, and in the north, the Forth Valley and Mersey Valley. The forests that mostly characterise Tasmanian wilderness at the present were largely not present, most of the land being covered by grass, heath and shrubs. Frigid moorland vegetated with herb fields, button grass swamps and conifers covered the areas between the high country and grasslands. The climate at the time was cold and wet, with short summers and long winters, and temperatures about 6° C lower than those of the present.

The migration ended at the foot of the glacial environment of Tasmania, in the coldest and most inaccessible regions known in the world, in a number of limestone caves in the central highlands and also in the wild southwest. Evidence has been found on the banks of the Maxwell River, at Warreen Cave, of human occupation that has been dated to between 38,800 BP and 41,000 BP. In the Forth River Valley near Cradle Mountain, people camped in Parmerpar Meethaner Cave that was located within 3 km of the glaciated highlands 44,200 years ago. The people occupying this caves spent the summers, in periglacial conditions, in the caves, as part of their seasonal strategy that moved from the highest, coldest altitudes in the summer to the lower altitudes during winter.

The hunters tended to use this wild, frigid land in a cyclical manner and according to the season, targeted selected resources. As Cane said (*the ice age settlers were mobile hunters, discerningly, intentionally and intelligently hunting easy prey in the glacial latitudes*'). They hunted a macropod about 1.5 m tall and about 20 kg, Bennett's wallaby (***Macropus rufogriseus***). The Tasmanian sub-species tend to flock on fertile patches of grassland in the moors that are tundra-like, and they have longer, shaggier hair than the mainland species. In the subalpine environment the fertile patches were of limited extent but they were maintained by regular firing which effectively tethered the wallabies to them, which resulted in 'managed' hunting, the hunters always knowing where the wallabies would be found in greatest numbers. They also hunted the wallabies selectively, taking mostly the older individuals, which would have lesser effect on the breeding population, and so maintaining this seasonal resource. The occupants also brought specific body parts of their kills back to their camp, apparently to get at the fat, cracking the skulls to get the brain and the leg bones for the marrow. The skins from these animals also had the winter coats of the thickest, highest quality furs to make into winter garments for maximum warmth.

It has become apparent that these hunters of the ice age were well aware of what they were doing as they managed this resource. Their hunting was not carried out in an opportunistic manner, they were managing where this resource was located, on the patches that were regularly maintained by fire, and had a 'harvesting' season when the furs were at their thickest. At first sight they may appear to have been opportunistic hunters taking animals where they could, but it seems they were actually approaching the task of hunting in a very methodical way, as Cane says, in a scheduled, cooperative, coordinated and clever manner. Though they might not have thought of it as 'scientific' knowledge of their target species, they obviously understood the animal ecology, breeding patterns and population dynamics of the wallabies. And as Cane points out these hunters were living 40,000 years ago in the southern-most inhabited location on Earth at that time.

See Aboriginal Occupation of Tasmania

Aboriginal Occupation of south central Tasmania in the Pleistocene - Palaeoecology

The populations of the Australian Aboriginal people in the Pleistocene have been characterised as being low density and widespread, with little variation between regions over large areas of the continent (White & O'Connell, 1982). The nature of the archaeological evidence, being geographically diverse and in most cases no more than a few material remains being found, tended to at least partially support these assumptions. According Cosgrove et al. (1998) contemporary demographic models (1998) suggest a narrow resource base as being used by Aboriginal populations in the Pleistocene; the groups were highly mobile, with the result that site occupation appeared to be ephemeral, which was reflected in the archaeological record. In a social context these groups are characterised as egalitarian, with less complex social networks than was the case in the mid-Holocene (Lourandos, 1983: 88; 1985: 398). According to this a trajectory exists of socio-economic complexity from foragers (Pleistocene) to collectors (mid-Holocene) (Lourandos, 1987: 158).

Cosgrove et al suggest that hunter-gatherer socio-economic organisation and change are inevitably unidirectional in that such notions where different behaviours over enormous lengths of time-scales have been blended, promoting ideas of modal behaviours though denying the existence of alternative behaviours that are systematic on a regional scale, and possess inherent variability. Cosgrove et al agree with the statement *'by equating foraging behaviour with egalitarian sociopolitical relationships, by merging the means of the two, we eliminate the range of variability present in each construct'* (Soffer, 1987: 492). They say that the range of variability associated with modern humans is greater than has been realised previously. Evidence has been found that there is not a 1-to-1 correlation between the advent of modern ***Homo sapiens*** and any particular classes of stone tools (Trinkhaus, 1986; Foley, 1987). It has been pointed out that, though the first people to arrive in Australia were essentially modern humans, the morphology and technology of their stone artefacts *'could come out of the African or European Lower Palaeolithic'* (Gowlett, 1987: 215), a pattern that had been recognised by early researchers (Jones, 1977: 190-1; White, 1977: 24). Observation that early Aboriginal colonists must have had an efficient marine technology prior to 40,000 BP [60,000 BP suggested by dating in NW Australia] to be able to cross the ocean gaps between the nearest island and the mainland of Greater Australia, thus extending the contrast (Jones, 1987), as well as possessing an artistic tradition that was probably older than 30,000 years (Dorn *et al.*, 1988; Nobbs, 1988). Direct implications for ideas of unidirectional trajectories result from these paradoxes, based on value-laden archaeological data sets and assumptions employed to explain changes of human behaviour.

The Tasmanian Aborigines have provided models for reconstructing human behaviour during the Pleistocene for more than 100 years, because of their isolation in the Holocene and their geographical position that is unique (e.g. Sollas, 1911: 70). Cosgrove et *al* say the practice has continued, in spite of good reasons to question it, one of the main reasons being the actual nature of human behaviour in Tasmania during the Pleistocene. South east Tasmania during the Holocene has been seen as a regional exemplar of what is likely to have been indicative of the character of the behaviour of Aboriginal populations during the Pleistocene, suggesting that the Kutikina Cave site (Liernan *et al.*, 1983) in south west Tasmania, of Pleistocene age, represents inland hunting, that is transient, is indicative of Aboriginal behaviour in the Pleistocene (Lourandos, 1985: 397).

There would be not much variation in the archaeological record between the 2 regions if this was actually the case. The actual situation as seen from more recent excavations in south east and south west Tasmania has demonstrated a degree of archaeological richness and variation not previously reported for any other part of Australia from the Pleistocene (Goede & Murray, 1977; Goede *et al.*, 1978; Murray & Goode, 1980; Jones, 1984; Kiernan *et al.*, 1983; Blain *et al.*, 1982; Jones & Allen, 1984; Jones *et al.*, 1988; Allen *et al.*, 1988; Cosgrove, 1989; Cosgrove & Jones, 1989; Allen, 1989; Allen & Cosgrove, 1989; Allen *et al.*, 1989). There are 41 sites, both cave and open sites, have been reported from these areas indicating that occupation of these zones was continuous from 30,000 BP to 11,000 BP. Of the more than 20 radiocarbon dates that had been reported from the eastern portion of Tasmania prior to 1987 all were 10,000 BP or younger. The Southern Forests Archaeological Project was initiated in 1987, with the specific aim of investigation the temporal paradox, as well as investigating, elaborating and verifying propositions resulting from previous research, especially at Kutikina Cave.

It has been found that the periglacial upland areas of Tasmania were settled by humans in the Late Pleistocene, at least 30,000 BP, 10,000 years earlier than had previously been believed to have occurred, from western valleys in the south west, based on preliminary investigations of archaeological sites in south central Tasmania. Findings and conclusions that had been advanced for the Nunamira Cave site and the ORS 7 site have been supported by findings from 2 sequences, Bone Cave and M86/2 site. Rich faunal assemblages of large bones that are identifiable, stone tools that are distinctive, and stone raw materials that are location specific, allow the sites from south-western Tasmania dating to the Pleistocene to be distinguished from other Pleistocene regions of Australia. According to Cosgrove et al, the eastern zone can be distinguished from the western zone in the archaeological signatures within the Pleistocene province. An archaeological basis has been established for examining the associations between sites within the province as well as across its boundaries.

The study site in south central Tasmania is at the division of 2 environmental zones in southern Tasmania, a fold-structured geology with a vegetation of temperate rainforest to the west, and to the east, a fault-structured geology with a vegetation cover of dry sclerophyll forest (Kirkpatrick, 1982) (Fig. 6a.1). The location is a central pivot from which the variability of south east and south west Tasmania can be compared and contrasted. A palaeoecological conceptual framework has been used because ethnographic or archaeological analogues for the Tasmanian deposits are unknown in the rest of Australia. Their conceptual framework was generated from earlier archaeological data, as well as information on soils, vegetation and animal ecology. Cosgrove et al hope they will be able to observe links and relationships between the archaeological record, that is static, and human behaviours that produced them, that are dynamic, by understanding some ecological aspects of the zone that were present during the Pleistocene.

Aboriginal Occupation of South Central Tasmania in the Pleistocene - A palaeoecological model (Cosgrove, Allen & Marshall, 1998)

A number of locations on the western coast of Tasmania have provided pollen data for analysis that indicates that the vegetation of the area was predominantly of an alpine-sub-alpine type of herb, heath and shrub species between earlier than 44,000 BP and 25,000 BP. The mean annual temperature was about $5°C$ lower than at the present at this stage, with a wet climate (Colhoun & van de Geer, 1986; Colhoun, 1995a; 1985b). The dominant species were wet herb and heath communities 24,000-22,000 BP, with increasing herb and grass pollen appearing after 22,000 BP leading up to the last glacial maximum at 18,000 BP (MacPhail & Colhoun, 1985; Gibson *et al.*, 1987), the geographical extent of these grasslands being important to the model, as Cosgrove et al described later. About 21,000 BP the tree line was depressed about 230 m on the west coast, when the temperatures have been estimated to have been about $6°$ cooler than the present average temperatures, and the climate was drier than the preceding period. Tree and shrub species were of increasing importance 14,000-11,000 BP, after 11,000 BP rainforest taxa became dominant (MacPhail, 1975, 1979; MacPhail and Peterson, 1975; Colhoun & Moon 1984), the climate at this period being warm and moist.

The vegetation cover in the east, 25,000-10,000 BP, is suggested by the pollen data, especially in the Midlands Valley, to have varied much less than it did in the west over the same period. It has been suggested that there had been a progression from grassy woodland to grasslands then back to grassy woodland in which ***Eucalyptus sp.*** was more dominant than in earlier periods (Sigleo & Colhoun, 1981). Alpine and sub-alpine grasslands were present at a lower altitude; at least 300 m lower than at the present altitude of about 1,000 m, on the southern edge of the Tasmanian Central Plateau (MacPhail, 1975: 299). At about 18,000 BP the climate was relatively cold, dry and windier, especially in north-eastern Tasmania, the average wind speeds being suggested (Allen *et al.*, 1988) to have been 8 km/hr higher than at present (Bowden, 1983). In south east Tasmania the development of sand dunes has been dated to about 15,000 BP, shortly following the suggested period of maximum aridity (Sigleo & Colhoun, 1975). It has been found that the formation of lunettes continued in north-eastern Tasmania up until about 8,300 BP (Cosgrove, 1985). According to Cosgrove et *al* low sea levels resulted in these changes, the precipitation gradient between east and west was increased by the interception of most of the moisture by the mountains of the west coast (Bowden, 1983). It has been estimated that the mean annual precipitation on the west coast would have been at least 1000-1500 mm, whereas on the east coast it would have been 300-400 mm, even if the annual rainfall was 50 % lower during the Last Glacial Maximum (Galloway, 1986). During the glacial maximum eastern Tasmania would have experienced periods of drought stress, evidence of which is seen in the building episodes of inland dunes and lunettes (Bowden, 1978a, 1978b, 1983; Colhoun, 1978, 1982; Kirkpatrick, 1986: 239). Cosgrove et *al* suggest that grasslands may have been restricted to areas with deeper soils by the climate of the area at this time that has been classed as glacial-arid (MacPhail, 1975) with higher moisture levels, areas with sandier substrates being more vulnerable to erosion.

The structure and distribution of exploitable energy, animal and plant, for hunter gatherers in the period before the Last Glacial Maximum to the period following it, were affected by the ecological variation (Foley, 1977: 71; 1981; Gamble, 1984: 224; 1986: 42, 64;

Jockhim. 1979: 84). In south west Tasmania, the distributions of productive grassy habitats are especially relevant for their suggested role in resource distribution and availability. Extensive areas of western and south-western Tasmania covered by open herbfield and steppe (Kiernan *et al.*, 1983: 30) have been described as a myth (Kirkpatrick, 1986: 235). He believes the dominant glacial vegetation complexes were almost certainly stunted woody, heath and sedge taxa, similar to those covering the alpine and treeless sub-alpine regions of the present, as a result of the soil infertility that is widespread in western and south-western Tasmania (Kirkpatrick & Brown, 1984; Kirkpatrick, 1986: 239). Chenopod vegetation and short alpine herbfields have been extensive only in the east and parts of the North West, as well as the western continental shelf that was exposed (Hope, 1978; Sigleo & Colhoun, 1981; MacPhail & Colhoun, 1985; Colhoun *et al.*, 1982).

The character of the rich deposits of Kutikina Cave has been found to be based on a general association between fauna and steppe (Jones, 1984; Kiernan *et al.*, 1983). Valleys overlying limestone, and on soils that are relatively fertile, are the only places in the interior of the south west where grass is likely to have been supported (Kirkpatrick & Harwood, 1980; Kirkpatrick, 1982: 268; 1986: 237; Kirkpatrick & Duncan, 1987).

Cosgrove et al have proposed an alternative model based on the requirements of, and the interactions between, the flora, fauna, soils, temperature and fire. The red-necked wallaby (***Macropus rufogriseus***) has been found to be the main animal exploited by humans in the south west of Tasmania (Kiernan *et al.*, 1983; Jones, 1984; Allen *et al.*, 1988). At the present this animal occurs in open shrubland and sedgeland in very low numbers, being no longer common in the vegetation complexes of the south west (Hocking & Guiler, 1982). It has been suggested that the sites in the south west were abandoned when invading rainforest replaced the grasslands about 12,000 BP with the resulting reduction or elimination of the wallabies (Kiernan *et al.*, 1983). An aspect of red-necked wallaby behaviour is that they are extremely sedentary, having a home range that averages 15-20 ha, very unusual for macropods. They usually remain in a particular area of their home range for about 2-3 years, eventually moving to another one less than 30 m away (Johnson,

1987: 131), the range changing little from season to season and from year to year. In contrast, red kangaroos and grey kangaroos on the mainland of Australia have home ranges of about 10 km^2 or more, and when they moved to a new centre of activity it is 900-1060 m away (Priddle, 1988; Priddle *et al.*, 1988). Another characteristic behaviour of red-necked wallabies is that most rest close to the edges of the forest where they have good protective cover, as well as escape routes and proximity to feeding areas (Southwell, 1987: 28; Johnson, 1987: 128). The major food source of these wallabies is grasslands and herbfields, which are essential for the support of large congregations of these animals (Jarman, *et al.*, 1987; Kirkpatrick, 1983: 75; Strahan, 1983: 239; Gibson & Kirkpatrick, 1985: 96; Southwell, 1987). They apparently graze over a wide range of altitudes, a high correlation being found between the grazing of the wallabies and the distribution of short alpine herbfields on snow patches at an altitude of 1200 m on Mt. Field (Gibson & Kirkpatrick, 1985).

Fertile soils and reliable drainage are a requirement of grasses and herbs (Kirkpatrick & Duncan, 1987; Bowman *et al.*, 1986; Ellis, 1985, 1986; Ellis & Gravely, 1987). In south western Tasmania grasses are longer found on the siliceous soils, being restricted to sparse individual clumps of refugia on outcropping limestone in the Weld River, Franklin River and Maxwell River (Kirkpatrick & Harwood, 1980; Kirkwood & Brown, 1987). Grasses from these refugia would colonise the soils that were deeper and more fertile of alluvial flats or ground on restricted limestone geology, which, unfortunately for the wallabies that grazed the grass, also provided caves and rock shelters? that could be occupied by human hunters (Kirkpatrick, 1986: 237; Middleton, 1979).

According to the authors, to understand the reasons the Aboriginal population of south west Tasmania abandoned the region at the end of the Pleistocene it is important to find mechanisms involved in the maintenance of grasslands in the long-term. It has been suggested (Ellis, 1985, 1986) that under model conditions when fire frequency increases on grasslands the result can be a grassland sub-climax, but a colonisation sequence from heathland, tea-tree to eucalypt, and possibly to rainforest, can result from a cessation of burning, as has been observed to have occurred in less than 150 years in parts of north-eastern Tasmania (Ellis, 1986). It has been suggested that in higher alpine areas, where plant cover possibly approximates palaeo-vegetation characteristics, in the short term fire increases the dominance of herbaceous species like poa grasses, though the shallow fertile soils are degraded in the long-term, while the deeper substrates may suffer less (Kirkpatrick, 1983; Kirkpatrick & Dickinson, 1984). The invasion of these grasslands by rainforest species at the end of the Pleistocene, about 12,900 BP, as the climate became wetter and warmer, has been the explanation of the disappearance of the grasslands at this time (Kiernan *et al.*, 1983; Jones, 1988).

Cosgrove, et *al*. claim that on anthropogenic grounds this is difficult to sustain, a significant point being the extreme fire sensitivity of rainforest, that can be effectively excluded from its former range by firing that is systematic and regular (Bowman & Jackson, 1981; Jarman *et al.*, 1982; Hill & Read, 1984). In recent decades large areas of Tasmanian rainforest have been destroyed in short periods of time by fires that were human-induced (Jackson, 1978: 98-101). There is uncertainty as to why in some areas, such as the Florentine Valley, that is a fertile area close to the eastern boundary of the south-western zone, grasslands were not maintained with fire, as they would probably have been able to be utilised well into the Holocene. It has been noted that at the present any fires in the Florentine Valley will be severe in summer when hot, dry, northerly winds are blowing (Gilbert, 1949). It has been suggested that the replacement of progressive grassland by eucalypt forest in the Florentine Valley resulted from the end of firing that had previously been carried out by the Aboriginal people until 200 years ago (Gilbert, 1959). The authors say this suggests that the abandonment that occurred 12,000 BP was probably of a single type of Pleistocene economic strategy that was centred on cave sites.

Cosgrove et *al* suggest that a large quartzite core and several hornfels flakes that were found in the Nunamira Cave (Bluff Cave), that were lying on the floor surface, could indicate that following the sealing of the surface by calcite about 12,000 BP the cave was used for ephemeral visits. Additional evidence that the area had been used by Aboriginal people is seen in open sites (Kiernan *et al.*, 1983: 28), but these sites were still to be investigated in 1998.

Cosgrove et al suggest that in the south west of Tasmania resource patch-richness, with sedentary animals and plant food being interspersed among low trees and shrubs in the river valleys, where the moisture input was consistent and effective, is indicated by the palaeoecology of the region to have characterised the region at any point in time (Kirkpatrick & Brown, 1987: 548). Contrasting with the south-western region, the south-eastern region was characterised by widespread grasslands, that were drier and drought-prone, and in which the resources were probably widely dispersed, and at times unpredictable, and distributed across the landscape more generally (MacPhaill & Jackson, 1978; Sigleo & Colhoun, 1981; Kirkpatrick & Duncan, 1987). These patterns are illustrated in Fig. 6a.2, Source 1.

According to the authors they have assumed that these conditions were not stable, almost certainly varying on micro-scales and meso-scales with time and from place to place, the magnitude of such shifts being unknown. Theories of ecosystem dynamics, both at the present and in the past, that involve complex influences that include climatic, edaphic and anthropogenic factors that contribute to variability in the long-term as well as the short-term (Kirkpatrick & Brown, 1984; Bowman & Brown, 1986; Foley, 1981; Pickett & White, 1985: 374; Delcourt & Delcourt, 1983: Dodson, 1989). The authors claim the basing of their model mainly on evidence makes it useful, and to a large extent being independent of archaeological data. They say it forms an ecological framework in which it is possible to investigate variability, inter-regionally as well as intra-regionally, and the concomitant behaviour of the humans in the regions in question.

See Aboriginal Occupation of South Central Tasmania During the Pleistocene

Aboriginal Occupation of South Central Tasmania in the Pleistocene - Archaeological deposits - artefact density
(Cosgrove, Allen & Marshall In Murray, 1998)
The extreme richness of artefacts in the deposits at Kutikina Cave have been emphasised (Kiernan *et al.*, 1983), especially when compared to the deposits in other Tasmanian caves from the Pleistocene, such as Cave Bay Cave and Beginners Luck Cave (Murray & Goede, 1980). The richness found in Kutikina Cave

appears to have been characteristic of many Pleistocene sites in the Tasmanian south west. In M86/2, 9,500 pieces of artefactual stone and more than 30,000 pieces of bone were found in 0.25 m^3 of the deposit that had been excavated. At Nunamira Cave more than 30,000 stone flakes were found at a density of 50-80 per kg of soil, as well as about 30,000 bone pieces in 1.0 m^3 of the deposit. In Bone Cave there was a similar amount of bone and more stone present in 0.8 m^3 of the deposit. According to the authors there are a number of possible explanations such as the caves being preferred to more open sites as they provide more protection from the cold, or under the palaeoecological model of the authors the prey animals tended to congregate in certain patches, and unfortunately for the animals, there were nearby caves the hunters could occupy, with the result that these caves were used more frequently or for longer periods.

In the deposits at Nunamira Cave the richest bone deposits were in the upper layers that dated to later than 16,000 BP and increasing to 13,000 BP. M86/2 was abandoned at 18.000 BP, the last glacial maximum, a time when occupation at Kutikina Cave, 5 km away, was at the peak of its intensity. According to the authors this suggests there is no necessary correlation between the cold and the level of occupation of the caves.

The distinctly lower density of artefactual objects at OSR 7, though the species list of animals represented in the deposits of OSR 7 is similar, but with minor differences, to sites that are further west dating from the Pleistocene, there are specific variations, especially considering quantities and processing strategies. Significant differences also occur between the technology and raw materials of OSR 7 and the stone tool assemblages at the sites in the south west. The authors suggest OSR 7 reflects an archaeological signature that is distinctly different from sites in the south west of Tasmania dating from the Pleistocene. It also supports the proposal that the eastern border of the south-western geographic zone is also a border between regions with different human behaviour during the Pleistocene.

See Aboriginal Occupation of South Central Tasmania During the Pleistocene

Aboriginal Occupation of south central Tasmania in the Pleistocene - Fauna (Cosgrove, Allen & Marshall in Murray, 1998)

The authors have made some tentative observations concerning the fauna associated with the sites under discussion.

They believe that the vast majority of the faunal remains in the excavated sites reflect human activity. At Nunamira Cave about 12,000 bones of small mammals, mostly whole and unburnt, have been found in the upper units that are believed to have come from owl pellets (Dodson & Wexler, 1979; Marshall, 1986; Hoffman, 1988), most being found below the overhang at the front of the cave that provides a suitable roost for owls. Also in the top levels of Bone Cave, a high proportion of the bone that was highly fragmented is suggested to have been the result of activity of the Tasmanian devil (*Sarcophilus harrisii*) (Douglas et al., 1966; Marshall & Cosgrove, forthcoming in 1998). It has been found that in deposits where there are hearths and numbers of stone tools, the indicators of non-human predators are greatly reduced or absent. In layers in which there is little or no evidence of non-human predators, bone and bone fragments display various indications of processing by humans such as burning, breakage that is patterned, transverse incisions indicating cut marks, and in the margins of some fractures, impact notches.

Most of the bone that has been interpreted as being the result of human activity in the south west Tasmanian caves being discussed here is from a single animal species, the red-necked wallaby, *Macropus rufogriseus*. Among the minor elements the wombat, *Vombatus ursinus*. The same 2 animals are also found to dominate the faunal remains in Kutikina Cave (Kiernan et al 1983; Geering, 1983). Other caves, such as M86/2, Nunamira Cave and Bone Cave, all contain among the minor prey animals a wider range of species than found in Kutikina Cave, such as platypus, emu, Tasmanian native hen and native cat. Also found in the deposits, though in small numbers, is the eastern grey kangaroo, *Macropus giganteus*, not found in this part of Tasmania at the present.

Emu eggshell, which has been found only in Nunamira Cave, is believed by the authors to indicate an expansion of grassy habitats after about 20,000 BP, as well as suggesting that humans were present at this site in late winter and early spring (Dove, 1925: 221-2, 300; 1926: 213, 290-1).

The authors suggest an increasing vegetation cover in this region in the terminal Pleistocene is probably indicated by the presence in the Nunamira Cave of the wallaby, ***Thylogale billardierii***, late in the sequence, and very late in the sequence at Nunamira Cave and Bone Cave, the presence of the ring-tail possum, ***Pseudochirus peregrinis***. According to the authors, a large difference in the environment in the Late Pleistocene and Holocene of central Tasmania and the south-eastern section of the mainland Australia is indicated by the absence of the ring-tail possum throughout most of these sequences, as it is ubiquitous in faunal assemblages on the mainland at this time.

The apparent differential representation of body parts of the red-necked wallaby in many sequences are believed to suggest that the animals were initially processed off-site, possibly representing differential treatment and its breakage, it remains to be tested if the pattern changed through time. At Nunamira Cave and Bone cave, about 25 km apart, the bone is more fragmented and more often burnt in the earlier layers, the average fragment weight increasing and the percentage of burnt bone decreasing over time. At Nunamira Cave, and at about the same time at Bone Cave, the changes occur 24,000-21,000 BP, a time when the cold was intensifying. The authors suggest more recent Bone Cave and Nunamira Cave configuration is reflected in the sequence at M86/2.

Wallaby marrow bones display a consistent and regular breakage pattern, the long bones being systematically smashed, producing helical fractures to the diaphyses, the metatarsals and phalanges being split longitudinally. Similar patterns are found in experimental and ethnographic studies of marrow extraction (Noe-Nygaard, 1977; Binford, 1981: 148-61; Johnson, 1985; Lyman, 1987; Todd & Rapson, 1988). According to the authors it was not clear at the time of writing [1998] what was indicated by the distinctly different patterns of bone refuse in the earlier and later parts of the sequence. This difference between the earlier and later layers of the deposits at Bone Cave and Nunamira Cave is not believed to be site specific, as the change occurs in the deposits at both caves, and it is not considered to be coincidental that the pattern of activity area changes at both sites, as both sites are small. Exploitation of different species between the 2 caves has been ruled out as a reason for the change, as the same species are involved throughout all the sequences. The authors suggest it may reflect a change in the general use of the sites through time, or possibly a change in the economic utility of red-necked wallabies or a specific change in the procedures followed in the processing of the animals that occurred over time. The authors suggest that an intensification of the marrow extraction processes over time might be seen as the reason for the change, a less efficient or less complete use of the marrow is not indicated by the burnt and smashed bones in the earlier layers of the deposits. They also suggest that if it is found that marrow bones were selectively brought back to the sites when the upper levels were being deposited, but not earlier than the change, this might imply that the marrow bones being targeted more selectively.

The remains of extinct megafauna animals have not been identified among the bone assemblages at these sites.

The model proposed by the authors suggests that at any one time in the Pleistocene the ecological make-up of the south west region of Tasmania provided an animal resource that was relatively sedentary and that was potentially concentrated. This appears to be suggested by the presence of high concentrations of smashed bones, derived mostly from a single species, the red-necked wallaby, in all sites that have been excavated. According to the authors, it is important that a juxtaposed mosaic of ecotones is predicted for the region by their model, a general expectation of a high level of species richness and diversity (Wiens, 1985: 184; King & Graham, 1981), especially in patches of grassy microenvironments that are well watered are surrounded by scrub and low lying trees. The authors suggest there could be an expectation that part of the range of habitats in the region would have been exploited by humans in the Pleistocene, and that some evidence of this would be found in the excavated sites, in the form of the remains of a number of species of animal. The only sites where this has been found to be the case, though to a lesser extent than expected, the systematically exploited species numbers being low, were at Nunamira Cave, Bone Cave and M86/2. An example is the low level exploitation of the emu at Nunamira Cave, where there doesn't appear to be a necessary correlation between the resources forming the subsistence base and the range of the available resources that are predicted.

The seasonal presence of humans in at least 1 site, which corresponds to the most stressful part of the year, late winter and early spring, is suggested by the presence of emu eggshell. It has been found that the diets of hunter-gatherers living at high latitudes, temperate, subarctic and arctic zones, become marginal and inadequate in late winter and early spring, especially when they rely on lean meat for energy (Speth & Spielman, 1983). At this time the physical condition of humans, as well as other animals, is reduced, as a result of higher metabolic rates, higher calorific requirements and a fatty acid deficit, especially in environments that are sharply seasonal (Speth & Spielman, 1983: 2). Reliance on a high protein diet, at a time when food plants are not available, can be detrimental to the physiology of hunter-gatherers (Speth, 1987; Noli & Avery, 1988).

The meat of kangaroos and wallabies is extremely lean and the fat deposits around the kidneys, as well as in the marrow and on the back and tail are limited (Sinclair, 1988; O'Dea, 1988). In female red-necked wallabies it has been found that in winter there is a significant drop in the kidney fat, the same effect being found in wallabies living in dry zones compared to those living in wetter zones (Driessen, 1988: 16). Towards the end of winter the males put on condition, presumably in preparation for the mating season (Driessen, pers. com to Cosgrove *et al.*). It has also been suggested by field studies that pasture quality was a factor in the deposition of kidney fat. Wallabies living in high rainfall areas, on ranges that are more fertile, appear less stressed and have a physical condition that is enhanced, according to the available evidence. In areas with lower rainfall the females have fewer young at foot than those from wetter areas (Driessen, 1988: 23). In west Tasmania during the Late Pleistocene, the moister habitats of the region have been suggested by the authors to possibly have been crucial in the aggregation of animals in the south west, as well as to the health of the animals.

Macropod meat has been found to have the potential to dilate blood vessels and increase blood flow in response to cold. Experiments with humans, in which the subjects ate kangaroo meat, found that blood levels of arachidonic acid were increased (O'Dea, 1988). It is believed that this acid 'modulates the thrombosis tendency by affecting the platelet aggregation and blood flow' (O'Dea, 1988: 42). The opposite effect was found in subjects eating lean southern fish; these subjects had reduced blood flow in response to cold. See Rocky Cape Food. It has been suggested by O'Dea that the presence in the blood of such long chain fatty acids (PUFA) may protect against thrombosis. It is not known if the Aboriginal population of Pleistocene Tasmania had metabolic rates that were inherently higher, as has been found at the present in Eskimo (Inuit) and Patagonian populations (Kirk, 1983: 158). This suggests it might have been advantageous for the Aboriginal population of glacial Tasmania to have had PUFA in their blood.

In the subantarctic environment that existed in Tasmania during the glacial phase the diet of lean meat would not provide all essential nutrients in late winter and early spring seasonal fluctuations, with the absence of plant carbohydrates. It has been suggested (Bowdler, 1981, 104) that the small daisy yam, ***Microseris scapigera***, may have been present in glacial Tasmania, as it presently grows in subalpine grasslands of Tasmania (Jackson, 1973: 71), though no evidence has been found in any of the sites of the use of plants.

The possibility of protein poisoning would be increased by the lack of animal fats and carbohydrates (Noli & Avery, 1988: 396). The intensive processing and extraction of marrow (see Fauna) has been suggested as a possible solution to this potential problem, bone marrow containing the essential fatty acids such as linoleic acid, which is used in protein metabolism, the fats and carbohydrates enhance the effects of protein-sparing (Speth & Spielman, 1983: 13).

In the sites that have been excavated some body parts of macropods are well represented and were systematically broken in the sites. These bones, wallaby tibia, femurs, metatarsals and humeri, are the bones that in ungulates, as well as kangaroos, contain relatively high levels of marrow (Binford, 1978: 152, 188; 1981: 150; O'Connell & Marshall, 1989; Jones & Metcalf, 1988). It has been suggested that at high risk times of year they might allow the bridging of the dietary gap between winter and summer. According to the authors it is not certain why there was preferential selection of the red-necked wallaby as the main prey species, as other larger species, such as the wombat, the pademelon, the emu and the grey kangaroo, that was much larger, all of which are species inhabiting the grasslands in the river valleys at the time, in particular the Florentine Valley, remains of such species being found in caves and limestone pitfalls. All these animals have long bones that would have made a good addition to those of the red-necked wallaby that was the predominant prey species. It has been suggested that the improved physical condition of the male red-necked wallabies feeding on better-watered pasture towards the end of winter may have been a key factor in the exploitation of this species. It has also been suggested that the unpredictable, nomadic behaviours of the larger animals, together with their larger ranges and their smaller group make-up, may have contributed to reduced hunting success (Horton, 1981: 23). The red-necked wallaby would seem to have been an attractive prey species, based on these criteria, being a more attractive investment of time and labour, as the hunting success with this species would probably have been consistent and predictable throughout the year, though it is not known if the animal composition and abundance was different during the Late Pleistocene.

According to the authors it is difficult to assess palaeo-diets, even with well-preserved food refuse in middens and the use of stable carbon isotope analysis of any human collagen that is present (Collier & Hobson, 1987). Study of the middens doesn't reveal the total and exact diet of the occupants of a site, only giving an indication of the foods eaten over long periods of time, and is not believed to give a complete picture of the economic strategy. Stable carbon isotope analysis of the collagen indicates the diet at a specific location. It has been suggested that wallabies may have performed the role of a food source that was relatively sedentary, tiding the people over stressful periods, such as the glacial winters, when food could be scarce, the dependence on wallabies being suggested as a glacial, middle-latitude animal correlate of *'low-key dependable vegetable resources'* (Bowdler, 1981, 100). The authors warn of the risk of overemphasising a diet of terrestrial animals, not recognising the role of marine and plant food in the diet, the role of these foods in the overall diet of the population of the south west during the Pleistocene being uncertain. The picture given by the food resources exploited is added to by the presence of stone tools, as they give clues to the processing and other activities that were taking place in these caves.

Information gained from the study of these sites indicates they were not used as part of a transient economy with limited activities (Lourandos, 1983: 88), rather they display a degree of structuring of their economy that has not been recorded from any other Pleistocene sites in Australia. These sites appear to indicate that the behavioural pattern in this region was unique, their signatures being different from those of sites in south-eastern Tasmania that have been dated to the Pleistocene. The authors suggest it is not reasonable to ascribe the behavioural pattern of the south west as a likely pattern in all Australian human populations of the Pleistocene (Lourandos, 1987: 158). According to the authors the residues of the south west differ from those found in inland karst caves that have been dated to the Pleistocene, that are widely dispersed around Australia. Examples of such caves are Cloggs Cave in Victoria (Flood, 1980: 254), Devil's Lair, Western Australia (Dortch, 1984), Walkunder Arch, north Queensland (Campbell, 1984: 176) and Colless Creek, western Queensland (Hiscock, 1984). In the Pleistocene, the cave deposits of south-western Tasmania differ in many ways from the sites mentioned above in other parts of Australia, being as different as are the Holocene sites in south-eastern Tasmania from those on the mainland of a similar age. The authors suggest the subtle differences between early Australian sites should be studied in more detail, and not the continued highlighting of the similarities of Late Pleistocene residues, 'and by implication the continuity and unidirectional vectors of Pleistocene human behaviour' (Cosgrove, Allen & Marshall in Source 1).

Aboriginal Occupation of south central Tasmania in the Pleistocene - Stone Industries

A high degree of variability has been found in the individual assemblages present at the sites in the study area, though the stone tool types that are characteristic of the 'Australian core tool and scraper tradition', that includes such types as single platform, steep-sided cores, horsehoof cores, and steep-edged, flat and notched scrapers (Bowdler *et al.*, 1970: 49-52) could be extracted from some of the site assemblages. A large amount of analysis will be required to quantify the material in detail, as some of the observed variability results from the availability and physical reduction of different raw materials. The focus here is on the similarities and differences between the assemblages that combine sites into a south-western Tasmanian Pleistocene province, though also indicating differences between them. According to the authors, as well as the distinctive pattern of exploitation of the fauna at these sites, there is also a distinctive pattern of the stone assemblages at the sites.

Similarities and differences between the assemblages are exemplified by the stone raw materials. Comprising 97 % of the stone used in the manufacture of artefacts at M86/2, quartz is the predominant raw material used in the western part of the Tasmanian south west, as well as very small amounts of chert, crystal quartz, hornfels and silcrete. At sites such as Nunamira Cave in the east the local availability of raw materials is reflected in the use of fine-grained cherts, quartzites, silcretes and hornfels, quartz being uncommon in this deposit. The river in front of Bone Cave was the source of raw materials used in the stone assemblages at that site, tools being predominantly of fine-grained quartzite, as well as some crystal quartz from the Weld Valley. Crystal quartz was brought to Nunamira Cave from the south and hornfels and silcrete at Bone Cave were sourced from the north as well as possibly from the east. According to the authors, it is indicated by preliminary identifications that local sources are predominantly used; raw material distribution similarities between these sites are expected to diminish with distance. When considering stone raw materials there is a stronger similarity between Bone Cave and Nunamira Cave than to the western sites, very small amounts of chert, hornfels and silcrete may possibly have come from the east. The authors suggest the movement may be incidental, and not deliberate, movement of the stone materials within the overall region, though eventually a measure of the association between sites, may derive from the number of these types of raw materials, that might in turn indicate the pattern of movement between sites of people using them.

It is believed the movement of Darwin glass, impactite, from Darwin Crater (Fudali & Ford, 1979) in the western part of the south west, to a number of sites up to about 100 km from the impact site was intentional. With the exception of OSR 7, Darwin glass has been found in sites located in 6 of the river valleys of the south west, and all sites that have been discussed here. 10 pieces have been found at M86/2, 5 at Nunamira Cave and 1 piece at Bone Cave, the site that is the greatest distance from Darwin Crater in which Darwin glass has been found.

A small, round type of thumbnail scraper found in Kutikina Cave (Kiernan *et al.*, 1983: 30) is commonly found in all excavated sequences, with the exception of OSR 7, none being found at that site. All specimens from the western sites have been made from milky quartz, and at Bone Cave and Nunamira Cave all specimens were made from fine-grained chert. Among the artefacts of the Australian Pleistocene stone industries it is an unusual type of tool that is likely to have restricted distributions, spatially and temporally, and distinguishes these assemblages from the Australian core tool and scraper tradition, as found in mainland Australia.

In the Kutikina sequence the first appearance of Darwin glass and thumbnail scrapers has been dated to about 17,000 BP (Jones, 1988: 36). The authors say that the suggestions that these introductions were simultaneous or an 'artefactual disconformity at the level of the assemblage' (Jones, 1988: 36; 1989, 770) that is reflected in the appearance of the thumbnail scrapers, is not supported by more recent evidence. The discrepancy between the dates of introduction of these items is suggested by the authors to be more likely to result from the inadequacy of the present samples than to be real temporal differences.

In the earliest levels of all these sites no Darwin glass or thumbnail scrapers have been found. In Tasmanian assemblages from the Holocene, such as Rocky Cape and **Sisters Creek** (Jones, 1965: 195, 197; 1966, 7), Darwin glass may have become inaccessible or simply dropped from the raw materials used.

A quartz thumbnail scraper has been found at Cave Bay Cave that has been dated to 19,000 BP (Bowdler, 1984, 122), and 18 thumbnail scrapers, 16 of which were made from quartz, in the **Green Gully** site near Melbourne in Victoria. Though poorly dated, these river terrace sites are believed to be more than 8,000 years old (Mulvaney, 1975: 172). Neither of these sites suggests other connections or is a reflection of behavioural patterns similar to those in the south west of Tasmania. In the context of the Australian Holocene, thumbnail scrapers appear more widely, though the authors suggest they might be separated from the Pleistocene groups (Wright, 1970: 1987).

In Bone Cave, at a level older than 23,000 BP, a single, atypical flake with denticulated edges was found that is the first indication of simple flaking by the pressure method known from Tasmania. In the Australian industries of the Pleistocene this technique is rare, though a piece that is very similar has been found, that dated to about 20,000 BP, at Burrill Lake Shelter on the coast of New South Wales, as has been illustrated (Lampert, 1971: 52). At this site 5 examples from the Pleistocene includes 3 that have double edges that have been called 'saws' (Lampert, 1971: 28). In Devil's Lair, in Western Australia, 2 have been found that dated to 12,000 BP (Dortch, 1984: 52). Other examples have been found that date to the Late Holocene (White & O'Connell, 1982: 70).

Chapter 3 - The submergence of the Bassian Plain – Bass Strait

Rising Water, Disappearing Continental Shelf (Cane, Scott, 2013)

The people who had occupied the continental shelf when it was exposed by low sea levels would have been greatly affected as the sea gradually covered their territory, disrupting the social structure of communities whose ritual politic was embedded in the land they watched being submerged. For those people who were responsible for that land their social and political consequences must have been devastating as their power to stop the sea rising was shown to be non-existent. There would probably have also been increasing tensions between the communities losing their land and those in neighbouring country. Those groups who lived on land that was centred on high ground on coastal hills and ridges, though they were on the continental shelf, would also have had problems as their country on broad plateaus and mountains would have eventually been surrounded by the sea as they became islands. They would have had no way of knowing if the high central parts of their territory would eventually be cut off from the mainland, or even be submerged, so not knowing if they should try to find space on the nearby mainland or trust that their upland home territory would be safe from the rising water and if there was enough remaining above water for them to survive if and when the rise stopped.

At some point the people living on the extensive plains of the continental shelf would need to make a decision on what to do about the rising sea level, move to higher ground or off the plain altogether. Once a peninsula became an island it would be necessary to decide if they needed to move to the mainland as the water gap was increasing and the island appeared to be getting further from the mainland, leaving the decision too late would mean they may be too far from the mainland to cross easily, and there was the problem of not knowing how high the water would rise. At some places such as east of Wallen Wallen Creek and Burrill Lake, and to the west of Mandu Mandu Shelter, the coast was more precipitous. At places such as these there wouldn't be much social and territorial change to cope with, as effectively they had always lived on the coast and the lateral impacts of sea level change would have been minor in the context of the vertical shores they encroached upon. These groups were not without risk from an insidious threat, there was always the chance that they could change from a coastal people to an island people before they realised what was happening.

That process of entrapment occurred in the Whitsunday Islands over a period of 2,000 years. About 10,000 years ago people had moved to higher ground on Hook Island, camping in a small cave in Nara Inlet with the rising sea a few metres from the entrance, at a time when the island was connected to the mainland by a long narrow peninsula, but 1,000 years later this peninsula was cut and over the next 2,500 years the peninsula became a chain of islands. For some time they travelled between the islands by watercraft to South Molle Island that was newly formed, to collect stone for tools. They may also have travelled to the mainland, though by the time the gap to the mainland had widened to more than 30 km it was too wide, which meant they were isolated on their own. They specialised as marine foragers and developed their own artistic tradition as well as a distinct social and linguistic identity. New tools were invented that suited their subsistence needs such as fish hooks from shellfish and turtle shell, bone and wood were fashioned into spear points, and nets and scraping tools. They hunted everything available in the sea - turtles, small pilot whales, fish, crabs and shellfish.

The Keppel Islands of the present were mountains on the exposed continental shelf and people stayed on them as the water rose around them, the settlement contracting up the mountains 5,000 years ago, and the inhabitants of the Keppel Islands could reach the mainland by taking a dog-leg route via the Pelican Island, as they were 13 km from the coast of the continent. There were not many trips to the mainland, though it could be reached the distance was large, the people on the islands becoming effectively isolated. These now-island people underwent the same process as animal populations do, becoming smaller and more inbred (the island effect), and their language began to change and new rituals developed. As with other groups of people who were isolated at this time they adapted their material culture to suit their new requirements, shields, ground-edge stone axes and boomerangs disappeared from their occupation deposits They also began making new tools such as fish hooks from turtle shell and coconut shell, stone drills for making fish hooks, yam-digging sticks, harpoons with detachable heads for hunting sea turtles and marine mammals. Their access to other islands and the sea was by communal logs that were paddled by hand.

According to Cane the people living on the coast of north Queensland at the time were impacted, though they were not devastated by the rising water, rather they were affected by the impact the isolation of parts of their extended society, as the people who once occupied territory adjacent to them were restricted to their islands. They would also have needed to adapt their material culture now that the coastal plain was gone, and with it rich hunting country, they were now living directly by the sea and needed to change their tools to take advantage of the new, different resource. They would still be able to see the smoke from the fires of those they were now just out of reach of on the adjacent islands.

The lateral encroachment of the sea would have been more noticeable to the inhabitants of the flatter coastal plains which would account for those living on high grounds escaping to the mainland before it was too late. Between 9,000 and 8,000 years ago people vacated sites on the western coast of the continent such as Noala Cave and the Montebello Islands. The inhabitants of the nearby Barrow Islands and the Recherche Archipelago, and further to the south, Rottnest Island apparently escaped to the mainland before they were cut off. The people living in the larger upland areas, promontories and peninsulas had more of a problem knowing if they needed to escape to the mainland; it may have appeared to them that their home territory was large enough to avoid being cut off, or at least being large enough to survive if they remained in their country. Cane[1] suggests other reasons why they would have been reluctant to leave, such as the possibility of regional territories being present on the soon-to-be-islands, and they had no way of knowing how much things would change if they stayed.

On the Bassian Plain people lingered as the water surrounded them, evidence of their decision to remain being a hearth found in Cave Bay Cave that has been dated to 15,400 years ago. As more people were crammed into the country the occupation intensified, the people of the plains were being forced to live in a country that was contracting as the area of the peninsula continued to diminish. By 6,500 years ago the peninsula was an island. As evidence of the most recent camp has been dated to 6,600 years ago is seems they escaped to the mainland just in time.

The occupants of Flinders Island apparently dallied too long being forced back into the uplands of this large island, about 1,300 km^2 in area, by the encroaching sea. It appears to have been known to the people of the plains that the sea was rising, as is suggested by the abandonment of the hills that formed the smaller islands before they were surrounded. On Badger Island and Prime Seal Island there is no evidence of human habitation after 9,000 years ago, at which time occupation appears to have ceased abruptly, though it had been occupied since the glacial maximum 21,000 years ago. Cane[1] suggests the decision to retreat to Flinders Island was a miscalculation, though at the time it probably seemed like a good idea. They could not have known that another climate change would make the island too small to sustain them all. It is not known how many of the people stayed as the island was surrounded by water, though managed to survive for 2,000 years after the sea level stabilised. Another unknown is what happened to them during those 2,000 years. Cane has suggested some possible scenarios such as a slow decline in population until there were not enough to survive genetically. Though he suggests it is unlikely they ran out of food, as not all the available resources were available to them, and being coastal foragers did not exploit near-shore resources that were available in near-shore areas such as abalone and crayfish. During the Holocene the climate became more variable with droughts becoming more common and extreme, so they may have died of thirst. There would have been no escape route available as the climatic conditions declined drastically in the Late Holocene. The water gap they needed to cross to escape to Tasmania would have been too difficult to cross as the tidal current in this water gap flows at 10 km/hour, one of the strongest currents in the world.

The same fate befell the people who retreated to Kangaroo Island, with the population moving to higher ground as the water encroached. This island had been a substantial promontory adjacent to the coast, and then about 6,400 years ago it became an island. At 4 times the size of Flinders Island it is a large island, though it was still not big enough. The inhabitants of the promontory and the surrounding plain had been there since 16,000 years ago. Then about 11,000 years ago they are believed to have retreated to the island as the sea encroached. At Seton Site on Kangaroo Island there is evidence of occupation that was more intense at this time, including more stone, bone and charcoal among which are 2 bone points that seem to have been used for working skins. After this time there is decreasing evidence of occupation, with only sparse scatterings of stone and shell to indicate a small population on the island. The youngest site to be found has been dated to 4,300 years ago, though regular burning continued until about 2,500 years ago, Cane suggesting the people may have lived on the island until evidence of regular burning ceases 2,500 years ago.

Chapter 4 - Material Culture

Aboriginal Weapons and Tools

Ground-Edge Axe – Oldest in the World Coincides With Human Colonisation of Australia

In this paper Hiscock et *al.* report evidence of the earliest ground-edge axe in the world, at 44,000-49,000 BP. The age of this axe coincides with the time when the Aborigines were still in the process of colonising the Australian continent. The discovery of ground/polished axes exemplifies the diversification of technological practices that occurred as modern humans dispersed out of Africa, as this type of axe has not been associated with the dispersal of ***Homo sapiens*** across Eurasia. Ground-edge axes have now been found in 2 colonised lands at the time humans arrived and Hiscock et *al.* therefore argue that these technological strategies are associated with the adapting of economies and social practices to new environmental contexts.

The evidence of ground-edge axes was uncovered in northern Australia dating to 44,000-49,000 BP. This age makes it the earliest evidence of a ground-edge axe to be reported in the world to date, and such evidence has implications for the dispersion of modern humans form Africa, as well as the nature of the first occupation by humans in Australia.

Australian stone lithic industries from the Pleistocene have, according to Hiscock et *al.*, been persistently characterised as being extremely and uniformly simple, being tools that were unstandardized and expedient, which means that the discovery of ground-edge axes in Australia is challenging.

Ground-edge axes have been reported across much of northern Australia that dated to the terminal Pleistocene, at Widgingarri 1 and Carpenter's Gap I and 3 in the Kimberley, Western Australia (O'Connor, 1999; O'Connor et *al.*, 2014) at Malanangerr, Nauwalabila 1, Nawamoyn, and Nawarla Gabarnmang, in western Arnhem Land (Geneste et *al.*, 2010; Jones, 1985; Schrire, 1982; White, 1967), and on Cape York, Sandy Creek (Morwood and Trezise, 1989). Hiscock et *al.* say these ground-edge axes were invented locally. In the islands to the north of Australia such ground-edge axes first appear in the Neolithic, also, there is no evidence that this technology was introduced to the Australian continent. The unanswered questions until now are when axes were invented, and in what manner did that invention relate to the colonisation process? In this paper Hiscock et *al.* present evidence for the production of axes close to the time of colonisation of Australia.

There are not large numbers of axes in assemblages as they are long lived. Therefore the early axe chronology cannot be based solely on recovery of whole axes, which are rare, and the discovery of the presence of such axes from well-dated excavations depends on flakes that have been removed from ground bevels on axes as they were being resharpened or repair of damaged and worn edges. The identification of axes that have been dated to 35,000 BP in Australia (Geneste et *al.*, 2010) has been based on such flakes with parts of a bevelled edge on them. There have been suggestions of even earlier axes from Madjedbebe (Malakunanja II) based on the presence of small flakes of volcanic material in sediments that were dated to more than 40,000 BP (Clarkson et *al.*, 2015). Hiscock et *al.* are cautious of this interpretation as the flakes lack diagnostic ground bevels (Clarkson et *al.*, 2105: 173). The repair of a bevel often involved removing a number of flakes before the edge was reground, and such a repair cycle may be repeated several times, the process making an order of magnitude more flakes than axes deposited in the archaeological record. It is, therefore, the polished bevel that defines specimens as ground-edge axes, and reshaping the flakes that remove the bevel as identifiable as the complete axe. The angle of ground bevels ranges from 60° to 100° (Dickson, 1981: 104), and the characteristics of the edge can vary significantly over the life of the axe as multiple uses and repairs are carried out on it (Kononenko et *al.*, in press). As this range of angles overlaps with the range of angles that are produced by core reduction they are not reliable as a sole diagnostic trait. The ground surface that is highly polished is the only morphological feature that is unique to axes. Extensive abrasion with another rock is used to make smooth surfaces which cannot be produced incidentally by other knapping actions such as the preparation of platforms. It has been shown by experiments that grinding basalt to a polished level takes from 1.5 to 5.0 hours depending on the abrasive agent that is used (Dickson, 1980). Hundreds of forceful strokes are needed to produce a smooth bevel, even under optimal conditions. This proposition is confirmed experimentally and it is indicated that though the smoothness of ground surfaces vary, they are always smoother than fracture surfaces. Hiscock et *al.* say the key indicator of axes they use is convergent bevels with high surface smoothness which is achieved by extensive abrasion, and this is applied to the identification of small flakes from axes that are produced by bevel reshaping.

Recent discovery of such flakes have demonstrated that axes were made in Australia at least 30,000-35,000 BP (Geneste et *al.*, 2010; Jones, 1985; Morwood & Trezise, 1989; O'Connor, 1999; O'Connor et *al.*, 2014). Evidence that has been presented in this paper from excavations at Carpenter's Gap Shelter 1 demonstrates that ground-edge axes were being made in Northern Australia more than 10,000 years earlier. This is the earliest evidence to be reported in the world to date of ground-edge axes, and it reveals that the first Australians were technological innovators who developed grinding and abrading as techniques to be used for shaping a range of new implements that included hafted ground-edge axes. Hiscock et *al.* argue that the evidence from Carpenter's Gap Shelter 1 shows that this kind of innovation arose as humans dispersed from Africa as they invented regional traditions as part of their adaptations to new landscapes.

Carpenter's Gap Shelter 1

Carpenter's Gap 1 (CG1) is among the oldest known habitation sites in Australia that have been dated by the radiocarbon technique. The first excavations at this site were carried out in 1992 and 1993 during which 5 1 m square test pits were dug to bedrock (Frawley & O'Connor, 2010; O'Connor, 1995). Square A2, which is close to the large rockfall that trapped the deposit within the upper part of the shelter, to produce the artefactual material that is discussed in this paper. Units average a depth of 2 cm in this site excavation but were dug within depositional units. A hearth 10 cm deep, e.g., would be removed separately from other sediments, to be treated as 1 stratigraphic context, though it would be divided into excavation units of 2 cm depth to enhance assessments of provenance.

The sediments have primarily accumulated in the shelter, dating from the Upper Holocene, as a result of *in situ* weathering of layers of softer sedimentary rocks that are embedded in the limestone reef the cave formed in, as well as a component of aeolian deposits (Vannieuwenhuyse et *al.*, in press), overlie sediments of Pleistocene age that have been dated to approximately 49,000 cal. BP through to approximately 18,000 BP). Assemblages of Holocene age were found to be restricted to layers 1-4, and most of the deposit accumulated prior to the LGM. Cultural material was deposited throughout the site, beginning in excavation unit 61, which was significantly below deposits dating to 44,000-49,000 BP. The axe fragment that was of the earliest age was recovered from excavation unit 52, near the base of the cultural sequence.

The specimen referred to in this paper as Carpenter's Gap Axe Flake 1 was recovered from Square A2 unit 52 was designated cg1/a2/52/1. A charcoal sample was also found with it and it was dated to 48,875-43941 cal. BP (WK-37976). Hiscock et *al.*, argue that the axe fragment and the charcoal sample are associated stratigraphically and therefore constitute evidence that the axe grinding technology that was employed in the manufacture of the axe at or immediately after the arrival of the humans in Australia.

Some have questioned the chronological integrity of the early Australian assemblages (e.g. Allen & O'Connell, 2003, 2014; O'Connell & Allen, 2014), their argument being that for older specimens their post-depositional relocation placed them in a false association resulting in radiometric estimates of an early age. The reply of Hiscock et *al.* is that though their critique is overdrawn (Hiscock, 2013), the possibility of movement should be examined for each deposit. The assemblages from the Pleistocene at CG1were evaluated to determine if they had been affected by vertical displacement by looking for size-sorting of artefacts within the lower deposit. This test of post-depositional movement of materials within archaeological deposits, as there are a variety of processes that act to lower small specimens and/or raise larger ones (Bocek, 1986; Cahen & Moeyersons, 1977; Hofman, 1986; McBrearty, 1990; Schiffer, 1987; Stockton, 1973; Wood & Johnson, 1978). Therefore, Hiscock et *al.* predicted that there would be smaller specimens in unit 52 and adjacent levels than in ones that were immediately higher, if there had been significant movement involving displacement of specimens into unit 52 from higher levels in the deposit. With this in mind Hiscock et *al.* examined the relationship between the size of artefacts and their depth for specimens in excavation units 45-60, which represents MIS 3 – the period prior to the Last Glacial Maximum (LGM). Using univariate GLM (General Linear Model) and non-parametric regression statistical tests established that there was no significant relationship between depth and artefact mass

($F = 0.043$, d.f. = 15, $p = 0.975$, $r_s = 0.011$, $p = 0.914$, $N = 100$),

maximum artefact dimension

($F = 0.882$, d.f. = 15, $p = 0.586$; $r_s = 0.079$, $p = 0.433$, $N = 100$) or

Flake percussion length

$F = 0.998$, d.f. = 12, $p = 0.477$; $r_s = -0.141$, $p = 0.384$, $N = 40$).

Hiscock et *al.* view the failure to find size-sorting as refuting the hypothesis that vertical movement of artefacts had occurred within the oldest levels of the deposit. Other lines of evidence are consistent with this conclusion. For example, excavation units 51-53 commonly contain basalt flakes, though they are rarer in high levels, 42-50, which indicates there is minimal 'reservoir' of similar specimens from which the axe flake, cg1/a2/52/1, could possibly have derived. Also, small and large artefacts, as well as the limestone plaque that was recovered from the base of the deposit, that was covered with ochre (O'Connor & Frankhauser, 2011), was discovered which was lying horizontally. Regular displacement of material is not suggested by these observations. As a consequence, Hiscock et *al.* were confident that this specimen is associated, stratigraphically and temporally, with the radiocarbon sample in that excavation unit, having an antiquity of 44,000-49,000 ca. BP.

Axe production demonstration

The interpretation that is offered by Hiscock et *al.* relies on reliable data as well as a clear identification of the technological character of the specimen in question.

Archaeological comparison

The comparative sample used by Hiscock et *al.* was comprised of artefacts from 3 categories comprising a total of 50 artefacts;

The specimen that was discussed in this paper, Carpenter's Gap Axe Flake 1,

11 axes and axe fragments recovered from sites in the Kimberley and adjacent regions, and

38 basal flakes that were not ground from levels 48-52 of CG1.

Included in the 3rd category were flakes which had surfaces that were weathered and slightly patinated.

Mean values for Ra ratios and Rzjis ratios differ significantly for basalt ground-edge axes and flakes with no grinding

(Ra ratios $t = -3.810$, d.f. $= 10$, $p = 0.003$; Rzjis ratios: $t = -3.089$, d.f. $= 10$, $p = 0.011$).

Contrasting with this the Ra and Rzjis ratios of ground-edge axes do not differ significantly from those of unground axes, and the specimen from excavation 52 of CGI that is reported in this paper

(Ra ratios $t = -0.541$, d.f. $= 10$, $p = 0.601$; Rzjis ratios: $t = -0.542$, d.f. $= 10$, $p = 0.600$).

According to Hiscock et *al.* these results are consistent with the proposition that the smoothing of the platform and dorsal surface is unlike the surface of basalt at Carpenter's Gap 1 that has been flaked or weathered and is indistinguishable from the ground faces of axes. Given that the morphology of the platform and its junction with the dorsal face of cg1/a2/52/1 is the same as is seen on the typical bevels of axes, and that abrasion, that has been extensive and laborious, has smoothed the basalt to the same extent as is observed on axes, the conclusion of Hiscock et *al.* is that Carpenter's Gap Axe Flake 1 (cg1/a2/52/1) must be a flake that has been removed from the polished edge of a ground edge axe.

Technological novelty and the colonisation of Australia

Hiscock et *al.* suggest that the date of the production of ground-edge axes is close to, and possibly immediately after, the age that has generally been accepted for the colonisation of Sahul (Hiscock et *al.*, 2008). It is now clear that ground-edge axes first appear in the archaeological record shortly after the landfall of the earliest colonisers. Therefore, there is now evidence of substantial technological innovation in the context of the process of colonisation of Sahul.

There is also a remarkable parallel, the first appearance in the Japan archipelago of ground-edge tools that coincided with the arrival of ***Homo sapiens*** in Japan about 38,000 BP (Takashi, 2012). The axes from the Pleistocene in Australia and Japan that are known of are distinctly differ distinctly in size and shape from each other, and represent separate technological innovations, and Hiscock et *al.* speculate that they both possibly built on grinding applications that were pre-existing such as the grinding of haematite for pigment or the production of bone tools. It is suggested that the timing of these innovations in 2 separate lands at the point of colonisation, that dispersing humans often innovated as they entered new territories, and not maintaining technologies that had been previously employed. Adjustments to provisioning and production systems that local materials were suited to, and the availability/costs of materials, as well as new economic and social systems in the new landscapes that were serviced by these novel technologies. It is suggested that something of the magnitude and structure of technological experimentation and innovation in Australia can be illuminated by describing the growth of regional diversity in the production of waisted axes and ground-edge axes.

Technological diversity and regional traditions

According to Hiscock et *al.* geographic variation and regional traditions of behaviour are evident in the technology of the modern humans who were colonising Sahul. The use of hafted ground-edge axes in northern Australia and flaked, waisted unground axes in Papua New Guinea, though the complete lack of axes in the southern $^2/_3$ of the Australian continent, epitomise this (Balme & O'Connor, 2014; Geneste et *al.*, 2010; O'Connor, 1999; 18, Summerhayes et *al.*, 2010). Around the time of colonisation these divisions originated and persisted through to the Holocene, by which time axes began to appear in the assemblages recovered from archaeological sites in most parts of southern mainland Australia and in New Guinea polished adzes are found in deposits. Hiscock et *al.* say these regional distinctions persisted for 40,000 years, which was presumably bolstered by distinctions in language and social views.

A new image of the dispersion of modern humans out-of-Africa is offered by the findings of the study that is reported in this paper.

Flexible and novel adaptations were displayed by cultural groups who occupied new lands such as Sahul and Japan, which is revealed archaeologically in the invention of new technological strategies, such as hafted, ground-edge axes. The construction of cultural differences between groups in different regions and the cultural distinctions formed at colonisation in some instances, were extremely long lasting. It was concluded by Hiscock et *al*. that with the dispersal of ***H. sapiens*** dynamic adaptive modification of cultural systems occurred in conjunction with the dispersal, which played a significant role in the successful expansion of modern humans around the world, as well as leading to a long-lasting differentiation of human societies.

Conclusion

The antiquity of the production of ground-edge axes in Australia has been progressively pushed back, which is a reflection of the increasingly sensitive dating techniques, as well as the gradual increase of archaeological sample sizes. Hiscock et *al*. conclude, based on their discovery of the specimen at Carpenter's Gap 1, which dated to 44,000-49,000 BP, that the production of ground-edge axes is broadly coincident with the colonisation of Australia by modern humans. It is suggested by Hiscock et *al*. that axe production was probably invented within Australia a short time after the first humans arrived in the continent, and they have noted 2 implications of this inference.

The emergence of novelty during the human global dispersal. With the continuing spread of humans, technology was not only losing the diversity it had evolved in Africa; it was also being transformed by invention of tools that were of entirely novel diversity.

The early invention of ground bevelled edges on axes from Northern Australia is a marker for regional behavioural distinctions that are long-lasting, demonstrating spatial differentiation in traditions and adaptive patterns beginning in the earliest period of exploration and settlement.

The technological elements of these regional distinctions persisted for 40,000 years, which indicates that these differences in technology were part of deep social and linguistic distinctions within Sahul.

The Spear and Spear Thrower

The favoured weapon of the Aborigines was the spear and spear thrower. The fact that they never adopted the bow and arrow has been debated for a long time. During post-glacial times the bow and arrow were being used in every inhabited part of the world except Australia. A number of reasons for this have been put forward, one of which was that the Aborigines were ultra conservative and incapable of change. This suggestion is now known to be wrong, they did adopt items such as the out-rigger canoe, and they obviously saw the advantage over their bark canoes, which were not suitable for fishing at sea. When the dugout canoe was adopted by them, being introduced by the Macassans, it allowed them to fish for dugong and turtle further out to sea.

The bow and arrow was assumed to be more efficient than the spear for hunting and fighting, but in Australia this doesn't seem to be the case. It has been suggested that bow and arrow were useful in places like New Guinea where the prey species were not very large. In Australia the animals hunted were often much bigger, several species of kangaroo grow to the height of a man, and their hide would no doubt be tougher than the smaller wallabies hunted in New Guinea.

It is not that they don't embrace change, they have been demonstrated to have been doing that since their first arrival in Australia, it is just that they have been very selective in what they take. If they don't see an improvement over something they already have, they reject the item. This characteristic of the Aborigines was commented on by Captain Cook.

Captain Cook saw the bow and arrow being used on an island close to the mainland at Cape York, as it was in the Torres Strait islands and New Guinea. But the Aborigines preferred the spear. And it seems they weren't the only ones to think it was a good thing to have. Spears and spear throwers were also appreciated by their neighbours. Cape York was the Switzerland of the prehistoric north, not getting involved in their neighbour's wars, but selling high quality weapons to all. It has been said that the spear and spear thrower were probably Australia's first export item. They had different points for different uses. The 2 main spears traded with the people of the Torres Strait islands were the fishing spear and the fighting spear. The fishing spear had 4 bone barbs. The fighting spear had a barbed bone point.

The people of the Torres Strait islands also used them for hunting dugong.

Death spear

All backed blades were microliths, usually less than 3 cm long, and all appear to have been used for a similar purpose. It has been suggested that their main use was in rows of barbs along the sides of death spears. These spears were deadly weapons, the barbs causing great blood loss in the victim, human in fighting, animal in hunting. It has been said that they usually couldn't be pulled out, needing to be pushed right through the body, which no doubt caused even more damage.

The death spears from museum collections have up to 40 barbs attached to grooves in the spear shaft with gum. These barbs are unbacked quartz flakes with no secondary working. Evidence from sites such as Sassafras and Currarong indicates that backed blades gradually disappeared about 2000 years ago, to be replaced increasingly by quartz flakes. It is thought that in earlier times backed blades were used as barbs on death spears, evidence for which is the large numbers of backed blades that have been found, the large numbers suggesting they were used for something other than spear points, with so many being used on death spears this could account for the high numbers found.

Spear thrower - woomera or atlatl

The antiquity of the spear thrower in Australia was pushed back to at least 40,000 BP (some have dates of 60,000 BP), making it possibly the oldest known use of a spear thrower in the world, when it was discovered that Mungo Man, Lake Mungo 3 (WLH 3), had severe osteoarthritis of the right elbow, spear thrower elbow, a sure sign that the gracile Skelton was indeed a man, right handed, and used a spear thrower for a number of years.

Points

Stone points are usually assumed to have been used hafted to the ends of spears. They have been found trimmed on one side (unifacial) or both sides (bifacial). Neither appears to predate the other, both have been found in the same level at sites such as the Yarar rock shelter in the Northern Territory. At the Yarar site, the majority of broken points were butts, broken tips being a minority. It appears the rock shelter was a place where spears with broken points were rehafted. Both types of points, which are believed to have been spear points, had similar dimensions of about 3.5 cm long. They are of a size that could be used on arrows, but no evidence of arrows has been found in Australia. At the time of the European colonisation of Australia spears were being used in north western Australia that had stone tips. In the Kimberleys, these spear points ranged in size from 3 to more than 10 cm long. Some spears from museums have 3 cm long bifacial points of which 2 cm of point protrudes from the hafting gum. It is assumed the use of very small points meant that the point would be less likely to break on impact than longer points.

The spear points from the Kimberleys are characterised by symmetrical, pressure-flaked bifacial points. These points may have been regarded more as ritual or status objects, as they were traded along the trade routes to distant tribes. After the overland telegraph was established the porcelain insulators became a sort after material for the construction of these points, along with glass. These high quality points were being used by the desert tribes 1000 km away in circumcision rituals.

Symmetrical, unifacial points, **Pirri points**, were characteristic of South Australia. They were apparently used only in the distant past, Aborigines believing they must have been used in the Dreamtime, because they had no knowledge of them. Points occur in a broad north-south belt across the continent. They were not present on the west coast and only a few are known from the east coast.

There may be a long continuity of technological tradition in the Kimberley, in grooved, ground-edge axes and serrated flakes. The Kimberley serrated spear points are renowned for their fine crafting and their symmetry. They were made by the pressure-flaking technique, fine flakes are removed by use of wood or bone. Prior to European occupation fine-grained stone was used. This type of leaf-shaped, bifacially trimmed spear points has been used for at least 3,000 years.

Throwing boomerangs

In other situations boomerangs were used as throwing sticks that could be thrown with great accuracy at high speed to knock out or kill the animal or human that was the intended target. The throwing boomerangs were designed to fly straight and fast by giving them an aerodynamic twist. Boomerangs were cut from branches that already had a bend, then carved, heated and twisted to give them the aerodynamic shape. In plan throwing boomerangs were asymmetrical, the longer end being used for leverage and the shorter end were weight and shaped to cart wheel the blade, enlarge the parameter of the blade and to increase the likelihood of a successful kill. Extremely hard wood was used in their construction which helped make them a deadly blade-like club. Cane[1] reports seeing a man hit on the head by one of these boomerangs who suffered severe brain damage, giving some indication of just how deadly they would have been in battle.

The technology of the Pleistocene displayed a high degree of homogeneity across Australia, but from about 5,000 years ago this homogeneity is replaced by a very diverse toolkit across the continent. Over the last few thousand years ground edge axes became widespread, replacing pebble tools and horsehoof cores as the tool of choice for chopping throughout the mainland, but in Tasmania it wasn't used.

Thumbnail scrapers, that were finely trimmed, first appear in some of the Pleistocene industries, becoming much more common in the small tool period.

Backed Blades

Backed blades, a distinctive tool type, are found in a belt across the continent from west to east south of the area of the tropical monsoon, with a few being found in Cape York in Queensland and the Top End in the Northern Territory. Artefacts from Miriwun in the Kimberly were claimed to be backed blades, but this is disputed, suggesting they were actually more likely to be a type of abruptly trimmed points.

Backed blades are flakelets, very small blades with an edge blunted by steep retouching. They appear to have been the Stone Age equivalent of a pen knife. There are 2 main types, Bondi points, first discovered on Bondi Beach in 1899, are slender, asymmetrical backed blades, the points of which are tapering with a length twice that of the width.

Geometric microliths are broader, and are found in a wide range of geometric shapes - trapezoids, triangles and half-circles.

All backed blades were microliths, usually less than 3 cm long, and all appear to have been used for a similar purpose. It has been suggested that their main use was in rows of barbs along the sides of death spears.

Backed blades with traces of hafting gum still present on the blunt edge have been found at Graman. Most of the geometric microliths found at Seelands have an end broken off. This is the type of damage that is expected if they were used as barbs on spears.

In historic times death spears were still being used across the southern part of the continent. This is the area where great numbers of backed blades have been found. In other parts of the continent the use of death spears and the presence of backed blades don't coincide so precisely. South of Sydney, more than 1000 were collected from the Curracurrang Rock Shelter. Thousands have been collected at Kurnell and around Lake Torrens in South Australia.

Both points and backed blades were also used in the construction of composite tools in which the flakes were attached to a tool, usually in grooves, held in place by hafting gum and twine. The small tool tradition allowed the development of the composite tool.

Cane

Backed blades first appear in the archaeological record 15,000 BP, the numbers and frequency of these artefacts increasing over time, and more appearing 9,000 years ago, and the numbers astronomically increasing 4,000 years ago, their production at some sites increasing by about 200 fold, and across the southern parts of the continent there were many thousands of them at some of the primary production sites

See Weapons

Wyrie Swamp tools

Adze Flakes

Unlike the adzes of the Pacific Islands and Asia, which were large with ground and polished edges, the Australian adzes were small pieces of flaked stone that were used as woodworking tools, used in a similar way to chisels. Up to the present the Western Desert people were still using adze flakes that had been gummed to the end of a wooden handle or spear thrower to work hardwood, such as mulga, to make such items as shields and bowls, etc.

There are 2 types of adze flakes, tula (a name used by the **Wongkonguru** people of the Lake Eyre area) and burren. On the tula flakes retouch and use-wear occur on the distal edge (opposite the striking platform). On the burren use occurs on the lateral edges.

Adze flakes have been found in 2 late Pleistocene sites in Western Australia, 10,000 year old Puntutjarpa and a single adze flake from Devil's Lair in the layer dated to 12,000 years ago. These differ from the usual adze flakes and it is believed they were used as scrapers, not for woodworking as the later adze flakes were used by the desert people.

The tula adze was used almost exclusively in the arid central Australia, only a few bifacial specimens being found at Caloola, which are believed to have reached there along trade routes, but were not widely used there. The burren adze occurs more widely from Cape York and along the east coast. It is believed the adze flakes may have been invented by the Aborigines of the central arid regions to work the desert hardwood of their territory.

Australian Pleistocene Technology

The Australian Aborigines had a varied tool kit during the Pleistocene, utilising stone, bone and wood. Pebble choppers, steep-edged scrapers, other types of scrapers, such as notched scrapers, and the bipolar technique was used to produce many small flakes and artefacts from quartz. A common use for these tools was the manufacture of other tools, such as making spears and implements for the processing of food.

Accumulating evidence is showing that there was an Australoid technological tradition, basically similar, whatever the raw material used, but with many local variations, across the entire Australian continent, that is distinguishable from the stone tool industries of Africa, Asia and Europe. The Australian Pleistocene tools have been called heterogeneous by some, homogeneous by others, and still others (Flood, 2004) see them as much more homogeneous than they were in the following Holocene, but with a number of regional variations on the theme of the old Australian core tool and scraper tradition. It seems the tool kit brought to Australia by the first immigrants may have been derived from elsewhere, but the Australian core tools and scraper probably evolved after their arrival, not by improvements being made by new tools being brought in at a later date.

At the time of first contact, the tool kit of the Aborigines was mostly comprised of artefacts made from materials other than stone, such as wood, bone, shell and plant material. Human hair was also used to make items such as twine. The direct evidence of the use of non-stone materials is mostly lost; these other materials don't survive well if they are not in constantly wet or dry conditions, such as dunes or peat bogs. Such conditions exist at Wyrie Swamp in South Australia.

Backed Artefacts in Southeast Australia - Changing Abundance Possibly Linked to Holocene Climate?

There has been much debate concerning the time of introduction, proliferation and decline of backed artefacts in Australia. The earliest known instance of backed artefacts in south east Australia has been dated to about 8,500 BP, then 4,000-3,500 BP they proliferated greatly and have been found in many sites, also occurring in large numbers in individual sites from that time. Their numbers declined markedly after about 1,500 BP, appearing to be completely absent by the time of European colonisation. According to Attenbrow, Robertson & Hiscock the suggestion that the increased levels of backed artefact production was triggered by a heightened foraging risk and/or a social reorganisation as a response to changing climate to a cooler, drier regime than at any other time in the Holocene, as well as intensified ENSO climatic conditions, has been advanced by models explaining their proliferation. The study by Attenbrow, Robertson & Hiscock develops this hypothesis, inferring the use of backed artefacts at Mussel Shelter in the Sydney Basin by an integrated analysis of use-wear and residue analysis. New insights have been provided by these inferences into the nature of evolutionary changes in the production and use of tools as a response to the period in which climatic conditions changed.

Artefacts

Arnhem Land Sites

A few sites in Australia had produced some remarkable discoveries long before their antiquity was revealed by new dating techniques. 2 main successive stone tool traditions were identified.

The earlier tradition was the chunky, steep-edged flakes and cores, found at Nauwalabila, in the 20,000 year old level, and at Ngarradj Warde Djobkeng (white cockatoo Dreaming), Kakadu in the basal level dated to 10 000 years ago,

The more recent tradition was characterised by 5,000 year old stone spear points.

An unexpected find in these sites was stone axes with grooves around their sides and ground edges in the Pleistocene levels. Prior to these finds, they had been found only in sites from the most recent few thousand years. Since then, the basal levels of other northern sites have been found to contain them, such as the Sandy Creek Shelter in Queensland.

A feature of the Australian ground-edge artefacts from Arnhem Land distinguishing them from those of Asian sites is that they are smaller, more properly called hatchets, for one hand use, instead of axes, for 2 hand use, as found in Asia. This indicates that they were probably a local invention. Other supporting evidence for them being developed in Australia is that the early use of hammer-dressing of ground-edge tools is confined to northern Australia.

Some of Australia's oldest grindstones have been found in Arnhem Land. 3 were found at Malakunanja II, the associated charcoal dating them to 18,000 years ago. 2 of them have flat to slightly concave grinding surfaces, one of them showing signs of being used to grind red and white ochre. The 3rd has a circular grinding hollow, about 10 cm wide, on one face. Similar grinding hollows have been found in the lower levels of Nawamoyn, and are common in Arnhem Land rock shelters. They were probably used for grinding ochre as well as plant food preparation, such as seeds.

The oldest known ground stone axe has been found in the Nawarla Gabarnmang Rock Shelter in Arnhem Land, in the country of the Jawoyn people. Dated to 35,000 years ago, it is currently the oldest known stone axe in the world.

Comparing earliest Australian stone tools with contemporary tool industries in Europe and Africa

Australian industries are distinctive, with some unique tools such as large, waisted axes and the horsehoof core, a single platform core often used as a chopper. There are also similarities between the Australian industries and the contemporary Mousterian industries from Europe and the Middle East, as well as to the Mesolithic of Africa, with the Levallois flake technique.

It has been suggested that if the 'Out of Africa' hypothesis is correct, the first arrivals in Australia would have had a basic tool kit that, like the marsupials, evolved in isolation. Some of their artefacts appear to have arisen by the process of convergent evolution, arriving at the same solution to a problem independently, while others were entirely local inventions.

One big difference between the development of the tools in Australia and Europe is that in Europe there was a creative explosion, whereas in Australia the process was much more gradual and incremental. Wobst has put forward a theory that Europe had 'Arctic hysteria', in which the explosion of new ideas was triggered by the need to find any way they could of surviving the Last Glacial Maximum.

In Australia there was no such need. When the northern hemisphere is glaciated Australia gets drier. Hunter-gatherers have been called the original affluent society. The Aborigines adapted to the changes as they occurred, their artefacts gradually changing as the need arose. In fact, they adapted so well to every difficulty presented by changing climate that they were indeed an affluent society.

It is now known that the Australian Stone Age was not a static period, the tools gradually evolving towards more effective, smaller and a greater variety of implements. Rhys Jones has estimated, based in the increase of average working length per unit weight, that stone tools became 8 times more efficient over a period of 25,000 years (Flood, 2004).

The occupation site at Wyrie Swamp that was covered by an expanding swamp became a peat bog that preserved the wooden tools, providing a very rare, if not unique glimpse of the non-stone part of the culture, showing that then, as at the time of first contact, tools of wood formed a big part of the tool kit. It shows that the digging sticks used by women, even now in a few places, were used thousands of years ago. It also shows that the barbed 'death spear' was not a recent invention, being used for thousands of years since some time in the Pleistocene.

On the driest continent on earth, with a climate that was too erratic over most of it for settled communities to become established, where the type of agriculture seen in other parts of the world could develop, they developed a tool kit to suit their needs. A kit that was easily transportable as they moved around their territory, never staying in one place long enough to exhaust the resources to the point where the environment could not recover by the time they returned. This tool kit allowed them to live sustainably for 60,000 years.

Aboriginal Stone Tools - Most stone tools observed being used were unrecognisable as tools - what are the implications?

Brian Hayden in Murray, Tim, ed., 1998, *Archaeology of Aboriginal Australia*, Allen & Unwin, discusses the attitude of the Aboriginals of the Western Desert to the making and using of stone tools. This aspect of Aboriginal life in the Western Desert has also been studied by a number of other authors (Gould, 1969: 81-3; Gould *et al.*, 1971: 163). Hayden observed a number of Western Desert men and women making and using stone tools as they remembered from their youth when such tools were being made and used in normal daily life.

When occupation sites are excavated the numbers and types of stone tools found are used to add to the knowledge of aspects of the lives of the people who made them, as well as to determine when the site was first occupied. A finding of Hayden and others who have observed the traditional making and use of stone tools is that many of the stone implements being used by the people would not be recognised as being a tool, most of the implements having not been altered for the intended purpose, simply being picked up from the ground because they were already of a type suitable for their use, such as a sharp edge, that would probably be blunted by any attempts at reworking, and they fitted the hand sufficiently well. With the exception of hafted adzes, the working of stone implements was rarely practiced, though in special cases they could make such tools when they needed to. One such rare case was known among the Warramunga and Walbiri, where knives with prismatic blades were made for trade.

Hayden found that there were no craftsmen specialising in making particular tools, everybody made tools as they needed them. Flakes were generally chosen from what was apparently a random group of flakes, the only criterion appearing to be their usefulness for the task at hand. A similar casual attitude to the selection of tools has been observed among the Nakako and Pitjantjatjara (Tindale, 1965: 146,160) and the Ngatatjara (Gould *et al.*, 1971: 160) where 'cores' were often seen to be 'flaked' by simply throwing them on the ground or 'smashed' in some other manner, or flakes were 'randomly' detached by a hammer stone. The resulting flakes would then be examined to choose a suitable one, the process being repeated if necessary until a suitable one was found. A similar method of flake production was also observed in the Kimberley (Hardman 1888: 59) and Tasmania (H. Ling Roth, 1899: 151; Hambly, 1931: 91). The variability in craftsmanship among individuals making wooden bowls (Thompson, 1964: 407) is suggested by Hayden to indicate frequent modest control over the working medium.

Hayden has stated that the biggest surprise was the lack of or rarity of tools that would be recognised as implements in archaeological excavations of occupation sites. At the beginning of his observations he saw Aboriginal people using only primary flakes for shaving and wood scraping, and chopping wood with unmodified stone blocks, none of which would be recognised as tools. This lack of retouched tools led Hayden to wonder if the knowledge of the making of retouched tools had been lost following epi-culture contact phenomenon. But a similar lack of unretouched stone tools in traditional use had been observed earlier (Mountford, 1941: 316; 1948; Tindale, 1941; Gould, 1969: 81-3; Gould et al., 1971: 163). The result was the proposition that one of the most primitive technologies in the world was used by the Pitjantjatjara, as they did not use retouched tools, exclusively using natural forms, apart from the hafted adze. After observing for some time Hayden found that retouched tools were indeed being used, but rarely. He suggests this may have been because of the reason suggested by Bordes, that the stone flakes are sharpest immediately after being removed from the core, any retouching tending to make them blunter. A similar reason was implied by Basedow (1925: 365). According to all informants, instead of retouching a primary flake they sorted through the flakes for a more suitable one, removing more flakes if necessary. They would often try several primary flakes before finding one they were satisfied with.

A similar behaviour had been observed among groups around Lake Eyre (1924: 91) "Casual stones are any that have a sharp edge. They are used for scraping. Directly they are blunt they are thrown away and another picked up. Sometimes they are chipped if the stone will keep its edge long enough to warrant chipping, but usually they are not kept." These observations substantiate those of later authors among groups from the Western Desert. The effectiveness of working edges were not always easy to gauge by visual examination, as there were occasional small, subtle variations of the stone surfaces of the working edge, several being tried before one was selected.

Hayden found it difficult to determine the criteria used to decide if a flake could be retouched, believing the decision was based on a subjective evaluation. Some retouched flakes were discarded immediately because the retouched working edge was unsuitable, though there were times when a resharpened piece would continue to be used. When the tool was retouched it was to restore the sharpness of a dulled working edge. He could see no indication that there was an ideal shape, classic form or perfect specimens, which are often spoken of by archaeologists and collectors. Among the traditional people of the Western Desert the most important attributes of a tool was its working edge that displayed a variable morphology, and whether or not it would fit comfortably in the hand so pressure could be applied. He suggests these attributes might become more patterned by habit and tradition, but admits there is no quantitative data to support his suggestion.

After viewing stone-using activities for a short time, another author has stated that the "Pitjantjatjara might vanish and no trace of them would be left behind" (Mountford, 1941, 1948). A similar situation has been reported from New Guinea, where it was suggested that the edge in hand held tools is the important variable for the makers and users of stone tools. His observations have been supported by Strathern (1969). Another factor that has been suggested to be involved in the decision of whether or not to retouch a tool is the availability of raw material. Hayden says for the technological projects he asked the people in the Western Desert to work on the assumption that there were always more raw materials available. He suggests it could be expected that where raw material was a limiting factor retouching would probably occur. At most camps visited by Hayden there were many flakes and a number of cores, (also Basedow, 1925: 364; Thompson, 1964: 406). It is known that in traditional societies Aboriginal people carried primary flakes and blocks of raw material when they travelled (Thompson, 1964: 405, Plate 34; Basedow, 1925: 364; Hayden, in press (1998)).

Another factor involved in the decision to retouch appears to be the availability of the raw material. Hayden found that less than 20 % of the rocks used for chopping wood were modified in areas where there were hard metamorphic rocks or igneous rocks available that had naturally acute edges. When flint nodules or opal were used for chopping wood, that usually lack acute, sharp edges, they were often flaked to get a sharp working edge, 90 % of such opal or flint implements were modified by the removal of flakes to get a sharp working edge. Of the flakes he observed being used for 'scraping' or shaving wood, less than 25 % had been retouched or otherwise modified, the primary flakes being sharp with no modification. The implements he observed being modified did not always display 'scraper' retouch. He suggests it might possibly be the case that retouching was carried out only when no suitably edged rock was immediately available, and with primary flakes, only when none of the flakes were suitable without retouching. He also suggests there may have been reasons for retouching that he was not aware of, as there is not much difference in the effort required to retouch or search through the primary flakes present.

Nearly all adzes had been retouched, probably because much more effort and time is involved in unhafting and rehafting than retouching the working edge. Some adzes were removed with no retouching, but in these cases it was because they broke or the particular implement was made of a rock that was difficult to resharpen. With regard to the resharpening and retouching of stone tools there appears to be a dichotomy between hand-held and hafted tools, the hafted ones being retouched but the hand-held ones only rarely being retouched because of special circumstances, such as unavailability of raw material with sharp surfaces. In general, hand-held tools appear to correspond to Binford's class of non-curated artefacts, the hafted tools corresponding to his curated class. Hayden suggests caution is required with making a one-one equivalence, as the transport and curation of unhafted flakes and 'scrapers' in bags has been well documented (W. Roth, 1904:20; Horne & Aiston, 1924: 109; Spencer & Gillen, 1927: 26).

Hayden has estimated the number of retouched tools used by a nuclear family group living a traditional life in the Western Desert in a year. According to Hayden, though it is inherently risky to make such an estimate, it was calculated to give some idea of the magnitude of the problem faced by archaeologists. The numbers are presented in Table 7a.1 in Source 1. The estimation is based on statements of Pintupi people and on his own estimates based on a family that were previously based a bit to the south of Lake Macdonald. They had a limited variety of wooden tools, and he believes many of the estimates may be on the generous side, in particular with the replacement of spear throwers, hardwood bowls of the women, and 25 spears on a yearly basis. He has calculated the number of tools that would be recognised archaeologically resulting from maintenance tasks, based on the actual retouched tools produced at Papunya settlement. If unmodified hand-held flakes are incorporated the numbers would be doubled, at least. He has assumed that all chopping tools are modified; though he says he has been liberal as in most cases this would be unrealistic.

He has calculated the number of tools produced per person per week at camps where informants were living 30 years previously, a time when they used only stone tools. They were using 2.5-10 flake tools per person per week (Hayden, in press 1998), totalling 130-520 tools per person per year. This agrees well with the estimates, and one of the sites was adjacent to a quarry where old adzes were probably discarded, and at other sites several spear throwers were manufactured by young men, which would have inflated the number of tools produced and used over a short period of time, so the estimates can be considered to be on the high side. The average production rate of retouched tools used by a husband and wife, their parents and non-producing children, about 150 per year ($\pm$ 50) and about 40 ($\pm$ 10) chopping tools being made, seems reasonable, assuming all chopping tools were modified. Many of these tools would be scattered at various places around the landscape, and the estimates could be reduced, in some cases considerably, by the lack of raw materials available.

Many of these archaeological tools will be only slightly superficially modified, many of the choppers having a single flake removed, and others may be 'used up', making them closer to the 'classic' type as considered by some archaeologists (e.g Fig. 7a.2, Source 1). Archaeological tools from the Western Desert are generally not of predetermined form, being the mechanical results of needing to create or sharpen a cutting edge one or more times. The factors that determine when any given tool is discarded, whether unmodified, 1 flake removed, 1 resharpening or multiple resharpenings, are the nature of the material, the potential of the particular tools to be resharpened, availability of raw material, and the point at which a particular task is finished. Archaeological 'tools' are the results of attempts to rejuvenate and pass through several stages. Hayden believes it is worth restating that habit or tradition may be an important factor in determining which implements have the best prospects of being resharpened, and the most frequently resharpening mode used.

Functions

One of the observations of Hayden's technological projects was that almost all use of retouched stone tools was for woodworking. This is in agreement with observations of Pintupi life 'certainly the main use of stone here was for shaping and maintaining wooden tools and weapons' (Long, 1971: 269). Hayden suggests there is little doubt that all or nearly all retouched stone tools were used for woodworking, though there may have been rare occasions when retouched stone tools were used, even made, for purposes other than woodworking, such as cutting meat or skins. No retouched stone tools were made in any of Hayden's technological projects, which included plant food procurement and processing. A similar conclusion was reached from information provided by older members of the Pintupi. Skins were not used for any purpose among the people of the Western Desert with whom Hayden worked. He suggests it is possible that retouched stone tools may have been used for purposes associated with skins in other parts of the country where the people used skins. Study of other hunter-gatherer groups around the world has found a similar association of retouched stone tools with woodworking. In other parts of Australia there are 4 references to the use of chipped stone tools for the gathering and processing of plant food.

The chopping up of fern roots with a unifacial implement was referred to by Jackson (1939). It has since been claimed that this is almost certainly unreliable (see Bancroft, 1894; W. Roth, 1901: 10).

It has been claimed that chopping implements might be used for digging holes for roots among peoples of the Western Desert. This observation is unique, the digging stick being the tool of choice for this purpose. Hayden suggests this was either a fortuitous occurrence or the detachment of roots, which is a woodworking function, in which a chopping tool was confused with the excavation part of the process.

Tindale observed a crude hand chopper being used to cut the husks from Pandanus fruit (Hale & Tindale, 1933: 114; 1934; 131). According to Hayden, this is ambiguous as it is not clear if the implement was made specifically for this purpose, or if any stone would have served the same purpose, the use of the chopper being a matter of convenience.

O'Connell has reported the former use of retouched blades to make spoons for eating tubers (O'Connell, 1977).

Hayden has said he has no knowledge from anywhere else in the world to indicate that chipped stone was being used for procuring or processing plant foods. Sickles were used by some cultures, but from the Palaeolithic, that pebble tools were being used almost invariably for the chopping up of plant food (Deevey, 1968: 286). He suggests the generalisation that retouched hand-held tools were used for woodworking, and possibly in areas where the people used animal skins, for skin working, is a good place to start analysis. Microliths are excluded from consideration.

When comparing woodworking and the cutting of meat, he suggests that the cutting of meat requires a sharp blade, as is best found in unretouched flakes, while sharpness is not usually important in woodworking. In practice, when an animal is being cut up any waste flake is habitually used to gut and open the skin. Among the Pintupi and Ngatatjara these flakes were rarely retouched. According to Gould:

'These knives are discarded after only a few uses, and no effort is made to resharpen them. Thus they rarely show much in the way of secondary trimming and could be difficult for an archaeologist to recognise once the gum handle has decomposed' (Gould *et al.*, 1971: 156).

The making of several retouched 'knives' among the Pintupi has been illustrated and described (Tindale, 1965: 114-19). Several factors make consideration of the representativeness of these examples difficult.

The larger flakes were never observed being used, and no specific use for them was given. The smaller 'knives' were described as being used to inscribe lines on wooden implements.

The original article was written in 1933, the 1965 article being a reconstruction of the field notes and memory. Hayden considers it puzzling, from a functional viewpoint, that the 'knives' were retouched before they were used. In the 1965 article it is implied that these knives often had one 'blunt, thick margin and a sharper, somewhat more arcuate one opposite' (Tindale, 1965: 141). These pieces may well be morphologically distinguishable, though they were retouched in a similar manner to scrapers and adzes that had not been used much. With the exception of instances where unmodified flakes were used for butchering, every major description of chipped stone being used in Australia, some form of woodworking has been mentioned much more frequently than any other activity. Evidence from Tasmania supports this conclusion.

Morphology

Choppers

The choppers for rough work were primarily unifacial, though there were also bifacial choppers. The modification of the choppers ranged from the removal of a single flake, multiple flakes removed around the periphery, to bifacial choppers, including large flake specimens. A fuller illustration of these tools can be found elsewhere (Hayden, in press (1998)). They differ little from the choppers found in abandoned camp sites throughout the Western Desert at the present (1998), and generally are of a similar size and weight to the Kartan heavy duty implements (Bauer, 1970). They were used to procure wood for all wooden implements, often being used to hollow out hardwood bowls, chopping out the spear-thrower interiors, thinning fighting spears, removing branches from the shafts of spears, starting nooks for spear barbs, and the initial spear point shaping. (Source 1, Fig. 7a.3, 7a.4). They appear to have been left at sites where the work was carried out, as also observed by Mountford (1941). They were often made of quartzites or other locally available rocks that are non-cryptocrystalline.

High quality cryptocrystalline rocks appear to have been carried around, when they were available, to be used as a source of raw material, as well as for chopping, possibly until the piece was exhausted (Thompson, 1964: 405; Hayden, in press (1998)). According to Hayden, while working with the 2 dialectical groups he worked with most, they had separate names for cryptocrystalline and non-cryptocrystalline rocks that were suitable for tool-making. The Pintupi called them kanti vs pilari, and the Yankuntjara called them kanti vs kaltjiliri. He reports witnessing on several occasions metamorphic rocks and quartzites, that were coarser grained, being preferred over fine-grained opal material. He noted that the finer grained rocks that he expected to be most sought after were not the rocks of choice, the coarser grained material being the preferred type. Some authors have regarded the Aboriginal people who had only metamorphic rocks to make their tools from as being worse off than those with cryptocrystalline rocks to work with (Stockton, 1972: 22), but the observations of Hayden and others suggest it is actually the other way around. Tools made from cryptocrystalline rocks are more aesthetically appealing, and their flaking properties are better, but they tend to shatter easier and become dulled more quickly when used for chopping hardwood. Hayden suggests the grain of metamorphic rocks may bite into the grain of the wood, being more effective in wood separation and detachment. Experiments have come to this conclusion (Crabtree & Davis, 1968: 428).

According to Hayden, there appeared to be a prohibition among the Yankuntjara against women using cryptocrystalline rocks. One of the women told him she had never used kanti (flint, chert, opal, etc.), but had used kaltjiliri, though kanti was regularly used by men for adze stones. In central Australia a similar prohibition has been reported (Spencer & Gillen, 1912: 373, 376). A preference for pilari, non-cryptocrystalline rocks was also observed among Pintupi women, as well as for using choppers, as opposed to adzes, for all woodwork. When hardwood was being thinned down, men would use adzes but women would use choppers, the women were observed to be clumsier at using an adze than the men. When making fighting sticks, digging sticks, sharpening the blades and smoothing the surfaces of bowls and fighting sticks, the women used grinding, telling Hayden they always used tjiwa (a small pounding slab made of sandstone) for these purposes. This appears to have probably been an alternative method of working with wood throughout Australia, including parts of Tasmania. The first report of its use was in the Western Desert (Basedow, 1925: 362), supported by observations (Finlayson, 1943: 79; Thomson, 1964; Horne & Aiston, 1924: 93). Murray didn't see any men grinding their wood implements.

Grainy choppers of chipped stone were observed being used by men and women, though women tended to use only such tools. It appears women rarely used adzes, whether by proscription or preference, using grinding to finish many of the tools they use. These heavy duty stone chopping tools tended to have high edge angles, with an edge angle mode of 75°.

An implication of this in the Western Desert is that women are not known to have made or used any type of chipped stone tool that is unique to women in the Western Desert. It would be difficult to detect the presence of women at an archaeological site, other than by the presence of small flat stones and hammerstones for pounding lizards and leaves for pituri ash burned (a *Nicotana* species), made more difficult by the use of these implements by single males. Hayden suggests the presence of grinding stones is probably the best evidence of women, so the absence of grinding stones as an indication of the presence of women is negative evidence, so is unsatisfactory.

Flake Tools

Hayden notes he was surprised at the morphology of retouched hand-held flake tools. Instead of the scraper-type of retouching he expected for the smoothing of spear shafts, only about 50% were of this type, the remainder being of an alternative type that achieved the same goal. An example is a single flake removed from the edge that created an archaeologist's 'notch' (the larger types, not the minute denticulations). The only difference between the use of the original flake and this is that there is a new edge to cut with that is sometimes more effective than the original edge (Source 1, Figs. 7a.5, 7a.6). Denticulates result from the repeating of such modifications. In one instance a flake was first resharpened with a notch, and then flaked back into a scraper. There didn't appear to be a regular pattern to the decision to use either the notch or the scraper retouch, though he suggests this could be because of his limited sample, they appeared to occur in free variation. A very small burin was found in an ethnographic excavation, and an old Pintupi man, Ngayuwa, claimed he had made and used it about 30 years earlier, saying he had used it for shaving down his spears. Hayden noted that the tone of the informant's reply suggested he was questioning why anyone would use a hand-held flake for any other use. The side edge of the burin was used in this case. In Australia, true burins are occasionally found (Mulvaney, 1969). According to Hayden, an informant claimed he had thought of it himself, not being taught by anyone, and it was about the only one he had made. While the credibility of the story was difficult to assess, he was observed to pick out a flake with a broken edge with a cross-section like a burin-blow edge from flakes he had been knapping for finishing spears. After carefully examining the piece he put it aside, saying it was a good one. When he used it as a flake shaver it proved to be very effective. It was the only flake he had picked out. At Cundeelee and Papunya, many of the primary flakes used had edges close to right angles. These flakes were never retouched. Prior to his observations the author had believed hunter-gatherers used real 'tools' for woodworking, now he was seeing broken flake edges and accidental right-angled edges being used for the same purpose.

He found that edges that were slightly less than right angles, with a flake body that was strongly buttressed, proved to be excellent, very efficient shaving edges that are slow to dull. The same results have been shown experimentally (Crabtree & Davis, 1968: 46). The same burin cross-sectional characteristics have been found to occur in many flakes with right-angled breaks or edges, characteristics recognised by the Western Desert people for use in shaving spears. The author suggests the scraper, notch, denticulate and burin may all be stylistic variations of the same functional type. These implements can all be used for finishing wooden shaft implements, especially spears, throwing sticks, digging sticks, adze shafts, and in parts of the Western Desert, spear throwers. The author suggests the different type of retouch may have been used for different activities, such as notches being used to sharpen spears, saying there is no ethnographic evidence, the frequency of hand-held retouched tools being too low in his study to reach any firm conclusion.

He observed flakes being used in a sawing motion in the making of barbs on 1 type of Pintupi spear, the karimpa (Source 1, Fig. 7a.8). These saw flakes were frequently changed, and of 17 that were used only 3 were retouched, 2 with notches and 1 with a scraper retouch. A notch on the end of a flake was mainly used for severing cross grain wood fibres in the barb nocks, not actually being used in a sawing motion, the other never being used. It has been noted that small resin-backed 'knives', 3 cm long, with an edge that was slightly serrated, was used effectively as a saw for incising decorative lines (Tindale, 1965: 147). An unexpectedly high number of saws the author observed being used carried an abrupt edge opposite the working edge, which was often cortex covered, the same characteristic being implied by Tindale for his 'knives'.

Vertically oriented rocks Brian Hayden in Murray, Tim, ed., 1998

Hayden observed non-retouched artefacts, in the form of flattish rocks, that were relatively large, that had been set on their edge in the ground, one in an ethnographic excavation and another in his technological projects. In both cases the vertical slab acted as a fulcrum, a pressure point for straightening spears. The part of the spear to be straightened was heated in ashes, and then placed on the apex of the vertical slab, the hands about 1 m apart on either side and downward pressure was applied. In the procedure observed at the settlement, the flat slab was a cinder block, while at the excavated site it was iron-rich metamorphic rock, about 20 cm long, and in cross section was approximately a scalene triangle. In other parts of the Western Desert, wooden blocks or 'Y' uprights have been observed performing the same function (Ackerman, 1974). It has been reported that at Isimila some hand axes were found set on the sides vertically in the ground, the function of which was unknown (Howell, 1961: 121). Hayden suggested that, based on the above observations, there is a strong possibility they were used for straightening spears.

Wear patterns

Wear patterns on all tools were examined, as the main concern with the archaeological identification of functions of stone implements. The author expected the stone tools to be abraded most by the hard wood, but it was found that the stone tools used to work on the hardwoods traditionally used by the people of the Western Desert displayed little trace of any distinctive or diagnostic micro edge wear, while the stone tools used to carve shields and bowls from the very soft wood of the bean tree (***Erythrina vespertilio***) appeared to dissolve the edge of the stone tools very quickly, with a high frequency of gloss and striations occurring. See Hayden & Kamminga (1973) for a fuller presentation.

Package of cultural Innovations (Hayden, 2008)

Klein (1992, 1995, 1999, 2000) has proposed the appearance of a "package" of traits at about 40,000 to 50,000 years ago, and the associated spread of populations into new areas, suggesting a strong association between human biological evolution and behavioural changes, resulting from a genetic mutation that proved to be a selective advantage, proposing that the mutation led to a neurological change that was the basis of innovative ability of modern humans. Further suggesting that this innovation allowed modern humans to replace nonhuman or near human populations in areas the modern humans moved into. Harold (1992) listed the changes in morphology that occurred in the transition from archaic to modern humans, and the subsequent behavioural changes.

Included in the "package" of cultural innovations were enlarged geographic range, expanded exchange networks, personal adornment, art, imagery, ritual behaviour, blade technology and worked bone. Also, Exploitation of resources that require specialised technology such as worked bone and other biological materials, and new lithic technologies that indicated an intensification of their economy.

The "package" was proposed to have reached western Asia and Europe with colonists 'out of Africa'. There was also a suggestion that the "package" was exported from Africa to the other parts of the Old World that included south Asia and Australia (Bar-Yosef, 1998; McBrearty & Brooks, 2000; Mellars, 2006a). The arrival of the "package" in Europe has been associated with the transition from the Middle to Upper Palaeolithic, and the first appearance of modern humans in Europe.

Habgood & Franklin have carried out a study on the archaeological record of the Late Pleistocene of Sahul, the combined continent of New Guinea and Australia during the Pleistocene, when sea level was much lower than at present. They have concluded that the archaeological record in Sahul does not support the arrival of the "package" ready formed, rather, that the components of it are seen to have developed gradually over about 30,000 years, and the various components first appear in occupation sites that are widely separated in space and time.

See Table of first appearance of components of the package in Sahul

Bone tools

It has been suggested that bone points, and other implements made from bone, that were recovered from M86/2 and Bone Cave were systematically used in some activities at some sites. Among the uses that have been suggested are skin processing, cloak toggles, marrow extractors and possibly spear points. In the deposit excavated at Nunamira Cave there were no bone implements.

Darwin Glass

This is a natural glass that if found on the west coast of Tasmanian south of Queenstown. It is named for the place it was first found, Mount Darwin in the West Coast Range. The meteorite impact crater that is believed to have been the source of the glass was given the name Darwin Crater. Small, contorted impactites of glass formed in the high-energy collision from melted rocks, occurring in small seams around the impact crater, about 25 km North West of Kutikina Cave. The Aborigines carried bags of this glass from the crater to Kutikina Cave where they worked it into tools

Darwin Glass fragments occur over a strewn field (area covered by the material from the impact) that covers an area of about 419 km^2. It is found at an elevation of 250 to 500 m, where it occurs beneath soil and peat together with fragments of quartz. Above 500 m the bedrock is exposed so the only glass found there is the occasional fragment. It is buried at elevations less than about 220 m.

It can be white, black, and dark or light green. It is found in twisted masses of up to 10 cm. Type 1 is white or light green, and type 2 is black or dark green. In the interior of the chunks the texture can be flowing, defined by lines of gas bubbles.

Darwin glass was used to make implements for at least 12,000 years in south west Tasmania. The earliest known instance of its use was at Nunamira Cave 27,770 BP. At some sites the use of Darwin glass appears to have increased immediately following the glacial maximum, which is believed to possibly be because of easier access when the glacial conditions ameliorated to leave a treeless expanse along the track to Darwin Crater. Darwin glass was transported to a number of caves of varying distances from Darwin Crater, 75 km to Nunamira Cave and 100 km to Bone Cave. These distances are the direct line distances, the actual tracks could have been as much as double these distances. As with thumbnail scrapers, there was no Darwin glass found at the ORS 7 site, 10 km further than Bone Cave from Darwin Crater. The track between both occupation sites and Darwin Crater would have been very similar, probably along the easiest line that is followed by the Lyell Highway at the present.

Stone Artefacts - Tasmania

Preliminary analysis of the stone artefacts from Tasmania has established a South western Tasmanian Pleistocene province. The distinctive assemblage of this area is reflected in the pattern of animals hunted in the area, as indicated by the animal remains found at the archaeological sites. It is believed the stone tools in this area may be a regional variant of the Australian core tool and scraper tradition.

There are steep-edged flat and notched scrapers that are characteristic of the tool and scraper tradition at Mungo. The raw materials used in the manufacture of the tools are linked to their availability in a particular area, quartz being most common in the western sites, but rare in the eastern sites. The richness and presence of thumbnail scrapers, that are common in Holocene deposits on the mainland, but rare in mainland sites dating to the Pleistocene, distinguishes the Pleistocene south western assemblages from the wider core and scraper tradition.

It is believed that thumbnail scrapers were used for butchering animals and processing plant material, and working with skin, bone, and wood. The **ORS 7** site, the most south-easterly site among the known occupation sites of south west Tasmania, is the only site where thumbnail scrapers aren't found, small numbers being found in all other sites in the south west.

Thumbnail scrapers were used as early as 24,000 years ago, but were more common from about 18,000 years ago, after the end of the glacial maximum.

In the south west of Tasmania, Darwin glass was used for at least 12,000 years, but its first known use was at Nunamira as far back as 27,770 years ago. At some sites the use of Darwin glass seems to have increased during and immediately after the glacial maximum, about 18,000 years ago. It has been suggested that the increase in use may have resulted from the treeless conditions on the path to Darwin Crater after the glaciers retreated but before the trees grew thickly. Nunamira was 75 km from the crater and Bone Cave was 100 km from it by direct lines, but the actual routes used are unknown, so the distance travelled is also unknown. As with thumbnail scrapers, Darwin glass has not been found in the OSR 7 deposit. OSR 7 is about 10 km further than Bone Cave from the crater. It has been speculated that the lack of Darwin glass at OSR 7, and probably also with lack of thumbnail scrapers, was probably a cultural difference, particularly as at this site there are other differences between OSR 7 and the other south western sites. There was also a lower number of artefacts, and big differences between the technology, raw materials, faunal quantities and processing methods.

It has been concluded that the OSR 7 site has a much different archaeological signature from the sites on the other side of what appears to be a boundary between the south western sites and those on the other side of the boundary during the Late Pleistocene.

Bone Artefacts-Tasmania

Bone points have been found in most Tasmanian caves in the south west, and in Cave Bay Cave. There has been some discussion about what these bone points were used for. One suggestion has been that they were used in the making of fur coats, as awls or reamers. In south eastern parts of the mainland, Aborigines have been seen using them to make holes in animal skins to sew them together with thread made from animal sinew. Study of bone points from Pleistocene sites in Tasmania, such as Warreen Cave and Bone Cave, indicates they may have been used for skin processing, cloak toggles, as well as marrow extraction and possibly as spear points. Use-wear evidence suggests the use of some bone points for skin scraping and making holes in dry skins.

An unexpected find was that they appear to have been used as spear points for hunting mammals, which suggests they were hafted to a spear. 2 fine points have been found with what appear to be signs of hafting marks on the bases. The type of tip damage seen on some points and use-wear evidence suggest they were used as spear points. At some sites points and spear shafts have been found and interpreted as being places where bone points were being hafted to repair spears. If this is the correct interpretation, it is the first evidence of a hafted tool in Tasmania from any time of the Aboriginal occupation of the island.

Kartan tool industry

The Kartan industry is characterised by the massiveness of its core tools. The dominant implements are hammer-stones and pebble choppers. The hammer-flaking technique is used to get flakes from one side of a quartzite pebble. The result is usually oval-shaped and a sharp edge is produced by trimming the margin. Many of the pebble choppers were perfectly symmetrical, finely-made by what must have been highly skilled craftsmen with a strong aesthetic sense. Another characteristic of the Kangaroo Island tools is the large, heavy, horsehoof core, but there are not as many of them as there are of the pebble choppers.

An occupation site was found at Seton Site, (the Seton industry), a small limestone cave near a freshwater lagoon, 8 km from the south coast, where dating has shown the site was occupied, at first sporadically, from about 16,000 years ago, and intensively at about 11,000 years ago, until the separation from the mainland at about 10,000 years ago.

Some believed that the island was abandoned once the sea level rose enough to make the crossing between the mainland difficult, but some coastal occupation sites have been found that have been dated to later than separation. Some of these sites contain small shell middens associated with flakes that have been dated to 6,000 years ago. Some inland stratified camp sites, such as Rowell's Site, dated to 5,200 years ago and Sand Quarry Site, dated to 4,300 years ago, contained small flints and scrapers.

Post-separation occupation was very sparse compared to the earlier Kartan sites and the many shell middens on the adjacent South Australian coast from the Holocene. Two explanations have been proposed for the post-separation sites on Kangaroo Island that a relict population survived for several thousand years before dying out; there were occasional, probably temporary, occupations from the mainland. The second option requires the possession of more suitable watercraft than was possessed by the Aborigines of the adjacent mainland in historic times.

It is now thought what evidence there is from ethnography, archaeology and palaeoclimate, points towards it probably being a relict population. If it was a relict population, the reason for their disappearance is unknown, but at best the population that could have been maintained on the island was never more than several hundred, small enough to be severely affected by natural disasters, and pollen evidence suggests the climate became drier.

At Lashmar's Lagoon a pollen core contained evidence of a change to drier habitat shrubs, and other evidence suggests there was a drying of the environment of the island between about 5,000 and 2,000 years ago, and that regular burning of the vegetation didn't occur after about 2,500 years ago. The early European explorers in Australia associated no smoke with no Aborigines, the practice of burning being so common in all parts of Australia.

It has been suggested that the original occupation of the island may have occurred about 60,000 years ago at a time of low sea level, then at the start of a later phase of higher sea levels they left the island before the water was too deep to cross, returning again at another time of low sea level, bringing the Seton industry tools with them, that had been developed on the mainland during the time Kangaroo Island was uninhabited, but failed to leave in time when the water again rose. The industries also differ in the stone used for their manufacture, Kartan artefacts being made from quartzite and Seton artefacts from quartz. It has been suggested the change in source material may have resulted from the quartzite beach pebbles being unobtainable when the sea rose.

The size difference between the Kartan and Seton industries is also seen on the mainland, the difference being that on the mainland there is a gradual reduction in size, as seen in the artefacts, from places such as Cloggs Cave and Burrill Lake, whereas the Kartan artefacts suddenly gave way to the much smaller Seton artefact.

The discovery of 24 very large waisted, flaked stone tools introduced another debate. These tools have been found in widely separated sites on the mainland, at Wepowie, in the southern Flinders Ranges, South Australia, as well as 80 found near Mackay, Queensland, at the foot of 500 m high Mt Jukes, about 6 km from the coast. Study of the artefacts from the Mackay site concluded that they were very similar to those being used on Kangaroo Island.

The function of these waisted tools is not known, but it has been suggested they are very similar to tools used for pounding sago in

New Guinea. Other suggestions have been for forest clearing and killing large animals caught in pitfall traps, as has been known from historical times in the Queensland rainforest, where pitfall traps were used to catch large animals which were dispatched with a large, heavy bladed stone axes, some of which were grooved, attached to very long handles of 'lawyer cane' that wrapped around the axe head and was bound with cane lashings (Flood, 2004).

Australian Pleistocene technology

Karta Culture on mainland Australia

Karta Culture on mainland Australia

Tools of the Kartan type have been found over an area of about 100,000 km² of South Australia and nearby coastal islands. Sites have been found, none of which was stratified, on Fleurieu Peninsula, Yorke Peninsula and Eyre Peninsula. Crude, heavily weathered stone tools were found at Hallett Cove. About 400 Kartan core tools have been found at this site that weighed up to 5.5 kg. The Kartan tools found in the sites around Hallett Cove, pebble choppers, horsehoof cores and hammer stones, were all made of locally obtained siltstone. The nearest site where better quality raw material, fine-grained quartzite pebbles, were situated, at the foot of the cliff, are believed to have been covered by a talus slope during the Pleistocene, when the sea level was low, the nearest source for such material available at the time being on the shore, which was much further away at the time.

Roonka Flat is another site where tools from the Kartan industry have been found.

Study of the industries of the Australian core tool and scraper traditions has indicated the Kartan industry to be more archaic in 2 characteristics, its large size and high ratio of core tools to scrapers. The core tools of the Kartan industry are much larger and heavier than those from any other industry, and there are many more of them compared with smaller tools. Kartan tools were made of many different raw materials, so it is considered their size does not relate to the raw material used. The waisted tools of the Kartan industry are believed to be of great age. They are even larger than the core tools from the same industry, averaging about 1.837 g compared to 882 g for the Kartan core tools (Flood, 2004). Another feature that is believed to indicate great age is that the waisted tools are usually bifacially flaked crudely, while the Karan tools are flaked unifacially. It is believed they may have either been hafted or used in a 2-hand grip.

The area around the mouth of the Murray River and the north east coast of Queensland, have the highest known concentrations of Kartan Culture sites. It has been suggested that the reason these 2 localities are the main sites of known Kartan Culture is that they are both on high ground, remnants of the continental shelf that are not presently submerged, suggesting that most sites from this age may be under the sea. A suggested reason for the concentration of Kartan culture on Kangaroo Island is that it is part of the continental shelf that is still above water and that is near the mouth of the Murray River, Australia's largest river.

See List of Occupation Sites in Australia - Chronological - Earliest date for sites, some estimated.

Aboriginal Shelter
In the Simpson Desert the use of wood for the construction of mia mias (humpies or wiltjas) by the Wangkangurru made it a valuable commodity. Mia mias were mainly made from gidgee.

Stone structures
Stone structures of Aboriginal Australia were well known in the 19th century, as can be seen from the ethnographic literature from that time. The known structures were of a number of types, stone-walled windbreaks, stone-walled residential buildings, stone foundations for houses and shelters, hunting hides, food storage buildings, as well as storage sites for sacred objects that must only be seen by fully initiated men.

Engineering works of stone were also known, such as marine and freshwater fish traps, canals, ovens, protective coverings for sacred objects and path liners. There were also stone layouts on the ground of geometric and abstract design that had spiritual significance. See Aboriginal Astronomy. Early references to stone structures were made by a number of authors (Worsnop, 1897; Kenyon, 1930).

An Aboriginal artist made drawings of stone houses still being used by Aborigines in the Australian Alps in 1840. In the Warringah area, north of Port Jackson, now the northern suburbs of Sydney, the stone bases of winter houses of the Gai-Marigal people could be seen, and would no doubt have been known to the early settlers of the Sydney area.

Basedow described a house with a stone roof being used by the Yaurawarka people from the lower Cooper Creek, Warburton Creek and the Strzelecki Desert in the north east of South Australia (Basedow, 1925, in Memmott, 2007). Basedow did not specify the type of stone but the description as slabs make it sound like slate. According to the description it may have been domed on a frame of heavy timber, the gaps between the slabs being plugged with clay.

The Gunditjmarra tribe of western Victoria were observed to be using structures of circular plan form with the entrance to the east.

Stone houses with a roof seem to have been first recorded in the ethnographic literature in March 1842 by George Robinson, Aboriginal Protector. He mentioned a village of the 'Nillen gundidj' clan in the Eumeralla River region, near Bessibelle. He described a number of houses of 2 designs, either stone or 'dirt'. The dirt houses he mentioned are believed to refer to houses with a domed frame covered with a sod cladding. This type of house was known to be in use in this region.

Historical records indicate that about 500 people lived in this village at times during the period of early contact. Robinson stated that the area was comprised of stony rises as well as swamps and thickly wooded areas. A number of circular stone walls were seen by a surveyor, Alex Ingram, as reported by Kenyon, in about 1898, around Mt Eccles and in the south of Lake Condah. An Aboriginal man at the Condah mission station told him they had been roofed like 'an ordinary hut', with boughs and bark. He was told by another man that his grandfather had spoken of 'decaying bark and sapling rooves on stone houses that had been on his property near Louth Swamp.

Among anthropologists and archaeologists up to the 1970s (Memmott, 2007), when the settlement at Lake Condah came to their attention, which eventually led to the Victorian Archaeological Survey 1992, the existence of stone houses wasn't well known. It has since been shown to be a unique region of stone structures. It is in an area of volcanic rocks, draining into Portland Bay, south western Victoria. It is open hilly, grassy areas, which are often treeless, with scattered stones and boulders, locally called 'stony rises', streams and swamps in the lower parts. The surrounding woodlands are comprised of stringy bark, manna gum, red gum, yellow box, sheoak and swamp gum. A number of swamps in the basalt lava flows are connected to each other by Darlot's Creek and the Eumeralla River. The lava flow, Tyrendarra Flow, is about 50 km long, from Mt Eccles and Mt Napier in the north, extending to the coast.

The Gunditjmara people's territory covered much of the drainage basin prior to contact, their modern descendants continuing to inhabit the area. This people made use of the plentiful supply of rocks to build stone structures that were integrated with the landscape. The complex of stone structures in the area have been studied by archaeologists for 30 years, but they are still to finalise their work to the point where they can reach a definitive conclusion on the use and purpose of many of the structures in the complex.

There is a degree of agreement between the archaeologists and the living descendants of the Gunditjmarra people that there is a complex system of creeks, ponds, dams, dykes, races, channels, weirs, traps and gates that have been engineered to extend, join and manage the wetlands with the aim of farming the short-finned eel, *Anguilla australis*. The structures they built were stone, stone-lined and earth. Openings were built into walls to hold conical eel traps made of plaited reeds, each about 3 m long and with a mouth about 600 mm wide, tapering to 100-125 mm. The eel harvest took place in the winter, possibly lasting as long as 9 months, as the result of engineering such a complex structure. At the time of year of the harvest, the area experiences 3-4 months of very cold weather, with intermittent frosts at night. They moved to the coast for the summer months, where they depended on abundant food from the sea and mutton bird chicks and eggs.

The eel harvesting technology sustained a large group of people who lived in sedentary/semi-sedentary huts and villages for up to 9 months each year. Throughout the cold, wet winters they worked at harvesting and smoking eels, but still had time for ritual and social activity, and no doubt enjoyed their summer holidays at the beach.

Information accumulated from Aboriginal, as well as anthropological evidence, suggests that local groups of the tribe each owned an estate, each of which contained a set of eel traps and the associated structural complexes, including a village. These estates were passed on to the descendants of the group owning each estate.

The smoking of eels in hollow trees has been demonstrated by Builth (2002). She has hypothesised they were for export, being traded to other parts of Victoria and as far as South Australia.

Archaeologists use the term when considering describing the development of a combination of intense exploitation of local resources and semi-sedentary village construction. This economic strategy is usually only applied at the intergroup level in Aboriginal Australia where sizeable gatherings are facilitated.

At a number of sites in western Victoria, such as Lake Condah (or Allambie), Wallacedale, Kinghorn, Darlot's Creek, Stony Rises, Toolonda, Mt Eccles, Mt. Napier, Gorrie Swamp, Lake Purrumbete (the south side), Ettrick, Homertown, Mt William, Lake Bolac and Salt Creek. These are sites where stone structures have been mentioned in the literature, places where it is believed intensification may have occurred.

The interpretations from the archaeological evidence has been disputed by Dr. Annie Clarke, in a paper 'Romancing the Stones', where she presents a systematic critique, suggesting alternative explanations for the circular stone remains. She suggests they may have been foundation walls for timber-domed structures, windbreaks or daytime hunting hides. According to her interpretation of the stone circles they were more likely to be a foundation to hold the base of the sapling ends in place for the construction of a domed structure. In other, less stony areas, the sapling ends would be inserted into the ground. In her paper she warned of 'romancing the stones', seeing the natural structures as being of human construction. Following the publication of her paper archaeologists were more reluctant to claim human engineering in the formation of some structures.

Further evidence for human involvement in the structures has resulted from the Victorian Archaeological Survey of 1992. Dr. Heather Builth (2000, 2002) has also provided evidence for the constructions being man-made. In a 40 Ha area at Darlot's Creek Builth has found at least 25 weirs and channels that had been constructed by the Aboriginal people, as well as the remains of 103 dwelling and storage structures that occurred in clusters, some of which had shared walls. She found that the stones of uniform size had been used in the construction of hypothesised shelter sites. Many of the stones averaged about 200 mm long by 100 mm in width and height. The areas surrounding these areas were found to be depleted in stones of the size used, the stones both smaller and larger being still present. The remains of the simple wall structures were all found to have an opening to the east or north east, away from the prevailing winds in winter. Among the structures she found was a 1 m high circular wall, 6 courses high, enclosing a space that was 2 m across. The height of the wall decreased towards the entrance, definite evidence of the presence of higher walled structures, as well as the windbreaks that were low.

Builth has identified a number of plan forms among the remains of stone structures:

Circles of various diameters, many with an average diameter of 2.5 m These circular structures were either isolated or in clusters of 4-5, in some of which was an internal pit that is believed to have been a hearth,

Up to 5 intersecting or interlocking circle segments in a structure of a cellular type

An oval exterior wall with an internal cross partition - a bicellular form

Single circular wall which had a small circular chamber attached near the entrance

A spiral wall enclosing a circular space. This type was known to the living Gunditjmara as a 'number 6' shape. It has been suggested this may have been a way of protecting the interior from wind of changing direction.

A normal circular wall with a smaller diameter circular wall attached at the entrance. It has been proposed that this may have been another way of protecting the interior from winds of changing direction.

See Memmott, 2007

There are other stone structures of shapes that were unlikely to have been used as houses, but their use is unknown at present. Builth has identified one such structure that is composed of 2 walls, at most 1 m apart, that were almost 6 m long. There is also a structure of a dumbbell shape; composed of 2 circles, the smaller having an internal diameter of 1 m and an external diameter of 2 m. 2 parallel walls connecting the 2 circles has been described as a narrow race that may have been a corridor.

Land was taken from the Gunditjmara in the 19th century by the colonists and they were eventually moved to the Lake Condah Mission where they remained from 1867-1918. They put up a fight against the invaders, carrying on guerrilla warfare 1834-1854. Many of the tribe now live in the towns of Heywood, Portland and Hamilton. They are keen to preserve and even re-develop the stone culture of their ancestors.

In the meantime, many of the stone structures have been damaged or destroyed, partly by walls being knocked over by cattle and the stones being taken to build walls around paddocks, as well as the squatters own houses. Hence the necessity for extensive archaeological work to gain a true appreciation of what has been lost over the years of destruction and neglect.

The roofing of the walls

As bark sheeting would not have been available in all parts of such a large area covered by the Gunditjmara country where the eel farming was practised, it is not certain what material they would have used to roof their houses.

A few of the methods proposed for roofing the circular walls, are based on methods observed in other parts of Australia, as well as by the squatters of the 1840s on the Gunditjmara land to roof their own houses. These are earth sods, thatched tussock grass and woven reeds with a clay or mud plastering. Sods could have come from many of the swamps in the area that dry out in summer, producing a thick green grass suitable for use as sods. High thick swards of kangaroo grass grew in the lava areas. Just to the north east and south of the eel harvesting area the use of grass thatching or sods have been reported. Where the camps were located near woodlands, the cladding could be supported by a frame of heavy limbs. It has been suggested a free-standing roof structure could have been made from reeds, if the required limbs were not available in the area. It is believed the same technology used for eel traps may have been used. The ethnographic literature reported these eel traps as being up to 3 m long. Grass or clay could have been used to cover such a framed structure.

Timber-framed domes western Victoria

In the 1840s villages of up to 30 domed winter (wet-weather) huts of a bee hive shape were observed that were waterproofed. A village near Caramut in south western Victoria that was observed in about 1840 was the site of the best example. These are illustrated as well as with written descriptions. The residences have been estimated to have been 3.0-3.5 m in diameter and about 2.5-2.8 m high with a 1 m high semi-oval opening of a vertical orientation. At the apex was an opening about 20.0-22.5 cm diameter, to let out the smoke from the fire. It was covered with a sod during rain. The interiors of the domes were on mounds of raised earth. The construction was of limbs with mud cladding. These structures were strong enough to bear the weight of a man, allowing men to climb onto the roof to carry out maintenance. There is some evidence that these villages were used at times of large social gatherings of the people from the surrounding areas, such as were held throughout Aboriginal Australia when rituals and ceremonies were held that involved a number of neighbouring groups, as well as when trade took place. As with other places where large numbers of people gathered for limited periods of time, it was a place where there was plenty of food and water, that would support a large population, at least for a limited length of time (Williams, 1984, 1987; Crichett, 1984). Apparently, a Stone Age convention centre.

At Great Swamp, Konnung-i-yoke, past Lake Linlithogow to the north of Mt Napier at the Grange, believed to be near Hamilton, according to the map, George Robinson saw a number of camps, describing one village of 13 houses. According to Robinson (in Memmott, 2007: 196):

"The Great Swamp is skirted by low hills and well grassed open forests. The natives are still the undisputed occupants, no white man having been there to dispossess them. The people who occupy the country have fixed residences. At one village were thirteen huts. They are warm and well-constructed. In the shape of cupola or kraal. A strong frame of wood is first made, and the whole covered with thick turf with the grass inwards. There are several varieties. Those like a kraal are sometimes double, having two entrances; others are semicircular. Some are made with boughs and grass and last are temporary screens. One hut measured 10 feet in diameter and 5 feet high, and sufficiently strong for a man on horseback to ride over."

Another observer writing of the same region, about the Wannon River area in particular, mentioned that sometimes porches were fitted that were often oriented to take advantage of gentle breezes from the north east.

James Dawson wrote of a standing architectural pattern in western Victoria, people living in base camps over-winter in tall domes with internal partitions. Each dome had a central fire as well as a separate apartment for each nuclear family, with a separate one for the single young women and a separate one for single young men. Small shelters, not as waterproof, but usually dome-shaped, were used when travelling or during fine weather, and windbreaks were also used, a separate one for each of the above-mentioned groups. The low dome was about 1 m high and at the front was a peaked ridge. Limbs were arranged in a 3/4 circle and bent in to support each other. There was an open wall on 1/4 of the plan.

According to Dawson, "habitations ...wuurns...are of various kinds and are constructed to suit the seasons. The principal one is the permanent family dwelling, which is made of strong limbs of trees stuck up in dome shape, high enough to allow a tall man to stand upright underneath them. Small limbs fill up the intermediate spaces, and these are covered with sheets of bark, thatch, sods and earth till the roof and sides are proof against wind and rain. The doorway is low and generally faces the morning sun or a sheltering rock. The family wuurn is sufficiently large to accommodate a dozen or more persons; and when the family is grown up the wuurn is partitioned off into apartments, each facing the fire in the centre. One of these is appropriated to the parents and children, one to the young unmarried women and widows, and one to the bachelors and widowers. While travelling or occupying temporary habitations each of these parties must erect separate wuurns. When several families lived together, each builds its own wuurn facing one central fire. This fire is not much used for cooking, which is generally done outside. Thus in what appears to be one dwelling, fifty or more persons can be accommodated, when to use the words of the Aborigines, they are 'like bees in a hive.'

He goes on to describe the houses as comfortable and healthy, saying they are occupied by the owners of the land in the neighbourhood. He said they were built on the edge of a lake, stream or 'healthy swamp', but they avoided places he described as a 'malarial morass' or beneath large trees that could fall or be struck by lightning. Gum trees are also prone to drop branches, even big ones, especially in windy weather. He said that whenever they left their house to travel they closed the doorway with bark sheets or bushes and placed a crooked stick above it pointing in the direction they intended to travel. He also said that as they left they always uttered the words that translate as "close the door and pull away".

According to Dawson even temporary habitations were dome-shaped. He said they were made of limbs, gum tree bark and grass, and not very waterproof, being erected with less care, and were smaller and more open than the permanent huts. These huts were not used for permanent or semi-permanent residences, only in summer or when they were travelling. They had a fire in front of a large opening on one side. A semicircle of small green bushes was often used as a windbreak in warm weather.

Women constructed the smaller shelters, but the men build the permanent shelters, all the men of the group helping. The men kept their smaller weapons with them when they entered the huts, leaving their spears standing on either side of the doorway for easy access if they are required at short notice. He said the huts were made of flat stones when wood and bark was not available, and the roof was made from limbs and thatch. Karn Karn was the name of a stony point on the southern side of a lake near Camperdown, the name translating as' building of stones', though no evidence of a stone building could be seen by Dawson.

Dawson said these buildings were cool in summer and warm in winter, making them better, at least in comfort, for the occupants than the wooden cottages used at the 'Government aboriginal stations'. A fire is kept burning 24 hrs/day in cold weather in the centre of the floor, only a small fire being required to keep the interior of the hut warm. He states that to keep a moderate steady temperature, the ends only of the sticks meet in the centre of the fire, and as they burn slowly away they are pushed inwards. Any other method would be a waste of fuel and would raise too much heat.

'In the event of the habitation being burned down by a bushfire, or occasionally accidentally - which often happens in the absence of the inhabitants - the debris are levelled, and a new wuurn erected on the same spot, which is always preferred...'

Dawson also refers to houses of stone walls roofed with limbs and thatch. A watercolour by George French Angas, painted in the 1840s, which is in the South Australian Museum, depicts a structure from Portland Bay in western Victoria. The structure appears to have a high, long-spanned roof, which was probably a permanent building, though the precise details of the structure are not clear. It is believed this type of structure was occupied in winter, a season that in this part of Australia is generally wet and cold. Woven mats can be seen in use.

The caption of the painting is:

'Native Encampment at Portland Bay. 'Cold Morning and his family: In the south western portion of the Province, and about the Portland Bay district, the natives build larger and warmer huts than those to the northward: the native name among the Portland Bay tribe for these huts is miam miam. The plate represents one of these encampments inhabited by a native who has assumed the ludicrous name of 'Mr. Cold Morning'. At the period of my sketch he was lying sick upon a round grass mat within the hut, and his wife, with a numerous family of dirty, naked, little 'Cold Mornings' were about him. Spears, shields and baskets were lying about on the roof of the miam miam, which was constructed of boughs of Banksia and eucalyptus, thatched with reeds and dry grass. The scene is in the woods near Portland Bay'. (from Memmott, 207: 198).

Ngalawuru or High Cliffy Island

This island is a member of the Montgomery Island complex, in the Buccaneer Archipelago, to the north west of the Kimberley coast about 10 km from the mainland. Evidence of stone houses has been found on this island by a post-graduate anthropologist from the

University of Wisconsin (Blundell, 1975) while carrying out research in the Kimberleys. The find was made at about the same time as the study at Lake Condah was being undertaken by the Victorian Archaeological Survey. The island was owned by the Yawijibaya people (Montgomery Islanders).

The climate of this region is of a semi-arid monsoonal type similar to that of Arnhem Land and Cape York, temperatures being high throughout the year, reaching as high as $30°C$ in the cooler months, the minimum temperatures hardly ever going below $18°C$. At nearby Cockatoo Island the mean annual rainfall is 919 mm. The seasons in this region are mostly the Wet and the Dry, with about 1 month of transitional conditions at the changeover. During the Dry, about May to October, the easterlies are the prevailing winds, rain usually not falling between July and September. During November the winds swing around to become westerlies, but fluctuating between easterlies and westerlies until December, when the westerlies become fully established and the Wet season begins, lasting until about March. At this very wet time of year campsite location is determined by the availability of shelter, and there is no shortage of surface water.

In what appears to have been a settlement of relatively high density, there are the remains of hundreds of stone structures. The island, about 15 m above sea level, is about 1 km long and at its widest point about 300 m wide, adding to the surprise of finding a settlement of what must have been many people. It has been suggested that the island was probably used throughout the year, though mostly as a camp during the monsoon season, as there is apparently no permanent water on the island. It would have been relatively free of annoying insects that are common at this time of the year on the mainland. The people are believed to have used rafts for crossing water prior to European contact. Their economy is thought to have been based on the availability of many birds' eggs, turtles, dugongs and fish. Quarrying was also thought to have taken place, the products being exported (traded) to the mainland. Evidence has been found of many stone walls of quartz sandstone that are laid out in a stretcher bond, of a rough type, up to 1 m high and up to 50 cm at the base. There was an opening for entry that was narrow, and the interior was about 3 m wide. The remains of fish and turtles, as well as stone artefacts have been excavated inside this structure suggesting it may have been a house (of domiciliary function).

It has been suggested that the circular wall structures were clad with spinifex (O'Connor, 1987, 1999). This and stunted eucalyptus and acacia associations were the only vegetation on the island. The soil is relatively thin on the rocky top of the island, so post holes would have been very shallow, probably too shallow to be of any use.

According to 2 of Blundell's informers, one of whom said they were windbreaks that were covered with paperbark, *Melaleuca sp.*, brought from the mainland on rafts, and spinifex, *Triodia sp.* Another informer believed they were wet weather shelters, as well as providing a way of hiding fires from view, as the island was prone to attack from parties of Worrorra who raided at night. This informer also believed the lines of stone probably had ceremonial associations. The island has been identified as 'the sacred place of the Yanjbai' (Love n.d., 68).

Photographs suggest that the walls with wide entrances were windbreaks and those with narrow entrances were probably roofed as wet weather shelters, in at least 1 case both types appear to form a complex. Whatever the roofing material used it would require some sort of frame to support it. A requirement for a roof in this location would be to withstand strong wind and heavy rain. A problem on the island was the lack of suitable timber, for both structures and firewood. If it is accepted that paperbark sheets were brought to the island by raft, timber could just as easily have been brought in by raft.

Georgina River

On the Georgina River, about 40 km south of Boulia, near the airstrip of Marion Downs Station (pastoral property), a village of 17 circular, or curvilinear enclosed, stone houses have been found. It appears each circular structure had an opening less than 1 m across on one side, and facing north. There are also a number of structures with a rectangular floor plan. The area of the internal space averaged 7.1 m^2. The structures were studied by Dr. Ian Davidson in 1989. He assumed they were huts. One had a collapsed group of gidgee boughs, that may have been either over it or above it, which suggests it probably had a roof structure. It is not known if they were being used prior to European contact.

Stone walled game hides

These hides or blinds used for hunting have been described from the Western Desert and Central Australia. They usually consisted of a section of dry-stone wall structure that often abutted a natural feature of the landscape, often near a waterhole. The area inside the hide, about 3 m wide, was usually cleared of stones to allow the hunters to sit comfortably as they waited. The rocks from the cleared area were used to build the walls of the structure, about 1.2 m high. These hides are mostly found in rocky high ground in arid sand country near waterholes where water is held for long periods because of the impervious rocks and some degree of protection from the sun. The animals hunted by this method were mostly kangaroos, wallabies and emus that came from the waterless sand country to drink. Such structures have been found near Yuendumu that were used by the Warlpiri. They were also found at Ampilatwaj, used by the Alyawarr on the Sandstone River in Central Australia.

According to Memmott, the best description in the ethnographic literature was written by Richard Gould (1968, 1977), an ethno-archaeologist working with the people of a dialect subgroup of the Pitjantjatjara language group, the Ngatatjara, from the Warburton and Rawlinson Ranges area in the Western Desert. He described a rock wall hide at Mularpayi, a part of the Barrow Range situated between the point of intersection of the borders of Western Australia, the Northern Territory and South Australia, and the Warburton community.

'The principal feature of the site is a 57 metre long gorge with unusually regular rock walls ranging from 1.8 to 4.5 metres high. The floor of the gorge slopes downwards to the entrance, while at the upper end there is a small but deep pool of freshwater. In a few places along the side walls of the gorge there are natural crevices large enough for a man to hide inside. The gorge is renowned among the Ngatatjara as a natural game trap and its use reflects similar practices at the 13 other sites visited during the survey ... on the north east rim of the gorge, 10.8 metres from the waterhole is a circular hunting blind constructed of local rocks piled neatly on one side in a row, with natural rocks comprising the back and sides. The blind is 1.8 metres in diameter; the rocks had been cleared from the interior and used in the wall construction. The earth floor of the blind contained a few pieces of butchered bone and some stone flakes. My Ngatatjara guides explained that the hunters crouched in the hides at night, waiting to spear kangaroos and emus as they approached the water. Once inside the gorge there was no escape except by means of the entrance. This route was usually blocked by additional hunters. Gould also described rock art, both secular and ritual, in the vicinity of the hide. There were small openings in the sides of the hides so the hunters could watch the game. They could also throw their spears through these openings, over the walls or around the outside of the hides. There were also bird hides from which the hunters catch birds through an opening in the roof.

Stone-walled bird hides
Darrell Lewis reported circular stone walls covered with a cladding of grass and spinifex on timber rails being used by bird hunters in the basin of the Upper Victoria River in the Northern Territory. They used a dead pigeon impaled on a stick that they poked through the cladding of the roof, attracting certain species of hawks and eagles to the bait by lighting a fire. When a bird lands to eat the pigeon the hunter grabs its legs and pulls it through the covering and kills it, then pokes the pigeon through the roof again to attract more birds. George Augustus Robinson described birds being caught by the same method at Macquarie Harbour in Tasmania in 1833, the birds being hunted were crows. In Tasmania the hides were made of pliable saplings. The stone-walled hides have also been reported from Esmeralda Station near Croydon, to the southeast of the Gulf of Carpentaria. These hides were similar to those structures being used as residential shelters in western Victoria and on High Cliffy Island, though they were smaller.

Covers protecting sacred objects
In Central Australia various tribes have retained their beliefs in ancestral Beings from the Dreamtime (Agterre) and creation myths of their ancestors. They believed that many sacred objects still contain the powers imbued in them by the ancestral Beings. These objects were often placed in clefts and holes in the rocks of the

landscape, and camouflaged with layers of stones. One of these sites is known to also have had a stone wall built around it. These sacred objects were taken out only when they were to be used in sacred ceremonies and rituals connected with the Dreamtime Being who left them for the people.

A sacred site, Lyabe, in the western MacDonnell Ranges in the Northern Territory, is believed by the Arrente to have been created by Honey Ant Beings, Yerrampe. The atywerrenge are sacred objects they left in a depression in a rocky part of the range. Surrounding this site are upright stone slabs that are said to be the transformed Ancestral Honey Ant Beings that were turned to stone at the close of the Dreamtime. A horseshoe-shaped stone wall surrounds the pit-like depression. The wall open at the western end, is about 1 m high and at the base is at least 1 m thick. The outer diameter of the wall is about 5 m, the 2 m-wide storage pit continues below the wall base. Honey Ant increase rituals were held at this site by the Arrente. The secretive nature of such sacred sites prevents more detail being provided (Memmott, 2007: 204).

The evidence for stone structures

According to Memmott (2007: 204) Worsnop was the first ethnographer to attempt a summary of the evidence for stone structures, including the lava flows region of western Victoria, in Arnhem Land and the Prince Regent River basin and stone arrangements for ceremonial purposes and the use of low walls.

The 2 examples of stone villages of a sedentary use, one in the Kimberleys and one in western Victoria, both used at times when resources were in plentiful supply, and on a regular seasonal basis. They reflect the process of socio-economic intensification. Evidence indicates they were used pre-contact, as well as for some time after contact. There is a high level of similarity between the structures on High Cliffy Island and the Lake Condah complexes of stone structures, as noted by O'Connor, stating 'these use the same walling techniques, are of approximately the same size and are clustered in the same way ... [and] are located immediately adjacent to a resource rich zone ...'. She noted that at Lake Condah fish traps were constructed, while the reef and rock pools at High Cliffy Island formed natural fish traps. The rock type differed between the 2 sites, those on High Cliffy Island being fractured, flat slabs of sedimentary rocks. At Lake Condah, the rounded, igneous rocks were of less regular shape. They used comparable architectural styles at both sites, adapting it to allow for the rocks available.

The structure of any roofing present has still to be determined, at least to the satisfaction of the scientific community, though there are a number of references to roofed walls appearing in the ethnographic literature. These often clearly describe huts with circular stone walls with roofs of various materials.

Whale bone house structures

Among many groups of coastal Aboriginal people whales were important in their economy and culture, particularly in the south and southeast of Australia. An example was the people of the Nullarbor Plain and the people of the coastline of the northern section of the Great Australian Bight. They identified with the Whale Dreaming (Burgoyne, 2000). Whale bones are known to have been used in the construction of coastal houses, as depicted in a painting by W. A. Cawthorne (1842) in which 2 whale bones are employed as a structural frame for an Aboriginal shelter. Around the time Cawthorne painted the scene he was writing a manuscript about the local Aborigines. In 1847 George Angas published a book, *South Australian Illustrated*, in which he included copies of Cawthorne's painting and his subjects, re-working them in his own style. The Caption included for his copy of Cawthorne's painting:

'Natives of Encounter Bay. The view here given represents a part of the shores of Encounter Bay with a native hut formed of the ribs of a whale. Numerous carcasses of whales being cast upon the shores adjoining the fisheries, most of the native huts are constructed with a framework of bones, the interstices being filled in with boughs and dried grass. The present group consist of a man called Ginnginnana, and his two wives, Kundarkey and Wuddagar, Kundarkey is chewing reeds, while her husband is twisting the chewed strips into a cord upon his thigh, for the purpose of being made into baskets and fishing nets, one of which lies on top of the hut.'

According to Memmott the location of the hut is suggested by the caption to be adjacent to an early European whaling station. In Tasmania there is evidence of the use of whale bones in construction of shelters in pre-contact times. In the 1820s, Jorgen Jorgenson described a house at Venable's Corner, on the North West coast of Tasmania, that is a sheltered bay:

'On the following day they reached the Venable's boat harbour. On passing along they observed a very neat and compact native hut. It bore all the marks of simple rudiments of Gothic architecture; it rose in the shape of an oblong dome, and might easily contain from sixteen to twenty persons. The wood used for the principal supports was bent into a curve, and seems to have been rendered hard by fire. It was uncommonly neatly thatched, and the door-way was about two and a half feet high. Necessity is the mother of invention, and therefore the Aborigines on this coast have been compelled to construct compact huts to screen from the inclemency of the cold, and the boisterous winds, especially where fuel is so scarce as it is here ...'.

Also in Tasmania, John F. Jones discovered a hillside camp site at Bluff Point on the same stretch of west coast as Sandy Cape. He visited the site in 1930 and 1945, finding on his second visit that the wind had eroded the site to reveal whalebone structures. He compared his findings with those described by Jorgenson:

'On the top I noticed, standing erect at the edge of one of the hollows, a portion of a rib of a large whale. On pulling it out of the sand I found it to be about [600 millimetres] long. The portion that had been exposed to the air had been decayed and the end that had been forced into the ground had been cut on two sides by a chopper by the natives. It was evidently part of one of the roof supports of the hut. Not far off I found a complete rib which showed little sign of decay having probably been uncovered more recently. It appeared that in one, at least of the ten huts that had been built on the hillock a whale's rib had been used for the support. I tried to realise the effect, I suddenly realised how Jorgenson's Gothic vault and dome might be quite comprehensible. The number of ribs with one end embedded in the sand at intervals around the hollow, with the other end gathered and fastened together over the middle of the hut would, when completed with light material and thatched, make a very perfect dome. Inside the dim light and blackened by smoke, the bones might easily be mistaken as wood while their smoothness and

evenness of the curve would give the impressions of timber that had been artificially shaped.' (Jones, 1946 in Memmott (2007: 207).

Dugong bone grave site at Stewart River

A grave site was recorded near the mouth of the Stewart River, on the east side of Cape York, in 1928-1929 by Donald Thomson, an anthropologist. It was constructed from the bones of 8 dugongs, and was also decorated with their bones.

'*The vertebrae and small bones were piled up on the centre of the grave and were completely encircled by the ribs arranged with vertebral (thick) ends inwards*'. At the head of the grave the dugong heads were placed facing towards the sea.

Spinifex houses of the Western Desert

In pre-contact times the people of the Western Deseret built their domed huts with timber frames with a cladding of spinifex (hummock grass) **Triodia spp**. The method used for collecting spinifex for cladding has been described '*squatting on the ground and leaning backwards, the weight of their bodies supported on their hands, they would thrust their feet forward, and using the tough callused skin of their heels, they would gouge the clumps out bodily complete with the roots*'.

According to Memmott the settlement patterns of the Aboriginal people of the western Desert were integrated with their social, economic and religious organisation.

Professor Bob Tonkinson has said '*Extending over a million square miles, the Western Desert ... covers a vast area of the interior of the continent. It extends across western South Australia into central and central-northern Western Australia (south of the Kimberleys) and south-western Northern Territory and it includes most of the hill country in northern South Australia. The area is marked by an overall similarity in both climatic conditions ... and physiographical characteristics. More important, however, is its delimitation as a distinct cultural area ... its Aboriginal inhabitants share a common language (with dialectical variations), social organisation, relationship to the natural environment, religion and mythology and aesthetic expression*. The term Western Desert, then, refers to both a cultural bloc and a geographical entity.

Features of the cultures of the various groups of Western Desert people that are shared or similar cover a wide range of activities such as camp layout, shelter construction and materials, there is some variation between the different groups.

In the part of the Western Desert comprising the northern section - the Gibson Desert, the Great Sandy Desert and the Little Sandy Desert, the Aboriginal inhabitants refer to themselves as Martu. These people now live in places such as Newman, Jigalong, Parnngurr, and on the Old Canning Stock Route, Kunawarraji. In the south and east, comprising the Great Victoria Desert and the Nullarbor Plain, they refer to themselves broadly as Anangu. This term includes people such as the Pitjantjatjara, Yankuntjatjara and other related dialects. These people mainly live in such places as Amata, Pipalyatjara, Fregon and Iwantja (Indulkana). The people identifying themselves as Western Desert people include the Kukatja, the Pintupi, and the Ngalia subgroup of the Warlpiri, as well as several other groups, inhabit the north-east part of the Western Desert. The northernmost parts are occupied by the Walmatjarri, and in the south west are groups such as Ngaanyatjarra, Mandjindja and Nyanganyatjara. They live in places such as Warburton, Wiluna, Kalgoorlie and Laverton (Memmott, 2007: 210).

The Giles weather station near the Rawlinson Ranges provides data that gives an indication of the range of temperatures that can be experienced in the Western Desert, which can range from below freezing in winter to occasional summer maximum temperatures of 46° C. The peoples of the area wore no clothes at any time of the year, cold or hot. In winter the only way they avoided the coldest times was with fire and shelters.

Very limited study of the ethno-architecture and camps of the area has been undertaken. The only study was apparently undertaken by an architect, Peter Hamilton at Mimili in the Everard Ranges in 1970-1971. He camped with them for more than 16 months. The Mimili settlement was on a flat, open area near a water bore. The surrounding country was rock outcrops in a large area of sand ridges. The shelters, called a Wiltja, numbered 19. The layout of the village was centered on a public space, around this common the village was divided into a number of living spaces, 'niches', each about 18.5-22 m^2. These were of a segmented design. Gender specific rituals were carried out in peripheral places around the edge of each living space. These places were also used for defecation. Each Wiltja, with its cleared space, was moved around a central point that was normally unchanging. A number of reasons were given for such moves, such as the materials had to be physically replaced, as with structural components that had broken, and disintegrating cladding, as well as a response to sickness.

Couples with children occupied 10 of the wiltjas. 6 were for childless couples. 1 had 2 widows, 1 contained a widower and 1 housed 5 unmarried adolescent men. The number in the settlement varied up to 84 during the period of study - individuals or families leaving for varying lengths of time from days to months. Hunting and rituals were reasons for leaving, as well as visiting relatives who had moved to the Indulkana settlement set up by the government, that was nearby. Fregon, Ernabella and Alice Springs were also places where relatives had moved to. The people were no longer living the free ranging traditional life, receiving social security payments and doing occasional stock work on the cattle stations. Tea, flour, sugar and tinned food had entered their diet. No traditionally living groups were studied in connection with their shelters.

Models of camp sites and architecture have needed to be pieced together from references in the literature from widely separated places throughout the Western Desert.

Because of the hostile nature of the environment of the Western Desert, the early contacts with Europeans were very limited.

Aboriginal Stone Arrangements

A number of stone arrangements have been found in Australia that show remarkable similarity to stone arrangements in Europe, but could be thousands of years older. In Victoria, the Wurdi Youang people built a stone arrangement, that was roughly egg-shaped, and with a diameter of about 50 m. Its major axis is east-west. 3 prominent stones, that are waist high, are at its highest point at the western edge. It has been found that, when viewed from these stones, some outlying stones to the west of the main arrangement appear to indicate the setting of the sun at times of equinoxes and solstices. The straight sides of the arrangement have also been found to point to the solstices.

The only prehistoric structures associated with religion that have survived are stone arrangements that are very difficult to date, but it is thought they have been part of Aboriginal culture for a very long time. There are a wide range of stone array types. There are circles, lines, corridors, single standing stones, and piles of stones heaped into cairns. The mythology and significance of these stone arrangements is unknown, to the local Aborigines as well as the researchers. Most of the sites haven't been used for an unknown number of years, possibly centuries. The only thing known about them is that they are connected with the Dreamtime stories, representing either totemic beings or enclosed areas where special events took place.

The only stone arrangement dated so far is in the Bay of Fires in north eastern Tasmania where a new arrangement was set up on top of an old one that had been covered by a shell midden and charcoal, it is 750 years old. This only gives a minimum antiquity for this type of prehistoric stone arrangement.

The stone arrangements were observed by the Berndts while many Aboriginal groups were still living in the old tribal way of life.

Chapter 5 - Archaeology of Australia

Sahul

Across monsoonal northern Australia there are sites that date from more than 40,000 BP, which includes Carpenter's Gap I, (O'Connor, 1995) and in the south central Kimberley, Riwi (Balme, 2000), in south western Arnhem Land Nawarla Gabarnmang (Geneste et *al.*, 2010), in northern Arnhem land, Malakunanja II, in northern Arnhem Land, Nauwalabila (Roberts et *al.*, 1990, 1994) and in northern Queensland, GRE8 (Slack et *al.*, 2004). Infrequent occupation in the earliest levels of these sites is indicated, and small flakes are predominant of which very few show signs of retouch.

There are sparse faunal remains in the deepest levels of these deposits, and not much on their identification has been published. A dense lens of freshwater mussels has been referred to at GRE8 (Slack et *al.*, 2004: 134) between dates of 40,000 and 32,000 cal BP. It has also been suggested that at Ngarrabullgan the faunal remains represent small to medium-sized animals.

In northern Australia many of the sites from the Pleistocene have been found to contain evidence of ground stone axes. At Nawarla Gabarnmang the oldest of these has been found that dates to 35,400 ± 410 cal BP. At about 2.4 x 4.0 cm (Geneste et *al.*, 2010: 67) it is a fragment that has been interpreted to have been flaked from a ground-edge axe to thin the side of the axe because of the convexity of the ground surface. At this antiquity not many complete axes have been found, but a deposit at Sandy Creek that has been dated to 32,000 BP has produced a quartzite waisted and grooved ground-edge axe (Morwood & Trezise, 1989). Deposits at Malangangerr, Arnhem Land, dating from 25,000 BP (about 29,000cal BP) have produced complete axes (Schrire, 1982). These axes have a thin edge that is produced by flaking bifacially and then grinding them (Schrire, 1982: 106). Manufactured grooves were retained by some axes, though they were weathered, that have been interpreted as being to facilitate hafting (Schrire, 1982, 107, fig. 27d, 241). Ground flakes have been found in deposits dated to 28,000 BP (about 33,000 cal BP) at Widgingarri Rock Shelter I (O'Connor, 1999, 75). At Nauwalabila I some dolerite flakes and objects have been produced by deposits dated to between 30,000 BP and 25,000 BP that are very weathered (Jones & Johnson, 1985, 217) but it is suspected they are ground-edge axe flakes (Jones, 1985, 297).

Stone axes from PNG are flaked rather than polished, which makes them different from axes found in Australia. Their probable use in hafts is indicated by a central indent or 'waist' that is often found on them. These 'waisted axes' are often found in locations in highlands and coastal areas on the mainland. Examples of these tools that dated to 42,000-35,000 BP (about 45,000-39,000 cal BP) have recently been recovered from several open sites near Kosipe at about 2,000 m (Summerhayes et al., 2010). The sites at Kosipe overlook a large swamp and remarkably they contain evidence of plant food exploitation that is well preserved such as charred ***Pandanus*** drupes, as well as starch from yams, which is comparable with ***Dioscorea*** (Summerhayes et al., 2010, 79). The Kosipe axes are believed to have been used for felling trees, as is the case with the much larger flaked and waisted axes at Bobongara on the Huon Peninsula, which in combination with firing was used to open patches of rainforest canopy to promote growth of useful plants (Groube, 1989; Groube et al., 1986; Summerhayes et al., 2010, 78). The Kosipe axes occur in a range of sizes and raw materials, while the waisted axes from the Huon Peninsula are massive. It has been suggested (Balme & O'Connor), that the axes form PNG were used for a variety of tasks, such as thinning smaller saplings, slashing undergrowth and ring-barking large trees, though it has been argued that the PNG axes were predominantly used for forest clearing. The smaller examples found near Kosipe may have been used for cutting timber for the manufacture of wooden tools such as the hafts of axes.

Some have claimed that the stones used for seed grinding may have been part of the stone tool technology that was associated with incursions into regions of semi-arid grassland in Australia during the Pleistocene. The excavation of grinding stones at Cuddie Springs, that were recovered from a level earlier than the level dated to 35,000 BP and which still had residues of plant use, is the main evidence for this (Fullagar & Field, 1997). It is, however, suggested by recent electron spin resonance (ESR) and uranium (U) dating of fauna, that there has been a considerable mixing at this site, the authors suggesting it may be necessary to confirm the Pleistocene age of the grinding stones from this site by further finds that are in contexts that are well dated.

Discussion

The variability of the environments that were occupied apparently rather quickly during the colonisation of Sahul indicate the flexibility of the technology that allowed adaptation from tropical rainforest in PNG to the sub-arctic conditions existing in Tasmania at the time. Balme & O'Connor suggest the tool assemblage could be described as Mode 3. But the trajectory from large thick flakes that were retouched to be used as scrapers, to a reduction in the tool size with smaller cores, fewer core tools and scrapers that were increasingly made on thinner flakes as previously proposed (Lorblanchet & Jones, 1979) has not held up. Some sites from the Mid- to Late Holocene had the most massive tools, and many of the other sites, such as Carpenter's Gap I and Widgingarri I in the Kimberley, in south west Australia Devil's Lair, and near Perth, Upper Swan have lithic assemblages that are almost exclusively comprised of small unretouched and irregularly retouched flakes (Dortch, 1984; Dortch & Dortch, 1996; O'Connor, 1995; O'Connor, 1999; Pearce & Barbetti, 1981). The same situation is found in sites such as Lachitu, the north coast of PNG (O'Connor et *al.*, 2011a), and Liang Lemdubu in the Aru Islands (O'Connor et *al.*, 2005; Hiscock, 2005), islands that in the Pleistocene were connected by land as part of Sahul.

Apart from axes recovered from sites in the tropical north of the continent there is very little specialised adaptation of stone tools. These axes appear to have been an Australian innovation as they are not known from the rest of the world at this time early in the colonisation of Australia. The examples known support the view that they were manufactured in different forms and different sizes for different uses, though only a few complete axes have been found. This appears to also be the case in PNG, where robust flaked and waisted axes have been found on the PNG mainland. Hitherto the focus of flaked stone assemblages in the Pleistocene has meant that variation in size of stone tool assemblages has been unrecognised in Sahul. Balme & O'Connor suggest the bone tools recovered from southern sites, which have been well preserved in caves, and organic technologies that have not been preserved, though their presence is indicated by other evidence, must also be added to these technologies that have been unrecognised. It is suggested that in the same sites in the south the importance of organic remains that have not been preserved cannot be underestimated. Where retouch has been identified on flakes from Sahul it is associated with woodwork, which indicates the importance this raw material has had since the earliest times. The macropod remains found in some of these sites may have been hunted with wooden spears. It is suggested wood may have been the technological equivalent of spears with projectile points, that are a marker of industries from the Upper Palaeolithic, as these spears have little technological advantage over wooden spears (Waguespack et al., 2009) in this region, The presence of hafted axes is evidence for the use of fibre for binding them by its association with watercraft (Balme, 2013), and suggested use in net making in western New South Wales, though it is possible animal sinew may have been used instead for the axes.

It has been suggested that all the stratified sites from the Pleistocene in Island Southeast Asia (ISEA) can be characterised as Mode 3 (O'Connor et *al*., 2011a). The island assemblages are very similar in many respects to the earliest assemblages known from Sahul, though they lack the large flaked and waisted axes from PNG, as well as the smaller polished-edge axes and hatchets that have been found in northern Australia. The island assemblages are also comparable with flaked lithic assemblages from South Asia that have been dated to approximately the same time (O'Connor et *al*., 2011a, online supplement). The faunal suits from the islands exhibit some distinctive characteristics, in terms of subsistence. There are a range of large mammal faunas in the Philippines, but once the early human colonists crossed the Wallace Line, they would have experiences serious challenges with adaptation in terms of animals available for hunting. The smaller islands in Wallacea would have especially presented problems with food availability as they have unbalanced and depauperate faunas. At that time Flores had a range of large animals that are now extinct such as stegodons, a large varanid and a large land turtle and giant endemic rats, and it is believed that at least some of these large fauna may have been present until about 18,000 years ago. A similar range of megafauna existed on Timor, though they appear to have been extinct by 42,000 years ago.

In the earliest levels of Jerimalai and Lene Hara there were small reptiles, bats and large rats. Small islands such as the Talaud-Sangihe Archipelago the faunal resources available to the early colonists would have been even more limited. Balme & O'Connor suggest that it should possibly be viewed in this contexts that the early people of East Timor developed their remarkable maritime skills.

Conclusion

Balme & O'Connor suggest it might be more profitable to view the lack of specialisation of stone tools as an adaptation to new, unfamiliar environments that were challenging, and not for evidence from Sahul and ISEA of a progressive loss of types of tool or cognitive continuity in flake production over time and space after the dispersal of modern humans out of Africa into India and eventually into Sahul. The early colonists would not have been required to find sources of fine-grained stone or material of a required size for the production of blades by the basic reduction repertoire. The colonists could have substituted organic materials for stone, or combined them with stone, when they needed to, or when the opportunity arose. The occupants of Golo Cave were making their sharp flakes out of *Turbo* shells, while in East Timor and Talaud they used small chert nodules, and in the earliest sites in the Philippines, the people appear to have relied wholly on expedient bamboo or other organic tools. The presence of fish hooks indicates the role of fibre in ISEA, and while strapped firmly to watercraft its critical role in the settlement of Australia and, according to Balme & O'Connor its probable subsequent use in Sahul, provides more evidence of the remarkable adaptability of the people in this region. The earliest assemblages in Sahul are now seen to be as diverse as the landscape and nothing like the uniformity previously believed. Source ?

Tropical and Arid Australia

Prior to the discovery of the sites of ancient habitation around the Top End it had been postulated by a number of researchers that the first Aborigines to arrive in Australia would have landed at places like Arnhem Land, Cape York or the Kimberly region, based on the proximity of these places to New Guinea and the islands of South East Asia. All 3 regions have now yielded evidence of Pleistocene human occupation. Some of the sites are in excess of 30,000 years in age. What has surprised archaeologists was the finding of Pleistocene sites in extremely arid parts of the Pilbara, Central Australia and even as far south as the Nullarbor Plain.

It seems that by 25,000 years ago there was already a well-developed inland economy based on macropods and emu eggs in the Pilbara, and in the Central Australian Ranges humans were present in the spinifex sand hills throughout the glacial maximum, the time of maximum dryness in the Australian inland.

Changing to a settled way of life would have been difficult at best, as the climate over most of Australia is too dry and erratic for dependence on crops, and as is now known, Australia has the most impoverished soils in the world. A nomadic lifestyle was probably the best option, as they could move around their territory, allowing other parts to recover before they returned.

Cape York Peninsula

At both Mushroom Rock and the 10 000-year-old layer at Early Man Shelter there were small rock fragments with grinding marks which hinted at edge-grinding in the late Pleistocene in Cape York Peninsula. This find considerably extends the time of the introduction of edge-ground axes in the region and in the continent.

Ground-edge axes have been found in a number of Pleistocene layers at sites in north Queensland, the Top End of the Northern Territory and in highland New Guinea - Kafiavana, Kiowa, Yuku, and Nombe, where a complete axe was found in a layer dated to 26,000-14,500 years ago. In Western Australia's Kimberly region, flakes showing signs of grinding were found in a 27,000 BP layer in Widgingarri 1, and the 18 000 year-old layer at Miriwun Shelter.

Fern Cave

Mushroom Rock

Nurrabullgin Cave

Sandy Creek Shelter I

Walkunder Arch Cave

Allen's Cave

Allen's Cave is near **Eucla**, about 80 km west of Koonalda Cave, in South Australia. After the first occupation of the cave there was a break when the cave was apparently abandoned, between 17,500 and 15,000 years ago. This coincided with a period of increased aridity and the accompanying sea level fall that caused the coast to retreat about 160 km further south. The Eucla-Koonalda region became a treeless plain. The estimated average annual rainfall at this time was about 160-180 mm. Allen's Cave was mostly abandoned during this time. Between 22,000 and 15,000 BP there was intermittent use of Koonalda Cave. It is assumed the people of the area moved south to follow the coastline, probably living on the exposed plain. The sea rose again about 12,000 years ago.

About 50,000-60,000 BP the roof of a bigger cave collapsed to form Allen's Cave. Over the following 10,000-20,000 years 1 m of deposit had accumulated by the time of the first signs of occupation. The evidence of occupation is irrefutable, though minimal, consisting of small unmodified flakes of chalcedony and 3 flaked limestone pieces, that were found wedged between rocks and sealed beneath a thin layer of gravel, that was then capped by a band of laminated silts that was 7 cm deep. A date of 39,850 BP (calibrated deviation of 36,750-42,950 BP) has been obtained for these silts, and the artefacts are obviously older, as the silts are Cane suggests the antiquity of the occupation is secure, based on the closed, compact association of the artefacts, the laminated silts and the adjacent rocks.

Bass Point

A midden site is on the southern coast of New South Wales north of Burrill Lake, near Shellharbour. The site is on a hill that has a sharp drop on the eastward side. This site was occupied sporadically from about 17,000 BP, the early stone tool industry being from 17,000 to 3,500 BP. Because of the steep profile on the seaward side of the hill it would have been about 30 km from the sea when the sealevel was low, but as the sea level rose it became a headland. In the upper levels of the site the midden included the remains of shellfish, seals, birds and land mammals.

Bass Point is one of 2 known open occupation sites dated to the Pleistocene on the east coast of Australia, the other being at Wallen Wallen Creek, southern Queensland.

Birrigai Shelter

This is a rock shelter formed by a large block of stone leaning against another. It provides shelter for up to 12 people, it is open at both ends so the wind howls through, which would make it a cold place, as it is high on the northern fringes of the Australian Alps in the Tidbinbilla Nature Reserve. When one end is closed off, it becomes a warm refuge from the cold wind. At the height of the Ice Age, when it was apparently being used as a summer camp, at least for hunting trips, at 730 m above sea level it would have been above the tree line. Based on paleontological and geomorphologic evidence it has been estimated the average annual temperature would have been about 7° C lower than at present. The climate at this site, near Canberra, would have been similar to the top of **Mt Kosciusko** of the present. It would have been very cold in winter, but in summer it would be habitable.

It has been dated to about 21,000 years ago onwards. This date was questioned, but other dates in the area of 18 000 BP make it more acceptable.

1.5 cubic metres of the floor of the rock shelter were excavated, producing evenly spaced small stone tools. Maybe it was the travelling kit of long-distance hunters. The Pleistocene tools are all quartz, flakes, chips, core fragments and bipolar pieces.

Microscopic analysis of the residue on the working edges of tools from a level dated to 16,000-21,000 BP, revealed residue. On the largest tool from the site, 5 cm long, a retouched quartz flake, was found plant residue. Another piece of quartz had step scarring and a residue of bone collagen, possibly a bone-scraping tool.

There is a definite hearth at the site, with a depression and hearth stones, so it was probably a ground oven rather than a warming-sleeping fire. Charcoal from this hearth dated to 16,000 BP. A piece of red ochre and a quartz core fragment were found near the hearth. The quartz core had blood and skin collagen on the edge, suggesting it was a butchering tool,

Another quartz bipolar has blood on it, but not on the working edge but on the side, just the spot where the user would have his thumb, and a missed blow would have hit it, 10 000 years ago, maybe evidence of a Neolithic industrial accident.

Bone Cave

This is 1 of 3 caves east of Acheron Cave, with oldest occupation levels of about 30,000 years ago, on rivers flowing to the southeast. It is in the Middle Weld Valley, at 400 m altitude.

This very small cave on the Weld River is of a vertical limestone type. The floor area is now about 9 m^2 with a height of 1 m. It was originally larger, but infilling has reduced the size. The oldest date, from charcoal at the base, is 29,000 BP. The cultural material in the top layer is 13,700 years old. After this time it was abandoned, the surface being covered with a layer of moon milk. In the small chamber, bone points, stone artefacts and burnt bone were found. An extremely rich deposit was excavated in a trench 2 x 0.5 x 1.5 m that contained more than 24,000 stone artefacts in the 0.8 m^3 extracted.

Human use appears to have been sporadic between about 29,000 and 24,000 years ago, the period of most intensive human use occurring after the glacial maximum, between about 16,000 and 14,000 years ago. The first thumbnail scrapers are found at about 24,000 years ago, becoming so common at about 18,000 BP that they make up a large proportion of the tools found from this time. Dated to sometime between 16,000 and 14,000 years ago, a single piece of Darwin glass has been found. Bone Cave is the occupation site that is the greatest known distance from Darwin Crater in which Darwin glass has been found, a direct line distance of 100 km, though the actual route followed between the 2 sites is much longer. (Jones 1989; Holdaway & Porch, 1996; Holdaway, 2004)

The most common material used for the manufacture of the stone tools is quartzite from the local area. The next most common are chert and quartz, and a small number of tools made from chalcedony, silcrete and hornfels. In the upper levels, dating from about 16,000 to 15,000 years ago, the percentage of quartz tools increases, as does the use of bipolar anvilling, which is the best method for fracturing the small water-rounded quartz pebbles. Large flakes made from quartzite and chert are common in all levels of the site. Many were steep-edged scrapers.

As at Kutikina, the red-necked wallaby is the most common prey species, and wombats are the next most common, but a wider variety of other prey was taken than at Kutikina.

The distribution of artefacts through time has been found to display 3 periods of occupation separated by long gaps over the time period from 35,000-10,000 BP. See Source 3.

A wallaby tibia bone was found that showed impact flaking along the crest made to extract the marrow, which is believed to be from the Holocene, less than 12,000 BP.

See also Stone Tools

Burkes Cave - Flaked Stone Assemblage Variation in Western New South Wales, Australia

A small section of creek terrace adjacent to Burkes Cave in the Scope Range, western New South Wales, was excavated by Harry Allen in 1970, which revealed a stratified deposit that was dated to about

2,000 BP by a single radiocarbon determination. An analysis of this stone artefact assemblage has not previously been fully published. In this paper the authors[1] describe the technological characteristics and composition of the stone artefact assemblage recovered from this important site and consider the similarities to and differences from other assemblages they have studied that were recovered from other sites in western New South Wales.

Burrill Lake Rock Shelter

Situated on the south coast of New South Wales, this large sandstone rock shelter was first occupied about 20,000 years ago. Examples of the Australian core tool and scraper tradition have been found at this site, such as horse-hoof cores. From about 5,000 years ago there is a change to the Australian small tool tradition, from this time backed blades have been found.

See Aboriginal Occupation of south central Tasmania

Cape Range Area, Western Coast Arid Zone, Western Australia

There are several sites on the western margin of the arid zone of Western Australian in the Cape Range area such as Jansz Cave, Mandu Mandu Creek Rock Shelter, C99 and Pilgonaman dating from about 35,000 BP (about 40,000 cal BP) (Morse, 1999; Przywolnik, 2005). Rare evidence has been found in these sites of the coastal life of the early settlers in the Pleistocene as a result of the rapid falling away of the coastal shelf in this area that meant that they were never more than 12 km from the coast, even at times of lowest sea level (Morse, 1988, 81). Stone artefacts representing a flake assemblage, with little retouch evident, is sparse in the earliest levels of these sites. Artefact dating to between 35,000 BP and 20,000 BP have been described, e.g. in Mandu Mandu (Morse, 1988, 43) (earlier dates than those published in 1988 are found in (Morse, 1993b) (about 39,600 - about 25,000 cal BP) as large flakes and flake pieces, of which only 5 are retouched. In the lowest levels of these sites faunal remains are poorly preserved, and fragmented marine molluscs, crabs, sea urchins and small arid zone marsupials have been found (Morse, 1988, 1999; Przywolnik, 2005, 190).

Cloggs Cave

This is a cave in a cliff near the Buchan - Orbost road in Victoria. There is a rock shelter outside the cave, the roof of which is blackened, apparently from the campfires of past inhabitants. A short passage leads to the inner chamber. This has a high cathedral-like roof and the floor is dry.

Excavation of the floor under the rock shelter showed that it had been used for tool making, and the basal layer was dated to the last 1000 years. Inside the cave excavations found that it was first inhabited by humans 17,000 BP. It was probably used occasionally, but not as a permanent campsite.

See Aboriginal Occupation of south central Tasmania

Colless Creek Rock Shelter

It is situated in Lawn Hill Gorge area. Traces of occupation more than 17,000 years old have been found on the Barkly Tableland in north-western Queensland. Colless Creek Rock Shelter is the only good rock shelter along 40 km of Colless Creek. It is deep and well-sheltered. The area, north-west of Mt Isa has spectacular gorges, permanent rivers and waterholes with plenty of fish, shellfish, Pandanus nuts and cycad palms.

The Colless Creek site is a very rich site, with an average density of 50,000 artefacts per cubic metre. There were 500,000 artefacts in the top cubic metre of the excavation. Occupation at Colless Creek goes back more than 17,550 years - the oldest date from shells on the site.

The conditions in the area of the site were considerably drier over the last 18,000 years than during the preceding phase. Human occupation is thought to extend back to about 30,000 BP, and possibly much further.

See Aboriginal Occupation of south central Tasmania

Cranebrook Terrace

This site is in the quarries near the Nepean River near Penrith, New South Wales. The original discovery at this site was a pebble chopper at the base of the gravels. Pumping of the site dropped the water table enough to allow investigation and bog-preserved logs were found. They were originally dated to 30,000 years ago. Later it was found that the logs had been contaminated by younger carbon in the ground water. The site has since been dated to between 43,000 and 47,000 years ago.

The Djadjiling archaeological site

The early settlement at this site records occupational intensity, when compared to a site such as Allen's Cave. At this site 664 artefacts have been recovered from the basal layers of the shelter as well as a small hearth, the artefacts are more than half of the total number of artefacts recovered from this site from the succeeding thousands of years of occupation at this site. This provides some indication of the patterns of settlement and the intensity of occupation from this time in the greater desert.

According to Law et *al.* the settlement of the arid zone during the Pleistocene is a prominent theme in archaeological research in Australia (Hiscock, 2008: 45-62; Hiscock & Wallis, 2004; Marwick, 2002a, 2002b; O'Connor et *al.*, 1998; Smith, 1987, 2005; Thorley, 1998; Veth, 1993, 1995, 2005). The inland region of the western arid zone in the Pilbara is of particular interest, which had in the past been believed to have been first occupied between about 26,000 and about 20,000 years ago (Brown, 1987: 27; Edwards & Murphy, 2003: 45; Maynard, 1980: 7). The region is suggested to have been occupied before $32,920\pm270$ BP (Slack et *al.* 2009: 34) by recent test excavations at Junkan-1 Rock shelter. This result is supported by the work of Law et *al.*, at Djadjiling Rock shelter as it demonstrates the presence of Aboriginals at the site at about 35,000 BP. This site is unique for its antiquity, and a large flaked stone assemblage has been recovered from the earliest occupation phase by excavations. Repeated early site use is demonstrated by evidence, and a sequence of occupation that was intermittent throughout the Pleistocene and Holocene. Law et *al.* present their preliminary findings in this paper.

Fern Cave

This is a large cave with 2 high-domed chambers, with an occupation site going back at least 26,000 years. There are a few heavily painted peckings on the wall adjacent to the excavation, that includes a series of loosely clustered pits, a star shape, and 3- to 4-? pronged motifs, resembling 'tridents' or bird tracks. These have been demonstrated to be similar to other peckings from Chillagoe, Mitchell-Palmer Region, Laura Region and Koolburra region, which are believed to be very old, based on the degree of patination and the nature of the superimpositions.

The lowest layer in this deposit has been dated to $26,010 \pm 410$ BP, but it is believed the deposit actually extends back to about 30,000 BP according to extrapolation based on the age-depth curve (David, 1991).

According to Laura Lamb her paper presents the results of a technological analysis of the assemblages from Test Pit 4 in Fern Cave in the south east of Cape York Peninsula. Investigation of David's 1991 claim that the stone artefact deposition rate at Fern Cave increased during the peak of the Last Glacial Maximum (LGM), about 20,890-17,200 BP was her specific aim in this study. Other claims made by David (1991), that deposition rates of other cultural components, such as mussel shell, remains of fauna, burnt earth, or ochre, were not investigated further in this study. More intense use of Fern Cave during the LGM was suggested by David (1991) to be the reason for the peak period of deposition and sedimentation.

Questioning of the use of artefact densities for the inference of site use intensity (Hiscock, 1981; Ross, 1985), their argument being that increased deposition rates may be the result of factors that are not related to the intensity of occupation of the site, such as changes in the processes of manufacture. They argue that because of this, an attempt should be made to determine the nature of the systems of lithic production by lithic analyses. This analysis has been designed by Lamb to test a number of issues associated with the increased production of flaked stone at Fern Cave. See Lamb, 1993.

Fern Cave is in Spring Tower, part of the limestone karst region of Chillagoe, north Queensland. There is permanent water, springs, within 2 km and 4 km of the cave (observations by Lamb; Robinson, 1982). Lamb suggests these springs may be important for understanding the occupation patterns of Fern Cave, as well as the Chillagoe region as a whole. The landscape where these water sources are located is at least 80 million years old (Willmot & Tresize, 1989). Lamb suggests this landscape appears to have been subjected to slow change during the human occupation of the continent, and the assumption that springs were in existence during the LGM seems reasonable to her (B. Bultitude, Queensland

Department of Minerals and Energy, pers. Com. To Lamb). The age of the springs was investigated by David et *al*.

David excavated Fern Cave over 2 field seasons, 1985 and 1989. The 1985 excavation was part of his Masters project (David, 1987). The aim of his research was to obtain a general sequence of occupation to ascertain temporal changes in 2 cultural phenomena, stone artefact characteristics and strategies of faunal exploitation in the Chillagoe region, the study becoming part of a broader regional archaeological project (David, 1987).

Fern Cave was included in David's doctoral research, because it contained engravings that were believed to date from the Late Pleistocene/Early Holocene period (B. David, pers. Comm. to Lamb). David obtained a radiocarbon date of 25,710 ± 400 BP on shells of land snails that were recovered from the 1985 excavation (Lab.no. Beta 30403). Later in 1985 the cave was re-excavated to find more evidence of the age of the occupation at the site. In 1989 David excavated 4 50x50 pits, one of which TP4) was analysed in this paper. According to Lamb there are 2 reasons for this analysis being restricted to TP4, there is a heavy encrustation of $CaCO_3$ on most of the material from the other excavated squares, and there were dates for material from other squares that were not encrusted in $CaCO_3$.

Stone Working Techniques

Strategies for the reduction of cores recovered from Fern Cave underwent changes over time, though the apparent rates of increases of deposition of stone artefacts cannot be said to result from these changes during the LGM. There are notable decreases in the bipolar technique use that is evident at this time and the evidence of core rotation also declines. It is implied by a decreased use of these reduction strategies at this time that people were actually obtaining fewer flakes per core in Phase 2 (about 20,890-17,200 BP) than in Phase 3 (about 25,710-20,890 BP), rather than more that would be necessary for them to contribute to the apparent increases in rates of deposition of stone artefacts in Phase 2. This trend was coincident with a shift in the procurement patterns of raw material, with the selection of chert increasing and quartzite decreasing from about 25,710-20,890 BP to about 20,890-17,200. Chert is available locally, being present within 3 km of the cave, while the nearest quartzite source is about 11 km away.

Aspects of Site Use

There is an increase in the proportions of artefacts that are heat treated from Phase 3 to Phase 2, and this trend is associated with an increase of flakes that were transversely snapped and flakes that exhibit edge damage (snap fractures). According to Lamb the increase in flake production, as well as the incidence of edge damage and snapping, was due to the effective tensile strength of homogeneous stone. When a flake snaps, transversely of otherwise, as a result of the flake being subjected to post-depositional forces, the archaeological record effectively contains 2 or more artefacts.

Core decortication, the initial stages of core reduction appear to have been carried out at Fern Cave during Phase 2. Previously, decortication was performed elsewhere. The steep increase in the number of flakes with cortex intact at that time, in spite of no significant change in the average or range of artefact sizes, is the strongest evidence for this view. It is implied by this that reduction behaviour changes and Fern Cave's position in the flaking systems' organisation may have contributed to the increase in the rates of stone artefact deposition at this site, especially when coupled with the possible effects of burning. Deposition rates still peak in Phase 2 even if heat-treated artefacts are eliminated from the sample. Increased rates of deposition of stone artefacts during Phase 2 are likely to be caused by other factors.

Significance Testing

When small sample sizes are used for tests of significance there is a tendency to obtain poor levels of statistical significance. Many of the results obtained using Fisher's Exact Test were not statistically significant. Statistically significant patterning is shown by only patterns of raw material (for statistical calculations see Lamb, 1993). Lamb draws some conclusions about site use trends that rely on 'substantive' trends, instead of statistically significant trends (D. Chant, Department of Education, University of Queensland, pers. Comm. to Lamb).

When an attribute or characteristic shows numerical variation between analytical units substantive trends exist. Until it is proven to be statistically significant any trend is substantive by virtue of quantitative variation. Lamb argues that it is valid to use substantive trends only when it is possible to demonstrate that a series of such trends has an association with each other and with a set of statistically significant trends. The result of this is that the interpretations and conclusions concerning aspects of site use are of a preliminary nature only.

According to Lamb substantive trends were used in this study with the proviso that in regards to Fern Cave more work needs to be carried out on the lithic assemblage.

Results – Discussion

During the peak of the LGM, about 20,890-17,200 BP, to local lithic resources from those that were relatively distant implies a size reduction of the catchment of raw materials, the size of the territory over which the inhabitants of the cave collected stone, and/or there was a reduction in the frequency of visits to the more remote parts of their country.

It is implied by the accompanying change is strategies of reduction that there was no shortage of resources or needing to be conserved as it appears the cores were reduced less in Phase 2. In Phase 2 chert was the predominant material being used, and there were large, exposed ridges from which the material could be collected relatively close to Fern Cave. Therefore by considering the increased use of chert and the accompanying change in reduction strategies, Lamb argues that the cave inhabitants increasingly used the abundant chert resources that are present near the cave at the height of the LGM, also suggesting that it may have been as a result of water being less easily obtained at that time.

A very small proportion of the lithic assemblage of each XU is made up by complete flakes in TP4. The XUs between radiocarbon dates were combined into 'dated phases', which were the basic analytical units used in this analysis, for the purpose of the analysis. This was done to increase the sample size of complete flakes, thereby making the observable trends suitable for significance testing. The trends that are finer-grained between XUs will not be observed, which is the limitation of this method (David?).

Ingaladdi Rock Shelter, Nimji

This rock shelter, west of Katherine in the Northern Territory, is situated around the large, permanent Ingaladdi waterhole, around which is a series of sandstone outcrops, and is the last in a series of permanent waterholes in the gorges along Price Creek. Past this point, to the east, the country becomes open and drier with black [soil?]. It is a large semicircular rock shelter in a weathered sandstone outcrop. The dark sandy floor, with stone artefacts on the surface, as well as ochre, it is situated within the Delamere Plains and Benches, on a sandy plain with hills to the north and south. The rock of the shelter is part of the Antrim Plateau Volcanics. More than 48 rock art sites have been found in the outcrops in this area.

This rock shelter provided the first firmly dated example of Aboriginal art. There are paintings on most of these outcrops, and on the back walls on some of the shelters are petroglyphs of animal tracks and human feet. There are also thousands of linear abraded grooves. In the 20th century similar grooves were made 80 km to the south of the rock shelter at Yiwarlarlay, as part of a rain-making ceremony. The ceremony was associated with the Lightning Brothers, multicoloured paintings of which are present at Yiwarlarlay.

Pieces of engraved rock were found on a 7,000 year old layer, and below a 5,000 year old layer. This gives the age they fell from the roof/wall, but a large bird track and parallel abraded grooves are common motifs from sites that are suspected to be from the Pleistocene.

The basal level of this site was dated to 6800 ± 270 by radiocarbon.

See Aboriginal Art - the Pilbara Engraved Stones

Jansz Cave, Cape Range Peninsula, Western Australia

At a small cave, Jansz Cave, just to the north of Mandu Mandu Creek Cave, on Cape Range Peninsula, located between Exmouth Gulf and the Indian Ocean, evidence has been found of people exploiting marine and terrestrial resources, Hunting kangaroos, turtles and fish and collecting emu eggs and shellfish at 40,000 BP[1]. This archaeological site, as well others such as Mandu Mandu shelter contains the oldest evidence known of marine subsistence in Australia, as part of a mixed economy that included Bandicoots, bettongs, and possums. In the base of the site there also are thylacine bones.

Jawoyn Country

According to David et *al.* there are a vast number of ancestral sites in the Jawoyn Country, with many located in extremely remote areas. As a result of their isolation many are in superb condition, and also because of the presence of art styles that are ancient, no longer being practised, and with no artefacts from the European contact period and no scenes that include Europeans at many of the art sites led the authors to believed many of the sites had not been occupied for hundreds or even thousands of years. There are also sites with known connections with ceremony and creation or Dreaming stories, and there are also art sites that include more recent depictions.

Up to the present there are 117 known site complexes that contain 921 sites and more than 44,000 individual artworks that have been recorded on the GIS database of the Jawoyn Association (e.g. Gunn et *al.*, 2010; Gunn & Whear, 2008). This paper presents the initial results of the excavation of the Nawarla Gabarnmang site, the first of 4 excavations that were carried out at the request of the Jawoyn Association.

The site was seen during a routine aerial survey of the Arnhem Land Plateau. The Jawoyn were enabled to learn the name of the site, which translates as 'place of hole in the rock', by anthropological work with senior Elders Wamud Namok and Jimmy Kalarriya, both of whom had visited the site as children. They had been told it was an important site where people camped on their way to ceremonies on Jawoyn Country, and also identified the Jawoyn clan Buyhmi as the relevant traditional site owner.

The ceiling of the site is formed of interleafed layers of sandstone and hard quartzite, each of which is of between 10 and 40 cm thick. Though poorly soluble, the compact bedrock has been subjected to strong chemical alteration between individual rock strata and along fissure lines, which resulted in dissolution of large parts of the site (Quinif, 2010). The hollowing of the site by the geochemical processes over a geologically long period of time has resulted in a grid-like matrix of cavities that are divided by remnant pillars, the cavities extending from floor to ceiling. There are accumulated sediments on the floor of the cavities and fragments of bedrock that have been exfoliated naturally and anthropologically. There is also evidence of past activity, and the pillars and flat surfaces of the ceiling have been extensively painted and quarried for stone artefacts.

In May 2010 work began on the archaeological excavations of the site, with 2 50 cm x 50 cm squares being excavated in an area of the floor that showed little or no disturbance of the surface (square A), as well as an area that was more open near the centre of the site (Square B). There is a lot of rock art near both these excavation squares. The squares were excavated in arbitrary excavation units (XUs) that followed the stratigraphy where it was visible.

Conclusion

David et al. concluded that at Nawarla Gabarnmang there is secure evidence of habitation at about 45,000 BP. Work is continuing on the levels that are earlier than 45,000 BP.

Jinmium Rock Shelter, Northern Territory 1,

The age of this site has been very controversial; the earliest dates not being accepted by most scientists.

In the Unit 1, lowest stratigraphical level, there were multi-platform quartzite cores, flakes, fragments, unifacially retouched flakes, and quartzite cobbles that had been used as pounding stones that still has starch residue on the working surfaces. (Fullagar et al., 1996).

A series of TL dates on quartz, 116,000* +/- 12,000 to 73,300 +/- 7,000. These are the earliest dates recorded for ochre. For a buried sandstone slab that has pecked cupules the earliest date is 58,000 +/- 6,900 BP & 75,000 +/- 7,000. All these dates are very controversial and are not accepted as accurate. Fullagar et a., (1996); sf, Roberts et al.,(1998); Watchman et al., (2001). 7 AMS dates on charcoal from the upper 2/3 of the deposit at Jinmium ranged from 1,1100? +/- 60 BP to 3,300 +/- 100 BP. A series of OSL dates from individual quartz grains from the deposit ranged from 300 +/- 30 BP to 22,000 +/- 1,200 BP. (Roberts et al., 1998). Among 16 AMS dates on oxalate in the crust covering cupules were 1,400 +/- 110 BP, and from 5,840 +/- 65 BP to 11,050 +/- 650 BP. The 11,000 BP date is considered inconsistent because the disparity "between the thickness of the crust and its age when compared with the other crusts in the Keep River region" (Watchman et al., 2000: 7). Watchman (2000); Watchman (2001).

Jinmium Rock Shelter, Northern Territory – Early Occupation of Northern Australia by Humans[4]

The Jinmium Rock Shelter is an archaeological site field code: Coornamu 1 or 'C1', NTMAG site number: 4767 0028) (129.2°E, 15.4°S) is located within 50 km of the mouth of the Keep River, in the north western corner of the Northern Territory.

The study area

This site that was excavated by Fullagar, Price and Head is situated on undulating sands gently sloping towards Coornamu Swamp and Sandy Creek, east of the Kimberley region between the Ord River and Victoria River. The region between the Ord River and the Victoria River is semiarid, with a warm, dry monsoonal climate that is characterised by a distinct wet season that occurs between December and April, and has an annual rainfall of 700-900 mm. The maximum daily temperature ranges from about 30°C to 35°C and a minimum between 20°C and 25°C (Stewart et *al.*, 1970).

The area of the Keep River is located within the Ord-Victoria geomorphic region, and is part of the Bonaparte Basin, and is younger than, and lies between, the Kimberley Basin to the west and the Victoria Basin to the east (Whitehead & Fahey, 1985). The area consists of estuarine deltaic plains, open woodlands and tall grass plains, with rugged sandstone hills and low hilly country. The 2 main stream systems in the area are the Keep River and Sandy Creek, both of which flow to the north into the Joseph Bonaparte Gulf. Included in 4 main Palaeozoic units are dolomites from the Lower Carboniferous (Burt Range Formation) and sandstone and conglomerate dating to the Upper Carboniferous, the Border Creek Formation, in which the Jinmium Rock Shelter formed. Surface occurrences on the Burt Range Formation include cryptocrystalline silica that is suitable for flaking, including cherts, silcrete and chalcedony. Quartz and quartzite are suitable for flaking, and several locations of prehistoric quarries have been documented by Fullagar, Price and Head.

The establishment of cattle stations in the Kimberley region on the 1880s marks the onset of European settlement history. Between 1909 and 1019 Legume Station began as an outstation of Carlton Hill. Stories that were documented (Shaw, 1981, 1986) indicate the Legume was an important location for Aboriginal law and the relations to land that were maintained throughout the pastoral period (see also Head, 1994b).

Archaeological work in the Kimberley and the Victoria River District that was previously reported suggests there were 2 distinct technological phases based on analyses of stone artefacts and an antiquity of at least 40,000 years (Bradshaw, 1986; Stokes, 1986; Dortch, 1972; 1997a; 1997b; David et al., 1990, 1991, 1994; Flood, 1970; Fullagar, 1995; Gregory, 1994; O'Connor, 1995). Thick notched flakes and adze flakes which marked the earlier technological phase is supplemented after the mid Holocene by a distinctive technology of making projectile points. There are 3 phases in the rock art styles that are recognised widely in the Kimberley to the north and west: a rock engraving tradition, which is suspected to be of at least Pleistocene age, as well as 2 main painting divisions: earlier Bradshaw figures and later Wandjina figures (Welch, 1993; Walsh, 1994). In this study Wandjina paintings have not been observed in the immediate area. Engravings and paintings have been recorded throughout the study area (McNickle, 1991) includes the Keep River region within the broader style of the Victoria River District where changing paintings styles have been documented (David et al., 1994) which have been related to changes in the signifying systems and land tenure the Late Holocene.

The Rock Shelter

According to a dreaming story the Jinmium site is connected to locations that have important economic and ceremonial resources such as swamp foods, ochre, stone and yams. Jinmium was a female ancestor-being who was once pursued by Djibigun, a male ancestor-being. A senior Gajerrong man and traditional custodian, and a senior Murinpatha woman and traditional custodian, have defined the area of the site, in terms of proximity to the main outcrop and sandstone stacks 20-40 m high. In the story Jinmium turned to stone at this location where Djibigun catches her and turns into a small bird, associated with 2 ochre sources that are nearby. Aboriginal camp sites, both prehistoric and historic, on the sandy ground are indicated by glass, stone and other artefacts that cover an area of more than 5 hectares.

The rock shelter C1 is formed by a large loose boulder with a sloping side embedded in the sand sheet within the Jinmium area, about 50 m from the main outcrop and sandstone stacks. It has many cup-shaped pits or cupules, some of which extend below ground level, several paintings, and a floor area of 24 m^2. Beginning in 1992, archaeological investigations to complement research into contemporary and historical resource management and relations to land were carried out (Head & Fullagar, 1991; O'Neil et al., 1993; Head, 1994a; 1994b). The specific objectives of the excavation can be summarised as the investigation of:

- The nature of Aboriginal camp sites associated with the pastoral industry (Head & Fullagar in press);

- The prehistory of Aboriginal landscapes (Fullagar & Head in press);

- And the role of stone artefacts in the gathering and processing of plant foods (Fullagar, 1993; Atchison, 1994).

Conclusion

To summarise, Fullagar et al. have presented evidence that humans had occupied northern Australia earlier than 116,000 ± 12,000 BP, with artistic activity that is inferred from ochre that dates from between 75,000 and 116,000 BP, and ground mudstone that dates from slightly later, and rock engravings dating to earlier than 58,000 BP. Fullagar et al. admit this scenario is highly controversial but needs to be further tested at this site as well as others. Fullagar et al. say the main reasons to support the TL ages in this paper are:

- The consistency of the stratigraphy of the TL ages;

- Young TL dates obtained from the top of the sequence, which suggests that the maximum error on the lower samples, if incomplete TL resetting was a problem, would be 2,000 years;
- In the younger parts of the deposit there is good correspondence between TL and radiocarbon ages;
- Archaeological integrity of the deposit, including trends in the density of different components.

Fullagar et *al.* say the only reasons to doubt the TL ages are the possibility of saprolite being contained in sample W1646 and foreshortened temperature plateaux on some, though not all samples. Fullagar et *al.* argued that the high temperature data from which the ages were calculated has not been affected by this foreshortening. They say that the ages cannot be easily dismissed, though also they cannot be accepted unequivocally.

In[3] the uppermost sediments seeds were noticeably weathered and below 40 cm the number declined, which indicated that this record was influenced more by factors of preservation than cultural processes (Atchison et *al.*, in prep.).

The Jinmium (C1) rock shelter excavations are at the base of an exposed sandstone boulder, and the sand sheet is located 10 m from the rock shelter (C1/IV). OSL and radiocarbon dating of the young sediments is supported by the seed and stone artefact chronology (Atchison et *al.*, in prep.), in spite of a disturbance or contamination (Roberts et *al.* 1998b). The published chronology of the sand sheet excavation (Fullagar et al., 1996) at Jinmium, unlike the rock shelter sediments, has never been revised. A TL age of about 76 ka BP at a depth of 6m was obtained for the sand sheet sediments between Jinmium and Goorurarmum (Ward, 2003; Ward et *al.*, 2005). Which lends support to the chronology determined by TL dating of (Fullagar et *al.*, 1996), which produced an age of 103 ± 14 ky BP at a depth of 5 m near the Jinmium site. It was noted by Fullagar et *al.*, (1996) that stone artefacts are present throughout the sand sheet deposit, though the initial presence of stone points, ochre and seed artefacts was dated to about 2.9 – 3.9 ky BP.

The extreme weathering that is characteristic of monsoonal climates in semi-arid areas will decrease the potential for preservation of artefacts and bias a record in a sedimentary sequence in favour of younger material. An example comes from excavations in the Jinmium Rock Shelter where in the uppermost sediments seeds were noticeably weathered and below 40 cm the number declined, which indicated that this record was influenced more by factors of preservation than cultural processes (Atchison et *al.*, in prep.). The lack of radiocarbon ages at depths greater than 150 cm in the Keep River region most likely is a reflection of *in situ* organic preservation resulting changes in the level of the water table.

* See Possible Global Ice Volume Changes and Geomagnetic Excursions and Earth Orbital Eccentricity

The Colonisation of Greater Australia in the Pleistocene - a Re-examination

Links

TESTS REVEAL TRUE AGE OF JINMIUM SITE

Optical and Radiocarbon dating at Jinmium rock shelter in northern Australia

Optical Dating of single and multiple grains of quartz from Jinmium rock shelter, Northern Australia: Part II, results and implications.

Juunkan-1

This is an ironstone rock shelter that faces south, approximately 25 m wide by 8 m deep, with a dripline (the lip of the shelter) about 8 m high. Features of the site are a higher collapsing chamber at the rear and an entrance area that is open and set at a slightly lower level and the 2 areas are separated by a lot of roof fall. The rear chamber has a floor that consists of soft sediment sloping down from the rear. Along the front of the site flaked stone material has been found, particularly in the western end of the shelter.

The first excavation at this site was a 1 x 1 m test pit in 2008 in the front chamber of the rock shelter. At 75 cm below the surface a solid roof fall or bedrock was encountered. There were 3 main layers that comprised the stratigraphy of the test pit: a topsoil of loose material above brown/grey sediment that was compacted containing many organic finds and below this a horizon of orange/brown material. At a depth of 40-50 cm there was a small lens of pink/white soft chalky material, and at the same depth were small charcoal lenses.

The results of 3 radiocarbon determinations show that the earliest evidence of discard at Juunkan-1 indicated that discard was occurring at a conventional radiocarbon date of 32,950 ± 270 BP (Beta 249759) at a depth of 60 cm. The accumulation of sediment and the discard of artefacts were very slow until a depth of 35 cm below the surface, which has been dated to 26,640 ± 160 BP (conventional radiocarbon age) (Beta-249758). From 35 cm below the surface it is proposed there was a generally more rapid rate of accumulation that extended to more recent times near the surface that has been dated to 760 ± 40 BP (conventional radiocarbon age) (Beta-249757) (740-760 ca. yr. BP).

From Juunkan-1 the total number of stone artefacts recovered was 32. Spits 1 and 2 (a spit is a unit of excavation in archaeology) contained the majority of these, and with only individual artefacts being recovered from lower spits. The oldest artefact recovered from this site was in spit 14, which was 70 cm deep, and below the layer that has been dated to 32,920 BP. All the flaked stone was recovered from the far south eastern corner of the test square. Slack et *al.* (2009) suggest it is likely that a greater assemblage size will be found with further planned extensions to the excavations.

As well as flaked stone there were 67 fragments of animal bone recovered from this site, 57 of which were identifiable. Among the species identified were bandicoot, kangaroo, wallaroo, native mouse, rat and 1 fragment of fish. With the exception of spit 9, animal bone from small to large species were recovered from most spits, with majority of bone being from medium-large species of macropod. The density of faunal remains is consistently small, apart from spit 12, where almost 50 % of the bone was found. All of the bone is highly fragmented and fragments of long bones accounting for 66 % of the bone that was recovered, followed by teeth (9 %).

A total of 9 bone fragments had been burned, of which 2 are calcined, which suggested they had been deposited in fire for longer periods of time. In addition to burning, taphonomic analyses have shown several specimens to have evidence of heavy mineralisation, which is potentially suggestive of greater time depth. The bone that has been recovered from Juunkan-1 unweathered, and has no post-depositional modifications on the surface that are obvious, which suggests an *in situ* deposition and rapid burial.

Activity of either humans or carnivores is suggested by the frequency of fragments of long bone shafts among the faunal assemblage. This assemblage is believed to have most likely been accumulated by humans as there are no animal gnaw marks on the surviving bones, together with evidence of burning from fire. It is difficult to draw conclusions concerning species utilisation changes and/or frequency diachronically. The extant faunal evidence, however, suggests both species and element frequencies remained constant throughout the spits that contained bone, showing no evidence of diachronic change. Also, spit 12, which associated with the oldest date (and possibly) with the oldest artefact, and it provides clearer evidence of early occupation.

Juunkan-2

This is a large cavernous rock shelter 50 m west of Juunkan-1. At this site there are 2 chambers that face to the south; a large western chamber that has very deep sediment and a roof that is at a cathedral-like height, and an eastern chamber that is lesser, smaller and largely not protected and with a floor of bare rock. The main chamber is 10 m wide and 10 m deep and its height at the dripline is 8 m. In the main chamber there are 3 general areas; in the western side, a scoured, rocky area there some plants where a hole in the roof has allowed some rain to enter, a main central area in which a large roof fall has resulted in the accumulation of extensive sediment, and at the eastern rear of the site, a raised area where bedrock is higher than in other areas, and where sediment accumulation is at its least.

A single 1 x 1 m test pit was excavated in 2008, as in the case of Juunkan-1. There were a total of 21, 5 cm spits excavated that concluded at about 1.05 m beneath the surface, where further excavation was prevented by large amounts of roof fall. Within the deposit were 5 stratigraphic units, which were largely related to changes in the weathering and minerals of the ironstone. There were 5 hearths recovered, and flaked stone at high frequency and animal bones were also recovered.

Dates of 470 ± 40 BP were determined for spits 2, 12 and 17 (Beta-247330) (540-490 cal. yr. BP), 16,160 ± 80 BP (Beta-247331) (19,490-19,080 ca. yr. BP) and 20,090 ±100 BP (Beta-247332). AMS techniques were used to obtain the lowest date of 20,090 BP and are derived from a depth of 85 cm beneath the surface. Neither the level of the lowest artefact nor a basal date for the site is represented by this date for the site. Slack et *al.* suggest the deposit at Juunkan-2 could be up to 0.5 m deeper than the excavations.

At this site 272 flaked stone artefacts were recovered from the test pit excavation. Spit 16 of the excavation was the only spit in which there were no artefacts, with spit 18 (at 90 cm depth) being the lowest recorded age determination of 20,090 BP. Unmodified flakes (95.2 %) dominate the assemblage, with a few flakes (4.4 %) and even few cores (0.4 %). The main raw materials used for the retouched artefacts are chert (n = 8), ironstone (n = 4).

The flaked stone assemblage was discarded at a low rate, though the rate remained steady throughout the occupation period, and then at spit 4, about 5,000 BP the discard rate increased fourfold. There doesn't appear to have been a hiatus in occupation or sedimentation at the site before, during or after the LGM, though it is limited by the sample size.

The assemblage is shown by the analysis of the richness and diversity of artefacts of raw material that the assemblage is comprised of 5 different stone types; ironstone, chert, quartz, chalcedony and siltstone. The assemblage was dominated by chert and quartz (55.9 % and 29 %), lesser amounts of ironstone (13.6 %), chalcedony (1.1 %) and siltstone (0.4 %). Slack et *al.* point out that it is interesting that in the lower spits ironstone is as dominant a raw material as chert and quartz until the massive increase in discard rates that occurred from about 5,000 BP onwards. At about 19,000 BP in spit 14 the first retouch in the assemblage is encountered, sharply peaking at about 7,000 BP in spit 5, the time at which the first evidence of backing is found.

Dominance of complete flakes (81.9 %) (n = 222), is shown by the fragmentation rate of flakes, with much lower quantities of broken flakes – distal account for 7.7 % (n = 2), proximal for 5.2 % (n = 14) and medial for 4.1 % (n = 11). Until split 3 at about 4,000 BP the ratio of broken to unbroken flakes is very low by which time the complete flakes account for 65.2 % (n = 43) and broken flakes account for 34.8 % (n = 23). Slack et *al* suggest it is probably the result of treadage, with the proposal that the shelter was used more intensively at this time during the Mid-Holocene El Niño arid phase that was experienced in Northern Australia.

Ironstone flakes dominated the assemblage until the Middle Holocene. According to Slack et al. these flakes were generally heavier and had a greater size range, especially between about 15,000 and 5,000 BP. Chert is the dominant raw material after 5,000 BP, with an average weight of the flakes much less than 1 g. It is generally the case that retouched flakes are heavier than unmodified flakes, and with ironstone the retouched flakes are generally significantly heavier.

Analysis of the amount of cortical surface remaining on the dorsal surface of the flake is said by Slack et *al.* to further support the relationships between the size of complete flakes and extent of their reduction. It is shown by this analysis that ironstone flakes are much more likely than chert to have more cortex, an indication that ironstone flakes have been reduced less than chert flakes. Also, chert and quartz flakes are much more likely than ironstone flakes to have smaller, more reduced platforms, as is evidenced by single and multiple flake scar platforms.

As well as the flaked stone, 857 animal bone fragments were found in the Juunkan-2 site, from a wide variety of species. There were small species such as native rats/mice, lizards and snakes, that made up the majority of the species recovered (61 %, NISP = 523). Medium-large macropods, kangaroos and wallabies, made up 30 % (NISP = 255), and the remainder of the assemblage comprised bird and fish fragments. Among the species identified are red kangaroo, common wallaroo, bandicoot, possum, pygmy possum, echidna, bettong, native mouse, rat, gecko, skink, small bird and fish, the bone fragments being recovered from almost all spits.

In the assemblage all the major skeletal elements are represented, and the fragments of long bone shafts contribute the highest number of fragments (NISP = 120). There are however, differences in the frequency of elements between the smaller and larger species. Limb bones dominate elements from the smaller species and they are largely unfragmented, a large proportion being of complete skeletal elements. The teeth are most frequently occurring with vertebra being the next most frequent. Contrasting with this, bones from medium-large individuals are highly fragmented and there is a heavy weighting towards fragments of the long bone shaft. The relative paucity of lower limb elements of macropods can probably be accounted for by the fragments of long bone shafts. Teeth from macropods that are medium-large display a mixture of tooth wear stages which range from unworn to extremely worn suggests a mixture of young and old individuals.

Evidence of burning is displayed by 7 % (NISP = 61) of the assemblage, of which 1/3 have been calcined, which suggests they were deposited in fire for longer periods of time following defleshing. The burned bones are from a range of species, and were not confined to any single class of individual. As well as burning, evidence of tooth marks are present on 5 specimens, and 5 fragments recovered from spit 15 show possible cut marks, including the sacrum, pelvis and fragments of long bones of a kangaroo. The faunal assemblage has been shown by taphonomic analysis to represent a deposit that is *in situ* with rapid burials, because the bones are not weathered and the surfaces of the bones show no physical evidence of either aeolian or fluvial transport.

Slack et *al*. (2009) suggest faunal analysis at Juunkan-2 may provide important diachronic information about subsistence strategies in the region. Medium macropods, wallaroos, were more common at the beginning of the occupation, and towards the end of the occupation the large macropod (kangaroos) frequency increased, though the majority of species and distributions of skeletal elements appear to have remained consistent over time. As burned and calcined bone, when considered in conjunction of the evidence of hearths, suggests that people were responsible for some of the faunal accumulation, the presence of macropods is therefore considered to probably be a cultural accumulation rather than a natural accumulation. A primary human role in the accumulation is further suggested by the heavy fragmentation of the lower limb bones of macropods, as well as possible cut marks. Yet further evidence that people were involved in the accumulation of bone is the presence of bone from species that are less common such as echidna and fish. It is rare to find preserved faunal remains in rock shelters, and it is suggested that further faunal analysis could potentially contribute significant information with regard to the exploitation of species in the Pilbara for which there is severe shortage of published data.

Kakadu, Occupation Sites, Along the Base of the Cliffs

Rock shelters have been found at the base of the escarpment at Kakadu, 8 of which contain evidence of occupation dating from the Late Pleistocene. The occupants of these rock shelters occupied the upland valleys and escarpments during the wet season, and then in the dry season they dispersed over the plains where they lived and hunted, just as their descendants living there did in the recent past. Being adapted to the local environment the ancient population used it intensively, and as part of their subsistence activities, burned the country as vegetation was cleared and the plains below were filled by sand washing from the cliffs. In the cooler, drier climate the bush was thinned as a result of the frequent burning.

Large numbers of stone tools have been recovered from the caves and outliers across the escarpment. At Nauwalabila more than 30,000 flakes have been found at a density of 12,000 flakes per m^3. Sequential occupation periods have been revealed by the deposition, with seasonal settlement and seasonal religious relationships with favoured locations being suggested across the millennia by pulses of stone artefacts and charcoal. Quartz and chert were used by the inhabitants of these caves to make woodworking tools and the preparation of food, and they brought volcanic rocks to the caves for grinding stone axes. Chips from ancient axes, dated to 30,000 BP, have been recovered from Nauwalabila, and other ground-stone axes, that are more than 20,000 years old, have been found at other sites along the escarpment. At Nawarla Gabarnmang, western Arnhem Land, a fragment of a ground-edge axe was found dating to at least 35,400 BP, making it the earliest-known ground stone axe in the world, in other parts of the world the earliest known axes of this type have been found in the Neolithic of Europe dating to about 25,000 BP. These tools were used for felling trees and serious wood working activities, their invention and use in Australia being a technological revolution.

Ochre was also being ground on mobile grindstones and in cupolas in the sandstone of the bedrock by the inhabitants of Arnhem Land. Indirect signs of the artistic temperament of these people have been found by their use of ochre crayons 20,000-30,000 years ago. A canvas for their artistic expression were the escarpments of Arnhem land where there are thousands of galleries, art being found in every cavity, recess, shelter and cavern. Up to the time of publishing of Cane's book more than 6,000 galleries have been recorded, though the total has yet to be counted. So far 923 galleries have been counted in Western Arnhem Land, with more than 44,000 individual art works being found. Compared with this the Palaeolithic art 'revolution' in Western Europe is comprised of 275 sites with a bit over 10,000 individual representations.

Kenniff Cave

This cave is situated in Carnarvon National Park, Queensland, a tableland of low relief that is dissected by steep-sided valleys in the Central Queensland Highlands. It is 700 m above sea level near the crest of the Great Dividing Range. The region of sandstone cliffs and gorges is rugged, with timbered hills and grassy plains. The cave is in Lethbridge Pocket, a sheltered valley, above Meteor Creek. Near the base of the Lower Jurassic sandstone cliffs are formed by the sides of the gorges, the Tertiary basalts that overlie these form a second, higher cliff. Outcrops of 'grey billy' silcrete are present at a number of places throughout the highlands (Finlayson & Webb, in press) in discontinuous layers up to 3 m thick at the top of sandstone that lies immediately beneath the basalt.

Ochre pieces that showed signs of use, scratched, smoothed and with longitudinal grooves were found, but according to Mulvaney & Joyce (1965:202) "*no utilised fragments were found below 4 feet*" dated to 4,000 BP (4,130 +/- 90 BP; GaK 523). The earliest date obtained at the site was $16,130 \pm 140$ BP (NPL 68) (Mulvaney & Joyce, 1965; Mulvaney, 1975).

Kenniff Cave is located on the south bank of Meteor Creek, in a sandstone cliff (fig. 1, Webb & Domanski, 2008). Silcrete is present beneath the ridge capping of basalt, and silcrete scree has choked part of Meteor Creek near the cave (Mulvaney & Joyce, 1965). There is a silcrete quarry a few metres from the cave.

The Kenniff Cave silcrete is uniform and light grey, with conchoidal fracture surfaces, fine-grained, grain-supported, consisting of sub-rounded to angular fine-sand-sized quartz clasts that are well-sorted. They have been cemented by syntaxial overgrowths and chalcedony in very thin layers around small voids (Table 1, Fig. 2 (B), Source 3), and microcrystalline matrix of quartz is virtually absent. The fine-grained silcrete at Kenniff Cave is considered to be high quality material that is relatively easy to flake by percussion knapping, that is indicated by the low fracture toughness (median 48 MPa.mm$^{1/2}$), that is comparable to Australian flint (median 58 MPa.mm$^{1/2}$), and Tibooburra microcrystalline silcrete (median 65 MPa.mm$^{1/2}$), (Table 3, Webb & Domanski, 2008). Kenniff Cave silcrete that is not weathered has a moderate compressive strength, a moderate index of stiffness, and a tensile strength that is considered low, the weathered material has much lower values of all these mechanical properties. The Kenniff Cave silcrete has compressive strength, index of stiffness and tensile strength values that are lower than those of Australian flint and Tibooburra microcrystalline silcrete, though they are much higher than those of medium-grained silcretes found in Australia (Table 2, Webb & Domanski, 2008). Webb & Domanski (2008) suggest these factors indicate that Kenniff Cave silcrete has enough compression-bending stiffness to maintain the directional stability of fracture propagation. They suggest that during fine retouching there would be a low frequency of step fracture terminations, the small number and size (0.5 mm) of the largest quartz clasts having little effect on the fracture direction.

A 3-part cultural history was revealed by Mulvaney's excavation of Kenniff Cave (Morwood, 1981, 1984). The core tool and scraper industry, all of which were varieties of flake scrapers, was the earliest phase found. In the mid-Holocene, the appearance of the small tool industry was a time of proliferation of micro-blade technology and backed artefacts, pirri points, elouras, tula and burren adzes. The recent industry was characterised by the Juan knife, though a number of tool types such as backed artefacts, dropped out of the assemblage.

Throughout the sequence at Kenniff Cave the predominant material used was fine-grained silcrete, referred to as quartzite (Mulvaney & Joyce, 1965) because of its high quality, as well as its close proximity. This lithology is suited to the manufacture of blade scrapers, which are commonly found in the early industry, as well as the blade-based implements from the mid-Holocene assemblages, including tools requiring delicate backing or semi-invasive retouching, as is shown by the mechanical properties of this rock type. The lithology that was used was not affected by the changes that occurred, technological and typological, in the cave deposits, because the versatility of the locally available high quality fine-grained silcrete was sufficient for the manufacture of both flake scrapers and blades/micro-blades.

Koolan Shelter 2

This site is located on a small offshore island, dating from at least 27,300 BP. The age of the first occupation of the site has been estimated to be about 30,000 BP. At this time there was relatively high sea level, which meant the sea would have been close to the shelter. The site shows a heavy dependence on seafood. Among them the mangrove clam shell ***Geloina coaxans***, were very common at this site. There was also pearl shell (***Pincruda sp.***) that occurred in late Pleistocene levels. A ***Geloina*** shell from here has been dated to at least 26,500 ± 1,050 BP. The site was 20 km from the coast. The presence of these shells is considered as evidence of long distance exchange or transport during the late Pleistocene (O'Connor, 1999).

Koolan Shelter 2 was abandoned by about 24,600 BP, probably as a result of increasing aridity, as the sea level dropped and the coast retreated about 220 km. The island became a peak in an inland range in the arid west Kimberley. People re-occupied the shelter about 10,400 BP, when the sea had returned, making the peak an island once more. The inhabitants seem to have followed the shore line as it moved towards the mainland and retreated again.

Kulpi Mara

There are Pleistocene sequences at this site. This is one of the 3 known Pleistocene sites in Central Australia. The sedimentation history and phases of occupation at the rock shelter have been clarified by the combination of 7 new radiocarbon dates and 4 dates that were obtained earlier. A number of pulses of occupation have been shown by the sequence with the earliest being between about 34,178 and 29,102 BP, and there were intermediate pulses when there was little use of the site, which contrasts with the use of the Puritjarra rock shelter, 165 km to the west, where the occupation was more or less continuous. It is suggested by these differences that intraregional variability of both the geomorphic settings and the occupational histories of sites from the Pleistocene and Holocene in central Australia and the Western Desert can be expected.

Optical Dating of Grave-Infill of Human Burials, Lake Mungo, Australia

Age constraints on Mungo I and III, the oldest human remains found in Australia to date, from Lake Mungo, western New South Wales, were based on the optical dating of sand from the same stratigraphic units as those which the remains had been inserted into, 42±3 ka, and the overlying sand, 38±2 ka, gave the age of burial as 40±2 ka. As the original site where the burials were found had been eroded away it was necessary to date the burials by this indirect method. When Mungo III was originally excavated blocks of grave infill sediment were collected for sediment fabric analysis which entailed impregnating the blocks of sediment with polyester resin, after which the blocks were sectioned for analysis, the remaining blocks being stored in a cupboard for the next 30 years. In this study (Olly et al., 2006) optically dated single quartz grains they extracted from the centre of one of the blocks of sediment and these grains were found to display a wide distribution of equivalent doses ranging from 0.0±0.3 to 43.7±8.3 Gy, indicating that light has not been excluded from all grains following excavation. According to Olley et al. their study has shown that the population of grains with the maximum equivalent doses indicate an age consistent with that of the previous study, which indicates that at least some of the grains have remained light-safe. (Olly et al., 2006) used linearly modulated optically stimulated luminescence to identify single grains that had remained light-safe, and these were found to have an age of 41±4 ka, representing a direct optical age for the grave-infill, consistent with the ages arrived at by the previous study of the same stratigraphic unit as that which contained the burial. Olley et al. suggest these results demonstrate the potential of the application of optical dating of archived samples of sediment that were not stored in a light-safe environment.

Continuity and Antiquity (R.M. & C.H.Berndt, 1964; Flood, 2004; Habgood & Franklin, 2008)

Evidence for the continuity and great antiquity of Aboriginal culture has been found at Lake Mungo and Malakunanja II rock shelter, 2 of the oldest known archaeological sites in Australia to contain evidence of Aboriginal occupation. The skeleton of a man buried at

Lake Mungo (LM3 or WLH 3) (either 40,000 or 60,000 years ago, depending whose numbers you believe) had his hands on his groin and had been covered with red ochre. Both the sprinkling of red ochre over the body as part of a mortuary ritual, and the apparent clasping of the penis at burial, were still being practiced at various places around Australia at the time of first European contact. The use of red ochre at both Lake Mungo and Malakunanja II, thousands of kilometres apart, though possibly of similar antiquity, indicate that long-distance trade routes were operating even at that remote time. At both sites the nearest deposits of red ochre was some distance away.

Another indication of the antiquity of the Aboriginal material culture was the presence of osteoarthritis in the right elbow of LM3 (WLH 3), a condition called woomera elbow or atlatl elbow, found only in the elbow of the spear-throwing arm of men using spear throwers. Their implements evolved over time, but the spear thrower was one tool that stood the test of time, still being used up to the present, though even it evolved. In parts of the interior where desert oak, a very hard wood, was used to make implements, the woomera became a multipurpose tool, a stone flake being fastened to the end so it doubled-up as a wood-working tool.

Lake Mungo – Evidence for Seed Grinding in the Pleistocene[27]

Archaeological sites at Lake Mungo, south western New South Wales, have often produced grinding stones and fragments, the function of which has been inferred mostly on the basis of grindstone morphology. The antiquity of the grinding of grass seed has been of particular interest, usually being associated with large sandstone dishes that are deeply grooved. Previously no compelling evidence of seed grinding before the Pleistocene/Holocene boundary has been found in studies of grinding stones from this region. One of the problems associated with previous studies of grindstones in this area has been that the grinding stones have been found on deflated surfaces making it difficult to determine their provenance and date. In this paper Fullagar et *al.* report a functional study of 17 sandstone artefacts that had been collected from the central part of the Mungo lunette and a suite of OSL ages have provided bracketing age estimates for the stratigraphic units. Of the artefacts tested 10 were attributed to Unit E that was deposited between about 25 ka and 14 ka, and 4 were attributed to Unit F, which was deposited about 8 ka. There are 3 artefacts from the Golgol lag for which the ages are not known. Use-wear indicates it is likely seeds were ground on 14 of the artefacts; the use-related residues include starch, cellulose and collagen. Fullagar et *al.* suggest the results of this study provide additional evidence for plant processing and seed grinding activities in Sahul during the Pleistocene.

Lake Mungo is a dry lake in semiarid south eastern Australia (Fullagar et *al.*, 2015: Fig.1) where archaeological investigations have identified some of the oldest burials, faunal remains, hearths, ochre, flaked artefacts and grinding stones that have been found in Sahul (Pleistocene Australia-New Guinea) (Bowdler et *al.*, 2003; Mulvaney & Bowler, 1981). In Sahul grinding stones were used for many functions, such as the production of ground-edge axes and hatchets; as well as for the processing of bone, shell, ochre, small animals, medicines, drugs, poisons and many other materials, as has been witnessed ethnographically (see Gott, 2002). The antiquity of the grinding technology, the emergence of seed grinding activities, and correlations with climate change with the consequent shifts in the availability of resources, have been key problems in the prehistory of Sahul. Cuddie Springs, in semiarid south eastern Sahul is the only site from which secure evidence for the processing and grinding of specific plant foods, such as tubers and seeds, in a Pleistocene context has been reported (Fullagar et *al.*, 2008).

Fullagar et *al.* present in this paper the results of a functional study of 17 sandstone artefacts, which included 8 refitted fragments, LMGS2-9, all of which had been collected from the central part of the Mungo lunette. Bracketing age estimates for the strata in this part of the lunette (Fitzsimmons et *al.*, 2014) has been provided by OSL (optically stimulated luminescence), thereby providing approximate ages for the associated artefacts from the late Pleistocene, which included fragments of grinding stones which have been documented within the mapped region (Fullagar et *al.*, 2015: Figs. 1 & 2; Fitzsimmons et *al.*, 2014; Stern et *al.*, 2013).

The ethnographic evidence and the archaeological significance of grinding stones in the local and regional Aboriginal economies have been described (Allen, 1974). According to Fullagar et *al.* there is a great deal of ethnographic evidence for the processing of grass seeds, which have been identified as a major subsistence base in arid regions of mainland Australia (Tindale, 1977). The archaeological significance and distinct morphologies of implements for grinding seeds in Central Australia, particularly the large dished millstones and mullers that were used for the processing of seeds have also been documented (Smith, 1985, 1989). Though when dealing with small fragments of grinding stones, which are the most common form that are recovered in archaeological contexts, it is not always possible to extrapolate the original shape or size of a grinding stone on the basis of morphology.

Also, Fullagar et *al.* say there is no evidence that suggests the grinding stones that were used in the Pleistocene are necessarily of the same morphology as those that have been ethnographically documented in Central Australia. Use-wear traces associated with residues are the best indicators of the function of an artefact.

Fullagar et *al.* say the aim of the study presented in this paper was to reassess seed grinding at Lake Mungo by adopting an integrated approach to the analysis of use-wear, optically and biochemically visible residues and microscopic technological features of sandstone artefacts that are associated with dated contexts.

Conclusion

A multidisciplinary study of Lake Mungo grindstones presented here has demonstrated that interpretable wear traces and residues are preserved on small ground stone fragments that were recovered from exposed surfaces of stratified, eroding landforms in semiarid Australia. The original morphologies of the grindstones are difficult to reconstruct from small fragments, but include concave, convex, facetted and flat surfaces, with many bearing similarities with ethnographic implements for seed grinding from Central Australia. The use-wear of 14 of the 17 artefacts recovered is consistent with the results obtained from experiments and ethnographic data indicating seed grinding (Fullagar et *al.*, 2015: Fig. 5). According to Fullagar et *al.* all the pieces of sandstone that were examined almost certainly derive from larger broken grinding stones that must have been carried into this landscape. Of the specimens studied 1 has wear that is poorly developed with uncertain function (LMGS12); 1 specimen (LMGS13) has no distinct use-wear; and 1 specimen (LMGS11) has evidence of plant processing, though not necessarily including seeds. Residues could be derived from use, though they were recovered in low abundance. Fullagar et *al.* suggest the poor residue recovery is probably the result of poor preservation after erosion from the depositional matrix. Fullagar et *al.* suggest variation in the observations of residue may in part be attributable to the difference between worked surface areas sampled by the researchers and methodical approaches. The majority of plant and animal tissues that were recovered have not been identified with taxonomic precision.

Compelling evidence from the results of this integrated approach to functional analysis has been provided that 14 of the 17 grinding stone fragments that were used in the processing of seeds. Multiple functions for at least 3 artefacts is suggested by the presence of other plant tissue and animal residues that include collagen. A precise provenance has been determined for only 1 of the grinding stones, though all can be linked directly with particular strata in the central Mungo lunette. Combined with the chronological sequences that have been established for units within the lunette (Fitzsimmons et al., 2014; Stern et al., 2013) the recent geomorphological study has provided strong evidence of a Pleistocene context (25-14 ka) for the fragments of grinding stones from Lake Mungo. Further support for the theoretical argument that the development of seed grinding may be linked with environmental stress that was associated with the LGM is provided by the use-wear and the residue traces indicating that seed grinding occurred during the Pleistocene at Lake Mungo (Edwards & O'Connell, 1995; Fullagar & Field, 1997: 302).

Fullagar, R., E. Hayes, B. Stephenson, J. Field, C. Matheson, N. Stern and K. Fitzsimmons (2015). "Evidence for Pleistocene seed grinding at Lake Mungo, south-eastern Australia." <u>Archaeology in Oceania</u> **50**: 3-19.

Malakunanja II (Madjedbebe) site in Arnhem Land associated with early colonisation

This is a shallow sandstone rock shelter near Ngarradji Warde Djobkeng and Ja Ja Billabong, south of Malangangerr. It has faded paintings on its overhanging walls. The first excavation found charcoal dating to 18,000 years ago. Associated with the charcoal were a grinding hollow and 2 flattish mortars, one of which had clear traces of ochre. There are many burials in this rock shelter.

Later excavations in the 1980s established Malakunanja as the oldest dated site in Australia. The first signs of human occupation appear 2.6 m below the surface. The layers showing signs of human occupation were TL dated to between 61,000 and 52,000 years ago. Humans apparently appeared abruptly dated to 61,000 +9,000/-13,000 BP. The sand below this layer was devoid of any signs of human activity. From a depth of 2.5-2.3 m there was dense occupation, from between 52,000 +7,000/-11,000 BP and 45,000 +6,000/-9,000 BP. More than 1,500 artefacts were found in the lowest occupation layer.

Artefacts included those made from silcrete, quartzite and white quartz, a grindstone, pieces of dolerite and ground haematite, chlorite and mica and red and yellow ochre. The researchers allowed for the earliest occupants to have trodden artefacts into the soft sand of the floor, putting the first occupation of the site at a conservative time of 52,000 years BP. Below the earliest occupation there was 2 m of sand that had been deposited gradually over a period of 110,000 years.

The presence of high grade haematite in this deposit indicates that long distance exchange or transport took place during the Pleistocene, as the nearest known possible sources for the haematite are long distances from the site (Jones & Johnson, 1985b; Jones & Negerevich, 1985; Chaloupka, 1993).

See Stone Tools

According to Roberts et *al.* (1994) the date of the first arrival of humans on the Australian continent has important implications for the debate on human origins. Later evidence for the timing of the entry of humans into Australia was provided by the optical dating of unburnt quartzose sediments from Nauwalabila I, Lindner Site in

Deaf Adder Gorge, and 70 km to the south of Malakunanja II. Optical dates were obtained from several stratigraphic levels in an excavation that was 3 m deep where flaked stone artefacts and ground pigments were found in a primary depositional setting. Dates of 53.4 ± 5.4 ka and 60.3 ± 6.7 ka bracket the lowest human occupation levels, and that there is good agreement between optical and ^{14}C age estimates has been demonstrated by the upper levels. Associated directly with the 53 ka level is a high quality haematite with ground facets and striations that indicate the earliest Aboriginals were already using pigments. Roberts et al. (1994) suggest evidence for the colonisation of northern Australia a short time after 60 ka should be seen in the context of this region being the likely entry route of the first human movement into Sahul.

Archaeology, chronology and stratigraphy[4]

As well as having been dated to more than 50 ka BP Malakunanja II in northern Australia also contains the largest assemblage of stone artefacts and other important archaeological components of any site known in Sahul, and these have never been described in detail, which has led to doubts about the stratigraphic integrity of the site. In this paper Clarkson et al. report their recent analysis of the stone artefacts and faunal and other materials that have been recovered from the site during the excavations in 1989, as well as the stratigraphy and history of deposition that was recorded by the original excavators. This study has demonstrated that the technology and raw materials of the early assemblage are distinctive from those recovered from the upper layers. In the early assemblage silcrete and quartzite are common raw materials, and there are also fragments of an edge-ground axe and ground haematite. The lower stone assemblage, which comprised a mix of long convergent flakes, some radial flakes that had platforms that were faceted, and many small thin flakes of silcrete that Clarkson et al. interpreted as thinning flakes. Occasional grinding of haematite and woodworking are indicated by residue and use-wear analysis, as well as frequent abrading of the edges of platforms on thinning flakes. This study led to the conclusion that there may have been a degree of overstatement in previous claims of displacement of artefacts being extensive and post-deposition disturbance. The earlier claims of human occupation 50-60 ka BP are supported by the stone artefacts and the stratigraphic details, and also showed that human occupation at this time differed from occupation in later periods. In this study Clarkson et *al.* discuss the implications of these new data for understanding the earliest colonisation of Sahul by humans.

Madjedbebe (MJB), or Malakunanja II, its previous name, has attracted much attention as a result of its claims of early human occupation at the site between 50 and 60 ka BP (Roberts et *al.*, 1990a). The scientific significance of the site was established by previous work at the site, especially in connection with an understanding of the timing of human colonisation of Sahul. A dense lower cultural assemblage, which includes evidence of early complex technological, subsistence and artistic behaviours, which has implications for understanding the economic and symbolic dimensions of the earliest societies to occupy Sahul. Thermoluminescence (TL) and Optically Stimulated Luminescence (OSL) ages of 52 ± 11 and 61 ± 13 ka BP brackets the lowest artefacts in the MJB site (Roberts et *al.*, 1990a). At Nauwalabila, a nearby site, similar OSL ages were found to bracket the ages of the lowest artefacts at between 53 ± 5 and 60.3 ± 6 ka BP (Roberts et *al.*, 1994; Bird et *al.*, 2002). Potentially, both of these sites predate Lake Mungo, Devil's Lair, Nawarla Gabarnmang, Riwi, Lake Menindee Lunette, and Carpenter's Gap 2 by 5-15 krs (Bowler & Price, 1998; Roberts et *al*, 1998; Balme, 2000; Turney et *al.*, 2001; Bowler et *al.*, 2003; O'Conner & Veth, 2005; Cupper and Duncan, 2006), which therefore increases substantially the period of human occupation.

Clarkson et *al.* refer to Sahul as a geographic terminus for migrating modern humans as they moved out of Africa along the southern arc through south and South East Asia. Modern genetic analyses also supports such a dispersal (Huoponen et *al.*, 2001; Macaulay et *al.*, 2005; Liu et *al.*, 2006; Sun et *al.*,2006; Friedlaender et *al.*, 2007; Hudjashov et *al.*, 2007; Oppenheimer, 2009, 2012; Rasmussen et *al.*, 2011), as well as remains of anatomically modern humans that have been recovered from sites such as Liu Jiung (Liujiang) in China, with an estimated age of 65 ka BP, in Laos at Tam Pa Ling, 46-63 ka BP, Borneo at Niah Cave, 40 ka BP, and in Australia, Lake Mungo, 40 ka BP; Shen et *al.*, 2002; Barker et *al.*, 2007; Demeter et *al.*, 2012; Veth & O'Connor, 2013). The possibility of contact and gene flow has been raised by an archaic species on Flores (Brown et *al.*, 2004), and an unidentified species of ***Homo*** in the Philippines (Mijares et *al.*, 2010) species of humans), as well as a modern human presence that was potentially sparse and patchy in the region before the colonisation of Sahul.

It is suggested by early dates for colonisation that before modern humans colonised Europe they had reached the end of the southern dispersal route, which means that the European Upper Palaeolithic would have had little to do with understanding on the development of modern technology and symbolic expression in South and South East Asia and Oceania (e.g. Brumm & Moore, 2005; Habgood & Franklin, 2008; Davidson, 2010; Langley et *al.*, 2011). The period of contact between humans and megafauna in Sahul would also have been lengthened substantially by a 'long' chronology for Sahul (cf. O'Connell & Allen, 2004) of 50-60 kyr, which would require further consideration of the nature of this interaction and role of predation versus climate change in leading to their demise.

An opportunity to examine closely the nature of the lithic technology that was employed by early colonists would also be made available by a colonisation date of 50-60 ka BP. It has been argued by Mellars and colleagues (Mellars, 2006; Mellars et *al.*, 2013) that modern humans left Africa with microlithic technology, artistic conventions, and bead-making technologies that were similar to those present in eastern and southern Africa after 60 Ka BP. In sites that have been dated to more than 40 ka BP there is, however, little evidence for this along likely dispersal routes between Africa and Sahul. There is another possibility, that when modern humans left Africa they had technology that was from the African Middle Stone Age (MSA), which included prepared core technology and projectile points, and that this technology is antecedent to those technologies that have been found in Southern Asia and Sahul (Clarkson et *al.*, 2012; Clarkson, 2014). The assemblage at MJB is suggested by Clarkson et *al.* to be ideal to investigate the nature of the earliest stone technologies in Australia, given the high density of artefacts and the presence of a stone technology that was hitherto not documented in the earliest occupation period in Sahul.

According to Clarkson et *al.* no detailed report or stratigraphy or assemblage at MJB has ever been published, in spite of the significance of MJB for addressing questions of chronology, origins of modern humans, and early complex behaviour. As a result of this there have been persistent concerns regarding the chronology of human occupation at the site and the extent of any post-deposition disturbance and movement of artefacts that may have obscured patterns of cultural change. In this paper Clarkson et *al.* address some of these concerns with a detailed examination of evidence, published as well as unpublished. The specific questions addressed by this paper are:

The chronology of the archaeological materials that were excavated in 1989,

evidence of change over time of human activities, stone artefact technology in particular, at the site,

and the implications of the stone artefact assemblage data for post-depositional disturbance and the movement of artefacts.

Clarkson et *al.* present new data on the chronology and stratigraphy of the site, the size and diversity of the lithic assemblage, and the change throughout the sequence at MJB in the pattern of technological change. A better understanding of the age and formation of this site, its stratigraphic integrity, the nature of the early lithic industry, and the subsequent technological changes over time was afforded by these data. Re-examination of the assemblage that was recovered during the excavations in 1989, as well as new information about the chronology, stratigraphy, biological components, and the changing nature of the deposition of artefacts, that were obtained from field records that had not been published, were the basis for this study.

Conclusion of Clarkson et *al.*

According to Clarkson et *al.* their re-analysis of data from the excavations from 1973 and 1989 at MJB shows that a detailed sequence of industrial succession and palaeoecological change, that overlaps with the regional pattern that is evident at other archaeological sequences in western Arnhem Land, has been preserved at this site. This study found that there is not much evidence that indicates the process of displacement of artefacts or post-depositional disturbance to the deposit that is exceptional at this site. It appears that any post-depositional movement had little impact on the integrity of discrete cultural units, even at the lowest occupation level.

The level of resolution in age estimation that can be achieved for the initial levels of occupation, particularly whether any material can be assigned with confidence to the period prior to 45-46 Ka BP, is the major outstanding issue. With regards to the first specific question asked in the introduction, a date of 50-55 ka BP, based on current evidence, is likely to be a conservative estimate of age for the lower occupation level at MJB. There is a dense horizon of debris of occupation at the 45-55 ka BP level, and there are in situ artefacts below this level. The status of MJB, as being among the earliest archaeological sites in Australia, is supported by the data that has been presented in this paper. The key issue, therefore is whether a series of luminescence ages that are provenanced more tightly, by the use of an OSL technique that reduces uncertainties on individual estimates of age and assesses if there is any mixing of sand from different levels, will provide a chronology that is sufficiently fine-grained to provide a high-resolution age-depth curve for level from 2.4-2.9 m below the surface. There is also a need to assess further intrinsic differences between the assemblages at the 45 ka BP levels and material recovered from earlier levels over a wider area of the site.

The cultural change over time, the second question, has been addressed by examining the assemblages below and above the lens at 2.39 m below the surface, which suggests the levels below 45 ka BP (i.e. below spit 40) display differences in raw materials used and technological composition, which includes a discrete and differentiable lens feature. The raw material preferences, for stone artefact manufacture, display stark changes over time, with quartzite and silcrete being dominant in the early phase and quartz and chert being dominant in the later phase. Technological changes are also associated with these raw material changes, such as ground-edge artefacts, convergent and radial flakes, and in the lower levels, thinning flakes, and points in the upper levels. One of the priorities for analysis of the 2012 excavation is further analysis of the spatial structure of the lowest level of occupation. Clarkson et *al*. described a major change in the use of the site with the appearance of a shell midden in the Holocene, which reflects adaptation to local variability in mangrove environments and/or a different utilisation of the landscape and the resources that were available after the rise of the sea level and landscape evolution that occurred in the mid-Holocene.

After the report of the brief excavation in 1989 at the MJB site, critiques of the MJB site to a large extent focussed on clarification of dating, artefacts and stratigraphy. Some of the original doubts surrounding the possible inversions and displacement downwards of artefacts have been allayed by this new analysis that is presented in this paper. Several issues that are critical to understanding the chronology, composition and formation of the MJB site were solved by re-examination of the unpublished ages, field notes and lithic assemblages from the 1989 excavations at the MJB site. With reference to the 3rd question about the implications for understanding post depositional disturbance and movement of artefacts of the archaeological data, there is evidence of major changes over time in the preferences for raw materials, which would not be visible if the deposit was greatly disturbed. There is also evidence that within 3 spits in the lower deposit which Clarkson et *al*. were able to refit flakes, which also suggests that these spits have not been highly disturbed. According to Clarkson et *al*. a robust response to concerns about the age and integrity can be provided only with field collection of additional material, though these results are insightful. The use of OSL dating at this site was one of its first applications of OSL dating for an Australian archaeological site, and since that time the OSL dating technique has undergone significant technological and methodological developments (see Jacobs et *al*., 2008, Wintle, 2008), therefore it is strongly suggested that MJB should be re-dated with modern luminescence dating techniques, as is presently being carried out on samples from the 2012 excavation.

Though much more will be revealed about the structure and formation of the deposit by the new campaign, as well as gathering a much larger sample of artefacts, it is possible to deduce from the 1989 excavation material that the site contains succession of industrial changes, a radiocarbon and OSL chronology that is consistent, a record of ecological changes in the Holocene that is consistent with the Arnhem Land sequence that has been documented at other sites, and the presence of artefact refits and cultural features in the lower layer. Though it should be expected that all sites show some degree of mixing which is consistent with deposition being in a predominantly sandy matrix, there is also no a priori reason to suspect that the artefacts at MJB are disturbed heavily or seriously mixed. Understanding of the formation and chronology will be enhanced by the results of the new dating campaign and the new geoarchaeological investigations, such as micromorphology.

Clarkson, C., M. Smith, B. Marwick, R. Fullagar, L. A. Wallis, P. Faulkner, T. Manne, E. Hayes, R. G. Roberts, Z. Jacobs, X. Carah, K. M. Lowe, J. Matthews and S. A. Florin (2015). "The archaeology, chronology and stratigraphy of Madjedbebe (Malakunanja II): A site in northern Australia with early occupation." Journal of Human Evolution **83**(0): 46-64.

Burial Practices in Western Arnhem Land, Australia – a Ground Penetrating Radar Study

Prior to new archaeological excavations being carried out at Madjedbebe (Malakunanja II) rock shelter, western Arnhem Land, Australia, a ground penetrating radar (GPR) survey was carried out. It was revealed by the GPR that there was subsurface patterning of rocks in the deposits in the shelter, and it was demonstrated by archaeological excavations that these were related to burials. Following excavation GIS (geographic information system) and statistical analysis elucidated further the relationship between the rocks and the human burials. An opportunity to test a method of identification of unmarked burials by the use of GPR in sandstone rock shelters, and document a marker for burial identification in the region was provided by this integration of mapping, GPR and excavation.

The density of burials tends to strongly correlate with population densities in Australia, and where burials may be found within residential spaces, the development of methods to detect burials is an area of keen interest for researchers as well as managers. A non-invasive way of investigating subsurface features is provided by geophysical techniques (Gaffney & Gater, 2003; Johnson, 2006; Witten, 2006), and therefore these techniques, especially GPR, are now very popular in projects where it is anticipated there may be burials.

It has been suggested (Conyers, 2006: 66) that the physical features that are frequently associated with burials that it is possible to identify by GPR include:

Sediment that has not been disturbed below and surrounding the shaft of a grave;

A coffin or human body as well as associated artefacts;

Sediment that has been used to fill the shaft of the grave that has not been disturbed;

Any surface sediments that have accumulated above the shaft and surroundings following interment (Conyers, 2006: 66).

Also of particular relevance are areas of compacted soil and void spaces, especially in Indigenous burials.

GPR sometimes produces false negatives or no results, and sometimes it produces false positives as a result of other sources of disturbance, in cases in which the graves are not distinguishable from the surrounding strata, therefore GPR is not a foolproof method of detection (Bevan, 1991; Dalan et *al.*, 2010; Davenport, 2001; Nobes, 1999). In Australian historical archaeology, burials that are unmarked are common, and almost exclusively unmarked in Australian Indigenous archaeology, and this presents specific challenges. The identification of these burials with GPR is often impeded by the particular form of these burials, such as bundle, cremation, limited grave goods, shallow depth, no coffin etc. (see Meehan, 1971) and the nature of sediments which are geologically ancient that the interment occurs into. Also, there can be significant "distortions" in the data for both the area that is disturbed of the grave shaft and areas that are not disturbed adjacent to the grave, where the sedimentary matrix is comprised of gravelly, shelly or sediments that are rich in cobbles, which adds to the complexity of the interpretation. The interpretation is often speculative, and excavations are only rarely carried out in order to confirm the specific nature of the anomalies that are identified by GPR, as a result of there being limited case studies with which the Australian results can be compared.

In this paper Lowe et *al.* detail how a combination of GPR and archaeological excavation was combined with a GIS approach to test and identify many unmarked burials in the context of a rock shelter. Statistical analysis was also used to test the results in order to confirm that the association that has been documented was deliberate rather than random. Across Arnhem Land burial methods are known ethnographically to include secondary burials in rock shelters, excarnation (removing the flesh from corpses), tree burial and hollow log coffins (Meehan, 1971), though as to why certain individuals might receive particular treatment there is little known evidence, and it is also not known if this changed over time. None have been reported from Lowe et *al.*'s study site, though several accounts have been documented in the region of the study.

Additionally, legal codes have changed over the last 30 years, which define Indigenous peoples as the primary rights holders with regard to decision making in respect to their heritage have been instrumental in improving relationships between archaeologists and the Traditional Owners, though they have also resulted in a lower number of burial sites being investigated in Australia. The Gundjeihmi Aboriginal Corporation (GAC) – which represents the Traditional Owners of the study area, the Mirarr, have granted permission to study the Madjedbebe rock shelter in Arnhem Land as part of broader heritage initiatives, with the result that was a rare opportunity to carry out a detailed geophysical survey, and then ground disturbance by archaeological excavations.

Madjedbebe site

This is a narrow rock shelter, that is a sandstone overhang that faces to the north west dating to the Pleistocene, located at the base of the Arnhem Land Plateau escarpment, about 40 km to the west of the

East Alligator River. The floor of the shelter is generally flat, sandy and mostly free of vegetation, and the wall contains a gallery of pigment art. At Madjedbebe the archaeological deposits comprise a thick shell midden unit that is about 70 cm thick dating to the Holocene, below which is a further about 3 m of cultural deposits from the Pleistocene (Kamminga & Allen, 1973). The subsoil parent material is mix of sand and silt that has weathered from the adjoining quartzose sandstone escarpment of the Kombolgie Formation dating from the Middle Proterozoic (East, 1996: 40). In this study it is only the shell midden unit that is of interest.

Madjedbebe has been investigated several times since its discovery in 1972 (Kamminga & Allen, 19723), and in 1989 (Roberts et *al*., 1990); the 1989 excavation yielded luminescence dates of 50,000-60,000 BP. Investigations involving small test pits revealed that within the midden unit there were burials present, though there were assumed to be only a few mainly secondary bundle burials (Smith, 1989). Concerns were raised by the prior identification of burials when the site was to be re-investigated; therefore a geophysical survey was conducted before work began on the excavation so the researchers would be prepared for what they might find.

The excavations carried out in 2012 recovered 17 individuals that coded as skeletal remains (SR) in various states of completeness. These burials were mainly primary interments (n=13) that had been dug into, or just through, the shell midden into the uppermost level of the sand unit on which the midden had been deposited. All the burials contained minimal amounts of grave goods, and the SR were found in both flexed and extended positions.

Rocks were found to be associated with at least 9 of the burials, which is a tradition that had been documented at the Nawamoyn site which was near the Madjedbebe site (Schrire, 1982). It was found that at Madjedbebe most of the rocks were placed on the individual's heads and, in 2 instances, rocks had been placed on the head and the feet (SR1 and SR5), and 1 burial (SR4) the rock placed only on the feet. Apart from 2 burials in a single grave, SR3 and SR14, the rocks were of a similar size in each burial, with an average diameter of 20 cm, a size which would allow the rock to be moved by a single person, though not likely to be moved by animal activity or bioturbation, as is indicated by the relatively intact and articulated bones in the burial. When these rocks were plotted during excavation it was revealed that they coincided with the burials, therefore when these rocks showed up in the GPR survey it corresponded with primary interments.

Concluding remarks

The importance of detailed recording of data and integration when attempting to investigate and map complex archaeological sites is highlighted by this excavation. This study demonstrates the potential value of GPR surveys, though GPR surveys have been extremely rare in rock shelter studies in Australia. The use of GIS in the integration of the results of GPR and excavations has proved to be very beneficial in the understanding of burial practices at Madjedbebe because of the specific way the individuals were interred at this particular site. The presence of many subsurface rocks of unknown origin was found by the initial GPR survey; they were subsequently identified by excavation to be associated with 17 burials, and it was indicated by statistical analysis that the association was deliberate, and therefore not random.

Lowe, K. M., L. A. Wallis, C. Pardoe, B. Marwick, C. Clarkson, T. Manne, M. A. Smith and R. Fullagar (2014). "Ground-penetrating radar and burial practices in western Arnhem Land, Australia." Archaeology in Oceania **49**(3): 148-157.

Links

Ngarrabullgan Cave, a Pleistocene Archaeological Site, Australia - New Optical and Radiocarbon Dates, Implications for Comparability of date and Human Colonisation of Australia

See Aboriginal Occupation - Populating the Continent - The Evidence

Mammoth Cave

At Mammoth Cave, in Western Australia, there is evidence of the bones, older than 37,000 BP, of megafauna animals being deliberately broken, cut and burnt, such as Zygomaturus.

Mandu Mandu Creek Rock Shelter

This shelter, on North west Cape, in Western Australia, has an occupation site dated to 34 000 years. It is in Cape Range National Park, facing west over the 1-km wide coastal plain to Ningaloo Reef. More than 500 stone artefacts were found in the upper layer, together with marine and terrestrial bone fragments and marine mollusc shells. In the lower, Pleistocene layer below a layer dated to 19 500 BP, were fish teeth and some parts of mollusc shells. The continental shelf is narrower here than in any other part of the continent.

The Pleistocene tools were mostly of poor-quality silcrete and limestone. The flakes of this age are much longer and thicker than in the later assemblages, and more cores and amorphous flaked pieces. In this Pleistocene assemblage the most recognisable tool is a 595 gram limestone horsehoof core. It was found about 10 cm below the 19 590 BP dated layer.

By the Holocene there is a noticeable change in the tools, now there is a higher percentage of re-touched artefacts and better quality silcrete. And distinctive artefacts such as adzes, and 1 tula, make their appearance after 2,400 BP. In the later assemblage there is a significant decrease in flake size.

This is the earliest-known evidence for the exploitation of marine foods in Australia. It is the first dated occupation on the large arid stretch of the West Australian coast. The aridness of the area was previously thought to have posed a barrier to occupation. This shelter was used intermittently until about 19,000 years ago when it seems to have been abandoned, probably because of increased aridity and retreat of the sea to about 10 km from the site. It was re-occupied about 2,500 BP. Extensive middens in the region have given earlier Holocene dates. At Woroora Midden dates of about 8,000 BP have been measured.

It seems likely that increasing aridity around 19,000 BP led to the abandonment of the Australian desert zone until the climate changed again in the early Holocene. A unique find for the Pleistocene in Australia was made in this area, 22 shell beads. They were made from small marine cone shells and were associated with the bailer shell that gave the date of 34,200 years. These beads show similar wear patterns to those on threaded recent shell necklaces. The only other decoration of this type from Pleistocene Australia was bone beads found in Devil's Lair.

Shell bead necklaces were common in recent Aboriginal Australia, especially in Tasmania. There is a very long continuity of Aboriginal decorative traditions.

The Miriwun Rock Shelter

This site on the Ord River was excavated in 1971 as part of an emergency salvage program before the area was flooded by the Ord River irrigation scheme.

Small tools were found in the upper levels of the site. In the dark brown lower levels, from 18,000 to 3,000 years ago, a distinctive early assemblage was found. The find included thick, denticulate or notched flakes, core scrapers and small blades, pebble tools and quartzite fragments that could have been part of grindstones or anvils.

Among the artefacts of this site were 2 flakes from below the 18,000 year-old horizon. They had been struck from tektites or Australites as they are known in Australia. 750,000 years ago a shower of tektites fell across Australasia. In Australia tektites are found in a swathe across the southern half of the continent, especially in Central Australia and southern inland parts of Western Australia.

One of the flakes was analysed and found to be from the Indochinite group, tektites from Indochina. This flake is the first of this type of tektite found in Australia. So there is the possibility, however remote, that this tiny flake was brought from Southeast Asia, as so far no unworked tektites of this kind have been found in Australia in association with occupation sites. The **Miriwun** tektite may be the first Asian artefact from the Ice Age period to be found in Australia.

There may be a long continuity of technological tradition in the Kimberley, in grooved, ground-edge axes and serrated flakes. The Kimberley serrated spear points are renowned for their fine crafting and their symmetry. They were made by the pressure-flaking technique, fine flakes are removed by use of wood or bone. Prior to European occupation fine-grained stone was used. This type of leaf-shaped, bifacially trimmed spear points has been used for at least 3,000 years.

A feature of the Ord River sites is that organic material if often well preserved. The occupants of the **Miriwun** site hunted a wide variety of animals from the region. Among them were many eggshells of the pied or semi-palmeted goose (***Anseranas semipalmata***), this bird breeds in the wet season, so the site may have been a wet season camp from the Pleistocene to the European era.

The rock shelters at Widgingarri 1 and 2 north-east of Derby on the Kimberley coast, are believed to have been used from about 28,000 BP. At this time they would have been more than 100 km from the coast. Occupation apparently ceased at about 7,500 BP. It is believed by some that the increasing aridity is the probable reason for the abandonment of the site.

Monte Bello Islands

Recent excavation on the Monte Bello Islands, now 120 km off the present Pilbara coast, has found evidence of Pleistocene occupation. 3 limestone caves have been excavated on Campbell Island. Cultural material was found and a marine shell at the base of the deposit in Noala Cave gave an age of 27,220 BP, at this time in the Pleistocene, when it was adjacent to the coast. The deposit shows the occupants were hunting kangaroos and other mammals on the surrounding plain as well as fish.

Retouched stone artefacts were of materials like metamorphic rock that is not found on the island. Between 8,000 and 7,500 BP the island was joined to the mainland at low sea levels. Soon after 7,500 BP they appear to have been abandoned. They were uninhabited islands 50 km offshore by 6,500 BP.

Mount Conner Artila

Aboriginal stories

In the Dreamtime stories of the local Aborigines it is connected with the feared **Ninya, or Ice Men**, the creators of cold weather. The Ninya are believed to have camped at Artila during the Dreamtime, but now they live about 25 km away to the north beneath a dry lake. The Aborigines believe that when deep cracks form on the soles of their feet they are caused by ice left in the grass by the Ninya. There is evidence on the coarse pebbles of the mesa that at some point in the past, presumably in the Pleistocene ice age, the area did indeed undergo some degree of glaciation. Maybe the dreamtime stories in this area are memories of the glacial phase that has been passed on through many generations. History remembered in stories.

Mt Conner, especially the caves, is a refuge to some rock-dwelling marsupials and bats.

Mt Newman Rock Shelter Orebody XXIX

The first of the sites found, overlooking the headwaters of the Fortescue River. Ash, charcoal and ochre were found at this site. 11 hearths were found, of these 1 was of the type typical of those used by modern Aborigines for baking animals. Most of the 400 artefacts found were simple flakes or re-touched pieces. 2 implement types were found - steep-edged scrapers and notched scrapers. Radiocarbon dates from the 1-metre deep excavation put it at more than 20,750 years old.

Nawarla Gabarnmang Rock Shelter

The oldest known stone axe with a ground edge has been found in Arnhem Land, in the country of the Jawoyn people. At 35,000 years old, it predates the earliest known stone axe elsewhere by about 5,000 years.

Nawarla Gabarnmang Rock Shelter in south western Arnhem Land has replicated a similar ancestral history as at Malakunanja and Nauwalabila. The last people to sleep in the cave were 2 old Jawoyn men who camped there when they were children; the first people to sleep there did so at least 45,000 BP. There are 2 entrances to the cave and about 2 m of head space over the living area that covers an area of at least 1,500 m^2. The flat ceiling is supported by 36 henge-like pillars of sandstone, each pillar having been painted, and the ceiling has also been painted, the overall appearance being stunning. The soft sandstone between the pillars has been removed by chemical weathering, as well as by human modification. The inhabitants removed blocks of rock to enlarge the already cavernous spaces. A labyrinth of interconnected space is formed by the linking of the caverns, the overall effect being an effective balance between space, ventilation and insulation, the overall result of the work of nature and human's modification is a cool place to live.

Stone tools were produced by flaking blocks that had fallen from the ceiling. Flaking off edges of some blocks was used to reduce them, while others were broken up and moved from the cave, apparently clearing it out of the way to allow movement, comfort and accommodation. It has proven possible to match some blocks that were deliberately removed from the ceiling to their original location. Having been removed intentionally they made extra space, enlarged the cave and exposed fresh surfaces that had not been weathered for the application of new frescos. Nawarla Gabarnmang has been described by Cane (2013) as 'an artefact of social and ritual endeavour: A cultural catacomb, a monument of structural engineering and an art gallery of unequalled magnificence. The physicality of the site and its cultural heritage exists as a testament to tradition, community, social cohesion, artistic brilliance and ritual activity. It is a monolithic statement of human aesthetic achievement and - a real stone henge, and a place of social, artistic and religious centrality that existed countless millennia before the first pillars of Stonehenge were erected in England'.

Earliest known drawing

The earliest known drawing in Australia is also found at this site, a charcoal drawing on a 2.8 x 3.5 cm piece of rock that has fallen from the roof. According to Cane the drawing is difficult to describe, it contains 2 crossed lines, the longer axis being straight and 1 side of the shorter axis is curved. The curved part is bulbous and has been filled in with a darker, heavier, application of charcoal, but the remainder of the drawing has faded beyond recognition. The rock fragment is between 15,600 and 45,600 years old, though Cane suggests the likely age is about 28,000 BP.

Also found at this site was a large ochre crayon with faceted sides of mulberry colour that matched the colour of the 'dynamic' figures that had been drawn on the walls of the cave. The sediments the crayon was found on dated to 15,000-25,000 BP. The 'Mimi' or dynamic art found throughout Arnhem Land, are believed by the Aboriginals to have been painted by the Mimi spirits. This art form is characterised by human-like figures, in which the Cane says movement is vibrantly expressed through pose and balance, describing them as delicate and bellicose, apparently depending on the mood of the viewer. *'The compositions effect a sensation of grace and agility through elongated limbs, refined body shape, alignment and contingent activity'*[1]. Cane describes the figures in the art as 'superb representations' of form and balance that creates an illusion of mystical momentum. Adornments are often added to the delicate beings, armlets, necklaces, headdresses, tassels and feathers, which enhance the illusion of fluidity that results in a sense of ancient fantasy. The figures are often active, holding, and in some cases throwing, a spear, holding a club, a boomerang or a hafted ground stone axe, and at the same time having great aesthetic appeal, and according to Cane they convey a lot about human attributes.

Most representations are of men with notable hairstyles, many wearing long plaits. There are also elaborate headdresses on the male figures and they wear hair belts with pubic aprons and bustles over their buttocks. On the rare figures that show their penis it is an explicitly sexual representation. The male figures wear necklaces, wristbands, pendants and armbands, and some have cicatrices which Cane suggests is an indication that scarification and body image manipulation has a long history. Representation of women is not common in this art, and when they are depicted they are typically running with a dilly bag and digging stick, and occasionally a firestick. Those depicted are mostly young women.

In the Kimberley the Gwion figures are believed to be more than 15,000 years old, making these the oldest known depiction of boomerangs and rich personal adornments such as tassels, armlets, fans, belts, bustles and elongated headdresses in the world. In the historic era in the Kimberley area men that were richly decorated and wearing elaborate headdresses of Gwion ancestry, and holding spear throwers and floral fans have been observed.

In the paintings people are depicted with single-barbed spears that were thrown by hand, as spear throwers had not been invented at that time, and they also carried boomerangs, which at the age of the art were the oldest known boomerangs in the world, their outlines being stencilled onto the rock face, and they are depicted in many forms, symmetrical, asymmetrical, hooked, large and small. Among these stencilled boomerangs are every type known of in Australia, a complete boomerang arsenal that may be as old as 16,000 years. A number of activities are depicted in the paintings, especially in a particular famous painting of an emu in the act of being speared in which both the bird and the man appear to be uttering a sound. According to Cane it is rare to find motion, emotion and voice in art, to the extent that it is almost unknown in ancient art, though in these paintings that are particularly old it is common, with tracks, splashes and dashes depicted emanating from the figures, perceptual cues to the sensory experience of the artist, sound and smell, speed and movement, fear and pain, shock and anxiety, being provided by their feet and mouths.

The Gwion or Bradshaw art of the Kimberley are regional expressions of the dynamic art of Arnhem Land. They have been dated to between 14,000 and 23,800 years old and overlay hand stencils that are obviously even considerably older. The Gwion are more solid than their counterparts in the north east, though they are equally as delicate and a bit more elaborate. They show similar aspects of humanity and material culture, such as barbed spears that are hand thrown, boomerangs, and dress, such as bustles, tassels and headdresses. All across the savannah lands of Australia they are part of greater artistic tradition embedded in accretions of ochre. There is an example in the southeast of Cape York where pigments were selected from local weathered rock, red haematite, yellow goethite and white kaolinite clays, that when applied to the local sandstone impregnated the rock leaving layers of ochre in fine mineral laminations, this art being 27,000 years old.

A long sequence of AMS radiocarbon ages from individual charcoal pieces that were adhering to stone artefacts back to $45,180 \pm 910$ cal BP during recent excavations art Nawarla Gabarnmang in Jawoyn country, south west Arnhem Land. This site represents one of the earliest sites in Australia to be dated by radiocarbon. In this paper the authors report on the initial results. According to the Bruno David, the author, old archaeological sites with ages at near the limits of radiocarbon dating have usually been the subject of heated debate concerning the actual antiquity of the site containing cultural deposits. Of the concerns raised 2 are the most commonly raised: the age reliability and the chronostratigraphic integrity of the associations between the archaeological materials, the sediments in which they are buried and dated materials. Some controversial cases have been mentioned by David, including Nauwalabila, $60,300 \pm$

6,700 to 53,400 ± 5,400 BP (Roberts et al., 1994), Malakunanja II, 61,000 ± 8,000 BP to 52,000 ± 8,000 BP (Roberts et al., 1990), Lake Mungo, 56,000 to 46,000 BP (Bowler et al., 2003) and Devil's Lair, 48,000 BP (Turney et al., 2001), and an even more controversial example is Jinmium, >116,000 ± 12,000 BP (Fullagar et al., 1996). Sites with younger ages tend to be less controversial, some of the earliest ones being Riwi, 41,300 ± 1,020 BP (Balme, 2,000) and carpenter's Gap, 39,700 ± 1,000 BP (O'Connor, 1995), the latter 2 being dated by radiocarbon. Any securely radiocarbon dated sites with an age of more than 45,000 cal BP is considered significant in securing progressively earlier ages for the origins of the Australian Aboriginal people. In this paper the authors report on such a site from the Jawoyn Country in western Arnhem Land.

Ngarrabullgan Cave

A Pleistocene Archaeological Site, Australia - New Optical and Radiocarbon Dates, Implications for Comparability of date and Human Colonisation of Australia

Site and Stratigraphy

Ngarrabullgan Cave is a rock shelter in Queensland. This is a large flat-topped mountain 18 x 6 km, 100 km west of Cairns, 200-400 m above the surrounding hills and plains and bounded by high cliffs. This cave, the largest archaeological site on the mountain, has cultural deposits that are more than 37,000 radiocarbon years old (David, 1993). At this site the deposits are very dry and there are few terrestrial mammals on the mountain-top that could have disturbed the sediments, and the strata integrity and preservation of organic materials, especially charcoal and microscopic residues on stone tools, are exceptional (Fullagar & David, 1997).

Dating

A good suite of radiocarbon determinations has been obtained at this site for which there are matches with 2 optically stimulated luminescence (OSL) dates, which Bruno et al., views as an encouraging sign that OSL dates are reliable. According to Bruno et al., humans first arrived in Australia in the period when dating is made difficult by the reduced reliability of radiocarbon dates near the limit of their reliability, dating relying more on a variety of luminescence methods.

Debate has continued concerning the time of arrival of the first humans in Australia since the determinations of OSL and TL dates of 50,000-60,000 BP from northern Australia (Roberts et *al.*, 1990, 1994b). Some have argued that the habitation of Australia took place in this time range (Chappell et *al.*, 1996; Roberts et *al*, 1994a; Roberts & Jones, 1994), while others argued that these dates are not correct, or are not directly comparable to radiocarbon chronology from other sites in Australia, arguing that there is no conclusive evidence that Australia was occupied before 40,000 BP (Allen, 1994; Allen & Holdaway, 1995). More recently TL dates of 116 ± 12 ka and beyond have been reported for sands containing artefacts (Fullagar et *al*, 1996) that have lengthened the disputed time frame, though there are some chronostratigraphic uncertainties making these results open to a number of interpretations. For the period beyond 30 ka there are no paired ^{14}C/optical dates available for Australia, partly as the result of the rarity of sites containing the appropriate sediments and charcoal. In Ngarrabullgan Cave* in north Queensland there are deposits rich in charcoal within a sandy matrix rich in silica that has allowed the obtaining of 2 Pleistocene optical age determinations.

* The spelling of Ngarrabullgan has changed over time (Nurrabullgin, Ngarrabullgin) as a result of instructions from elders of the local Aboriginals.

The deposit in the rock shelter is shallow but finely stratified, with 27 distinct strata over a depth of 43.5 cm, the cultural material being in the top 35.7 cm. The dates obtained for the site are 21 ^{14}C dates (accelerator mass spectrometry (AMS) and 4 radiocarbon dates by beta-counting.

Paired age comparison

The best estimate of the optical age of sample ANU.sub.OD122a is 34,700 ± 2,000 BP, which is about 2,200 years older than the mean ^{14}C age of stratum 3, which is about 32,500 BP, a similar degree of underestimation for the 40,000-30,000 BP period has been previously reported. On the basis of coral ages, ^{234}U/^{230}Th (Bard et *al.*, 1993), TL on fireplaces (Bell, 1991) and burnt flints (Boeda et al., 1996), and geomagnetic intensity variations (Guyodo & Valet, 1996; Laj et al., 1996). The AMS ^{14}C ages for stratum 3 are consistent with the optical date, this agreement indicating that the 2 time clocks are broadly comparable over at least this time period (Smith et al., in press). It is implied that the 60,000-50,000 BP dates from TL and optical methods from sediments that were unheated from Malakunanja II (Roberts et al., 1990) and Nauwalabila (Roberts et al., 1994b) do not equate with the ^{14}C dates from less than 40,000 BP, as was suggested (Allen, 1994). The implication of the luminescence dates from Malakunanja II and Nauwalabila I, coupled with the results presented in this article, is that the prehistory of Australia is much older than 39,700 ± 1,000 BP, currently the oldest reliable radiocarbon evidence of the human presence in Australia (O'Connor, 1995).

Thermoluminescence Dating of Flint from Palaeolithic sites - Advantages and Limitations

For the dating of Palaeolithic sites, thermoluminescence (TL) has been widely used. The underlying assumptions of this method of dating are not considered to be trivial, though the basic principle of TL dating is simple. The external dose rate is one of the major sources of error, contributing to the denominator of the age formula to a varying degree; therefore the amount of its influence on the dating result is variable. According to Richter the aim of this paper is to enable the evaluation of TL age determinations of flint that has been heated, with some of the parameters used for the determination of age and some of their relationships being discussed. It is shown that for heated flint the reliability of the TL results depend on the proportion of the various dose-rate parameters, and the importance of these in the evaluation of ages. Richter discusses the limitations of the method as well as its advantages, the dating of 2 Near Eastern Palaeolithic sites, Rosh Ein Mor and Jerfal-Ajla, being used as examples.

Conclusions (Richter (2007)

For any chronometric dating of an archaeological site the accuracy is most dependent on the relationship of the sample to the archaeological event (association), but it is also dependent on the environment of the deposition and the quality of the samples. The precision of a result of dating is dependent on the latter 2 as well as on the method being used. The making of a number of assumptions are required by all dating methods, and it is necessary that these be carefully evaluated for each individual site.

To establish the elapsed time since the last time the object, such as a flint, has been heated; dating by thermoluminescence is a useful tool. The direct association of the event with past activity of humans on a linear timescale, and its lower vulnerability to variation of certain parameters that are unknown, are advantages of TL over other methods. It is necessary to take great care in the evaluation of TL dates and when publishing the results of dating certain standards need to be met. Included among these are the presentation of glow curves, heating plateaus and D_E plateaus, growth curve(s) (including correction for supralinearity) and the determination of the alpha sensitivity of each sample, and it is required that equal care be taken in the evaluation of parameters that are prone to variation over time. Results of TL dating that have large components of external dose need to be evaluated critically, with great care being taken when the models used and errors associated with this component are considered. γ- or α-spectrometry should be carried out on sediment samples to obtain at least the information on the state of the equilibrium of the U-chain for the more recent history of the external radiation field ($D^*_{\gamma\text{-external}}$). The sum of the 2 constant dose rates ($D^*_{internal}$ and D^*_{cosmic}) contribute largely to the total dose rate, making such dating results less vulnerable to variations, providing confidence in TL dating as a powerful tool for dating Palaeolithic sites.

Puritjarra Cave Rock Shelter

With the excavation of Puritjarra Cave Rock Shelter, almost at the dead centre of the continent, it was shown that people had already occupied the site by 22,000 years ago. This is a very large rock shelter in hard red sandstone cliffs, 45 m long and 20 m high, with a shaded floor space of 400 m². Later it was shown to go back to about 32,000 BP. The site was occupied up to the 1930s when the people moved onto mission stations and rations depots in the western MacDonnell Ranges.

The deposit is formed of 3 stratigraphic layers that are well-defined. Layer 1, composed of loose, gritty, light-brown sand (Munsell colour 5YR 5/8), that extends from the present surface to 42 cm in which there are rock fall lenses, intact hearths, charcoal, flaked stone artefacts, grindstones, ochre and emu eggshell. The site has evidence of a major occupation increase in the region over the last 1,000 years, such a change being shown in more detail at other sites (Napton & Greathouse, 1985: 90-108; Smith, 1986: 123-30).

The Puritjarra site is close to the only permanent water in the Cleland Hills, near the eastern end of the Western Desert, about 320 km west of Alice Springs. The area is made up of spinifex grassland and mulga woodlands around the central ranges. In an area with an average rainfall of less than 350 mm/year, the ranges act like an oasis, with permanent springs, waterholes, deep rock 'reservoirs' and soakages in creek beds. All the rivers of the area, such as the Finke, flow only after rain, or even after heavy rain, but there are usually some water holes and soaks along their otherwise dry beds.

There is a large array of rock art, stencils, paintings and Panaramitee-style engravings. This type of engraving is also present at the nearby Thomas reservoir site. 11 m^2 of the site were excavated. Charcoal provided 12 radiocarbon dates, and 6 TL dates from the sediments. The base of the lower level has a preliminary date of 30,000 BP.

The site was first occupied for a short period well before 22,000 years ago. The first long period use began about 22,000 BP. This appearance of artefacts is marked by the presence of charcoal and 10 pieces of high-grade red and purple ochre, 60 stone flakes, including a single large steep-edged tool, and about 200 small pieces of flaking debris.

Between 22,000 and 13,000 years ago the shelter was used occasionally, only a few artefacts being added per millennium. The uppermost layer is formed of loose, gritty sand with cooking hearths, charcoal and flaked tools, many grindstones, ochre and emu eggshell. There are no grindstones in the Pleistocene layer. This spans 6,000 years. It shows that in the last 1,000 years there was a large increase in occupation of the region. Chemical analysis of the red ochre, found in layers dated to between 32,000 and 13,000 years ago, at this site have placed its source in the Karrku quarry, 150 km away, indicating that some level of mining was already taking place in the Pleistocene (Smith, 1996; Smith et al., 1998; Gibbs & Veth, 2002).

The 22,000-year-old occupation level coincides with the onset of major aridity. This is probably the beginning of a pattern of land occupation where reliable water was of major concern. From 22,000 to 13,000 years ago there was repeated, light use of the site, probably related to the fact that this was the height of full glaciation. The repeated use of the Puritjarra site, as well as its location away from major corridors, indicates there may have been a resident population in this refuge area.

In levels dating to between 32,000 BP and 18,000 BP, in the centre of the shelter floor, small fragments of ochre were found that weighed 0.1 g. From 13,000 BP onwards, larger amounts of ochre were found in deposits against the walls adjacent to a panel on the wall of stencils and paintings. The earliest identifiable [ochre?] was found that came from this period. It was a piece of very fine-grained yellow pigment, 10 mm across, that is believed may have been a droplet of thick paint that had been moulded on a small brush (Rosenfeld & Smith, 2002). It contained about 30 % organic matter, which is consistent with it being prepared paint (Smith, 1989; Rosenfeld & Smith, 2002).

Wallen Wallen Creek

Wallen Wallen Creek is on **North Stradbroke Island** 6 km south of Dunwich, Brisbane, at the foot of a high sand dune that is about 400 m inland from the present coast. When the sea level was about 150 m lower than present, about 20,000 years ago, the site was first occupied near the base of a well-vegetated sand hill near a water course. At that time North Stradbroke Island was part of the mainland, the site is believed to have been a stopover between the coast, about 12 to 20 km further to the east, and the present mainland. This site has been dated to the Pleistocene, and is the first evidence of Pleistocene occupation of the east coast north of Sydney. The finds in this site lead to the conclusion that there was continuous occupation for the duration of the Pleistocene, followed by a dramatic increase in occupation in the Late Holocene. The site on the west coast of the island was in use sporadically for more than

20,000 years. The 2.5 m deposit has produced charcoal, animal bones and stone flake artefacts.

The upper levels of the site indicate it was used more intensively in the last few thousand years, as indicated by a large increase in the quantity of artefacts found in the deposit. There was apparently a big increase in use of Moreton Bay islands. Over this period there was a large increase of shell middens on other sand islands, such as Fraser Island and Moreton Island, indicating a greatly expanded use of the islands by the Aborigines.

In the most recent levels of the site the people were eating shellfish, fish and dugong at the site.

It is 1 of 2 open Pleistocene sites known on the east coast of Australia, the other being Bass Point occupation site, north of Lake Burrill near Shellharbour in New South Wales.

Widgingarri 1 & 2

These sites were situated on the coast of the Kimberley region of Western Australia. They would have been about 100 km from the coast when occupation is believed to have begun about 28,000 years ago. These sites appear to have been abandoned about 7,500 years ago, thought by some to most likely be because of increasing aridity.

A ground sea urchin spine and pearl shell (***Pinctada sp.***) were found in levels that have been dated to about 18,900 +/- 1,800 years ago. A minimum age date of 28,060 +/- 600 years ago was obtained from a ***Geloina*** shell (O'Connor, 1999).

Widgingarri 2

The site was 200 km from the coast at the time of occupation. The presence of marine shells here suggests the existence of long distance exchange networks/transport in the late Pleistocene.

There were 25 nodules of ochre in this deposit, red, yellow and orange, that were in dated levels between 28,060 +/- 600 BP and 18,900 +/- 1,800 BP. (O'Connor, 1999, Table 5.17).

Willandra Footprints

The footprints that are 20,000 years old, found at Willandra Lakes are important for a number of reasons. There are more footprints at this site than all other known footprints from the Pleistocene of the entire world combined. One is notable for its size, 29.5 cm long. It was apparently made by a very tall man running fast, estimated at about 37 km/hr, in the range of Olympic speeds. Track Way 4 is special for another reason, because of 7 men running parallel, evenly spaced like on a running track, and curving apparently like a running track, there is a 1-legged man, and only the track of his right foot is visible. It has been speculated that they may have been running to cut off an animal they were hunting from escaping. The possibility of 20,000 year old Olympics has not been considered. Other tracks are of a man with several children. Many of the tracks appear to have been made by 1 or more family groups, some running, and some walking.

The footprints have been preserved because they were made in a magnasite magnesite pavement when it was wet, then soon after was covered and dried out.

The WLH50 remains are of a very large man that is believed to be more archaic than any other Aboriginal remains, said to be even more robust than *H. erectus* from Java, possibly as the result of a blood condition that is believed to have protected the people of Java from malaria.

Keep River Region, Eastern Kimberley, Australia – Comparative Occupation Records

In this paper Ward considers the occupation record of the Keep River region in the eastern Kimberley, and whether archaeological records are preserved equally within regions as well as between regions. Evidence from archaeological sites, luminescence and radiocarbon dating, were used on 8 rock shelter sequences which contained occupation sequences dating from the Late Holocene (5,000-0 years BP), though occupation as far back as 18,000 BP was found from sand sheet sequences based on luminescence dating and archaeological evidence. Ward questions to what extent the representative records from the eastern Kimberley, as well as the adjacent western Kimberley, Victoria River District and Arnhem Land regions can be compared, given that such different chronologies can be produced by work in rock shelters and sand sheet excavations. Ward also argues that it remains unclear whether apparent intensification in the Holocene is actually a product of cultural change or of research and preservation, in the absence of comparative chronostratigraphy, of rock shelters in particular.

The Keep River cultural province is in the eastern Kimberley adjacent to, and possibly related to the cultural provinces of the western Kimberley and Victoria River Districts (Taçon et *al.*, 1999) and Arnhem Land (Lewis, 1988). In the Keep River region the relative occupation age compared to these adjacent cultural provinces remains in contention (Fullagar et *al.*, 1996; Roberts et *al.*, 1997; Watchman et *al.*, 2000). Arnhem Land is considered to be the location of the earliest evidence of occupation (Mulvaney & Kamminga, 1999), though the previous age determination of about 60,000 BP (Roberts et *al.*, 1998b) is now being questioned, with a younger age of about 45,000 BP being proposed (O'Connell & Allen, 2004). The earliest evidence of occupation in the western and eastern Kimberley is about 40,000 BP (O'Connor, 1995) and about 20,000 BP respectively (Dortch & Roberts, 1996). Ward suggests that before any comparisons are made regarding occupation between regions it is important to consider if archaeological time periods are preserved equally within regions (Waters & Khuen, 1996), as comparisons between regions may be only random.

In this paper Ward compares the record of occupation in sedimentary sequences from 5 rock shelters with the sequences from 3 sand sheets located within the Keep River region. The sand sheets link the escarpments to the rock shelters, and the research was concentrated at 5 sites known in Aboriginal tradition as Jinmium, Goorurarmum, Punipunil, Granilpi and Karlinga. Geochronological determinations that were derived from recent (Ward, 2003; Ward et *al.*, 2005) and research that had been published previously (Fullagar et *al.*, 1996; Head & Fullagar, 1997; Atchison, 2000), and included dating by radiocarbon, thermoluminescence (TL), and optically stimulated luminescence (OSL). According Ward full site descriptions can be found in the earlier publications, and a discussion of the sedimentary and archaeological records (Ward et *al.*, 2004). Keep River current data have been integrated into the records of occupation in the eastern Kimberley and Arnhem Land.

Keep River archaeological records – review of archaeological excavations

Sedimentary stratigraphy of sand sheets and rock shelters are typically comprised of loose surface sands that is charcoal-enriched, which overlies sands that are slightly more compact, which in turn overlie rubble and/or a bedrock base. Among the cultural materials are flaked and stone points, charcoal, processed seeds, ochre, bone, and glass. Stone points recovered in the Kimberley region have been dated to about 3,000 BP (Attenbrow et *al.*, 1995; Fullagar et *al.*, 1996: 764). For the excavations at Jinmium, Granilpi and Punipunil full details of the chronometric, sedimentary and archaeological records can be found in (Fullagar et *al.*, 1996; Atchison, 2000; Atchison et *al.*, in prep.) and for excavations at Goorurarmum and Karlinga (Ward, 2003; Ward et *al.*, 2004, 2005).

The Karlinga (Karl-1) rock shelter is situated at the base of a sandstone cliff, and is sheltered behind several boulders. At 27 cm depth an age of 18,400 ± 1,400 BP was found by OSL dating of sediments was obtained. As with the sediments from the Jinmium rock shelter (Roberts et *al.*, 1999), the sands were thought to probably include 'saturated' quartz that was derived from slow disintegration of the overlying and surrounding bedrock (for more details see Ward, 2003; Ward et *al.*, 2004), which is why this estimate is not considered to represent an occupation age. This age of 18,500 BP is also inconsistent with:

1 Estimates of radiocarbon age younger than 1,000 BP obtained from charcoal samples from the same sediments,

2 with other luminescence and radiocarbon ages for excavations in rock shelters in the Keep River region,

3 and with the presence of flaked stone and Kimberley points.

The location of the Karlinga sand sheet excavation is about 500 m from the site in the Rock Shelter. At this site the sediments are not affected by contamination from the bedrock as there was no contact with the underlying rock. At 240 cm depth an age of 18 ± 6,00 BP was obtained by OSL dating, and for the surrounding sediments TL produced a similar estimate (see Ward, 2003; Ward et *al*, in review, which represented a minimum age for the beginning of formation of the sand sheet (Ward, 2003). Immediately above and below the 2 cobble layers the highest density of stone artefacts, which included stone points, were found dating to about 2,500 BP by OSL and 900 BP respectively.

At the Goorurarmum excavation site (Goor-2) is in an elevated rock shelter, and the adjacent sand sheet (Goor-1) is about 20 m in front of Goor-2. Within the rock shelter the sediments produced a similar age by OSL of 500 ± 140 BP and ages of 300 ± 70 BP by radiocarbon. According to Ward these recent estimates of age are younger than that indicated by the presence of stone points at the profile base, which indicates that either the points or the older sediments containing them have been moved or reworked. Dated by TL to 14,300 ± 400 BP at a depth of 220 cm, the lowermost sediments of the adjacent sand sheets are significantly older. Below these sediments is indurated (hardened) or bedrock horizon which according to Ward may represent a surface dating to the LGM. The inversion between the OSL age of 4,300 ± 100 BP at 180 cm and the TL age of 6,100 ± 100 BP at 155 cm, assuming there are no errors in the dates, indicates secondary mixing. The upper metre of the sediment sequence contains the greatest density of artefacts which includes charcoal, stone points, and bone.

Within a cluster of boulders on the north western side of a large sandstone outcrop is the location of the Granilpi excavation site which displays extensive rock art (Taçon et al., 1997), while Punipunil is a long narrow rock shelter within a sheltered gorge (Atchison, 2000). Early to Mid-Holocene ages for the sequences were obtained by radiocarbon dating of fruit tree seeds at both Granilpi and Punipunil rock shelter excavations (Atchison, 2000). The Jinmium (C1) rock shelter excavations are at the base of an exposed sandstone boulder, and the sand sheet is located 10 m from the rock shelter (C1/IV). OSL and radiocarbon dating of the young sediments is supported by the seed and stone artefact chronology (Atchison et al., in prep.), in spite of a disturbance or contamination (Roberts et al/. 1998b). The published chronology of the sand sheet excavation (Fullagar et al., 1996) at Jinmium, unlike the rock shelter sediments, has never been revised. A TL age of about 76 ka BP at a depth of 6m was obtained for the sand sheet sediments between Jinmium and Goorurarmum (Ward, 2003; Ward et al., 2005). <u>Which</u> This lends support to the chronology determined by TL dating of

(Fullagar et *al.*, 1996), which produced an age of 103 ± 14 ky BP at a depth of 5 m near the Jinmium site. It was noted by Fullagar et *al.*, (1996) that stone artefacts are present throughout the sand sheet deposit, though the initial presence of stone points, ochre and seed artefacts was dated to about 2.9 – 3.9 ky BP.

Comparison of sequences of sand sheets and rock shelters

If the 18.5 ky BP estimate for the Karlinga rock shelter, and accepting the young Holocene chronology from Jinmium, the sedimentary sequences of the Keep River region rock shelters all have an age of mid-Late Holocene (7,000 – 0 BP). Contrasting with this, the adjacent sand sheets are comprised of sediments and associated cultural sequences which are much older, providing a possible record of human occupation that extends back to 18 ky BP. Also, greater vertical accumulation of Holocene age sediments and archaeological deposits are provided by the sand sheet excavations. Ward suggests that it appears to be likely that the absence of earlier occupation within the rock shelters is due to the geomorphology of these rock shelters being insufficient for the accumulation and preservation of sediments and archaeological material in the long term compared to the adjacent sand sheets, rather than reflecting any absence of earlier human occupation.

The situation where deposits are deeper and older outside rock shelters compared to within rock shelters has been noted previously at Native Well I, Queensland, where respective ages of (6,100 BP and 11,000 BP) (Morwood, 1981). According to Ward, in this as well as a number of other excavations where the deposit extends out past the dripline of the rock shelter, there has generally been minimal comparison of cultural deposits (e.g., Flood, 1970; Smith, 1989) and of sediments and chronology (e.g. Jones & Johnson, 1985; Allen & Barton, 1989; Morwood et *al.*, 1995) between the rock shelter and the area outside it. The excavation records of the Keep River region indicate greater preservation of older sequences may sometimes occur in the open sites, though enclosed rock shelters may provide greater preservation potential for older sequences (Lourandos & David, 1998). In the Keep River region the rock shelters that have young ages have ages from the Late Pleistocene for cultural deposits in the sand sheet area that is immediately adjacent. There are examples of sequences dating to the Pleistocene within rock shelters, such as Narrabulgin (Ngarrabulgan) (David, 1993), Carpenter's Gap (O'Connor, 1995, 1996) and Riwi (Balme, 2000), though the absence of a wider contextual chronostratigraphy limits interpretation of these older sequences.

Eastern Kimberley, western Kimberley and Arnhem Land – representative records of occupation

Ward suggests re-evaluation of the representative records of occupation for the eastern Kimberley, and the adjacent western Kimberley and Arnhem Land regions, given the age discrepancy between the rock shelters and adjacent sand sheets. It has been noted that there is a lack of high quality stratigraphic information and $\delta^{13}C$ values as a guide to a material being dated. Here the extent to which the datasets are comparable is the important consideration in the regional chronological comparisons. The quality of the dating results are referred to elsewhere (for reviews see Frankel, 1990; Allen, 1994; Roberts and Jones, 2001).

Rock shelters have comprised more than 80 % of the archaeological excavation sites in the Keep River and surrounding region that have been published, and contain a freshwater or terrestrial record. Most of these sites are of Late Holocene age, with the earliest evidence of occupation dating to 4,000 – 3,500 BP. In the Victoria River District all the sites excavated have been rock shelters, all of which are dated to the Holocene. The vast majority of archaeological investigations in Arnhem Land have also been rock shelters (Taçon & Brockwell, 1995), which apparently indicates that there was an accelerated increase in the number of these beginning at the close of the Pleistocene (Morwood & Hobbs, 1995).

In the western Kimberley the **Wundadjingangnari**, **Idayu** and **Goalu** are the only open midden sites, the remaining 11 archaeological sites are rock shelters that contain terrestrial and estuarine records. All 3 midden sites are located in the Mitchell Plateau where the entire record of occupation is of Holocene age. For the coastal midden sites along the South Alligator River most sites are younger than 6,000 BP (Woodroffe et al., 1988). It is not clear, however, whether the greater abundance of these Mid- and Late Holocene middens indicate a change in human occupation, or the younger material has been preferentially preserved after the stabilisation of the sea level to current levels (Woodroffe et *al.*, 1988: 101). There are no published dated midden sites, or evidence of a marine economy, in the eastern Kimberley.

The occupation sequence extends into the Pleistocene in other parts of the Western Kimberley, but it comprises a period from about 17 – 13 ky BP which has been regarded as a cultural hiatus (Veth, 1995; O'Connor et *al.*, 1999). Evidence of a continuous cultural presence for the past 40,000 years is apparently provided at Carpenter's Gap (McConnell & O'Connor, 1997: Balme, 2000) in spite of the hiatus above the levels from the LGM. It is still not clear whether each of the major chronological hiatuses that have been documented in each of these excavations actually represent a 'cultural hiatus' during which the site was not often used and there was a low level of sediment accumulation, or represent a natural hiatus during which any sediments that had been deposited in the Late Pleistocene-Early Holocene were removed by geomorphic processes (Wallis, 2001: 105).

It is apparent that in all regions of north western Australia, whichever was the case, most of the sites that have been excavated have been rock shelters, the majority of these being of Holocene age. Whether the records that resulted are comparable regionally depends mainly on the identification of the natural processes, e.g. physical conditions, or cultural processes, e.g. movements of populations, which Ward suggests may explain the temporal distribution patterns (e.g. Feathers, 1997; Parkington, 1989; Ward and Larcombe, 2003). In Arnhem Land, e.g., it has been documented (Woodroffe et al., 1988) how the geomorphological development, associated with rise in sea level of the South Alligator River had influenced the distribution and preservation of shell middens, with the oldest being radiocarbon dated to $6,215 \pm 100$ years BP. Ward suggests that it is possible that the similar temporal distribution of midden records in the western Kimberley may be accounted for by a similar geomorphological history. More generally, in the unconsolidated soil profiles that are typical of northern Australia, the limited resolution of archaeological and environmental records often result in an approach in which temporal distribution patterns are used to identify cultural processes (Parkington, 1989; Holdaway & Porch, 1995).

Before making comparisons between site types it is first necessary to normalise them to equivalent sites that are not occupied or another measure of frequency or common datum. It may only be possible to make comparisons between different sites if the associated *processes* which are responsible for those shared patterns can be demonstrated (see Ward & Larcombe, 2003). There are 3 different types of archaeological site which have been compared (Lourandos, 1997: 225), rock shelter, shell middens and earth mounds of south western Victoria and south eastern Australia for the past 12,000 years and Lourandos (1997: 225) argues for a significant increase in the use of the site and establishment since 3,500 years BP. In the absence of normalisation, however, the frequency of sites may be a reflection of the greater perseveration of younger, and probably shallower, site assemblages. That is, the trend that is shown by the different types of site can also be explained by natural processes rather than by cultural processes, and these are not necessarily the same for each site. It is argued (Lourandos, 1997: 225) that before the terminal Pleistocene when the sites first become visible, the climate was drier, with the landscapes open and semiarid, the resources were dispersed and therefore the populations of the Aboriginals were also relatively more dispersed. There would inevitably have been poorer preservation of these earlier sites. It is also argued (Lourandos, 1997: 226) that after 2,500 BP the appearance and increase in earth mounds associated with wetlands is a reflection of more intensive use of the sites. Ward suggests that it may also indicate that the survival in such environments of earth mounds might have been limited to 2,500 years because in the words of Lourandos *"no equivalent sites existed in prior times"*.

When considering the distribution of archaeological sites Ward suggests questioning if the same patterns were present in occupied and equivalent unoccupied sites. It may be questioned, e.g. whether the absence of sediments of Pleistocene age in rock shelters is also observed in rock shelters that contain no evidence of occupation. It may be possible in some cases to compare equivalent sites, such as bird or animal midden sites and midden sites that were man-made. According to Ward it may require closer cooperation among sedimentologists and archaeologists during the planning of excavations, and interpretative stages (e.g. Ferrand, 2001) to answer such questions.

Intensification and the Holocene record

It is generally regarded that the Middle to Late Holocene period is one in which there was increased cultural change as indicated by alterations in stone artefacts (new types), greater processing of plants, development regionally of art styles and an increase of occupation of older sites (Hiscock, 1984). Qualitative change can be observed in the nature of plant processing (Atchison, 2000; Atchison et *al.*, in prep) and a reduction of stone tools (Fullagar et *al.*, 1996, Boer-Mah, 2002). It is, however, not certain whether the *qualitative* changes that were apparent in the number of archaeological sites and deposits in the Holocene are actually the products of 1 or more (1) cultural change, (2) research and/or (3) preferential preservation.

It is indicated by previous research in the Keep River region, in terms of cultural change, that there was an increase in the number of sites where rock art was preserved from about 4,000 BP (Watchman et *al.*, 2000; Ouzman et *al.*, 2000), at about 3,000 BP the introduction of stone points (Fullagar et *al.*, 1996: 764; Atchison, 2000; Boer-Mah, 2002: 38) and archaeological evidence of the processing of fruit seeds from at least 3,500 BP (Atchison, 2000). It is also indicated by palaeoenvironmental evidence that there was significant human interference of wet and dry rainforest in the late Holocene, 5,000 – 0 BP (Head, 1996). Though there are therefore clear indications of cultural change, Ward suggests there are also natural processes which may have influenced these records. Such as, e.g., in some of the sand sheet profiles in the Keep River region with the mean grain size decreasing as a result of illuviation (deposit of illuvium) as the finer material is concentrated in deeper horizons. A similar redistribution of cultural material may be indicated by a similar pattern with depth of mean grain size and numbers of artefacts (2 – 4 mm fraction) in the same profile. A similar pattern in the distribution of artefacts and bioturbation in sandy deposits in western Illinois has also been observed (Van Nest, 2002). It has been argued (Michie, 1983: 23) that the formation of the archaeological record is wholly attributable in some sandy areas to a dynamic system of bioturbation and gravity (see also Leigh, 2001). A need to distinguish between process-related and product-related attributes of a site, and to differentiate cultural from natural processes is indicated by these results (see also Waters & Kuehn, 1996; Ward & Larcombe, 2003).

The bias towards Late Holocene timescales, in terms of research, has been indicated by a greater representation of rock shelter sites in the published records than open sites (see Smith & Sharp, 1993; Ulm in press). Similar findings come from South Africa (Parkington, 1989), where it was considered that the extreme bias that was found in the distribution of radiocarbon dates towards caves or rock shelters mainly represented patterns of cave use that was changing, and not of prehistoric settlement in general. In the case of thorough regional surveys it was indicated (Parkington, 1989: 215), that a chronological data base could be made more relevant if the set of open site assemblages is considered. Within the regional area of interest a chronographic survey of rock shelters that were unoccupied would also provide an indication of whether the patterns that were observed in the unoccupied rock shelters were representative of natural or cultural processes. The extreme weathering that is characteristic of monsoonal climates in semi-arid areas will decrease the potential for preservation of artefacts and bias a record in a sedimentary sequence in favour of younger material. An example comes from excavations in the Jinmium rock shelter where in the uppermost sediments seeds were noticeably weathered and below 40 cm the number declined, which indicated that this record was influenced more by factors of preservation than cultural processes (Atchison et *al.*, in prep.). The lack of radiocarbon ages at depths greater than 150 cm in the Keep River region most likely is a reflection of *in situ* organic preservation resulting from changes in the level of the water table. It has also been observed at Nauwalabila (Fifield et *al.*, 2001) that radiocarbon ages were not reliable beyond this depth, which was coincident with the appearance of pisoliths (aka a pisoid, a concentric sedimentary grain >2 cm diameter formed as a concretion) of a prior water table that was fluctuating. There may therefore be environmental factors, past or present, limiting the age-depth range of radiocarbon dates, and in some cases this may be avoided by choosing sites at higher elevations.

Whether variation in the sedimentation rate is due to natural or cultural processes, they are an important consideration when the site use intensity is being evaluated as a function of the artefact density or fauna density (Ferrand, 2001: 547). In the Keep River region, increasing rates of sedimentation on sand sheets from less than 10 cm per 1,000 years in the Pleistocene to more than 20 cm per 1,000 years in the Holocene is a major factor in the preferential preservation of Holocene records (Ward, 2003; Ward et al.,. 2004). At Nauwalabila I in Arnhem Land, a similar site, it was also noted (Hope et al., 1995) that there was a progressive increase in the accumulation of sediment, from <1 cm/1,000 years in the Late Pleistocene-Early Holocene, prior to the past 2,000 years when it ceased completely. Exposure time and increased potential for preservation may be reduced by high rates of sediment accumulation, which may explain the observed increased artefact rates of accumulation per unit time (see also Ferrand, 2001; Ward & Larcombe, 2003).

In the eastern Kimberley region the predominantly Late Holocene record of occupation may reflect real cultural changes, though the effects of research bias towards rock shelter sites and the limitations that have been imposed by preferential preservation in semi-arid sandy environments must be considered further before interpretations of human behaviour can be further considered. Between rock shelter sites and over Holocene time periods regional comparisons may be valid, though it is not known if there is a comparable record for the Late Pleistocene of occupation in the sand sheets to those preserved in the Keep River region. According to Ward these sampling and taphonomy issues are not limited to north western Australia, also existing in north Queensland (Ulm in press), and in South Africa (Parkington, 1989) and North America (Marshall, 2001). Therefore the re-examination of regional datasets and deciphering the relationship between absence of evidence and evidence of absence in the archaeological record that has been preserved remains important.

Ward's conclusion

There is evidence of occupation in the sand sheets dating to the LGM in the Keep River region, though in the rock shelters only Holocene sequences are preserved. An important consideration when making comparisons within and between regions is that different geomorphic environments can produce different records of occupation, as data about land use by humans can be overlooked when the targets for analysis are restricted to select types of site. According to Ward the research and preservation bias of rock shelters of Holocene age is apparent across northern Australia, and has been the basis for many theoretical discussions concerning intensification in the Holocene, as well as abandonment and/or gaps in the record of rock shelters. Across north western Australia further excavation at locations at sites outside and away from rock shelters, even at sites where there is no indication on the surface of artefacts, might test these theories. Greater consideration needs to be given to processes of site formation which may have influenced the temporal distribution of archaeological sites and deposits. In many cases a multi-disciplinary approach to other possible explanations for change should be considered before cultural regional chronological patterns are considered.

Mining and quarrying - The Nullarbor Plain
Koonalda Cave, in the Nullarbor Plain

This cave, in the South Australian section of the plain, opens at the surface by a 30 m deep sinkhole that is 85 m in diameter. The sinkhole gives no indication of its presence from the surface until it is approached close enough to be seen as a large opening flush with the surrounding plain. The walls of the sinkhole are sheer vertical sides or undercut for about 20 m down from the surface. From that point a steep slope continues to the main chamber. This chamber, about 70 m below the surface, is huge, 60 x 90 m, and the domed ceiling is about 45 m above the floor. 2 passages lead from this main chamber, one of which leads to 3 underground lakes.

Archaeological significance
Radiocarbon dates for Koonalda Cave, on the Nullarbor Plain, South Australia, shows it was occupied by 24,000 years ago. Allen's Cave was occupied by 25,000 years ago. TL dates for the occupation levels where charcoal didn't survive are 34,000 years. Preliminary optically stimulated luminescence (OSL) for Allen's Cave has a date of 34,000 ± 7,000 years 1 m above an artefact, so presumably the

artefact is much older. Similar dates have been found at Koonalda Cave.

Koonalda Cave is a crater-like doline (limestone sinkhole) in the karst of the Nullarbor Plain. It was used as a flint mine, quarrying being carried out underground, often in places with no natural light, the resulting flint nodules being transported elsewhere for manufacture of tools. In the first dimly lit chamber of the cave, which was 100 m from the surface and 70 m below ground level, there were hearths, charcoal and mining residue. Later excavations found that flint mining had been practiced between 24,000 and 14,000 years ago. Charcoal has been dated to between $23,700 \pm 850$ BP and $13,700 \pm 270$ BP, and a layer that dated to $19,900 \pm 2,000$ BP (Wright, 1971a).

There were 2 major attractions in this cave, reliable water and a plentiful supply of flint.

Mining & quarrying in Prehistoric Australia

The earliest evidence of mining and quarrying from Sahul, as noted by Habgood & Franklin in their study, was at about 24,000 years ago. During the Late Pleistocene, there doesn't appear to have been much stone mining and quarrying being carried out in Australia. The probable reason is that raw material was easily found in the local area or from short distances away. Many of the stone implements used at that time were simply naturally shaped pieces of fractured rock found on the surface of the ground or river stones (Hiscock, 1996; Hiscock & Allen, 2000). Obsidian was being transported to the offshore islands of the Bismarck Archipelago from New Britain in the Late Pleistocene, at that time part of the Australian continent, at a time of low sea level. The recipients fashioned the obsidian into the implements they needed (Allen et al., 1989; Summerhayes & Allen, 1993; Gosden, 1995; Fredericksen, 1997; White & Harris, 1997).

Most of these quarries seem to have been used for the acquisition of raw materials for implements such as stone hatchets (Hiscock, 1996; Smith, et.al., 1998; Gibbs & Veth, 2002).

There are known sites of extensive ochre mining from the late Holocene, such as at Bookartoo (Parachilna), South Australia,

Wilgie Mia, Western Australia, and the Campbell Ranges, Northern Territory (Hiscock, 1996; Mulvaney & Kamminga, 1999).

Koonalda Cave is the oldest dated stone quarry known from Sahul. This cave was being mined between about 24,000 and 14,000 years ago (Wright 1971a). Another very old mine, as indicated by indirect evidence, is Karlie-ngoinpool Cave, Mt Gambier Region, where silicate mining is believed to have occurred in the late Pleistocene (Bednarik, 1984).

At the Puritjarra rock shelter, ochre has been recovered from layers dated to 32,000 - 13,000 years ago. This ochre has been sourced to the Karrku quarry, about 150 km from the Puritjarra site. This indicates that larger scale ochre mining was taking place in the Pleistocene (Smith, 1996; Smith et. al., 1998; Gibbs & Veth, 2002). Ochre is believed to have been extracted on a small scale throughout Sahul during the late Pleistocene.

Spongolite was quarried at Rebecca Creek, on the west coast of Tasmania, 100 km from the Rocky Cape caves where it was used in the manufacture of stone implements.

Aboriginal Flint Mining

There doesn't seem to have been many instances of major stone mining in Australia during the late Pleistocene. The raw material for their stone culture at the time seems to have come mainly from local sources, most of the artefacts being made from naturally-fractured river pebbles picked up from the ground (Hiscock, 1996, Hiscock & Allen, 2000). Only about 1/3 of known stone quarries in Australia contain evidence of mining during the Pleistocene, most being from the Holocene, where they have been dated. Mostly they appear to show material was obtained for exchange, the oldest known dated site in Australia being Koonalda Cave.

Flint mining was found in Koonalda Cave on the Nullarbor Plain where the mining has been found to have occurred between 24,000 and 14,000 years ago.

Ochre Mining

Ochre was one of the most important commodities passing along the trade routes of Australia, partly because it was used for decoration of bodies, artefacts, cave wall painting, but most importantly it was an essential part of decoration for important ceremonies. The places where the best ochre was mined, such as the Yarrakina red ochre mine where the sacred iridescent ochre was mined at Parachilna in the Flinders Ranges in South Australia, were busy centres of trade, people travelling from as far away as western Queensland to trade for the ochre.

The ochre miners crushed the soft rock and made it into a paste by mixing it with water, though sometimes it was mixed with the fat or blood of animals such as fish, emus, possums, or kangaroos. Orchid juice was sometimes used as a fixative. The paste was rolled into small balls for trade.

There are a number of ochre mines known around Australia.

Mt Rowland, Tasmania

At this mine the women were the miners. The red iron ore was levered out with a pointed stick as a chisel and a stone as a hammer. They squeezed into narrow crevices to get at the ochre. One instance is known of a woman getting stuck in a crevice, having to be pulled out by the legs. The ochre was carried away from the mine in kangaroo skin bags.

Wilgie Mia (Wilgamia)

This mine is north west of Cue in the Weld Range, Murchison district, Western Australia. The mine was on the northern side of Nganakurakura Hill. An open cut mine had been dug out of the hillside that was 20 m deep and 15-30 m wide. A cavern opens from the pit and the miners tunnelled out many small caves and galleries as they followed the red and yellow ochre seams.

The mining method here was to hit the rock with heavy stone mauls and dig the ochre out with fire-hardened pointed wooden wedges. To reach seams that were too high to work from the floor they erected pole scaffolding. The ore was processed at the top of the northern slope were the ochre was extracted, crushed, had water added, then rolled into balls for trade.

Wooden wedges and stone implements have been found in the strata of the cavity floor. Dating has placed the wooden implements at 1,000 years ago, but the huge amount of material removed from the mine, estimated to be as much as several thousand tons, indicate that mining has probably been going on for much longer. The mine was still being worked as late as 1939.

Of the ochre pigments, the red variety was the most valuable in pre-contact Australia. And when it is found in a place associated with an important Dreamtime being, as the Wilgie Mia site is, being associated with the a giant kangaroo that was speared by Mondong, the spirit being. The kangaroo was said to have made its final leap to what is now Wilgie Mia, the red ochre is said to be its blood. Yellow and green ochre were also mined here, the yellow being the liver and green the gall of the great kangaroo.

The aborigines feared the ochre mine, the only people allowed to enter were the elders, stone piles being placed to mark places where the uninitiated could not go. The miners were not allowed to take mining implements away from the mine, and when leaving had to walk backwards, brushing away their footprints as they went to prevent Mondong from following and killing them.

This red ochre was much sought after all over Western Australia, and is even said to have been traded as far as Queensland. The mining activity was organised to a level that was not usually attributed to Aborigines.

Karrku Quarry

This quarry is situated 150 km from the Puritjarra Cave Rock shelter, about 320 km west of Alice Springs, is the source, as determined by chemical analysis, of the red ochre found in layers at Puritjarra dated from 32,000 to 13,000 years ago.

Late Pleistocene

Ochre recovered from sites all over Australia dated to the late Pleistocene are thought to possibly indicate the occurrence of small scale ochre mining before the close of the Pleistocene.

Rock Art

A notable find in the cave was Pleistocene rock art, finger markings on the wall, 300 m from the entrance, where there was no natural light. The graphic markings on the walls that resembled the macaroni or meander style of the earliest European cave art.

Different parts of the cave walls have different textures, the wall markings varying with the texture. A part of the cave known as the art passage has very soft and friable walls, the colour and texture being compared to that of compacted talcum powder. In this part of the cave a finger touching the wall leaves a mark. Other parts of the cave have walls that require pressure with a stone or stick to mark them with fine incised lines.

In places, large flat areas of wall are covered with random crisscrossing parallel finger markings. There are large groups of vertical lines, and occasionally horizontal lines, as well as some definite patterns, such as in the form of regularly spaced grids or lattices. There are 2 sets of 4 concentric circles about 20 cm wide. A unique design is a herringbone pattern that is 120 cm long, with 74 diagonal incised lines, above which are 37 short finger markings. The numbers of lines are believed to be deliberate because the number of lower lines is exactly twice the number of upper lines. It has been assumed that there is possibly some symbolic significance attached to this design.

In places there are more modern markings, graffiti, which allow the comparison of the old with the new. The new markings show much sharper lines on the ridges than the older markings. It is believed the art is probably more than 20,000 years old. Charcoal found just below the surface in the passage leading to 'the squeeze' has been dated to 20,000 years ago. It has been suggested the charcoal might have come from the torches used by the people who marked the wall; the wall above the charcoal was covered with incised markings.

In a cavity 15 m below a massive rock fall there are markings on the wall that are believed to be very old, but no dating has been possible. There is a platform high in the dome of a large chamber containing a lake that is reached through 'the squeeze'. There are more markings on a part of the wall that can no longer be reached from the platform, part of the platform having fallen into the lake after the markings were made. This contributes to the circumstantial evidence that the markings are very old, probably being of similar age to those that have been dated to between 15,000 and 24,000 years ago.

There has been some dispute over whether the markings on the walls should be regarded as art of had some other purposes. Among the suggestions for alternative causes of the markings are sharpening bone points, guiding the miners to the flint veins. Counter arguments have been put forward. Why would they sharpen bone points in darkness? If they were mining guides, why did they occur only in some parts of the cave, whereas the flint veins occur in all parts of the cave?

Another explanation suggested is that they are simply the expression of the common human attraction to marking blank spaces. Graffiti has been around for a very long time, having been found made by Romans and Vikings, and was probably made by many others from the distant past. It has been documented all over the world, and has been suggested as the urge that led to art everywhere.

It has been suggested that the markings may have been associated with rituals, as could be expected to have occurred with initiations, which are always conducted away from prying eyes of the uninitiated, or connected with the mining of the flint.

Another cave has been found on the Nullarbor Plain, in Western Australia, that is being studied that has not been damaged by modern graffiti. The markings in this cave are similar to those in Koonalda Cave.

Markings are found on the walls of Kintore Cave in the Northern Territory, Orchestra Shell Cave in Western Australia.

A date from charcoal found beneath a concentration of finger marks, which may have been the remains of a torch, in a dark part of the cave gave a date of 19,900 +/- 2,000 BP. (Maynard & Edwards, 1971; Wright, 1971a; Mulvaney, 1975).

Colonisation of the Arid Zone

Temperate Australia

Western Australia - Upper Swan River site
This is an open-air campsite on an ancient floodplain along the upper Swan River. It has been dated to 38,000 BP. Among the artefacts found at this site were flakes made from a distinctive chert containing fossils. The same chert has been found in a number of other Western Australian sites with ages in excess of 4,600 BP, and the probable source of the chert was subsequently found in drill cores from the seabed off the coast, on the continental shelf that would have been dry land when the first people arrived in Australia. It appears to have been a toolmaking site. About 900 artefacts had been

found at this site by the time of writing, mostly of deeply patinated dolerite. 75 % of these finds are stone chips less than 15 mm long. 37 tools have been found that were retouched or showed evidence of use-wear. The tools of small size were also found in the Devil's Lair deposit, also in Western Australia.

Small scrapers were included among the artefacts in this site that were manufactured from quartz and quartzite. Wear was found on the edges of pebble fragments. It is believed this was a tool-making site that has been relatively undisturbed, based on the presence of chips, cores and conjoins (stone flakes that can be fitted together). The site is now controlled by the local Aboriginal community.

Devil's Lair

This is a cave in the far south west of Western Australia, 5 km from the present coast and 20 km north of Cape Leeuwin. At the time of low sea level it would have been about 25 km from the sea. Its single chamber has an earth floor that is covered by flowstone, a sheet of stone, about 20 cm thick, which occasionally forms on the floors of limestone caves. The upper levels contained large numbers of bones from the Tasmanian devil, hence its name. It was originally excavated by palaeontologists looking for animal remains, as these are common in limestone caves. Once it was realised there were artefacts in the cave, excavations were taken over by archaeologists. Possible artefacts and a human incisor were found. The artefact-containing lower levels have been dated to about 33,000 BP.

Bones of a wide range of animals were found, some charred, and in one case in an intact hearth, indicating that it wasn't the kill of a predator. Some of the bones, of giant kangaroos, ***Protemnodon & Sthenurus***, had been cracked and a couple have possibly been used as tools. If this proves to be true it will be the first definite evidence from Australia that the early inhabitants hunted megafauna. See Cuddie Springs.

A number of limestone plaques have been found in this deposit. B3651 has a geometrical design, a trapezoidal shape, formed of intersecting incisions. This plaque was found in a hearth that has been dated to between 12,900 and 13,200 years ago. It was originally dated to $11,960 \pm 140$ and $12,050 \pm 140$ years ago. These original dates have since been rejected, being replaced by $13,050 \pm 90$ years ago. Plaque 3652 came from a layer dated to between 24,950-26,050 years ago. The original date for the site, 20,400 ± 1,000, has been replaced by 25,500 +/- 275.

According to Turney et.*al*. (2001) 4 independent dating techniques, OSL, ESR, U-series dating of flowstone and ^{14}C dating of the carbonate in emu eggshells, all agree with the chronology that indicate the site was occupied by about 50,000 BP.

The lowest level of the site dates to 31,400 ± 1,500 BP and the most recent to 30,590 ± 1,810 BP. Fragments of red ochre have been found in the deposit, one of which came from a hearth that was originally dated to 27,700 ± 700 BP. A number of large ferruginous nodules of ochre were found, one of which weighed 13 g. It is believed these nodules were brought to the cave by the occupants, but smaller nodules are thought to have possibly washed into the cave (Dortch & Merrilees, 1973; Dortch, 1984; Dortch & Dortch, 1996; Dortch, 2004).

See Aboriginal Occupation of south central Tasmania

See Table of notational pieces

Tasmania - Cave Bay Cave

This is a large sea cave in Cave Bay on Hunter Island, 6 km from the north western tip of Tasmania. The occupation at the site has been found to extend back 23,000 years. The oldest occupation level found was at about 22,759 years ago. Over the following 2,000 years 0.5 m of ash accumulated, containing some bone points and stone tools, and smashed, burnt animal bones.

The implements found here, of both stone and bone, are similar to those from the mainland during the Pleistocene, but are the forerunners of those that were to be developed in isolation in Tasmania. A 9 cm long bone point from the shin bone of a macropod found in association with charcoal was dated to 18,550 years ago. Other bone points were similar, but dated from 6,600- 4,000 years ago.

At the time the cave was being used the sea would have been about 30-40 km away, the view from the cave being across the wide Bassian Plain. The remains found in the lower levels of the cave are believed to be the result of occasional occupation by hunting parties.

In the levels dating from the ice age, have been found brush wallaby, barred bandicoot, tiger cat, native cat, and the Tasmanian pademelon and wombat. These are all extant animals, though the wombat and native cat are not found in later sites. And they are not present in historic times on Hunter Island.

The early occupation of the site apparently occurred spasmodically, and for short periods. This was followed by a period of heavy rock fall, thought to be from the peak of the last glacial phase about 18,000 years ago. It is believed it may have been caused by water freezing in cracks and crevices, which led to the opening of the cracks enough to cause the rock slabs to be pried loose.

The sea reached its present level about 7,000 years ago, and from 18,000 years ago till that time the cave was apparently deserted. From that period there is only 1 small isolated hearth that has been dated to about 15,000 years ago. This indicates that during this period the main occupants were owls and carnivores, though humans were occasionally present. The presence of owls is indicated by many intact small animal bones that are indicative of the presence of regurgitated bones from owl pellets. The presence of the Tasmanian devil is indicated by the many macropod and possum bones that had been chewed into fragments.

When the sea was near its present position, about 6,000 years ago, the cave is occupied again, as shown by the presence of the remains of marine shellfish, which would have been easily found along the now nearby water's edge, suggesting that the occupants now had a well-developed coastal economy. The contents of these more recent levels are similar to the middens from the lower levels at Rocky Cape South that has been dated to about 8,000 years ago.

The base of the dense shell midden at Cave Bay Cave has been dated to about 6,600 years ago, contained the bones of small macropods and mutton birds, the shells of rocky coast species and some fish bones. Bone points, stone tools, quartz and quartzite flakes, and pebble tools have been found in layers older than 4,000 years.

Bowdler has interpreted this midden to mean that the cave was occupied by people who had a well-developed fishing economy that had been moving further inland as the edge of the sea progressively encroached on previously dry land, and the site at the time of the upper levels of occupation would probably have been on a Hunter 'Peninsula', the link to the Tasmanian mainland being severed as the sea continued to rise, It was then on Hunter Island. The cave was apparently abandoned for several thousand years, only being occupied by people from Tasmania again about 2,500 years ago.

A macropod femur was found that has groups of grooves and scratches on its surface. It has been dated to between $15,400 \pm 330$ and $20,850 \pm 290$ years ago. There was also a broken swan tarsometatarsus that had deep incisions and an 'embayment' into the bones where grooves are visible. There is a gloss over the ridges. It was found in a shell midden dated to $6,640 \pm 100$ and $3,960 \pm 110$ years ago (Bowdler, 1984) (from Habgood & Franklin 2008).

A deposit dating to $22,750 \pm 420$ BP contained quartz fragments with adhering ochre. (Bowdler, 1984)

See Aboriginal Occupation of south central Tasmania

The South West
Kutikina Cave "spirit" (Frazer Cave)

This is a large cave, 170 m deep in the side of a limestone cliff, 35 m from the eastern bank of the Lower Franklin River, 10 km from where it joins the Gordon River. It is about 40 m above sea level.

The cave floor covers an area of about 100 m^2 covered by up to 2 m of bone debris in which tools and fireplaces have been found. About 250,000 bones and about 37,000 stone flakes have been found in less than 1 m^3, leading to the estimate of an average density of 70,000 artefacts and 68 kg of bone per cubic metre (Flood, 2004). It has been suggested that about 20-30 people camped in the cave for a few weeks every year, probably while they hunted in the area, before moving on. It was in this way that Aboriginal groups tended to not overexploit any one area. In some parts of the cave there are small openings in the roof. Beneath all of these openings, "skylights", were found a mass of stone-working debris, apparently they were utilised as the places with the best light to work on tool making, including some bone points.

There was a thin white layer of calcium carbonate (moon milk) covering the floor of the cave. Below this was a layer about 30-40 cm thick of interleaving hearths. This layer was darker than others because of the amount of charcoal, ash and burnt earth from the small depressions where the cooking fires had been. The top of the hearth layer has been dated to 14,840 ± 930 years ago. The layers below the hearth layer, that continue down to the bedrock, contained limestone blocks that had fallen from the roof and mixed among them were stone tools and charcoal that allowed dating of the oldest occupation layers in the deposits to about 20,000 years ago. The conditions that led to the formation of the layers containing the limestone blocks probably resulted from the freezing conditions of the ice age.

It has been suggested the stone tools are characterised as a regional variant of the Australian core tool and scraper tradition of mainland Australia from the last ice age. Features include steep-sided, domed horsehoof cores with a single striking platform, and steep-edged, notched and flat scrapers. Quartz and quartzite are the main materials used. Darwin glass, a natural glass, was also used for making cutting tools.

Analysis of the cutting surfaces of Darwin glass tools has revealed traces of collagen and crystallised haemoglobin, that further analysis showed was from the red-necked wallaby, aka Bennett's wallaby, ***Macropus rufogriseus.*** Haemoglobin crystals are unique for each animal species. In this case the haemoglobin crystals proved to be identical to that of the living species. So at least 1 use of Darwin glass was for butchering animals, but it is believed there were multiple other uses for it. It is believed the small flakes may have been used like a modern penknife.

99 % of the artefacts from the lower layers, between about 19,000 and 17,000 years ago, are made of quartzite. There is a change of the dominant material to 99 % milky quartz. These tools were now fashioned by the bipolar hammer and anvil method. This method is usually associated with the manufacture of tools from hard, intractable quartz. The sediments from 17,000 to 15,000 years ago contained the largest concentration of archaeological debris (Ransom et al., 1983; Jones, 1989). It was from this period that Darwin glass makes its first appearance at the site, as well as other new tools. There is also an increase in the amount of bone of the red-necked wallaby and wombat.

160 very small thumbnail scrapers, round-edged tools about the size and shape of a human thumbnail, mostly about 20 x 15 mm and about

8 mm thick. Some are even smaller, 11 x 7 x 5 mm. This type of scraper was common in the small tool tradition from the Holocene on the mainland. Prior to their discovery in south west Tasmania they were almost unknown among Pleistocene assemblages. There is no evidence that the Pleistocene scrapers were ever hafted to a handle. It is believed detailed study will disclose differences between the thumbnail scarpers scrapers from the Pleistocene and those from the Holocene. At Kutikina Cave all the known thumbnail scrapers were made of quartz and produced with the bipolar method, though at other sites chert and Darwin glass were also used in the manufacture.

Functional analysis of the thumbnail scrapers from Kutikina and Nunamira Cave has concluded that they were hand held, showing no traces of hafting or use-wear. The backing was apparently the curved, steep retouched edge, apparently to prevent cutting the hand of the user, and all residues are found on the other, cutting edge.

Comparison of the residues on the thumbnail scrapers with that on the cutting edges of tools from the large flake industry in lower levels found that they had a similar use, both showing a similar broad range of functions. 30-40 % of both tool types had traces of butchery on their cutting edges, bone-working 20 %, plant working of various kinds 15 %, woodworking 10 % (Flood, 2004).

There were also bone points from wallaby fibula, but not many animal bones are known to have been modified, though there are 250,000 pieces of animal bone known from the site, giving information about the diet, environment and way of life of the occupants of the cave. Bone preservation is not common in archaeological sites, and even when it is preserved it is difficult to distinguish between the prey of humans and animals that died there at times when the occupation site was not being used by humans. In the case of Kutikina Cave there is no doubt as many of the long bones have been smashed for marrow extraction, marrow being an important source of essential fatty acids, and have often been charred. And not all body parts are present.

Among the animals represented by the bones, red-necked wallabies represented 75 %, wombats 12 %, and a combined fraction of 15 other species, 13 % (Flood, 2004). Red-necked wallabies that were obviously so common in the area during the Pleistocene prefer open shrubland and sedgeland habitats, grazing on grasslands and sedgelands and herbfields. Their presence in the area of Kutikina Cave during the Pleistocene fits with the area as it would have been at the time the cave was occupied, with rainforest present only in sheltered valleys along rivers. In present-day south west Tasmania few red-necked wallabies are found in the rainforest.

At a time when the annual average temperatures were about $4°$ C, $6°$ C lower than at the present, rainfall was about half the present level at about 1,500 mm/year, and glaciers flowed down the high mountain valleys. There would have been grassy plains from the forest edges where the wallabies could feed.

As with the hunters in the Northern Hemisphere at this time, the Tasmanian Aborigines occupied deep caves to avoid the freezing conditions of the ice age. The Kutikina Cave remains have been compared with those of the caves of southern France. They had similar tools, cooking methods, and the hunting strategies. The main difference was the prey, reindeer in the France and red-necked wallabies in Tasmania.

Karta: Island of the Dead - Kangaroo Island

This is a large island, 150 by 50 km, which has been separate from the mainland for nearly 10,000 years. It was called the 'Island of the Dead' by the tribes in the southern part of the Australian mainland around the Murray River, probably because a creation being from the Dreamtime, Ngurunderi crossed to the island, from where he travelled to the Milky Way. The spirits of the dead of a number of tribes were believed to follow his track to the afterlife in the sky. See Kangaroo Island Mythology.

On the island there is plenty of evidence of occupation in prehistoric times. It is separated from South Australia by Backstairs Passage. This body of water would be very difficult to cross in canoes. It is subject to strong currents, heavy tidal swells and steep breaking seas. The first evidence of Aboriginal habitation on Kangaroo Island was the discovery of hammer stones at Hawk's Nest near Murray's Lagoon in 1903. In 1930 more stone tools were discovered and excavation was proposed. It was based on the finds at Kangaroo Island that the first suggestion was made that colonisation by Aborigines might date from the Pleistocene. The Aborigines on the nearby mainland had no water craft capable of making the dangerous crossing, having only rafts and bark canoes that were propelled with poles.

The method of transport to the island used by the original occupants had been puzzled over, the conclusion being that they probably reached the island at a time of low sea level. The occupation was thought to have probably occurred a long time ago, as indicated by the archaic nature of the tools, no similar tools being found on the mainland from more recent times. Further support for this conclusion was the fact that the dingo never reached the island, as was the case with Tasmania. Also, no small tools have been found that were used at more recent times on the mainland.

An indication of the length of time since the isolation of the island by rising sea levels is that many of the animals and plants of the island have evolved a subspecies related to those on the mainland.

Fieldwork in the early 1930s near Murray's Lagoon, a land-locked freshwater lake, revealed some hammer stones and some massive pebble implements. Subsequent exploration revealed the presence of 47 camp sites on the island; by 1958 the number had risen to 120. There were hundreds of pebble choppers, horsehoof cores and hammer-stones. The tool industry was named the Kartan, after the name for the island among the mainland Ramindjeri tribe.

Most of the Kartan tools have been found in ploughed fields where they have been brought to the surface by the ploughs. Some tools have been found in areas where the land is covered by near-impenetrable scrub, but in the past, when the climate was different from the present, especially when the vegetation was probably being controlled by fire-stick farmers. Some have been found on a high ridge above Murray's Lagoon that was apparently the water's edge, about 5 m above the present water level, indicating that at the time of occupation the climate was different from that of the present.

The nearest source of quartzite for the tools found at Hawk's Nest is about 35 km from the site on the north coast of the island. Together with the lack of flakes and debris from the manufacture of the tools at the site the tools were found, this indicates that the tools were prepared elsewhere, probably at the source of the raw material.

Pleistocene Dates

Chapter 6 – Human Remains in Australia

Mungo Man - Willandra Lakes Hominid 3 (WHL 3) See Willandra Footprints

On 26 February 1974 an eroding gravesite was discovered in the shifting sands of a lunette around Lake Mungo in the Willandra Lakes World Heritage area in western New South Wales. The human skeleton, named Lake Mungo 3 had its fingers interlocked over the groin. The bones had been coated in red ochre at the time of burial, which is thought to be the earliest use of ochre for this purpose.

The skeletal remains found at Lake Mungo have recently been dated by 3 different methods, uranium series, electron spin resonance and optically stimulated luminescence, to arrive at a new, older, age of 62,000 years +/- 6,000 years. Previously it was thought to be 30,000-40,000 years old.

As any humans arriving in Australia could only have landed in the north, and Lake Mungo is in the far south west of New South Wales, a great distance from the north coast of Australia, the first arrival must have been prior to 60,000 years ago.

Writing in *Archaeology*, May/June 2003, Dr Jim Bowler, the discoverer of Mungo Man, has claimed that 3 different labs have now revised the date back to 42,000 BP.

Whether Mungo Man was 40,000 or 60,000 years old doesn't change the arrival date of humans in Australia while the Malakunanja II and Nauwalabila I sites in Arnhem Land remain dated to 60,000 BP. These sites are well inland of the actual landing sites that would have been on the continental shelf at a time of low sea level, so presumably the time of the first arrival would have been even earlier.

Mungo Man, LM3 (WLH-3) has been claimed to be the oldest modern human skeleton from which mtDNA has been recovered. see Genetic Evidence

The skeleton was of a gracile type, and identified as a male by the configuration of the pelvis and thighs, but also because the positioning of the hands suggest they were holding the penis, interesting because this placement of the hands has continued until historic times. Other features indicating that the skeleton was of a male are the angle of the sciatic notch, a large femur head, and an estimated height of 170 cm (5 ft 7) compared to the estimated height of 148 cm (4 ft 10) for Mungo Woman. Another feature of this skeleton was the presence of a condition called woomera elbow or atlatl elbow, in the right elbow, that is, severe osteoarthritis believed to results from the action of throwing spears with a woomera for a number of years. This condition occurs only in the dominant spear throwing arm. This means that at 40,000 (or 60,000) years old, it is the earliest known use of a spear thrower.

Red ochre powder had been scattered over the body at the time of burial. The fact that ochre was used in the burial indicates that trade routes must have been operating even at this remote time, as there are no known sources of ochre for long distances around the burial site.

According to the authors[3] burial seems to have been carried out by humans for a very long time in island South East Asia and Australia, being a feature human behaviour since not along after the first signs of their arrival in the region. The burial at Lake Mungo, that was associated with red ochre, is a notable example (Bowler et *al.*, 2003; Habgood & Franklin, 2008), and the burials found at Willandra Lakes, that were later (Grün et *al.*, 2011) and at Roonka (Robertson & Prescott, 2006).

Among the earliest known evidence of symbolic activity is the use of exotic ochre at Lake Mungo (Allen, 1972; Bowler, 1998), as well at other sites in Sahul, and throughout the Pleistocene pigment provides the most abundant symbolic evidence. At Lake Mungo the early use of pigment is suggested to possibly be the most significant of these sites as a result of its use in the WLH3 ritual extended burial and the transport of ochre over a distance of about 200 km to the burial site (Bowler, 2003). Dating to about 40,000 years ago, this site was the oldest known cremation in the world, as well as demonstrating the ritual complexity of the early inhabitants of southeast Australia (Bowler et *al.*, 2003).

At Lake Mungo the imprints of shafts are the earliest known evidence of the use of wooden projectile technologies that date to about 25,000 years ago (Webb et *al.*, 2006). Also at Lake Mungo, as well as other sites such as Riwi, dating from 36,000 to 40,000 years ago, is the first known evidence of long-distance social interaction or exchange, examples being marine shells, shell beads and ochre that were transported for distances of more than 200-300 km (Allen, 1972; Balme, 2000; Balme & Morse, 2006).

It has been shown by conjoining flakes onto horsehoof cores that prior to 40,000 years ago at Lake Mungo blades had been removed from the site (Shawcross, 1998).

Lake Mungo 3 (WLH 3) western NSW

An extended burial that has been dated by OSL to 40,000 ± 2,000 years ago. The remains were covered with red ochre. The nearest known sources of ochre are in the Manfred Ranges, 100-200 km to the North West, suggesting the existence of long distance exchange or transport in the Pleistocene (Bowdler & Thorne, 1976; Bowdler, 1998; Westaway, 2006).

On 26 February 1974 an eroding gravesite was discovered in the shifting sands of a lunette around Lake Mungo in the Willandra Lakes World Heritage area. The human skeleton, named Lake Mungo 3 (WLH 3) had its fingers interlocked over the groin. The bones had been coated in red ochre at the time of burial, which is thought to be the earliest use of ochre for this purpose.

The skeletal remains found at Lake Mungo about 20 years ago have recently been dated by 3 different methods, uranium series, electron spin resonance and optically stimulated luminescence, to arrive at a new, older, age of 62,000 years ± 6,000 years. Previously it was thought to be 30,000-40,000 years old.

As any humans arriving in Australia could only have landed in the north, and Lake Mungo is in the far south west of New South Wales, a great distance from the north coast of Australia, the first arrival must have been prior to 60,000 years ago.

See Genetic Evidence see Mungo Man

Lake Nitchie Burial

At Lake Nitchie, dated to 6820 ± 200, by bone collagen, in western New South Wales, a burial of a man in the lunette of the lake had a very large pierced tooth necklace. The necklace was made of 178 Tasmanian devil teeth. The teeth would have come from 47 individual devils, now extinct on the mainland. If it was common for the teeth of Tasmanian devils to be used in such large necklaces, maybe it contributed to the demise of the devils in the mainland. Individual teeth are pierced by a hole that was ground and gouged - a very labour-intensive job. So far this necklace is unique in Australia, present or prehistoric.

An unusual feature of this burial was that the body had been compressed into a shaft-like pit. Ochre pellets were found in the pit. The man lacked his 2 front teeth. Tooth avulsion, knocking out of 1 or 2 of a novice's upper incisors, was practised as part of an initiation rite among some Aboriginals. This is another skeleton that has been classified differently by researchers; some say it is robust while others regard it as gracile.

Lake Tandou Skull

In 1967 a skull from the Pleistocene was discovered in the Willandra Lakes region at Lake Tandou, 150 km North West of Lake Mungo. It was on the surface of the lunette of the lake, in association with a shell midden. The shells dated to 15200 ± 160 BP.

It is believed to be a man about 20-25 years old (Leonard Freedman & Marcel Lofgren, 1983). The cranium was considered similar to skulls from Lake Nitchie and Keilor in overall 'size' and 'shape', but the Kow Swamp 1 is of markedly different 'shape' and 'size' from the other 3 skulls. Each of the 4 skulls is markedly different in equal proportions from those of recent skulls of Murray Valley people in 'size' and 'shape'. (Leonard Freedman & Marcel Lofgren). According to Freedman & Lofgren, "Tandou fits the 'gracile' group well but its cranial vault bones are very thick, as are those of the so-called 'robust' crania".

West Point Midden

This midden, 60 km west of Rocky Cape, is one of the largest occupation sites, and one of the richest known in Australia. It is in the form of a grassy hill from which the view to the east is over reefs, bays and islets, and to the west are swamps and tea tree scrub. The base is a pebble bank covered by a dune, above which the midden rises 6 m above the surrounding flat land. The midden is 90 m long and 40 m wide, on top of which are about 8 circular depressions, each about 4 m wide and 0.5 m deep. It is believed these were the bases of dome-shaped huts that were known to be present at a number of places in Tasmania in historic times. Such huts were built of a framework of pliable branches, at least sometimes of tea-tree branches, thatched with bark, grass or turf and lined with skins, bark or feathers (Flood, 2004).

Many huts of this type were seen on the west coast in the 1830s, many of which were grouped into villages, especially where they were close to freshwater and good foraging areas, as was the situation at West Point Midden. Near the site was what is believed to have been an elephant seal colony, though elephant seals now come no closer than Macquarie Island to breed. Elephant seal pups were being eaten at West Point between about 1,800 and 1,300 years ago. The hunting of elephant seal pups would have been in summer when they breed.

Seals were a major food source for the people at West Point, together with abalone, other shellfish, wallabies, small mammals and lizards. There were only 3 fish vertebrae known from the 75 m^3 of the deposit.

It has been estimated the site was probably occupied for several months each year by about 40 people, probably over the elephant seal breeding season, for about 500 years. It is believed that the men hunted the seals and the women dived for shellfish. At present seal colonies are attractions for white pointer sharks, so they probably patrolled the waters at the same time the women would have been collecting shellfish.

At places like West Point the division of labour of hunter-gatherer people seems to have been a bit skewed in favour of the men, at least for the part of the year they occupied the huts. At this site the hunting seems to have consisted of strolling to the local seal colony, clubbing a young seal or 2 and taking it back to the camp. In stark contrast, "the women's work was never done". The women were observed by a number of Europeans diving for shell fish. When they dived they had rush baskets suspended from their necks that they filled with shellfish they pried from the rocks with small wooden wedges. They collected crayfish, even when the sea was rough, by diving up to 4 m, sometimes pulling themselves down along the strands of giant kelp, where they pulled the crayfish from under rocks and flung them onto the shore. It was commented on by a number of European observers that the women were excellent swimmers who could hold their breaths for long periods.

Another popular food source was mutton birds that nested in burrows on offshore islands such as Trefoil. The women swam 1-2 km across the sea to these islands to drag the nestlings out of the burrows. The mutton bird's flesh was very oily, making them an energy-rich food. At the time of contact some men couldn't swim, all the swimming connected with foraging being done by women. It has been suggested that the reason the women did all the swimming may have been because the women had a larger amount of subcutaneous fat that partially insulated them from the cold water in these southern latitudes. The swimmers rubbed their bodies with the fat of seals or mutton birds mixed with red ochre, to aid in the insulation. G. A. Robinson was told by a woman that in the west, where shellfish were an important food source, the women excelled at swimming and diving, but in the east, where shellfish were less important, they excelled at climbing after possums (Flood, 2004).

The division of labour on the Australian mainland was different; here the men climbed after possums, cutting toe holds into the trees to assisting climbing. In Tasmania the women contributed much more to the survival of the group than the men, much more than in other parts of Australia where the division was more equal. As well as providing most of the food, they carried the spears and game, as well as the babies, toddlers, and all the gear when travelling. Added to this, they mined the ochre. Robinson reported witnessing a group of Aborigines that were caught by a sudden storm. The men sat down while the women built huts over them (Flood, 2004).

More than 30,000 stone artefacts have been recovered from the West Point midden, mostly steep-edged scrapers that are believed to have been used to make wooden implements such as digging sticks, spears and clubs. As with the upper layers at the Rocky Cape sites, there are no bone points present.

West Point Midden - Human Remains

The West Point midden also contains the first prehistoric human remains that have been found in Tasmania. One molar among the several teeth found in the midden had severe erosion of the root indicating periodontal disease. There was a small cremation pit at the base of the midden and 2 other small cremation pits in the middle that have been dated to about 1,800 years ago. The pits were about 45 cm wide and 30 cm deep in the sand or the sandy midden. The bodies appear to have been burnt, the bones broken, and then buried with the ashes in small pits.

A number of wallaby foot bones and the talons of a large hawk were found in one pit, and a 32-shell necklace of pierced shells was found in another. These were apparently grave goods, providing evidence that the burial practices of Tasmanian Aborigines and the necklaces worn by them in the 18th century had continued for at least 1,800 years. At Lake Mungo cremation was also practiced 25,000 years ago. It seems the burial practices may have been taken to Tasmania with the first arrivals there.

The human remains in West Point Midden are fragmentary, but display strong similarity to modern Aborigines from mainland Australia. A burial has been found in a sand dune near the Mount Cameron West engraving site, in which a woman's skull was set upright, facing north east and 2 long bones crossed in front. On the western side were a series of carbonised remnants, believed to have been poles that had been set in the sand to form a wooden 'wigwam'. Similar structures had been observed on Maria Island, off the north east coast of Tasmania by Francois Peron, where they were erected over burial pits. Dates obtained from the carbon of the poles, and flecks found associated with the skull, were 4,260 +/- 360 years ago. These remains show signs of being partially cremated after death, after which the bones had been smashed. Her teeth showed signs of chronic periodontal disease and molar wear, but there was no tooth decay (Flood, 2004). The skull was of Tasmanian type, but was within the range of variation of the Australian mainland Aborigines.

Variability

The Willandra Lakes Hominids
By 1989 1350 individuals had been discovered in the Willandra Lakes region. Among the remains from this region there were both robust and gracile forms of both sexes. There was also a variety of burial practices, cremation, inhumation and bone smashing.

Willandra Lakes Hominid 50

In 1980 the skull and some arm, hand and foot bones were found on the surface near Lake Garnpung, not far from Lake Mungo.

This skull and limb bones, the 50th find of human remains from the Willandra region, Willandra Lakes Hominid 50 (WLH 50), is the most significant of the finds in the area. It is believed the bones eroded out of the Mungo sediment, but as they weren't in situ in their original site, or which layer, is not known. The author of the paper to be published on the detailed analysis of the remains describes it as "much more robust and archaic than any Australian hominid found previously ".

An unusual feature of this skull is its preservation; the bone has been completely replaced by silica, the same process as opalisation. It has been said that this man is so robust he makes the Kow Swamp man look gracile, quite a statement, given that the most extreme of the Kow Swamp skulls was more robust than *H. erectus*. The cranium is 210 mm long and very wide. The average thickness of the cranial vault bone is 16 mm. There is a continuous torus above the eyes formed by the massive brow ridges, and a flat, receding forehead. The occipital region of the skull is even more archaic than the other features, displaying substantial cranial buttressing. The neck muscles are huge and the extremely wide skull with the greatest width occurring very low in back view. The width difference above and below the ears is much greater than in any modern people. Combined with these extremely archaic features is a very large brain. With an endocranial capacity of 1450 ml it is much higher than the average of 1300 ml for modern skulls. Like the Kow Swamp people, the skull is flask-shaped from above, all the rugged features in the Kow Swamp people are much more pronounced in this skull. It is unfortunate that the face, jaw and teeth of this skull are missing. Enough of the rest of the body was found to suggest that his body was equally as massive as the skull. The surviving elbow bone is enormous.

The small amount of bone remaining gave an electron spin resonance (ESR) date of 29,000 +/- 5,000 BP, and more recently an OSL dating of 25,000 BP was measured. Some believe that it is more likely to be closer to 35,000 BP at least. There is disagreement about the connections between WLH 1 and WLH 50. Some claim it is simply not possible to have WLH 50 descended from people like WLH 1 because of the extreme difference in proportions as well as the form of the two. The skull bones of WLH 50 is 15-19 mm thick, those of WLH 1 is 2 mm thick.

Chris Stringer of the Natural History Museum in London took detailed measurements of WLH 50 and concluded that when the size was taken into account it was of modern type, but in shape it is closer to the Skhul-Qafzeh crania than to the other Australian samples. It now appears that the individual may have had a genetic blood disorder that in Indonesia, where it is believed the Aborigines came from, helps protect against malaria. One feature of the cranial thickening in WLH 50 is that it differs from other modern Aborigines, in that whereas it is common for the modern male Aborigine skulls to have some thickening in parts of the cranial vault, WLH 50 had it over the entire vault. If WLH 50 did in fact have a blood disorder it might mean that he was one of the earliest arrivals from Indonesia as there was no malaria in his new home it would be eliminated from the gene pool over the millennia since his arrival in Australia. As at least some of the oldest dated sites in Australia are of a gracile people, maybe he was among, or descended from, more recent arrivals, that still carried the blood disorder that was lost from the gene pool of people who had been in Australia longer, where there was no endemic malaria.

The confusion over the actual dating of the skull, the silica replacement of the bone indicating a very long burial, while the dating was difficult because of the isolated position of the skull, with no possibility of dating associated material, allows some to hold the view that it may actually be more than 35,000 years old.

Australoid variability (Flood, 2004; Habgood & Franklin, 2008)

It has been established that there was a large amount of morphological variability among Pleistocene Australians, from the gracile to the robust at the other end of the continuum. It has been suggested that the morphological variability among the late Pleistocene populations of Australia resulted from genetic mutation, drift and selection, as the migrants moved into new environments.

The present Australian Aborigines are among the most morphologically diverse peoples in the world. Now that a lot of evidence from the Pleistocene in Australia has been studied it seems that diversity has been present a long time, in fact it was more pronounced in the past.

Joseph Birdsell and Norman Tindale proposed 3 migrations during the Pleistocene of Oceanic Negritos, Murrayians and Carpentarians. The Tasmanians were considered by them to be Oceanic Negritos, based mainly on their small stature and spiral hair. 12 Aboriginal tribes from the rainforests of north Queensland were also believed by Birdsell and Tindale to be of this type. Analysis of skeletons of these people failed to show any Negrito components among the rainforest Aborigines. Genetic studies have shown that pygmy peoples are not racially distinct from other non-pygmy groups, but rather are more probably adaptations to their environment.

In Tasmania analysis of skeletal remains from 3 sites, King Island, West Point Midden and Mount Cameron West, show no differences between them and contemporary Pleistocene peoples in the mainland. Any differences between modern Tasmanian Aborigines and those on the mainland are now believed to have arisen during the 10,000 years of isolation from the mainland after the sea rose to cover the plains joining the island to the mainland.

Birdsell's Carpentarians are now thought to have resulted from mixing with non-Aboriginal peoples from the north. People from Indonesia, e.g., Macassan traders, had been trading with the Aborigines long before the arrival of Europeans in Australia.

There is still no general consensus among anthropologists on most features of Australian Aborigines, apart from 2 facts, they are *Homo sapiens*, and there was a great deal of variability among the Pleistocene populations. They are yet to explain large amount of cranial variation in Pleistocene populations, and the more archaic appearance of some early Australian *Homo sapiens*.

Coobool Creek Crania - Human Remains

In 1950 126 crania were found on the surface at Coobool Crossing on the Wakool River between Swan Hill and Deniliquin in the Murray River Valley. Bone from one of the skulls, Coobool Creek 65 (LLO-416), gave a uranium thorium date of $14,300 \pm 1000$ BP. Studies comparing the Coobool Creek skulls with other populations from the Murray River Valley show affinities between the Coobool Creek population and that of Kow Swamp, but not with any other known populations. The results of this comparison, particularly the form and thickness of the cranium, as well as tooth size, have led Brown to conclude they were a single Pleistocene population that was homogeneous. Thorne has pointed out that as the site was undated, the remains having been found on the surface, suggesting that because of this it could be possible that the remains were from burials that took place over a period of 20,000 years, and not a single population from the closing stages of the Pleistocene. Thorne and Webb still support a modified 2-population theory, but Brown and Habgood and others have questioned the 2-populations theory, basing their conclusion of the Coobool Creek material and a number of comparisons between gracile and robust forms.

Cossack Skull

This extremely robust skull was found near Cossack in north western Western Australia, nearly 5000 km from Lake Nitchie and Kow Swamp. The skeleton was at the base of an eroding coastal dune. The dune was formed when the sea level reached its present height, so it cannot be more than 6500 years old. The skull is from a man who was about 40 when he died. He had a large, powerful build. The forehead slopes backwards, and the skull is very thick. This man has the most sloping forehead, and is the longest, dolichocephalic, skull ever found from an Aborigine, past or present. He was missing his right front tooth, which was probably knocked out during initiation.

The Cossack man resembles the Kow Swamp man, and both differ from modern Aborigines in Western Australia. This find demonstrates that the robust type of Aborigine was widespread across Australia, and lasted right up to post-glacial times.

It has been suggested that the long, sloping foreheads, extreme frontal recession, to be technical, as seen in skulls from Cossack, Cohuna and Kow Swamp, might have been artificially produced. The practice of binding the heads of children to produce this effect in adults was used by a number of people around the world. It wasn't common among Australian Aborigines.

There are only 3 known examples in Australia of this practice among Aboriginal groups. There are no artificially flattened skulls in museum collections in Australia. The 3 known groups are in

Victoria, Cape York and Mabuiag in the Torres Strait. It is not known which method was used in Victoria. In 1852 the practice was observed in Cape York. In this case the mother pressed on the forehead with one hand while pressing on the occipital region with the other. The skull was longer and wider than it would normally have been.

It has been suggested that the high, flat sloping foreheads could have resulted naturally from mixing of gracile and robust types. Similar foreheads have been seen on some Aborigines from Central Australia who have not had their skulls deformed.

Keilor Skull

In 1940 a skull was unearthed in a Victorian quarry near the junction of **Dry Creek** and the **Maribyrnong River**, 2.5 km north of Keilor and 16 km north of Melbourne. It was found that the skull was contemporary with fauna from Keilor Terrace. The skull was encrusted by a 2 mm thick layer of carbonate. Once the crust was removed it was discovered that the skull was filled with yellow silt like loess. This proved to be identical with silt of the upper part of Keilor Terrace. The carbonate encrustation could only be accounted for by a zone of secondary carbonate deposition in the silt.

The cranium showed signs of being rolled in a water course, as had the Talgai skull, roughly contemporaneously with the deposition of the sediments. Therefore it wasn't from a later burial into the sediments. Chemical analysis of the skull demonstrated that its chemical composition was similar to that of the faunal remains in the same terrace, suggesting that the skull was *in situ*.

Radiocarbon dated the skull and a femur to about 13,000 BP. The skull has a full, rounded forehead and lacks the prominent brow ridges and projecting jaw found in the Talgai and Kow Swamp skulls. Some classify it as gracile, while others disagree, describing it as robust.

Excavations at Keilor Terrace has uncovered in the base of the D clay, the remains of extinct megafauna and some stone tools. There was disagreement about the stone objects found actually being stone implements. But an examination of the site turned up an unmistakable flake in the D clay. So there is some evidence for human activity at the base of the deposit. Radiocarbon dates have been found that place the lower levels of the D clay to 36,000 BP, but it is believed it could be as old as 45,000 BP.

In the mid-1960s it was thought Talgai and similar skulls represented an earlier, archaic form of ***Homo sapiens***, appearing similar to the fossil skulls from Java. The picture was complicated by finds at Lake Mungo and Kow Swamp.

King Island Skeleton

A skeleton was found in a cave on King Island, Tasmania, in 1989. It was radiocarbon dated to 14270 +/- 640 BP (ANU-7039). At that time the cave would have been on the side of a plateau overlooking a plain. King Island was at the time connected to Tasmania and the mainland by dry land. It would have been about 20 km from the sea. It is the oldest evidence known of the physical form of the early Tasmanian Aborigines, as well as of the burial customs, secondary burial, and the use of ochre in what are believed to be burial rites. (Flood, 2004).

The remains were discovered by Robin Smith and studied by Thorne *in situ* with the permission of the Tasmanian Aboriginal Centre, after which it was reburied. It is the oldest evidence known of the physical form of the early Tasmanian Aborigines, as well as of the burial customs, secondary burial, and the use of ochre in what are believed to be burial rites. (Flood, 2004). It is believed the burial was of the secondary disposal type, the bones being collected in a pile and covered with a pile of rocks in the cave. No artefacts were found with the remains, but small pieces of ochre were found in the cranium and femur. It is not known if the ochre had been added at the time of the secondary burial or if it had been on the body and hair prior to decomposition, as had been recorded by explorers. The ochre must have come from some distance from the site. The explorers Baudin and Peron reported the bodies being covered with ochre.

The bones were carbon dated from charcoal that was found adhering to some of the bones. The remains found were a cranium, mandible, a femur, fibula tibia, some vertebrae, and a number of other fragmentary bones. The bones were believed to be of a man about 25-35 years old at the time of death. The fully rounded cranium and flat face, that was flat and not prognathous and there was no brow ridge development, all leading Thorne to conclude the remains were of a gracile man.

The sex of the remains was later challenged by Peter Brown, but according to Flood the scale in the photos taken in the field confirms Thorne's findings that they were the bones of a man. The head of the relatively short femur is 49 mm in diameter, placing it outside the range for women.

This burial was apparently of the secondary disposal type, the bones being collected in a pile then covered by a pile of rocks inside the cave. There were small pieces of ochre on the cranium and femur, apart from these there were no grave goods. It is uncertain if the ochre was placed on the bones or had been on the body prior to decomposition, as had been recorded by explorers. A skull and a number of other bones were found. The skull was from a man about 25-35 years of age, and was of a gracile type. The fact that this skeleton was of the gracile type has been claimed by some as further evidence that the most southerly people were of the gracile type. This would imply that the first of the people to arrive in Australia were gracile, the later arrivals being more robust.

The form of the femurs, short and robust with big heads, is similar to that in modern people living at high latitudes or elevations, e.g., Inuit and Sherpas. It is an adaptation to the cold. These people had been living in Tasmania for 35,000 years and appear to have become short and stocky by 14,000 BP, adapting to life in the cold Roaring Forties latitude.

This burial is the oldest evidence of the form of the earliest inhabitants of Tasmania. It also provides evidence for the early use of secondary disposal burials and probably the use of ochre in burial rites.

Study of the skeletal remains from King Island, as well as from other Tasmanian sites such as those at West Point Midden and **Mt. Cameron West** show that there were no differences between those of Aborigines from the Australian mainland and those from Tasmania in the distant past. Any differences noted since European contact has now been attributed to changes that took place over the 35,000 years the population of Tasmania, that was relatively small, was isolated from the rest of Australia, and being completely cut off by rising sea levels about 10,000 years ago. The changes that took place are in the direction of adaptation to life in a cold climate.

Kow Swamp

Kow Swamp, in northern Victoria, had a lake-full stage from the end of the Pleistocene to early in the Holocene, at which point it covered about 25 km^2 to a depth of 3-4 m. Wind-blown sand from the beach of this lake-full phase formed a low dune on the southeast shoreline, known as the **Kow Sand**. It was in this dune that the burials were situated.

In 1968 excavation of a site on the edge of Kow Swamp, not far from that of the Cohuna skull, uncovered a partial skeleton, the other half of which was already in the National Museum of Victoria, which had led to the search for the remainder of the skeleton. This Skelton was named **Kow Swamp 1**. By 1972 the skeletons of nearly 40 individuals had been uncovered around the edge of Kow Swamp, mostly along the eastern shore, in a narrow belt of lake silt. This silt was partially overlain by a crescentic sand dune (lunette). Radiocarbon dates from bone and charcoal associated with the burials; show that the burials span a period from about 13000 to 9500 BP.

The graves were in relatively soft silt and sand. The preservation of the skeletons was enhanced by the formation of carbonate crusts on the bone, in some cases up to 1 cm thick. Construction of an irrigation ditch through the site has disturbed some of the burials. Differential mineralisation allowed the disturbed skeletons to be reassembled because of the slightly different colours of the different skeletons.

Some of the undisturbed skeletons displayed a variety of orientations of burials, some stretched out on their backs, some on their sides, some were in a crouched position, one facing downward and forward, the knees drawn up to the chest with hands in front of the face, some were tightly flexed, with the body on its side or back, and there was 1 cremation.

This is the largest single population burial site in one locality of the late Pleistocene in the world. They were of men, women, juveniles and infants. Kow Swamp is thus of great importance to world prehistory.

The enigma of Kow Swamp is that the skulls are younger than those at Keilor and Willandra Lakes, but appear much more archaic. The people at Kow Swamp had large, long heads with very thick bone, up to 13 mm thick. Their faces were large, wide and projecting, with prominent brow ridges and flat, receding foreheads. From above they show a pronounced inward curvature behind the eye sockets, giving the skull the appearance of a flask. They had enormous teeth and jaws, some even larger than Java Man, *Homo erectus* (Previously called **Pithecanthropus**, from the middle Pleistocene of **Sangiran**.

Teeth are usually the most resistant body parts found in excavations of animals, but at Kow Swamp the teeth are not well preserved, few being found with their enamel crows still intact. Some of the damage to the teeth was caused by post-mortem erosion, but as well as that, the teeth of all adults display pronounced wear. It is thought it was probably the result of using grindstones to crush seeds, the stone particles in the ground seeds being responsible for the large amount of wear on the molars.

Only 1 individual at this site is of advanced age. The first molars of nearly all adults show such severe wear that the roots are exposed and worn down half way to their ends. As a result many individuals had chronic periodontal disease.

The appearance of the skulls at Kow Swamp suggests they were physically similar to those at Cohuna and Talgai. This contrasts strongly with the more gracile appearance of the inhabitants of Keilor and WLH 1 (LM1) & WLH 3 (LM3). The gracile people lack the flat, receding foreheads, pronounced brow ridges, massive jaws and thick bone of the Kow Swamp people.

Several of the Kow Swamp burials included grave goods. One body was placed on a bed of mussel shells; others included ochre, shells, marsupial teeth and **quartz artefacts**. One body was covered with powdered ochre. The same had occurred in a 40,000 year earlier burial at Mungo, showing a long continuity of customs, even though the people were apparently physically different.

Most of the grave goods were utilitarian, but one burial from Kow Swamp, about 12,000 BP, had a **band of kangaroo incisor teeth** around the head, traces of resin on the teeth suggesting that they were originally stuck together. In the 19th century, **Central Desert** Aborigines wore a head band of kangaroo teeth, plant fibre and resin. Kow Swamp possibly dated to as early as 22,000 BP. At least 40 individuals were buried with grave goods, some of which were mussel shells, **stone artefacts**, **marsupial teeth** and **ochre**; The Cohuna cranium came from the Kow Swamp site. It has been dated to between 14,000-9,000 BP, but it has been suggested it may be between 22,000 BP and 19,000 BP, (based on OSL dating); KS1 has been dated to 10,070 +/- 250 BP (ANU-403b); KS5-13,000 +/- 280 BP (ANU-1236); KS9, 9,300 +/- 220 BP (ANU-619b); KS9, 9590 +/- 130 BP (ANU-532); KS14, 8,700 +/- 220 BP (ANU-1038); KS17, 11,350 +/- 160 BP (ANU-1235); The **Kow Sand** where KS9 was buried, gave OSL dates of 14,400 +/- 800 BP & 19,000 +/- 1,100

BP. The **Cohuna Silt**, containing the burials of KS1, KS5, KS14 & KS17 gave an OSL date of 21,600 +/- 1,300 BP. (Thorne & Macumber, 1972; Brown, 1987, 1989; Pardoe, 1988, 1995; Stone & Cupper, 2003).

OSL ages for the Kow Swamp people

Stone & Cupper (2003) obtained OSL dates for the Kow Swamp sediments that differ from the radiocarbon ages previously obtained for the site. According to the calibrated ^{14}C ages the Kow Swamp people occupied the site in the period 15-9 ka. According to the single aliquot OSL ages they actually occupied the site during the Last Glacial Maximum, LGM, 22-19 ka. The authors[4] suggest Palaeoenvironmental reconstruction supports the OSL dates for the Kow Swamp people, as the shoreline silt, the location of most of the burials, was deposited at a time of high lake levels between 26 and 19 ka. According to Stone & Cupper (2003) there were few remaining robust people by the time the lunette formed after 19 ka, Stone & Cupper (2003) suggesting climate change may be the explanation for the demise of this unusual genetic population.

Oldest Human Remains in Australia (Cane, 2013)

The Willandra Lakes in the central south east of Australia is a system of freshwater lakes to the west of the Lachlan River situated between the Murray-Darling Basin and the fringe of the desert. These Lakes were full between 50,000-60,000 years ago, though at the present they are dry. They covered an area of about 1,000 km^2 and were about 10 m deep. When the Aboriginal people encountered these lakes they camped along their margins and exploited the plentiful resources of the lakes, frogs, fish, yabbies, and shellfish. It is not common to find burnt bone around the lakes, but the few found indicating they were hunting bettongs, bandicoots, quolls, wombats, possums, small wallabies and eastern grey kangaroos and eastern red kangaroos. It is common to find burnt-out wombat burrows around the lakes, indicating that an ancient wombat hunting technique was to burn out or smoke out wombats from their burrows. They also hunted emus and collected their eggs, and starch grains found adhering to the stone implements proved to be starch from sweet potato. The earliest signs of settlement around these lakes, though slight, indicate that humans were present around the lakes between

45,700 - 50,100 BP (with a statistical variance suggesting the lakes could have been occupied 43,400 - 52,500 BP), The artefact densities increase over time, peaking between 43,000 and 45,000 years ago, and it has been assumed that the human population also peaked at that time.

A burial has been found in the sand dunes near the lake that contained the remains of an old man, often called Mungo Man. His skeleton had remained undisturbed for at least 38,000 years and possibly as much as 42,000 years. The age of the man at the time of death has been estimated at about 50. He was buried in a grave that was 80-100 cm deep with his hands clasped [clasping his penis See Mungo Man]. Red ochre covered his head, chest and groin, the quantity being used was enough to stain the surrounding sand. The author[1] raises some questions such as how the ochre was applied. Was it rubbed into the skin of the man post mortem? Was it a decorative part of an ancient shroud? Was it sprinkled over the body? And where did the ochre come from?

The nearest source of ochre is 200 km away to the North West in the Olary region, South Australia. People must have travelled 200 km to the mine or traded for it. Whichever way they obtained the ochre it would have entailed human effort and organisation. Cane suggests the generous application of the ochre indicates some degree of emotional attachment and/or the high status of the man. The application of the ochre certainly implies some form of ancient funeral rite involved in his burial, the decorative treatment possibly suggesting concern for the afterlife. '*The sense of ritual attendance, the decorative consideration and careful placement of the corpse implies grief, communal concern and reverence*' (Cane, 2013). The importance of the burial is not only that it may be the first of its kind in the world, but that it also displays recognisable human emotions, creating an empathetic link with this ancient community over a period of 40,000 years.

The old man had an arthritic elbow, atlatl elbow or spear thrower elbow, an arthritic condition that results from years of throwing spears, an overuse injury that probably caused some degree of pain in his later years. The wear pattern of his teeth suggests he used them to strip plant fibres, possibly for the construction of nets, baskets or dilly bags. Cane has observed desert people using their teeth to strip bark from herbaceous desert shrubs for use in the making of sandals to protect their feet from the hot desert sand in simmer, possibly he had made sandals for the hot dunes of the Willandra area. He also had no lower canine teeth, indicating that he may have had them removed as part of the initiation rites when he was a young man, if so it is the earliest known initiation ritual in the world. There are also the remains of a young woman who was buried around the same time, though the burials are not related. She was 148 cm tall, 4'10", and lightly built. Her head was oval, with a delicate, fine-featured face and small teeth, the gracility suggesting to Cane that she was pretty. She had been cremated, following which her bones were smashed and placed in a small burial pit. Her burial is reminiscent of traditions of the desert where the dead are buried, leaving their spirits to roam until past scores have been settled. At this time friends and family try to disguise themselves in an attempt to avoid spiritual retribution. At this time they shave off their hair and remove all attachments to the life of the deceased in an attempt to avoid attracting the attention of the wandering spirit. The remains are eventually exhumed, the skeleton is smashed then reburied, as the spirit is now at rest and the people can carry on with their lives.

This woman is the earliest known incidence of cremation in the world. These are the earliest known traditions that were developed to deal with grief. Life and death at Willandra Lakes allows us to see how significant the ancient human response was, and the use of ritual to the way people dealt with the loss by way of considered burial.

Chapter 7 - Aboriginal Culture

Aboriginal Inhabitants of the Lamington region-south east Queensland-northern New South Wales

At the time of European settlement the area of what is now the Lamington National Park was inhabited by Aborigines of several tribal groups, the Birinburra, Kombumerri, Wanggerriburra and the Migunberri. They were of the Yugambeh Language Group. Other members of the group lived in the Gold Coast and Tweed areas, including the hinterland, from about the Logan River to the Tweed River. Prior to European settlement, the aboriginal people had been living comfortably in the area for thousands of years, needing only a few hours of the day to collect enough food for their group. In fact, in the early days of settlement, the Europeans only survived because of the trade in food with the Aborigines.

Aboriginal Tribes of the North Queensland Rainforest

In 1941 Tindale and Birdsell identified what they termed a Tasmanoid group living in the rainforests of North Queensland. This group was comprised of about 12 tribes that were described as small or pygmoid in stature, with crisp curly hair, physical characteristics that led Tindale and Birdsell to believe they were similar to Tasmanian Aborigines. Because they had territories near Lake Barrine, they were also called Barrineans. Both Tindale and Birdsell believed they represent '*a separate small-framed type of modern man forming one of the earliest stocks in southern Asia*' (Tindale, 1974:89). They suggested they may have represented the 'first wave of the Aboriginal occupation of Australia' (Dassett, 1987).

The tribe comprising Tindale's Tasmanoid group are: Ngatjan, Mamu, Wanjuri, Tjupkai, Barbaram, Idindji, Kongkandji, Buluwai, Djiru, Djirubal, Gulngai and Keramai.

Tindale & Birdsell noted a number of cultural characteristics that were shared by the tribes, a patrilineal moiety system, or a 4-class system, partial mummification of the dead, carrying the skull and jaw bones of the dead for long periods before disposal by burning, food cannibalism, large decorated fighting shields, the wearing of beaten bark blankets, fig-tree baskets sewn with lawyer cane, specialised food collection and preparation, such as leaching alkaloids from toxic nuts (Tindale & Birdsell, 1941).

An American anthropologist, Lauristan Sharp, studied the Aborigines in North Queensland in 1933 and 1935. Sharp divided in excess of 100 tribes into 9 groups based on combination of totemic traits. Dixon (1976) classified Aboriginal groups on the basis of linguistic groups.

The statement concerning Dixon's work, at the 1993 Julayinbul Conference, a tribal elder of the Ngadjon-Jii, Ernie Raymont, shows that the Aboriginals don't always agree with the categories they have been assigned to by non-Aboriginal experts. He stated, 'He found that we're all one people but our language was just slightly different and...all that time we were thinking we were all strangers and we were all enemies and that's the attitude I was brought up when I was a kid in the camp in Malanda from the old people... So it's only in the last 10 years that Professor Dixon went amongst our people and wrote books about it, that we have come together and started talking to one another and all these years we thought we were all enemies talking different tribal dialects.' (Rainforest Aboriginal Network 1993; 23) (Stork & Turton, 2008).

Aboriginal Tribal System

A tribe, in the Aboriginal context, is a group of people related by actual or implied genealogy, a common language, occupying a recognised tract of country where they hunt and gather food. The characteristic that differentiates their tribal system from that of other such systems is their powerful connection with the land they occupy. The land they occupy was travelled by their spirit ancestors in the Dreamtime, when the places were named and their laws and traditions were given them by the Dreamtime ancestors. These same ancestors formed the various landmarks and totemic sites as they travelled around the territory. The boundaries between tribal territories are not always immutable, in some cases they overlap at places along the boundary, and some tribes can have totemic or Dreaming centres in a neighbouring tribe's territory, which they are considered by both tribes to own. It is not known how long it took for the tribal boundaries to become established, but by the time of white occupation the territories had long been established. After all, they had 60,000 years to get it right. The boundaries were apparently to some extent elastic, some tribes being allowed to hunt on the territory of neighbours in times of drought in their own country, at least in some cases.

Tribal territories varied in size, depending on the productivity of the country, the central Australian tribes occupying semi-arid to desert country, need a much larger territory to survive than those in highly productive areas such as wetter coastal areas, so the inland territories are larger to allow for this. Fighting between tribes was not unknown, but in no case could this fighting be caused by, or lead to, the taking over of the territory of one tribe by another. Neither side would consider that situation. To the Aboriginal tribal person, the land they were born in is part of them, their spirits were believed to reside in places like sacred waterholes or other places when a person died until it entered the body of a pregnant woman and was reborn as a baby. So the lack of the possibility of acquisition of a neighbour's territory by any tribe removed an excuse for war that was present in other parts of the so-called civilised world. Even when the tribes did have wars, there were often stylised substitutes for outright war that minimised death or injury. Another case in which they had customs, that would seem to be more civilised than those of the rest of the world, where wars have always been fought over anything that a powerful leader considered a good excuse to gain extra territory.

The meanings of tribal names were not always known, even to members of that tribe. The name of the Dieri of Lake Eyre means simply 'man' - implying the other tribes were lesser beings. Some examples of tribal names are the Walang or Gunbalang. The 'Bat' people' lived among the caves on the northern Arnhem Land coast. The Maijali or 'Stone country' people lived south of Oenpelli. The Gunwinggu or Winggu, 'Fresh Water' people of western Arnhem Land. In west-central Northern Territory there were the Lungga or 'Long faced' people.

The various tribes mingled to varying degrees with their neighbours. Some interacted easily while a few kept themselves relatively isolated because they were not tolerant of the neighbours' customs. Such groups kept to themselves, restricting the choice of marriage partners to within their borders. But even these isolated groups did occasionally meet with their neighbours for the purpose of trade and the ceremonies that took place when neighbouring tribes joined to participate in large ceremonies connected with the dreamtime beings, usually when paths of one or more of these dreamtime beings crossed through the territory of more than one tribe. The groups that imposed this isolation on themselves had a harder time than the less isolated tribes accepting the forced contact with European settlers.

In some parts of Australia, neighbouring tribes formed varying degrees of alliance, in some cases crossing each other's tribal lands almost at will, intermarry and coming together to perform large secular ceremonies, as well as the religious ceremonies that other neighbouring tribes combine for. Examples of these multi-tribe groups are the Pidjanga-speaking bloc and the 'Narrinyeri' Confederacy.

The Pidjanja-speaking bloc included tribal lands of the member tribes that extended across the Great Victoria Desert, through the Musgrave Ranges and the Everard Ranges, along the Canning Stock Route to the country of the Wailbri (Warlpiri, Warlpiri) and Waneiga around Tanami and the Granites.

The 'Narrinyeri' Confederacy included such tribes as the Wakend, Tangani, Jaraldi, Tatiear and Ramindjeri. On the northern Australian coast, between the Daly River and Fitzmaurice River, were the 'Bringkin' groups.

While the tribe was a linguistic and territorial unit, that united all its members, in everyday life it was the smaller groupings within the tribe, the clan, horde and family unit that took part in the daily life activities, food gathering, feuding, fighting, hunting and fishing.

Clan members trace their descent from a common ancestor. In places such as eastern Arnhem Land, the line of descent is through the father's line, while in other places, such as western Arnhem Land, it is the mother's line. Each clan belongs to a special district within the tribal country. Each clan usually has its own rituals or songs. Members of a clan usually find their husbands and wives in other clans, usually within the same tribe. Members of a particular clan are usually expected to not marry other members of their clan. The extended family of parents and children, and often including other relatives, is called the horde by anthropologists.

A moiety is a term used by anthropologists to describe the practice, in nearly all tribes in Australia, of dividing each tribe into 2 groups for social and ceremonial purposes. It was usual for people to marry someone from outside their own moiety. The children may belong either to the moiety of the father or their mother, depending on whether the local group recognise their descent through the mother or the father. This system is at least partly totemic in nature, as it is often extended to include other animate and inanimate things, as well as the people. In some areas the moieties can be further divided into sections and sub-sections, where special marriage rules apply, as well as grouping various relatives in different ways.

To the Aborigines, the social organisation in their system was known to every member of every tribe, but to outsiders it is often extremely complicated and riddled with hidden difficulties and contradictions, making it difficult to master.

Intellectual Aristocrats - Claude Levi-Strauss

The famous anthropologist Claude Levi-Strauss called the Australian Aborigines 'intellectual aristocrats' among early peoples, based on outstanding features of traditional Aboriginal Society such as sophisticated religion, art, social organisation, an egalitarian system of justice and decision making, complex, far-reaching trade networks, and the demonstrated ability to adapt to, and survive in, some of the world's harshest environments. (in Flood, 2004).

As mentioned in Flood (2004), the Aborigines were still being characterised as '*unchanging man in an unchanging environment*' in the 1920s. Since then evidence has been accumulating, especially from archaeology, that the reverse is actually true. Some features of their culture were indeed conservative, such as some burial practices, such as where men were buried clutching the penis. This has been observed in the 18th century, and has since been found in burials such as at Lake Mungo, where the burial of WLH 3, dated to about 60,000 years ago (or 42,000 BP), had his hands in a position consistent with this practice. But they have adapted to extraordinary climatic changes. At the time of their arrival in central Australia the lakes of the centre were vast stretches of freshwater, the remains of large fish caught in them being found in middens near the lakes. Since then, the lakes dried up, the people, along with the animals, moved away from their dependence on the lakes, shifting to such food sources as grass seeds and the marsupials that had also adapted to life without much standing water.

Aboriginal culture has been shown by archaeological research to have been evolving for at least 50,000, and more probably 60,000 years, to suit the situation they find themselves in at any particular place and time. Whether rainforest or desert, they flourished wherever they went. Rather than being unchanging they have shown themselves to be masters of adaptation. Aboriginal society has the longest continuous cultural history in the world.

The stone constructions for eel harvesting in south-western Victoria and fish trapping at Brewarrina are examples of engineering practised by Aboriginal people. These constructions demonstrate they had the ability and the knowledge of their environment and the animals they hunted to plan and successfully build large scale permanent structures where the environment was reliable enough to make the work required worthwhile in the long term, and where there was a need, as in the case of the Brewarrina fish traps, to catch large numbers of fish when they were available in times of drought. The processes used for preserving eels demonstrate they knew how to preserve food when required. With regards to activities such engineering structures, mining, quarrying, permanent or semipermanent huts, when the conditions permitted, where they could they did.

Present-day research has found 16 refuge sites occupied by red kangaroos during drought, 10 of which were sacred sites associated with Ara, the red kangaroo from the Dreamtime. Among the Aborigines, hunting was prohibited in these sacred sites, and for some distance around them. Conservation being practised many thousands of years before the word existed, also a clue to how these "primitive" people survived, sustainably, on the driest vegetated continent on earth. These sacred sites would now be called a network of conservation reserves in prime habitat. Further evidence that, rather than being unchanging people, they had adapted extremely well to the very harsh conditions of central Australia.

Some features of Aboriginal society that were unknown at the time of European colonisation were a sophisticated religion, complex social organisation, art, and knowledge of astronomy. Some that were observed and commented upon in journals by a number of early colonists, such as agriculture, aquiculture, mining of ochre and stone, engineering (see Brewarrina fish traps) and the building of semi-permanent or permanent huts in small villages in places where the climate and food supply were reliable enough to sustain such settlements was not widely known or ignored. The complexity of the religion, mythology and ritual was at an even higher level than first appears, because of a deeper level of symbolism and meaning known only to fully initiated men. In the most sacred rituals carried out by the fully initiated men, song, rather than narrative, is the medium used to tell the stories. Key words or references were used, instead of full descriptions. Any man that was not fully initiated, or women and children, would not appreciate the full meaning even if they overheard the songs, as the associations of each word must be known to fully understand the story being told. In north-eastern Arnhem Land a word used in everyday speech can have several sacred equivalents with slightly differing meanings, as well as a further series of 'singing' words'. See Aboriginal Mythology.

The complex nature of their spiritual life can also be glimpsed in the beliefs and stories about the Land of the Dead, some of which have a theme somewhat like that in Dante's Inferno, and the crossing of a river, or stretch of sea, with the help of a boatman (canoe man) to reach the final abode of the spirits of the dead, as seen in Greek and Roman mythology. Some of the ideas expressed in their belief of the Afterlife can also be seen as not too dissimilar from those expressed in the belief systems of some of the present prominent religions, such as Hinduism and Buddhism, such as the cycle of life. In southern Australia, at least some of the tribes apparently had a single omnipotent 'God', known by a number of names among the different tribes, such as Bunjil, Baiame and Daramulun, as do some of the modern religions such as Christianity, Judaism and Islam, and they even had stories of a flood caused by Kaboka (thrush) that killed most of the population, the few who survived climbing onto Mt Dromedary, predating the Biblical flood by many thousands of years, as did the flood in the Epic of Gilgamesh, that also predated the Biblical flood, but only by a couple of thousand years.

More evidence of the complex nature of Aboriginal societies can been seen in the illustrations in William Blandowski's book,

Austalien Australien in 142 Phorographischen Photographischen Abbildungen nach zehnjarigen Erfahrungen - Australia in 142 photographic illustrations from 10 years' experience. See Josephine Flood, Archaeology of the Dreamtime, JB Publications, 2004

Aboriginal Tribal Groups (language groups)

There were many tribal groups in Australia at the time of European colonisation, not all survived that first contact, whether by being displaced or decimated by introduced disease.

The Afterlife in Aboriginal Australia

Ideas about the afterlife were fairly similar over much of Aboriginal Australia, though the details varied between areas (Elkin, 1954: 319). There were basic similarities throughout Aboriginal Australia, though there was no single uniform belief about an afterlife. A person's actions during life had no bearing on the wellbeing of his spirit in the afterlife; there is no hell or heaven, as referring to a place where only those who were 'good' during life were allowed to enter. The uncertainty as to whether a dead person's spirit is allowed to enter the Land of the Dead is based more on whether they display physical signs of having taken part in certain rites, such as initiation, and to whether or not the mourners have carried out the appropriate mortuary rites correctly. The sanctions applied here are usually very vague.

One belief that seems to be universal, or at least almost universal throughout Aboriginal Australia, is the indestructible nature of the human spirit, though there are occasional statements to the contrary. The spirit of a deceased person is believed to retain the individual identity of the person immediately after death, but generally this is a temporary state. The loss of personal distinctiveness, or separateness, is not seen as the destruction of the spirit. It is perceived as one approach to the concept of immortality, regardless of whether or not reincarnation is involved.

The concept of the Eternal Dreaming was basic to the view of the world held by people throughout Aboriginal Australia, as well as a person's relationship to the social and physical environment. The span of a person's earthly life is a framework for explanations for the meaning of life that are based, generally, on a body of belief, more or less systematised, centring on birth, death as a transition, and rebirth. Death is seen as a transition rite ensuring the continuance of the cycle, the main emphasis being on essentially an unchanging panoramic view of life.

The Land of the Dead was fairly consistently defined as being in the sky, the sky-world, in a particular place, such as Bralgu, or even in a particular direction. A dead person's spirit could be seen as either residing with, or merging with the great creative or ancestral beings. They could also be believed to return to a totemic site that was intimately related to them. This was widely believed among the tribes of Central Australia, whether or not they believed in a single spirit or multiple spirits of a person after death. Concerning the Aranda, it has been suggested that "*death to him is the last great catastrophe which leads to the eventual complete destruction of his own body and of his own spirit*" (Strehlow, 1947: 42-6). The western Aranda believed the spirit goes to the island of the dead in the northern ocean, where lightning during a storm finally destroys it. According to Strehlow, the Aranda had no hope of a future life; still, every person is an incarnation of a totemic being. Death is the destruction of the body but not the spirit, this returns to its source. Like the totemic beings, it is indestructible. Even though in the Dreamtime stories they were sometimes "killed" or "died", their spirits remained part of the Eternal Dreaming stream, which included human beings. The Aranda believed in the spiritual essence residing in the sacred tjurunga of each person. There is still the nucleus of unborn spirits awaiting rebirth. The spirit or part of the spirit, of a dead person returns to its totemic site until it can be reborn.

Aboriginal Agriculture

One of the features of Aboriginal Australia that has been wondered about is that for the whole of their presence in Australia, possibly more than 60,000 years, the inhabitants never adopted agriculture or domestication of animals, remaining one of the few places in the world sticking with their traditional hunter-gatherer way of life.

Many reasons have been put forward for the lack of agriculture in Australia, but it is only recently that it was realised that they did in fact practice a form of agriculture, firestick agriculture. They not only used fire to hunt, setting fire to grass to chase out animals to aid in hunting, but regularly burnt limited areas to increase the availability of new grass to feed the animals they hunted, maintaining the populations of their prey species sustainably for many thousands of years. Not only did they maintain their hunting lands in the condition their prey species preferred, they are also thought by some authors to be possibly, at least partially, responsible for the spread of dry eucalypt forests after their arrival, because this type of vegetation is fire-resistant.

The pig has been present in New Guinea for about 10,000 years, and definitely by 6,000 BP. Pigs were not endemic to New Guinea, so must have been brought from Indonesia, but never reached Australia. Agriculture has been present in New Guinea since at least 9,000 BP, but was not taken up in Australia. By 6,000 to 5,000 BP the inhabitants of New Guinea were living in semi-permanent villages, cultivating and sometimes irrigating endemic and imported crop plants, and raising pigs. But not in Australia. One of the reasons suggested for the lack of agriculture in Australia was the lack of contact where these practices could be learned. Obviously there has been contact with people practicing agriculture for many years. Even in New Guinea it wasn't practiced intensively, more as an adjunct to hunter-gathering. Regarding hunting in New Guinea, compared with Australia, there is a paucity of mammal species, and those present, such as wallabies, are smaller than the very abundant kangaroos in Australia. This gap in the food supply in New Guinea is filled by pig raising.

On the northern Torres Strait islands the mix of agriculture and foraging was similar to that in southern New Guinea, but moving from north to south of these islands the mix gradually changes until by the islands in the south it was the same as in Cape York, there was no agriculture, subsistence was based entirely on foraging.

There is also a difference in the islands of the western and eastern parts of the Torres Strait. In the west the islands are mostly high volcanic islands with surrounding reef and shallow seas with plentiful fish and shell fish, turtles and dugongs, as well as plant foods like yams and mangrove fruit. On these islands there was normally no agriculture, though some yams could be planted for periods when there was a temporary leaner time. On the smaller, lower islands in the east the surrounding seas are not as bountiful as around the western islands and agriculture was practiced extensively.

Based on the presence of agriculture only on the islands where a comfortable living could not be depended upon, it seems that agriculture is not the lifestyle of choice, being resorted to only when necessary for survival.

One of the main differences between the early civilisations in the Middle East where many of the plants and animals were originally domesticated was that in the Middle East the opportunity to move to a different location if food was in short supply didn't exist, either because of the lack suitable land or unfriendly neighbours. In Australia in hard times the people simply moved to another area, unencumbered by large amounts of baggage that sedentary farmers needed, and moved more frequently than they would in better times, and the neighbours tended to be more accommodating. In the harshest environment in Australia, if not the world, the Western Desert, the inhabitants often travelled 400-500 km, especially during drought. The people of this area have been known to cover an area of 2,600 km^2 in 3 months.

A feature of the food exploited by Aborigines is that they eat a wide variety of food, never being dependent on a single or a few food types. This is a problem with sedentary farmers when times are bad, they can't easily move to a new area or exploit a new food source. Studies of Aborigines in their environment showed that when one usual food supply wasn't available at a particular time, such as a drought, they shifted their foraging to other plants and animals, and often moved to a different part of their range, or even into a neighbouring group's range, were they were permitted to hunt until times improved in their own area. Their lack of material goods made such travels easier, just taking the bare necessities for their survival, their travelling kit. An advantage of the nomadic way of life that was not appreciated by most Europeans is that they are not vulnerable to starvation because of the failure of a single crop, as has occurred even in historical times among settled peoples.

Unlike farming peoples they did not use times of plenty to store food for leaner times, and, as occurred with the civilisations of the world, increased food availability allowed larger populations, which makes the people more susceptible to food shortages. In Aboriginal society the population size was aligned with the food supply in the leanest time, such as winter in the southern parts of Australia, the good times being a time for get-togethers, corroborrees corroborees, art and dance, etc.

Studies of the foraging of Aboriginal people found that in times of plentiful food it took only a couple of hours a day to gather enough food for the group for that day. In the Western Desert it only took the women less than 7 hours to gather enough food for the group, even in drought, and the men always hunted meat for the group. By moving around their territory on a regular basis they allowed each part of their range to recover before returning, unlike farming practices that are much harder to maintain sustainably without input such as fertilisers, particularly when the population grows and more food needs to be produced.

Archaeological evidence has shown that the same species of plant and animal have been eaten for a very long time. The nomadic way of life was apparently adopted soon after arriving in Australia when they had worked out what was needed to survive in this very inhospitable continent. Apart from their possible contribution to the demise of the megafauna, they seem to have done a remarkable job of living sustainably for a very long time, much longer than the existence of any civilisation anywhere on earth, and without the periodic collapse of civilisations, at least partly through over exploitation.

In 1770 Captain Cook wrote of the Aborigines he encountered.

'From what I have said of the Nature of New-Holland they may appear to some to be the most wretched people upon the Earth, but in reality they are far more happier than we Europeans. They live in a Tranquillity that is not disturrb'd by the Inequality of Condition: The Earth and sea of their own accord furnishes them with all things necessary for life, they covet not Magnificent Houses, Household-stuff & ca, they lie in a warm and fine climate and enjoy a very wholesome Air, so they have very little need for clothing and this they seem to be fully sensible of, for many to whom we gave Cloth & ca to, left it carelessly upon the Sea beach and in the woods as a thing they

had no manner of use for. In short they seem'd to set no Value upon any thing we gave them, nor would they part with any thing of their own for any one article we could offer them; this in my opinion argues that they think themselves provided with all the necessarys of Life and that they have no superfluities'.

The attitude of the Aboriginal people to the agricultural practices of the white settlers on their land can be seen from the statement of an Aboriginal woman in Arnhem Land when watching a Fijian missionary working in his mission garden who became concerned that a few of his plants had died. *'You people go to all that trouble, working and planting seeds, but we don't have to do that. All these things are there for us, the Ancestral Beings left them for us. In the end, you depend on the sun and the rain just the same as we do, but the difference is that we just have to go and collect the food when it is ripe. We don't have all this other trouble.'*

In areas such as the Daly River, they avoided exhausting yam beds, always leaving enough scattered plants to provide the next season's crop for harvesting. This sort of attitude was actually widespread across Australia. Their intimate knowledge of the plants and animals on which they depended allowed them to avoid overexploitation of any particular food source. This aspect of their culture was overlooked by nearly all the Europeans who came in contact with them. It allowed them to use the same plants and animals continuously for about 60,000 years. Instead of hording food in times of plenty they realised that by avoiding overexploitation of a food resource in times of plenty they ensured the continuance of the food resource for the future. There were a number instances that were observed of this practice in various places. One example is Aborigines observed to refrain from killing stingrays for food because it was the breeding season for stingrays.

By treating their environment as a big garden that didn't need cultivation they had to make use of the food that was available at any particular time, but by doing this they were not continually fighting against the climate and the soils as European agriculture did, with its boom and bust cycles as droughts and floods came and went. They successfully lived with the environment for thousands of years, taking what it offered and not trying to grow crops or animals that were not adapted to the harshest and most variable climate on Earth.

In 1941 the husband and wife anthropologists, the Berndts, listed some of the food plants and animals the local Aboriginals used in the area immediately around the Ooldea Soak and mission in arid central Australia, country that to Europeans looked too desolate to support anyone. The food items they counted were 18 varieties of mammals and marsupials, 19 birds, 11 reptiles, 8 insects, 6 water roots, 17 varieties of seed, 3 vegetables, 10 fruits and berries, 4 other plants and fungi, and a variety of eggs.

Some important food sources

In some instances the Aborigines in various parts of Australia encouraged the production of certain food species of plants, with fire as usual, and in south-western Victoria they built structures to assist in the capture of eels that come close to the accepted meaning of agriculture, or aquaculture. On the Barwon River near Brewarrina the local Aborigines built stone fish traps to take advantage of the occasional abundance of fish during floods when they were more abundant than at other times.

They used fire to encourage the production of cycad fruit and daisy yams, removing competing plants. The Anbara of Arnhem Land dug the yam tubers out but left the top of the tuber attached to the plant, and the tubers subsequently regrew. They also planted yams on offshore islands for a reserve.

Yams, Fruit trees, Millet harvesting, Food storage, Eel harvesting

Fish traps, The biggest Estate - Millet Harvesters.

The one native cereal grain in Australia, wild millet (*Panicum decompositum*), was one of the main foods in arid Australia. There was also a closely related species of *Setaria*; relatives of these Australian plants were the plants from which the domesticated European common Panicum and Italian millet (*Setaria italica*) were derived.

Harvesting cereals was mostly an adaptation to survival in arid central Australia where the annual rainfall was 300 mm or less. In wetter areas to the north, where alternatives such as fruit, nuts and tubers, were available, seeds were a minor food source, if collected at all.

The Bagundji (river people) occupied the semiarid areas in the Darling River Basin. Along the banks of the Darling River they had a riverine economy mostly based on food from the river, fish, shellfish and ducks, as well as bulrush roots. These foods were in shorter supply in winter, so at this time of year the people separated into smaller groups and moved out away from the river. They collected wattle seeds and flax seeds and hunted emus by luring them with a horn that sounded like a female emu then trapped them in nets. They also caught kangaroos by driving them into nets with beaters or fires. In winter rainwater pools were utilised for drinking water, but when they were away from the river in summer they depended on water in some plant roots and carrying it in kangaroo skin bags.

The main plant food in summer was native millet which seeds between December and March. The seeds of the millet don't all ripen at the same time, an adaptation to the erratic climate. This was a problem for harvesters who wanted to gather large quantities at a time. The problem was solved by harvesting the grass while it was still green, but after the seeds were full but not ripened. The grass was stacked in heaps to dry and ripen. When it was needed the heap was threshed, all the now ripe seeds falling to the ground in the one place making it easy to gather.

The explorer Sir Thomas Mitchell reported in 1835 as he passed down the Darling "*the grass had been pulled, to a great extent, and piled in hayricks, so that the aspect of the desert was softened into the agreeable semblance of a hayfield ... we found the rick, or haycocks, extending for miles . . . the grass was of one kind, a species of Panicum . . . and not a spike of it was left in the soil, over the whole of the ground . . . The grass was beautifully green beneath the heaps and full of seed*". It was July when Mitchell travelled along the Darling; the hayricks he saw were actually in-field storage of seeds that had been harvested at least 3 months previously.

Cereal grasses were harvested by pulling the plants up by the roots and either pulling the stalks off or gathering the seeds into a bark dish. The latter method was the method used in central Australia. A stone reaping knife was used in the area around Cooper's Creek in south western Queensland, as was used by the early cultivators in the Middle East. Knives used for reaping can be distinguished by the 'use-polish', a sheen they have on the edge of the implement.

The stones used for grinding seeds are different from those used for grinding other food, being larger, flatter and smoother. It has been suggested they should be called millstones because they are used to make flour. These are the type of grindstones found at sites in the Darling Basin. A study of the grindstones found in New South Wales in the Australian Museum, Sydney; show a correlation between the distribution of these grindstones and the harvesting of millet.

The Mungo people ate fish, shellfish, and small mammals, birds and emu eggs 30,000 years ago. After the lakes dried up about 15,000 years ago, they ate the same food but it now came from rivers, but now with the addition of grass seeds. At sites dated from after the drying up of the Willandra Lakes millstones are found in the middens. The diet based on fish, shellfish, small mammals and grass seeds were still the basic diet in the 19th century.

In New South Wales the semiarid basin and humid western slopes of the interior had a similar environment to areas where cultivation developed in Mesopotamia and Mexico. There were also plants such as millet that were potential crops for cultivation. But cultivation never developed in these parts of Australia. One reason may be the erratic climate, where droughts were common and often severe and long lasting. It might also be because the Aborigines could always move to a different part of the territory and shift their foraging to a different set of their wide variety of food items. If they cultivated in such an unreliable climate they would be tied to their crops however long the drought. Even with more efficient food storage methods than they had it would have been difficult, and probably impossible, to store enough to sit out the frequent droughts.

Abrupt Change in Vegetation in South East Australia Following Megafaunal Extinction in the Late Quaternary

Coinciding with the spread of humans across the Australian Continent there was a substantial mass extinction of the marsupial megafauna (Bowler et **al.**, 2003) across the continent between about 50,000-45,000 years ago (Roberts et al., 2001; Grün et al., 2010). There were also large shifts in the vegetation types across Australia at about this time, though it is uncertain if these changes resulted from the use of fire by the humans (Turney et al., 2008) - which then contributed to the extinction event - or whether the loss of the megafauna grazers (Rule et al., 2012; Flannery, 1990) resulted in the vegetation changes. In this paper the (dos Santo et al., 2013) reconstruct past vegetation changes that occurred in south east Australia by the use of the stable carbon isotopic composition of wax **n**-alkanes produced by higher plants and the use of the accumulation rates of levoglucosan, a biomarker, to determine the levels of biomass burning from a well-dated sediment core obtained offshore from the Murray-Darling Basin. Their results indicated that the abundance of C_4 plants was 60-70 %, which is generally high, from 58-44 ka, and the abundance of these C_4 plants declined to 30 % by 43 ka and there was an increase in the burning of biomass. The transient shift in the vegetation continued for 3,000 years following the period of human colonisation and directly following the extinction of the megafauna that occurred between 48.9-43.6 ka (1). (dos Santo et al., 2013) concluded that in this region the extinction of the megafauna was not caused by the vegetation shift. They suggest their data are consistent with the hypothesis that the vegetation change was the consequence of large marsupial browser extinction, and these vegetation changes led to the fire-prone nature of the Australian landscape.

Bogong Moths *Agrotis fusa infusa*, Noctuidae

During winter the bogong moth larvae, black cutworms, feed on broad-leaved plant seedlings over a wide area from southern Queensland to South Australia. In spring they migrate to the Snowy Mountains and Victorian Alps where they aestivate in caves throughout the summer, from November to February. They tended to crowd together in rock crevices and cover walls. It was at this time of year that the Aborigines used to congregate to feast on the roasted moths. They are also an important part of the diet of the Mountain Pygmy Possum (***Burramys***). Later in the year they return to their breeding grounds to reproduce.

They accumulate arsenic in their tissues from the soil their food plants grow on and this has been found to be accumulating in higher levels in the caves where they hibernate from the bodies of those that die during aestivation. There is now concern it could affect their predators such as the Mountain Pygmy Possum.

Fire-Stick Farmers

See Desert mammals and fire see The Biggest Estate on Earth

A lot of the vegetation that was encountered by the first Europeans in Australia was actually an Aboriginal artefact. The Aborigines had used their fire-sticks to change the vegetation of the continent to suit their requirements.

Fire had a number of functions in Aboriginal culture. One use was for signalling, the once well-known smoke signals in movies. Another was for clearing tracks through the bush and keeping poisonous snakes away from them, making it easier to move through the bush. This function of fire was used regularly to keep tracks clear in thick bush in the Blue Mountains and the dense tea-tree scrub in western Tasmania. It was also used to keep tracks clear through the tall tropical grasslands of Arnhem Land. And all across the continent fire was used to flush animals from grass to make them easier to hunt.

It was also used to encourage the kangaroos and other prey animals to congregate on the areas of fresh vegetation sprouting on the areas they had burnt. Fire also encouraged the regrowth of eucalypt trees and edible plant food such as bracken, from which the roots, young leaves and shoots could be eaten. The ash from the burnt areas was a fertiliser for the regrowth as soon as it rained.

Extensive, regular burning altered the environment, increasing the area over which they could find food. One of the places where they had an enormous effect was on the west coast of Tasmania, converting the fire-sensitive rainforests of southern beech, *Nothofagus,* which was a relict of Gondwana, from mixed eucalypts and rainforest to scrub and eventually to heath and sedgeland. Since the end of burning in these cleared areas the rainforest is reclaiming its habitat.

In 1827 the explorer Henry Hellyer came across open grasslands among the rainforest in the highlands of northern Tasmania. He called them the Surrey Hills or Hampshire Hills after the countryside of England. The European colonists found that these grasslands were ideal for sheep, but they found that once the Aborigines had been moved from the area and the regular fires had stopped, sour grass and scrub replaced the open grassland and sheep farming ended about 1845. So European agriculture lasted 18 years, whereas the Aborigines who lacked agriculture, had used the same land for many thousands of years.

The fire-stick methods of the Aborigines increased the amount and diversity of food available. The rainforest was not rich in food plants and animals. The heathland and wet scrub and grasslands that replaced it provided plenty of animals and food plants. Two of the staples of temperate Australia were grass trees and bracken. Bracken colonises burnt forest, so rapidly provided food after the burning. The pith at the centre of the grass tree was eaten by the Aborigines.

One the reasons fire-stick farming was so successful over such a vast range of environments is that the farmers adapted the fire regimes to suit individual areas.

Unlike the fire regime in Tasmania, where the rainforest was cleared by fire to allow food plants to grow, the Anbara from Arnhem Land use a variety of burning regimes that avoided the rainforest patches because they provided many food plants that were susceptible to fire, not regenerating after burning. Among the Anbara there are strong ritual prohibitions against burning jungles that are the home of spirits that would blow smoke into the eyes of the fire lighters and blind them. Soon after the wet season fire breaks about 1 km wide are carefully burnt around these thickets. This protects the jungle thickets from the fires set to burn off the surrounding grasslands in the dry season, in June and August.

The Anbara say that fire is necessary to clean up the country; they regarded unburnt grassland as neglected. At least once every 3-4 years the grassland, eucalypt woodlands and savannah in their territory is burnt. The same pattern of regular, low intensity burns were carried out all over the continent prior to European colonisation. The result was that high-intensity fires that burnt the trees as well as the litter and dry grass were avoided, and the food supply was maintained.

It can now be seen as ironic that the same Aborigines, who were regarded by the white settlers as ignorant nomads, admired the Australian parklands and open woodlands that were actually created with the fire-sticks of the ignorant nomads.

Aborigines never put out their fires, camp fires were left burning, as were signal fires, those lit in sequence to indicate the direction travelled by humans or kangaroos, or hunting fires. They lit fires so apparently casually that they have been called 'peripatetic pyromaniacs'.

A mosaic pattern of burning was practiced in desert regions in winter; parts of the area were burnt. In spinifex grasslands, the spinifex is burnt and the cleared land is colonised by other desert plants that provide more food than areas dominated by spinifex. One of the plant species that replaces spinifex under these conditions is the wild tomato. These are the most important fruits of the desert people, they are very nutritious, and are high in vitamin C, and they remain edible for long periods on the plant. Another plant that replaces the spinifex is the wild banana, its leaves, fruit and roots are all edible.

In Arnhem Land Aborigines are known to have aimed their fires in particular directions. In the Western Desert, the inhabitants were observed burning patches of grassland, and although they appeared to be lighting them randomly, the resulting fires never entered previously burnt areas that were producing food, so they were apparently not as random as they seemed.

It has taken 200 years for the fire-stick to be recognised as the agricultural instrument that it had been for up to 60,000 years or more before European colonisation.

The Fire-Stick Farming Hypothesis

For a long time burning by Australian Aboriginal people has been believed to be a strategy for managing food resources, though this hypothesis has never been tested by quantitative analysis. In this paper Bird et *al.*, (2008) combine contemporary ethnographic observations of Aboriginal hunting and burning with analysis of satellite images of anthropogenic and natural landscape structure to demonstrate the processes by which the vegetational diversity of the arid-zone is shaped by Aboriginal burning. A greater diversity of successional stages is contained in anthropogenic landscapes than under a lightning fire regime, differences being in scale rather than kind. According to the authors the scale of the landscape is linked directly to foraging for small prey that burrows, such as monitor lizards, which is a specialty of Aboriginal women. Small animal hunting productivity is increased by the maintenance of small-scale habitat mosaics. There are implication of these results for understanding the unique biodiversity of the Australian continent, through time and space. Anthropogenic influences on the habitat structure of palaeolandscapes, in particular, are likely to be localised spatially and linked to less mobile, "broad-spectrum" foraging economies.

Food Preparation – Poison

The fruit of the cycad *Macrozamia* was exploited as an important food source in spite of its being highly toxic and carcinogenic. The Aborigines had developed methods of removing the toxins that allowed the cycad fruit to become a rich food source. Different groups had different methods of removing the toxins, but they all achieved the same end, an edible, sustaining, fruit.

In one method the kernels are cut open and the toxins are leached out in water. When the process had been completed the kernels were ground into a powder like flower and baked to make cycad bread.

Other groups used a method involving fermentation, leaving the kernels in large containers, or in some cases pits, where they remained for several months. The process is complete when the kernels have frothed or become mouldy.

However processed, the toxin-free cycad seeds are a rich food source, and they are produced in large numbers on each plant. It has been estimated that cycads can produce more food per hectare than many cultivated crops. The increase in area and productivity of cycads is an example of why the Aborigines could be called fire-stick farmers, not simply hunter gatherers; they used fire to remove competing plants from around the cycad stands. In fact, the cycad stands were not natural; they are an agricultural crop, though they weren't recognised as such until recent times. The Aborigines had learned that by regular burning of the area around the stands they increased the production of seeds much above the natural level. Burning could also be used to produce a heavy crop that ripened at the same time so they could be used as food source for the large gatherings at times of big ceremonial events, when a number of groups came together.

Cycads were used in this manner, providing food for large gatherings of hundreds of people at ceremonies that could continue for weeks or months, in Arnhem Land and the Carnarvon Ranges.

The processing of macrozamia has apparently been known of since at least the late Pleistocene, evidence of processing having been found at a number of archaeological sites. Among the sites where evidence of exploitation of *Macrozamia* has been found are the Carnarvon Ranges, dated to 4,000 years ago, Native Well I and II, dated to 10,000 years ago, Jiyer Cave in the north Queensland rainforest, dated to about 4,000 years ago.

Evidence has been found at Cheetup Shelter, near Esperance in Western Australia, that cycad seeds were being detoxified in pits lined with grass-tree leaves in the Late Pleistocene. It has been suggested that the process of detoxifying the seeds may have developed independently in a number of areas, based on the fact that more than one process was used.

In the Blue Mountains area, at sites such as Noola and Capertree III, there was an increase in use from between 3,000 and 4,000 years ago, associated with the use of cycad nuts and the small tool tradition. The same is seen in the Carnarvon Ranges. At both places occupation occurred on a lower level prior to this time, possibly even intermittently.

Other foods

Concentrated sources of food occurred at the sites of the big rituals, such as the northern tablelands of New South Wales. Overall, this was not a good place for food, and it was cold and windy, but the area had a single major food item that was abundant, the mirr'n-yong or daisy yam (*Microseris scapigera*). In other places the tubers of this plant were heavily used by the Aborigines as food. An example is known of an eyewitness of the use of the daisy yam as seen by Governor Hunter in 1793 on the banks of the Hawkesbury River near Sydney. It was said that where the Aborigines had been digging these yams the land could look similar to a ploughed field. On the tablelands they probably also caught kangaroos with fixed hunting nets made from *Kurrajong* bark.

The daisy yam was another food source that the fire-stick farmers 'propagated' with fire, using the fire to expand the area covered by this plant.

Food Gathering - desert country

In the desert areas it was necessary for the people to camp in any given area for no more than a few days because the women soon gathered the available food within walking distance of the camp and the men hunted the animals, such as kangaroos, near the camp or water hole. The remaining kangaroos soon move to more distant feeding areas.

In his book (2) Mountford describes some of the food collection methods in the area of the Musgrave Ranges. There are a number of rocky hills separated from each other by open grassy flat areas. Euros live on the hills and are well adapted to the area, being coloured similar to that of the rocks, which make them difficult to see when they don't move. They are also very agile, moving around the rocks too fast for the men or their dogs to run them down. They shun the open spaces between the hills, only venturing out on the flats to move between hills. When they do so they tend to follow familiar paths. The hunters make use of this behaviour to hunt them. Some hunters wait along the path with their spears ready to throw while the remainder of the hunting party act as beaters, moving from the far side of the hill they are working on driving the animals to another hill along the known track by lighting the spinifex as they go. The spearmen make use of another behaviour of the euros, as well as other kangaroos. When they are being chased by a predator they tend to only keep track of the area in front of them and behind them, not noticing any potential threat to the side unless it moves. The men along the track wait motionless until a euro is in range, when they hurl their spear. The spear usually doesn't kill, but slows the animal down enough to be caught and killed.

The red kangaroos remain on the open plains, so another method is used to hunt them. As with the euros, they don't recognise threats that are not moving, so the hunters move a few steps closer every time the kangaroo lowers its head to feed, remaining motionless as soon as it raises it head to look around, making use of any tree or bushes to get as close as possible. They continue this slow process until within range of the spear. As with the euros, the spear slows the animal enough to be caught. They also hunt the red kangaroo along known tracks used by the animals travelling between favourite feeding areas, using the same methods as for euros, stationing men along the track while the rest of the hunting party disturb the feeding roos, shepherding them towards the track where the men are waiting with their spears ready to throw.

Food collected by women

While the men are hunting the larger animals the women gather other foods such as cereals, fruit and small animals. Among the seeds they gather are munyelroo (a species of portulaca, acacias of various kinds, especially mulga (*Acacia aneura*), the desert kurrajong, and dig up various types of tubers and the roots of some trees.

They also collect the fruit of species such as wild peaches (*Eucarva persicarius*), wild oranges (*Caparis Capparis mitchelli*), figs (*Ficus platypoda*), black plums, and galls on mulga and bloodwood trees.

Among the small animals they collected were lizards, bandicoots, snakes, rabbits, witchetty grubs and termites.

When collecting wongona seeds the women rake the seeds and dust into small piles that are placed in a wooden dish. The seeds and dust are placed on a flat rock or patch of hard ground. When enough have been collected they winnow the mixture until it is mostly seeds and the coarser sandy material that remains. The seeds are them place in a wooden dish that is rocked in a particular way, that Mountford says few men seem to be able to master. The result is that the clean seeds collect at the lower end while the rest moves to the higher end. The seeds are then placed on a bark sheet or hard ground then the process is repeated until they are satisfied that the seeds are as clean as they can be. The seeds are then ground into flour with a grinding stone, which is mixed with water, formed into a small cake, which is then buried in the hot sand and ashes of a camp fire until cooked. The result of all this work is a small cake about the size of a saucer.

Under their system of division of work the food provided was the more reliable, the hunters were not always successful, and often had to travel long distances from the camp, which meant the women could always be depended on for keeping the group going until the hunters were successful, even though the food they collected was not always plentiful or tasty.

According to Mountford, when a hunter brought a kangaroo he had caught back to camp he dropped it at the feet of one of the people then went and sat in the shade of a tree. The person the kangaroo was given to, cooked it and distributed the meat to the rest of the group, keeping the favourite parts, the liver, heart and any other favoured bits. The hunter received the least favourite bits, the ribs, head and neck. When another hunter brought in food another day it would eventually be the donor's turn to receive the animal.

This system ensured that all the members of the group received a fair share of any food that was available. Mountford suggests there is a less obvious basis for the method of distribution of the food provided by the hunters. The old men are the custodians of the sacred knowledge and ceremonies, and control the enforcement of laws and customs. If the hunters decided who they presented their game to they would have the opportunity to gain power and favours from others, and could gain control that was usually held by the old, fully initiated men. A skilled hunter could gain control of the group, whatever his age. As the food distribution system worked the hunter had to be satisfied with gaining prestige as a great hunter, someone to be admired, but without the power to control the group.

Eel Farming

In south-western Victoria there was a large area covered by small rivers, swamps and wetlands that in the winter wet season became a huge area of marshes. These marshes were the feeding area for a 1 m-long Australian eel (*Anguilla australis occidentalis*). In spring the eels moved along the rivers from the sea to their feeding grounds, returning to the sea to breed in autumn.

To exploit this abundant seasonal food source, the Aborigines constructed an elaborate system of traps and even canals that were on a scale that could be considered to be engineering. Among the sites where these structures were built of stone and still remain are Ettrick (Mainsbridge Weir site), Lake Condah, Toolondo and Mt William.

A detailed study of the trap network has been carried out at Lake Condah; the publication they produced is *Aboriginal Engineering of the Western Districts of Victoria.* The study found many stone races (above ground canals), canals, and stone walls, up 1 m high by 1 m wide made from black volcanic rocks that are common in the area. These walls were often more than 50 m long. Channels had been dug into the basalt bedrock that were up to 1 m deep and extended for up to 300 m.

Apertures were built into the walls for the placement of eel pots or eel nets, and traps were built across the stone races and canals. Eel pots were made of bark strips or plaited rushes; they had a hoop of willow at the mouth. They tapered to a narrow exit where the eels could be grabbed as they emerged from the trap.

The system of traps was built on a number of levels to take advantage of different water levels in the lake, and was designed to operate whether the water was rising or falling.

At Mt William and Toolondo there was a system of water control that connected 2 lakes in 2 different drainage basins that were connected by 400 m-long channels dug out through the low divide between the 2 basins with digging sticks, allowing the water to flow in either direction. The system not only allowed the eels to occupy a larger area, and the channels were places where they were easy to catch, but it was designed in such a way that it coped with extra water during floods and retained water like dams in drought.

Later research that included computer simulation concluded that the eel trap systems were in fact part of a huge area of modified land, up to 100 km^2, where there were a number of weirs, channels and dams, that were probably a giant aquaculture project, growing eels that were smoked and traded along the trade routes. The oldest dates recorded for the area is at least 8,000 years ago. So aquaculture has been practiced in the area for at least 8,000 years. Near a lot of the eel traps were burnt-out hollow trees. Soil samples from the base of these "smoking trees" were found to contain traces of eel fat.

Associated with the eel business were permanent or semi-permanent houses, with a stone base.

The local Aborigines, the Gunditjmara, are unsurprised by the discovery, they say they still use the traps, and still weave the eel traps. It seems no one thought to ask them, they say they have always known that their ancestors were not nomadic. The only thing they didn't know was just how old the traps were.

Fish Traps at Brewarrina

Aboriginal shelters - villages among the eel harvesting structures.

A number of references in literature, such as the journals of explorers and a number of other people that were written in the 19th century, describe stone structures, as well as structures from other materials or combinations of the various materials, built by the Aboriginal inhabitants at various places around Australia.

George Augustus Robinson

The country at Kilgower is but slightly elevated above the sea. Kilgower is on the [blank(Moyne)] or Port Fairy River ... He ... took me to a very fine and large weir and went through, with several other of the natives, the process of taking eels and the particular spot where he himself stood and took them. I measured this weir with a tape, 200 feet, five feet high. It was turned back at each end. The eel pots are placed over the holes and the fisher stands behind the uere.roc or weir and lays hold of the small end of the arrabine or eel pot, And when the eel makes its appearance he bites it on the head and puts it on the lingeer or small stick with a knob at the end, thus or, if near the bank, he throws them out. The fishing is carried on in the rainy season. Arrabeen or eel pot made of bark or plaited rushes with a ... round mouth and having a small end to prevent the eel from rapidly getting away.

These yere.roc or weirs are built with some attention to the principles of mechanics. Those erected on a rocky bottom have the stocks inserted into a groove made by removing the small stones so as to form a groove. The weir is kept in a strait line. The small stones are laid against the bottom of the stick. The upright sticks are supported by transverse sticks, resting on forked sticks as shown above. These sticks are three, four or five inches in diameter. Some of the smaller weirs are in the form of a segment or circle. The convex side against the current. Robinson 30/4/1841 in Clark, 2000b: 157-158 in the Report to Aboriginal Affairs Victoria).

James Dawson - possible first hand description

*The small fish, 'tarrapatt,' and others of similar description, are caught in a rivulet which runs into Lake Colangulac, near Camperdown, by damming it up with stones, and placing a basket in a gap in the dam. The women and children go up the stream and drive the fish down ... Eels are prized by the Aborigines as an article of food above all other fish. They are captured in great numbers by building stone barriers across rapid streams, and diverting the current through an opening into a funnel-mouthed basket pipe, three or four feet long, two inches in diameter, and closed at the lower end. When streams extend over marshes in time of flood, clay embankments two or three feet high, and sometimes three to four hundred yards in length, are built across them, and the current is confined to narrow openings in which the pipe baskets were placed...Lake Boloke is the most celebrated place in the Western District for the fine quality and abundance of its eels; and, when the autumn rains induce these fish to leave the lake and go down the river to the sea, the Aborigines gather there from great distances. Each tribe has allotted to it a portion of the stream, now known as Salt Creek; and the usual barrier is built by each family...For a month or two the banks of Salt Creek presented the appearance of a village all the way from Turreen Turreen, the outlet of the lake, to its junction with the Hopkins (*Dawson, 1881, in the Report to Aboriginal Affairs Victoria).

George Augustus Robinson - early site descriptions

[Mt William Region]

<u>*? passed several dieks dug by the natives for draining several small lagoons into the large ones for the purpose of catching eels, etc. These channels were from a foot to 18 inches deep and from one to 300 yards in length*</u> (Robinson, 8/7/1841 in Clark 2000b in the Report to Aboriginal Affairs Victoria).

[Near Mt William]

At the confluence of this creek with the marsh observed an immense piece of ground trenched and banked...which on inspection I found to be the work of the Aboriginal natives, purposefully constructed for catching eels... These trenches are hundreds of yards in length. I measured in one place in one continuous tripple line for the distance of 500 yards. These treble watercourses led to other ramified and extensive trenches of a most tortuous form. An area of at least 15 acres was thus traced over...These works must have been executed at great cost of labour...the only means of artificial power being the lever...This lever is a stick chisel, sharpened at one end, by which force they threw up clods of soil and thus formed the trenches, smoothing the water channel with their hands. The soil displaced went to form the embankment...This description of work is called by the natives <u>cro.cup.per</u>, i.e. Bennewongham [said so].

The plan or design of these ramifications was extremely perplexing and I found it difficult to commit [to] paper, in the way I could have wished, all its various form and curious curvilinear windings and angles of every size and shape and parallels, etc. At intervals small apertures left and where they placed their arabeen arrabine or eel pots. These gaps were supported by pieces of the bark of trees and sticks. In single measurement there must have been some thousands of yards of this trenching and banking. The whole of the water from this mountain rivulet is made to pass through this trenching ere it reaches the marsh; it is hardly possible for a single fish to escape. I observed a short distance higher up, minor trenching was done through which part of the water ran its course to the more extensive works. Some of these banks were two feet in height, the most of them a foot and the hollow a foot deep by 10 or 11 inches wide. The main branches were wider.

Around these entrenchments were a number of large ovens or mounds for baking, there were at least a dozen in the immediate neighbourhood (Robinson, 9/7/1841 in Clark 2000b in the Report to Aboriginal Affairs Victoria).

Alexander Ingram - early site description
At the south-western portion of Lake Condah is situated one of the largest and most remarkable Aboriginal fisheries in the western district of Victoria. The position has been very well chosen, as the small bay is the lowest point on the western side of the lake. Owing to the peculiar formation (open trap scoriae) along the eastern, southern and part of the western sides of the lake, the water sinks very rapidly and becomes very low during summer months, but as it receives the drainage of a large extent of country the water rises very

quickly during winter, and first flows into the scoriae at the point named, which has been facilitated to some extent by the channels formed by the Aborigines for trapping eels, trout, etc. These channels have been made by removing loose stones and portions of the more solid rocks between the ridges and lowest places, also by constructing low wing walls to concentrate the streams. At suitable places are erected stone barricades with timber built in to as to form openings from 1ft. to 2ft. wide; behind these openings were secured long narrow bag nets made of strong rushes...There are also numerous smaller fisheries constructed in suitable places in small bays and outlets where the water sinks into the trap scoriae down along the margin of the valley of Darlot's Darlots Creek. Across this valley, at suitable places, were erected large barricades constructed with strong forked stakes, horizontal spars, and vertical stakes strengthened with piles of stones; openings were also left in these (Ingram in Worsnop, 1897: 104-105 in the Report to Aboriginal Affairs Victoria).

George August Robinson

Led our horses into the stony rises: masses of larve large?, steep stone - horse could barely walk - plenty ash hills, round sharp layrs layers?, plenty huts of dirt and others built of stones...At the native camp they had oven baking roots...Stone houses...stone weirs...Mt Napier bore north and Mt Eels WNW (Robinson, 20/3/1842 in Clark 2000c: 42 in the Report to Aboriginal Affairs Victoria).

Fish Traps at Brewarrina
ngunnhu   See The Stone Fish Traps of Baiame

These fish traps consist of stone walls about half a kilometre long in the Barwon River, a tributary of the Darling. The Aborigines say they were built in the Dreamtime by Baiame and his 2 sons Boomaoomanowi and Ghindaindamui. They are known to be very old; some even suggest they may be one of the oldest human constructions in the world. The traps were built on a section of the river bed that covers a bedrock outcrop. Their use was first reported by European settlers in the 1850s.

According to the stories of the Ngemba people, Baiame and his sons built the traps when there was a drought and Gurrungga, the waterhole at Brewarrina, dried up, leading to possible famine. It has been said that the placement and method of construction demonstrated an understanding of fish biology and the hydrology of the river, representing an engineering method no longer practised.

Yams

Yams are a high-starch food that is an important food source in tropical north Australia, as with the Anbara of Arnhem Land. The Anbara dug the tubers out but left the top of the tuber attached to the plant, and the tubers subsequently regrew. The same harvesting technique was practiced in other parts of Arnhem Land and Cape York. The plants were marked to show ownership. They increased the numbers of yams available by planting them on offshore islands as a reserve. It was almost agriculture but took less effort.

Native Doctor Initiation

Across Australia the initiation of a native doctor was broadly similar with some variations between areas.

Wuradjeri

An example is among the Wuradjeri, where a person is eligible only when he is considered a social adult. A requirement for a boy to be accepted for initiation is that he must have shown a leaning towards the 'profession' throughout his early life (Berndt & Berndt, 1964), as well as being close to a reputable practitioner who guides him through a probationary period, instructing him and even taking him 'in spirit on his teacher's nocturnal wanderings' (Berndt & Berndt, 1964). At a later point he is given an assistant totem (bala) that is sung into him. He is then taught the songs and rituals that will release it from his body when it is required. Baiame tells his father or his father's father in a dream, often after several years, that he is now ready for initiation. The postulants with their guardians are taken to a place that is sacred to Baiame where Baiame appears to them after singing. His appearance is the same as normal people, but light is shining from his eyes. Sacred water, gali, imbued with great power, issues from his mouth, which is said to be liquefied quartz crystal. When it falls on the postulants it enters them. After a while feathers appear, then Baiame departs. Several days later Baiame teaches them to fly when the feathers have grown into wings.

Baiame teaches them how to use quartz crystals and sings a piece into their foreheads to give them x-ray vision. He sings fire from his body into their chests, telling them to sing away their wings and return to their guardians. The final rite is when he returns and removes a thick sinew cord (the maulwa cord used by doctors for a number of purposes) that he sings into each of them. Before they return to the camp as doctors they spend a period of time trying out the powers. Variations on this theme were recorded by Howitt (1904, 355-425, Elkin, 1945).

Dieri

A special experience was thought to be involved in a person acquiring the power to perform beneficial magic as well as sorcery among the Dieri (Berndt & Vogelsang, 1941). If a man wanted to be a doctor after subincision he could be trained by a gungi, a practitioner. After completing the training with a gungi he becomes a gungi when he receives the power from gudgi, a spirit. The gudgi can assume various shapes such as an animal or even a willy-willy (whirlwind). The willy-willy is disliked, and sometimes feared, by a number of tribes, including the Dieri. Howitt (1904: 446) reports seeing a man chasing a willy-willy, trying to kill the gudgi with boomerangs. The man said later that he had fought with this gudgi, which had growled at him. He died a short time later. The Dieri refer to the 'making' (Berndt & Berndt, 1904) in which a postulant who has been specially decorated, is taken to the bush by a gungi, where he spends some time in seclusion and meditation. His parents mourn him as he leaves the camp. It is said his old life is forgotten. The spirit visits him while he is in trance, replacing his mind with a gungi mind. The spirit returns to perform certain rites the following day. The next day the spirit completes the making by giving him powerful gifts that he can use for magic. As a result of the making he is said to be reborn, having had a spirit snake inserted into his stomach by the gungi during one of the rites. He is believed to then visit the sky world. Gungi can fly to the sky world by a hair cord where they drink water that gives them power (Siebert in Howitt, 1904: 359).

Ngadjuri

The native doctor candidates of the Ngadjuri from central Australia has to endure a similar experience, seclusion, meditating, talking with spirits, trance and visions. He is considered to be dead during the seclusion part of the initiation, being reborn when it is completed, as a mindaba (doctor). Among the Ngadjuri, women can also be initiated as mindaba, with powers equal to those of male mindaba.

There are at least 2 main waterholes in the Great Victoria Desert that are connected with initiation of native doctors (gingin) (in Berndt (1964), Berndt, 1942-1945; see Elkin, 1954; 284-94), gabi Djabudi, to the west of Ooldea and Lake Darlot, Western Australia. Both of these waterholes are associated with Wanambi, the Rainbow. At the start of the initiation the man is led away from the camp by gingin. His relatives and close friends wail for him as though he had just died. He was said to be going to receive power, daramara ('cut into pieces'). He was blindfolded at the waterhole and led to the edge of the water, where he was said to be swallowed whole by Wanambi, then the gingin return to the camp. The gingin brought food to the snake a bit later, and then when he eats it, he expels the postulant into the air so that he falls to earth in a nearby rock hole. The gingin search the rockholes until they find him, now in the form of a small boy, which they carry as they fly back to camp.

The next is the stage of the fire rite, in which the child is placed in the centre of a ring of fires, the heat of which causes him to grow to adult size. After a period of meditation, the next stage is the use of an eradji australite in the ritual dislocation, or 'cutting', of all his joints. A meban, a small pearl shell disc, is placed in each cut. These shell discs have life-giving powers so revive his limbs. They are also put into the man's ears and jaw which is said to allow him to speak all languages, which allows him to speak with the spirits. He is enabled to see with x-ray vision, as well as the power to divine, by the placement of a shell disc into his forehead. A shell disc in his stomach is believed to make him invulnerable. When he is aroused he has completed his training and initiation. On his return to the camp all the initiated men throw spears at him, which are said to bounce off him because he is protected by the life-protecting meban.

Birrundudu
In this tribe in the Northern Territory the native doctor initiation is very similar to that of the Ngadjuri, but in this case it is said the native doctors and the postulant fly on the Rainbow.

In the eastern Kimberleys, the Rainbow Snake and the spirits of the dead give a sorcerer his knowledge (Kaberry 1939: 213,217). Among this people a woman may not be a sorcerer, though she may use poison revenge, by using a white substance. There is often an association between the Rainbow Serpent and other snakes.

Gunwinggu

The spirits of the dead are the main source of power among the Gunwinggu from western Arnhem Land, the native doctor having one or more spirit familiars, which provide advice and information he needs. In some cases the power is received by him directly, which allows him full use of the power. It was said that usually a man becomes a margidjbu (native doctor) while hunting alone. In this case he receives the power from the ghost of a close relative, such as his mother or her brother, his father or his father's brother, his son or his brother's son or one of his immediate grandparents. When this occurs he is believed to have collapsed to the ground and is too weak to move other than to nod his head, staring at the ghost. The ghost then tells the man it has come to give him the power to become a margidjbu. The ghost inserts a small rod like a miniature spear into the man's head and breaths power into all the openings of his body, and tells him to use the power for healing. At this point the man can't speak, only nod, and the ghost breathes more power into him that allows him to stand, though at first he moves slowly as though he has just woken up. Once a man has been made a margidjbu the power cannot be revoked by the ghost who gave it to him, even if they later argue. Some margidjbu were believed to have more power than others. Such powerful margidjbu were said to heal the sick by following the patient's spirit in a dream, catching it, and returning it to its body, which was said to be useless without its spirit. Alternatively the margidjbu may take the sick person to the land above the clouds, again in a dream, where he can heal the patient.

There are a number of things a margidjbu should be capable of, such as having knowledge of diagnosis and healing using physical means like massage, bathing and 'medicine'. Another requirement is that the patient must be co-operative and have confidence in the doctor, who must also have confidence in his own abilities. Sometimes a margidjbu would reject a case because they claim they were brought in too late, or simply because the patient or his relatives didn't cooperate. One method of judging if it was too late or not was to tug on the patient's hair; if it came loose easily they were considered to be untreatable. Occasionally a doctor was rejected by the patient because their fee was too high.

Other authors writing on this topic are Roheim (1945), and Spencer and Gillen (1938: 522-33), suggesting 3 distinct schools in the making of medicine men (native doctors). In one of their categories the rites are performed by iruntarinia, who are spirit doubles of tribal ancestors. In this type of initiation the postulant's tongue is pierced by the spirit. An example of this ritual is seen in a photo by Spencer and Gillen which shows a man with a hole in his tongue. There are other rituals, some involving taboos. Occasionally women are initiated by this method.

In another category the rituals are carried out by orancha urantia?, mischievous spirits associated with the time of the Dreaming. This series of rituals is used to initiate both men and women.

The third type of initiation is by other native doctors. With this initiation crystals removed from other native doctors are inserted in holes made under the fingernails of the postulant. He also has his tongue cut. There are also taboos involved.

Beneath all the methods of magical initiation is the theme of ritual death and rebirth with new powers and the ability to do the work of a native doctor. Common to all these is the belief that he has received these powers through a mystical experience. In different areas the native doctor has been attributed different sets of powers. He can have the power of foretelling the future, making rain, curing the sick, using his power to divine a murderer, and having the power to defend against magic.

The native doctors used a number of objects as well as using spells and rituals to cure the sick. These objects included australites, pearl shell, quartz crystals, bones and stones (Berndt & Berndt, 1964). The various native doctors used a number of techniques, some of which would probably work without any physical treatment, even on modern non-Aboriginal people, as they used the power of suggestion, or the placebo effect. According to Berndt & Berndt, (1964), some of the methods used were slight-of-hand, ventriloquism, massaging and sucking. Steaming over medicinal herbs was used by the doctors along the lower reaches of the Murray River in South Australia.

They used small pearl shell discs for divination, and for healing they depended on their x-ray vision. According to Berndt & Berndt (1964) there were a number of powers that these men were believed to possess by their patients, in different combinations in different places and practitioners of differing experience and reputation, included hypnotic power, supernatural abilities such as thought transference, clairvoyance, and mind reading. Some were believed to produce a magical cord, in some cases from the navel, or an assistant totem in the form of a spirit familiar. Some were believed to have the power to speak with ghosts and spirits, fly or travel at super human speeds, become invisible, change into smoke or wind, or into an animal such as a reptile, and create illusions.

In western Arnhem Land, some of the practitioners with the highest reputations were believed to be able to do such things as use the swarm of flies around their bodies to disguise their approach to another person without being seen. They could also attack an enemy by sending swarms of stinging insects, to at least make him uncomfortable.

Elkin has given examples of activities, such as among the Wuradjeri, in demonstration ceremonies during which a native doctor lay on his back beneath a tree, produced his maulwa cord by singing it out as a spider produces threads of web, then use it to climb to the top of the tree.

Aboriginal Mortuary Rites - Disposal of the Body

There are a number of ways of disposing of a body, different areas preferring a particular method, though sometimes more than one method could be used in any given area. Among the methods of body disposal were burial, exposure on a platform or a tree, desiccation-mummification, cremation, in a hollow tree, a construction that has been called a coffin, burial cannibalism, reburial or secondary burial (see King Island). As the various methods are not usually mutually exclusive, the bones may be collected then either carried around or reburied. The body could be placed on a platform until it decomposed following which the bones were re-collected and placed in a cave or a hollow log.

An instance of one form of this practice was told to my family by my great grandmother. After arriving from Ireland in 1882 they settled in Maryborough, Queensland. My great grandparents befriended some of the local Aborigines and one particular woman they often invited to their home was known as Kitty Biglip, because of an ornament she wore in her lip. I don't know if any of the family knew her Aboriginal name. My family sometimes invited their Aboriginal friends to Sunday dinner (midday). One day after her husband died Kitty arrived with his bones in a dilly bag; I think it was carried around her neck, but I'm not sure. I don't know if that was the normal practice among the Aborigines in the **Maryborough** area (MHM).

In the Grampians area of Victoria, the **Mukjarawaint** left a corpse in the camp for a few days, then the body was bound with the knees drawn up, the elbows against the sides and the hands on the shoulders. It was then placed in a hollow tree (Howitt, ibid., 453, 459).

The corpse was bound in the same way by the **Kurnai**, but they carried the bound body around for some time before being placed in a hollow tree.

The Yerkla-mining (Eucla) were said to never bury their dead, the dying person being left beside a fire, the rest of the people in the camp moved to another camp (Howitt, ibid., 450).

Rock shelters were used instead of hollow trees on the **Keppel Islands**. On the smaller islands around **Broadsound** the people were said to take their dead out to sea in canoes and throw them overboard (Roth, 1907, 398).

If an unauthorised trespasser was killed in the northern Kimberleys, the local people place the body in a hole dug in a termite mound. The termites soon repair the damage and there is no evidence that could lead an avenging party to the culprits (Basedow, 1925: 206). The Berndts reported hearing of this practice in the **East Kimberleys**.

When a baby died in the western Arnhem Land, its body was placed in a **termite mound** so the bones would quickly disintegrate freeing its spirit to return to the same mother to be born again. Sometimes the mother would carry some of the baby's bones around with her so that its spirit could enter her to be reborn.

It was reported by Roth (1897: 165; 1907: 395) (believed to be referring to the Boulia area of Queensland) that a person sentenced to death by the tribal council for a serious offence was obliged to dig his own grave.

When men were killed in tribal fighting, their bodies could be left where they fell, broken spears or boomerangs being left nearby to indicate how they died.

A man speared for breaking a sacred law could be left where he fell, in parts of the **Northern Territory**, Daly River and **Arnhem Land**. This punishment not only deprived him of his life, but also the usual mortuary rites, that could be considered the most serious part of the punishment.

In South Australia, among the people on the Lower River Murray, after a body had been smoke dried it was treated as if it had been repossessed by its spirit when it was used in the inquest rites.

In Queensland, the **Wakelbura** carried around the remains of close relatives, though during ceremonies it could be placed against a tree, a red band tied around the bundle in the position of the head, as though it was watching the dancers (Howitt, 1904: 473).

Among the **Gadjalibi** and neighbouring tribes in north-central Arnhem land, where the corpse, usually a man but occasionally a woman, would be painted and decorated as though it was a participant in the mortuary ceremony, designs in pipeclay on the face and a small red basket hanging from the neck. The body was tied to a pole in a sitting or standing position as the relatives sing and dance in front of him, calling out to him to join in. In particular, those to whom he was a mother's mother's brother or a sister's daughter's son joke and laugh at him, telling him to get up and join in the dancing. This is his last chance to return, though only a symbolic chance, as they show they are willing to accept him back but it is his choice not to return. 1 or 2 days later they wrap the body in preparation for either burial or platform disposal. After some time the bones were collected, and kept for some time before the final ceremony. During the final part of the process the bones are shown and presented to his closest relatives, and possibly his wife.

The spirits on this island of Bralgu send out **Morning Stars** to different parts of Arnhem Land as they dance. In the **Dua moiety** mortuary **Ritual of the Morning Star** a large pole is used on which are feathered strings and balls of seagull feathers to represent the stars. The actions of the living people in this ritual was said to be an imitation of that carried out by spirits of the dead on **Bralgu**.

Aboriginal Mortuary Rites - Cannibalism

The Australian Aborigines were not generally cannibals, in that they did not kill people to eat. Where cannibalism does occur it is in a ritual context, if the reports of early workers in the field are accurate. Burial cannibalism, in a number of forms, occurred fairly commonly in Aboriginal Australia. In parts of Queensland it occurred in connection with mummification, before the body was exposed on a platform (Elkin, 1954: 513), as occurred among the tribes of south west of the Gulf of Carpentaria, and in the northern part of the Kimberleys, occasionally. In north east South Australia, it was part of the interment ritual (see Elkin, 1637: 283-5). In the Liverpool River area of western Arnhem Land, only a small part of the body was eaten, but only by specified relatives.

The **Maung** of **Gilbert Island** and the nearby mainland have been reported to have occasionally cut up a corpse, though only specified kin were permitted to eat the flesh of the dead person. Inedible organs are placed in a hole and a fire was lit to destroy them. The heart liver and kidneys were placed in another hole and buried. A larger hole was dug where the flesh was cooked. The flesh is shared out among certain kin, though not those of the territorial group, the **namanamaidj**, of the deceased. Those eating the flesh were believed to gain strength from it. The hunting ability of men was believed to be enhanced by carrying around dried pieces of the flesh. The head was left on a pole to dry, after which it was carried around as a memento.

A mother of a stillborn child or a child who died early, was said to eat the flesh of the child, in the expectation that it would make it easier for the spirit of the child to enter her body and be reborn. It has been suggested that the anointing of the bodies of mourners with exudates from decomposing bodies, as was practised in many parts of Australia, can be seen as being similar to cannibalism (Elkin, 1954: 313).

Ritual cannibalism has been reported to be widespread in North West central Queensland (Roth, 1897: 166), where a child's body could be eaten by its parents and siblings. Not all of Roth's accounts were well documented. An example he gives is the **Kalkadoon**, who were said to eat any corpse, even where there were visible signs of **venereal disease** (**STD**s). He did specify that he knew of no case where a person was killed with the intention of eating them. In north Queensland, on the Pennefather River, an early stage in cremation ceremony of a young man, the soles of the feet and the flesh from the front of the thighs are baked in the ashes after being cut into small pieces. One or more of his sister's sons would then eat them over a period of 2-3 months (Roth, 1907). Those eating these pieces are prohibited from speaking until they can identify the 'murderer', after which he can speak to reveal the name. The dead man's fibula is used to make a death charm of bone needles. This charm can then be used by his sister's son or his mother's father's brother's son to avenge his death.

In the Brisbane area, a native doctor singed the body hair from the body at a large fire, leaving the beard and head hair unburnt, while other members of the group sat around their own fires. 3 other native doctors dance toward the corpse, while each holds a stone knife in his mouth. If of a man, the corpse was placed face down on the ground, women were placed face up. The skin is removed as a single piece, including the fingers, toes, ears, etc. It is then spread on spears near a fire to dry. After the internal organs, including the entrails, had been removed, the body was then cut up and shared, and after roasting, was eaten, except for certain parts that were destroyed in the fire. Some relatives, mother, widow or sister keep the collected bones. After placing the pelvis in a bag it is used to identify the 'murderer' (Roth, 1907: 398-401). The process is finalised by placing the skin and bones in a hollow tree.

The explanations for these procedures are the participants don't fear the dead person's spirit, so can immediately dispose of the body. Secondly, the corpse is prevented from decomposing by the procedures followed.

Aboriginal Mortuary Rites - Cremation

Cremation could be either the final rite of disposal of a corpse, or it could be the only rite. Several examples were reported from North Queensland (Roth, 1907). In 1 example from the northern part of Cape York Peninsula, a young man had drowned and his body had been recovered and cremated. The head, a fibula and some other parts, that were not specified, were not burnt. By not burning some of the bones the dead person was prevented from returning.

In the area of the Lower Tully River, the dead person was tied up in a particular way then cremated, interred, desiccated, or parts of the body could be eaten. According to Roth, it appeared that specific ritual accompanied cremation only if the dead person was of high status. If the corpse was of an ordinary person the body was simply thrown onto a pyre and cremated without ritual, after which the female relatives searched the ashes for relics.

It is suspected there may also have been more complicated procedures. In one instance reported, the skin and hair had been removed from a corpse and the hands were tied together. A man carries the body on his shoulder while others follow. When they reach the designated spot in the bush they prop the body against a tree and heap up some wood. The ceremony that follows includes a song about the coming inquest. This inquest takes place after the body has been taken to another place where it is placed on its back and the native doctor sits astride it. He made a number of incisions, removing the stomach, wrapping it in a paperbark, or in the bark blanket of the deceased. The identity of the murderer was divined using the stomach, after which it was buried, and the corpse was then cremated on the pyre.

Cremations were reported at **Kew** and **Geelong** in Victoria. In those areas it was said the body would be cremated if there was no time to dig a grave to bury it, when the deceased was a married woman, or an elderly person who had been strangled because they were physically of no further use. The latter reason, if true, would be very unusual in Aboriginal Australia (Howitt, 1904; quoting other sources). There are very few cases of old people being killed in Australia.

Among the Victorian tribes, a body could be placed on a funeral pyre with its head to the east, and the belongings associated with the person were also placed on the pyre. If the deceased was a woman, her husband collected her bones after the body had been burnt, which he pounded into a powder to be carried around his neck in a possum skin pouch, either until he remarried or the pouch wore out, when it would be burnt (Howitt quoting Dawson).

In another instance, when the corpse was believed to be that of a headman, the bones of the lower leg and forearm are removed and cleaned, after which the body is bound in a flexed position then wrapped in a rug. It is placed in a hut with a smoking fire. While there it is fanned to keep the flies away, and after an unspecified length of time it is placed on a tree platform. Eventually it is cremated, after which the bones are pounded into powder then kept in small bags.

At Mt Macedon, the King River, Ovens River and the Murray River the people are reported to have cremated their dead, the bones being gathered and placed in a hollow tree (Howitt).

Cremation was practiced by the **Katungal** (associated with the **Yuin**) in the **Port Jackson** area. In this area cremation was used for stillborn babies or very young children.

Aboriginal Mortuary Rites – Desiccation

In parts of northern and eastern Queensland, the Darling River Basin and the Murray River Basin, the Lakes District of the lower Murray River and the middle north of South Australia were found various forms of desiccation (Elkin, 1954: 313). A desiccating corpse was seen as far west as Ooldea in 1941 by one of the Berndts, they presumed it had come from eastern Australia. On occasion an incision was made through which the internal organs were removed, the cavity being packed with grass etc. The body was then dried in the sun or over a fire. Following this it was bound and usually painted, then carried around by the mourners, eventually being placed on a platform in a tree or in a cave, or sometimes it was buried, cremated or put into a hollow tree.

Sometimes corpses were smoke-dried by the people at Encounter Bay and on the lower Murray River (Taplin & Meyer, in Woods, 1879: 21-1, 198-200.) According to Taplin, the people constructed a special bier with a slow fire under it, and then arranged the corpse on it in a sitting posture with the arms outstretched. The hair is removed when the skin blisters, after which they sewed up all body apertures. The smoke-drying is carried out by men who have inherited the position of smoke-drying corpses. They then rub the corpse with grease and red ochre and place it on a platform in the same sitting position, but inside a hut. It dries gradually over a slow fire as the loudly grieving mourners brush away the flies with long whisks. The mourners eat and sleep either beneath or next to the platform. It is wrapped in a specially prepared mat when it is dry and kept in the hut. According to Meyer, the corpse is placed between 2 fires. The heat from the fires, combined with the heat from the sun, causes the skin to loosen after a few days. At this time the term the Aborigines used to refer to Europeans was used to call the corpse, because it is the colour of Europeans. For the rest of the process, most of the description by Meyer agrees with that given by Taplin. The body is carried around for several months after it is dry, then finally left on a platform to disintegrate. Sometime later the skull is taken by a close kinsman and used as a drinking vessel (Tindale, 1938; Massola, 1961).

The **Marinoa Maranoa People** dried the corpse on a platform over a fire, and then carry it around for a long time, then the liquid exuding from the corpse is collected and rubbed over the bodies of young men to pass on the good qualities of the deceased person to them (Howitt, 1904: 467-8).

The **Kurnai** wrap a corpse in a possum skin rug, and then tie it in a bark sheet, then build a hut over it. The relatives mourn in this hut by wailing and cutting themselves. The body is unwrapped and examined after a few days, and then a close kin-father, mother or sisters plucks the hair and preserves it. They then re-wrap it and it is not opened again until it is well decomposed, at which point the fluids exuding from it are used for anointing. Sometimes they hasten the drying by removing the internal organs, then carry it around until it is a "bag of bones", when it is either buried or put in a hollow tree.

The same topic in relation to north Queensland has been discussed by Roth (1907). In Cape York, corpses were disembowelled and desiccated (Haris Harris, 1912). According to McConnel (1937) the body is cremated and the mourning dances continue until the food dues are settled. Accompanied by rhythmic movements and mourning songs, food payments are made to the dead man's brothers, sisters and father by the widow and her brothers and sisters. Wrestling matches are held between 'brothers' on the day of the cremation, and eventually the mourners turn their backs to the funeral pyre as the body is cremated.

In the area of the northern part of Cape York, the body is typically bound to a pole erected on 2 forked sticks, particularly if the deceased person is a young man, either covered with bark or a dilly bag may be placed on the head. Certain parts are kept and carried around as relics, or eaten ritually, the remainder of the body being burned.

Desiccation is a very elaborate process in the area of the Russell River, the 'mummy' being ornamented. At places such as **Miriam Vale**, the corpse was sun-dried on a platform, and then placed in a hollow tree through an opening that has been cut in the tree. 'The classic form of mummification was practised in the Torres Strait region and possibly spread down into eastern Australia '(Elkin, 1954). According to Elkin, when a body was preserved in other parts of the world it was to preserve the corpse as a home for the spirit. In aboriginal society it was seen as a temporary abode of the spirit until the mourning was complete, and if the death had been avenged, after which the body could be disposed of to free the spirit to allow it to find its way to the abode of the spirits in the Land of the Dead, in Aboriginal Australia this usually meant it could return to a sacred water hole, or some other sacred place, to await a suitable pregnant woman who it could enter as the spirit of her unborn child. see Aboriginal Afterlife

Aboriginal Mortuary Rites - Interment

Interment was by far the most common method of disposal of a corpse in Aboriginal Australia, though sometimes only part of a sequence. In the Ooldea region, bodies have been observed in which the hair had been removed and shaped into a coit-shaped object, then doubled up and bound (Berndt & Harvey Johnston, 1942; R. & C. Berndt, 1942-5). The corpse of a man would be prevented from throwing a spear in the afterlife by having his spear arm tied to his side. The body was then carried to a selected site where it was placed on a bed of leaves in a round shallow grave, the head facing the east. It was then covered with leaves and bushes, and finally logs, but not with sand or earth. Nearby a conical mound was built that was named after the Moon. **Moon** had been the first man to be killed in the Dreamtime. After a period that ranged from 3 months to about 2 years, the burial party returned, comprising the people who originally placed the body in the grave, and removed the remains. The actions of the burial party could then involve removing the bones, cleaning them and replacing them in the grave, or they could rub their bodies with the exudate. They then filled in the grave with earth and sand and covered it with heavy logs.

In the south eastern parts of Australia, New South Wales, Victoria and eastern South Australia, grave mounds were constructed. Sometimes the bones were later moved to another site. One instance was observed in which the bones were moved to a side chamber of the same mound. Among some tribes in south western Australia, and in north western New South Wales and south eastern Queensland, mythogically mythologically significant conventional designs are carved into trees around the grave. In western **Arnhem Land**, grass or paperbark figures are placed near a deserted camp after a death, with one arm pointing to the new camp, the other to the corpse that was usually on a platform. In parts of South Australia, such as the **Adelaide**, **Gawler** and **Gumeracha** districts, the corpse is interred in an upright position, wrapped in a wallaby rug that is packed with leaves and boughs. At the head of the grave, earth or stones are arranged in the shape of a crescent (Howitt, 1904).

Among some tribes, such as the **Tongaranka** of western New South Wales, the corpse was placed in the grave in a sitting position, and the person's belongings were also placed in the grave. The nearest male relative of the deceased person stands by the grave that was still open, and was struck by the edge of a boomerang several times until blood dripped onto the corpse. The grave was then filled in. The dripping of the blood has been suggested to be a propitiatory rite, possibly to appease the spirit and, in the event of it being accused of sorcery, to assure its innocence. It has also been suggested that it may be connected with rebirth, at least of the spirit, as blood symbolises life.

Near the **Darling River**, on the upper Murray River, the **Wiimbaio** wrapped the corpse in a rug or blanket and placed it into a 6 ft hole, which is then packed with twigs and bark, after which it is covered with sand. The grave is then covered with a pile of wood, above which rushes or soft grass are heaped, tapering at the top, being held together with old netting or string. Fires are kept burning on either side of the grave to keep the dead person warm.

Near **Swan Hill**, on the **Upper Murray River**, among the **Wathi-Wathi** the headman was buried in a cleared area that had been fenced with logs and brush. The grave was covered with bark sheets in the form of a hut, including a ridge pole in the centre.

In western Victoria, the **Wotjobaluk** tied the corpses, with crossed arms and knees up to the chest, after placing his spear thrower on his chest he is rolled up in his possum fur rug. In this case the grave was oblong, a layer of bark on the bottom, covered with leaves and strands of possum pelt. The corpse is then placed in the grave. The body was then covered with a lot of leaves and pelt, above which is more bark. After the grave is filled with earth, logs were then placed on top to prevent dogs from digging up the body. A nearby fire is kept burning. The next day an oval-shaped clearing was prepared around the grave, in which are parallel soil ridges. Earthworks over certain graves have been reported (Worsnop, 1897), though the Berndts were uncertain how accurate these reports were.

Corpses were buried in a horizontal position among the **Laragia**, usually being placed on their right side, with the head on the hands and the legs up against the trunk, covered with bark sheets and grass, and finally with earth, though a small gap is left at the side for the spirit to leave and return if it wants to (Basedow, 1925).

Among the **Dieri**, food was placed at a grave of an influential man. In winter a fire was kept burning to keep him warm. The corpse was wrapped in a rug or net, its big toes tied together. It was buried after it was asked to name the person responsible for its death (Howitt, ibid. 448).

The **Port Jackson** tribes practised canoe burials in which a body was placed in a canoe that was prepared specially for the burial, together with a fishing spear and spear thrower and waistband. The canoe was carried to the burial site on the heads of 2 people (Howitt, Quoting Collins)

The Aranda seated a corpse in a round hole, with its knees drawn up to its chin. The earth that fills the hole is mounded up over the grave, with a depression of the side facing the deceased person's totemic territory. In particular, the sacred site associated with the conception of the person. It was believed the spirit spent part of the time until the final mourning ceremony watching over close relatives, the rest of its time being spent in the company of its spirit double, its **arumburinga** that lives in the dreaming site. The depression allowing easy access for the spirit (Spencer & Gillen, 1938).

The most spectacular burial sites in Australia were on **Melville Island** and **Bathurst Island**. Above a grave, a mound is heaped with stringy bark sheets (Spencer, 1914; Mountford, 1958). Tree trunks are carved into large grave posts, 3-4 of which are erected as part of the first mourning ceremony that takes place several months after the burial, and about 12 are later added at intervals.

The **Gagadju (Kakadu)** wrapped the body in paperbark, and then took it into the bush to where a trench had been prepared with a thick layer of grass and leaves. It was placed on its right side, its legs bent back at the knees (Spencer, ibid., 240-9). It is then covered with another layer of grass and leaves, then earth is built up into a small mound over the grave, then stones are heaped on it to prevent dogs from reaching it. After the burial is complete, the bark that was used to carry the body to the bush is used to wrap the person's belongings, which are taken back to the camp, where they are placed in a tree. A purification rite is then carried out in which the belongings of all the people in the camp affected by the death are smoked and water is poured over the heads of the men. The possessions of the deceased person, as well as the burial covering, are burnt. The men are then painted with charcoal and older men eat lily-seed cake. There is then a second sequence in which the personal belongings of all the camp members are placed in 2 heaps, one for women and the other for the men. The women wear armlets and the older men eat more lily-seed cake. All the men who had previously painted themselves black, with the exception of the immediate kin of the deceased person, now painted themselves white. After some time a third sequence takes place in which belongings and food are brought, and all are painted in red ochre. The men speculate about who was responsible for the death, then, after the women and children have returned to camp, the men eat then arrange bundles of spears on the ground, and the sequence is finalised by the bartering of the spears.

Aboriginal Mortuary Rites - Platform and Tree Disposal

This has been called delayed disposal. As soon as a person dies in north eastern and north-central Arnhem Land, the body is covered with red ochre. The clan and linguistic group totemic patterns are painted on the face, chest and abdomen of the body. The painting is done so the spirit beings in the Land of the Dead can easily see to which clan or sacred well the deceased person belongs (Warner, 1937/58: 416). Most of the hair is cut, to be woven into a hair belt interwoven with feathers later, the remainder is covered with white clay. All the belongings of the deceased person are arranged about the body, as well as sacred feathered string and carved objects, as part of the first mortuary ceremony. Later, the death messengers will take these carved objects to notify kinsfolk in distant places of the death of the person. At the time of the first mortuary ceremony a feast was held. During this feast no food is set aside for the spirit, in the hope it will be compelled to leave the earthly surroundings it is familiar with. To assist in the driving away of the spirit, the mourners brush themselves with smoking green leaves to purify themselves. A platform is constructed and the body is carried out into the bush and placed face-up on a specially prepared platform. If the diseased is a woman, models of her children, grandchildren or other close relatives, in paperbark or bound grass, are placed on each side of the body. The deceased is assumed to have been killed by someone, and the fluids dripping from the platform are used to divine the identity of the person responsible for the death. Other rites are carried out later (Warner, 1937/58: 412-33).

The upper Georgina district of Queensland

The dead person is placed on a platform, wrapped in a net, and covered with sticks and bushes, along with his or her possessions (Roth, 1897, 165-6; 1907). The tribes around the Brisbane area also sometimes practised platform disposal. It was a common method for persons considered 'unimportant'. According to Roth, the genitalia are removed to prevent the spirit from having sexual relations with the living"; the body is tied up and placed on a platform that has been constructed in the bush, the feet towards the west. The dead person's belongings are stuck into the ground and a small fire is lit under the platform so that the spirit can hunt and cook its own food. The identity of the murderer is revealed by divination, the area around the platform being inspected for footprints on the following day. 2-3 months later the bones are collected, some being burnt and others tested to confirm the murder's identity.

In northern New South Wales, the **Wollaroi** people sat beneath the platform as fluid drips from the corpse, rubbing it over themselves to gain strength. Once the flesh has decomposed away, the bones are buried (Howitt, 1904; 467). Examples of tree and platform disposal are given in which the bones are finally buried (Spencer, 1914; 249-52).

The **Waramunga** build a small platform in the branches of a tree, eventually burying all but the smaller arm bones, they used these in sorcery (Spencer & Gillen, 1938; 498).

In the eastern Kimberleys, the corpse on the platform in a tree is covered with paperbark, branches and stones, the remans being left on the platform until only bones remain (Kaberry, 1959: 212-14).

It has been observed that this form of disposal was practised throughout the north western part of Australia, in Arnhem Land, and from Wyndham to Darwin, south to about the centre and eastward into Queensland. It is always associated with bone collection, as well as the subsequent mourning rites, and the rites associated with an inquest.

Aboriginal Totemism

Totemism in Australia is linked to the Dreamtime - the time before time - the time outside time - the time of creation, when the ancestral beings, the totemic ancestors, roamed the land, giving birth to the people of the various totemic groups and naming the animals, plants, landscape features, etc.

It has been described by Elkin as '...a view of nature and life, of the universe and man, which colours the Aborigines' social groupings and mythologies, inspires their rituals and links them to the past. It unites them with nature's activities and species in a bond of mutual life-giving. And that it is a 'relationship between a person or a group of persons and (for example) a natural object or species, as part of nature'. It is a worldview in which a human is an integral part of nature, not distinct from other natural species, sharing with them the same life essence.

In the Dreamtime, the formative period, the various species had not fully assumed the shapes they have today. Their physical manifestations were more fluid. They could manifest themselves in the human form or that of a particular species of animal. A goanna ancestor could look like a man, but potentially change to look like a goanna. This is the basis of the connection between the living people and the ancestral being, the person having a connection with the type of goanna represented by the ancestor.

Individual Totemism

Only 1 person is involved in a special relationship with some natural species, or a particular member of that species. The relationship is a personal one, which is not usually shared or inherited. Though there are actually cases of inheritance, as among the **Wiradjuri**, in which a youth may be given a totem during his initiation. There is also a form of '**assistant totemism**', in which a totem animal may serve as a familiar, or 'second self' for a native doctor. There is another form among the Wiradjuri, a native doctor may take a 10-12 year-old-child from the main camp and 'sing' the assistant into him (**bala** or **jarawajewa** - 'meat' or totem within him, or the 'spirit animal'. In that case the bala is of patrilineal descent. It is widely distributed throughout New South Wales. Native doctors have spirit snakes in central, north and north-western Australia, associated with the Rainbow Serpent. The patrilineally inherited totem serves as an assistant in its physical as well as its spiritual form, among the **Jaraldri** on the Lower Murray. There are some songmen in western Arnhem Land who specialise in gossip songs, dealing with contemporary people. These songmen usually attribute new songs with a non-inherited familiar, a spirit or creature that reveals itself in a dream.

Sex Totemism

Each sex can have an emblem, such as a bird or animal, which usually signifies solidarity of that sex as distinct from the other. Injuring or killing the sex totem animal is like challenging or attacking that sex associated with it. An example was observed among the **Kurnai** of Gippsland. Among these people the emblems of the sexes are 2 different birds, one for each sex, who regard them as elder brother for men and elder sister for women. In this society marriages take place by elopement, and the girls can refuse a suitor. Conflict among the male-female totems helps overcome shyness of young people of marriageable age. Older women can kill a male totem and display it in the camp. This enrages the men and fighting takes place between young men and women. Later a young man can meet a young girl and call her by the female totem name, asking what that creature eats. Her reply can be something like, 'she eats kangaroo', or 'she eats possum.' This is a formal offer and acceptance of marriage, and the young couple elope. This system is usually associated with the south-east of Australia, with matrilineal moieties and matrilineal social totemic clans. It did exist in other places.

Moiety Totemism
This is widespread across the continent, but is most marked in the southeast and the south west. In many cases it is expressed through other forms of totemism. For example, in north eastern Arnhem Land the social and natural environment and the mythological constellations are distributed between the two moieties. There are hundreds of objects which could be termed totemic; these could be divided into major and minor totems. In western Arnhem Land, the matrilineal moieties are divided into phratries, each of which is associated with one or more totems.

Section and Subsection Totemism

In aboriginal Australia, some tribal groups are divided into 4 or 8 categories, based on the lines of indirect matrilineal descent. One or more natural phenomena, representing its members, distinguishing them from others, can be identified or linked to a particular category. In the eastern Kimberleys there is a totemic bond of kinship, and they adopt a ritual attitude towards the totem. In north eastern Arnhem Land, several totems are associated with each subsection. Some examples are, **wamud** is associated with the **wedge-tailed eagle**, **buralang** with **rock kangaroo**, **heron**, **albatross** and **wallaby**. The subsection system is relatively new to this region, so is not tightly integrated with the cult totemism of the clan-linguistic unit. In the eastern Kimberleys, north of **Balgo**, narangu - the subsection totems were treated more like namesakes, having no taboos associated with them. They weren't treated with respect.

Clan Totemism

A clan is a group claiming common descent in the male or female line. They share a common relationship with 1 or more natural phenomena. For the members of this unit, the clan, the totem is a symbol of membership of the unit. It is recognised for the members of this clan and those of other clans. This totem has strong territorial and mythological ties associated with it, and it is believed that it can warn them of approaching danger.

Some distinguish between matrilineal social clan totemism and patrilineal clan totemism. Matrilineal clan totemism is widespread throughout eastern Australia - Queensland, New South Wales, western Victoria and eastern South Australia. There is also a small area in the south west of Western Australia. The general translation of the word for this totem is 'flesh' or 'meat' - the person is 'of one flesh' with his totem. The totems connected with matrilineal phratries of western Arnhem Land are not the centre of cult life, and the members of the phratry don't have a special attitude towards it. The totems of the matrilineal social clans are the centre of cult life. An example among the **Dieri** is the mardu. It is really an **avunculineal** (of the mother's brother's line) cult totem. Patrilineal clan cult totemism, bindara, is also found in this tribe. Patrilineal clan totemism was present in parts of Western Australia, the Northern

Territory, Cape York, coastal areas of New South Wales and Queensland, central Victoria, along the lower Murray and the **Coorong** district and among the Lake Eyre groups. The best example was among the Jaraldi, **Dangani**, etc. and north eastern Arnhem Land. In eastern Arnhem Land a combination of aspects, including non-totemic, were associated with the clan. A clan has several totemic cults, and these can be associated with more than one linguistic group. In central Australia totemic combinations were apparent but less strongly so.

Local Totemism

With this people of a particular site or locality share a common totem, that is not connected with kin relationships or descent. The totem/totems were connected with the site. This is totemism that is determined by the locality in which a child was born, such as the Great Victoria Desert, among others. In such a case this is also birth totemism. Births nearly always occur in the local territory of the father, so it is patrilineal local (cult) totemism. The main difference between local and patrilineal cult clan totemism is that descent is not a major factor - though there was a tendency for it to become patrilineal. A good example existed among the **Aranda**, where it is the conception, not the birth, which determines local totemic cult membership. A person associated with a particular site that has mythological associations has therefore a direct link with the totemic being connected with that site. People connected with a particular site share a bond.

Conception Totemism

Conception totemism can be identified with local totemism. The place a mother first realises she is pregnant determines the child's ritual (cult) totem, according to the totemic or other connections with that site, as among the Aranda. It can be near a track followed by a being from the Dreamtime, a waterhole or other landscape feature formed in the Dreamtime by the various beings inhabiting the area at the time of creation. It is preferably associated with the ritual or cult totem of the father, though this is not essential.

In some areas a man can find a spirit child in a dream or vision before the mother knows she is pregnant, he may 'know' a spirit child is to be incarnated in his wife. The child may appear in conjunction with a natural phenomenon, often one connected with the father, with his country, or his social unit. This is the child's conception totem. If a mother becomes sick after eating a particular food and later dreams of a spirit child, the food will be considered the conception totem, the child having entered her body with it, or taken the shape of the food. In some cases the spirit may not be connected to the totem. In north eastern Arnhem Land the totemic affiliations are oblique, even though it takes the form of some natural species, and is not directly significant to the resulting child. The spirit centres at which unborn children live in the Great Victoria Desert are not totemic, though spirit beings from the Dreamtime put them there, so they have indirect associations with the dreamtime. Spirit children were made by the Rainbow Serpent in the eastern Kimberleys, in the anthropomorphic form. At **Balgo** they are directly totemic, being associated with mythological sites.

Birth totemism
In this form of totemism the place where a child is born determines its ritual or cult totem, rather than its place of conception. Men in the Great Victoria Desert tried to make sure their wives gave birth in their own country, preferably at a site near a track of the Dreamtime being most closely associated with him.

Dream Totemism
This overlaps other types of totemism - individual and/or assistant totemism, conception, or birth. In dreams a person can be consistently represented by a natural phenomenon which he is known to have a close link with. He can identify himself with a totemic being, either human or other form, in his dreams or dreams of others, the actions of the being and his. A dream totem, not identified as being his other self, may perform certain services in a dream. Spirit familiars of western Arnhem Land songmen and the spirit assistants of native doctors are examples of this. In the first example a person may appear in his dream-shape even after death. A person's ritual or cult totem is the one most often appearing in this way in many parts of Australia. This is the case in north-eastern Arnhem Land, but not in the Great Victoria Desert, though here the same word is used for totem and dream.

Multiple totemisms

Multiple or **classificatory totemism**, may be associated with other types of totemism, moiety, clan, section, subsection, phratry or local totemism. The known universe, or major aspects of it, is categorised on this basis. The main totem is regarded with a special attitude, and to all secondary totems classified with it. This form is common. An example from north-eastern Arnhem Land is:

'The Djanggawul sisters and brother walked along the east coast until they came to **Ngadibalji**, where they saw a mangrove bird. Here the brother left his hair belt: It is now a sandhill. On the sandhill were the tracks of wild duck, which were eating wild peanut roots. On the opposite side was a large barren sandhill; and on the surface of this were goanna tracks and the tracks of many birds. A tree with inedible 'apple'-like nuts was growing there too; this is a sacred bullroarer tree. Here the Djanggawul paused and heard the cry of the black cockatoo. Here too is the sacred waterhole which they made, and beside which they camped.'

Although the Djanggawul are not really totemic they might be the major totem. Men or women belonging to this site would also have a secondary totem, not actually graded as such, mangrove bird, hair belt, wild duck, nut tree, and black cockatoo. He might claim any one of them as his totem, which implies association with all of them.

'The **Wadi Gudjarra** (Two Men), in the course of their wanderings across the country, reached gabi (waterhole) Bindibindina. Here they made camp, ate berries, and picked flowers to put in their hair. They also made bindi, sharply pointed sticks with bunched shavings at one end, which they used for decoration. They prepared feather down for putting on their bodies: some of it fell from their hands and became stones. They drew blood from their arms and some fell on the ground and became red ochre...'

The major totem here would be the Wadi Gudjara; and a man or woman belonging to that site would have all the other totemic affiliations as well.

Totemism - 2 Major Categories

All these totemic forms can be classified into 2 categories - social & ritual or cult.

Social totemism has an emphasis on the social dimension; totemic affiliation depends on membership in a particular social unit defining a person's totemic relationship to everyone in that social unit. Social totemism is usually of matrilineal descent and is concerned with the ordering of things like marriage and sexual relations. There are sanctions against marrying a person from the same totem, the rule of totemic exogamy being supported by stories from the Dreamtime. A person may not be allowed to kill or eat the totem animal, because it is of the same flesh as that person. It can be considered an elder brother or sister, or even a guardian, of the person in question. The closeness of the association is demonstrated by the use of the term flesh.

In **ritual totemism** or **cult totemism**, the totem is not regarded as 'flesh' or 'meat', so there are no prohibitions on killing or eating it. This variety of totemism was widespread across Aboriginal Australia. **Matrilineal cult totemism** was observed in Cape York, but in most cases it was patrilineal. **Totem exogamy** is not considered important. In parts of the Western Desert it may actually be preferred by a man, to have a wife of the same totem as him. There are sacred sites in the territories of all the tribes that are connected with beings from the Dreamtime. These can be waterholes, rocks, hills, trees, or caves in which there are paintings in ochre or blood. A number of fully initiated men are responsible for the care of the sacred site. The birth or conception totems of these men give them the right to this position. These men are responsible for the myth and ritual connected with the site, leading or performing the rites associated with the site.

Totems are not always exogamous; when social totemism, not cult totemism, is involved they are more likely to be exogamous. In cult totemism, and to a lesser extent in other forms, even when a man identifies with a totem he can still eat it casually without sacramental intent.

Nearly every Aboriginal society had some form of food taboos, and many of them are not connected with totemism. A person's relationship with the totem should not be viewed in isolation. A totem represents a wider range of associations, a person and his/her totem share what can be called a sacred quality because their relationship is part of a broader relationship with the totemic ancestral beings from the Dreamtime. The totem serves as a link between the human world and that of the Dreamtime, so that the person is, in a sense, one with the ancestral beings. The totem also symbolises the concept that these Dreamtime beings are sometimes reincarnated through human beings.

Social Organisation and Structure

Cycle Aboriginal of Life

For the Aborigines life began when the child's soul/spirit leaves its spirit home, such as a waterhole, and enters the mother's body, through the mystic experience of the father or one of his relatives, where it dwells in the material substance in the pregnant woman to become a person.

The next stage in a boy's life is initiation, or the age-grading rites. These rites can be in the form of a series of rites throughout his youth. For girls the next stage is puberty, with associated rituals that are often colourful and always socially significant.

Age-grading mechanisms separate the men from the women, the men taking part in or being initiated in particular ceremonies which exclude women, and girls being initiated into the women's ceremonies that exclude men.

The passage from childhood to near-adulthood takes place through age-grading or puberty rites, or some kind of initiation.

When she reaches puberty a girl may go to her husband, though she may already be living with him, but not yet as a wife until puberty. The further learning the girl receives in social and ritual life is more informal than with boys, who undergo a series of stages on the way to becoming a man, always associated with definite rituals. For a boy the series of rites he undergoes marks his gradual acceptance as a practicing member of the most important cults of his tribe. Not all reach the ultimate goal at the top level of the cults, the level he reaches in dependent on the force of traditional life, the strength of his convictions, and the quality of his teachers.

Among the Aborigines, both men and women have a complex social and ritual life. Besides their small immediate family, they are also members of larger, less personal units - the clan, the tribe, linguistic group, and moiety. They are also members of totemic system involving a scheme of ceremony, mythology and belief that they feel a direct and active responsible for. As a boy passes through the various stages of initiation he participates in an increasing amount of community life, becoming gradually more fully involved in the way of life of the tribe, which, unsuspected by all but a few of the white settlers, was very structured and complex.

The Aborigines believed that men and women start off as spirits, taking on their materialistic form at birth, returning to the spiritual existence at death, when their spirit returns to the spirit home to await its next incarnation, when it enters a pregnant woman to be reborn.

Aboriginal Kinship Systems
Summary

In Aboriginal Australia kinship, one of the most complex systems in the world is the basis of all social interaction. The kinship system of a particular tribe or language unit controls the network of interpersonal relationships, in that the tribe guides its members in their interactions with other tribal members. Kinship pervaded every aspect of social organisation and structure.

There are 10 points that are regarded as important about the Aboriginal kinship system.

Kinship is an integral part of the total social organisation. The tribal members are sorted into categories with names used in each tribe. Relatives-in-law are often placed in the same categories as consanguineal relatives, though qualifying names can be given to them. Ideally, husbands and wives are related to each other as kin, though it can be in a classificatory sense rather than real kinship.

Classificatory kinship is used throughout Aboriginal Australia. For example, if a man addresses another man with a particular kin term he will use the same kin term for his full brother. A kin term applied to a woman will also apply to all her full sisters. This system is a formal structure, in the implementation of it in actual cases differences are recognised and in practice the equivalence is rarely exact or complete, at least as it refers to adults. Attitudes varied according to the closeness of the ties. A person's father was never confused with a nominal one, or of an own brother being confused with a classificatory one such as a father's brother's son or a mother's sister's son. In some cases there may appear to be almost complete identification, as between a man and a person he calls his 'own' son, but he can explain the relationship by saying, for instance, that the boy's father is his own close brother, and that he has helped to rear the boy as his own. The social aspect is all important. Opposite sex siblings are equivalent for other purposes. In some systems a man uses much the same terms for his sister's children as she does. They may reciprocate, using terms that associate him socially with her. Correspondingly, both siblings may use identical terms for his children. An example comes from north-eastern Arnhem Land. In this system a man calls his own children gadu and they call him baba (baba is also a term for father in Cantonese and Mandarin, the different Chinese dialects placing different emphasis on the first and last parts of the word. (Did Zheng He's fleet visit Arnhem Land on his voyage to South East Asia?), and his sister mugal-baba; a woman calls her own children wagu, and her brother uses the same term for her children.

Some relationships are thought of as being more binding than others. This is the case with same sex siblings, where conflict is ideally at a minimum - though brothers may compete for the same women and this situation is exacerbated in many areas by the levirate (The passing of a widow to her dead husband's younger brother). In some parts of Australia sibling rivalry is much more apparent than in others. It is generally modified or kept under control by common religious interests which are of dominant concern. Sisters are often close friends and this was often reinforced when they were also co-wives. Competition for husbands or sweethearts is less noticeable between sisters, at least partly, because they can and may share the same husband. A man can have multiple wives if he wishes, and his circumstances permit it. In all such families there can be only 1 man. As a result there is likely to more competition among men. Children of same sex siblings are classified together, while opposite sex siblings may be distinguished by different terms. The local group organisation is underlain by the structural principle equivalence of same sex siblings. Thus for this purpose, a man's father's father, father's father's brothers, father, brother's brothers, brothers, father's brothers' sons, sons, and brothers' sons are classified together. The same applies to his mother, his mother, mother's brother, mother's brother's son, etc.

The statuses of mother's brother and father's sister are an extension of the sibling relationship. This status involved special obligations and responsibilities in nearly all Aboriginal societies that could be combined with avoidance taboos. Such persons often have an important role in the initiation rituals of their brother's son or daughter, or sister's son or daughter. There is often great attachment in the relationship between a man and his father's sister. But there are often taboos of some kind between the man and the wives or husbands of these kin. This is usually because of their role in providing for their actual or classificatory nephews, or husbands for their nieces. This is the case whether or not cross-cousin marriage is preferred. The kin positions of the mother's brother and the father's sister are pivotal and crucial.

The relationship between people from different generation levels is not simply an extension of the parent-child bond. It signifies a difference in status and authority, if not in age, in terms of superordination-subordination. That is, it suggests horizontal stratification on the basis of status and kinship positioning. People related to each other as grandparent and grandchild are often drawn closely together for certain purposes, as those of succeeding generations are for others, and this is often reflected in the terminology used. This is usually a symmetrical relationship, in contrast to the possibility of asymmetrical relations for those under (4). It usually signifies mutual aid and respect, in the case of the grandparent, a teaching-learning relationship. But it can also mean that in some cases a person may marry into the generation of a grandparent or grandchild. Generation levels in this sense are not reckoned in terms of chronological age. They are formal divisions based on relative status. For example, when a man marries for the first time in his 30s, has several children, and whether or not he marries in between, takes another wife later at the age of about 50 or 60. If he married his first wife when she reached puberty she may still be bearing children. There may be a gap of 20 years or more between surviving children of one mother and father and it may be even wider between the children of one father and different mothers. In other societies around the world this is not an uncommon situation. In this case polygyny and the classificatory system complicate it. To at least some extent there would be 'equals' within a person's own generation level - brothers and sisters, cross-cousins, age-mates, etc. Some with authority over him, directly or indirectly, would be included in the generation level above him - father, mother, father's sister, father's sister's husband, mother's brother, mother's brother's wife, possibly mother-in-law, father-in-law, etc. Deference, and in some cases avoidance, are relevant here. In some systems a degree of constraint is present in some relationships, even within his own generation level, as in the case of a wife's brother, or a sister's husband. Constraint or partial avoidance can be the rule between a man and all the women he calls sisters. Relations usually revolve around superordination-subordination in the generation below. A person's own children, brother's children (classified as his own), sister's children, etc. In some areas avoidance relationships are present, usually between a man or woman and the men they call daughter's husband. Formally, a man might be a generation level above his wife's mother. For example, if he marries his father's sister's daughter's daughter's daughter. That is, kin positioning and generation level represent only one aspect of status relations.

Reciprocity in marriage is part of the wider principle. Betrothal arrangements underline the fact that marriage is not simply a relationship between 2 people or nuclear families. In all tribes, in one way or another, there are structural implications. Those receiving a wife must make a repayment, at the time or at a future date, and the repayment doesn't have to be in kind. Men exchanging sisters or women exchanging brothers, as in bilateral cross-cousin marriages, is the simplest arrangement of this repayment. This can mean that a mother's brother's wife is actually a father's sister. Maternal and paternal cross-cousins are often terminologically equivalent. The same principle applies when the marriage is between 2 moieties, different clans or local descent groups. It is at least potentially implicit in the section and subsection system. There may be a delay in this reciprocity. Marriage reciprocity also involves the exchange of gifts as well as of men and women. There are also rights and privileges, obligations and responsibilities associated with the exchange. Where elopement is not institutionalised it represents a threat to this system. It upsets the balance of relationships between the persons or units involved and in that particular cycle of marriage arrangements.

The basic kinship is the nuclear family, as well as being the basic social unit. With its core of husband and wife or wives it is also the usual medium of achieving sexual satisfaction. The structure of the majority of Aboriginal kin systems allowed for the opportunity for both men and women to find extra-marital sexual partners on a transient-mundane or transient-ritual or even romantic basis. This was achieved with the potential replacement of spouses, as well as allowing for parent surrogates. Extra-marital relations conventionally fit into this broad framework. In some places, as with the Dieri, the provision of secondary wives and as in western Arnhem Land the provision of secondary husbands.

Kinship is always involved in interpersonal relationships. Usually kinship doesn't indicate relationship between groups or classes, simply between persons within those social groups. In north-eastern Arnhem Land the relationship between mada is an exception. Kinships are usually oriented genealogically with respect to any given person. Almost every person in that particular society can be expected to have a slightly different perspective within it.

There are a number of factors that distinctive patterning is dependent on:

a. The number of kinship groups distinctly recognised and terminologically separated out. In some cases, as among the southern Aluridja, the few terms used do little more than indicate sex, generation level and marriage relationships. The people of north eastern Arnhem Land had 25 main terms.

b. The preferred marriage type and the series of reciprocal exchanges associated with it.

c. The question of socially acceptable alternative marriages that could entail the rearrangement of personal genealogies and kin alignments, with the associated reshuffling of terms.

d. The question of irregular marriages that are thought to be wrong but not crucially wrong and those that are consistently condemned, and in the old tradition subject to severe sanctions, such as unions considered to be incestuous.

e. Factors influencing the range of marriage choice and the terminology used, such as local descent group, moiety, subsection, section and exogamy.

f. The method of distribution of responsibilities, rights and duties among various types of kin.

g. The form of totemism present in the area.

h. The fact that kinship systems were often modified to accommodate introduction of section or subsection system.

i. Questions of descent.

Descent is central to reckoning the kinship system, relationships to and through one parent in terms of unilineal descent is emphasised. Overall kinship is bilateral. Recognition of descent in terms of other social categories can also be bilateral. Usually one is selected over the other, or one is made subordinate to the other.

The Individual

The individual person in Aboriginal society tends to follow the rules, marrying a person from the group he or she is supposed to choose a husband or wife from, but there are instances where these rules were not followed. In most cases, the couple need not worry about trouble from the rest of their groups, as long as they were not incestuous, which in Aboriginal society extended to tribal family members as opposed to actual family members. There was a strong taboo concerning interaction between a man and his mother-in-law, as well as all her tribal sisters. With the exception of times of ceremonial licence they were not permitted to speak to each other, or even approach each other. Strict though this prohibition was, it has been known to be circumvented.

Just like other societies around the world, not all people take part in sacred ceremonies, some take a strong interest in the whole ceremony, singing, dancing, rituals, and try to learn as much as they can about the beliefs and rituals. Others just like the singing and dancing, taking as little part in other aspects of the ceremonies as they can get away with.

In some tribes, men could have as many wives as they wanted; some took full advantage of this situation, while others preferred only 1 wife. So as with every other culture in the world, people are not all the same.

Law and Order

Offences within the tribe or clan

Offences against property

Offences against the person

Embryonic court

Trial by ordeal

Inquest

Feud and Warfare

Maintenance of Order

Capital Punishment - Ritual Killing

In all parts of Aboriginal Australia government was mostly loosely organised and informal. As with all parts of Aboriginal society, the laws and rules of behaviour were set in the dreamtime by the ancestral creation beings who are said to have given the people the laws they were to live by.

In most of traditional Aboriginal Australia the loyalty was locally based, to the land and the people they know. Strangers were regarded with suspicion, so the further apart 2 tribes are, the more the mutual distrust. At times of great ceremonial occasions, and when trading, these attitudes were put aside as they were expected to be on friendly terms for the duration of the ceremonies or trade negotiations. Neighbours who shared beliefs, as when an ancestral being was believed to have travelled through the territories of both during the dreamtime, shared the associated ceremonies and were friendlier than if they believed they were connected to the wanderings of different creation beings.

Nowhere in Australia were there any wars over territory, unlike elsewhere in the world where it is a feature of human life that goes back a very long way, though they did have quarrels and fights, sometimes on large scales, but never to take over a territory. They felt a connection to the land of their territory, the resting places where their spirits waited to be reborn were on the land. When they did fight there were rules to cover the fighting and peacemaking after it.

The rules given to them by the ancestral beings that formed the basis of Aboriginal life, the rituals they performed collectively, such as the movements of a particular dreamtime being through their territory, constantly reinforced the social identity and solidarity of those taking part, as well as introducing the religion and rules to the young. Their way of life had a religious basis, being based on the teachings of the dreamtime beings.

Not all actions of the dreamtime beings are expected to be followed, being more actions to avoid. In the Djanggawul stories the brother and his 2 sisters commit incest. Other stories deal with murder, adultery, and theft.

In the dreamtime the ancestral beings prescribed the roles of men and women for all aspects of life, sacred and secular, marriage, child bearing, death as well as the economy of the group. They also warned of the consequences if the taboos and avoidances were not adhered to. The dreamtime beings were law-givers, but were above the law, in some of stories about them they tell what to do and in others what not to do. In some cases the meanings of their statements are inferred by the stories and songs associated with their rituals.

In some cases acts that were not normally permitted assume a sacred quality, as in fertility rites in which sexual association between people who normally must avoid each other.

Some of the rules given by the ancestral beings have a practical purpose, as when it helps the people in a particular environment to survive. The fact that it is viewed as sacred, having been given by an ancestral being, gives it authority, though it may be the accumulated wisdom of generations of ancestors who learnt the hard way how to survive in a particularly harsh environment.

Conformity

Children growing up in a particular tribe would usually accept the teachings of their tribe without question. The only problems would come when they had contact with other tribes with varying views on some part of their tribal beliefs. In practice, not all behaviour dictated by the ancestral beings was strictly adhered to by all. Some variation was tolerated as long as it was on a matter of lesser importance. But there were limits beyond which it was not permitted to stray, especially with the actions that were considered more important.

When deciding if an action was to be tolerated or not the older people, the elders, were considered to be the most knowledgeable, though there was no defined official, the person who would usually be regarded as a person of final authority on such matters would be an older man who was fully initiated, so would have the most knowledge of the rituals associated with the dreamtime, and hence the actions of the ancestral beings, as well as a lifetime of practical experience. Other members of the tribe could make their point, but the final word would come from the unofficial leader.

Discipline for minor offences & children

For children and for minor offences, discipline was usually maintained by the immediate family. Childhood was generally a time of permissiveness, the rules of their society being learned by example and informally, such as being told and shown things as part of daily life, rather than formal lessons. They were told what to do without explanation, and if they disobeyed too much they could be slapped. Severe punishment was extremely rare.

For boys, the permissiveness ends when they reach the age of their first initiation, their discipline is no longer in the hands of their immediately family. Through the various levels of initiation they are taught the rules as well as the rituals they are expected to perform, and the way they are to act in adult life. This period of initiation varied across the country, in some places it involved physical operations, such as sub-incision, in others there were only the introduction of food taboos.

Puberty is the time when girls are introduced to the ritual life of the group, as when she is taught in a more formal way the rules she is expected to follow.

Positive Sanctions

Children are gradually introduced to the rules they are to follow and the things they are not to do from an early age. There are stories told that illustrate to the young the actions that are considered inappropriate, such as a mother-in-law abusing a son-in-law, who are expected to avoid each other.

Adultery is not allowed, but some release from this taboo is allowed in some rituals and in the practice of wife-lending, probably in the hope that such permitted extramarital relations will head off straying. But elopements and adultery did occur.

Rewards for conformity could be in the form of ritual and secular leadership, though over conformity was not liked, sometimes leading to criticism. Or simply as social approval.

Negative Sanctions

In this category are such things as ridicule, the role of a man in the punishment of his biological or classificatory sister, fear of supernatural punishment, fear of sorcery, the threat of physical violence, and worst of all, killed and not being accorded usual mortuary rites. The forms of negative sanction used in different parts of Australia, the order of importance of the different sanctions, varied across the country.

Ridicule

This form of sanction is powerful, but doesn't always work because it can often cause or exacerbate quarrels. This form can sometimes be used against people who have no control over their actions, such as the deaf or those with mental problems. It can sometimes lead to partial ostracism, and very rarely to complete ostracism. Many people with mental or physical impairments are cared for by other members of their family and group. Swearing or the use of obscenity is also in this category, but it can also be dangerous, as in some rare cases it has been known to lead the immediate killing of the speaker (Berndt & Berndt, 1964). Malicious talk about a particular person could be used to change the behaviour of people who thought it might affect them, but it could also cause trouble.

The brother-sister taboo

Where this was used, in some parts of Australia, a man could be expected to discipline any of his sisters, whether biological or classificatory, for such things as using bad language or if she neglects her work, family or ceremonial duties or for fighting.

The possibility of supernatural punishment for offences such as breaching some taboos or sacred laws, or for failing to perform certain songs, dances or ritual correctly. Kaberry, 1939, said it was difficult to assess the degree to which the Dreaming (ngarunggani) is used as a sanction and threat of supernatural punishment for the breaking of taboos. Examples were sore eyes as punishment for associating with a tabooed relative, incest could lead to death immediately or in the near future, and a malignant disease could develop if tabooed food was eaten, such as the animal or plant associated with a person's totem. The threat of supernatural punishment was associated with straying from the patterns of behaviour as set down by the spirit beings in the Dreamtime. Some threats were in the form of 'If you do this, which is wrong, the great Djanggawul, Ngurunderi, or some other spirit being will punish you' (Berndt & Berndt, 1964). Mostly they were less explicit 'If you do this, which is wrong, you will become ill and die' (Berndt & Berndt, 1964). If they failed to heed the decrees of the spirit beings they knew what to expect.

The fear of sorcery was a powerful force keeping people on the straight and narrow. It appears retaliation by sorcery could be incurred by minor fences. Fear of being a sorcerer was also present. If a person has a misfortune or gets sick of even dies, a person known to hold a grudge against him could be accused of sorcery. Suspicions of this kind were not always associated with claims of the person holding the grudge using magical rituals.

When writing about the area around Oenpelli, Berndt and Berndt state that if a woman has a lover or lovers over a long period of time without her husband's approval, and he dies she may be accused of being responsible for his death, either by weakening his heart, or being careless about his belongings, that were subsequently taken by a sorcerer. Men usually keep track of their wives' affairs, if he knows about them unofficially he may retain the right to find out about them officially if he decides it is time to stop them, possibly because they are becoming too frequent or blatant. The threat of a husband's 'dreaming' of a wife's affairs, with the subsequent arguments that would follow, tended to keep the straying wife's affairs to a reasonable number.

The threat of physical violence
Some breaches of accepted behaviour could incur punishment that could involve death or injury. As with the infamous 'witch trials', in

some cases this was occasionally used to settle a grudge, while appearing to maintain conformity to the rules of the tribe.

The threat of not only being killed but being denied funerary rites

This was a serious punishment, involving the spirit of the offender as well as the body. The Aborigines believed in re-incarnation, the spirit travelling to a resting place, such as a waterhole, while it waited for a woman it could enter to become a baby and be born again. The threat of not having the funerary rites after a person's death would have been a powerful deterrent, as it could prevent, or at least make difficult, the return of the spirit to the waterhole. When this punishment was carried out the relatives were prohibited from handling the body, if they ignored the prohibition they could be condemned to the same fate.

Offences within the tribe or clan

There are 2 main subcategories in this category, sacred and secular. The sacred law is considered the most important, involves regulations, codes, and behaviours based on the supernatural. It has a religious connotation similar to the concept of sin. The other category is of offences against people or property. Not all offences are as clear cut as those at the extremes; many tend towards one extreme or the other, depending on their seriousness. Some offences such as incest come under both types of rules, traditional and supernatural. In practice, less serious offences are not usually covered by both category of law.

Sacred law

Appropriate punishments for breaches under this category of law were decided upon by ritual leaders in secret meetings. The maximum punishment for some of these breaches could be death. 2 or more ritual leaders may take action themselves or delegate it to another man. He was not always told immediately what they expect him to do, and they may coerce a man more subtly. One example was that a man may be given tabooed food to eat, after which he was told to kill a certain person. In Arnhem Land there was a form of compulsion in which a sacred object was placed on a man's head, the man could not then refuse to carry out their instructions to kill another man.

Occasionally, when wider repercussions might be involved, as when the act that was actually mainly personal vengeance, supernatural sanctions could be used to disguise the real motive for the act. Another method, which was used in the Daly River area, was to throw a stone spearhead into a sacred ring while chanting ritual invocations. This placed an obligation on all initiated men to co-operate.

There was a report of this being used at the end of the 19th century, at the time of early contact with European settlers. In the newspapers it was reported as the 'Copper Mine Massacre'. According to the report, a man who thought he had a grievance against the settlers had carried out this ritual, compelling all the initiated men to take action on his behalf by invoking sacred law. This case is an example of how supernatural authority could be invoked to take physical action against a transgressor against sacred law.

Kaberry (1939) makes the same point "when some laws are disobeyed, punishment is inflicted by the old men who are concerned with maintaining the status quo and conformity to tradition. They are the instruments of justice...." (Berndt & Berndt, 1964). On rare occasions, when women or children intentionally or unintentionally see sacred objects or rites they are prohibited from seeing, they are usually speared immediately.

Punishment involving death for a serious offence against sacred law by any method that achieves the end is used. A marked man may be speared in the back while hunting, with no warning. Whichever way a man is killed there should be no redress and no feud should follow, as it is capital punishment, just as in many modern countries.

The same punishment by group action can be carried out against a member of the tribe who refuses to respond to the usual sanctions, persisting in spite of repeated warnings. If he continues to ignore warnings he risks being declared to be uncontrollable, a menace to any people he comes in contact with, and could be killed. An example of such rebellious behaviour could be a young man who wouldn't keep away from other men's wives, and especially if those men were ritual leaders. They can invoke capital punishment even if he doesn't break any sacred law. A man who elopes with his wife's daughter or a close mother-in-law incurs the same punishment. As it is 'state' sanctioned punishment it is with the approval or passive consent (at least in public) of the group. Women have little if any say in the punishment, and may not even know what is about to take place.

Offences against property

In traditional Aboriginal Australia this type of offence was rare. The land occupied by the tribe or clan is not transferrable, hence the lack of war for conquest. The land is seen as being held in trust by the living for the members of the unit from the past, present and future. They think of themselves more as being owned by the land, rather than them owning the land. This must have been one of the most difficult things for the tribes all over Australia to understand after European colonisation, that any person could claim that they owned land. And they believed that the connection between them and the land was supernaturally sanctioned, having been decreed by the ancestral beings from the Dreamtime. The same attitude applied to ochre mines and stone quarries.

It was almost unknown for small items of common use to be stolen, such as digging sticks, baskets, mats, wooden dishes, fishing spears, though kinship obligations meant that they could be borrowed. Dogs were regarded as almost members of the family. As a result an offence against a dog was a serious matter, with possible violent repercussions. In a Dreamtime myth from western Arnhem Land a man's special pet dog was unknowingly killed and eaten. His reprisal was severe, wiping out several large camps.

In north eastern Arnhem Land there are 2 known examples of ritual stealing. In one connected with the making of the Dua moiety feathered string. The making of string or twine was women's work, whereas the men were responsible for adding the coloured parakeet feathers. In this case sorcery is used to steal the string they were to add feathers to. The method of procurement of the string by the men is based on the dreamtime story where men stole the sacred rangga from women in the Djanggawul myth.

The other example is connected with the wuramu ceremony of the jiridja moiety. A carved wuramu figure, a 'collection man', was carried through the main camp, the men in charge of it taking everything portable within reach. Both are socially approved forms of stealing.

Maintenance of Order

The maintenance of law and order, social solidarity and cohesion are matters of local control. The sanctions applied by a clan, tribe or linguistic group were usually applied within the group. There can be exceptions, as when more than 1 are involved, being linked by a common culture pattern or close trading links, or share a common sacred and ceremonial bond. A stranger from a different linguistic group, who had no other links to the group, had no ritual status within the group. If the group accepted him as a member, attaching him to a kinship group, he could never be viewed as being as closely related as those from within the group.

The maintenance of order in pre-contact times had very limited, local application. Authority was limited and was overridden by claims of kinship. These factors determined justice. The desire to retaliate in kind is the first reaction to injury, but other factors come into play, such as why that particular person was injured or killed, what were the circumstances? Who was he and who were his kin? Who else is interested in the matter? The identity of the aggressor or aggressors, and his/their kin, and the reason for injuring the man. When these questions are asked, others are involved, becoming part of the decision making. When these questions are considered the precedents for the action taken in previous similar cases is discussed. At this point it is the basis of law and regulation. In all parts of pre-contact Aboriginal Australia there were a number of mechanisms for dealing with such situations - the council, the meeting, the magarada or ordeal, armed combat and duel, and the inquest. All these mechanisms are available for the resolution of disputes. The authority system was not strong enough to impose its own penalties, but some have seen indications that it may have actually been much stronger than appears at first sight.

Allowing for the overriding nature of the kinship system, evidence has been seen of a comparatively weak authority and of government, in that law and order are kept within limits. In Aboriginal society the level of self-help is higher and the lack of a central authority is lower than in most other societies.

Generally, in Aboriginal Australia, the people tended to respond to legal action with physical aggression, though a lot of the retaliation involved mostly magic or sorcery. Though this could be as physically damaging as physical violence, as in the case of a person dying because they strongly believed that someone had 'pointed the bone', 'a thought spear', at them, considering it just as deadly. Generally, there appears to have been a tendency towards resolving serious disputes and avoiding escalating them.

Controls operate in regard to sanctioned retaliation in such a way as to restrict the spread of violence and keep the number of killings as low as possible. The influence of kinship can contribute to the spread of violence, but also has an even stronger influence in resolving conflicts.

See Capital Punishment - Ritual Killing

Aboriginal Embryonic Court

In most parts of Aboriginal Australia meetings for more or less formal discussions were held at irregular intervals to settle grievances, though the basis of legal procedures was self-help. When different tribes come together for ceremonies, as when they carried out the rituals associated with the wanderings of the Dreamtime beings that crossed the country of all the tribes at the gathering. There were few other times, apart from trading trips, when several tribes came together. These were usually times when fighting was avoided, but sometimes, after the main ceremonies were complete, fighting did break out, but more often it was at these large gatherings that inter-tribal disputes were sorted out.

Agreement on the ways and means of keeping social order wasn't restricted to within a tribe or linguistic group, it also applied to neighbouring tribes, or parts of them, sharing a common mythology and ritual. These meetings were significant because they provided a means of social control, but they weren't judicially-based bodies, which didn't exist in Aboriginal Australia. The relatively weak political organisation, concentration on self-help and the use of sorcery made it difficult for a formalised law system to develop.

Though formally constituted courts never developed in traditional Aboriginal society, less formal and less systematic councils existed that carried out much the same function.

The councils of the **Jaraldi** and **Dangani** people of the Lower Murray River, and some others, appear to have come closest to a formalised court system. The **tendi**, a council of elders was presided over by the **rupelle**, negotiators and tribal spokesmen, or patrilineal headmen, who could settle disputes with neighbouring tribes or clans. Offenders were brought before such councils for trial. Women played a prominent part.

There are a number instances of these tendi that have been observed by researchers, as by Taplin and the other by R.M.Berndt (Berndt & Berndt, 1964). Taplin described one he witnessed. There were 2 clans involved in the dispute. The members of the 2 clans sat facing each other, members of other clans gathered around their rupelle. A general discussion began the tendi during which accusers and defendants had their say and witnesses gave evidence. In this case there was no decision on the case (Flood, 2004). In the case witnessed by R.M.Berndt, a judgement was made and punishment was imposed.

Howitt reported what appears to have been a similar situation in eastern Australia, involving tribal councils headed by a leader (Howitt, 1904). The **Wuradjeri** people had a system where a headman could summon people to consider what should be done in cases of murder, abduction of women, adultery, and raids on other tribes or of raids by other tribes (Berndt & Berndt, 1964).

The headman settles all arguments and disputes among the **Gournditch-mara (Gunditjmara)** tribe. In these instances it seems almost anyone could be present. The situation was different among the **Dieri**.

The Dieri deliberations took place at special closed meetings which were attended by the heads of the local totemic groups, fighting men, native doctors, and elders of some standing (Gason in Woods, 1879). These meetings could deal with murder, breaches of moral code, offences against sacred ritual, and even disclosure of the secrets of the tribal council or initiation rituals to uninitiated people. If a person is found guilty of a major crime an armed party (**pinya**) is sent by the headman to kill him.

It appears these tribal councils composed of elders or important men, or leaders of tribes, clans or local groups, and ritual leaders, were fairly common in traditional Aboriginal society. They were usually very informal and didn't consider all types of problems, and didn't always act in a judiciary capacity.

Among the **Pitta Pitta** from the Boulia district of Queensland, the camp council "will take upon itself to mete out punishment in crimes of murder, incest," (Roth, 1897), and indiscriminate use of weapons in the camp. Murder and incest incur a death sentence, and the condemned person may be required to dig his own grave. For the indiscriminate use of weapons the punishment was to be crippled with knives.

According to Spencer and Gillen, 1938, when a meeting is called to deliberate on an offence the headmen consult with the elders. If the accused person is found guilty of a major crime he will receive the death penalty, in which case the elders organise an **ininja party** to carry out the sentence.

According to Kaberry (1939), among the people of the eastern Kimberley, "the horde and not the tribe [and not the local kinship group, (Berndt & Berndt, 1964)] is the political unit," that is concerned with government and administration. The headman and the elders have the authority, though men make the decisions. The headman arranges when and where the meetings are to be held, "He and the elders conduct the proceedings centring round the ceremonies" and dispute settlement. Grievances are thrashed out at these meetings. Many of the lesser charges are the responsibility of the relevant kinship groups

In north eastern Arnhem Land, the **bugalub** is the procedure for settling minor grievances. It resembles the **garma** mortuary rites described by Warner (1937). To clear up a dispute or disagreement, and restore equanimity, it can be set in motion by a person of either moiety. An instance that was observed was a man from Elcho Island who had been taken to the Darwin hospital with a severely injured hand. On his return he called a bugalub. An area of ground in the main camp is cleared and surrounded by mounds of sand, and a hole dug in the centre of the area that represents a sacred waterhole associated with the holder of the rite. The singing, accompanied by clapping sticks and didgeridoos, are 'outside' versions of the secret-sacred 'inside' songs, but with the same associations. As each song in the series is sung, a woman jumps up and dances. The next part of the ceremony is when the person, usually a man, but sometimes a woman, enters the 'waterhole'. Invocations are called to the spirit beings associated with the site, as water is poured over the person in the 'waterhole'. The ritual washing is believed to heal dissension and encourage goodwill between the participants. The healing of minor breaches by contact with the sacred world and ritual provides popular entertainment for the people not directly involved with the incident.

Among the Dieri and neighbouring tribes, the kopara, is mostly designed for the same purpose, but with economic overtones.

Aboriginal Inquest

After some deaths inquests were held, usually by a native doctor, who claimed that, by divination or other means, he can determine the person or persons responsible. Some deaths were followed by an inquest, and some, but not all, inquests were followed by retaliation.

One of the methods of determining a person responsible for a death among the people of the Lower River Murray was for a relative to sleep with his head on the corpse. By this means he hoped to dream the person responsible, the 'murderer' (Taplin, in Woods, 1879). The following day the corpse is carried on a bier, while the man who slept with his head on it and others surround it, suggesting likely names. If the men carrying the bier feel a movement of the corpse towards a person who calls one of these names, that is accepted as confirmation.

The **Jupagalk** believe that after a man dies, the spirit of the murderer can be found in the bush nearby (Howitt, 1904). If no native doctor is available, the **Wurunjerri Wurundjerri** sweep the top of the grave clean, look for a small hole, and insert a stick, The direction in which the stick slopes indicates where they should look for the murderer's spirit.

Another method was used at **Port Stephens**. Here 2 men held the corpse on their shoulders while a 3rd man strikes it with a green bough, all the time calling the suspects' names. If the correct name is called, the corpse shakes, on which the bearers also shake.

Among the **Chepara**, it is the native doctor who sees the murderer in a dream.

In some tribes, such as the **Bigambul**, the corpse is asked the person who caused its death.

Among other tribes, such as the **Turrbal**, the native doctor makes a track on the cleared ground under the mortuary platform and interprets the identity of the murderer.

The **Wakelbura** loosen the earth immediately below the platform to make the slightest mark visible, examining the site intermittently.

In the eastern and northern Kimberleys stones are arranged beneath the mortuary platform or tree. The direction the sorcery came from is determined by which stone the liquid from the decay of the body falls upon. (Basedow, 1925, Kaberry, 1939).

The Bad and **Ungarinjin** (Elkin, 1954) establish the guilt then older relatives of the dead person paint the skull and some of the bones with red ochre and blood and bury it in an ant heap with fire. By singing over it they hope the murderer will sicken and die.

A method that was sometimes used to narrow down the range of responsibility for a death among the people of the Western Desert was carried out when the people from an area came together after an interval when a number of people died. Usually on a dark, still night, a small firestick was prepared for each person that died. As the names of the dead are taboo, each stick is identified by marks representing the section and subsection and local affiliation. Each stick, in its turn, is held up, if the sparks are carried up and move a long distance, it means that the responsible person is from another country in the direction in which the spark has moved. If sparks travel only a short distance and extinguish quickly the guilty person is nearby. Also in the Western Desert, the bones may be exhumed several months after burial and examined, divination being used to determine the killer.

The people of north-eastern **Arnhem Land** say the spirit of the murderer hovers near the corpse, where it can be identified by a native doctor (Warner, 1937/58). They use the liquid from the mortuary platform for divination, or the native doctor placed an arm band belonging to the dead person, or some of his hair on a stick that he watches, then suddenly hits it with a 'spirit bag' to catch, or at least identify the spirit of the murderer as it jumps from the stick.

According to Warner, (1937/58) and Spencer and Gillen, (1938) a man may whisper the name of his killer to the native doctor as he is dying, though the killer can also be determined by examining the grave.

At Laverton, a corpse could be examined for signs of magical choking, and the native doctor determines from the smell, roughly where the murderer can be found (Elkin, 1954). Elkin has discussed some of them.

When revenge is being considered, inquest is the first step, and it can be simple or elaborate, immediately after death or delayed. An explanation of events is given, the people most closely related to the dead person must then weigh up the situation and decide if they want to proceed to the next stage, revenge.

The procedures for settling differences or identifying sorcerers tend to be fairly formalised or conventionalised. But leading up to them, or at the same time during the proceedings there was often a lot of informal discussion, both men and women loudly voicing their opinions in the main camp. Just after an offence has been committed, when feeling is still running high, the arguments could lead to fighting. Arguments and discussions could continue for weeks, or even longer. In the end it is the older men and women who have a final say.

In north-east and north-central Arnhem Land, these strong grudges often led to a lot of dramatic gestures. A man with such a grudge, after painting himself with ochres and carrying a bundle of spears, one of which is fitted into his spear thrower, displaying that he is ready to back up his claims with force if necessary. His supporters may also be armed. The defendant and his supporters may also be armed. They may in engage in long verbal battles for many nights. These arguments may include long monologues loaded with mythical allusions. This situation could continue until a settlement was reached by compromise or bloodshed, though it often faded away after some time, only to be resumed later. If a man is so enraged that he wants to do more than just talk, the conventional outlet for him may be to try to frighten or startle his opponent. This was called the **maragaridj** or **mari** (anger or angry). The aggressor would work himself up to a near-trance-like state with threats and boasting about what he is going to do. Eventually he grabs his weapons and with a spear in the thrower held above his head ready to throw, he charged across the open ground toward his opponent, shouting and cursing him. Part of the show was an old woman, a close female relative, possibly a father's sister, who made a show of trying to restrain him. The best places for such a show were a wide open space where there would be no distraction from the drama of the charge. Men seen to do this had eyes that appeared glazed but they didn't always intend to spear the opponent, often aiming their spears to just miss the target. Things didn't always go to plan. Sometimes the woman who was supposed to try to restrain him would be unprepared when he charged or the victim could completely ignore him. Such a situation was seen to occur when **Old Wonggu** was singing and clapping his sticks at a mortuary rite. A **Groote Eylandt** man ran at him with his shovel-nosed spears but **Old Wonggu** carried on his singing and clapping as though nothing had happened.

Feud and Warfare

In traditional Aboriginal society, warfare was armed conflict by the members of one social unit, it could be a tribe or clan, or in the name of the unit, against another unit. Feud, though it may have wider implications, involving many people, was armed conflict between family groups or kin groups. Feuds sometimes became warfare. Howitt describes incidents of armed combat and duelling. He also reported that a **blood feud** could spread, eventually involving an entire tribe (Howitt, 1904).

Some feuds in western and eastern Arnhem Land went back a number of years, attempts at peacemaking failing repeatedly.

Basedow (1925) divides Aboriginal warfare into 2 categories, inter-tribal fighting and intra-tribal (or inter-clan) feuding. He claimed inter-tribal fighting was common in the early days of contact, but the number of such instances that were actually inter-tribal fighting has been disputed, though some instances are supported by other observers. It is believed that in most cases incidents that were described as inter-tribal warfare were actually armed expeditions that were socially sanctioned for a particular purpose, such as to avenge a death, or to punish an offender.

Howitt (1904) and Gason (in Woods, 1879) described a **Dieri** armed party (pinya). The pinya were given the task of dealing with the man by the headman when a man is condemned to death by a special council. The men taking part in the pinya wear a white headband, their beards are tipped with human hair, and diagonal red and white stripes were painted across their chest and stomach. When they reach the camp of the condemned man they ask for him. The people of the camp know the reason for the demand and usually hand over the man for justice. He is taken by the hand, they announce his sentence, and then lead him aside and he is killed by one of the pinya with a blow from a large boomerang. Howitt reported a case where a man who was apprehended by the pinya men pointed to his elder brother to take the blame, because an elder brother should ideally protect his younger brother. In some examples sorcery could be used instead of physical violence.

In 1953 a man from Arnhem Land was accused of an incestuous relationship. Before his trial he fled the camp, automatically incurring the death penalty. He was taken to the Darwin hospital where tests failed to find any reason for his sickness. He believed he would die because he had been '**bone pointed**'. On the 5th day he died, not believing that 'western magic' was strong enough to overcome the power of the 'bone'.

Among the Aranda the avenging party is called atninga. They are usually formed following a quarrel between 2 groups, often over women or a death suspected of resulting from sorcery (Spencer & Gillen, 1938). According to Spencer and Gillen, the atninga enter the camp of the accused man fully armed, but don't usually resort to physical violence, attacking only with words, and things settle down after a while, though occasionally there is fighting. Sometimes the atninga hide and wait for their victim who they then spear. One case is known of where the men of the atninga were offered women in the ordinary way. They indicated their hostile intentions by rejecting the women. They reached an agreement after a couple of days, in return for the death of 3 men, the 3rd man had boasted of killing a man from the tribe of the atninga, the local men would be unharmed and help the atninga men. 2 of the accused men were speared through trickery but the 3 rd grew suspicious and left the camp. The avengers danced around the bodies while the others watched passively. The actual killers were called immirinja and the decoys were called alknalarinika. When the atninja returned to their camp they were greeted by old women dancing and waving their fighting clubs.

It was fairly common to send women to a camp of visitors whose intentions were uncertain. It was usually done as a friendly gesture to appease an enemy. But sometimes it was used to put the visitors off their guard and so vulnerable to an attack. Sometimes members of avenging parties captured the wives and daughters, and occasionally sons, of the men they killed. A number of such instances were mentioned by Howitt (1904). On the Hunter River, the Geawegal keep captured women of the correct intermarrying group. Many cases of similar events have been reported, such as from the Maryborough region of Queensland, south east South Australia, south western Victoria, the Yorke Peninsula, and Gippsland. It is now believed that many of these reported captures were simply examples of the custom of marrying by capture; the party of men go for a woman, not as revenge, but as a marriage custom.

In the Western Desert the wanmala is the equivalent of the atninja of the Aranda. It was most commonly used to avenge a sorcery death or to track and kill a runaway wife and her lover. A native doctor or sorcerer summoned several men who went into nearby bush and painted themselves and prepared their special wibia shoes. These shoes were usually made of woven human hair and included other items such as bird feathers. They left little or no footprints. Once they are ready there is a short ceremony in the main camp in which the women sit beating time for them while they rattle their spears and wave them about. As they leave the camp they fling spears as they go. They also have other ceremonies that foreshadow the fight which will take place on reaching the victim's camp. They sing songs of the mythical Wadi Banbanbalala, **Bell Bird Man**, who 'makes wanmala'. Even in normal life people hearing a bell bird can feel uneasy, saying there must be a wanmala nearby. The elders carry bundles of spears on the wanmala journey.

According to traditional accounts they enter the victim's camp stealthily, and taking the victim by surprise, surround him, hold their spears ready as the old men sing a traditional song, and kill him as the final word is sung.

On Bathurst Island and Melville Island, the Tiwi duel to resolve disputes. If the duels don't resolve the dispute, full scale fighting between 2 groups of armed men may occur (Hart & Pilling, 1960).

In north eastern and north-central Arnhem Land the most highly organised warfare in all of Australia took place (Warner 1937/1958). The fighting unit here is the clan or linguistic unit, the most usual source of trouble is the killing of a woman. A point that has been supported by the findings of Berndt and Berndt is that most of the fighting takes place between neighbouring clans of the same moiety. Warner comments that "feuds between clans of opposite moieties are more likely to die out for lack of the stimulus provided by competition for women. Such clans are likely to allow a magarada to be held . . . ." and "kinship solidarity extends warfare but also has the opposite tendency: that of limiting its scope when it has reached very large proportions. All the clans are interrelated, and generally many will find their loyalties divided . . ." In this region the main aim of fighting is to cause the enemy to suffer the same injury it has inflicted, an eye for an eye.

Warner has named at least 6 categories of armed attack, not all of which are normally considered warfare. For example, the magarada is mainly settlement by ordeal, though at times it can lead to further fighting. Camp fights (Nirimaoi julngu) are based on adultery accusations, and is mostly loud talking rather than physical fighting that could lead to death. In narub or djawald a victim is killed or wounded while sleeping. Responsibility for this is ascribed to the clan as a whole, regardless of the fact that no sanction was obtained by the men involved prior to the event. Miringu (maringo, death adder, according to Warner) is much more like the normal sense of warfare. It is usually caused by an inter-clan killing. The members of the miringu party carry out magical rites, such as going through the motions of finding and spearing the victim's image that has been drawn on the ground or moulded from clay and identified by name. A bone from the dead man is used to show them the direction they should take. They move off to the victim's camp in a snake-like formation. They surround it in a way prescribed by tradition, and then kill him, and possibly others as well.

The miringu is analogous to the wanmala of the Western Desert, the pinya of the Dieri and the Atninga of the Aranda.

In north eastern Arnhem Land there are 2 other types of fighting, the milwerangel, that involves a number of clans, is pre-arranged, and the gainger, on a regional basis, is on a larger scale, and is very rare. It results from high levels of anger that has been building over long periods of feuding, and according to Warner is intended to be 'a spear fight to end spear fights', and hopefully bring peace to the whole area. Magical rites precede the gainger in which the spears of each moiety are symbolised by special decorations. These are later sent out as an invitation and challenge. The number of deaths resulting from this type of fighting, in which any ruse is permissible, was expected to be higher than with any other type of warfare. Even with this type of fighting the number of deaths would not be expected to reach more than about a dozen.

Capital Punishment - Ritual Killing

At Narrabeen on the northern beaches of Sydney a skeleton was found that was 3,700 years old. The man, who was about 35 years old when he died, at the height of the production of backed blades, which was near the peak of the sea level rise following the closing of the glacial period. Associated with the body were 14 artefacts, 12 of which were backed blades which display damage as either spear barbs or knives. Of these 1 that is believed to have been an awl for skin working, appears to have been carried in the man's hair at the time of his death, another was wedged in his spine. He had been speared in the back, the spearing striking him just above the left hip, passed through the small and large intestine, and possibly the kidney, eventually lodging in his spine. He was also speared from the front, and then killed on the ground with a club to the head, possibly by a stone axe, and speared in the skull, after which he was left on the sand dune.

The time of this man's death puts it at a time of high conflict, a time when backed blades were being used in conflict, and at a time when there were extreme social and environmental circumstances, which the death has been associated with, as there was social change occurring and increasing social proscription This was a time when sea levels had reached their peak and increased territoriality and social conflict was at its highest point. In that particular area there was an increase in rock art, as occurred in Magnificent Gallery in Queensland, which Cane[1] suggests may indicate social and territorial adjustment, the diversity of engravings at this site appearing to indicate territorial division, a time when a number of factors were impacting the population of the continent, highest sea levels, diminished territory, variability of the climate, all impacting on population pressure. At that time conflict was a national characteristic, with evidence of violent disputation across populated areas such as the Murray River that Cane[1] suggests bordered on organised warfare.

The manner of killing of the man at Narrabeen bears a remarkable similarity to a judicial killing, a ritual execution, of a man who had committed a crime for which the guilty person could receive a death sentence. In pre-contact Australia this was a normal part of the social justice system. Therefore this killing may be seen as less of an indication of the brutal nature of a murder as part of territorial conflict and more as the process of a justice system that was unflinching in its application. Cane[1] reports a similar incident he was told of in which a man who was widely said to have too many wives lost his temper when one of his wives ran off with her lover. Her husband tracked down the pair 100 km away and killed the man. He was found guilty and a party of senior men from all the surrounding districts were sent to execute him for his crime. All in the party were required to take part in his execution, possibly so blame could not be placed on any individual, and anyone who might think of taking revenge would be similarly treated.

Aboriginal Trade

In Aboriginal Australia trade and ritual were closely linked. An example is from western Arnhem Land, where various tribes regularly gathered to perform dances and songs and to exchange goods. The value of the exchanged good was enhanced by the associated rituals. People hunted for food during the days or weeks the ceremonies took to complete, but some food that could be stored was gathered in preparation for the festivities. At the times of these large gatherings trade was not the only activity, differences were settled, ideas exchanged, old friends were greeted and new friends were made. It was also a time for betrothals and marriages to be arranged, as well as the more holiday type activities, dancing and singing and love making. The usually complicated network of taboos of who could make love with who were relaxed, and all but the very young and very old participated.

The people of western Arnhem Land had 6 principal trade ceremonies, each associated with a particular area. The *djamalag* had a strong emphasis of sexual licence, but also was important for trade and reinforcing intertribal friendships. The culmination of the ceremonies was the ritual presentation of trade goods such as shovel-bladed and serrated-headed spears from the east.

In the *rom* distinctive emblems are sent to invite the visitors who perform special totemic dances, and again the culmination is the exchange of goods.

The *midjan* involves a different series of dances from the sea coast. Hanks of twine made from the hair belonging to their hosts have been prepared by the visitors; they are given goods in payment for these.

The *wurbus* is a series in which the main interests of the people are special breast mats and baskets. In the concluding rituals, after the dancing, eggs are given as part of the trade exchange. It is thought that these eggs may have been connected with magical increase.

The dancing and most songs in this ceremony are about the normal daily life of the people.

The most spectacular of the events is the *njalaidj,* which closely resembles the sacred dances of the *Kunapipi*. It is commemorated in many myths. The traders connected with this event brought red ochre that was highly prized for its use in cave painting, and special stone spears that can only be made by these people.

On the Daly River, south of Darwin, trade took place at occasions when neighbouring tribes gathered for other reasons such as initiation or sacred ceremonies, the exchange of trade items were not actually associated with ceremonies as the those from western Arnhem Land were. On the Daly River and in north eastern Arnhem Land each man and woman had a special trading partner in a complex network of gift exchange.

A vast network of trade routes criss-crossed the Australian continent prior to white settlement, after which the trade contacts were soon broken. Pearl shell was traded from tribe to tribe to the Nullarbor Plain. Native tobacco moved from the central ranges to the south of the continent, while wombat fur for twine making moved from the south to the north. Stone spear heads were traded from the central Australian quarries to the tribes of Arnhem Land. By the 1930s, when much of the anthropological work was being carried on in the places like Arnhem Land, the trade routes were much diminished.

There is evidence from Pleistocene occupation sites that long distance trade routes existed throughout Australia.

Aboriginal Art

There are thousands of rock art sites throughout Australia, most of them in the north of the continent. The high interest in rock art is partly because many of the art sites are of prehistoric origin, so are windows, if not clear windows, on prehistoric life. Some of the petroglyphs and hand stencils have been there since the Pleistocene, and some of the paintings may be as old.

George Grey was the first European to record the huge Wandjina figures of Western Australia, paintings of such quality and aesthetic accomplishment that he didn't believe they were the work of Aborigines. For over 100 years the Aborigines were not credited with the best of the art, the thinking being they were simply too primitive to have accomplished such an artistic feat. The best of the art works were attributed to any people who someone thought might have passed by Australia, the lost tribes of Israel, Egyptians, Romans, Greeks, Hindus and even LGM, visitors from outer space. In the 1970s Aboriginal art was finally recognised for what it was, aboriginal art of world quality.

Rock Art

This includes graphic markings on cliffs, cave walls or rock surfaces. It can be of a number of forms, painted, drawn, stencilled, imprinted or carved. The art of the Aborigines, as with the art other pre-literate societies elsewhere in the world, played a completely different role in Aboriginal society than it does in modern societies, where it is viewed for aesthetic pleasure in places like art galleries.

Archaeology in Europe started much earlier than in Australia, where real archaeology had its beginning as late 1929. European archaeology divided the rock art into 2 categories, parietal art, found on the walls of caves. Mobiliary art was the portable art found on pieces of carved or engraved stone, as well as on bone of fired clay. In Australia, mobiliary art is almost unknown; by far the largest majority of art in Aboriginal Australia was of the parietal kind.

The carvings that occur on rock surfaces in Australia, either in caves or cliff faces, or even on isolated rocks, are usually referred to as petroglyphs, though sometimes called engravings, are carvings on rock surfaces made by an implement, of which there are 2 basic methods. One of these is abrasion, which includes rubbing the implement on the surface or drilling by applying pressure to the implement. Images produced by this method are in the form of scratched grooves or rubbed or drilled areas.

The other is percussion, in which the pressure is applied vertically by hammering. The resulting designs are in the form of pits in the rock that may be joined by lines. The percussion method can be by hammering the rock surface directly with the rock or in a method similar to using a chisel, the implement being struck with a rock while being held against the rock. Petroglyphs produced by the hammer and chisel method have sharper edges, and the lines are more precise and are deeper than those produced by the direct percussion method, where the outline is usually more diffuse.

Age of Petroglyphs

Some of the first petroglyphs found appear to be very old, being of the footprints of what is thought to be extinct animals such as ***Diprotodon***. There are also no dingo tracks on these very old carvings, which are very common on later carvings from later than 4,000 years ago when dingoes were introduced into Australia. Another indication of great age is the presence of a thick sheen of desert varnish.

Other indications of great age are the presence of rock art in places that are now inaccessible, such as petroglyphs on cliffs at Red Gorge in the Flinders Ranges, South Australia, where erosion and a rock fall has occurred since they were made. Some designs on the cliff face are incomplete, the remainder of such designs being found on rocks in the gorge. Some of the designs that are still on the cliff have large cracks running through them.

In 1929 evidence of the antiquity of some rock art was found at Devon Downs Rock Shelter, an engraved slab was found buried between 3 and 4 m below the surface.

The first firm date for Aboriginal art was found at Ingaladdi Rock Shelter, Northern territory. An engraved slab was found between layers dated to 7,000 and 5,000 years ago.

In Early Man Shelter in far north Queensland, the back wall is covered by a diagonal frieze that continues below the land surface, and below the occupation site that has been dated to 13,000 years ago.

Pleistocene rock art was found deep within Koonalda Cave on the Nullarbor Plain. On the walls 300 m from the entrance, where sunlight never reaches, were found graphic markings that have been compared to the macaroni or meander style patterns seen in the earliest European cave art.

Cave wall markings have also been found at Kintore Cave in the Northern Territory and Orchestra Shell Cave in Western Australia.

New Guinea 2 Cave in the Snowy River Gorge near Buchan, Victoria, also has wall markings thought to be about 20,000 years old.

Finger marks and petroglyphs in 3 succeeding styles have been found in more than 25 caves in the Mt Gambier district of south-eastern South Australia.

Petroglyphs of what some believe to be the Panaramitee style, have been found at the Sandy Creek Shelter 1 site that appears to be associated with a 32,000 year old occupation.

The Panaramitee Tradition is the name proposed by Lesley Maynard for a 3-part sequence of patterned variation she observed within the known rock art of Australia.

Petroglyphs have been found at Cleland Hills, about 320 km west of Alice Springs. There are 16 that appear to be human faces; the remainder are tracks and circles.

There are petroglyphs on the walls of a gorge at Durba Springs, Western Australia.

There is a large rock carving of the constellation, called by the Aborigines the 'Emu in the Sky', which is formed of dark clouds rather than the stars as in most other constellations. It is in the Elvina Track Engraving Site in the Kuring-Gai Chase National Park, Sydney, New South Wales.

In his book, *Australian Mammal Extinctions*, Chris Johnson refers to paintings of kangaroo tracks that show a single large toe, which is believed to represent an extinct Sthenurine kangaroo.

Long-beaked echidnas, mentioned by Murray & Chaloupka (1984), have been depicted on cave walls that show 2 species, the short-beaked and the long-beaked forms. The long-beaked form went extinct on the Australian mainland but survives only in New Guinea at the present.

In a cave in Arnhem Land, an ancient cave painting of a ***Palorchestes*** that has mud-dauber wasp nests built over the pigment, and had subsequently been fossilised by the water running down the cave walls. These nests have been dated indirectly, giving a minimum age for the painting of the ***Palorchestes***. At 40,000 BP, and possibly older, it is one of the oldest known cave paintings in the world.

A petroglyph found at the Panaramitee North site in the Olary area of South Australia bears a strong resemblance to the skull of ***Quinkana fortirostrum***. The petroglyph is now in the South Australian Museum. Great age can be inferred for this petroglyph by the thick layer of desert varnish covering it.

Some paintings in Arnhem Land (Johnson, 2006) depict animals that closely resemble thylacines, with stripes, and other animals that lack stripes and a tufted tail, tail butts clearly demarcated from the body, with broad paws and limb proportions that are very similar to those of the marsupial lion (Thylacoleo). According to Murray & Chaloupka, the painting of one of these animals appears to be dead. They suggest it appears as though a dead animal may have been laid out for the artist.

There are early paintings of animals with short legs and large bodies that are believed to have been diprotodonts on rock walls in the Kimberley (Johnson, 2006).

A number of limestone plaques have been found in Devil's Lair deposit. B3651 has a geometrical design, a trapezoidal shape, formed of intersecting incisions. This plaque was found in a hearth that has been dated to between 12,900 and 13,200 years ago. It was originally dated to 11,960 ± 140 and 12,050 ± 140 years ago. These original dates have since been rejected, being replaced by 13,050 ± 90 years ago. Plaque 3652 came from a layer dated to between 24,950-26,050 years ago. The original date for the site, 20,400 ± 1,000, has been replaced by 25,500 ± 275.

Hand stencils have been found in Wargata Mina Cave in south west Tasmania that date from the close of the Pleistocene ice age.

Bradshaw figures

Pole Art

Visual Art

Arkaroo Rock

See Nawarla Gabarnmang Rock Shelter

Rock Art

Age of Petroglyphs

Aboriginal Art - the Pilbara **Engraved Stones**
The Pilbara is a rock pile facing the sea that dovetails with the desert, the constituent rocks being iron-rich granite that has been dated to more than 3 Ma. The rocks have rusted brown over time as a result of their age, and have also weathered round and been fractured to square shapes that gives then an artificial-looking appearance, forming extensive piles of rock that were used by humans to form, according to Scott (2013) the greatest art gallery in the world by abrading, bashing and hammering (pecking). There are engravings all over the Pilbara, such as at Woodstock Station on the Yule River, where there are more than 3,000 engravings on 200 boulders, and on the Burrup Peninsula there are more than 10,000 engravings. At some other places there are individual locations with more than 1,000 engravings as well as many other art works throughout the greater region, with possibly a total 1 million engravings, more art here than at any other place on Earth. The artistic technique involved cutting through the rusted skin of the rocks thereby exposing the fresh surface of inner rock, soft yellows and brighter orange, and 'wondrous abstractions'[1] were carved in contrast to the darker patina

of the rocks. The author[1] suggests the Pilbara people were engravers, 'the best, the most prolific and the most accomplished of their time'[1].

The earliest known of these petroglyphs consist of lines and geometric patterns, various figures and terrestrial animals that are engraved deep into the rocks. The engravings are so old that their abraded surfaces have long since returned to the weathered stain of the rocks on which they were engraved. The actual age of these art works has yet to be determined, though it is safe to say they are very old, probably at least 25,000 years old. Among these ancient engravings there are some that are younger which lack the veneer of age and display marine animals dating from the time when the rising sea level stabilised 7,000 BP. By this time the engravings are of many kinds of track, artefacts of predictable kinds such as spears, shields and boomerangs, wondrous kinds of figures, such as **Murujuga Man**, with antennae, huge genitals and strange projections from their heads, and in various positions, such as running, fighting, hunting, dancing and having sex.

There is a panel that the author[1] describes as of particular interest, which stands out among this sea of fine art. It is believed to be about 3,000-4,000 years old, but its notable feature is that it conveys something about the nature of human society in the more distant past. This comparatively small panel consists of a triptych formed by a repeated pattern of figures on both sides of tracks that they appear to be following. As the engraved line is aligned vertically it gives the appearance of figures climbing. The focus of each panel is the engraved line, possibly a track, a branch or an imagined pathway, and the figures face each other along the engraved line. The figures appear to hang, rather like leaves to a branch, as they are attached to the engraved line by their left forearms, though they could be leap-frogging, swinging or dancing, or possibly climbing or crawling. All the figures are in-filled, stylised and variable, suggesting men, women and children, as well as strange human-like figures. The entire composition also hangs, as it aligned but otherwise disconnected from anything but imagined surroundings. There is a small circular head detached from the body of each figure. Though in all respects it is motionless and meaningless, it conveys movement and meaning. It immediately conveys ritual and dance in the context of the Wati Kutjara (The Two Men) and Tjukurrpa to senior Aboriginal leaders from Australia's western deserts.

In this collection of art that is otherwise diversified the 'climbing men' stand out as a result of their peculiarity and singularity, and also because there is another similar panel of them in the Little Sandy Desert more than 600 km to the west, that would be described by the Aboriginal people as 'the same but different'. In this panel there are 2 figures, one of which is filled in, that faces the viewer. This one looks like a man and is half-way along an engraved line that it is attached to by its left foot and hand, and the suggestion it is climbing results from its position. There is a second figure that is represented in profile that appears to be stepping or walking while leaning slightly forward. In this panel the track is more elaborate being comprised of 2 parallel lines, that make its appearance path-like, that ends in a circular 'head' with a banded neck and linear protuberances. There are 11 pecked dots adjacent to the path on either side of the path and the figure sits to the left of the path approaching one of the 11 pecked dots.

According to the Cane[1] the engravings are clearly part of the same tradition, though there are stylistic differences displayed by them. A common cultural tradition across a large socio-geographic area is suggested by the similarity of engravings, there being a covert relationship between subject, society and space. That the people of the Pilbara shared the same religious beliefs with the people from the Little Sandy Desert, viewed the world in the same way, expressing it accordingly, is suggested by the relationship between geography and style. It is indicated by the concordance of their artistic symbolism that they followed similar codes of social conduct and religious attendance, though the people of these 2 different locations may never have met. It is suggested by the 'climbing men' that there was a large-scale relationship across vast areas about 4,000 BP. Common traditions that necessarily imply broad-ranging social traditions, such as similar language, kinship, religion and territorial protocols, are suggested by the similarities of the engravings. In the Western Deserts of Australia traditional society is configured in the same way at the present, and it is suggested by the 'climbing men' that it was similar in the past. Current traditions with ancient roots and great geographic meaning is implied by the analogous relationship between the Wati Kutjara, its ritual meaning and the 'climbing men' - the past lives on in the present.

The small figures of the 'climbing men' therefore have big implications. Beside the 'climbing men' is what the author[1] calls the even greater, older and more widespread artistic tradition, the 'Panaramitee'. The Panaramitee, that has been found throughout Australia, from the Pilbara to Cape York margins then south to the Flinders Ranges of South Australia, is characterised by symbols that would be widely familiar and that are ubiquitous in Aboriginal art of the present, such as tracks, lines and circles that are painted in various combinations. Across most of the continent there are many thousands of these symbols that comprise the Panaramitee tradition, with sites in central Australia where there are 2,000-3,000 of these engravings. At the Sturts Meadow site in north western New South Wales there are more than 18,000 of these motifs on rocky outcrops. There are more than 20,000 engravings at 20 sites in the Olary area of north eastern South Australia. The geographic spread appears to have been across the arid zone and its edges at a time in the distant past when that particular environment was more extensive than it is at present. Scott (2013) suggests that the universality of artistic creation implies social accord, in an established population of Australia with shared traditions across the continent by the Late Pleistocene. In the earliest phases of human settlement there were human sketches and by the Late Pleistocene there is textured and patterned infill, it has become the art of all people across Australia. The author[1] describes this as 'the art of the ancients within which there is general and regionalised uniformity that suggests social coherence and communication on a scale that spans the continent. The art speaks of an ancient society of image-makers with imagined realities and diverse symbolism that was at once provincial yet set within a coherent social universe'.

It is not yet known how old the Panaramitee art tradition is, though great antiquity is always implied and there is nothing that appears to be older than it, but its antiquity remains elusive. As recent imagery is often superimposed on it, this suggests its possible age. The old, weathered nature of the engravings covered by the dark covering of desert patina and the mineralised coatings of 'desert varnish' suggest great antiquity. The fact that it is found in north western Tasmania suggests it arrived in Tasmania prior to the closing of the land bridge that occurred 14,000 years ago, though there is no reason to suppose that the tradition is defined by this event. The greatest antiquity is of 9,000 BP for it, its presence at sites of greater antiquity, such as at the Puritjarra Rock Shelter in central Australia suggest it may also be of the greater antiquity of the site, though at present the evidence is circumstantial.

Archaic design and composition implies great antiquity, as well as its presence in areas where the people of the present no longer recognise either the design or composition, it is obviously a tradition that has long been forgotten and of a culture before remembered time. At a site in an isolated range, Yiripanta Range, in the remote eastern margin of the Great Sandy Desert, the country having being occupied until 1985, there is a series of rust-coloured panels with ancient circular and linear engravings. The people who had lived there until 1985 didn't know who made them and couldn't interpret them. More recent engravings had been cut into the patina and superimposed the older engravings, though the author[1] suggests these petroglyphs appear to be attempts to copy the older engravings rather than renewing them as is often done. He suggests the new attempts appear more scratchy, frail and tentative than the older artistic traditions. The older petroglyphs at this site suggests that at Yiripanta Range the Panaramitee art was more labour-intensive and difficult to produce than the present art in the same part of the desert, which is mostly sweeps, smears, washes and dots of charcoal, ochre and pigment, and the ancient petroglyphs are more substantial than the intaglios superimposed on them. It is believed the older art had more time and resources spent on it than on the modern art, which is ephemeral, in the region. It has been estimated that the 18,000 engravings at Sturts Meadow took a year to complete. It is implied that the older, more substantial art tradition suggests there was a more substantial human presence in the area, therefore a more productive subsistence environment than the region is at the present. A sense of enduring human presence at the time the art was produced is conveyed by the physicality of the art, though there is a lack of confirmatory evidence from that period.

At the Early Man site in Cape York engravings have been found that are covered by sediments dated to more than 14,000 BP, and the art continues below this and the age of them is not known. In the Sandy Creek site in Cape York an ancient panel of rock art has been reported, and it has been found that in Ingaladdi in the Victoria River district engraved rock fragments had fallen from the cave walls into the sediments. The sediments have been dated to 5,000-7,000 BP, but the age of the engravings is unknown. Engravings at several locations across southern Australia are suggested by mineralogical examinations to be 25,000-40,000 years old, though these estimates have proven to be complicated and have been contested.

The Panaramitee are considered by archaeological intuition to be ancient. The pan-continental parity of the Panaramitee reinforces the breadth of tradition as a substantive feature of Australian society in the Late Pleistocene, as does the artistic specificity and geographic disparity of the 'climbing men' which points to social networks on a regional scale that is defined by common artistic and religious traditions, that is, a single people who are firmly established in a single country. The Panaramitee tradition is described as art of homogeneity with regional variation that indicates ancient traditions, social commonality, as well as emergent autonomy across the continent in the very ancient past.

Archaic Faces Panaramitee Tradition

The Panaramitee Tradition included the first known representation of the human face in the world, according to Cane (2013) there are virtually no faces portrayed in prehistoric art anywhere else in the world. In antiquity the main artists painted the animals they hunted though not other humans, any images that include them are portrayed in part as headless figures, any images that include representations of humans lack heads, though they sometimes have hair or headdresses. In contrast the human face is the most common representation in Western art of the present.

In Europe the Venus figurines are the best known and earliest representations of humans that were carved between about 22,000 and 16,000 years ago, and they are abstracted images of women with enlarged proportions - large buttocks and huge breasts. Heads are rarely found on these figurines, and when they are there is no face. Another phase of human representation followed the Venus figurines about 12,000 years ago, a tradition in which the human representations were depicted in concerted action, such as hunting and fighting, though the faces are still lacking, apparently the painters were not concerned with individuals or personality, rather expressing a broader social consciousness in which people were represented similarly regardless of their age or gender. According to Cane the evolution of human representation has been interpreted as mechanistic representations of demographic and social circumstances. The homogeneity of the earlier figurines is seen as pointing to open social networks, mobility and low population densities (societies of similarity). The variability and complexity on a regional scale of the later action figures indicates closed social networks and higher, more sedentary, competitive, self-defining populations - societies of difference. Cane says it is not until late in human history that the human face emerges in the West, less than 5,000 years ago. The first such representations of the human face were in places such as Egypt with, as the Cane describes them, lifeless faces in Egyptian sarcophagi or the cold marble eyes of early Greek statues.

In Australia things were different within the Panaramitee Tradition where faces were engraved in the very early phases of human history, at least 10,000-15,000 years before any representations of faces appear in the rest of the world. The earliest human faces known in the world first appear in arid Australia across the desert from the Burrup Peninsula to the Calvert Ranges in the Gibson Desert and Cleland Hills of central Australia, across an area of about 666,000 km^2. The faces are engraved in stone and have pecked eyes that are surrounded by concentric circles, with mouths, noses and ears set in heads that are heart-shaped. It is suggested by associated weathering that they are from 25,000-10,000 years old, though their actual age is still to be determined. The earliest dates for them are circumstantial which suggests they may be from 29,700-37,700 years old.

According to Cane (2013) the engravings of faces are expressive, in some cases being comical in their ability to express their feelings and moods such as surprise, happiness, anger, horror, frustration, distress, stupidity, annoyance, and disillusionment. Cane suggests it is clear that the engravers of these faces at disparate locations were capable of expressing feelings and empathising with the feelings of others. These faces convey the first notions of personality anywhere in the world, where people are portrayed as individuals within the society and environment to which they belong. *'The engravings thus imply the emergence of subjectivity through the embodiment of self and the singular expression of human identity and personality in the context of society and its geography'* (Cane, 2013).

With these engravings, the representation and composition of these faces at distant places across the vast expanses of desert imply, as do the engravings of the 'climbing men', that the engravers belonged to the same social system, a system that was probably defined by mobility, communication and religious conformity, and within this system the artistic representation of faces suggests that a regional social identity had developed. Distinctiveness within the greater social context is implied by the recognition of the human face necessitating the realisation of other people in this social relationship. Therefore engraved faces allude to both an emergent sense of self and an emergent sense of difference on a regional scale, and possibly competing political and territorial perspectives in the larger landscape of society. The result is that the archaic faces paint a portrait of nomads with a common culture, as well as a regional identity that is emerging.

Iconic Imagery – The Development of Rock Art Across Northern Australia

According to Mulvaney a date of sometime prior to 45,000 BP is generally agreed upon for the peopling of Sahul, and by 30,000 BP most parts of the continent being colonised. All parts of Sahul where the first settlers left their mark there is rock art, which comprises both engraved and painted images. Mulvaney asks the question "*Did this artistic endeavour come with the people or was this an expression of being in Sahul?*" There are aspects, such as cupules and hand stencils, which have parallels in other parts of the world, though there are other aspects suggesting separate artistic traditions and conventions present which have continued ever since. There is a vast body of rock art, spread across an area of more than 1 million km^2 (386,000 miles^2), that extends in an arc for more than 2,000 km from the coast of the Pilbara through the Kimberley and into Arnhem

Land, which demonstrates the existence of differentiation in the symbolic structuring of people's lives at a relatively short time after the beginning of colonisation. Mulvaney contends that this supports the notion that within Sahul regionalisation is not simply a Holocene expression.

Elvina Track Engraving Site
There are many different types of engravings at this site, off the Elvina track

Elvina Track Engraving Site

Aboriginal Pole Structures
The large jelmalandji that are constructed as part of the rituals of the **Kunapipi**, that occurred throughout the regions of Arnhem Land and the Roper River and the central west of the Northern Territory (R. Berndt, 1951*a*), are included in this category of art. They were about 15-25 ft high, the centre being about 2.5 ft wide. Wads of grass and paperbark were tied with twine to the solid pole, the outer surface being bark. Arm blood and red ochre are smeared on the bark to form a meandering pattern, with bird down or wild cotton stuck onto the designs. The Rock Python, Julunggul or the Rainbow, was the symbolic basis of this design. The swallowing of the Wawalag Sisters at Muruwul, the sacred site, by the Python is symbolised by a bunch of white cockatoo feathers on top of each pole.

There were usually 2 such structures (Berndt, 1651*a*: Plate VIII) beside the ganala, a crescent-shaped trench: the gulwiri (the wild coconut) palm is represented by the second. Gadjeri, the Fertility Mother, and Gadjiri or Kunapipi and the Rainbow Snake are said to be represented by the jelmalandji in the central western parts of the Northern Territory. Pearl shell eyes, as well as other decorations, have been reported being used on a jelmalandji structure from the latter area.

The northern Aranda used a tnatantja pole (nurtunja). The most common form comprises from 1 to 20 spears that have long bunches of grass bound to them with hair girdles, rings of downy feathers, in a design that varies, are stuck onto the structure with blood, sometimes with a few tjurunga suspended from it, and eaglehawk feathers are used to decorate the apex. Some are described and illustrated, and some detail of the associated rituals were provided by Spencer and Gillen (1938: 253-55, 298-300, 345-6, 360-4, 627, Figs. 63, 64, 68, 81, 82).

Poles were discussed, including one associated with the bandicoot totem, red and white down was stuck on with blood in alternating lines (Strehlow, 1947: 23-5 *et passim*). Experiences of the ancestral bandicoot are recorded in the associated myth. In this myth a great tnatantja sprung from amongst a bed of purple flowers growing over the Ilbalintja soak, it was a living creature with smooth skin like that of a man, and it was swaying above him (Strehlow, 1947: 7).

Others described had lines of down that symbolised the wattle tree roots that ancestral women were digging amongst in their search for ants (Spencer & Gillen, 1938: 325).

The kauaua ritual pole of the Aranda was required to be cut down and must not touch the ground as it was taken to the camp (Spencer & Gillen, 1938: 364, 370, 629; Strehlow, 1947: 77, 111). Human blood was smeared all over this pole, or it could be substituted by red ochre. The top of this pole was adorned in the same manner as the heads of the participants, as it represented a human head.

Poles were used in many ceremonies and rituals, non-sacred as well as sacred, over most of northern Australia. Decorated sacred forked poles were used in western Arnhem Land for usually men, but sometimes women, to climb and call invocations. One variety was the djebalmandji, associated with the Kunapipi. Along the north coast of the Northern Territory other poles, as well as hollow logs, were used in mortuary ceremonies. On Bathurst and Melville Islands the bugamani poles, grave posts, were large, heavy logs that could be up to 18 ft long (Basedow, 1913; Spencer, 1914: 230-9; Mountford, 1958: 60-121). According to Mountford these poles were regarded as gifts to the dead rather than a memorial. The shapes of the designs painted on the trunks vary, and according to Mountford there is almost no reference to myths or totemic localities. The upper parts of the poles have been variously associated with forks or limbs of trees, women's breasts, rocks, windows and doors. Some take the shape of human figures. According to the Berndts, they were told that the shapes of the poles were highly conventionalised, and represent human beings, that the

Berndts consider to be plausible when they are compared with Mountford's collection of figures (Mountford, 1958: Plates 36-41).

The banumbir, the Morning Star of the Dua moiety or the 'Macassan' mast of the jiridja moiety, decorated poles are used in eastern Arnhem Land (Warner, 1937/58: 412-49; Elkin, Berndt & Berndt, 1950: 92-100.) The 'Macassan' mast was intended to be a replica of the mast of a Malay prau, the symbolism being that the living were farewelling the dead as the Macassan praus raised their masts and spread their sails as they set out for home across the sea.

Bark coffins were painted with the clan designs of the dead person. In the final stage of some mortuary rites red ochre was rubbed on the collected, cleaned bones, after which they were placed in a hollow log resting on either 1 or 2 forked sticks. The mouth of the log was cut to shape and designs to symbolise an association with the mythology of a type of fish, animal, natural object or feature. Some Dua moiety designs represent a whale, sawfish, porpoise, shark, wild honey, snake and stone. The jiridja moiety have a different range of designs, featuring such things as a ship's funnel, mast, cloud, a different kind of wild honey from that of the Dua moiety, and various fish. Red ochre completely covers the log and it was painted with clan designs. As the log was between 12 and 20 ft. long, the designs were painted by several artists. One term for the hollow log is a laragidi. It is left to stand in the main camp until it rots away once the bones are in it and the rituals are complete. Log coffins were reported in western Arnhem Land (Elkin, 1954: Plate opposite p. 254, is of such as log coffin in use at South Goulburn Island).

Aboriginal Astronomy

It has been suggested the Australian Aborigines may have been the first astronomers (Haynes, 1992). A number of stone arrangements have been found in Australia that show remarkable similarity to stone arrangements in Europe, but could be thousands of years older. In Victoria, the **Wurdi Youang people** built a stone arrangement, that was roughly egg-shaped, and with a diameter of about 50 m. Its major axis is east-west. 3 prominent stones, that are waist high, are at its highest point at the western edge. It has been found that, viewed from these stones, some outlying stones to the west of the main arrangement appear to indicate the setting of the sun at times of equinoxes and solstices. The straight sides of the arrangement have also been found to point to the solstices. They had differentiated between planets, stars and constellations, and they used the sky as a calendar to plan their year, when to harvest their various food sources, when to move camp as the season was about to change. And they knew the connection between the Moon and the tides. They had myths to explain the effect the Moon had on the tides, they knew what tides to expect by observing the Moon. They had a sound knowledge of the cyclical phases of the Moon. They used this knowledge to plan when to move to new sites and to hold their big ceremonies, when many people would gather and need a large, assured food supply for the duration of the rituals, which could last for weeks or months.

An astrophysicist studying Aboriginal Astronomy has found an impact crater in Palm Valley that was about 280 m wide and 30 m deep, about 130 km south west of Alice Springs, Northern Territory, that was connected to a story from the Dreaming of the local Arrernte people. According to the story, a star fell to earth at Puka, the approximate site of the crater. The crater is heavily weathered and no fragments of meteorite were found, but a small amount of shocked quartz was found. The only 2 ways this material forms is by nuclear explosions and by meteorite impact.

About 170 km west of Alice Springs, at Gosse's Bluff, is another impact crater, in this case associated with a dreaming story of a 'cosmic baby' that fell to earth. As both craters are millions of years old it is not possible that they were witnessed by humans. It seems the people may have learned to associate craters with impacts of objects from space. There are some craters at Henbury, about 70 km from Palm Valley, that are about 4,000 years old, these could have been witnessed by humans. The tribal elders know Dreaming stories about the Henbury craters but they are considered sacred and secret.

In the north, when Scorpio was visible in the morning sky in early December the people of **Yirrkala** knew that the Macassan Traders were due to arrive on the northern shore. On nearby Groote Eylandt, in the Gulf of Carpentaria, they knew that when 2 stars in the 'sting' in Scorpio's tail appeared in the evening sky at the end of April the wet season would soon end and *marimariga*, the dry south east wind, would soon come. Mountford (1956), Crawford, (1668), Dreaming the Stars.

Confirming the suspicions that these stone arrangements may have had astronomical significance, other stone arrangements have been found in Victoria that also appear to point to the cardinal points.

Ngaut Ngaut is a site north of Adelaide on the banks of the Murray River in South Australia. At this site the **Nganguraku** people had engraved a rock with a series of dots and lines. The traditional owners say it represents the cycles of the moon, but as the early Christian missionaries banned the speaking of the language, as well as the initiation rites, during which much of the oral tradition was passed on to younger generations, the oral tradition has been mostly lost.

The Kuwema people near Katherine in the Northern Territory used the rising of Orion early in the morning in winter to know when dingoes were breeding, so pups would soon follow, in this case as a food source. (Harney, 1959).

The Yolngu people in the Northern Territory call the constellation of Orion Djulpan. According to a Yolngu story, 3 brothers went fishing but could only catch kingfish. As they were of the Nulkal totemic group (kingfish) they were prohibited from eating this fish species. One got so hungry that he ignored the ban on eating his totem fish. Walu, the Sun woman, punished him by making a waterspout that carried the canoe to the sky where it became Orion's belt, but to the Yolngu the 3 stars representing the belt were the 3 brothers in their canoe. The Orion Nebula was a fish on a line from the canoe.

The emu in the sky. At the Elvina Engraving Site in the Kuring-Gai Chase National Park, Sydney, is an engraving of the emu in the sky, a constellation recognised by many Aboriginal groups across Australia, that is formed of dark clouds in the Milky Way, rather than the stars as in most constellations. When the constellation is above the carving in the rock the local Aborigines knew it was time to collect emu eggs.

The people of the Torres Strait islands use their constellation of Tagai, a warrior, to tell them when it is time to plant their crops. When his left hand, the Southern Cross, is about to enter the sea the first rains of the wet season are coming.

Links

Australian Aboriginal Astronomy

Rocky Ways to secrets of the Sky

Australian_Aboriginal_Astronomy - wikipedia

Aboriginal Astronomy - Questacon

Aboriginal Astronomy - Neilloan

Emu Dreaming

Aboriginal folklore leads to meteorite crater

Emu Dreaming: An Introduction to Aboriginal Astronomy by Ray & Cilla Norris

Cosmogenic Mega-tsunami in the Australia region

Dreaming the Stars

Australian Aborigines the first astronomers

Sources & Further reading

Jennifer Isaacs, Australia Dreaming: 40,000 years of Aboriginal History, New Holland Publishers, 2005

Australian Aboriginal Astronomy – Overview

There are still some Aboriginal cultures in northern and Central Australia that have retained almost all of their culture and language from pre-contact times, still conducting initiations where knowledge is passed down the generations. Most of the detailed information has been obtained from some of these, in particular the Yolngu and Wardaman peoples. In this paper only the material that is not considered to be secret and sacred by the traditional Aboriginal owners is considered. .

In the song, stories, art, and ceremonies of many traditional Aboriginal cultures celestial objects feature, the Sun, Moon, planets, stars, the Milky Way, as well as the dark clouds within it (Stanbridge, 1861; Mountford, 1956; Haynes, 1992; Johnson, 1998; Cairns & Harney, 2003; Norris & Norris, 2009; Norris & Hamacher, 2009; 2011; Hamacher & Norris, 2011a). For example, included in the Aboriginal "constellations" are the Southern Cross, the meaning to different Aboriginal groups might be seen as the footprint of an emu, a stingray, or a possum in a tree. Alternatively, in many different Aboriginal groups Orion symbolises a young man or group of young men, chasing the Pleiades (7 sisters). The "constellation" the emu is another that is well-known (Cairns-Harney, 2003; Massola, 1963), consists of the dark clouds within the Milky Way, which is important in many different Aboriginal groups throughout Australia.

The deeper understanding of the sky, such as the explanation of the tides, eclipses, the motion of the Sun and Moon, and the ability to predict the rising and setting places of celestial bodies in the sky also had practical applications for navigation and time keeping (Cairns & Harney, 2003; Clarke, 2009), discussed in greater detail by Clarke (2014).

The Sun, Moon and planets

It is shown by many Aboriginal people that they sought to understand the motion of the celestial bodies, and to place them in a framework that was self-sufficient that described the natural world. The motion of the Sun, e.g., is described by the Yolngu people as being caused by the Sun-woman, Walu, who lights a stringy bark tree each morning, then carries across the sky to her camp in the West (Wells, 1964). The lunar phases represent the Moon-man, Ngalindi, being attacked by his wives wielding axes who cause the lunar phases by slicing pieces off him.

Solar eclipses were widely viewed as a bad omen, though good evidence exists that shows that at least 3 Aboriginal groups, the Euahlayi, Yolngu and Warlpiri people, each from a different state of Australia, recognised an eclipse for what it is, a conjunction between the Sun and the Moon (Hamacher & Norris, 2011b). In all of these 3 cases they were seen as mating between the Sun-woman and the Moon-man, and in one account, the Warlpiri, adding a bit extra, the Sun-woman was sent away by the sky spirits for trying to seduce the Moon-man. In many other Aboriginal groups an eclipse was recognised as something covering the Sun, but thought that it was a hood or cloak. As a total solar eclipse is seen in any one location every 3 or 4 generations, this implies there was a remarkable continuity of learning in these explanations.

Lunar eclipses were also interpreted widely as something covering the Moon, though there is only one case in which it was attributed to the relative positions of the Sun and Moon (Hamacher & Norris, 2011b). Others have thought of the Moon-man being covered by shadow of a man walking in the Milky Way. It was widely believed that the red on the Moon during a lunar eclipse was blood on the face of the Moon-man.

The Yolngu noticed that tide height varies depending on the phase of the Moon, and the highest tide, a spring tide, occurs at the time of a new moon, an association that was not noticed by Galileo. The Yolngu noticed this connection and devised an explanation for the phenomenon. Their explanation, which was based on the filling and emptying of the Moon as it passed through the ocean at the horizon (Berndt, 1948), differs somewhat from that of modern science, though it is suggested by Norris & Hamacher that it is a good example of an evidence-based approach to understand the world in a cultural context.

Similarly, it was noticed widely that the planets move differently from the stars. E.g. the Yolngu noticed how Venus was always low in the sky, and close to the rising or setting Sun. Their explanation for this was to suggest that Venus as a morning star was attached by a rope to the mythical island of Baralku in the east (Norris & Norris, 2009; Allen, 1975), which prevented her from rising high in the sky. Venus as an evening star was held down by a rope connected to the "spirits of the West" (Berndt, 1948). Norris & Hamacher also suggest that it is possible that the zodiacal light, which is easily seen in Arnhem Land, was believed to be supportive evidence for this rope.

Orientation and Prediction

For several Aboriginal groups, most notably the Warlpiri people, the concept of cardinal direction is important, as much of their cultural lore is based on cardinal directions (Pawu-Kurlpurlurnu et al., 2008), which are largely determined by the rising and setting Sun. The dead are buried facing to the east in some Aboriginal cultures (e.g. Mathews, 1904), and initiation sites are often oriented north-south (Fuller et al., 2012). It has been shown (Hamacher et al., 2012) that a sample of linear stone arrangements is oriented north-south with an accuracy of a few degrees.

There are 3 techniques that have been suggested as possible methods of determining the cardinal directions:

This would involve the use of so-called "magnetic" termite mounds, but this couldn't have been used as this type of termite mound that is elongate and is aligned north-south, and has an accuracy of $10°$ as they are found only in the Northern Territory (Grigg & Underwood, 1977). Therefore they could not have been used as they are a long way from the boras and stone arrangements which are in the south of the continent. Astronomical observations are involved in the other 2 techniques.

From a given viewing position, a stone or stick could be placed on the ground in the direction of the setting Sun. The ends of the lines that result will indicate the position of the Sun at the solstices, and the midpoint between the ends indicates due west. It has been shown (Ruggles, 1997) that variations in the height of the horizon limits the accuracy of this technique, but this is not likely to limit these measurements, as the accuracy being cited is here is of the order of a few degrees. It is noted that the solstitial positions at Wurdi Young are indeed marked with due west being marked between them.

The position of a circumpolar star, such as those within the Southern Cross, similarly may be marked by placing a stick or stone vertically below the star at various times through the year. Due south will be indicated by the midpoint of the line that results.

The Wurdi Youang stone ring is the best example of astronomical alignments (Morieson, 2003; Norris et al., 2012), where there are several east-west indicators that are accurate to a few degrees, as well as outliers and sections of the ring that are straight and indicate the setting position of the Sun in midwinter and midsummer. It is indicated by a Monte Carlo analysis that these alignments are not likely to be due to chance. This the only known Aboriginal site that indicates significant astronomical positions on the horizon other than the cardinal points, and, as long as it is not a statistical freak or a hoax, suggests that there may be other such sites that are yet to be discovered.

Archaeoastronomical significance

There is unequivocal evidence that Australian Aboriginal people possessed a deep knowledge of the sky, and were aware of many celestial phenomena. Evidence has also been found that interest in the sky went beyond this, to the extent that they were trying to understand the mechanisms behind these phenomena, and how they fitted into a world view that was self-consistent.

A sparsity of data hinders these studies. With the exception of comets (Hamacher & Norris, 2010), there is only a single known example of a transient phenomenon that has been incorporated in to a traditional Aboriginal oral account (e.g. the Great Eruption of η Carina: (Hamacher & Frew, 2010), and attempts have been made to link stories of stones from the sky with meteorite events that are known of have not been successful (Hamacher & Norris, 2009).

There is also a danger that an interpretation from the point of view of Western culture may be imposed on it. An example is that it has sometimes been stated that careful measurement is alien to Aboriginal culture, and it has sometimes been asserted until recently (e.g. Blake, 1981) that there is no Aboriginal language that has a word for a number greater than 5. There is no basis in fact for this latter assertion, though it appears to reflect a combination of post-colonial prejudice and a lack of understanding of number systems.

Relying only on evidence-based studies is the best way to avoid such cultural bias, in either direction.

Norris, R.P. and **Hamacher, D.W.** (2014). Australian Aboriginal astronomy: an overview. Handbook of Archaeoastronomy and Ethnoastronomy, Vol. III, edited by Clive Ruggles. Springer-Verlag, pp. 2215-2223

Records of Supernovae in Indigenous Traditions?

In this paper, traditions of Australian Aboriginal people are explored for possible descriptions of novae/supernovae. There are currently no conformed accounts of supernovae in indigenous Australian oral or material traditions, though representations of supernovae may exist in Aboriginal traditions.

Australian Aboriginal people have a detailed knowledge of the night sky, as do many indigenous cultures around the world, using their knowledge for navigation, calendars and time keeping, when to gather particular types of food, ceremonies and social structure (e.g. Cairns & Harney, 2003; Frederick, 2008; Hamacher & Norris, 2011a; Johnson, 1998). Involved in the sky knowledge is an understanding and explanation of the motions of planets, relative to the positions stars, lunar phases and tides, and the position of the rising and setting Sun throughout the year with respect to the landscape (Hamacher & Norris, 2011a; Norris & Hamacher, 2009; Norris et al., 2013). Explanations of transient phenomena are included in this knowledge, such as meteors, comets, eclipses and aurorae (Hamacher & Norris, 2010, 2011b, 2011c; and Hamacher, 2013, respectively). Oral traditions and material culture were the forms by which this knowledge was passed down through successive generations (Clunies-Ross, 1986).

Scientific information explaining the natural world in terms of cause-effect is contained in astronomical traditions of indigenous people. This scientific information, which was based on observation and deduction, was used for predictive purposes. Australian Aborigines linked lunar phases to tides and this knowledge was used as a guide for deciding when to fish, and their traditions also contained an explanation of how and why the Moon was connected to the tides (e.g. Johnson, 1998: 27,37). The Arrival of winter in the Central Desert was signalled by the heliacal rising of the Pleiades (Tindale, 2005: 374), while the rising after dusk of the celestial emu indicated that the emu eggs would be ready to collect (e.g. Fuller et al., 2014). Also, transient phenomena, rare or common, were often linked to special events on Earth. An example is the sudden flash of a meteor may coincide with a death in the community, or the appearance of a comet or an eclipse might coincide with a famine, drought or a battle (Johnson, 1998:86-89).

One account confirms the sudden brightening in the oral traditions: the 'supernova-imposter' eruption of Eta Carinae in 1843. The Boorong people of western Victoria, Australia, witnessed this event and incorporated it into their oral traditions. Stanbridge recorded the required data, such as the physical appearance of the star, its position in the sky and catalogue number during the outburst of the star. The Great Eruption of Eta Carinae was not, however, a real supernova or nova.

One story has been identified as indicating the appearance of a new star in the sky. This story of "The Fisherman Brothers" is from the Yolngu people of Arnhem Land, Northern Territory, Australia (Wells, 1873: 31-36).

According to Hamacher this paper establishes criteria that are necessary to identify novae/supernovae in oral traditions or material culture. He also suggests that attempts at linking oral traditions or material culture to novae/supernovae are worthwhile. Understanding of cultural astronomy and indigenous knowledge traditions will benefit from the identification of these phenomena in oral accounts or material culture. Also, astronomers could be led to supernovae remnants that have been unrecorded.

Hamacher, Duane W., 2014, Are supernovae recorded in indigenous astronomical traditions? Journal of Astronomical History and Heritage, 17(2), 161-170 (2014).

Aboriginal Astronomical Traditions, Ooldea, South Australia, Part 2: Animals in the Ooldean Sky

A relationship between animals in the sky and the behaviour of their terrestrial counterparts is demonstrated in Aboriginal Indigenous Astronomical traditions. Leaman et al. investigated the relationship between animal behaviour and stellar positions when these relationships are not described specifically in the written records, in their continued study of Aboriginal astronomical traditions from the Great Victoria Desert, South Australia. A methodology was developed to test the hypothesis that the position in the sky of the celestial counterparts of an animal at particular times of day predicts the behaviour of the terrestrial animal. Of the 12 stellar (i.e. non-planet or non-galactic) animals that were identified in the Ooldean sky 9 were analysed and a close connection was demonstrated between the behaviour of the animal and stellar positions. Leaman et al. suggest the possibility that this may be a recurring theme in Aboriginal astronomical traditions, which requires further methodology development.

A wealth of traditional knowledge of the night sky has been revealed by the study of astronomical knowledge and traditions in Australian Aboriginals. It has been found that calendars and economics of food are closely integrated with astronomical traditions (Frederick, 2008; Johnson, 1998; Sharp, 1993) which often involved animals and their behavioural habits. It is common across Australia for oral traditions to describe animals in the skyworld (Stanbridge, 1861) and the world (e.g. Kelly & Milone, 2011: 499; Urton, 1981). Constellations, asterisms, individual stars, star clusters, planets, nebulae and other celestial objects may represent these animals. Celestial animals are commonly linked to behavioural patterns of the terrestrial counterparts by Australian Aboriginals, such as mating, birthing or brooding their young (Cairns & Harney, 2003; Johnson, 1998; Stanbridge, 1861). In part, these traditions serve as a guide for noting the time of year when particular food sources may be available.

According to Leaman et al. this paper continues on from a study of Aboriginal astronomical knowledge carried out near Ooldea in the Great Victoria Desert, South Australia (for the first part see (Leaman & Hamacher, 2014). Most of this information comes from Daisy Bates, an amateur anthropologist (Bates, 1904-1935; 1921a; 1921b; 1924a; 1924b; 1933; 1938) as well as Ronald and Catherine Berndt, professional anthropologists Berndt, 1941; Berndt & Berndt, 1943, 1945, 1974; 1977). The primary information that was used in the paper was derived from Daisy Bates in a story she had recorded about the Orion and the Pleiades, a constellation and a star cluster (Bates, 1921b; 1933). Many animals in the Ooldean sky were described by Bates, though no details were recorded concerning animals and their celestial counterparts. In most cases the stories only mentioned the type of animal that was represented by each of the celestial object, and their major or minor role in the narrative.

In this paper Leaman et al. tested the hypothesis that each animal in the Ooldean sky is associated with a celestial object that is used to predict the breeding habits of these animals, such as mating, birthing, egg incubation, brooding and fledging the young. Therefore the study investigated whether the heliacal or acronychal rising or setting, or meridional transit, predicted the breeding habits of the respective terrestrial counterparts.

Animals of the Aboriginal skyworld

The realm of the skyworld has topography that is similar to and as real as the terrestrial landscapes below, according to the cosmology and cosmography of Australian Aboriginals (Clarke, 2007/2008; 2015b). The skyworld realm is inhabited by plants, animals and celestial beings, each of which is represented by celestial bodies (Clarke, 2014b; 2015a; 2015b; Leaman & Hamacher, 2014), or other prominent features in the night sky, such as the prominent dark bands of the Milky Way (e.g. see Fuller et al., 2014a; 2014b).

In the foundational work by William E. Stanbridge (1820-1894; 1861) on Aboriginal astronomy in western Victoria he recorded some of the astronomical traditions that were given to him by the Boorong, an Aboriginal clan belonging to the Wergaia language group that lived near Lake Tyrell. Included in his papers are several animals that relate to stars. The star Vega (α Lyrae) is an example, that is called Neilloan in the Wergaia language, was linked to the mallee fowl (Leipoa ocellata), a megapode that is the size of a chicken and lives on the ground where it builds its nest mounds when Vega rises at dusk (acronychal rising). These birds are laying their egg clutches when Vega is high in the sky at dusk (dusk meridian crossing), and the chicks begin to hatch when Vega sets at dusk (heliacal setting). Similarly, Arcturus, a star (α Boötis), Marpeankurrk in the Wergaia language, is related to the wood-ant larvae, which are plentiful for only a couple of months each year, August and September, the time when Arcturus is visible in the evening sky. These associations were built on to construct a detailed picture of the night sky of the Boorong, in which complex calendars are noted that are related to seasonal behaviour of animals (Morieson, 1996; 1999).

A definitive link between animal behaviour and the positions of their celestial counterparts, particularly at dusk and dawn, has been found by recent studies of Aboriginal astronomical knowledge (e.g. Cairns & Harney, 2003; Frederick, 2008; Fuller et al. 2014b; Hamacher, 2012). Aboriginal people know emus are laying their eggs, an important food source, when the dark emu in the Milky Way, from Crux to Sagittarius, appears in the evening sky (Fuller et al., 2014a; Norris & Hamacher, 2009).

In Aboriginal traditions such examples are common, though most of the traditions that were collected by early anthropologists do not provide much of this sort of information. In this paper Leaman et al. explore animals in the Ooldean sky searching for connections with their terrestrial counterparts, such as patterns of annual breeding behaviour in order to understand better the nature of Aboriginal astronomical knowledge.

Animals in the Ooldean sky

The Kokatha traditional country is where Ooldea is located (Gara, 1989). Ooldea Soak was a permanent water source which made the area around the soak an important drought refuge and meeting place in which trade and ceremonies took place, not only for the local people, but also for many Aboriginal language groups (Bates, 1938; Gara, 1989; Tindale, 1974). Activities that were associated with the Trans-Australian Railway were causing major disruption to traditional lifestyles of these peoples at the time Daisy Bates visited Ooldea (Bates, 1938; Brockwell et al., 1989; Colley et al., 1989), an important disruption was the establishment of more permanent camps, with diverse peoples of the region living in close proximity to each other. Leaman et al. suggest that this may be the explanation for blending that occurred of the vocabularies from different language groups in the word list of Daisy Bates (e.g. see Bated 1918), and in the skylore which she recorded in the Ooldea region (Bates, 1921a; 1921b; 1924a; a?924b;1933. In this paper Leaman et al. have adopted the term 'Ooldean sky' to describe the skylore of the region that was linguistically blended at the time of its recording, instead of attempting to disentangle Bates' records.

Several animals in the Ooldean sky are noted in records provided by Bates (1904-1935): the Australian bustard, Black Cockatoo, Dingo, Emu, Grey Kangaroo, Owlet Nightjar, Crow, Redback Spider, Red Kangaroo, Thorny Devil lizard and the Wedge-tailed Eagle. Most of the animals are related to stars, star clusters and asterisms, or to the dark band of the Milky Way (see also Leaman & Hamacher, 2014). The Red Kangaroo and the Grey Kangaroo are exceptions, being related to the 'morning' star and the 'evening' star respectively. Bates identifies these as the planets Jupiter and Venus respectively, though it is not clear if she was misrepresenting Jupiter as the morning star (as Venus is called both the morning star and the evening star), if Jupiter was prominent in the morning sky at the time Bates recorded the relevant astronomical traditions. There is no time stamp for when Bates recorded these traditions, though they are in the notes from Ooldea, where she lived and worked from 1919-1935. On many occasions Venus and Jupiter would both have been bright in the early morning sky during that 16 year period. The Black Cockatoo is related to both Antares and Mars. According to Leaman et al. planets are not suitable for denoting annual seasonal change on earth, though they may be used to reference longer climatic cycles, such as droughts, floods ENSO-driven events, etc.), so Venus, Mars and Jupiter will not be connected regularly with the annual seasonal cycles of any animal.

It is not known which exact star that represents baba the dingo father in the sky. It has been described as being the 'horn of the bull' (Bates, 1933). It is argued (Leaman & Hamacher, 2014) that it could be either the star β Tauri or ζ Tauri, though this is not certain, and Aldebaran (α Tauri) is already ascribed to a major character in the narrative.

Terrestrial behaviour of Ooldean sky animals

The Australian Bustard – Vega

Gibbera is the word for what is called in Central Australia the bush turkey. The Aboriginal people in the Central Australian deserts use the term 'bush turkey', or 'brush turkey' colloquially to refer to the Australian Bustard (**Ardeotis australis**). This is not to be confused with the Australian bush or brush turkey (**Alectura lathami**), which inhabits more temperate, wet tropical areas, The Bustard is an important source of food for the Aboriginal people (Ziembicki, 2009).

The breeding cycle of the Australian Bustard varies throughout its range across Australia and it is believed to be linked closely with weather and seasonal patterns, especially rainfall frequency (Ziembicki, 2009; 2010; Ziembicki & Woinarski, 2007: Fig. 2)

Populations are transitory and migratory in arid areas, such as exist at Ooldea, as the numbers fluctuate as a response to habitat and the availability of food in wet/dry years (Ziembicki, 2009). At Ooldea breeding generally occurs from May to August, peaking slightly in June (Ziembicki, 2009). The incubation period for the chicks is 23 days (Beruldsen, 2003).

In Early August the acronychal rising (AR) of Vega and setting at sunset (HS) by mid-November, and it crosses the meridian (reaching its maximum altitude) at dusk in the northern sky in late September. Therefore, during the entire mating season of the bustard for most regions in Australia, the star is prominent in the evening sky, with peaks occurring close to the dusk meridian transit (Mdusk). Regarding the mallee fowl a similar relationship is given with the star Vega in traditions of the Wergaia of western Victoria (Stanbridge, 1861).

According to the population survey that was carried out in 2007-2009, the breeding cycle in the Ooldea region can occur earlier, from May to July (Ziembicki, 2009). In this case, mating, laying and hatching correspond to acronychal setting (AS) of Vega, and during the star's acronychal rise (AR) fledging takes place. It is likely that the actual breeding patterns around Ooldea are highly variable, and wetter years may be more typical of other regions as the population of bustards is transient and highly dependent on rainfall. Leaman et al. relied on data supplied by Ziembicki (2009) for this study as there was a lack of other reliable data.

Altair, the Crow Mother and Delphinus, her Chicks

The star Altair (α Aquilae) is Kangga Ngoonji, the mother crow, and the stars of the constellation Delphinus are her chicks Nyumbu. Kangga (or Kaanka) is the name for the Torresian crow (**Corvus orru**) (Reid et al., 1993). It is believed that this species is not likely to be the species referred to in the story of Bates, as it is not usually found south of the Birksgate Ranges, which are located to the north east of the Great Victoria Desert. The Little Crow (**Corvus bennetti**) is a species that is similar in appearance, and it is found in the area around Ooldea, and it is easy to mistake it for the Torresian Crow. Though Wangarangara, the Pitjantjatjara name is usually specific to this species, it is possible that around the time Bates was recording her story the name Kangga Ngoonji was used for it, especially if her informants were less particular about distinguishing between the 2. Another species with a similar appearance, the Australian Raven (**Corvus coronoides**) is also found around Ooldea. It's range is a thin stretch of land across the Nullarbor and in the desert regions of South Australia (Beruldsen, 2003).

The breeding season is similar for all 3, whichever species is referred to in the account by Bates, ranging from July to September, and the incubation period for the eggs is about 20 days. Within 45 days the chicks are fledged, though the mother continues feeding them for up to 4 months (Beruldsen, 2003).

The crows begin laying their eggs in late July, and at this time the acronychal rising (AR) of Altair occurs. The eggs are hatching by early August and the brighter group of stars in Delphinus (the chicks) rise at sunset (AR). Altair crosses the meridian in the sky after sunset (Mdusk) by October and most of the chicks have fledged by this time. Altair (mother crow) and Delphinus (celestial chicks) set at dusk (HS) in December, as the last of the chicks are starting to leave the nest. Leaman et al., suggest it is worth noting that Altair and Delphinus first set in the western sky at dawn (AS) during the very start of the breeding season in July, to reappear in the eastern sky at dusk (AR). The result of this is that there are 2 possible, and sequential, connections to indicate the start of the breeding season.

The Emu (Coalsack Nebula)

The head of Kalia the emu (**Dromaius novaehollandiae**) is the Coalsack Nebula, a dark absorption nebula bordering Crux, Centaurus and Musca resembling the profile of the head and beak of an emu. In December and January emu breeding pairs form, then in late April to Early May they begin mating, continuing through to June (Eastman, 1969). The emu lays a single egg every day until all are laid. It can take as much as much as 3 weeks to complete the clutch and the size of the clutch varies between 5 and 20 eggs. The eggs are incubated for 56 days (Eastman, 1969; Reid et al., 1993). The male emu raises the chicks for up to 7 months. The prime predator of emu chicks is the wedge-tailed emu (Reid et al., 1993), which Leaman et al. suggests may be another reason the Wedge-tailed Eagle is in Crux, which is adjacent to the celestial emu, which is its natural prey in both the celestial world and the terrestrial world.

The head of the emu's association with the Coalsack has been found throughout Australia (e.g., Cairns & Harney, 2003, Fuller et al., 2014a; Stanbridge, 1861; Wellard, 1983). In many Aboriginal traditions it is the head of the emu with its eye being represented by the star BZ Crucis ($m_v = 5.3$) Hamacher, 2012). The emu can been in profile stretching from the Coalsack to the centre of the Milky Way Galaxy in Scorpius, Ophiuchus and Sagittarius, the galactic bulge outlining the body of the emu. Similarly it was claimed by Bates (1904-1935: No. 25/308, p.13) that the "...long dark patch in the Milky Way ...[is the] emu father ..." in the traditions of another desert community. The criterion used for single celestial objects is not applicable, as the emu is traced out by a large part of the sky. Similarly, it was excluded by Leaman et al. from analysis for the study. However, they reiterated that the rising of the celestial emu at dusk is at the time of year when emus are breeding and egg-laying (e.g. see Fuller et al., 2014a).

The Black Cockatoo – Antares

Antares (α Scorpii), a red giant star, is Warrooboordina, the red-tailed black cockatoo (**Calyptorhynchus banksii**). The red-tailed black cockatoo is the only member of its genus, **Calyptorhynchus**, which is found in the Central Desert. These parrots occur through the Musgrave Ranges, near the northern extent of the country of the Anangu-Pitjantjatjara- yankunytjatjara (APY), though the range of its distribution does not extend as far as the Ooldean region, which lies about 480 km to the north, that Leaman et al. suggest may be because of the lack of mature River Red Gums along the major water ways, this particular tree being required for nesting sites by the red-tailed black cockatoo. A clue to why it is connected to the bright red star Antares is the red on the tail feathers of this cockatoo. They breed from March to September (Forshaw. 2002) incubating their eggs (Kurucz, 2000) for about 30 days. The inland subspecies **Calyptorhynchus banksii samueli** also breeds in March, though it has a peak in July (Higgins, 1999; Storr, 1977). Fledging occurs a median of 87th day from hatching, with the chicks being fed by both parents for a further 3-4 months after leaving the nest (Higgins, 1999).

The crossing of the meridian at dawn (Mdawn) of Antares coincides with the beginning of the breeding cycle and in early May the acronychal rising (AR) coincides with the first egg clutches hatching. Soon after the acronychal setting (AS) in mid-June the breeding cycle peaks. Antares crosses the meridian and is almost at the zenith after sunset (Mdusk) by mid-August, towards the end of the breeding season and the beginning of the fledging.

Another name for the red-tailed black cockatoo was Kogolongo in the traditions that were recorded by Bates, and was represented by the planet Mars. Leaman et al. suggests the red feathers in the birds' tail are almost certainly the connection of both objects to this bird. It is most likely that their relationship to each other is due to the ecliptic passing through Scorpius, and sometimes Mars comes to within a few degrees of Antares. This occurred 10 times in the evening sky between 1919 and 1935 in:

September 1922 (angular separation 2.7°)

March 1922 (5.4°)

July 1922 (2.4°)

February 1924 (4.9°)

January 1926 (4.7°)

December 1927 (4.4°)

December 1929 (4.2°)

November 1931 (3.9°)

October 1933 (3.8°)

September 1935 (3.1°)

It can be reasonably assumed that the red colour of Mars and Antares, as well as their occasional close approach, are the reasons for Antares and Mars both being associated with the red-tailed black cockatoo, though there is no clear time-stamp to indicate when Bates recorded the story.

The Owlet Nightjar (Canopus)

The star Canopus (α Carinae) is Joorr-Joorr, is the Australian owlet nightjar (**Aegotheles cristatus**), which occurs throughout the

Australian outback wherever there are tree hollows or rock crevices are present which are suitable for the birds to lay their eggs. According to Leaman et al. the name of the bird is onomatopoeic, mimicking the sound of one of its repertoire of nocturnal calls. This, as well as other calls that are commonly used by this species have been described as sounding similar to 'laughs' or 'chuckles' of humans (Higgins, 1999).

The owlet nightjar breeds mainly from October to January and it has an incubation period of 18-29 days, depending on temperature (Brigham & Geiser, 1997). By late October the chicks form the first clutch of eggs hatch and are fledged by about 1 month later. The birds also hibernate (torpor) from May to September (Brigham et al., 2000).

The crossing of the meridian at dawn (Mdawn) of Canopus in mid-October and acronychal rising (AR) occurs in late October, and Canopus is high in the sky at dawn, which coincides with the beginning of the breeding season. In the "Orion story" (Leaman & Hamacher, 2014) Joorr-Joorr observes Nyeeruna's attempts seduce and impress the 7 Mingari sisters, who are represented by the Pleiades, laughing at the Nyeeruna's humiliation by Kambugudha, represented by the Hyades. Most chicks are fledging by early December, and begin using the 'churring' adult call (Higgins, 1999), and Orion is rising at dusk. An increase in vocalisation overall is led to by a combination of fledglings calling and a seasonal spike in the vocal activity of the birds during the warmer nights of summer (Schodde & Mason, 1980). Leaman et al. suggest this may explain why Joorr-Joorr laughs at Nyeeruna in the "Orion Story" (Leaman & Hamacher, 2014).

The heliacal rise (HR) of Canopus occurs at the time the owlet Nightjar begins a period of torpor, which is another interesting celestial correspondence. During the onset of spring the lifecycle concludes, which coincides with the heliacal setting (HS) of Canopus.

The Dingo (Achernar)

The star Achernar (α Eridani) is Ngurunya, the mother dingo (**Canis lupus dingo**). The dingo breeding season generally begins in March in most parts of Australia and gestation lasts between 61 and 69 days

(Corbett, 1995), and the first litters are whelped from May to July (Catling et al., 1992). Dingoes have been observed with pups throughout the year (Purcell, 2010: 43), which suggests the breeding cycles are also likely to be influenced by seasonal availability of food resources due to the cycles of weather and climate, though in the Central Desert there is a distinct breeding peak in March,

In March the breeding season peaks which corresponds with the heliacal rising (HR) of Achernar in the southeast. The dingoes begin whelping by June, Achernar sets at dusk (HS) and at dawn the Pleiades rise at dawn (HR). The Pleiades kept a 'tribe of dingoes' with them to keep the men away, so dingoes are related to the Mingari women of the Pleiades (Bates, 1933). The helical rising of the Pleiades indicated the beginning of winter and the time for the Aborigines to start the harvest of the dingo pups among the Aboriginal cultures of the Central Desert e.g. Clarke, 2007/2008; Mountford, 1956; 1958).

The Thorny-Devil Lizard (Pleiades)

The Pleiades (M45 open star cluster) are Yugarilya, the 7 Mingari sisters. The sisters become frightened and transform into the thorny-devil lizard (Moloch horridus) as Nyeeruna (Orion) tries to seduce the sisters (Leaman & Hamacher, 2014). The thorny devil is their totem animal and plays a central role in the narrative.

The lizard, also known as the 'thorny dragon', is 20 cm long with conical spines and camouflaged skin (Browne-Cooper et al., 2007). The female lays a clutch of 10 eggs in a burrow about 30 cm deep between September and December (Pianka, 1997). After incubating for 3-4 months (ibid.), the hatchlings crawl out of their burrow.

The crossing of the meridian at dawn (Mdawn) of the Pleiades coincides with the beginning of egg-laying. The acronychal rising (AR) of the Pleiades 2 weeks prior to the emergence of the first clutch of lizards from their nests in early December, which is followed by the acronychal setting (AS) closer to the actual time of hatching, and the last hatchings taking place just before the helical setting (HS) in April.

The bustard is the most important predator of the thorny devil lizards (Pianka & {Pianka, 1970). Leaman suggests that this predator-prey relationship may be seen in the interaction between the counterparts in the sky: as Vega (the Bustard) disappears from view in the north west sky, the Pleiades (the thorny-devil) 'safely' emerge soon after in the north east. This scenario is similar to the Greek mythology portrayal of the eternal pursuit of Orion and Scorpius.

The Wedge-Tailed Eagle (Crux)

The 4 brightest stars of Crux are seen as resembling the footprint of Waljajinna, the eagle-hawk, or wedge-tailed eagle (**Aquila audax**), which is represented by the stars of the Southern Cross constellation (Crux). This association is present in the astronomical traditions of the Arrernte and Luritja communities in the Central Desert (e.g. Maegraith, 1932; Mountford, 1976).

The wedge-tailed eagle, one of the largest birds of prey in the world, is common across the Ooldean region. The breeding season begins in March to April and continues to September, though a majority of the eagles laid their eggs in July (Olsen, 1995; 2005), and the eggs are incubated for 45 days.

The number of eggs in a clutch is normally 2, though only 1 of these survives to fledge from the nest. The stronger chick usually out-competes the weaker sibling for food, and sometimes the weaker chick is killed by its stronger sibling, a phenomenon known as Cainism. On a worldwide basis, for eagles of the **Aquila** genus this is a common action (Olsen, 1995; Simmons, 1998). The weaker chick usually doesn't live longer than 20 days after hatching. Fledging rates vary between 75 and 95 days, depending on factors such as the availability of food and nest disturbance (Marchant & Higgins, 1993).

At dusk Crux is at its highest altitude in the sky (Mdusk), and α and γ Crucis cross the meridian at close to the same time in June, which coincides with the peak in breeding and laying. This also coincides with the time of the hatching of the first clutch of eggs that were laid in late March, at which time the siblicide process is usually complete, with the surviving chick on the way to fledging. The breeding peak then carries over to a hatching peak in mid- to late-August, which coincides with the heliacal rising (HR), and a fledging peak in mid- to late-November, just after the heliacal setting of Crux (HS).

The Redback Spider (Arcturus)

Arcturus (α Boötis), a red-orange star, is Kara, the redback spider (**Latrodectus hasseltii**). Though it was identified in some of Bates' records as the blue star Rigel (β Orionis), Leaman et al. suggest this was probably a transcription error in her notes (see Leaman &Hamacher, 2014) for justification for this conclusion).

Redback spiders, less common in desert regions, mate throughout the year. The breeding rate increases as the temperature rises, peaking in summer (Forster, 1995). Sexual activity of the redback spider has been shown by studies near Perth, Western Australia, to peak in late November (Andrade, 2003). The spiderlings may emerge from their egg sack in 11 days after the eggs were laid, though their emergence is also temperature dependent, and the time before they emerge may be increased by cooler temperatures.

The breeding cycle peak of redback spiders in late November result in the emergence from the egg sacs of the spiderlings in early- to mid-December, closely corresponding with to the heliacal rising (HR) of Arcturus.

Leaman, T.M., **Hamacher, D.W.**, and Carter, M. (2016). Aboriginal Astronomical traditions from Ooldea, South Australia, Part 2: Animals in the Ooldean Sky. Journal of Astronomical History and Heritage, Vol. 19(1), pp. 61-78.

Bora Ceremonial Grounds, South East Australia – Astronomical Orientations

It is indicated by ethnographic evidence that bora (initiation) ceremonial sites in south east Australia, which are typically comprised of a pair of circles connected by a pathway, are symbolically reflected in the Milky Way by the 'Sky Bora'. It is also indicated by this evidence that the time of year when the initiation ceremonies are to be held is signified by the 'Sky Bora'. Archaeological data was used to test the hypothesis that Bora grounds in south east Australia have a preferred orientation to the position of the Milky Way in the night sky in August, when the plane of the galaxy from Crux to Sagittarius is roughly vertical to the south west in the evening sky. This was accomplished by measuring the orientations of 68 bora grounds by the use of data from the archaeological literature and site cards in the New South Wales Aboriginal Heritage Information Management System database. The study found that there is a preferred orientation to the south and south west, which is consistent with the Sky Bora hypothesis. It was shown by Monte Carlo statistics that these preferences did not arise by chance alignments, but were deliberate.

Notice to Aboriginal and Torres Strait Islander Readers

This paper discusses bora ceremonies and contains the names of people who have passed away. The exact locations of these sites are concealed in order to protect them. The co-ordinates provided are within 10 km of the site and are used only to demonstrate the general distribution of known bora grounds in south east Australia.

In traditional Aboriginal cultures throughout Australia young males are taught the laws, customs and traditions of the community, undergoing a transition ceremony from boyhood to manhood. A 'rite-of-passage' event is often included in this ceremony, in which the initiated males undergo some form of body modification (Jacob, 1991), which in south east Australia typically involves tooth avulsion (e.g. Berndt, 1974: 27-30). There are many names for this ceremony, but it has come to be generally known as Bora' in Queensland (Qld) and New South Wales (NSW), the name used by the Kamilaroi whose country is in north-central New South Wales (Ridley, 1873: 269). Bora grounds are generally comprised of 2 circles of differing size, one large and the other small, that are connected by a pathway. The larger circle is the public space, and the smaller circle that is some distance from the larger circle is restricted to elders and initiates. When colonists first settled the Sydney region Bora ceremonies were one of the first Aboriginal cultural activities to be described by the early colonists (Collins, 1798: 468-480; Hunter, 1793: 499-500). In this discussion information about Bora ceremonies will be limited to the ceremony itself, because they are culturally sensitive ceremonies.

A variety of evidence in the anthropological literature (e.g. Berndt, 1974; Love, 1988; Winterbotham, 1957) indicates a connection between bora ceremonies and the Milky Way and that ceremonial grounds are oriented to the position of the Milky Way in the night sky at particular times of year.

In this paper Fuller et al. used ethnographic and ethnohistoric literature to explore connections between bora ceremonies and the Milky Way. They then used the archaeological record to determine if bora grounds are oriented to the position of the Milky Way at particular times of year. Monte Carlo statistics were used to find if these orientations were deliberate or resulted by chance.

Bora Ceremonial Ground

Across south east Australia the layout of bora grounds are similar, with only minor variations from region to region (Bowdler, 2001: 3; Mathews, 1894: 99). The grounds have been described as consisting of 2 rings of different sizes which are connected by a pathway in several reports (e.g. Black, 1944; Collins, 1798: 391; Fraser, 1883; Howitt, 1904; Mathews, 1897a). There are some places where bora sites where they have 3 or more rings (Steele, 1984; Bowdler, 2001). Each ring is bordered by raised earth or stone, and the area within these rings is cleared of debris and the earth is stamped until firm. The larger, public ring has a typical diameter of 20-30 m. The smaller, sacred ring, where body modifications take place, is generally 10-15 m across, and this is restricted to the initiates and elders. A pathway that ranges from a few 10s of metres to a few 100s of metres in length connected the 2 rings. An Aboriginal man from Marulan, New South Wales, stated in 2004 that the parts of many such sites were destroyed immediately after the ceremony to conceal their location (Hardie, 2004). This would explain why some of the reports of bora sites that were reported in the Archaeological literature feature only a single ring, the smaller one having been destroyed.

It has been found that bora grounds are distributed throughout south east Australia, covering most of New South Wales and southern Queensland, and may extend into South Australia (Howitt, 1904: 501-508) and northern Queensland (Roth, 1909). Near Sunbury, Victoria (Vic), ceremonial rings have been found which may be bora grounds, though there are no ethnographic records attesting to their use for ceremonies (Frankel, 1982). A western boundary for bora which runs from the mouth of the Murray River to the Gulf of

Carpentaria has been cited (Howitt, 1904: 512). It was noted by Mathews (1897b: 114) that the bora can be found across ¾ of New South Wales and for some distance into western Queensland, with a boundary that extended from Twofold Bay near Eden, NSW in the south, to Moulamein, NSW in the west, and Barringun, Queensland, to the north. The geographical area covered by this paper includes distinct language groups, each of whom may have a separate culture and traditions, and to aggregate the data from such a wide area may be misleading. However:

Some commonality in culture is implied by the existence of similarly constructed bora rings, and

Any preferred orientations arising from a single group will be diluted by aggregating orientations from a large geographic area, rather than forming a correlation of spurious significance.

The bora ceremonies were, according to Love (1988), held predominantly in August each year, though a variety of dates have been reported by other authors including March-May (Winterbotham, 1957), April-June (Mathews, 1894: 99), May-July (Mathews, 1894), August (Needham, 1891: 70), September-November (Winterbotham, 1957), and October-December (Mathews, 1894). It is indicated by this that in some cases, the date of the bora ceremony is influenced by a number of variables, including the availability of food and water or having a sufficient number of boys to be initiated (e.g. Mathews, 1910). Though these factors vary across the region, in this study the hypothesis proposed by Love (1988) has been tested, Love having presented evidence that the association of the bora ceremony with the night sky and the orientation of the Milky Way, suggesting that most initiation ceremonies occur around August.

Anthropological Support for an Astronomical Connection

It has been well established that the night sky plays a significant role in several Aboriginal cultures (e.g. Cairns & Harney, 2004; Johnson, 1998; Norris & Hamacher, 2009; Hamacher, 2012). Dark spaces within the Milky Way are as significant as bright objects in the Aboriginal astronomical traditions. There are 2 animals that symbolically link bora ceremonies with the dark spaces of the Milky Way. A spiritual serpent, the 'Rainbow Serpent' that was known across Australia was one of them, that was traced out by the curving dust lanes of the Milky Way. It has been explained (Needham, 1981: 69) that in the Hunter Valley among Aboriginal communities motifs of this spiritual serpent were represented in the bora ceremonies and during the ceremony information about the serpent was recounted. The emu was the other animal, which is also traced out in the dust lanes in the Milky Way (Norris & Norris, 2009). It has been argued (Love, 1988: 129-138) that in south east Australia the emu was an important part of the bora ceremony, as did Berndt (1974: 27-30), as male emus brood and hatch the emu chicks and rear the young (Love, 1987). This is symbolic of the initiation of young boys by the male elders.

An illustration of the night sky and the associated stars in local Aboriginal astronomical traditions was provided (Needham, 1981). Altair, as the 'All Father', is cited in this illustration, which provides the positions of the celestial objects in August, the month during which the Aboriginal initiation ceremonies were held (Needham, 1981: 70). In August the Milky Way stretches across the sky from north east to north west in the early part of the night sky. An Aboriginal religion that was based on a deity that was variously described as Baiame, Bunjil or Mungan-ngaua (Henderson, 1832: 147; Howitt, 1904: 490-491; Ridley, 1873: 268) was referred to in many early reports. These names translate roughly as 'father' or 'father of all of us' (Howitt, 1904: 268). Baiame gave his son, Daramulan, to the people and it is through Daramulan that Baiame sees all, according to Frazer (1883: 208) and (Howitt, 1884:458). At the bora ceremony Daramulan is worshipped (Ridley, 1873:269) and Daramulan is believed to come back to Earth by a pathway from the sky (Fraser, 1883:212). It was reported (Eliade (1996:41) that Baiame 'dwells in the sky, beside a great stream of water' (i.e. the Milky Way), and there are various reports (e.g. Berndt, 1974; Hartland, 1898; Howitt, 1884) that Baiame's wife, or in some cases Daramulan) is an emu. There are reports from various cultures across south east Australia of Daramulan, Bunjil and Baiame, which result in variations of these reports. They share some features, however, such a close connection between bora ceremonies and the Milky Way.

Hypothesis testing

In order to focus the discussion, the study was concentrated specifically on the hypothesis that had been advanced by Love (1987, 1988), his argument being that bora ceremonies were held in the Milky Way, referred to as the 'Sky Bora', by the ancestral spirits in the heavens. The work of Love was based, in part, on another author (Winterbotham, 1957), who obtained information from a Jinibara man from south east Queensland. Bora circles, according to Winterbotham (1857:38), were always oriented towards points on the compass, with the larger circle to the north and the smaller one to the south. In this rule they conformed to the position of 2 dark (black) spaces (circles) – the Coal Sacks in the sky.

According to Love (1988:130-131), the Sky Bora was identified by the Jinibara account with the Emu in the Sky (Gaiarbau et al., 1982:77; Winterbotham 1957:46). The 'Coal Sacks' or Mimburi, which were referred to, are a dark absorption nebula that borders the western constellations Crux (Southern Cross), Centaurus and Musca, which represents the head of the emu, with the eye being represented by the star BZ Crucis. The neck is represented by the dust lanes running through the stars Alpha and Beta Centauri, and the galactic bulge, which is near the intersection of Sagittarius, Scorpius and Ophiuchus, represents the body. This area is the centre of the Milky Way galaxy. The legs are traced out by the dust lanes along the Milky Way through Sagittarius. The motif of the celestial emu is present across Australia (e.g. Cairns & Harney, 2004; Norris & Hamacher, 2009:13; Stanbridge, 1861:302; Wellard, 1983:51).

According to Winterbotham the dark nebulae were also known by other Aboriginal groups, such as the Badjala people of Fraser Island and the adjacent mainland, who knew them as Wurubilum, and the Wakka Wakka people near Murgon, Queensland. This concept was not restricted to south east Australia. It has been explained (e.g. Smith, 1913) that the initiate is left tied to the ground until the Milky Way is visible during an initiation ceremony in Western Australia. When the Milky Way is visible the initiate is asked if he can see the 2 dark spots, and he is released when he can see them. Fuller et al. suggest that though this account is not from the area where the study was carried out it may be similar to the example that Gaiarbau described.

According to Gaiarbau the bora ceremonies were only held when the celestial bora rings returned to their 'proper points of the compass' (Winterbotham, 1957:38). In south east Australia the Milky Way is visible in the clear winter sky about an hour after sunset. As seen from south east Australia an hour after sunset, the orientation of the plane of the Milky Way changes from near vertical in the south-south east in March to horizontal across the southern sky from east-south east to west in June and back to vertical (but inverted) in the south west in September. The Galactic bulge and the Coalsack (celestial emu) cannot be seen together in the sky (perpendicular to the horizon), but stretches from south to east.

In August an hour after sunset is the only time the Sky Bora can be seen in the sky together vertically aligned to the horizon, or later in the night as the year progresses. The Galactic plane, stretching straight through the celestial emu, is vertical 1 or 2 hours after sunset in August, and later in the month this occurs later in the evening. The azimuth is about 213° (south-south west) at this time.

It is expected that the orientation of each bora site, from the larger circle to the smaller circle, would be oriented to about 213°, if the hypothesis of Love is correct, which corresponds to the time the ceremonies are held in August. It was claimed (Needham, 1981:70) that in the Hunter Valley (NSW) the bora ceremonies were held in August, which is a time when the Milky Way was vertical in the south-south west, which agrees with the expectation.

It has been reported by other researchers that bora ceremonies in Queensland and New South Wales are held at various times of the year, as noted previously (Winterbotham, 1957; Mathews, 1824:99). According to Fuller et al. bora ceremonies could be held at times of the year that have little or no connection with the position in the sky of the Milky Way, even if the ceremonies are linked symbolically to the Milky Way. It has been claimed (e.g. Mathews, 1894:128) that the direction of one bora ring to the other depends entirely on the conformation of the country in which the ceremony is being held. It is expected that there would be a roughly uniform distribution of the orientations if the bora grounds are not oriented to any particular object or direction. If at least some bora grounds are oriented to the position of the Sky Bora it would be expected that a preference would be found for south-south west orientations when overall distribution of bora grounds examined at.

Conclusion

It was shown by this study that there is a preferred orientation to southerly directions for the bora grounds that were studied, and these orientations are not the result of chance, but were deliberate. It is not known for sure why this is so, though it is consistent with the Love hypothesis that there is a preferred orientation for bora ceremonial grounds in south east Australia to the celestial emu in the Milky Way in the south-south-westerly sky. During the month of August the celestial emu is in this position in the sky in the evening, the time during which it has been claimed (Winterbotham, 1957; Needham, 1981) that the bora ceremonies were held. It has been shown (Hamacher et al., 2012) that linear stone arrangements in New South Wales also have a preferred orientation to the cardinal points, especially north-south orientations. Many stone arrangements are ceremonial sites, which lends support to the claim that orientation is an important factor to Aboriginal people when they were laying out ceremonial sites.

Though the Love hypothesis is supported by the analysis by Fuller et al. it is not definitive evidence of the bora grounds being oriented to the Sky Bora. It has been stated by some researchers, such as (Winterbotham, 1957; Mathews, 1894) that across Queensland and New South Wales many bora ceremonies were held at various times throughout the year, which do not correspond to any particular orientation of the Milky Way. There is, however, strong evidence from ethnography that the Milky Way is associated with the bora ceremony and it is considered likely by Fuller et al. that some ceremonies were timed, and the sites of bora grounds oriented, so that the vertical Milky Way was visible above the path connecting the 2 circles during bora ceremonies. Fuller et al. say that to understand these links additional research is necessary and they are engaged in such research projects exploring this.

Fuller, R.S.; **Hamacher, D.W.,** and Norris, R.P. (2013). Astronomical orientations of Bora ceremonial grounds in south east Australia. *Australian Archaeology*, No. 77, pp. 30-37.

Australian Aboriginal Astronomy – Wurdi Youang – a Stone Arrangement with Possible Solar Indications

Wurdi Youang is an Aboriginal stone arrangement in Victoria, Australia, that is in the shape of an egg. This paper presents the results of a new survey of the site which show that the major axis aligns to within a few degrees of east-west. The survey confirms a previous hypothesis that it aligns with the position of the setting Sun on the horizon at the equinox and the solstices, and also shows that 2 independent sets of indicators align with these directions. It is shown that these alignments are not likely to have arisen by chance, and that the stone arrangement builders appear to have deliberately aligned the site on positions that are astronomically significant.

Aboriginal Astronomy

It has been well established that in many Australian Aboriginal cultures the night sky plays an important role (Stanbridge, 1861; Mountford, 1956; Haynes, 1992; Johnson, 1998; Cairns & Harney, 2003; Norris & Norris, 2009; Norris & Hamacher, 2009, 2011). The sky is used to regulate calendars, and mark the time of year when particular foods become available, as well as being associated with traditional songs and ceremonies. There were also practical applications of the sky in navigation and time keeping (Cairns & Harney, 2003; Clarke, 1997), and there is also some evidence for meaning in astronomical phenomena, e.g. eclipses, the motion of the planets and tides (Norris & Hamacher, 2009). In ceremonies and artefacts, such as the Morning Star pole used in Yolngu ceremony (Norris & Norris, 2009; Allen, 1975), and in depictions in bark paintings of constellations such as Scorpius (ibid.), astronomical themes are also widespread. It is not well-established if any measurements were ever made of the positions of the celestial bodies, also if there is any reference in the ethnographic literature to the solstices or equinoxes.

Norris et al. suggest it is not wise to assume similarities between the approximately 400 different Aboriginal cultures in Australia, though it is important to acknowledge that there are some similarities in some cases. E.g. the association of Orion and a young man, or a group of males, and the association of the Pleiades with a group of girls, are present in many Aboriginal cultures across Australia. In this paper the focus is entirely on the Wurdi Youang Stone Arrangement, the Wathaurong people, and similarities with any other Aboriginal cultures are not assumed, though we refer to them to set the context.

Stone Arrangements

Several Aboriginal cultures across Australia constructed stone circles that were of many different morphologies, such as circles, lines, pathways, standing stones, and cairns (Enright, 1937; Towle, 1939; Palmer, 1977; Lane & Fullagar, 1980; Frankel, 1982; Attenbrow, 2002). Some of the arrangements are believed to have had practical purposes; such as fish traps, land boundaries, while others had ceremonial purposes, such as initiation, or burial. Stone artefacts are often found associated with stone arrangements, such as rock engravings, scarred trees, and axe grinding grooves (e.g. Lane & Fullagar, 1980; Lane, 2009).

Stone arrangements vary in size from 1 m to 100 m, and local rocks are typically used in their construction, and are small enough to be carried by 1 or 2 people, though larger rocks are occasionally found that weigh up to 500 kg (Lane & Fullagar, 1980; Long & Schell, 1999). Ceremonial stone arrangements are commonly located on ridges and hill tops that have a panoramic view of the surrounding landscape (Hamacher et al., 2012). It has been suggested (McCarthy, 1940) that the surrounding landscapes were incorporated into the stone arrangements that were used for ceremonial purposes, and that they may indicate the direction of a landmark, or mimic a land feature.

According to Norris et al. there are 30 stone arrangements that have been recorded in Victoria (Marshall & Webb, 1999), though more are known to Norris et al. and it is claimed (Lane, 2009) that there are actually hundreds in western Victoria. There are no known ethnographic records or oral histories about these arrangements, and Norris et al. suggest this may be because they are considered to be sacred and secret to Aboriginal communities.

Wurdi Youang

The Wurdi Youang stone arrangement is also known as the Mount Rothwell Archaeological Site. It is located between Melbourne and Geelong, near the small town of Little River, and in 1977 it was declared a protected site by the Victorian Archaeological Survey (AAV Site No. 7922-001). The Wathaurong people, known also as the Wada Wurrung, are the traditional owners, their land extending to the west from the Werribee River to Fiery Creek beyond Shipton, and northwards from the south coast to the watershed of the Great Dividing Range north of Ballarat. The precise location is not given in this paper to protect the site, though access may be granted after gaining the permission from the traditional owners via Aboriginal Affairs Victoria.

Wurdi Youang consists of about 100 basalt stones that are roughly egg-shaped, about 50 m across along the major axis, which is aligned east-west. The stones are of a range of sizes from small rocks about

0.2 m in diameter to standing stones up to 0.75 m high, some of which appear to be supported by trigger stones. It has been estimated (Lane & Fullagar) the combined mass of the stones to be about 23 tonnes. They don't appear to be part of the bedrock, so potentially moveable.

A group of 3 large stones, about 0.6m high, are particularly prominent at the western end of the stone arrangement. These stones are at the highest point of the stone arrangement, the land on which it is built sloping downwards from the western end to the eastern end, a total fall across the arrangement of about 4 m.

There are no known eyewitness record of the construction of the stone arrangement or use by the Wathaurong people, the site is considered to have been constructed by Aboriginal people for the following reasons (Aboriginal Affairs Victoria 2003):

There are similar stone arrangements that are known of in Victoria, though none are known that resemble exactly Wurdi Youang (e.g. Massola, 1963);

The arrangement is on a property owned by a single family since the area was first settled, and a European origin of the arrangement is ruled out by family tradition (Lane & Fullagar (Fullagar?, 1980);

There are no known counterparts of the arrangements among colonial structures: it is located on rocky ground of no known agricultural or commercial value, it would not have been suitable for defining the boundaries of a sheep dip, sheep pen, or cattle dip, and evidence does not exist that it ever formed part of a fence or building (Lane & Fullagar, 1980);

Among the Wathaurong owners there is traditional knowledge regarding the sanctuary of the site (Marshall & Webb, 1999).

Also, the Wathaurong owners have found aboriginal artefacts on the site.

It is not known when it was constructed. It is believed the Aboriginal people have occupied the area from about 25,000 BCE (Clark, 1990) to 1835 when they were displaced by European settlers (Clark, 1995). The name "Wurdi" has been suggested (Morieson, 1994) to mean "plenty of people", and Youang means "bald" or "mountain", which has been presumed to relate to the nearby mountain range that was called "You Yangs". It has been suggested (Morieson, 2003) that the name "Wurdi" may be related to a word from the Woiwurrung "Wurding" which means abalone, which refers to the shape of the stone arrangement possibly being in the shape of an abalone shell, or possibly another mollusc, in which case the site may possibly have been used for increase rituals. These suggestions may, however, be weighed against the distance of 18 km between the site and Port Phillip Bay, where abalone could be found, the nearest major body of salt water.

Around the Wurdi Youang the vegetation is low and scrubby at the present, though it may have been much higher prior to European occupation, possibly even obscuring the view of the setting Sun. Norris et al. also note the common practice among Aboriginal people around the continent of clearing the land by fire periodically when necessary, as part of the standard Aboriginal land management practices (Clark, 2007; Gammage, 2011), so Norris et al. say it is equally possible that the vegetation was removed. They also suggest any such growth would need to have been cleared in those directions if this site was used to observe the position of the setting Sun.

The Morieson Hypothesis
It was suggested (Morieson, 2003) that 3 small outlying stones, the "outliers", indicated the position of the setting Sun at solstices and equinoxes when they were viewed from 3 prominent stones at the western apex. The Morieson hypothesis is specifically that the outliers were placed deliberately in their locations to indicate the position on the horizon of the Setting Sun at the equinoxes and solstices. The primary aim of this paper is to test the Morieson hypothesis.

There are significant differences between the results of the only 2 surveys of this site that were available, which suggests that at least 1 of them was seriously flawed, in spite of the potential importance of this site to knowledge of pre-contact Aboriginal culture. Also, the outliers that were proposed by Morieson were not included in either survey, so a new survey was required to test the Morieson hypothesis. There is also a previous survey that Norris et al. were made aware of after the new survey was completed.

Secular Changes in the Sky

Relative to the stars, the Earth's axis of rotation processes in a complete circle of 23.5° radius over a period of about 26,000 years. This motion, the 'precession of the equinoxes' causes the apparent position of the stars to move by 1° every 72 years from the viewpoint of the observer. The position of the stars would be significantly different from the present if the site had been used thousands of years ago. Therefore the position of the setting of a star on the horizon changes relatively rapidly over time, and a stellar alignment from 2,000 years ago could differ from that of the present by almost 30°.

Also, stars move relative to their neighbours as they are not stationary. This effect, 'stellar proper motion', results in the apparent position of the stars shifting relative to each other over time. An example is the Southern Cross, which would have looked significantly different 10,000 years ago.

The declinations of the Sun and Moon, and therefore their positions of rising and setting, are not affected by precession. The apparent declination of the Sun is, however, affected by a much smaller effect, the 'nutation' in the obliquity of the rotational axis of the Earth, which varies by about 2.4° over a period of 41,000 years. Such variations will have no measureable effect on these alignments, because the alignments that are discussed in this paper are accurate to a few degrees.

The date of construction of the stone arrangement has no measurable effect on the rising and setting positions of the Sun.

The aim of this paper was to test the Morieson hypothesis.

A simulation was run 10,000 times and the results imply that the likelihood of the Wurdi Youang stone arrangement occurring by chance is 0.25 %. Norris et al. say they recognise that this is not a precise calculation, and that their simple approximation to the site geometry introduces the possibility of bias, though this process nevertheless provides a rough estimate of the likelihood that the alignments are produced by chance alone.

They concluded therefore that it is extremely unlikely that the outlier stones happen to indicate the astronomical alignments by chance, and that the alignments were almost certainly deliberate human constructions to indicate the equinoxes and solstices.

Newly Identified Alignments

Another prominent alignment, as well as the Morieson hypothesis, is the major axis of the stone arrangement, which lies roughly on the east-west axis. A prominent viewing position would be either the centre of the stone arrangement or the eastern apex, which is the lowest part of the arrangement. Roughly the same place on the horizon is indicated by both these viewing points, which is due west of the site, or the setting of the equinoctial Sun.

According to Norris et al. it is important to consider if there are any prominent alignments at the site. There are 2 straight sections to the east of the ring that are included in the egg-shape of the stone ring which also constitute prominent alignments. Norris et al. consider that these prominent alignments in the stone ring would also be chosen as the only prominent alignments by an unbiased observer, whether they look at the plan or visiting the actual site. Only the western-facing direction of the alignment is considered in each case, as the site was built on a slope rising to the west, so the westerly lines point to the horizon, while the easterly counterparts point down into the valley. There is a relatively straight section in each case, the precise direction being poorly defined, as it depends on the choice of stones to be included (e.g. in a least squares fit) and as a result of damaged stones. The direction of each straight section is, however, roughly parallel to the Morieson alignments, when the directions of the equinox and the solstices are superimposed on the ring and on the Morieson alignments.

The Gap is at an azimuth of 272° and an elevation of 2°, from a viewing height of 1.6 m, from the eastern vertex of the stone arrangement, as defined by the intersection of straight lines (Norris, Norris & Hamacher 2013, Fig. 8). There the Sun would set at equinox directly behind the 3 prominent stones at the western apex of the arrangement, when viewed from the vertex, and would be visible briefly through the Gap before setting, which would be dependant of the exact position and height of the viewer. Norris et al. point out that these directions are not adjusted to fit the ring, being defined astronomically. The diagram in (Norris, Norris & Hamacher 2013, Fig. 8) shows that the straight sections of the ring are well aligned to the astronomical directions as the Morieson alignments, though the straight lines are not well defined, and not exactly straight.

If the outliers are included as prominent alignments, and the viewing position is the same as Morieson, Norris et al. consider that there are 7 prominent alignments:

The 3 noted by Morieson,

A 4th over the new outlier,

The major axis of the ring, and

The 2 sections of the ring that are almost straight.

Conclusion

The Morieson hypothesis that the position of the setting Sun at the solstices and equinoxes is supported by this detailed survey of Wurdi Youang. The likelihood of this occurring by chance was shown by statistical analysis to be extremely low. Also, the straight sides of the arrangement were found to indicate the solstices, and the point where the Sun sets at equinox is marked by the 3 prominent stones at the western apex of the arrangement, when viewed from the eastern apex.

In this paper there are no assumptions made concerning the viewing position, as the aim of the study is to test a specific hypothesis that has been made about viewing position. The many other possible sight-lines have been tested by Monte-Carlo analysis. It has been shown that the viewing position and the orientations suggested by Morieson are significant, and are not likely to have arisen by chance.

The age or purpose of the stone arrangement is not known, though it can be said with reasonable confidence that these alignments were intentional, while Norris et al. are careful not to claim that this is an "Aboriginal observatory", as there are no known ethnographic or oral histories that explain the purpose or use of the sight. There are plans for further research to determine age of the site, as well as to search for similar sites elsewhere.

Norris, R.P.; Norris, P.M.; **Hamacher, D.W.**, and Abrahams, R. (2013). Wurdi Youang: an Australian Aboriginal stone arrangement with possible solar indications. *Rock Art Research*, Vol. 30(1), pp. 55-65.

The climate in Aboriginal Australia - Yarralin

Yarralin (Walangeri) is an aboriginal community 382 km south west of Katherine in the Northern Territory, 16 km west of the Victoria River Downs cattle station on the banks of the Wickham River. It is not far from the Victoria and Humbert Rivers, the Gregory national Park and Jasper Gorge.

In the book, Windows on Meteorology, Australian Perspective, Deborah Rose reports some insights into the holistic and systemic nature of the understanding of the natural world held by the Aboriginal people during conversations at the site she studied, Yarralin on the Wickham River, 15 km upstream from the Victoria River Downs cattle station. For the Aboriginal people the meteorological systems are the result of the interactions of many parts of their natural environment, and they include humans in that interconnected system. See Jones (1985), Rose (1987) and Stevenson (1985).

As with other cultures, the Aboriginal people have based understanding of the climate on detailed observations through time and assumptions regarding how knowledge is acquired and the ideas resulting are accepted as true. July is the coldest month at Yarralin, at this time of year the daily temperatures range from about 11° C at night to about 29° C during the day. The country is very desiccated by the end of the dry season, in about October or November, the major water bodies being the only water sources that haven't dried up, and the ground is dry and cracked, with sparse dry vegetation.

Sometime from October to December the build up to the wet season is characterised by humid heat. It is a time when there is often a build-up of clouds and violent thunderstorms, though not always with rain, often only dust is stirred up. The winds are erratic and turbulent at this time, often occurring with short storms. The actual times when the seasons change varies from year to year, the wet season usually beginning in about January and lasting until about April.

At this time of year turtles form a large part of the diet of the people. Also at this time the monsoonal rains occur, sometimes at a number of times throughout the Wet, though not all the time, and the actual amount of monsoonal rain can vary greatly from flood-causing rain to no monsoonal rain at all in the Wet. The result is that the season can vary, from comparatively dry to flooding, from year to year. The median annual rainfall at Yarralin is about 600 mm. The temperatures are usually about 41-42° C, or possibly a bit higher, between about October and February, with high humidity. The result is that the area has been estimated to be the area with most heat stress to humans in all of Australia (Lee, 1969).

At Yarralin the people divide the year into seasons that accord roughly with the Wet and the Dry that are normally used for this part of the country. The Dry is known as the 'cold time', makaru, 'cold'. In the season of the build-up they have a season called ngarap that translates as 'more hot and hot'. The mayiyul is the Wet season, the name is believed to refer to the relationship between rain and plant growth.

To the people at Yarralin the weather is made by 2 of the Beings from the Dreamtime, the Sun, who was also the source of heat and light, though he had human form at that time, and the Rainbow (Rainbow Snake, Rainbow Serpent, Great Serpent) was associated with rain. The many Rainbow Snakes, that are usually inhabitants of waterholes, are referred to collectively as Rainbow.

The people of Yarralin apparently regard the Sun as predictable, unlike the unpredictable rain and wind, that they take more interest in as these interfere with sunshine. They refer to the rain by a number of terms, one for rain in general, yipu, as well as terms for different types of rain, rain in cold weather, rain in hot weather, the first rain after the very hot time of year, and the smell of the first rain. They also differentiate different colours of rain associated with matrilineal defined people. Conceptually, rain is associated with all water, differently coloured rains being linked to different coloured river water. The Rainbow Snake is responsible for both different coloured rains in changes in the colour of river water. The Rainbow Snake embodies the interconnected, complex ideas about water.

Rain occurs when the Rainbow Snake receives messages from a number of animals such as flying foxes. During the Cold Time, the Dry Season, they feed on the nectar of a number of species of trees, such as **Eucalyptus terminalia** and **E. confertifolia** in the bush, moving to roots in pandanus along the rivers when the flowers dry up. This tells the Rainbow Serpent that the land is getting hot, which means the vegetation is drying and food is becoming scarce in the country. On hearing this news he rises high into the sky and releases thunder, lighting and rain. At this time tadpoles hatch and frogs call to the Rainbow Snake to send down more rain. The Yarralin people told Rose that when the first rain falls the moisture rises to the sky to make more rain, and as the clouds form, the Rainbow Snake walks the sky at this time, more clouds forming from the ascending moisture for it to walk on.

The people believe that in bad years when the rain fails it is because someone has done something that broke the chain of messages that took the message of the hot, dry conditions to the Rainbow Snake, so he doesn't known to bring rain. It is believed that the tribes to the west have some control over the amount of rain received at Yarralin, the western people being able to 'hold back the rain'. If the people at Yarralin decide the lack of rain is caused by the westerners, they take their own measures to bring on the rain, usually making use of calcite crystals, 'rain stones', as well as songs. These actions are only a last resort, as they believe the laws governing the weather system were designed to benefit all living things. It is only after long deliberation by the elders that an attempt to interfere with the natural system is made.

The wet season usually lasts until about March or April, by which time the watercourses and waterholes are filled and the vegetation is sprouting. If the rain continues too long there is a danger of flooding, possibly on a large scale, bringing the possibility of disaster. When the country is saturated the west wind usually realises there has been enough rain and breaks the back of the Rainbow Serpent, that then returns to the waterhole and the wind switches to an easterly wind, and the sun returns to prominence in the sky, no longer blocked by clouds. If the rain continues and it is decided assistance is required to get the system back in balance, the wind and sun are invoked by special songs and actions to bring about the end of the rain until the proper time for them to return.

In the culture of the people at Yarralin the basis for the cycles of the weather involves behaviour of the animals, plant growth cycles, and all the other elements of the Earth and atmosphere, including humans. They believed that each part of the system must be balanced by the other parts for life to continue and flourish.

In their daily lives they knew from animal behaviour when the time was right to collect particular types of food. An example is crocodile eggs, that are not always laid at a particular time, all that can be said according to the western calendar is that they are laid at some time between late August and late September, maybe. At Yarralin it is known that the crocodile eggs are ready to be collected when the march flies begin biting.

The daily life of most Aboriginal people throughout the continent has been described by some anthropologists as 'original affluence', a term that applies to most hunter gatherers (Sahlins, 1972). Materials for tools were easily available, and those that were not found nearby could be obtained by trade, often from long distances away. They ate a wide variety of food that was healthy and nutritious and was available in sufficient quantities, often because of their intimate knowledge of their environment and the behaviour of all the plants and animals, especially their prey species. Captain Cook commented on their diet, saying they ate healthier food than many in Europe at the time. Their knowledge of the animals in their environment extended to the feeding and breeding behaviour, when and where they drank, even their reproductive systems, and when the different foods were available, which also applied to plants. Their long-term survival in such a challenging country, in such a wide variety of climatic conditions, was largely based on knowledge. A veritable knowledge-based society.

In the absence of writing, this accumulated knowledge was passed down the generations in the form of songs and dances, as well as their mythology in which the knowledge for survival was given more significance by being associated with various beings from the Dreamtime. Mostly it was passed on in the everyday life of the people, the young learning the skills of hunting, fishing, tool-making, etc., from the adults as they went about their daily business, with as much instruction as was required from the people who carried out the various tasks. All Aboriginal people of Australia were aware of the necessity of allowing breeding populations of animals to remain, and they tried to assist this reproduction by performing rituals at special 'increase sites'. These rituals were carried out to assist increase the numbers of the plants and animals they depended on.

According to Rose (1997), as well as the connection between march flies and crocodile eggs, there were many other 'messages' their knowledge of their environment allowed them to pick up, such as :

The falling of flowers of the jangarla tree into water told them the barramundi were biting;

green flies arrive - certain species of figs are ripe;

cicadas are singing - turtles are getting fat;

brolgas return - the dark catfish become active and the river will soon flow again.

They also had knowledge of the connection between the various constellations in the night sky and the activities of their food species. They could tell from the position of the Pleiades when dingo pups were born, the coldest time of the year, so know when they would mature.

Among the Yarralin people the Earth, the atmosphere and all living things, as well as the weather and climate with their variations, are part of a single living system that must be kept in balance. This knowledge gained through close observation over long periods of time, and the use of intelligence to make the connections between the various aspects of the system, was probably the basis of their use of the environment in a symbiotic way rather than a disruptive way, as has happened in Australia since they were displaced.

Tropical North

A brief study at Milingimbi was the basis of seasonal calendars across northern Australia.

Throughout the tropical north of Australia there are 6 major seasons that are generally recognised by the aboriginal people of the area, with minor transitional seasons at the turnover between the main seasons. The major seasonal divisions apply across the coastal and near coastal areas of the north. Differences in latitude are the main reason for timing of the successive seasons, though the timing differences are only slight.

The main seasons correspond roughly to the western calendar used by non-Aboriginal Australia.

Dhululdur - the pre-wet season - October to November

Barra'mirri - the growth season - December to January

Mayaltha - the flowering season - February to March

Midawarr - the fruiting season, this includes March - April

   Ngathangamakulingamirri - the 2-week harvest season in April

Dharratharramirri - the early dry season. It includes - May to July

   Burrugumirri - sharks & stingrays give birth - July to August

Rarrandharr - the main dry season - August to October

The seasons were documented in the area of the Arnhem Land coast (Stephen Davis in Webb, 1997, Fig. 5.1)

As with the people at Yarralin, the people of the north regard the environment as an integrated whole, incorporating all components, including humans. Among the Yolngu of northern Arnhem Land the thunder of the wet season is the voice of the giant Rainbow Snakes speaking among themselves. Lightning is spat out by one of these Snakes when he raises himself high above his waterhole when he is disturbed by humans.

The large-scale features of the tropical weather systems have been integrated into the cultures of Northern Australia, being seen as signs of the changeover between the seasons.

Along with the change to the following season comes not only changes in climatic conditions, but a new suite of flora and fauna. Seasonal changes are heralded by changed direction of prevailing winds, the names of some seasons being taken from the name of the prevailing wind at that time. The growth season, from December to January, takes the name Barra'mirri, Barra meaning ' north west monsoon' and the possessive suffix mirri - the season possessing the North West monsoon.

The growth and flowering of certain plants, as well as animal behaviour, tells the Yolngu the season is changing. They also know from the first appearance and movement of particular stars, planets and constellations that the season is about to change. The Yolngu recognise the 3 stars in Orion's belt as 3 men, Birrupirru, Djandurrngala and Ngurruwilpil paddling a bark canoe across the sky. Collectively they are known as the constellation of Djulpun. When Djulpun appears in the western sky the storms knock down the dry grass in the early dry season. The Yolngu begin burning the grass that remained following the main burning in the early dry season when Djulpun rises in the east in the night sky. It is the time to hunt goannas, wallabies and bandicoots, as they are fat and in good condition at this time.

In the pre-wet season, the 'male' thunder that is heard rumbling in the distance in the afternoons was believed to shrink waterholes. The clouds begin to build, building more each day, and the weather becomes hot and humid.

The night sky is well known to the Yolngu, they have myths associated with many constellations. When a shooting star is seen to fall in the 'wrong direction' it portends a death, possibly of a close relative. At night the coastal Aboriginal groups navigate at sea by the constellations as well as by sea wave patterns and wave swell. During the day they navigate by using the columns of cumulus clouds, as well as wind and wave direction.

On Bathurst and Melville Islands the Tiwi divide the year into 6 main seasons, the names being based on the type of rain most characteristic of each season.

Jamutakari - the wet season is made up of 3 main seasons

Wirriwinari - the dry season - is made up of 2 main seasons

The early dry is when cold weather and early morning fogs appear. Large-scale burning is carried out in the main part of the dry season.

Tiyari - the pre-wet season - the 6th season. Humidity increases and thunder storms build at this time. As the seasons change the main food sources change, travel is aided and the people know when various ceremonies are to be held.

To the south of the tropical coastal regions, in the arid regions to the south of the monsoonal belt, the plants and animals are more widely scattered and fewer in number, and the people are also fewer, the groups being widely scattered, needing a much larger area to find enough food. In the arid parts there are fewer changes of season. Among the Warlpiri of the Tanami Desert 3 main seasons are distinguished.

Another group from the arid zone, the Anmatjerre of central Australia, also have 3 seasons. This group divide the year up according to seasons based on rainfall, wind direction and temperature.

Utunakindja - early summer rain - plants flower, winds are from the north. The mid-summer rains come late in the season and wild fruits grow.

Alurrpakurla - the last rains with the south wind as winter approaches

Alurrpanda - the time of cold winter rain

Unlike in the tropical north there are no known transitional seasons recognised by the people of the arid zone, though there are some brief seasons within the main seasons.

Central Australia

Unlike just about anywhere else on Earth, the arid zone of central Australia does not have truly cyclical seasons, or even in a predictable sequence. Sometimes a season may simply not occur in a given year. They are more like recognisable patterns that usually recur at irregular intervals, (Robert Hoogenraad & George Jampilinpa Robertson in Webb, 1997).

In a region with such an irregular and unpredictable climate it was more important than in most places for the Aboriginal people of this arid area to have a thorough knowledge of the indicators of approaching seasonal changes, as such changes bring with them changes in the amount and type of food available and the availability of water.

The indicators they watched for included temperature, the direction and type of prevailing winds, the type of the cloud formations and the direction they were coming from, day length, the direction in which the sun rose and set and the position and movements of the constellations and planets. Changes in animal behaviour, such as when goannas hibernated, and the flowering of particular plants was also of use in knowing the type of conditions they should be preparing for.

The calendar used by the Warlpiri had the following seasons

Uterne - hot season - summer

Uterne urle - hot season forehead - early summer

Alhwerrpe - cold season - winter

Alhwerrpe urle - cold season forehead - early winter

Ulpulpe - seasons after rains, when plants flower and seeds grow - spring

See Fig. 6.2 Webb, 1997). Because of the erratic nature of the climate of the arid zone the people of the area regard the calendar that was designed for teaching purposes as a general guide, in the real world the seasons cannot be so easily ordered.

Over the 60,000 years, or maybe longer, that the aboriginal people have occupied Australia they accumulated enough knowledge of the erratic climate and the unusual biota to survive sustainably up to the present. A much better record than the agriculturally superior people who took over 200 years ago, and who continue to degrade what little productive land there is on such an arid, soil-impoverished, salt-encrusted continent, of which deserts cover more than half, and desert sand dunes are still expanding. And this knowledge was passed on without writing, in the form of mythology and songs, an oral history into which was incorporated the knowledge of how to survive in the most extreme environments in a land of extremes. Their mostly strict adherence to their traditions in everyday life has been criticised as being conservative and unchanging, but the climate over much of Australia is such that straying from 'the way things have always been done' could be fatal.

Indigenous weather knowledge

William Blandowski

Also known as Johan Wilhelm Theodor Ludwig von Blandowski, Wilhelm Blandowski, Wilhelm von Blandowski, William von Blandowski. William Blandowski lived in Australia between September 1849 and March 1859. His contributions to natural history and his illustrations of Aboriginal life he recorded on his expeditions were largely ignored for a time as a result of what has been called his difficult personality. One cause of problems was his descriptions of some species he collected and named after various prominent people, describing one as a slimy fish that lives on the mud. Other scientists took offence, believing he was describing the person he named the fish after, as well as the fish.

This book provides a glimpse of Aboriginal life about 60 years after the start of European colonisation, and before their culture was studied systematically. Their culture was already changing as a result of the presence of white settlers over increasing areas of their country; the tribes nearest the main settlements would probably have been losing their cultural identity at an increasing rate. By the time attempts were made to record their culture much had already been lost, much of the information gathered from the settled areas would have depended on the memories of those among the Aboriginal People who were old enough to remember life before they were dispossessed. In more recent times it depended on memories of stories from childhood of the 'old days', as remembered by the old people telling the stories, often from stories they had been told, not of their own experiences. Not the best way to gather information on a rapidly vanishing culture.

His illustrated encyclopaedia, with its visual account of the natural history, and daily life of Aboriginal people he witnessed on his travels, was published in 1862 in Gleiwitz, now Gliwice, Poland. He called it Australien in 142 Photographischen Abbildungen nach zehnjarigen Erfahrungen - Australia in 142 photographic illustrations from 10 years experience. The photographic illustrations referred to in the name refer to the process of reproduction of the drawings.

The sketches that became the basis for the illustrations in the encyclopaedia were made during explorations along the Murray River and Guichen Bay, the first of which was from February-May 1850, along the Murray to Lake Bonnie, near Barmera, then down along the river to Encounter Bay. His next trip, in January 1851 took him down the Murray to Wellington and Goolwa, then to the south east along the Coorong as far as Robe and Guichen Bay (Darragh, 2009), then on to Mount Gambier (Allen, 2010).

According to Allen (2010) the most remarkable aspect of the book is that the Aboriginal story is told through illustrations. The book is in the form of a visual narrative, from descriptions of the bush in Australia to all aspects of Aboriginal life through to mortuary rituals. The animals and plants he portrayed in the book are depicted, mostly, in their association with the Aboriginal people, in a way that Allen describes as a 'humanised natural history'. Blandowski said of the changes that had taken place between 1850, when he first travelled along the Murray, and 1862, when he published his book:

'...if you compare the state of Australia now with what it was only a single lifespan ago...There are burgeoning cities with steadily growing populations and productivity where Aborigines once had their endless hunting grounds, where they staged their festivities with games and dancing, fought and settled sometimes bloody tribal and personal battles. Now only the melancholy old recall those former times and mourn their loss ... another lifespan and only a few will be left...'(Blandowski, Australia, postscript, in Allen, 2010, p. 11).

Many illustrations are based on scenes he witnessed on his expeditions on the Murray River in 1856-7. The illustrations depicting hunting methods provide a glimpse of one aspect of Aboriginal life that is not normally found elsewhere, the people having been moved away from their traditional country where the hunting took place. These, and the illustrations of many aspects of Aboriginal domestic life, give a more complete picture of the Aboriginal People, one that was not known to many at the time, a situation that was not helped by Blandowski's work not being published in English.

Mutzel's compositions were based on field sketches by Kreft. The montages he produced allows many domestic activities to be depicted in a single illustration, and according to Allen (2010), these provide insight into daily life in Aboriginal camps, activities that would have been occurring all over the continent, though with different detail in different parts of the country. In one illustration, the removal of bark from a river gum, the depiction matches the written description given by Kreft in his published account of 1866 (Allen, 2010). Allen suggests that the illustrations 'provide insight into the ordinariness of Aboriginal life, a quality that connects us with Aboriginal people. This is most apparent in the small details, such as girls hugging each other (illustration 29), boys playing football (illustration 41) of 2 boys with a dog (illustration 68)'.

According to Buchan (2005) European Australians thought that because there didn't appear to be any form of government among Aboriginal Peoples it meant they had no society, as occurs in all civilisations. He quotes an opinion from colonial Australia by David Collins who reported a statement by Mathew Flinders '... the native depends on his fiz-gig or spear for support, depends on his single arm, and requiring not the aid of society is indifferent about it, but prowls along, a gloomy, unsettled and unsocial being.'

The illustrations in Blandowski's book gives lie to this belief, which was apparently widely held, and no doubt still held by some, of the type held by Flinders. According to Allen (2010), the terms that translates as a tribe of brothers, a kindred, or a clan, is used by Blandowski in the postscript of his book.

A number of aspects of Aboriginal society rarely mentioned elsewhere, and possibly not widely known of, such as the playing of games and competitive sport in Aboriginal Australia pre-contact and for some time after, at least with regard to the areas visited by Blandowski. These are depicted in illustrations 41, 97-9, and 103-5. This provides a view of Aboriginal society that fits with more recent accounts, that was apparently unknown to most in colonial Australia. If the extent of it had been known at the time there might have been some opposition, at least from 'outsiders', to the way the Aboriginal People were treated.

Allen refers to Blandowski's visual sense as is related in Blandowski's report of a case of a mother-in-law avoidance being observed. 'A mother-in-law being descried approaching, a number of lubras formed a circle around the young man, and he himself covered his face with his hands; - this while it screened the old lady from his sight, served as a warning to her not to approach, as she must never be informed by a third party of the presence of her son-in-law' (Blandowski, 1855).

By the time of Blandowski's travels along the Murray aboriginal society had already been changing for some time. Their toolkit had changed, now including firearms, iron-tipped spears and fishhooks. In 1866 Kreft wrote that many ancient cultural and social practices were still followed according to the traditions of the people. They retained their custom of sharing, and followed the taboos on names and foods, and fights still broke out over broken marriage contracts and freedom to camp on the frontages of rivers and lakes. According to Kreft the Aboriginals tried to maintain a hybrid economy (Altman, 2001).

Kreft witnessed an initiation ceremony in March 1857, as the Murray expedition approached Mondellimin (Kreft, 1866). According to

Kreft, the young men taking part, in what was said to be an 'attenuated' ceremony, said the only reason they cooperated was because they needed to be initiated before they could marry, not because they believed in the old traditions.

Blandowski believed there were only minor differences in ceremonies across the continent. He therefore based his illustration of one such ceremony that had been observed at Farm Cove, Sydney, 60 years earlier. The account of the ceremony was taken from '*an account of the English colony of New South Wales (1798) by David Collins*'. The illustrations were based on, and acknowledged, engravings by Thomas Watling (1798, plates 1-8., c.f. Australia illustrations 85-93, 125. '*This ceremony is known about because of the recall of Sir Maria Collins*' (Caption 94).

33. A drawing by G. Mutzel, based on sketches and written descriptions by Kreft and Blandowski. Water collecting in the Desert. '*Along the Darling River and in the area north west of it towards the Cooper and Victoria rivers, grow two types of small plants - Panicum and Portulacea - with lots of black seeds similar to our poppy plants. The women collect great amounts of these seeds in the skins of smaller kangaroo species for the winter - the only known case of Aborigines preparing for the coming months - in the foreground a woman is grinding these seeds into a pulp; behind her another woman is cleaning the seeds in a small trough by blowing on them. These seeds have become known as 'Nardoo', the food Burke & Wills were eating in their last days but which, because of its low nutritional value failed to save them from dying of starvation. On the left, there are different kinds of fishing spears and a very dangerous throwing weapon which can be thrown for a short distance through the enemy's chest.*'

37. A drawing by G. Mutzel. Australians catching fish at night on the Murray River. This scene is similar to one, 'Night Fishing on the lakes in Gippsland' that was in the book published by Haydon (1846). '*The fisherman puts wet clay on the canoe, lights a small fire on it, and with a torch in one hand and the spear in the other standing in the canoe floating downstream, he waits for the large fish weighing approx. 80 pounds that the Europeans call carp.*'

38. Composite by William v. Blandowski, based on a sketch by Blandowski. Aborigines at the coast fishing while the tide is out.

'They wait for hours without turning a hair, holding a spear ready to attack their victims. Area around St Kilda near Melbourne.'

40. Composition drawn by G Mutzel, based on sketches by Kreft and Blandowski, and written accounts. Fishing. *"In April the Murray River bursts its banks as the snow in the high alpine mountains melts. This is when the good season for the Aborigines starts. The small side arms of the river are closed off with sticks, leaving just a small hole in which to place the net. This net cannot be seen at night. Towards morning it is usually filled with fish. When they have a big catch a mature woman eagerly swings a piece of wood on a string above her head which makes a buzzing sound still audible at great distance. The Aborigines believe that with the help of the sound they can hinder the devil from taking their fish; more likely is it that it is an invitation for distant friends to come and eat fish. In the background one can see the camp, the 300 feet high, white jagged chalk banks indicate the lower reaches of the Murray River. The vegetation consists of* **Eucalyptus populifolia***, which at this time, produces the edible, Psylla which provides the Aborigines with adequate sugar. It tastes similar to manna.'*

41. Domestic occupation of the summer season on the lower Murray River. Composition by G. Mutzel, based on sketches and written accounts of Kreft and/or Blandowski. The scene is of men and women chewing bulrush roots for fibre to make nets. A woman is making twine by rubbing fibre on her thigh. There are also men making and using the long nets. There are men bringing fish to the camp, silver perch and eel-tailed catfish. Boys are seen playing a ball game, marn grook (marngrook).

'The Aborigines living at the confluence of the Murray and Darling Rivers live mostly on fishing and bird catching, using almost unbelievingly large nets. - In the foreground on the right is a group of men knitting nets: behind them is a family returning home laden with fish. On the left a family is eating a root dish called "Vangall" (Typha), next to them is a woman making string for nets out of the fibres of the root. - A group of children is playing with a ball; the ball is made out of Typha roots; it is not thrown or hit with a bat but is kicked up in the air with the foot. Aim of the game: never let the ball touch the ground. In the background a fishing net is being laid out to dry.'

A number of the illustrations depict the hunting of various animals, different hunting techniques being employed for each.

51. Emu Hunt, Composition by Mutzel, based on sketches by Kreft and/or Blandowski. It depicts brush or nets being used to drive the emus towards the hunters.

'The emu, the Australian ostrich, is watched by the Aborigines at places where it looks for water, and they observe where it came from and where it goes. They then enclose this spot with large, strong nets or surround the favourite spots of this animal with brushwood fences. The hunters wait singly or in groups in a hideout for two to three days, until the emu comes looking for water, then they jump out with their dogs and kill the animal one way or another.'

In other places they used different methods for hunting emus, better suited to the different situation.

52. Composition by Mutzel, based on sketches by Kreft and/or Blandowski.

*'In the clay area where **Eucalyptus marginata** grows in quantity, the Aborigines have developed a clever method for catching emus. They clasp branches in front of them and sneak up on the birds until close enough to spear them.'*

The Biggest Estate on Earth: How Aborigines made Australia see Fire-stick Farmers

In his book[1] Bill Gammage uses a variety of sources (1500 in the selective bibliography) in support of his proposal that prior to European settlement the entire land surface of Australia was managed as though it was a single giant estate that the Australia of 1788 was made by the Aborigines. The entire population of the continent did their bit on a local scale to maintain the productivity of the land at a maximum, given the extremely erratic climate and in many places the varying degrees of aridity, and the extremely impoverished soils over most of the land. He has gathered many written reports of Europeans, including Captain Cook, who personally witnessed many parts of the country before it was affected by the spread of colonisation. He also has included paintings, sketches and photos of various areas as they were when first encountered by the colonists (or invaders, depending on whether your choice of weapon was a gun or spear).

At many places in Australia travellers in the early times after European settlement described the unexpected and unexplained scenes they found as having the appearance of a "gentleman's park". Those cited in the book are:

H.T. Ebsworth - New South Wales - Port Stephens

John Hudspeth - Tasmania - the Jericho Valley

Alexander Buchanan - the west side of the Murray below the Big Bend

John Glover - Tasmania - describing a scene he painted 'my harvest' from a hill above his farm.

John Michael Skipper - South Australia - Onkaparinga - describing the painting, the view south of Adelaide.

Edward Snell - Willunga.

William Light - Aldinga - describing the painting 'View at Yankalillah'.

Martha Berkeley - Adelaide - describing the painting 'Mt Lofty from the Terrace'.

A recently arrived immigrant - Adelaide - early days of settlement.

John Fawkner - Melbourne.

John Lancey - Flemington hills north of Melbourne Swamp.

Sydney Parkinson - Bank's draughtsman on the Endeavour - describing the country seen on excursions along the east coast.

Charles Sturt - South Australia.

Thomas Walker - Omeo Plains

Joseph Maiden - Dorrigo - New South Wales.

Robert Dawson - New South Wales - Port Stephens.

One of the witnesses the author[1] cites in his book is Captain James Cook as he sailed the Endeavour along the east coast of Australia. He noticed a remarkable thing that I have not seen remarked on in any books I have read. The trees '*had no underwood*'. On the 1st of May he wrote '*made an excursion into the country which we found diversified with woods, lawns and marshes; the woods are free from underwood of any kind and the trees are at such a distance from one another that the whole country or at least a great part of it might be cultivated without being obliged to cut down a single tree*'.

Joseph banks was also surprised by what he saw *'The country tho in general well enough clothed appeared in some places bare. It resembled in my imagination the back of a lean cow, covered in general with long hair, but nevertheless where the scraggy hip bones have stuck out further than they ought accidental rubs and knocks have entirely bared them of their share of covering.'* According to Banks the hill tops were bare, though trees were present on lower slopes, though they *'were very large and stood separate from each other without the least underwood'*. Banks' draughtsman, Sydney Parkinson, agreed with Banks *'The country looked very pleasant and fertile; and the trees quite free from underwood, appeared like plantations in a gentleman's park.'*

As they travelled further north to the Whitsunday Islands, Cook noted *'land on both the Main and islands ... diversified with woods and Lawns that looked green and pleasant'*. There, 100 years later G.S. Nares, a naval commander, named GN Grassy Island, because it was grass-covered and had a few trees on its summit. At the present about half the island is tree-covered. Nares saw other islands in the Whitsundays that were grassy, but they are now all wooded apart from where they have been cleared. Cook summed up of the Australian east coast on 23rd of August *'It was clothed with woods, long grass, shrubs, plants &ca. The mountains or hills are chequered with woods and lawns. Some of the hills are wholly covered with flourishing trees; others but thinly, and the few that are on them are small and the spots of Lawns or Savannahs are rocky and barren'*. Cook spent 7 weeks at what is now Cooktown, as well as other landings along the east coast so his observations are not solely based on what he saw from the deck of the Endeavour as it passed north.

While camped by the Endeavour River, Cooktown, Cook wrote in his journal that he climbed Grassy Hill on the 19 June, getting clear views along the coast, seeing other grassy hills, calling them barren and stony, according to the author[1] some are stony but none are barren. Cook wrote on 19 July *'I had an extensive view of the inland country which consisted of hills and vallies and large plains agreeably diversified with woods and lawns'*. He also wrote of the diligence of the people who made them.

'I have observed that when they went from our tents upon the banks of the Endeavour River, we could trace them by the fire which they kindled on their way; and we imagined that these fires were intended in some way for the taking of the kangaroo .... .'

'They produce fire with great facility, and spread it in a wonderful manner ... from the smallest spark they increase it with great speed and dexterity. We have often seen one of them run along the shore, to all appearance with nothing in his hand, who stooping down for a moment, at a distance of every fifty or a hundred yards, left fire behind him, as we could see first by the smoke, and then by the flame ... We had the curiosity to observe one of these planters of fire, when he set off, and we saw him wrap up a small spark in dry grass, which, when he had run a little way, having been fanned by the air that his motion produced, began to blaze; he then laid it down in a place convenient for his purpose, inclosing it in a quantity of grass, and so continued his course'.

These descriptions of the supposedly untended bush along the east coast, as well as other places described by explorers and others further inland, are indeed curious as the author[1] suggests. Who would recognise any of these places at present, at least those that haven't been disturbed since the Aborigines were replaced in such areas, from the descriptions reported by people seeing the areas before white settlers had changed them. As there are so many similar descriptions, often by people such as Cook and some of the well-known explorers who were noted for their keen observation and the accuracy of their reports, as the author suggests, how can they all be wrong?

It is known that the Aboriginal people all over Australia used fire to manage their land, burning in patches so there would always be food in the form or newly sprouted grass that the animals they hunted preferred, as well as cover for these animals around these patches of fresh food. See Fire-stick Farmers.

In many places around the continent white settlers and explorers noted the presence of grass 'lawns' where there are now trees, as well as open forests with no undergrowth that are now dense forests. When travelling south of Hobart Abel Tasman noted they saw land *'pretty generally covered with trees, standing so far apart, that they allow a passage everywhere ... unhindered by dense shrubbery or underwood*. This area is now dense forest, and Gammage, (2011) asks why not then? There were dense forests in 1788, thick scrubs, impenetrable eucalypts, walls of rainforests, but as the author[1] says *'this only sharpens the puzzle, for often they gave way abruptly to grass'*.

The book is based on, according to the author[1], 3 facts about 1788:

About 70 % of Australian plants require fire, or at least tolerate fire. Critical knowledge in the management of land in Australia was knowing which plants need fire, when to burn and how much to burn. With this knowledge decisions could be made as to which patches should be burnt and which not to burn, the result being that grazing animals could be attracted to places where the people wanted them to go by the provision of their preferred food and the type of shelter they required nearby.

As there were no serious native predators the grazing animals could be shepherded by the humans, their only real predator. Australia was the only continent on which such a situation prevailed.

There was no wildness. The beings from the Dreamtime had 'given the laws to the people'; the laws including an ecological philosophy that was enforced by religious sanction, the people were compelled to care for all their country.

These ecological laws served them well, allowing them to live well, and sustainably, for unknown thousands of years since the ecological knowledge was accumulated and became the basis of managing some of the most difficult country in the world to survive in.

They were instructed by their law to leave the world as they found it. Static means were not imposed by this 1788 practice. The same goal was achieved by many variations of the apparently conservative practices to suit the local erratic climate and their management was active rather than passive. An overriding concern of their management was to remain alert to the changing seasons and conditions and to maintain a balance of life. A difference between the Aboriginal people of 1788 and the white colonists was their world view, believing themselves to be part of nature, not separate and with a God-given dominion over it. They believed that it was just as important to maintain all other animals and plants as to maintain their role in the environment, as all were equally part of it.

What appeared to the settlers as random burning that the Aborigines used to hunt was in fact part of the well-planned and precise management on a fine-grained local level. Gammage says burning must be predictable to be effective. They needed to plan where to burn and where not to burn and to space the burnt patches appropriately to achieve the desired goal. The burning pattern varied according to climate and vegetation type, different vegetation types requiring different burning patterns. Gammage suggests it is an impressive achievement to successfully manage such diverse material; 'making from it a single estate was a breathtaking leap of imagination'.

At least one of the settlers, Edward Curr, who had been born in Hobart in 1820, had an inkling of this achievement. He became a pioneer squatter and knew some of the Aboriginal people who had retained their old culture and values, and in the decades of their dispossession he studied them closely, as well as their country. He remained in Victoria for 42 years, after which he wrote '*it may perhaps be doubted that any section of the human race has exercised a greater influence on the physical condition of any large portion of the globe than the wandering savages of Australia*'. According to Gammage he knew when he wrote this that it would strongly contradict the European beliefs about 'primitive' people to link 'wandering savages' with an unmatched impact on the land, deliberately defying the European convention that nomadic people had little if any influence on the land. He suggests there are some scientists who are reluctant to accept that the Aborigines could have had such influence on the land, arguing or assuming that only nature made the landscape of 1788, possibly by lightning fires.

According to Gammage there is no evidence that lightning started most bushfires in 1788, 'nor that it could shape plant communities so curiously and invariably as to exclude human fire impacts. At the present estimates of fires started by lightning vary from 0.01 % in Tasmania to 30 % in Victoria. Gammage suggesting the figure for Victoria is overestimated when compared with 7-8 % for southern Australia, and the highest is for the north, 18 %. Western Queensland is the only part of Australia where it is believed by researchers that lightning is a major cause of fires, at 80 %. He suggests the number of lightning caused fires would have been even lower in 1788 because there were so many fires started by humans that there would have been little fuel on the ground to sustain lightning fires. He suggests that if the distribution pattern of plants was the result of lightning fires now as well at the time of first contact it should be the same then as now around towns and farms, but it isn't.

Some researchers are beginning to believe that pre-contact fires were possibly important in distribution of plants, possibly explaining it. It was known by some, such as Thomas Mitchell and Ludwig Leichardt that the Aborigines burnt grass to attract the animals they hunted, though it wasn't until the 1960s that some began to believe that there was more system and purpose to the burning than merely random fires. The extensive degree to which the land had been changed by pre-contact fires has been shown by a number of people, from different perspectives, such as R.C. Ellis, Sylvia Hallam, Bill Jackson, Rhys Jones, Peter Latz, Duncan Merrilees, Eric Rolls, and Ian Thompson, are mentioned in the book, as well as others.

The people doing the burning worked with the country wherever possible to emphasise or mitigate its natural character, in some places nothing else being possible. There wasn't much they could do about mountains, rocks, rivers and most swamps, but they sometimes found a way, they dammed rivers and swamps, cut channels through watersheds. See Eel Harvesting. Fire was used to replace a plant community with a different one.

Their management involved controlling which plants and animals flourished in the managed area. They managed their country for plants, knowing which plants grew where and which they needed to transplant and care for. They knew which plants were preferred by the animals they hunted and managed the land in such a way that the animals' favourite food was associated with the shelter they preferred and the safest scrub. By establishing a circuit of these places they were able to use one until either the animals moved on or the patch needed burning when they shifted their hunting to the next managed area, moving along in the circuit as necessary. This system made the whereabouts of their prey species predictable so that their hunting was not merely haphazard as is usually believed. This system of management made their food sources both predictable and abundant. They had the worst climatic and soil conditions of any continent but they not only survived, they maximised the productivity of their country to such an extent that they needed to spend only a few hours each day gathering food, leaving them plenty of time for a complex social and ceremonial/religious life.

This method of management differed from that of farmers in that the scale of land management in pre-contact Australia was on a much bigger scale, a particular clan spread the resources over a very wide area, which provided some insurance for the hard times such as the common and unpredictable droughts, which were often broken by flooding rain. They also formed alliances with other clans that could be hundreds of kilometres away where they could trade or where they could seek refuge in the worst of prolonged droughts. In central Australia rain is erratic and when it does come is often on limited areas, so that part of a clan's territory could receive rain while other parts remain drought stricken. In seasons that didn't suit farmers, such as droughts and floods, the managed system of the Aborigines was more predictable than farming. Under this system of management they had abundance, not just mere subsistence.

Gammage summed up the rules of Aboriginal management pre-contact:

'Ensure that all life flourishes

Make plants and animals abundant, convenient and predictable

Think universal, act local'

Though the local group in any region would have known and been familiar with the practices of only their neighbours and any other tribes they came in contact with along their trade routes, the same practice of using fire-sticks as the main tool for managing their local country was used by all the tribes across Australia. This management was "coordinated" by the stories and rituals that had been handed down from the Dreamtime, not by a continent-wide deliberate scheme that all took part in.

Each local area was managed in basically the same way as each other, though with adjustments to suit the local area, based on local knowledge, as there was a great variety of environments occupied by the Aboriginal people in different parts of the continent

Gammage has listed a number of changes that have occurred since 1788.

Water sources have been constricted by the compaction of the soil by the hooves of the settlers' livestock and the speeding of water.

In pre-contact times there was more water to ameliorate droughts (more soaked into the soil), spread resources, allowing people to walk over more of Australia. They expected to be able to care for their country even in arid areas, and expected its plants and animals to be sustainable indefinitely.

The Aborigines had management opportunities that were rare in Europe, as grass was widely available even in hard times. Grass could be burnt at almost any time, apart from the wet season, secure in the knowledge that it would re-shoot green. They knew they could expect the fresh grass to attract the herbivores and their predators, especially in summer. At the present this is a time where grass is scarce and what animals there are, are stressed. The presence of grass at all times allowed them to manage it in such a way as to help the animals they depended on for food to survive. It also made them abundant, convenient and predictable.

Salinity is now spreading because of the removal of much of trees, saltbush and perennial grasses since first contact.

Prior to European settlement the Aboriginal people used almost all plants for some purpose. The loss of many species since first contact masks the degree to which resources were connected and how widespread they were.

Gammage explained how this system of care for the environment provided the people with food sustainably.

The people were taught by the Dreaming why they must care for the world as it needed to be maintained and the land taught them how. They were taught by the first that maintaining their country was compulsory, the other made the maintenance rewarding in the form of the continued availability of food and materials for other uses. The groups, usually family groups, were small, said by John Oxley to be indicated by their abandoned camps to be about 6-8 individuals. Each group had its country to live in and care for, and every country was surrounded by other countries, none of which were dominant over any other countries, that resulted in a continuum of countries across the entire continent.

If the population of a country went too low to adequately care for it there were people from other countries who were qualified to take care of it. In the north, at least, there were specialist managers who could advise on the use of fire to manage a country. Then there were elders in neighbouring countries who could help, having a working knowledge of the country and its Dreamtime stories, often by dropping hints on what needed to be done.

There are many more quotes from the early colonists and explorers in the book.

See Fire-stick Farmers

The Dingo

The conclusion arrived at by Prof. Macintosh of Sydney University after studying dingos for several years is that its origins are enigmatic. Gollan concluded from his study of the dingo that it is most closely related to the Indian pariah dog, those from Burzahom in Kashmir, and especially with the domesticated dogs found in the ruins of Harappa of the Indus civilisation that date from about 3500-4000 years ago. Corbett concluded, based on a study of Asian canid skulls that the dingo is almost indistinguishable from those of wild dogs from Asia and Southeast Asia, all of which descended from the Indian wolf (***Canis lupus pallipes***).

Some believe that the dingo, that was brought to Australia about 4000 years ago, was domesticated or semidomesticated in Australia, the feral population descending from these original dingos. Among the aborigines, especially women who had recently lost a child or couldn't have children or were past child-bearing age, the pups were often taken from the wild as substitutes for children because of the requirement of the harsh environment to keep the population low. Childless women often carried a dingo pup wrapped around their waist. In the desert the nights are often cold, especially in winter the night temperatures can go below freezing. The dogs also took the place of blankets under these conditions. In the desert areas of Australia very cold nights are called a "5-dog-night".

Burials of dingoes have been found in middens at a number of places, such as Kioloa and Murramarang in New South Wales, in Victoria at Mallacoota. The fact that some dingos were buried indicates that they were often valued. The dingos that lived with the Aborigines were taken from the wild as pups and eventually returned to the wild.

It appears to be at the time the dingo is thought to have arrived in Australia that the native carnivores such as the thylacine and Tasmanian devil became extinct on the mainland, only surviving in Tasmania where the dingo never reached.

The Dingo - Domesticated Dogs

The associated technology and timing of the death of the Narrabeen man, whatever the context or reason for his death, suggests, according to Cane[1], a general conclusion: that there was a particularly turbulent time in the middle of the Holocene. The indication from the archaeological evidence is that people were seeking efficiencies and security in a time of social adjustment, at a time when territories were being redefined, and congruent with the rising sea. It was a time of social evolution, and their technology was also evolving, and around the continent the people were on the move. The available space was being demarcated more rigidly and most resources were being exploited more efficiently. It was at this time that mechanisms of food storage were developed, food was domesticated and its production was improved. Around the world people were experiencing the same problems, becoming more sedentary, and more aware of the limits of their territory and necessity rights, and they developed ways of protecting both. Around the world populations of humans were experiencing the problems, the loss of land, increased isolation and geographic fragmentation. It was at this time that the Americas were separated from the Euro-Russia continent. In Indonesia to the north of Australia the loss of land was even more extensive than in Australia. Though Australia lost about 1/3 of its land mass Indonesia lost about 2/3 of its land mass. In ancient Indonesia the vast glacial landmass was reduced from 6 million km^2 to less that 2 million km^2 across 13,000 islands. This must have had a large effect on the populations of humans around Indonesia, probably with some of the displaced people moving to Australia.

Evidence has been found of at least 2 such migrations in the Holocene. The first of these occurred about 7,000 BP, and among the people arriving from Indonesia was at least 1 person who was carrying a neurodegenerative disease, Machado-Joseph disease. The only part of Australia where this disease is found at present is in communities in eastern Arnhem Land. This disease, that it localised to Groote Eylandt in the Gulf of Carpentaria and Yirrkala on the Gove Peninsula, which indicated that the people from Indonesia arrived at this place and have remained there.

The second migration was at about 5,000 BP. It is known this migration arrived at that time because it was then that the dingo, or Asian dog, arrived in Australia. The dingoes quickly spread across Australia by 3,000 BP, an all-purpose dog; they soon became family pets, hunting companions, as well as food. Based on genetic studies they appear to have been domesticated dogs from south eastern Asia, the Australian population appearing to have descended from a few individuals that arrived with the 5,000 BP migration. Soon after the arrival of the dingo the mainland population of thylacines were extinct by about 3,300 years ago. Cane[1] suggests the disappearance of one and the arrival of the other are probably linked, directly, as the dingoes hunted in packs, possibly outcompeting the thylacine, and indirectly as an added strain in a continent already under strain from a changing climate and more effective predation and the likely conjunction of people and dingoes in hunting teams.

Chapter 8 - The Baiini (Bajini) and Macassans

These were people who appear to have come to northern Australia before the Macassans. They arrived in sailing ships (lolperu) long ago, some say maybe in the Dreamtime. According to the Dreamtime stories of Djankawu and Laindjung, they came across them on their travels. The stories tell that **Djankawu** and his sisters met the **Baiini** and traded with them, including beautiful feathered string. According to the story, after the Baiini left Djankawu found the spoon the Baiini had used to stir fires used to cook trepang. The spoon was blackened and he liked it so he took the colour for his own, using the black in the painting of designs. **Laindjung** also met the **Baiini**, eating some of the rice they grew.

It is believed to be more likely that the arrival of the Baiini was much more recent than the Dreamtime, probably no earlier than the 15th century, hundreds of years ago rather than thousands of years ago. There appear to have been 3 main points of contact between the Aborigines of north Australia and other peoples, brining alien influences. At Cape York, where the contact and influences were from New Guinea by way of the Torres Strait islands, Arnhem Land and the Kimberleys of the north west. According to Berndt & Berndt (1954) the people of Arnhem Land may have had more intense contact over a longer period than any other group in Australia. In their songs the people of eastern Arnhem Land tell of the arrival of people in ships from the islands to the west, in what is now Indonesia, beyond the Arafura Sea and the Timor Sea. They sing of the golden brown bodies of the new arrivals, as well as their women. The songs tell of the stone houses the Baiini built, the cloth they wove and dyed their gardens and the fish-spearing method that was apparently different from that of the Aborigines (Berndt & Berndt, 1964).

Unlike the Macassans, who came only to collect trepang, never setting up permanent camps with crops, apart from dropped tamarind seeds that sprouted, the trees still grown around their camp sites, the Baiini brought their entire families and built houses of stone and ironbark. They planted rice in Warrimiri (Warramiri) country and

Gumaidj (Gumaitj) country. The rice is birida (husked rice), called Luda by the Baiini.

The thing that appears to have been remembered the most about the Baiini was the beauty of their women, who had lighter skin than the locals and wore multi-coloured sarongs. It seems the men were hardly noticed, most of the stories are about the women and the things they did. It seems their every activity was watched with interest as they wove cloth on the looms they brought with them, from yarn they dyed in many colures in pots. The Yirritja people at Yirrkala carved the same designs on the figures they carved of the Baiini people that the women had on the cloth. The cloth was called jalajal by the old Baiini and liba by the Macassans. The design, darabu, was a pattern of coloured triangles that was used in many combinations.

Many stories of the Yirritja are about the Baiini women and every activity they carried out. Some stories tell of the Baiini men's activities, such as fishing, hunting with harpoons and traps, but it is the beauty of their women that was apparently most noted and is best remembered.

Evidence of the Baiini presence has been found along the coast of north-eastern Arnhem Land and the nearby islands, in places such as Blue Mud Bay and Elcho Island. A number of rocks are said to be wrecked Baiini boats, their anchors, or places where incidents involving them took place.

Near Trial Bay there is a waterhole that is said to represent the vagina of a Baiini woman who had sexual intercourse there. A large rock near Cape Wilberforce on Jamanga Island represents a boat the Baiini pulled up on to the land. Another place situated on the mainland near Pobassoo Island, it is said a group of Baiini rested in the shade of the boijama tree with their anchor being represented by a nearby rock. There are a number of other places the Aborigines associate with the Baiini mentioned in Jennifer Isaacs book, *Australian Dreaming: 40,000 years of Aboriginal History*.

The story relating the departure of the Baiini from Arnhem Land says that the Baiini headman saw smoke rising in the direction of Celebes and decided to go there. In Milingimbi a story called *Macassan and Dog give each other fire* gives a very similar account of the departure of the Macassans. According to this story, a long time ago a Macassan man came to the mainland by prau, landing at a place called Bambal, about 8 km (5 miles) from Elcho Island. On arriving on the shore he built a house for himself by driving bamboo poles into the ground. Then he planted rice (berratha), making holes with a stick that he poured the seed rice into, and when he finished his work he sat down. As he sat there a dog came to him and they talked to each other. The white man (Macassan) it is said offered matches to the dog, but the dog said he didn't need them because he had firesticks, duttji.

As they sat there the Macassan man saw smoke rising in the direction of his home, Murrunydjura, Guwalilnga, and Dhangarrpura. He worried that his home was burning so pulled out the uprights of his house and departed for his home. According to the story the post holes are still there and the rice turned into shell middens.

After the Baiini left the rice fields were abandoned and the type of grass that grows there is now used as food for the Aborigines of the area. The local people eat the roots of these grasses, or bulrushes, and say they are food that was brought by the Baiini (Isaacs, 2005).

Macassan Traders

People from Makassar, now Ujung Pandang, in the south west of Celebes, now Sulawesi, came to get trepang. They visited the north of Australia for at least hundreds of years, though probably much longer, fishing for trepang - sea cucumber - and trading with the Aborigines. These visitors contributed to the language, art, economy and genetics of the northern aborigines. The contact has left its mark on both sides of the Arafura and Banda Seas.

It is uncertain when the journeys began from Makassar to the place they called Marege, apparently on the north coast of Australia. It is thought the trepang trade may have begun in 1720, though some think it began closer to 1400. The voyagers visited places from the Kimberleys to Mornington Island in the east of the Gulf of Carpentaria. Trade dropped off towards the end of the 19th century as a result of the imposition of duties and licences by the Australian government. The last prau left Arnhem Land in 1906.

In 1803 Mathew Flinders met the Macassan trading fleet at what is now known as Nhulunbuy on his circumnavigation of Australia. As a result of this meeting settlements were established at Melville Island and the Coburg Peninsula. The trepang gathering fleets were sent from Macassar every year by Chinese trades in Macassar who shipped the trepang to China where they were used for soup and as an aphrodisiac.

The trepang were processed and dried before being taken back to Makassar. At Port Essington, Groote Eylandt and Snuru Bay there are still stands of tamarind trees brought by the Macassans and the remains of trepang processing plants from the 18th & 19th centuries.

The processing of the trepang involved boiling, gutting, recooking with mangrove bark to add flavour and colour, then drying and smoking. The naturalist said of them they looked like *'sausages which have been rolled in mud and then thrown up the chimney'*. He probably didn't taste them.

The Macassan contact with the aboriginals of the north had a profound effect on their cultures. The visits are still remembered through oral history, songs and dances and paintings on rock and bark.

The length of the processing required long stays on the coast. The camps set up by the Macassans had large boiling-down cauldrons, smoke houses and wells. The traces of these camps can still be seen on the coast of the Kimberleys and Arnhem Land. The remains include broken pottery and glass and stands of tamarind trees that sprouted from the seeds dropped by the Macassans who ate the astringent fruit. These Macassan camps were situated in places that could be defended, on small islands or promontories. It seems they felt the need to protect themselves, so presumably they believed there was a chance of aggression from the Aborigines. Historical records in Indonesia report a number of massacres of the crews of the praus.

The Macassans exchanged goods such as knives, tobacco, cloth, rice and alcohol, for the right to fish for trepang, which can be collected at low tide, and employed Aboriginal people. Some Yolngu communities changed their economies from being land based to being largely based on ocean fishing for dugong and turtles. This was made possible by the introduction of Macassan sea-going dugout canoes to replace the bark canoe.

Some Aboriginal people accompanied the Macassans on their return voyages, also remembered are the abductions and trading of Yolngu young women, and the introduction of smallpox.

And a Macassan pidgin became the lingua franca of the north coast, both between the Aborigines and the Macassans and between different Aboriginals that spoke a different language, having been brought into closer contact with each other as a result of the Macassan sea-going culture. Some Macassan words are still present among the Aboriginal languages along the north coast. Some examples are rupiah=money, jama=work, balanda=white person, originally from Dutch to the Macassan language "Hollander".

The Macassan praus were of about 25 tonnes, and they all carried seagoing dugout canoes that were used for fishing. Unlike the legendary Baiini, they did not bring their women. The fleets of praus were comprised of from 30 - 60 boats, each with about 30 crew, staying in Australia over the Wet Season in December and returning to the Makassar about 4 or 5 months later.

Though these visitors are usually referred to as Macassans, there were actually a number of different groups trading and fishing for trepang, each with distinctive praus. Another group trading along the north coast was the Bugis, also from what is now Sulawesi. The Aborigines recorded the different prau design of the different groups, the Bugis praus had a bow that bent down and had an eye painted on each side to allow it to find the way more easily, while the bow of the Macassan praus pointed up.

There are songs and stories about all parts of the praus, such as the rigging, the sails, even the wind in the sails.

In stories told by Aborigines, such as the one told by the Gumatj clan from Yirrkala, the first contact with the Macassans is apparently recorded. According to the story the first the Aborigines knew of the Macassans was when they saw 2 praus approaching Port Bradshaw. Most of the people scattered further inland, while some stayed to watch these strange things from the thick vegetation. 2 young boys had not heard about the praus and were fishing with spears in the mangrove swamps. The praus anchored at Daneia, in a tidal creek, at which point 2 young Macassan boys left the prau to collect shellfish. The Aboriginal boys heard the Macassans and crept closer, watching the Macassans. The Macassan boys eventually saw them and both groups watched each other for a while before they all began talking. The Macassans gestured that the Aboriginal boys should go with them to visit their father. At the Macassan camp the men were divided into 2 groups dancing and singing, which they apparently did before they begin collecting trepang. The Aboriginals thought it was like the moieties of their people.

The Aboriginals hid behind a tree while the Macassan boys told their father and he and another man came and grabbed the boys, taking them back to the camp. They were eventually given food and taught to smoke a Malay pipe and then allowed to return to their own camp. When they told their people about the Macassans many others went and made camp near the Macassan camp. According to the story the father of the 2 boys was named Dainasi, and the names of the captains of the praus were Gurumola and Wonadjei.

Along the northern coast of Australia, wherever the Macassans traded, the local people have stories about their first encounters.

Chapter 9 - Aboriginal Mythology

Myths - The body of mythology providing relatively standardised expression.

Rituals (rites) - Organised action, more or less conventionalised, that express the mythological features

Material objects or representations - they symbolise or represent certain animals or spirits, human body parts, etc.

Local sites - country associated with various beings - myths and rituals are always localised to some extent

Mythology

Myth Content

Myths connected with the sky and constellations

Myths that may be oral history

Myths of the Dieri See Increase Rituals

Rainbow Serpent

Mt Beerwah

Ninya, the Ice Men see Artila (Mt Connor)

Itakaura - Chambers Pillar

Mythology ofKata Tjuta

Mythology of Lake Eyre

Mythology of the Nullarbor Plain

Mythology of the Simpson Desert

Mythology of Uluru

The 3 Sisters - the Blue Mountains

Noatch - dead body or corpse

Mulka - Bates Cave, near Waver Rock

Arkaroo - The Flinders Ranges (Gammon Ranges)

Wonnaira - the Kimberley

How water became salty

Mandya

Arkaroo

Wuriunpranilli (Wuriupranili), the Sun Woman

Megafauna and the Dreamtime

Creation Myths

Djanggawul Sisters

Waramurungundju

Wawalag (Wagilag, Wauwalak) Sisters

Jingana, the Mother - West of Maningrida, central Arnhem Land

Central Australia

Uluru (Ayres's Rock)

Urdlu & Mandya - creation of Lake Frome and how it became salty

Eastern Australia

North eastern Arnhem Land

North eastern Australia

South eastern Australia

The Kimberleys

Tnorala, a star ancestor

Great Ancestor Spirit (all-father) of South eastern Australia

Mythology

Ritual and mythology complement each other but never completely coincide. Rituals involve acting out events or instructions expressed in the myths, mythology substantiating, justifying or explaining a range of rituals. The most common content of myths has to do with matters that are of great importance to humans, life, death, fertility and relations between people and nature. The Aborigines had a subsistence economy, being totally dependent on animals and plants provided by nature, with no crop plants or domesticated livestock to fall back on. Being subsistence hunter-gatherers, they depended entirely on being able to find food every day. So increase rituals would be expected to be part of their religious life, performing ceremonies believed to ensure the continuance of their food supply, the availability of water, etc.

The word myth can be used in 2 ways, one is to infer that the story isn't true, the other, that is used here, refers to a narrative or story or series of songs that have religious significance, enshrining a special body of beliefs, or expressing instructions from certain divine beings. As with the myths of other religions, the stories are believed to be true by the followers of this religion. Aboriginal **Dreamtime stories** are no less provable than the mythology of any other religion. And as with the archaeological support for the biblical stories, the Dreamtime stories of northern Australia, such as the Djanggawul sisters and brother, archaeology is suggesting that the Aborigines did in fact arrive by canoe from the north.

In Aboriginal Australia all the stories are not connected with religion, many are ordinary camp stories, some are told to children, which may be outlines of the main stories from their mythology. The most important religious stories are known only to the fully initiated men who are responsible for the care of the sacred sites and objects connected with the totems whose myths they are responsible for. They may not be allowed to tell others the stories, or in some cases, they are the only people who are permitted to recite it. This applies in north east Arnhem Land, the eastern Kimberleys, Central Australia, and north western South Australia. Among the **Aranda**, only the men belonging to a certain part of their country, who own the myths associated with it, are permitted to repeat them, and to perform the associated rituals. Men from other parts of the territory must get their permission before they are allowed to recite them or perform the rituals, and they need to have a very good reason for asking. The 'real' owners may dance while others assist them by decorating or making sacred objects, and sometimes with the singing.

Part of the community, such as children, may not know the major myths. In areas where boys undergo the first part of their initiation at a young age, they may be introduced to the stories earlier, and may be told more of the stories associated with their totems and their country. There are some stories that women are not allowed to know, in some cases, even when the stories relate to them. There are also a few which are known only to women. Usually, most adults have some knowledge of the main totemic and sacred sites in their territories, and the main Dreamtime beings associated with them, if not all the sacred stories. Among the Aranda the women are not initiated, so never get to share in the mythology of the tribe. They are never told any sacred stories. The women are prohibited from seeing the sacred ceremonies. In reality, the women got to know something about the mythology, but not officially.

The sacred versions of stories usually contain much more detail than the widely known version, including the explanation of the symbolism. Nearly every story has no version that is accepted as the only correct version. Within certain limits, variation is allowed, even with personal interpretations. When men of a local group tell a totemic story, even one very intimately associated with them, they often tell slightly different version of it. The agreement between these versions is more likely to agree, at least on main points, if a number of them are present. The versions given by each man when they are not together varied more, at least with the minor points.

Sacred myths don't take the form of spoken narrative over most of Australia. The songs used to tell the myths give key words or references rather than full descriptions. The meaning lies in the associations of each word, so simple translation is not enough to convey the full story. In north-eastern Arnhem Land a word used in everyday speech can have several sacred equivalents with slightly differing meanings, as well as a further series of 'singing words'. These types of songs are usually sung in a special sequence during sacred rituals. Specific localities often have sacred myths and corresponding actions connected with them. Sacred objects are sometimes associated with these localities. Songs are an aid to remembering the details. Sites having some importance, such as waterholes in the desert, a place with an unusual feature, like a special rock formation or an oddly shaped hill are connected to a myth or part of a myth. Usually the only places that don't have some story associated with them are places of little interest, like barren places.

Myth Content
Most religious stories have as their main theme the wanderings and activities of various beings, in this case, the Dreamtime beings. These wanderings usually take them over a number of areas, not just the one held by the people with a particular dreamtime story. Another characteristic of these stories is that the being often arrives from another area or leaves across another area, or sometimes both. They tended to move along a route that took them along a series of

waterholes, rivers or crossed the country to the next. They did various things at the places they stopped at along the way, such as putting water in a waterhole, creating people or animals and plants, and they often meet other Dreamtime beings, creating various natural features, naming the places and plants and animals, singing songs and instituting rites to be followed by their descendants.

The tracks followed by the ancestral beings in the Dreamtime trace many routes that spread across the continent when viewed together, each group of people having part of the travels in their mythology. As these routes crisscross the whole of Australia, often crossing each other, it has been suggested that maybe they have a basis in fact, representing the trade routes between the tribes. It is known from archaeology that goods from one area have been found on the other side of the continent. While it is unlikely that people walked across the continent, it is much more likely that these goods were traded along established trading networks. Far-reaching trade links seem to have existed in Australia for a very long time.

An example of the widespread nature of the Dreamtime stories telling of the wanderings of the Dreamtime beings is the **Kunapipi series**. Along the various tracks it is said to have followed, its name changed several times as it passed through the territory of about 35 tribes. According to the Dreamtime stories, it travelled North West from Roper River through Rose River to Yirrkala and Milingimbi, North West along the Wilton River to the Liverpool River and Oenpelli, it turned westward to Katherine, then swinging North West again to Daily River, then southwards to Tennant Creek. From Newcastle Waters it turned west and south west to Stuart Creek. More tracks lead up to the Victoria River and Fitzmaurice River, another track leading to Wyndham. As it crossed into the different territories, its name changed and parts of the local mythology was incorporated into the story.

In other Dreamtime stories the **Wadi Gudjara** travelled across almost the whole of the Great Victoria Desert and the Western Desert. Its travels took it through the territories of dozens of local groups, speaking 25-30 dialects. No local descent group, clan or dialect unit owns a complete myth, each group owning only part of the full myth, the part of the being's crossing through their territory, so they can only perform the rites connected with its actions in their country. Occasionally the members of several local groups came together to perform the rights or dances connected with the being, each group doing only that part of the myth that belonged to them. Because of the widespread nature of the travels, the complete myth would never be performed, because the owners of the separate parts are too widely separated to come together.

It is difficult to get reliable information from writings of the early observers of much of the southern parts of Australia, the first part of the country to be colonised by Europeans, and the first parts where the Aborigines were detribalised, by one method or another, so that much of their culture was lost before it could be properly documented. Some of the early writers paid too little attention to what the people actually told them, and some omitted or glossed over things they considered distasteful, obscene or shocking. Much of the information gathered in the southern parts depended on memory and hearsay, because the cultures were no longer functioning.

If information had been gathered systematically, information from the southern parts of the country might have been very interesting. What there is gives glimpses of what seems to have been a mythology that differed from the parts of the country where more accurate recording took place. At least some of the tribes of the southeast of the country were reported to have believed in a male god, a supreme being. In 1904 Howitt spoke of an 'All Father', suggesting that **Nurrundere (Ngurunderi)**, **Nurelli (Nepele)**, Bunjil, **Mungan-Ngana**, Daramulun, and Baiame (Baiami) 'all represent the same being under different names'. Too little is known about the mythology and ritual associated with them to be sure if they had 1 Supreme Being. Among the **Kamilaroi** Baiami was believed to have created everything. Among the **Yuin**, Daramulun lived on the Earth with his mother, **Ngalalbal**. *'There were no men or women, only animals, birds, and other creatures. He placed trees on the earth. Then Kaboka, thrush, caused a flood which destroyed all but a few of the people Daramulun had made, They crawled out of the water onto **Mt Dromedary**, Daramulun went into the sky, where he now lives, looking down upon the affairs of men'*. Such a fragmentary outline could have easily been influenced by alien contact (not of the UFO type).

In 1943, the Berndts were unable to get the details of the Baiami myth, he was still well-known, but was alluded to mainly in the context of initiation and magic. And also his appearance during certain rites. The emu was under his direct protection, so there were probably totemic affiliations. His wife, Guriguda, mother of Wakend, the Crow, left the Earth in the Dreamtime, going up into the sky to Wandanggangura, the place beyond the clouds..

See Baiame

This seems to be fairly typical for southeast Australia, where the totemic aspect does not seem to be stressed in this context. Shape-changing ancestral beings are common in northern South Australia, Central Australia and central Western Australia, to the Southern Kimberleys. The human elements appear to dominate in some cases or circumstances, the non-human in others. The essential qualities of one of these characters are assumed to be constant, whatever form he adopts, his words and actions carrying equal weight. Examples are the great **djundagal snake** who travelled through the east Kimberleys; **Bangal**, the creator Bat also in the east Kimberleys. There is also the **Moon Man** of the **djanama** subsection, with his many wives, all *nawala,* who today are the dark patches on the moon's face. These mythical figures are more than human. The final change from human to non-human shape results from a climax, either the end of a myth, or an episode in a myth, though sometimes it is the other way around.

The muramura beings were well-known among the **Dieri** and Lake Eyre area. In the Dreamtime, these beings wandered around the area creating and instituting the rituals. In one of the myths about these beings, in the beginning the earth opened in the middle of Perigundi Lake and a number of *mardu* (matrilineal clan totem) emerged. After lying in the sun for a while until they were strong, they stood up as men and spread out across the country.

People of the Western Desert say there are still wandering *djugurba* beings like those among the Dieri. They are part human and part animal - reptile, bird, etc., but they are thought of as mostly human in the mythology. The **Wadi Gudjara**, Two Men, are among the most important. One was called Gulgabi or Milbali, the white goanna; the other was Jungga, the black goanna. On their travels they created many local sites and instituted a number of rites. Njirana and

Julana are names used interchangeably for the ancestral man and his penis. There were also many others, Wadi Malu (Kangaroo Man), Minma Waiude (Possum Woman), Wadi Gulber ('Blue' Kangaroo Man), Minma Nganamara (Mallee-hen Woman), Wadi Galaia (Emu Man), Minma Mingari (Mountain-devil Woman), and Wadi Bera (Moon Man). The mythology associated with all of them is very long, mostly in song versions.

The total myth is made up of hundreds of incidents. In one story the Wadi Gudjara, Two Men, chase Minma Nganamarra, Mallee-hen Woman, to obtain her eggs. Wadi Bera, Moon Man, seduces one of Wadi Gudjara's women at Mindel-jari, they later castrate him and his severed penis is metamorphosed into a stone.

The Rainbow serpent is a common theme over much of Aboriginal Australia, being known by various names, but is always associated with water or rain. In some areas it is male and in others is female. Its link with sacred ritual varies widely throughout the country. The Rainbow is called **Wonambi**, living in rock pools and billabongs, in major parts of the Great Victoria Desert. It plays a major part in the initiation of native doctors. It is associated with rock paintings, and with rain and spirit children in the Kimberleys. He is always male and maybe associated with the **Lightning snake** in eastern Arnhem Land. Among the Maung of Goulbourn Island in western Arnhem Land it is male. It is sometimes male but more often female among the mainland Gunwinggu. Ngaljod (Ngalyod) (Ngal- is a feminine prefix) is one of her ordinary names. She is believed to bring floods to drown people who break certain taboos and children who refuse to stop crying. In myths she can be summoned by people who want to destroy a whole camp and suicide at the same time. Menstruation and childbirth are associated with her. She may also take different forms in different contexts. She made all living things, the first creator, in one version.

Most ancestral beings have mixed human and non-human forms in the desert areas and central Australia. They are more often human only in form on the northern coast, but they are associated with a large variety of totems, directly and indirectly. One of the major myths of the Gunwinggu of western Arnhem Land involves a woman, most commonly known as Waramurungundju, though she was also known by other names.

East from the East Alligator River, a lot of the country consists of river gorges and creeks between rocky hills and sandstone ridges. The rock formations can be spectacular, so it comes as no surprise that many have been connected to various Dreamtime beings in mythology. A recurring theme in the mythology of the area is the Rainbow, Ngaljod. In many stories she swallows the various beings, vomiting up their bones which turned into the rocks. In the translation of these stories the term used to describe these events is that 'they came into dreaming'. Among the Gunwinggu, the term *djang* is the term used for this kind of representation. A *djang* is an object, creature or spirit containing some power or essence that derives directly from the Dreamtime. Taboos cover some *djang* sites, they are said to be dangerous to certain parts of the community, such as women, children or in some cases everyone but the very old. Some are avoided by all members of the group, being considered too dangerous for anyone to go near. The term -djamun, set apart - not for everyday use, is used by the Gunwinggu. The term is also used for sacred rites and objects, the men's sacred dancing ground, and food to be used for ritual consumption. The *djang* are mostly of minor importance compared to beings such as Ngaljod. They are connected to specific localities, and have a limited range of influence, some more widely, e.g., Wuragag, Tor Rock, a prominent landmark. People knowing the name of a feature of the landscape, not directly connected with the person or their family, often don't know the myths associated with it.

In western Arnhem Land, the ubar, a long wooden gong shaped like a hollow log, is one of the most sacred objects. Among the Gunwinggu it is the uterus of the Mother, sometimes identified with Ngaljod.

The mythology surrounding the ubar is a bit different among the Maung of Goulburn Island. The ubar is still the uterus of the Mother, but more emphasis is placed on its phallic aspect. The ubar is also the penis of the male Rainbow Serpent.

The Djanggawul, or Djanggau, sisters, usually in conjunction with their brother, are 2 principal Fertility Mothers in north eastern Arnhem Land. The elder one is Bildjiwuraroju, and the younger is Miralaidj.

The mythology connected with them tells how the 2 sisters and their brother Djanggawul, and in some versions a companion, Bralbral, came across the sea from the north-east. After pausing for a while at Bralgu, an island somewhere in the Gulf of Carpentaria, near the home of the Dua moiety dead. Then they followed the path of the sun to the east coast of the mainland.

The sun is female in this area, and is connected with the 2 sisters. In other areas it is considered male. At Millingimbi the sisters are called 'Daughters of the Sun'. They symbolise the sun with its life-giving properties. In other parts of Australia this concept is not found to the same degree, in places like the central deserts where the sun's heat can be dangerous. On the north coast the north west monsoon brings heavy rain during the wet season, making surface water very plentiful.

An example of the things the Djanggawul siblings brought with them, objects or emblems having symbolic associations, the emphasis was on fertility. One of these objects was a round plaited mat rising like a shallow cone to a peak in the centre.

There are several versions of the Djanggawul cycle, owned by the Dua moiety men, though *jiridja* men participate in the ceremonies. This cycle was probably the most important in north eastern Arnhem Land.

Myths connected with the sky and constellations

Emu in the sky
The emu in the sky. At the Elvina Engraving Site in the Kuring-Gai Chase National Park, Sydney, is an engraving of the emu in the sky, a constellation recognised by many Aboriginal groups across Australia, that is formed of dark clouds in the Milky Way, rather than the stars as in most constellations. When the constellation is above the carving in the rock the local Aborigines knew it was time to collect emu eggs.

The head of the emu is the Coal Sack, the dark area near the Southern Cross, its neck passing through the stars called the pointers and the body is in the constellation of Scorpio.

The male emu is of significance to the Aboriginal elders because like the male emu, that hatches its mate's eggs and the cares for the young until they can fend for themselves, the elders carried out the initiation ceremonies that guided the boys into manhood.

The Milky Way

Examples of **Dreamtime stories about the Milky Way** come from South Australia and north eastern Arnhem Land.

In the South Australian story **Jooteetch**, the native cat, had a wife, **Wej**, the emu. One day **Wardu**, the wombat, walked into Wej's camp while Jooteetch was out hunting. He seduced her and when the sun went down she told him to go because her husband would kill them both if he caught them. Wardu go up to go, but first he covered Wej with red ochre, which is precious, that was used for ceremonies. She told Jooteetch she found the ochre but he didn't believe her. He had seen Wardu's tracks and made her tell him the truth. He told her to make a fire, then grabbing her, threw her into the fire. She flew out of the fire and right up to the sky. She became the dark patch in the Milky Way known to the Aborigines of the area as **Wej Mor**.

In an example from north eastern Arnhem Land, the story from the Dreamtime when animals and men were all one people, Walik, the crow, and Bari Pari, the cat, built a fish trap on the beach. On the first day the trap caught **Balin** the barramundi, and some of his friends and relatives. Walik and Bari pari decided to have a dance ceremony to show their happiness at catching so many fish. As they danced Balin called out to other clans to come and help him. When they came they speared and ate Balin and all the other fish. When the crow people and the cat people came to collect the fish all that was left was Balin's bones on the sand.

They said they had to fight the people who ate the fish, but first they buried the bones because he was a friend and totem, as they would not have eaten Balin. They planted a hollow pole, painted it, put Balin's bones in it, and set it in the sand. When they caught up with the people who had eaten the fish they had a fight, but they were losing because there were too many people in the group who ate Balin. The cat people and the crow people decided to fly up to the sky with the pole containing Balin's bones, camping beside the river that flows across the sky. The twinkling in **Milnguya**, the Milky Way, is really the many camp fires and the small spots on the cats. Walik the crow and the pole containing Balin's bones are also there.

Swimming in the river is Ying-arpaya, the great crocodile, the spines on his back and the curve of his tail are marked by big stars.

Wuriunpranilli, the Sun Woman

The peoples of northern Australia have an explanation of why there is night and day. They say the Sun is the light from a torch made from the stringy bark tree that is carried by the Sun Woman, Wuriunpranilli. When she wakes each morning she makes a small fire, this is the dawn glow on the horizon. She then decorates herself with red ochre, some of which gets onto the clouds, resulting in red sunrises. As she is getting ready for her journey across the sky the birds start calling to wake the people for the day's activities. She lights her giant stringy bark torch from the small fire, then begins her journey across the sky. When she drops below the western horizon she puts her torch out and applies more red ochre in the glow from her smouldering torch, which again often gets onto clouds to give red sunsets.

During the night she walks through the tunnel connecting her evening camp to her morning camp. At this time the birds stop calling until she wakes them next morning.

Kangaroo Island Mythology

Ngurunderi

Ngurunderi was a creation being in the Dreaming of the tribes of the lower Murray River, lakes and Coorong of South Australia. These tribes believe that the spirit follows the path taken by Ngurunderi to Naroongowie (Kangaroo Island) after death, where they travel to the Waleruwar (the spirit world) in the Milky Way.

One of the stories of **Ngurunderi** is about his pursuit of 2 of his wives who ran away.

2 of his wives ran away and he followed them across **Lake Albert** and along the beach to Jervis Bay where he saw the 2 women wading across the shallow channel that connected Naroongowie to the mainland. He punished them by ordering the water to rise up and drown them. The rush of water carried them back towards the mainland. They tried to swim against the current but drowned. Their

bodies are now 2 rocks off Cape Jervis that are now called The Pages or the Two Sisters.

He swam out to the island, and as it was a hot day, for shade, he made a she-oak tree that was the largest in Australia. He tried to sleep under the tree but the wailing of his drowning wives kept him awake. He walked to the end of the island where he cast his spear into the sea. The rocky reef that resulted is still there. He threw away all his weapons and moved to his home in the Milky Way, where the people who follow the laws he gave them will join him when they die. It is said that anyone who sleeps under a she-oak tree will hear the wailing that kept Ngurunderi awake.

Baiame See Sky Heroes

The Kamilaroi believed that Baiame created everything. When studies were undertaken at Menindee in 1943 it was not possible to gather much detail of the Baiame beliefs. His wife was said to be Guriguda, the mother of Wakend (the crow). One night she was sitting in the same camp as her son Wakend and his wife were eating together. Wakend would give nothing to his mother. Guriguda was angry, but Wakend grew tired of her constant grumbling and speared her in the knee. Instead of pulling out the spear he left it in the wound and it was on this that she climbed to Wandanggangura in the sky, the place beyond the clouds. Guriguda resembles an ordinary woman, but instead of skin she is covered all over with quartz-crystal, and as she turns rays of light flash in every direction. Her assistant totem (called *jarawajewa*. the 'meat which is within') is the emu, so that she and the emu are identified

There is a more complete myth among the Ngurunderi of the lower Murray River in South Australia. This is a version from an old man, Albert Karloan, who has since died, who was the last of his people to be initiated.

The ancestral hero Ngurunderi paddled his bark canoe down the small creek which was later to become the River Murray. He had come from the Darling, following the giant Murray cod. As this fish swam, its tail swept aside the water, widening the river to the size it is today. When Ngurunderi paused to rest, the cod swam on into the Lake, and he gave up all hope of catching it. Then he thought of his 'wife's brother', Nepele. Quickly getting into his canoe he quickly rowed to Bumongdung, and from there called out to Nepele, who was sitting on a red cliff named Rawugung, Point McLeay. Nepele pushed out his canoe, rowed it to some shoals, and waited with spear in hand. The cod swam down towards Nepele, who speared it opposite Rawugung and placed it on a submerged sandbank there. When Ngurunderi arrived they cut the cod into many small pieces, throwing each into the water and naming the fish it was to become. Finally they threw the remaining part into the lake saying, 'Keep on being a Murray cod.'

Ngurunderi continued his travels. Eventually he reached Bumongdung, where he disembarked and pulled up his canoe: his footprints are still there. Carrying the canoe he walked to Larangangel, where he left 2 large mounds of freshwater mussels. One day, on his way back from granangung, he saw some people at a place called Ngirlungmurnang. They were frightened of him and hid in the reeds. But Ngurunderi could hear them whispering, and he transformed them into a species of blue bird. At this juncture Ngurunderi's 2 wives appeared. They were at Gurelbang cooking the dugeri (silver bream), taboo to women, and the breeze from that direction carried the smell to him. Having no further use for his canoe, he stood on the 2 mounds of Larangangel, and lifting it up, placed it in the sky where it became the Milky Way. He then set off for Gurelbang. In the meantime, the 2 women, thinking Ngurunderi might smell the fish, had made their escape on a reed raft, poling their way across Lake Albert to Thralrum, on the western side. There they left the raft, which was metamorphosed into the reeds and yaccas found at that point today, and continued down into the Coorong.

When Ngurunderi reached Gurelbang and found them gone he too made a raft, and followed them into the Coorong. Here he met a malignant spirit named Barambari. Ngurunderi asked whether he had seen the 2 wives. But Barambari started a quarrel and speared him in the thigh. Ngurunderi laughed, pulled it out and threw it away. Then he threw his club, knocking Barambari unconscious, and thinking he was dead turned to go. But Barambari regained consciousness, and manipulated his magical spear-thrower in such a way as to stop Ngurunderi from walking on. Ngurunderi returned and killed him with his club. He lifted some large gums and other trees, piled them into a heap and set them alight, then lifted Barambari's body and placed it on top of the blazing pyre so it would be completely consumed. Turning around he tried again to walk away, but again could not do so. He picked up all the congealed blood and threw it on the fire, and after that he was able to continue. At Wunjurem, he dug a waterhole in the sand to get fresh water, kneeling down to drink he put his head against the sand, and this impression was transformed into rock.

Eventually he came to Ngurunduwurgngirl ('Ngurunderi's home'), where he lived for some time, giving up all hope of finding his wives. Later he continued his wanderings down the coast along **Encounter Bay**, and after a number of adventures was about to cross over from the mainland to Kangaroo Island when he saw his wives starting to do so. It was possible, at that time, to walk across to the island. When they reached the centre Ngurunderi called out in a voice of thunder, 'fall on them, you waters'. Immediately the sea rose and they were drowned; but they were metamorphosed into Meralang 'two sisters', now called **The Pages**, north east of **Cape Willoughby** on Kangaroo Island. Ngurunderi then went to Kangaroo Island, called Ngurungaui, meaning 'on Ngurunderi track', referring to the path taken by all spirits on their way to the spirit world. He made a large Casuarina tree, under which he rested. Then he walked down to the western side of the island, and threw away his spear into the sea; rocks came up at that place. Finally he dived into the sea to cleanse himself of his old life, and went up into the sky, Waieruwar, the spirit world. But before disappearing he told the Jaraldi people that the spirits of their dead would always follow the tracks he had made, and eventually join him in the sky-world.

In parts of southeast Australia **Baiame** is said to have 2 wives and several sons. It is said he returned to earth for the **bora** or great **initiation ceremonies**. His voice could be heard in the sound of the **bullroarer** that warned the women and children to stay away from the sacred, secret initiation ceremonies. He is believed to resemble a human, but knows all and sees all. Even after the great Boras finished they say he still watches over his people.

Baiame - How Swans Became Black

Baiame the Great Spirit lived on a mountain at the end of the world, and beyond that mountain was a land that was inhabited only by women who were skilled weapon makers, spears, boomerangs and nulla nullas. In this land there were no animals so the women traded the weapons for food and skins with men. The transactions always took place in the same fashion; the men piled skins and meat on the edge of a deep lake on the far side of a wide waterless plain. They did this because they were forbidden to cross the lake. When they left the water's edge the women paddled across the lake and took the food and skins, leaving weapons in their place that the men then returned to collect. The men continued to trade in this manner, in spite of the difficulty of reaching the lake, because the weapons were of such high quality that any man owning such weapons gained prestige.

Wurrunah was a man who decided not to conform to the traditional ways of his people and defy the rule of not crossing the lake. He told his 2 brothers that they shouldn't have to take just what the women gave them, as they were only women, men should be their masters. He decided to show them how women should be treated. "Men are always more clever than women," he continued, "if a man is weak and not determined women weaken him with their wiles, but a strong, determined man will always win."

He decided to gather a number of men he could trust, then taking only live animals they had tied up they carried them across the plain to the edge of the lake. Wurrunah led the way with his brothers, followed by the other men, each carrying a live animal on their back. Wurrunah gave instructions when they reached the lake's edge. His plan was to turn his 2 brothers into white swans who would swim out onto the lake. When the women saw them, not having seen anything like them before, previously having seen only wahn (crows) that lived on the sides of Baiame's mountain, they would get into their canoes and try to catch them. As this was happening, he would go around the lake and collect all the weapons in the women's camp.

He conjured up all his magic and turned his brothers into swans and they set out across the lake. On seeing them the women jumped into their canoes and tried to catch them. When Wurrunah reached the women's camp he gathered up all the weapons and headed back with his heavy load. At this point the women saw him and headed for the shore as fast as they could paddle. He shouted loudly to the men on the far side of the lake to release the animals, which they did, and as he expected, the women headed for the far side of the lake, jumping out of the canoes to chase all these animals they had never seen before. The trick worked exactly as Wurrunah had planned and he distributed the weapons to the men who each headed back to his own country.

Wurrunah was so elated at his success conquering the women with his cleverness he felt power flowing through his body. He looked up at the mountain peak where Baiame was said to live and in a mood of defiance started climbing up the sacred slopes. Before he got very far dark clouds gathered around the peak and lightning flashed. A spear-point of light struck him, causing him to fall back to earth, bruised and weakened. His hard-earned power drained away, and with it his magic, leaving no one who could change his brothers back to men. Unable to help his brothers he gasped for breath as he wearily headed for the wide plain on his way back to his country.

As this was going on, Mullian the eagle-hawk soared above him and spotting to the 2 white dots on the lake he swooped down to investigate. He was so enraged that they had invaded Baiame's preserves he attacked the swans tearing their feathers out their bodies. They cried out to their brother as they drifted along. The crows, the birds called wahn, had nested on the slopes of the sacred mountain, under the beaks of the eagle-hawks, their enemies, heard the swans calling for help as they sank in the water. As they had also rebelled against Baiame, they took pity on the swans and plucked feathers from their own bodies and spread them over the swans until they could float and swim again, and they swam ashore.

Baiame was amused by the temerity of the crows and because of their kindness to the swans, allowing the swans to live and decreeing from that time all Australian swans would be black.

Bunjil the Great Eagle Hawk

This is the ancestor spirit among the **Kulin** of Victoria. Bunjil created the environment and all the plants and animals that live in it, including humans. He also taught the people how to survive in their country, and how to make the weapons and tools they used, and gave them their laws.

Bunjil had 2 wives and a son, **Bimbeal**, the rainbow and his wife is the second rainbow that is sometimes seen. When Bunjil finished creating the earth and the people and animals he decided to go to the sky with his family. He told **Bellin Bellin**, the musk crow, who is responsible for the winds, to open the bags he kept the wind in and let out some wind. Bellin-Bellin opened 1 bag and the wind that rushed out uprooted huge trees and blew them into the air. But it wasn't enough, so Bunjil told him to let out more wind. This time Bellin-Bellin opened 2 bags and the wind blew Bunjil and his family into the sky where they became stars watching his people from the sky.

The Djanggawul cycle

The rituals connected with this cycle belong to the *Dua* moiety, but *jiridja* take part in it. The Djanggawul sisters or Djanggau sisters, Bildjiwuraroju is the elder, Miralaidj, the younger, are the principal Fertility Mothers in north eastern Arnhem Land. The Dreamtime story of their arrival has them coming from across the sea to the north east with their brother Djanggawul, stopping for a time on the island of Bralgu, which was said to be somewhere in the Gulf of Carpentaria, near the island of the dead of the *Dua* moiety, before continuing on to the mainland in a bark canoe, following the path of the rising sun, landing on the east coast. In some versions there was also a companion, Bralbral.

In this area the sun is regarded as female, and the 2 sisters are associated with it. At Milingimbi some versions of the story call them the 'Daughters of the Sun'. In this region the sun, which the sisters symbolise, is endowed with life giving properties, essential for the life of all living things, including humans. This attitude towards the sun was common in the north which is in the monsoon belt. In the harsh, arid interior, the sun was thought of as being not quite so benevolent.

The Djanggawul siblings brought with them a number of symbolic, sacred objects, the main emphasis being on fertility. One of these objects was an ngainmara, a symbolic uterus, a round, plaited mat, the centre of which rose to a peak, forming a shallow cone. These were probably the most sacred of the items brought by the Djanggawul, but they were not used in rituals, instead being used, mainly by women and children to shelter from rain, mosquitoes and midges while sleeping. They were also used to cover women and children during parts of the men's rituals they weren't allowed to see. *"It was not unusual a few years ago to see dozens of them scattered here and there in a beach camp, each sheltering a woman or child"* (Berndt & Berndt, 1964).

The ngainmara the Djanggawul brought with them contained a number of sacred *rangga* emblems, some of which related to animals, plants or trees that became totemic as a result of their association with the Djanggawul. One of the objects was a sacred dilly bag, a symbolic uterus. There were lengths of string to which were attached feathers of lindaridj parakeet. They represented rays of the sun, or in some contexts, an umbilical cord. There were also special patterns that were used ritually by different clans and linguistic units.

The principal role of the Djanggawul was as creators. The first human ancestors of the north-eastern Arnhem Land people were said to be born from the Sisters, or taken from the ngainmara mat or sacred dilly bag, later applying the finishing touches such as separating the fingers. They started the practice of childbirth as it has been ever since. They put the animals and plants in the area for the people, special sites as reminders of their physical presence in the area. They also instituted the biggest rituals, the Dua moiety nara. After many more adventures, they went towards the setting sun along the coast (Warner, 1937, 1958; Berndt, 1952a).

In north east Arnhem Land, a story tells how the Djanggawul sisters came to Marabai, built a shelter in which they hung their dilly bags, or long baskets, that were filled with the sacred emblems. While they were away collecting mangrove shells, their brother and his companions, men whom had been made by the sisters (in some versions of the story they were their brothers, 'fathers' and 'fathers' father'), stole the baskets. The sisters were warned that something was wrong by the whistle of the djunmal mangrove bird. They returned to their shelter to find their belongings were gone, and the tracks of the men who had stolen them on the ground. They followed the tracks but soon heard their Brother beating his singing sticks, and when they heard the men singing they fell to the ground and began to crawl. They were not frightened of the men, but were too afraid of the power of the sacred songs to go near that place. As well as the songs and sacred emblems, the men had stolen the power to perform the sacred ritual, a power that previously belonged only to the sisters. The men had nothing before they stole the ritual. The elder sister said...Men can do it now, they can look after it...We know everything. We have really lost nothing, because we remember it all, and we can let them have their small part. Aren't we still sacred, even if we have lost the baskets?..' (Berndt & Berndt, 1964).

Dhurramulan

Dhurramulan was believed to be the All-Father among some of the tribes of New South Wales, while other believed he was the half-brother or other close relative on Baiame. It was said he had only 1 leg and lived in trees and had a voice that was the sound of distant thunder. He was believed to have taken boys from their families to initiate then, to teach them the ceremonies of the tribe, leading them through the bush with a rug over their heads so they didn't know where they were going, and then he hit them on the back of the head, knocking out a front tooth. Then he threw the boy into the fire to scorch off all his hair. Sometimes he even burned a boy to ashes, but revived him with sorcery. He gave them a type of wood lizard that they had to eat raw.

He eventually entered different trees where he remains, coming out only during initiation ceremonies. A bullroarer, called **Dhurramulan**, is made from a piece of wood cut from one of these trees and the sound it makes when swung around represents his voice. He was believed to be a shape changer, being able to change from the size of a small animal to that of a giant. He was said to like to live on the variously shaped bulges on the stems of eucalypts.

Great Ancestor Spirit - South Eastern Australia

Throughout New South Wales and Victoria there was a common belief in a great **All-Father**, a supreme being, like a male god, known by different names in different areas. The most common name in Victoria was Bunjil and in New South Wales, as Baiame or **Dhurramulan**. The **Great Spirit Father** or **Great All-Father** is credited with creating most of the environment and with giving the

Aboriginal people their laws and culture. He is often believed to have lived on the Earth, before rising to the sky from which he can watch over the events of the Earth. The people of south-eastern Australia believed he returned to Earth during the Bora, or initiation ceremonies, his voice being the sound of the bullroarer that warns women and children to stay away from the ceremonies. Baiame has 2 wives and a number of sons. He is said to be a supernatural being that is omnipotent and saw everything that happens.

The term All Father was used by Howitt (1904), who suggested that all the names used by various tribes of southeast Australia for a male supreme ancestral being were referring to the same being. These names are **Nurrundere (Ngurunderi)**, **Nurelli (Nepele)**, Bunjil, **Mungan-ngaua, Daramulun (Dhurramulan)**, and Baiame (**Baiami**).

The Great Serpents - Rainbow Serpents

There are stories of great snakes from the Dreamtime throughout Australia. The giant serpent of North West Australia is known by 2 different names to different tribes. The country of this legendary snake is the northern areas where the torrential downpours of the wet season swell the rivers, sending them rushing through the gorges they have cut on their way across the plains to the sea. The sinuous tracks of these rivers, such as the Alligator River and the Liverpool River, and deep waterholes are believed to be the abode of the great serpents, in particular, the powerful Rainbow Serpent. It is associated with the wet season storms that bring so much water to the rivers, changing dry river beds to raging torrents.

The Gunwinggu call the Rainbow Serpent Ngalyod, while the Miali call it Borlung. Whatever its name, it is believed to inhabit deep permanent waterholes. Some groups say it is male, others that it is female, still others say it is male with the breasts of a woman. It is greatly revered and feared, being spoken of in lowered voices. There are not many stories of great deeds performed by the Rainbow Serpent, those there are mostly tell of its physical attributes and the ways it uses when it seeks vengeance on anyone who makes it angry.

The Ubar ceremonies of western Arnhem Land were associated with the Rainbow Serpent, the cylindrical wooden drum being beaten rhythmically to represent the voice of **Waramurungutidji**, mother of the serpent. One of the stories of the Ubar ceremonies associated with the Rainbow Serpent is that of **Yirawadbad**, who is sometimes said to be the husband of **Waramurungutidji**. In this story the serpent is a male.

Ngalyod

To the Gunwinggu, the **Rainbow Serpent** is Ngalyod, the great creation mother from whom the first people were born. She is the great creator, ever since the Dreamtime, because she brings the Wet Season after the long Dry, which rejuvenates the land with plants and animals flourishing. After rain she stands on her tail to reach high into the sky.

Ngalyod is a harsh mother, punishing severely those breaking her taboos or failing to observe the rituals associated with her Dreaming sites. She gave the people their laws and taught them the ceremonies they must perform, punishing any law breakers, becoming furious and keen on vengeance if the laws and ceremonies are not observed.

Borlung

Borlung is always male, and sometimes he is referred to as the son of **Ngalyod**. As with **Ngalyod**, he is seen as a rainbow in the sky, sometimes over water, and even in the spray from a waterfall. The **Dalabon** believe there are many Borlung, and they believe the Borlung are strongly linked to fertility. The Borlung snakes are common in waterholes, and one must enter a woman if she is to conceive. When a person dies, the spirit will change back to a Borlung and return to the waterhole to await another woman it can enter as the spirit of the baby. In central Arnhem Land, west of Maningrida, the Rainbow Serpent is usually called Borlung.

Among the people of this area, in the **Goregun**, the beginning of time, there was **Jingana**, the Mother. Jingana grew 2 large eggs in her belly, one becoming the male serpent Borlung, the other a female, **Ngalkunburriyaymi**, had an appearance more like that of a fish. When represented in paintings, Ngalyod and Borlung are usually given snake forms, Jingana usually has a composite hermaphroditic appearance, having a head ornament of white cockatoo feathers, a beard, a serrated back like a crocodile, and her chest has a prominent bulge like a brisket bone.

Jeedara

The **Mirning people** were the occupiers of the Nullarbor Plain, mostly in the south near the coast. They are not thought to have moved far into the central parts of the plain. The deeper caves were believed to be the home of Jeedara, a water serpent. According to their Dreamtime stories he was chased by Yugarilya, the Pleiades, pushing up the Bight cliffs and hiding in the caves. The air rushing in and out of blowholes was said to be his breath. They feared the places where he lived because he seized anyone he found in his territory. Evidence of their presence in some caves is seen in caves such as Koonalda Cave.

Kimberley Snakes

Great Serpents - Eastern Australia

Arkaroo - Gammon Ranges

Giant Serpents - Eastern Australia

The serpents in various stories are endowed with a wide variety of temperaments in various parts of the continent, some being so belligerent that the people cannot approach the waterholes where they live, whereas others they can. Fire is a deterrent, being used to allow people to camp near waterholes that are known to be the home of a serpent. The beliefs of different parts of Australia vary as to the connection of the snakes with fertility and spirits of children. Among the Wiradjuri of New South Wales, the serpent created the ceremonies and inspires artists.

According to the stories of the Wiradjuri, The **Wawi** is serpent-like, lives in waterholes on the Darling River, where it burrows into the banks. The Wawi's wife and children live in a nearby camp. The only person who can go near the Wawi is a clever man ('doctor'), who must paint himself all over with red ochre. To find Wawi, the man watches for a rainbow after a thunder-shower, finding the place where the end of the rainbow is over a waterhole, which tells him the home of the Wawi. He dives into the water and is taken to the hole of the Wawi where he is taught a new song for corroboree. When he returns to camp he goes into the bush with a few other clever men. They strip pieces of bark off the trees and paint different patterns on them with earth ochres. These bark paintings are taken to the corroboree ground where all the men sing the new song as they dance. The Wawi can change his size from a few inches to very big. One of the ancestors of the Wawi is a black streak in the Milky Way towards the Southern Cross.

There are stories of giant beings that are described either as serpents of crocodiles. The confusion of form is similar to that of the **Borlung** in Arnhem Land. There is the story of a great hunter, Toolalla of the Barwon River, who decided to kill the powerful snake to remove the menace to his people. He was unsuccessful, having to run for his life, taking refuge in a very tall tree until the serpent returned to the water. It is said the serpent is in the water of Boobera Lagoon when it is swollen by floodwater. It was said this serpent couldn't travel on dry land, digging into the bank of its waterhole when it wanted to travel, the water following and carrying it along the trench. The large number of shallow channels around Boobera Lagoon were said to be these channels dug by the serpent.

An example of giant serpents in Queensland comes from the Bloomfield River. This serpent is **Yero**, inhabiting long, deep pools connecting the waterholes and rapids of a stream known as the Roaring Meg, which flows to the river from rugged mountains. Yero is described as having the appearance of a giant eel or serpent with a striped body and a large head with red hair. It was said that if a man entered the water of one of the waterholes he will be pulled about by **Yero**.

There is a similar description of a supernatural water snake with a head of hair like a mane. He is said to be associated with quartz crystals at the ends of rainbows that were said to have come from the great serpent's body. The native doctors use them for their magical power.

The **Bunyip** was another being that was feared by the people of South Australia and Victoria. Like the great serpents, it lived in waterholes. The **Arkaroo** were ancestors of the **Flinders Ranges** people who appear to have had a serpent-like appearance. Also in Victoria, was a giant snake called **Myndie**, who had been created by Bunjil, the Great Creator, to be the keeper of his laws. Myndie was the enforcer, punishing law breakers. Like some other great serpents he could vary his size at will. He lived in a waterhole near **Puckapunyal (Bukara-Bunnal)**, but could climb trees, where he used his tail to grip branches like a ring-tailed possum.

The Wilpena Pound Serpents

According to the stories of the **Adnyaantana** (Adnyamathanha) **people** of the Flinders Ranges, at the end of the Dreamtime the bodies of 2 Arkaroo were changed into the steep walls that surround Wilpena Pound, their spirits became large, multi-coloured creatures with manes and beards that inhabit a waterhole at the entrance to the pound. It is said that during the Dreamtime the 2 Arkaroo heard that the first circumcision ceremony was to be held at Wilpena Pound in the Flinders Ranges. They decided to destroy the people so they travelled to the Pound and waited until the ceremony was finished. They surrounded the people who had gathered for the ceremony and used very powerful whirl winds to sweep the people into their mouths. The only survivors were **Wala** the wild turkey, **Yulu** the kingfisher and the initiate.

See Yamini, Rainbow Serpent, Atherton Tableland

Tagai the Warrior

Tagai was a warrior who came to Earth to fish. Also in his out-rigger canoe were Zugubals, beings who assumed human form when they were on Earth. On one fishing trip they were catching no fish so Tagai, the best of the fishermen, decided to walk on a nearby reef to look for fish. He took a long time and his crew got very hot. They tried diving into the water but decided that the only thing that would cool them down was to drink fresh water, but there was none available. They got so thirsty they drank the supply of water Tagai had stored in coconut shells for the trip. When Tagai returned he killed them all for taking all the water for the trip. Because they were Zugubals, he returned them to the sky in 2 groups. One group became Usal (the Pleiades), the other Utimal (Orion). He was still angry at them, so he banished them to the northern sky, telling them to keep away from him. Whenever they want to visit the eastern sky they must warn Tagai they are coming with thunder and lightning. When he hears this thunder and sees the lightning he moves below the western horizon.

Arkaroola, SA (the place of Arkaroo)

Mountain scenery at Arkaroola, northern Flinders Ranges Sillers Lookout (left), Arkaroola, northern Flinders Ranges

Arkaroo was a great serpent from the Dreamtime who lived in the Gammon Ranges south of Arkaroola. According to the stories about him among the **Adnyamathanha** people, he felt very thirsty so slithered down to the plains and drank Lake Frome and Lake Callabonna dry. When he finished drinking he went back to the Gammon Ranges, his long body gouging out the bed of **Arkaroola**

Creek and a number of waterholes at places he rested along the way as he moved. The large volume of salty water he drank gave him a terrible bellyache. The Aborigines believed that was the cause of the rumblings coming from beneath the ground in the Gammon Ranges, where he has slept in **Yacki Waterhole** since that time, every time he moves around in his restless sleep the water in his belly sloshing around rumbles. The water emerging from this spring is just below boiling point.

An alternative explanation is that the sounds result from minor tremors along fault lines produced by earth movements associated with readjustment of the crust after uplift of the area.

Paralana Hot Springs is one of the most important of the waterholes left by Arkaroo. The local Aborigines used it for cooking and bathing, especially as is was said to cure minor aches and pains. According to the dreamtime story it wasn't originally hot but in the Dreamtime 2 young men fought over a girl, the winner plunging the firestick he used to vanquish his rival into the spring where it heated the water, remaining hot to this day.

The Adnyamathanha Aboriginal people lived in the region before the arrival of Europeans.

Kimberley Snakes - The Kimberley (Rainbow Serpent)

In the Kimberley region there are myths associated with snakes as are found in other parts of northern Australia such as Arnhem Land, where the snakes are connected with water and thunderstorms, and also with the spirits of children and fertility, their images being found on the walls of many caves and rock shelters. In the Kimberley these snakes have a number of names, **Ungud, Lu, Lumeri, Lumuru**. They may appear as a rainbow or a whirlpool in the sea.

In the Kimberley, the mythology tells of great pythons that travelled from the east to the west, the tracks they made becoming the rivers of the area. On their travels they reached the north west corner of the Kimberley then travelled south along the coast until they reached the **Worora** country. The **rock python** travelled from the east to the sea. The snake took babies with her, and she became very tired and the babies were crying, so she lived in the **Mandangary Cave** (the Gum of the Kurrajong) on **Gibb River Station**. She painted herself on the wall of the cave, and after resting, travelled to **Manning Creek**, where she stayed on the cave wall.

In the most north-westerly part of the Kimberley region the Rainbow Serpent is replaced by the **Wandjina (Wondjina)**.

Wonnaira from the Kimberley

Mala the hare-wallabies and Kurpannga the spirit dingo
Pitjantjatjara-Yankuntjatjara, of central Australia

A party of Mala, hare-wallabies, travelled from their country to the north west of Mt Liebig to Uluru for an initiation ceremony. The route they followed became a line of bare rock on the north west corner or Uluru. The women set up a separate camp with their children and foraged from it every day. As the ceremonies were taking place an old man was sent to make sure the women didn't see the secret, sacred, ceremonies, that were 'men's business'. It was believed that if the women saw the rituals it would break the power of the Ancestral Spirits.

The rituals were performed on a bare patch of ground; this ground had been transformed into the back wall of a deep, cylindrical cave on the side of the rock. The cave is considered so sacred that women are not allowed to even look in the direction of the cave when they pass. The Wintalyka, Mulga-seed men, from the Petermann Ranges sent the messenger Panpanpanala to Uluru while the rituals were in progress to invite the Mala people to a ceremony. The Mala were asked to bring some decoration materials so they could use some of them. This made the Mala men so angry they sent back some white ash and a discourteous reply.

This made the Wintalyka very angry, so they asked their sorcerers to devise a revenge for the insult. Kurpannga, a giant, malevolent Spirit dingo was conjured and they sent him to Uluru. He looked like a dingo with not much hair and had very sharp teeth, and the singing of the sorcerers made him want to fight and kill strangers.

Kurpannga arrived at the Mala men's camp at midday when they were all asleep, except for Lunba, the old kingfisher woman, who was on watch. She warned them of the approach of Kurpannga but he killed 2 men before the rest of the Mala escaped to the east with their sacred emblems. The camps of the participants in these events, the sites of their battles and deeds were transformed into boulders and natural features of the rock at the close of the Thjukurpa (Tjukurpa), the Dreamtime. The main camp of the women and children is a large cave on the north west corner of Uluru. The erosion patterns are the transformed features of the women.

A long, curved line of caves in an eroded section of the northern and north western walls of the rock was the young men lying on the ground as the older men decorated them for the ritual. The bark brush used to apply paint in ceremonial designs is a now dark water stain on the rock face.

The use of Ayer's rock as a tourist attraction has caused a lot of stress to the local people who still regard it as sacred.

The mythology of Uluru

The mythology of Kata Tjuta

Megafauna and the Dreamtime

Among the stories from the Dreamtime of the Aborigines in many parts of Australia are references to giant animals that in many cases can be traced to fossils of animals that formed the megafauna of Australia. There are also mentions in some stories of what appear to be a time before much of the country reached the arid state it is now in.

In the Aranda stories of the giant kadimakara there is what could be an oral tradition of the coming of the dry times to central Australia. In places that are now desolate, such as the Willandra Lakes and Lake Eyre, the country was much different when the Aborigines first arrived there. At that time the lakes were full and there is evidence of Aboriginal camps beside the lakes.

The kadimakara story speaks of a time when the climate of the area was much wetter than at the present, and the clouds were thick and the ground was covered with vegetation. At that time, the sky was held up by tall gum trees. In this sky-land lived monsters called kadimakara. Often the smell of fresh vegetation enticed them down from their home, climbing down the gum trees to feed in the lush vegetation. The last time the kadimakara came down to earth they were feeding on the plants when the 3 gum trees that had been supporting the sky fell and they were unable to return to their land. They roamed the country and wallowed in the marshes of Lake Eyre until they died, their bones still being present where they died. With the fall of the 3 gums the sky became a single continuous hole, 'Pura wilpanina' (great hole). In times of prolonged drought the Dieri held ceremonies at the bones of the kadimakara to ask them to intercede with those who remained in the sky land and control the clouds and rain.

The lakes of central Australia never refilled permanently after the last glacial maximum. At most, they partially fill after heavy monsoonal rains in their northern catchments, but soon dry out again once the floods diminish and the extremely high evaporation rates of the hot, dry areas takes its toll.

The oral traditions of the Aboriginals allow a glimpse of what they might have thought and fragmentary evidence of ancient art allow some insight into what they saw. According to the author[4] tradition is embedded in art and art is embedded in stone all across the Australian continent. Among the examples of stone art is some of the oldest art in the world, the images of ancient animals transcending time to give a secular appreciation of the environmental, emotional and spiritual cognisance of the first human inhabitants of Australia. On the Arnhem Land Plateau in northern Australia, rock paintings, of which 126 are known so far, represent animals that have been extinct for thousands of years. The age of some of the paintings are believed to be between 40,000 and 50,000 years old, which would make them the oldest paintings in the world. The ancient artists obviously had an eye for natural details when they skilfully painted emotive testaments to animals that have been extinct for at least 45,000 years, in washed combinations of iron oxides applied and diffused in rock faces of quartzite that are now encased in silica. The rare art works depict deceptively loose representations of animals that no living person has seen, though confidence in the reality of the animals is gained from the details depicted in them. A good example is a representation of a thylacine that can be immediately distinguished by the details depicted. Details such as the long slender body, the tapered head, the accentuated length, the accentuated length of the tail, that is recurved, bent backwards and down, that is about 1/3 the length of the body, obvious stripes on its rump, the marsupial arrangement of the genitalia in which the scrotum is above the penis which bears backwards and projects beneath the base of the tail. The author[4] described the artist as both an artist and a naturalist. In 1 representation that captures a reproductive rarity, a female has 4 young suckling in a rear-facing pouch. There are also sketches of Tasmanian devils that are just as distinctive, one painting shows a hunter with a boomerang about to strike a Tasmanian devil. These animals were present on the Australian mainland until fairly recently, the Tasmanian tiger being present until about 3,000 years ago and the devil about 400 years ago.

Long-extinct animals have also been similarly depicted in the galleries of Arnhem Land. A full-scale drawing of the long-extinct **Genyornis**, the giant goose-like bird, that is unmistakable, with a tailless rump and massive legs with large heavy feet with 3 rounded toes (which differ from the toes of emus that are pointed). The pose of the bird is heavy, being overweighed towards the head, possibly because the artist wanted to portray its solid appearance, the shape of the head, the blunt beak and the long neck. There appears to have been stripes on the bird's legs and neck, and it appears to have a crop, unlike an emu or cassowary.

There is also a **Zaglossus**, a giant long-beaked echidna that is now extinct, that is distinctive in having a long, narrow, tapering head that is down curved, marked curvature of the back and a tail that is broad and ventrally directed. There are 2 paintings of **Thylacoleo**, the marsupial lion, that show particular attention to detail, one of which appears to be of a dead animal, with its limbs seeming to hang with the feet pointing down as if the painting was of a dead animal, as if it was of an animal that was laid out for inspection. Our knowledge of the animal is increased, as the only knowledge previously held comes from fragmentary skeletal remains. It has an aquiline head, at the end of the tail was a hairy tuft, around its eyebrows, chin and nose were long stiff hairs, on the body were vertical markings resembling fur, long legs with elongated 5-fingered paws, short rounded ears and a rump that terminated abruptly at the base of the tail.

In the Kimberley there is another painting of **Thylacoleo** (34), that the author[4] describes as tiny but a detailed masterpiece in ochre. The animal is striped and appears to be very large compared to the person that is painted beneath it. It has a long tail and massive forelegs and shoulders. The person shown beneath it appear to be either spearing it or fending it off as he holds the barbed spear in both hands. There is no spear thrower and the man seems to be jumping, and the spear is bending as if he is lunging up at the animal as it leaps down from above.

A ***Palorchestes***, a large bull-like animal has also been painted that was thought to be like a giant tapir. The considerable detail of the animal shows that it had an earless head directed upwards, with a line suggesting a mouth, projecting tongue adjacent to which what appear to be small leaves or insects have been painted. It had angled heel joints on short legs and notable claws on its feet, what appears to be a shoulder mane or shaggy long hair and long coarse hair on its back, which is represented by concentrations of dots, and a tail that was short and broad. Adjacent to this painting there is a remarkably similar version of the same animal that could possibly be a joey (a pouch young). It is a refinement of the larger and is suggested to be part of a deliberate composition. Both paintings appear to be dead (35).

"Art is a subjective representation of biology (at the time) and oral tradition is a metaphysical interpretation of that biology over a long period of time) (Cane, 2013).". Maybe these narratives are a mechanism of history as well as a means of understanding. Maybe the religious narratives of the first settlers are more than sacred mysticism, but historical memory encapsulated in tradition that is ritualised (36). The ancestral accounts of the arrival of the first settlers consistently recorded a familiar story. In various parts of Australia the stories of the arrival of the ancestors in Australia all have a similar theme, though the details often differ. In Queensland 'gales brought us here'; In New South Wales 'ancestors came from a land beyond the sea'; in coastal Arnhem Land 'great Djan'kawu came from an island far across the sea . . . in his canoe with 2 sisters; and in Kakadu, 'the lightning man...entered the land on the northern coast' (37). According to Cane (2013) when the ritual enhancements are removed they are effectively stories of colonisation. They tell of the arrival in Australia of people from across the sea, settlement, occupation, growth of population, regional expansion and diversification.

Cane suggests religious belief could be thought of as faithful tradition and encapsulated history held 'true' over vast periods of time, mythology in action, where natural phenomena of supernatural dimensions are embodied in the traditional story. He also suggests an instructive parallel is provided by Western religious tradition. The fundamental truth of the historical experience is not diminished by the tradition being embellished through the mythology.

Therefore the nature of oral tradition does not deny the foundation behind the mythology it conveys, and neither does the passage of time. It is possible to see seeds of historical truth in Aboriginal mythology while remembering its mystical illumination. The widespread nature of mythology relating to a giant snake makes the general point, whether it is the Rainbow serpent of the north or the Wanampi in the desert, from which the giant snake of the megafauna acquired its Latin name. The artistic representation in Arnhem Land dates to at least 8,000 years ago, though the most recent was painted in 1965 (39). One painting of the being central to this ancient oral tradition is 6.5 m long. The serpent symbolises fertility through propagation, progeny and precipitation. Behind the visual imagery, rhetoric and ritual the mythology in the desert is always and everywhere the same. It refers to a large, dangerous snake that inhabits waterholes and caves that punishes transgressors, and those at most risk are children. The account is a superstition in regard to permanent and ephemeral waterholes and as integrated religious narrative across vast areas of country. Stories tell of the serpent being pursued by 2 great figures, the Wati Kutjara, literally 'Two Men', anthropomorphic sand goannas, from the Kimberly to the Great Australian Bight, where the many limestone caves are home to this subterranean monster, the penultimate refuge of Wanampi, which re-emerged in central southeast Western Australia where it is Waugle (Woggle, Wagyl) in the Nyoongar mythology in the Swan River.

The narrative in the southern deserts that is the most secret and sacred relates to a giant goanna, that Cane (2013) suggests is reminiscent, to say the least, of **Megalania**, that is at the core of the famous Red Ochre Dreaming of the arid zone of Greater Australia. The particular religious narrative, Tjukurrpa is very significant so that the associated ritual objects are so precious that they are transmitted from community to community with great care, deliberation, reluctance and ceremonial duty. There is cyclical movement of the ceremonial expression around the desert in a very slow manner, so slowly that the ritual cycle may take 20-30 years to complete (41). The ceremonies have cycled once through the desert since they last went through the Everard Ranges in 1968.

There is a myth that describes central Australia as a place that was once well-watered and fertile in which Kadimakara, a monster, lived in the treetops. The story describes how the landscape dried up and the monster died, and how its bones accumulated in the mud around the edges of the lake (42), just where the bones of **Thylacoleo** as well as those of other megafauna animals are present so abundantly at the present. Cane[4] suggests the narrative may be recent enough for the fossils of the present to be interpreted, or old enough to explain how they got there.

The religious narrative relating to Wati Marlu, the giant transformative kangaroo, Cane describes as the greatest, and possibly the most defining religious narrative of the arid zone. The story is told across the Kimberley all the way across the southern deserts, to the margin of the Pilbara, the edge of the Nullarbor Plain, and through the central ranges towards Lake Eyre where it encounters another signatory story about another fearsome kangaroo. Giant kangaroos and a giant bird (possibly **Genyornis**) are also spoken of in stories by the people of the Lachlan and Murrumbidgee Rivers (43). A giant 'emu' is spoken of in another signatory story of the southern deserts, and there are extraordinary engravings of the tracks of giant flightless birds that are remarkably similar to those of **Genyornis**, in the Keep River district of the Northern Territory, that are believed to be a recent visualization of ancient Aboriginal thoughts (44).

It seems there might be some reality as the basis for the mythical accounts of colonisation, monster reptiles and giant marsupials. Is it possible the suite of giant and frightening animals covered in Aboriginal mythology is based on natural history or simply an extraordinary coincidence? It seems reasonable to allow that there was probably great long-lasting social, psychological and spiritual effects on the people who first explored this unique, often bizarre land, especially as they were unexpectedly encountering megafauna for the first time, among which were some very large and dangerous predators they would need to develop some defence against if they were to survive (45). Cane suggests it is entirely possible that biological and psychological effects of first settlement resonated in social psychology and spirituality of later radiation. When the elaboration is removed the remainder could be expected to be based on the reality of the megafauna, which in some cases would be truly horrifying to new arrivals armed only with spears.

Megafauna dreamtime stories

Giant eagle

Giant emu

Giant Frogs

Giant kangaroos

Yamuti (Adnyamathanha people)

Rock art

Diprotodon

Giant kangaroo (***Sthenurus***)

Long-beaked echidna (***Zaglossus***)

Palorchestes

Quinkana

Thylacoleo (marsupial lion)

Artefacts associated with Megafauna

Cuddie Springs

Coral Bay, Western Australia

Devil's Lair

Mammoth Cave

Possible events recorded by Dreamtime stories

See Aboriginal Occupation of Greater Australia

Giant eagle - Mullyan

The people of the area between Brewarrina and Walgett tell of a Big Dry, when times were very hard. They camped at **Greeah**, one of the last remaining of the waterholes. The people had camped under some giant gum trees that grew around the waterhole, and in the tallest of these trees, **Mullyan** the eagle had its nest. It hunted animals to feed its young, but when its usual prey became scarce during a long drought it started taking babies from the mothers in the camp below. Using their spears to protect them against attack from above the men cut the tree down. The eagles were killed and the base of the tree went into the waterhole, the water flowed along it to the where the nest was. The bones of the animals that had been eaten by the eagles sunk into the sodden ground of what they called Cuddie, 'natural water'.

Giant emu in the Dreamtime

The **Wotjobaluk** tribe of western Victoria had a Dreamtime story of a giant emu. **Ngindyal (Tchingal, Ngindual)** was a giant sorceress who had the shape and feathers of a giant emu, which was said to have killed and eaten many people. In her large nest at **Wambagruk** she laid a single enormous egg. One day a crow disturbed her and she got up and chased him. He slipped into a gap in the side of a mountain but Ngindgal split the rock with a powerful kick. The crack she made is now called **Rose's Gap**. As the crow ran from mountain to mountain she kept cracking the rock with her powerful kick until he reached his spirit waters were she could not follow, so she went back to her nest.

The crow met the **Bram-bram-bult brothers** near Jeparit and told them how he had escaped the Ngindual. They wanted to avenge the deaths of many of their people that she had eaten so they asked the crow to show them where she was. Eventually they saw a bright star that the crow said was her eye as she sat on her nest.

When they came near they encircled her, the younger brother standing in front of her and when she leapt up to attack him the elder brother threw his spear, hitting her in the breast, on which the younger brother threw his spears. Eventually she lost so much blood that she was weakened and ran off in the direction of the **Horsham Plain**. When the lark, **Witygurk**, saw her approaching pursued by the Bram-bram-bult brother he took a bough to conceal himself and when she was in range he threw his spear hitting her in the chest. This final spear killed her.

The brothers then split all her feathers down the middle, piling one half on the left and the other on the right. One pile of feathers was converted into a cock emu and the other into a hen, and their magic also changed Ngindyal's habit of laying only one egg so that emus now lay many. All emus now have double feathers, each having 2 independent shafts.

The people then gathered at **Wambagruk** to collect Ngindyal's egg, but none could lift it. When **Babim'bal** the wattle-bird came he put it in his bag and carried it to the Horsham Plain where it was cooked and the people feasted on it. According to the story the nest can still be seen at **Wambagruk**.

Ngindyal is now the black patch in the Southern Cross and the crow is Argus, still some distance from his pursuer.

Giant Frogs in the Dreamtime

The **Dieri** people from the area near Lake Eyre had a story of 2 giant frogs from the Dreamtime. These 2 giant frogs, who were men at that time, left their country, **Maluka**, near where Mataranka is now, to go on a long walkabout. They travelled north to the Katherine River. There they met 2 other frog men from a different country who were also on a walkabout, and camped together. **Koit-nong-me**, the elder of the 2 frogs from Maluka asked the other 2 frogs to get them some water. He told the other 2 frogs that they were young men and he and his companion from Maluka were old men frogs, so they should carry water for the older frog-men.

The 2 young men refused to carry water for the older frogs so the 4 frog-men began to fight. Koit-nong-me and his companion killed the 2 young men and began walking back to their own country. Sometime later men from the country of the 2 dead frogs found their bodies and took them back to their country. These frog men gathered an army then set out for the country of Koit-nong-me and his tribe to make war.

When Koit-nong-me heard about the army that was heading for his camp he also formed an army of his tribe. The 2 frog armies met on the plain called **Jartee-kunder-wenai**, near the Katherine River. The 2 frog armies formed long lines across the plain facing each other, and an old woman sat on her own on the plain watching them.

The battle began; they attacked each other with stone-headed spears and shields, clubs and stone axes. All the frogs on both sides were killed and lay on the plain in lines and heaps, where they were turned to stone, and the old woman also turned to stone. They can still be seen today on the plain in lines of stone and the old woman who was also turned to stone is still there.

The remains of giant frogs from the Pleistocene have been found in fossil sites such as Riversleigh in Queensland.

Giant Kangaroos in the Dreamtime

In western New South Wales there is a story of the Dreamtime that may be telling of an encounter between Aborigines of the Dreamtime and giant kangaroos. The story is set where the Lachlan River and Murrumbidgee River meet. It tells of a group of people resting in the heat of the day when they see a mob of giant kangaroos approaching. They are afraid and disperse into the bush. The kangaroos killed many by crushing them with the powerful arms. The headman survived and called together the survivors and they devised a defence against these fearsome roos. They made spears, clubs, boomerangs and shields, and the women made bark cradles to carry their babies so they wouldn't get lost when they rushed to escape the roos. The cleverest of the men was **Wirroowaa**. He thought they needed to call on the help of the **Great Spirit**, but to do this he needed to paint his chest with white clay. The clay had to be collected from the banks of the riverbed, but the giant kangaroos were camped there. He killed a brown-banded goanna that he found under a hollow log and smeared its fat all over his body, then rolled around in the dust until he was the colour of the ground. Carrying some branches in front of him to complete the camouflage he crept to the river and collected the clay without being seen. This was the first time camouflage had been used.

A breeze started blowing that got stronger the closer he came to the river. In the strengthening wind 2 sticks were rubbing together and eventually became hot enough that a spark jumped from them to dry grass that caught fire. He quickly rubbed the white clay on his chest in sacred designs that summoned the Great Spirit who told him to keep to the open treeless places. It was already too late for some who had been caught in the fire, but the rest of them gathered in an open clear space. They saw the giant kangaroos on the horizon but when the kangaroos saw the fire they were driven back.

The headman was dying so Wirroowaa painted him with the white clay so the power of the Great Spirit would be with him. He told the people that one day the giant kangaroos would be overcome and told the men to carry spears and clubs and to use bark to make shelters from the hot sun and to make shields.

Depicted in Rock Art

In his book, *Australian Mammal Extinctions*, Chris Johnson refers to paintings of kangaroo tracks that show a single large toe, which is believed to represent an extinct sthenurine kangaroo.

Ochre mine at Wilgie Mia

The Giant Kangaroo speared by Mondong, the blood from which became the red ochre at Wilgie Mia, where the kangaroo landed with its last leap, the liver becoming the yellow ochre and the gall becoming the green ochre.

The Yamuti

Chris Johnson relates a story in his book, *Australian Mammal Extinctions,* of the Adnyamathanha people from the Flinders Ranges, of a Dreamtime mammal called Yamuti (Tunbridge, 1991). He was bigger than any other native mammal, and was dangerous. There is a definite element of fear in the stories, as there is in other stories of the megafauna of the dreamtime. According to the story he ate people. It was believed that he couldn't raise his head enough to look at the sky, so children who came across a Yamuti were told to climb a tree. The Yamuti was also believed to have sometimes taken the form of a giant kangaroo. It is difficult to associate this description with any single megafauna species, making it sound more like a combination of several species, but there remains the fear of a dangerous predator, whether it was a real creature, a mixture of real creatures, or simply a creation to scare children into behaving themselves. A characteristic of the animal in the story does actually coincide with the suggestion that diprotodonts could probably not raise their heads.

They believed the diprotodont remains from Lake Callabonna were those of the Yamuti. Maybe in life the diprotodonts might not have been the gentle giants they are often thought to be, bull elephants in musth can be extremely dangerous. Being around an elephant in musth can easily lead to death.

Land of the Dead

In Aboriginal Australia there were a variety of beliefs concerning death and an afterlife among different tribes and in different parts of the continent. Tribes also often differed, even from their neighbours, in how many spirits were left when a person died, each spirit taking on a different role. Those groups that envisioned a place where the spirits of the dead went often differed as to where that place was, in most areas it was a sky-world, in some it was simply 'in the west'.

Along the Lower Murray River, a hero from the Dreamtime, **Ngurunderi**, travelled for a time on Earth then travelled to the west with his children (Meyer & Taplin, in woods, 1879: 55-62, 200-1, 205-6). When he noticed that 1 of the children was missing, he tied a rope to a spear and threw it in the direction in which he thought the boy would be. The boy grabbed the spear and his father pulled him to safety. Among the people of the Lower River Murray and Encounter Bay, there was a belief that Ngurunderi's sons continued the practice, throwing spears to dead Aborigines to guide them to the Land of the Dead. When the spirit of the dead person arrives Ngurunderi allocates him a place to live. The newcomer weeps and the tears or lack of tears indicates the number of wives he left behind. If tears flow from only 1 eye he has left 1 wife, if from both eyes, 2 wives, if tears stop from 1 eye but continue from the other, etc., he is allocated the same number of wives in the Land of the Dead. In this version, the old are young and the sick are healthy.

In another version, he told the people he was going first and they would follow him later, then **Ngurunderi** dived into the sea at the western end of Kangaroo Island to "cleanse himself of his old life (Berndt, 1940b: 182), then went up into the sky (**Waieruwar**-the **spirit world**). From that time the spirits of the dead follow **Ngurunderi**'s track, spending time on Kangaroo Island before cleansing themselves in the sea prior to following him to the sky where they live with him. In this area, the platform the body is placed on is in the shape of a raft, the craft to transport the spirit of the dead person to **Kangaroo Island**.

Among the tribes in the area between **Botany Bay** and the Victorian border, a place where the spirits of the dead departed for the Land of the Dead was a rock on the eastern side of **Coolangatta Mountain** (Mathews, 1899: 5, 30-5). From this point the gap to the Land of the Dead is bridged by an invisible tree. As they pass along this tree they must undergo several tests, especially fire. When the spirit reaches the other side he must undergo further tests before settling in with his kin who had died before him.

Spirits of the dead are believed to travel to the sky, remaining with the creative beings, the beings from the Dreamtime, over a large area of eastern Australia, as well as some parts of the west and North West (Howitt, 1904: 434-42).

Examples include the **Wiimbaio** from the area around the Murray River-**Darling River** junction, on the Victorian side, where the spirits are believed to travel along a particular track (Howitt, 1904: 434-42).

The **Theddora** from New South Wales have a similar belief. A neighbouring tribe, the Ngarigo, believed that after the spirits travel to the sky they meet **Daramulum** (son/brother) - of Baiame (Baiami) (Howitt, 1904: 434-42).

Among the **Wuradjeri (Wurundjeri)** and their neighbours, the spirits of the dead are believed to climb a cord into the sky to be with Baiame and the other totemic and ancestral beings from the Dreamtime in **Wandanggangura (Wantanggangura)** (Berndt, 1947). In the beginning, the ancestral beings are believed to have passed through a fissure to enter **Wandanggangura**, and since that time the spirits of the dead have to follow the same path through the fissure. The barrier they must pass consists of 2 continuously revolving walls through which a small aperture appears from time to time. There are 2 guardians of this aperture, on one side sits **Moon Man**, and on the other **Sun Woman**. Moon Man has a penis that is so long he carries it wound around his waist, while Sun Woman has a long **clitoris** covering the fire from which daylight and sunshine emanated. The spirit must remain unafraid to pass any further. If he does, he is confronted by **Ngintunginti** and **Gunababa**, 2 ancestral men from the Dreamtime. The spirit must remain silent as the men cross-examine him. They begin to dance in front of him, each with an erect penis, singing humorous songs, during which he must not smile or show any reaction. This test passed, 2 women dance erotically in front of the spirit, as with the 2 men the spirit must remain completely unresponsive. According to the Berndts, this is similar to experiences native doctors have said they experienced, claiming they had travelled to the **sky world**. All tests passed, the spirit is permitted to meet Baiame and **Gurigada**, his wife, who has a body like rock crystal (Berndt & Berndt, 1964).

Among the Wuradjeri, each person is believed to have 2 spirits, a harmless one, **warangun,** and **djir**, a malignant one. The **djir** lives independently but affects the **warangun. It is the warangun** that eventually travels to the sky world. The Djir is connected with the initiation of native doctors.

Spirits of the **Kulin** and **Wotjo** are said to ascend into the sky along the "bright rays of the setting sun" (Howitt, *ibidi*, 431).

Among the **Kamilaroi**, the spirit goes to **Maianba**, the dark patch in the Magellanic clouds, the endless water or river.

The **Milky Way** is the path taken by the spirits of the dead among the people in the area of the Herbert River in north east Queensland (Howitt, *ibidi*, 431).

Among the **Dieri** each person has 3 spirits or souls, 1 of which travelled to the sky world.

In the eastern Kimberleys, the Land of the Dead is in the west. The spirits were believed to return occasionally to the country and to the graves in the gorges where their bones had been placed. In this case the afterlife "does not offer compensation and benefits to those who have been denied them during their lifetime" (Kaberry, 1939: 210-11).

On **Bathurst Island** and **Melville Island**, the **mobadidi**, the spirits of the dead, return to their birthplace at various totemic sites "where they maintain self-contained communities and continue to behave in much the same way as living people (Mountford, 1958: 61-3). When a small child dies, it is a **mobadidi,** for the duration of the mourning, after which it returns to the mother to be born again. When adults die they become young again. Mountford does not specify if they are reborn (Berndt & Berndt, 1964).

In western **Arnhem Land**, the **Gunwinggu** believe that the spirit goes to the sky-world, sometimes known as **Manidjirangmad** (Berndt & Berndt, 1951a). On reaching the sky-world, the spirit meets **Gunmalng** or **Margidjbu**, general terms for a powerful being, who knocks out the middle teeth of the spirit. If the gum bleeds, the spirit is returned to the body which revives. If the gums don't bleed, the person is deemed to be really dead, and the spirit continues along a special path to **Manidjirangmad**. Along the way the spirit disturbs a white cockatoo. The sound of the cockatoo alerts the wife of the guardian that a new spirit has arrived. Feeling sorry for the dead person, she distracts her husband by offering to delouse him, allowing the spirit to pass by. She tells her husband she can see a spirit coming, but waves her free hand to signal the spirit to take another road. She tells her husband she has seen the spirit, but when he jumps up grabbing his spears, it is too late.

The spirit next comes to a large camp of people eating fish. When they see the new spirit they weep because they feel sorry for him. The weeping rouses another guardian who asks why they are weeping. They tell him they are weeping for fish. If the guardian knew the new spirit had arrived he would cut the spirits legs off. When the guardian goes back to sleep, the spirit continues on, and on reaching a river, calls for a canoe. The canoe keeper brings an old canoe for the spirit if is a man, then beats the spirit all the way across to the far side, the real Land of the dead. If the spirit is a woman, he brings a new canoe, lifts her into it and paddles gently across the river, in the expectation of being paid for his trouble with coitus. There are many people in a large camp on this side of the river (Berndt & Berndt, 1964).

Among the Maung, the story has a similar ending. The spirit was believed to go to Andjumu, a billabong near the mission station. Here the spirit waits until a canoe takes him to North Goulburn Island. Walking along the beach the spirit reaches 2 high sandhills, One each for men and women. Climbing the appropriate sandhill, the spirit calls out "We are here!", while facing in the direction of Wulurunbu Island, far away to the north east. When Jumbarba, a giant, who was sometimes identified with a falling star, hears the spirit calling he brings his canoe. In the canoe he has a fighting club with which he beats the spirits of men all the way. As in the version of the Gunwinggu, he treats the spirits of women gently for the same reason. After death the spirits of people are young, regardless of their age at death.

Among the Gunwinggu and Maung, it is assumed that at least part remains in the country of the dead person. The Berndts say there is a lot of uncertainty regarding exactly which part returns to its own country. In a number of rites and invocations of various kinds there is the assumption that the spirit returns to its home site that it belongs to, a waterhole or another dreaming centre, whether it is the place of conception or birth. Ideally this can be in the father's Namanamaidj country. The unattached spirits were believed to be at least potentially malicious, like the non-humans, spirits of the region, and they are unpredictable. One of the terms used for them among the

Gunwinggu is mamu that was sometimes used for both a corpse and a non-human spirit. Like the corpse, they are said to smell like a decaying body. The opinions on their appearance vary, but they seem to be similar to skeletons from which most of the flesh has decayed. This is the basis for the unpredictability, as the lack of a brain makes it impossible to come to amicable terms with them, as they can't think. The spirits of the newly dead are said to be the most dangerous of all, as they strongly resent their changed state, especially when they see living people enjoying life, and worst of all is seeing married couples making love. In their fury they could try to destroy the couple.

In some ways, the range of views on the north eastern side of Arnhem Land display some similarity with the overall picture, but each moiety has its own Land of the Dead. Much information on this point is contained in stories and songs, but here also they don't all agree on specific details. It is often said that after death the spirit of the dead person takes 3 shapes, dividing into 3 parts. One of these returns to the totemic centre, such as a sacred waterhole, to await rebirth. The **mogwoi**, another part, is a trickster spirit that is also bound to the locality, but is much more mobile. It is the third part that goes to the Land of the Dead, to merge with the creative beings and the spirits of the dead. The spirits of the newly dead are said to be present when the djungawon rituals are performed, being in the rangga objects that are used in the rituals (Warner, 1937. 1958: 280-1). It was believed that even if the spirit goes to the island of the dead, or they are taken to a totemic site on the back of a whale, they return to the rangga. This applies to both men and women. According to Warner, the local people said that a woman becomes a **birimbir** spirit **wongar** (Dreaming). Her spirit could go to the same well as that of a man, and like the spirit of a man, her spirit could return to the rangga.

The Land of the Dead of the Jiridja moiety is **Badu**, a collective name that includes several of the Torres Strait islands, as well as the southern coast of New Guinea (Berndt, 1984b). In other versions it is **Mudilnga**, an unidentified island to the north east of the **Wessels**. This island could be included in the **Badu** complex. This island has villages, coconut palms and exotic food, and there are freshwater streams that cross the beach that is fringed with coral reefs. On this island there are a number of spirits whose job it is to look after the spirits of the dead. These spirits are known by many names, one of which is **Duriduri**, also known as **Duradjini**, **Giluru**, **Wuramala** and **Babajili**. She is associated with the turtle, and his body, distended from overeating, is covered with cloud designs. There are also 2 other **Guldana** (**Kultana**), also known by multiple names, the husband lights large fires on Mudilnga to guide the spirits of the dead to **Badu**. In his free time he hunts stingrays in the mangrove swamps, while scratching mosquito bites. His wife spends much of her time in the forest fringing the beach gathering wood and jungle foul eggs.

After the wet season, when the North West monsoon has finished and before the southeast trade winds begin, various items wash up on the beaches around Cape Arnhem and Yirrkalla. Among these items are coconuts, breadfruit, Pandanus cones, long seed pods, as well as timber and the occasional canoe. The people in these areas believed these to be gifts from the **jiridja spirits** to the relatives who are still living. They also believe the north east winds and the clouds are also gifts to them from the **jiridja spirits**. The living send the spirits of their dead by performing the mortuary rites and singing the appropriate songs.

For the Dua moiety, **Bralgu Island** was the location of the Land of the Dead. This island, the identity of which is not known, was visited by the Djanggawul on their journey to Australia by canoe (Berndt, 1952a). It is the abode of some of the beings of importance to the **Dua moiety**, who administer tests to newly arrived spirits as they arrive there. The spirit of a newly dead person of the Dua moiety is ferried to the island by **Nganung**, the paddle maker. The spirits on this island send out Morning Stars to different parts of Arnhem Land as they dance. In the Dua moiety mortuary Ritual of the Morning Star a large pole is used on which are feathered strings and balls of seagull feathers to represent the stars. The actions of the living people in this ritual are said to be an imitation of that carried out by spirits of the dead on **Bralgu**. The spirits on Bralgu send out strings with the stars attached each night and pull them in again as daylight returns. The stamping of the feet of the dancing spirits on Bralgu raise clouds of dust that rise to the sky, changing to clouds they blow over the mainland.

The spirits of the dead pay the canoe man when they reach Bralgu, then carry on along the track through the Bralgu swamp yams, the food of the local spirits. The guardians are alerted to the arrival of a new spirit by the birgbirg bird (Australian bustard), then receive and test the spirits as they arrive. They check his teeth to make sure 1 has been removed and look to see if his nasal septum has a clear aperture. If he fails this test he is sent back. If he passes this test, he must pass unflinchingly as he is threatened with spears. The 2 spirit women stop digging bualgu and tempt him. If he passes all the tests he joins the other spirits and ancestral beings.

From some parts of Aboriginal Australia there are stories of living people having visited the Land of the Dead, not all voluntarily. There is the story of Red Man (he had been painted with red ochre after his death) from the Lower River Murray in South Australia. He had been placed on a platform with a slow fire beneath. The next day he revived and told the story of his travels to the home of Ngurunderi.

Native doctors were said to visit the Land of the Dead occasionally (Elkin. 1945). In eastern Arnhem Land, a man called Jalngura visited Bralgu (Warner 1937/58: 524-8). The Berndts heard the same story in 1946 at Yirrkalla and in 1961 on Elcho Island. According to the story told to the Berndts, a yam leaf blown by the Dua wind landed near Jalngura. As he looked at it he decided to travel to the Land of the Dead. Building a canoe, he fitted it out for the trip, and then he told his wives and children where he was going. He left from Bremer Island, paddling for several days until he came to Bralgu. To gain extra power he rubbed himself with sweat, then picking up his basket and special cylindrical spear thrower, which had a fringe of human hair at one end, of a type first made by the spirits on Bralgu. The spirits greeted him as a friend. A bird flew across his path, calling his name in his language as it passed. They gave him yams, and when he finished they gave him clapping sticks. He sang for them while they danced. Then he was given 3 young girls who he slept with. The spirits offered to let him see the Morning Stars, demonstrating how they were sent out each night and brought back each morning, but the old woman who kept them hidden in a basket at first refused to show him. He kept asking to see them, and eventually he sang a magic song and she relented, taking the balls of feathers attached to strings out. He immediately recognised them as those his people used in the Morning Star rituals. He sang the Morning Star cycle, the old woman sending out the 'ball' stars to different places over the mainland to his accompaniment, and he named each as it was sent out. As the light began to return to the sky the old woman pulled the stars back in and put them in her basket. As he prepared to return home the old woman promised to keep sending out the stars each night and he promised to return eventually with his wives and children. As he left for home, with his canoe full of gifts from the spirits, his spirit wives came to the beach and cried for him. His family were waiting for him on the shore of the mainland. That night, as he was having intercourse with one of his wives, he broke his back and died. It was said his back had been weakened by paddling too much, but the real cause was that his spirit wives had taken his soul.

Memories of the Great Flood - The flooding of the Continental Shelf

At times when the water was rising rapidly, a rate of up to 1 m/week has been suggested; at this rate the Nullarbor Plain lateral territory could be lost at the rate of 2-3 km in a human lifetime. At this rate a favourite hunting place could be lost in single season. The result of this would have been territories lost which would result in the alteration of subsistence regimes, and places of spiritual significance and religious pathways all being lost. It is suggested by Cane that when the sea was rising rapidly as much as 5 km of land could have been lost across the northern coasts of the Australian continent in a year.

Cane[1] suggests that the more than 500 myths about great floods may have their basis in the rising seas as the sea level rise was a global phenomenon and must have had a big impact on human populations around the world, possibly leading to the inclusion of a cultural memory in the myths. If this is the case it could explain the Australian narratives and possibly the story in the bible of Noah's flood, as it would also have affected the people of the Middle East as much the early Australian settlers. According to Cane these narratives invariably account for sea level rise in the context of land lost that existed before the flood. They all account for the rise of the sea level in the context of the previously existing land, they are myths of palaeoenvironmental context that concern less about the formation of the sea as it is seen and understood in the present and more about how the sea changed through antiquity. Joined together they form a body of religious law that Cane[1] says must be 6,500 years old and possibly up to 10,000 years old, which makes them among the oldest known parables in the world.

The accounts from Australia are typically associated with the flattest parts of the country; the places where the greatest impact of the rising sea was felt, as well as being the areas where the rising water could most easily be seen: the Gulf of Carpentaria, coastal Arnhem Land, the Bassian Plain, The Nullarbor Plain and Rottnest Island (Balme & Morse, 2006). The formation of the Gulf of Carpentaria is described as occurring when a raft was dragged across the land which made a channel that filled with seawater. There are 2 mythological accounts on Groote Eylandt that relate to the Tjukurrpa of the desert that reveal connections to the desert when the Gulf of Carpentaria was land. The formation of Elcho Island was said to have resulted from a stick being pushed into the ground after which the sea rushed in and separated the island from the mainland. Long periods of rain are said to have caused the sea to rise and this threatened to extinguish fire that had been maintained by mythological beings.

On the southern coast of the continent the story tells how children found a sacred object on the Bassian Plain causing the land to give way and the sea rushed in with the loss of many lives. The narrative of the formation of Port Phillip Bay describes the area as being a flat, fertile plain that was inundated when a large storm blew up and the sea flooded in. Between Fleurieu Peninsula and Kangaroo Island Backstairs Passage was formed when Ngurunderi, a being from the Dreamtime, ordered the water to rise and drown 2 of his wives who had run away from him. A great flood is spoken of in the stories of the formation of Spencer Gulf. Near the Swan River a great fire swept across the adjacent ancient plains which caused the earth to crack allowing the sea to flood in which isolated Rottnest Island from the mainland (Flannery, 1994).

On the Nullarbor Plain all the Tjukurrpa relate to the emergence of the sea. The Wati Kutjara myth ends abruptly where the 2 men went into the water, via a soak at the Head of Bight. The two men became pillars in the sea, 1 of which recently fell over. According to another story fire is almost extinguished by the rising water, as occurred in the analogous account of the formation of Joseph Bonaparte Gulf, while the aunt of the 2 men who saved it sat cross-legged pushing up a barrier attempting to stop the sea rising any further. Another story describes how a large number of mythological birds, that embodied the people of the Sun and the Shadow, crossed the desert to build a rampart of spears. The desiccation across the desert is related in the first part of the story, the second part concluding with attempted containment of the great flood following it. According to Cane the story of the attempts to stop the rising sea is replete with consequences and desperation, with people and animals dying, land being lost and country submerged. It is a story of distress that the attempts to stop the water would fail. There are also other sequential components in the story describing the re-watering of the desert, of rock holes being filled and the emergence of underground water that supports human life at the present. A story of prevention and rectification, that completes the Tjukurrpa previously described about the desiccation of the desert that had previously taken place. All this mythology is consistent with what has been found about the changing climate of the Holocene.

Mythology of Kata Tjuta 'the place of many heads'

Some stories from the Dreamtime of Kata Tjuta (The Olgas).

Wonambi, the mythical snake

The **Pungalunga** men of Kata Tjuta

Aboriginal mythology of Lake Eyre

The formation of Lake Eyre is connected to the travels of a Dreamtime being in the form of a kangaroo in Tjukurrpa. The Dreaming path across the desert areas taken by the kangaroo is considered very important by the Arabana tribe. Most of the songs relating the exploits of the kangaroo are sacred, secret, 'men's business', not allowed to be told to the uninitiated or women. The story of Wikunda is not included among the secret stories so can be told.

Wikunda hunting the kangaroo that became Lake Eyre

An old woman was hunting and saw a huge kangaroo in the distance. Wikunda, a young boy jumped out of her belly and chased the kangaroo to the west. When his spear finally struck it he thought it was dead and put it on his fire and went to sleep. When he awoke the kangaroo had gone. Wikunda tracked the kangaroo for many days. As he travelled, his path crossed that of an old man with his dog. The kangaroo was finally killed with the help of the dog and Wikunda gave the old man the meat for he only wanted the skin. Wikunda took the skin back to the east and, east of Anna Creek, he threw the skin down. The skin then changed, becoming Lake Eyre. Wikunda can still be seen as a boulder on the shore of the lake he made.

Mythology of the Nullarbor Plain

The Sun Mother

The Earth was completely silent and dark and the land was barren with nothing moving on it. A beautiful woman, the Sun, was asleep in a cave beneath the Nullarbor Plain, and the Great Father Spirit woke her and told her to leave her cave and stir the universe into life. Darkness disappeared when the Sun Mother opened her eyes, her rays spreading all over the land. When she took a breath the atmosphere changed and a gentle breeze blew, the air gently vibrating.

Once she was out of her cave she went on a long journey, going across the barren land from east to west and from north to south. Grass, shrubs and trees grew wherever her rays touched the ground and the land became covered with vegetation. The Sun found living creatures in each of the deep caverns of the Earth, that had been sleeping, as she had been, for unknown ages. She awoke the insects and told them to spread throughout the grasses and trees. Then she woke the snakes and lizards and many other reptiles that slithered out of their deep hole. Mighty rivers flowed behind the snakes that teemed with all kinds of fish and water life. Then she called for the animals, the marsupials and many other creatures, to wake and make their homes on the Earth. The Sun Mother told all the creatures that the days would sometimes change from wet to dry and from cold to hot, she made the seasons. One day as all the animals, insects and other creatures watched, the Sun travelled far in the sky to the west and the sky shone red, and darkness returned to the land when she sank from view in the west. Being alarmed the creatures huddled together in fear. Sometime later a glow began on the eastern horizon and the Sun rose smiling into the sky once again. By this means the Sun Mother had provided a time for rest for all her creatures by making this journey each day.

Mythology of South Eastern Australia

The sky heroes

Baiame and the origin of the Narran Lake

The stone Fish Trap of Baiame See Fish Traps at Brewarrina

Baiame's Camp

Baiame's Bora

Dhurramulan

Bunjil, the Great Eagle Hawk

The Bram-bam-bult Brothers

Aboriginal Beliefs Connected With Uluru (Ayer's Rock) Kunia & Liru

All parts of the rock of Uluru were believed to have been created in the Dreamtime by about 10 Dreamtime spirit people. Most of the southern face was created by the battle between the Liru (poisonous snakes) and the Kunia (carpet snakes). Minor parts of the southern face were created by 2 other totemic creatures, Linga (sand-lizard) and Metalungana (sleepy-lizard). The north western corner and most of the northern face were created by the activities of the Mala (hare-wallaby) people. Parts of this section of the rock were created by a number of other Dreamtime creatures, Linga (sand-lizard), Tjinderi-tjinderiba (willy-wagtail woman) and her children, the Yulanya. Kulpunya (the spirit dingo), who destroyed most of the Mala men and their families, and Lunba (kingfisher woman), who tried to protect them.

The formation of the western face has 3 other totemic beings associated with it. Kandju (sand-lizard), the creator of the Kandju soak and the surrounding topography. Itjari-tjari (marsupial mole), created a number of caves and potholes on the surface of the western side. The camps of the man and woman, Kaldidi, were transformed into a boulder pile on the south western corner.

The Carpet-snakes, Kunia (Kunyia), and the Venomous snakes, Liru

During the creation (Tjukurrpa) times many of the Woma (*Aspidites ramsayi*), the non-venomous snakes, and Kunia (the carpet-snake *Liasis childreni*) lived at Pugabuga, an unlocalised place to the east of Mt Conner. Pugabuga would probably be a water body of some sort, as snake beings, especially non-venomous species, from the Dreamtime are almost always associated with water.

After a while, the snake people became dissatisfied with the surroundings at Pugabuga and travelled west. When they arrived at Maratjara, a spring near the deserted station, Lyndavale, the snakes divided into 2 parties. The Woma, who now live only in the sandhill country, stayed near Maratjara. The Kunia continued on until they came to a large, flat sandhill in the centre of which was Uluru water. Others, mostly old people, women and children stayed at either the south eastern corner or in Tjukiki Gorge on the south side.

Those Kunia people were transformed into natural features at the end of the creation period. The Kunia women sitting in their camp became large boulders in Tjukiki Gorge. Their wooden carrying dish became a tall conical slab of rock at the head of the gorge. Their pubic hairs became the low bushes on the floor of the gorge, and their camp fire became Kapi Tjukiki, the Rockhole. The Kunia women were transformed into the larger boulders on the south eastern corner of the rock and the smaller boulders are their children. The camps of the women are now large caves and the camps of their children are the small caves.

A long boulder on the plain around Uluru was a Kunia woman and smaller boulder her children. An old Kunia woman and old Kunia man lying asleep in the sun became another long boulder. The deep ridges on the sides of Uluru were once the tracks made by the carpet snake people as they travelled to and from the Uluru Waterhole. The gutters on the sides of the rock were the beards of the old men. The caves in the face of the cliff were places where the Kunia people had camped. Smaller circular depressions on the summit of Uluru were the places where one or another of the carpet-snake people rested during Tjukurrpa in what was then the soft sand of Uluru. At that time things were going well at Uluru, every day the women gathered yams, grass seeds and fruit and the men hunted kangaroos, emus and wallabies and other animals.

At the same time as the carpet snake people were living at Uluru, a party of young and old venomous snake-men, the Liru, led by Kulikudjeri, were travelling around the Pitjantjatjara country, causing a lot of trouble with the other spirit beings. The Liru came from the west and made their camp on the southern end of Kata Tjuta. The huge dome near Mt Olga, the highest point of Kata Tjuta was the camp of the old Liru snakes, and a group of lower domes to the east were the camps of the young snakes. The black water stains and the vertical red and green lichen on the face of the 1500 ft high rock face were the body decorations of the old Liru men. After a while the younger snake-men wanted to cause more trouble so left the camp at Kata Tjuta and went to Uluru to attack and kill the harmless carpet snakes, leaving the older Liru men in the camp at Kata Tjuta.

The young Liru men approached Uluru from the south west carrying spears, spear throwers, stone knives and wooden clubs. The desert oaks on the sandhills are the metamorphosed bodies of these men. The Liru men gathered on 2 stony pavements about 400 m from Uluru. The men on the nearest pavement attacked the carpet-snake people camped at Uluru water. The tracks of these attacking men were transformed into the deep gutters on the south western face of Uluru. The Kunia men and women living on the southern side of Uluru quickly retreated to the east when the men on the second pavement threw their spears at them. At the close of the creation period the holes in the soft sand where these spears landed were transformed into potholes on the face of a vertical cliff and the rocks at its base.

There is a large split boulder on the southeast side. In time, a Kunia woman, Minma Bulari (Minma = married woman), gave birth to a child at this place. The boulder has been hollowed out into a small cave about 9 ft (3 m) in diameter. There is a smaller cavity within this cave that has a small entrance leading to the larger cave. In Tjukurrpa times the cavity was Bulari's womb, and its opening was the woman's vagina and vulva. The lighter marks at the opening and on the pavement are the knee-marks of the woman who assisted with the birth. The infant became the irregularly shaped rock near the mouth of the cave, and Bulari's carrying dish is a hollowed boulder nearby. After the birth, Bulari's body contracted so rapidly that she split open, as mud in a waterhole does when it dries.

There is a shallow cave to the east of the Bulari stone with a number of aboriginal paintings on the walls. The 2 irregularly-shaped stones in front of the cave were Bulari sitting on the ground with the infant resting between her knees. Pregnant women now try to give birth in the cave in the belief that the snake-woman, Bulari, will assist them have an easy delivery.

As the Liru men approached her camp, Bulari picked up her baby and walked towards them spitting out a lot of arukwita, the spirit of disease and death. The arukwita killed many of them, those that weren't killed continued approaching her while shouting insults and threats to her and the other carpet-snake people. Bulari retreated towards Mutitjilda Gorge. Caves high on the cliff face on the southern side of Uluru are the open mouths of the shouting Liru men. A large square boulder behind Bulari's camp is the body of the leader of the Liru men.

Kulikudjeri, the leader of the Liru fought Ingridi, a young man who was the son of the Kunia woman at Mutitjilda Gorge. They stood face to face and gashed each other's legs with their stone knives. The western face of Mutitjilda Gorge is the transformed body of Kulikudjeri; the 2 long vertical fissures are the cuts made on his leg by the stone knife of Ingridi, the longer one when the knife was sharp and the shorter one when the knife point had broken. Though wounded, Kulikudjeri continued fighting until he gashed the leg of Ingridi so badly that he bled to death. The bleeding carpet snake man crawled to the east then returned and made his way to the Mutitjilda water where he rested. He became delirious from blood loss and pain and crawled to the right. The track he made is now the stream that flows into Mutitjilda water. 3 rockholes mark the place where he died high on the side of the rock. The water in Mutitjilda and the rock holes were the blood of Ingridi. It was believed that if "Kuka-kuka" was shouted loudly from the head of the gorge the spirit of Ingridi, which was believed to reside in the upper rockhole, could be enticed to send water to Mutitjilda waterhole below.

The people of the Aboriginal tribes living in the area have dreamtime stories about every nook and cranny of the rock. One story is about the Windulka (mulga-seed men), who came from the Petermann Ranges. By coincidence, the story told by geologists is that it was sediment from the erosion of the then much higher Petermann Ranges that were consolidated to form the rock of the future Uluru hundreds of millions of years ago. The geological explanation has since been updated and the sediment that formed Uluru is actually from the south.

Mala the hare-wallabies and Kurpaanga the spirit dingo

Kandju and Linga, the lizard men - Pitjantjatjara-Yankuntjatjara, of central Australia

Lunkana, the sleepy lizard men - Pitjantjatjara-Yankuntjatjara, of central Australia

Willy Wagtail Woman - Pitjantjatjara-Yankuntjatjara, of central Australia

Wanambi (Wonambi)- the mythical snake - Pitjantjatjara-Yankuntjatjara, of central Australia

Mythology of Kata Tjuta 'the place of many heads'

Mythology of the Simpson Desert

Among the Wangkangurru the Dreamtime is called the History Time. The native wells were all connected with 1 or more of the ancestral beings from the History Time, travelling past the wells as they travelled across the country. As with Dreamtime stories elsewhere in Aboriginal Australia, they were associated with various features of the landscape.

Among the wells of the Simpson Desert that were associated with more than 1 myth was Balcoora, being passed by several of the History Time beings, the Two Boys, the Two Carpet Snakes and the Two Men. The Eastern Simpson Desert Rain History includes Perlanna Well and Kilpatha Well. Some wells were important in particular myths, such as Beelaka Well that was associated with the Wadla Grinding Stone History, and Beepla was one of the most important sites in the Crane and the Waterbirds myth. The ritual centre for the Acacia Seed History was at Pudlowinna (or Pulawini, Pulawani) Well.

The Two Boys
In the mythology of the Wangkangurru people the myth of the Two Boys is one of the most important. The Two Boys who lived with their mother at Dalhousie were rainmakers who spent their days catching small birds. While chasing birds they gradually ended up in the Simpson Desert. Here they met the Karanguru people, to whom they gave feathers from the birds they caught, initiating the cult of the Warrthampa, linking the Karanguru of the east with the Wangkangurru. Parra-Parranha Well (the long one) in the central Simpson Desert is the main centre for rituals connected with the Two Boys. Lindsay called it Burraburrinna.

Wurru the Ancestral Crane
This myth is centred on the Palthirri Pithi grindstone quarry in the Peake and Denison Ranges, west of Lake Eyre. The Crane, as well as all the other birds in the area, was trying to catch the Two Big Fish. The Crane lost interest in the Two Big Fish, becoming more interested in his 2 daughters-in-law. The Fish escaped. The birds then followed the Macumba River and the Diamantina River to the Simpson Desert. The Crane could think only of his daughters-in-law so he decided to kill the rest of the birds that were with him. Near Kallakoopah Creek he made the weather very hot and windy by singing songs, leading all the birds to areas where he knew there was no permanent water.

After returning to one of the waterholes to drink he created a very big dust storm as they approached Beelpa Well. To prevent the birds smelling the water he forced them to burrow into the sand on the northern side of the well. The Crane dug in the well until the water reached his neck. On returning to the other birds he begged them to cover him with cool sand because he was exhausted by the heat and lack of water. The other birds now became suspicious of his intentions, though they continued on north until, as they approached the well at Toko Range, they could smell water though were getting very weak and were almost blind, ignoring the Crane when he tried to persuade them to burrow into the sand. In their frenzy they were changed into Waterbirds.

In the lighter vein of this story the Crane made suggestive gestures to his daughters-in-law as they travelled along. An evil spell was left at Beelpa Well because of what Crane did there. The Crane and the other birds are said to be a number of white limestone boulders that can still be seen on a sandhill north of Beelpa Well.

Ancestral Rain Histories

In the Simpson Desert there are 4 Ancestral Rain Histories linking the Wangkangurru with their neighbours in the west, the Arabana and the Lower Southern Aranda, and their eastern neighbours, the Karanguru and Ngamini. Ilbora on the Finke River is the beginning of the Western Rain History, extending into the Western Desert. Boolaburtinna Well and the surrounding area is the centre of the Rain Histories from the central part of the desert. Perlanna Well, Kilpatha Well, Yelkerrie Well, and Lake Mirranponga Pongunna are associated with the Eastern Simpson Desert Rain Histories. According to Irinjili, the Rain travelled all over Wangkangurru country in History Time just as clouds still travel about anywhere, so the 4 Histories are closely linked.

In the desert between Wolporican Well and Boolaburtinna Well, 2 knolls, low gypseous hills, the Approdinna Attora Knolls, were said to be near an important ceremonial site, the hills being landmarks that warned all but the fully initiated elders to approach no further, as told to Ted Colson on his desert crossing in 1936, though he later doubted the accuracy of the information he was given in respect of these particular knolls.

As with other tribes, the country of the Wangkangurru was crossed by trade routes, often following Dreaming tracks of the ancestral Beings, with the result that they were mythologically significant. The Wangkangurru obtained stone from the Palthirri Pithi quarry, their red ochre from Parachilna in the Flinders Ranges. Fragments of bailer shell found at Boolaburtinna Well and Perlanna Well suggest the trade routes stretched all the way to the far northern part of the continent. Dolomite axes were obtained from the Mt Isa area and pituri, a narcotic plant, the leaves of which were chewed, came from western Queensland. There were small pieces of shell of freshwater mussels found at Murraburt Well and Beelpa Well. Again, indicating long trade routes.

Myths that may be oral history of actual events

The Aboriginal people from the area around Lake Eacham have several versions of the story of the formation of the lake. Aborigines would have been living in the area prior to the eruption, so whether or not the stories are the actual events passed down the generation for more than 10,000 years, the eruption was probably seen by their ancestors.

In one version, 2 young men who had not been initiated so weren't supposed to be hunting, tried to spear a wallaby but missed and hit a tree. When they pulled the spear out it had bits of a witchetty grub on it, so they cut the tree down to look for more of the grubs. This made the Rainbow Serpent (Yamini) angry. The sky turned orange and the ground under the camp opened and everyone in the camp was sucked in. The place where the camp had been became Bana Wiigina (Lake Eacham). (Warren Cannendo, Ngadjon-Jii)

Aboriginal Religion

Aboriginal religion had no manmade structures for religious ceremonies; they used features of the landscape for their rites and ceremonies, e.g., Uluru (Ayer's Rock).

They believed that when a person died the spirit left the body and travelled to a place like a waterhole to await rebirth. The complex rituals to protect the living from any anger the dead person may have harboured towards the living and to expedite the journey of the spirit to the spirit home, a waterhole, or offshore island.

They followed a totemic system; each person was associated with an animal or a natural feature of the landscape. Every person has a totem, usually an animal, and those of that totem are responsible for the rites necessary for the continued abundance of that species. The sites for the increase rites of each species are marked by a pile of bones of that species.

Examples of these increase rite sites were found in the Northern Territory, in Sleisbeck Cave was a star-shaped pile of crocodiles bones, and a grouping of emu skulls was found at Ingaladdi.

In many ceremonies an integral part of the ritual was elaborate drawings in the sand. On Bora grounds of New South Wales, mythological figures up to 10 m long were moulded in earth or clay in the centre of the Bora ring. The sand or earth sculptures were not intended to last a long time. The most common form of Bora ring was a double circle surrounded by low earth banks and a path, also bounded by an earth bank, connecting the 2. One of the rings was for all the people, including women and children participated in the corroboree, then the young men being initiated were led by the elders along the connecting path to the other ring where only initiated men were allowed to go for secret rituals like tooth avulsion or circumcision. At least in some places a form of birth control was practiced where a **subincision** was performed, the urethra was cut open for a short distance from the head of the penis. When they had intercourse some of the semen exited this opening so reducing the efficiency of fertilisation. It wasn't intended to be for birth control, it was connected with ritual symbolic representations of menstruation, but some suggest it may have had this unintended side effect.

The trees surrounding these Bora ceremonial grounds are often have geometrical designs carved into them. Trees with these carvings on them are called dendroglyphs, those that have had bark removed for the manufacture of canoes or other artefacts are called a scarred tree.

Carved trees were often associated with burial and initiation rites. Initiation trees usually have the carving in the bark, but those carved as burial trees the carving is extended to the sapwood or even the heartwood.

These carved trees seem to be restricted to the areas inhabited by the Wiradjuri and Kamilaroi peoples in eastern, central New South Wales and south eastern Queensland.

These designs were usually geometric and linear patterns cut with a stone hatchet. The motifs include concentric lozenges, diamonds, circles and spirals. The motifs resemble those on skin cloaks and to decorate wooden weapons. It is thought the designs carved on a tree near a grave may indicate the totem or kinship affiliations of the dead person.

A guide for Sir Thomas Mitchell, Yuranigh, died in 1850 near Molong in New South Wales, and was buried according to traditional custom. Four trees were carved near the grave, and the site is marked by a tombstone erected by Mitchell.

Some of the most elaborate grave ceremonies in Australia were carried out by the Tiwi from Bathurst and Melville Islands about 80 km north of Darwin at the junction of the Arafura and Timor Seas. During the Pukimani ceremony they carved large grave posts that were intricately decorated, each one taking months to finish. These posts were erected by the grave during the long mourning ceremony, while dancers in elaborate body decorations drove the spirit of the dead person into the bush, miming events of the person's life. After the ceremony the posts were left where they were put, and allowed to decay naturally, no further interest being taken in them.

Two major Kunapipi ceremonies were carried out in 1972-73, by the Gidjingali of Arnhem Land involving between 200 and 300 people. It was estimated that the work involved in these ceremonies totalled about 400 human weeks of work. Three months after the event Rhys Jones visited the site of the great ceremony and wrote that 'visiting the great camp of Ngaladjebama three months after the religious climax there, all we saw, was the wind, whirling red dust over midden debris, and strips of paperbark rustling against bleached poles of collapsed hut structures. The investment had been into the intellectual and not the material sphere of life.'

The only prehistoric structures associated with religion that have survived are stone arrangements that are very difficult to date, but it is thought they have been part of Aboriginal culture for a very long time. There is a wide range of stone array types. There are circles, lines, corridors, single standing stones, and piles of stones heaped into cairns. The mythology and significance of these stone arrangements is unknown, to the local Aborigines as well as the researchers. Most of the sites haven't been used for an unknown number of years, possibly centuries. The only thing known about them is that they are connected with the Dreamtime stories, representing either totemic beings or enclosed areas where special events took place.

The only stone arrangement dated so far is in the Bay of Fires in north eastern Tasmania where a new arrangement was set up on top of an old one that had been covered by a shell midden and charcoal, it is 750 years old. This only gives a minimum antiquity for this type of prehistoric stone arrangement.

Ranges on the east coast and religion

At Armidale on the northern tablelands of New South Wales, another part of the Great Dividing Range, the area was cold and windy. A single occupation site has been found above 1,000 m in the area. In this bleak region art and ceremonial sites have been found, such as many bora grounds and stone arrangements.

It has been suggested that the high country could have had religious importance among the people of the area. The belief in a sky god, a supernatural ancestral being, Daramulan (Durramulan) or Baimai (Baiame) occurred over much of eastern Australia. High, isolated sites were favoured for the initiation of boys. Women and children were excluded from these ceremonies; they were "men's business". The women usually had their own ceremonies from which males were excluded.

The Kunapipi

When the Kunapipi was brought to Oenpelli, western Arnhem Land, sometime between the late 1950s and the early 1960s, songs were included with it that could magically protect people, men and women, experiencing the rites for the first time. As part of the rite the spirit of snake or small parrot was sung into the backs of their heads that would warn them if anyone tried to sneak up on them to perform sorcery or harm them. This particular complex of Kunapipi is occasionally identified with Ngaljod, the Rainbow. She is a woman, and a snake, and is capable of taking other shapes. The Berndts were unsure how literally the women of the part of Arnhem Land being studied took the conventional accounts of her appearance, as well as what happens on the men's' sacred grounds. They say it seemed many of the men believe such accounts are factually true, as well as symbolically true.

The Kunapipi ranged over a wide region, throughout Arnhem Land, either side of the main road to Darwin as far as the outskirts of Darwin, west to the Daly River, Katherine River and Victoria River, and coming in contact with the Galwadi-Gadjeri series of the central western deserts. As a result, the Kunapipi constellation is fluid in many respects. The core, however, is persistent. The objects used are all very similar, wherever the rituals take place, as are the rites, myths and songs. There is always a dominant emphasis on birth or rebirth. The men pass through the 'mother place' (the sacred ground) to be reborn.

The Kunapipi is usually held in the dry season when there is a plentiful supply of food. The people believe that this food supply has resulted from the performances of the previous year, and are preparing for the arrival of the wet season with its renewed growth of food for the next dry season. The rituals may last from as little as 2 weeks to as long as several months, and before they begin messengers are sent out to notify other groups of the impending ceremonies. Before the invited people arrive the hosts go out into the bush and prepare the ritual ground, as well as making a bullroarer, anointing it with blood while singing. The first rites take place in the main camp a while later, in which the men sing 'outside', camp versions of the Wawalag and Kunapipi songs as the women dance, singing non-sacred *garma* or clan songs. These activities could continue for weeks.

Then one evening the voice of Julunggul, the rock python or Rainbow is heard, the bullroarer. The Kunapipi leader calls out an answer, as do all the women, the way the Wawalag sisters cried out when Julunggul came near them. At this point the young boys about to be initiated, who have been prepared, smeared with arm blood and red ochre, are led out of the main camp to meet Julunggul, to be swallowed by him. This is intended as an offering which persuades Julunggul to return to the sacred ground and avoid the main camp. Women wail for the initiates as though they were dead. This continues until the last of the boys has been taken to the sacred ground. Singing and dancing continue intermittently throughout the night, the women some distance from the sacred ground, answering the calls of the men and the sound of the bullroarer. The dances performed are connected with the animals the Wawalag Sisters tried to cook, but when ordered to by Julunggul, escaped and plunged into the waters of Muruwul. The sacred ground was in the shape of an elongated triangle, and is intended to resemble the body of Julunggul. The *nanggaru* hole at its apex is Muruwul,

The men dance towards the main camp from the sacred ground carrying lighted paperbark torches. Along the way women are crouched under conical mats and 2 old women walk up and down calling out the names of food items the women may not eat at this time, and reciting parts of the Wawalag story. Men of the *jiridja* moiety dance around the women concealed by the mats. They represent Julunggul smelling the blood of the Wawalag, but as there is none they go away, after being given food by the women.

By now the visitors are arriving. Women make more food gifts. The men begin digging the *nanggaru* on the sacred ground. In all the following dances the participants, who represent various totemic creatures, enter this hole, most being arranged in pairs of male and females, and simulate mating. The possum dancing is the most important series, in which the men have long bark penises protruding from their hair belts. These rituals continue until a large crescent-shaped trench is dug, over a period of several weeks. This represents the *ganala*, the uterus. In the western Arnhem Land Kunapipi the walls are marked with a snake design. When completed, snake totem actors dance or writhe in the hole, which is followed by the 'mating dance', and some other dances.

As these rituals are proceeding 2 large *jelmalandji* emblems, each about 12-40 feet long, are being prepared.

Aboriginal Division of Labour in Ritual

The sex of the participants in a particular ritual is an important consideration, but does not constitute the sole determinant of where the ritual lies on the sacred-mundane, or sacred-profane, continuum. The extent of participation varied among groups throughout Aboriginal Australia. It also depended, in part, on the degree of mixing of the sexes in everyday life, outside the immediate family and kin relationships. Men and women sat separately during large-scale gatherings in the Western Desert, for example, though there were casual comings and goings. The patterns of ritual participation tended to reflect the degree of mixing seen in daily life. Among the people of areas such as Melville Island, and possibly the Lower River Murray, the level of sex-based restrictions was much lower compared to groups in other parts of Australia.

Ritual performances can generally be grouped under a number of headings, each representing a particular point on a continuum. There are rituals restricted to men, rituals in which men play the major part at a particular place with the women playing parts, usually subsidiary, usually at a different place and sometimes at a different time. There were rituals in which both men and women participate in the same ritual at the same place at the same time. There were also rituals in which the women took part but from which the men were excluded. This coincides with the 'control' dimension only at the extremes, determining who is in a position to order or urge others to participate, using sanctions when necessary. The women have full control only in the last category.

The Berndts suggest 'participation' should be interpreted as referring to a wide range of possibilities on a passive-active continuum, that includes facets of seeing, hearing, uttering or performing various actions. Women are allowed to witness some rituals or parts of rituals, though were not permitted, or expected, to do more than watch. They may be allowed or expected to contribute to the ritual by being painted with appropriate designs or to observe particular food taboos if a close relative, such as a son or brother, is undergoing some stage of initiation. In some other rituals they may be permitted to take part in the singing in part or all of the ritual, but are prohibited from taking part in the dancing. For some rituals they were permitted to hear the singing, sometimes from close by, at other times from a greater distance. Even when they became very familiar with the songs they were not permitted to sing them. There was also a separate men's vocabulary, the words of which the women were not permitted to use, even if they knew them, except in a crisis.

Catherine Berndt reports hearing an unfamiliar word during a loud exchange between some men that were nearby, while present with a group of Western Desert women at an evening camp ceremony. On asking the meaning of the word she was told that it was a daragu word, a men's word, which women weren't allowed to use. Catherine Berndt reported that when there were no men present the women sometimes used the men's words as swearing on occasions, as when they burnt themselves.

There were special dancing grounds for men among many groups that have a variety of names that the informants translated to English, such as ring place, centre place, men's shade or shelter, Big Sunday ground, etc. Women are not normally allowed to enter these grounds, where the sacred rituals are performed by adult men. The 'work' associated with these places is mostly done by men. In some Areas, men and women both use a word that loosely translates as 'work' to describe what men do on these ceremonial places. In north east Arnhem Land the word is 'djama'. The rituals performed on these sacred grounds are intended to promote the welfare of the whole community. The co-operation of the women is essential in almost every case. In some rituals the only role of women was as an audience, probably at least partly as someone the men can show off in front of, or possible keep secrets from, according to the Berndts. But in most cases their active participation is required in particular roles. If the women don't perform their part of the ceremony correctly the men's 'work' will be wasted. In Arnhem Land the women had a very important role, collecting enough food for the large gathering so the men can concentrate on perfecting their performance.

Many of the rites that women are excluded from include symbolic imitations of physiological functions of women. These functions are natural to women but need to be imitated in ritual form by the men. The practice of subincision is regarded as analogous to menstruation in women. In some areas circumcision is seen as a ritual representation of the severing of the umbilical cord that is, separating the boy from the influence of his mother to make him an independent man. There were many other examples of feminine functions being ritualistically imitated by men during various religious ceremonies.

Mythology tells that many of the sacred objects restricted to men were originally owned by women, or in some cases destined to be owned by women. In one way or another the men got control of them and never returned them to the control of women.

Increase Ritual

The Dreamtime beings have decreed the behaviours of their descendants, including the rituals, instructing the people on what should be done, sometimes how it should be done, implicitly or not. In many rituals there is also a practical, immediate aspect; the love-magic rites of the women are of this type, having the immediate aim of attracting a sweetheart or keeping a husband interested. This is one of a broader complex connected with the Dreamtime beings such as Chickenhawk, the Munga-munga girls (fair haired), Possum and even the Rainbow. Relations between men and women are regarded as vital to fertility. The Berndts report a woman saying when the *djarada* had come to Katherine in the Northern Territory, through Willaroo from the Victoria River country, *'When we sing about chickenhawk eggs and snake eggs, things like that, we want that chickenhawk, that snake to have plenty of eggs, plenty of young: and women too, plenty of babies. If some women want to sing for sweethearts, they can sing. But some want to sing for Dreaming. Some of us don't want to sing for sweethearts all the time; we like to sing for Dreaming.'* The various facets are apparent in the songs comprising this particular *djarada*: love magic, reference to actions first performed by the mythical sponsors, e.g., the encounter between the Munga-mungas and the night owl; and then fertility increase aspect.

Straight-forward increase rites are much more common, most of which are connected with the aforementioned cult totems. Rituals performed to maintain or renew the numbers of a particular species are carried out by men associated with that totem, sometimes with the assistance of others performing in subordinate roles. Totemic increase rituals were carried out throughout Aboriginal Australia. The complexity of the rituals varied from place to place, in some areas with a simple ritual, the performers may not be painted or decorated, and no special objects were used.

From Kaberry (1939: 203), "As the totemic ancestors passed through the country they left stones or sometimes a tree, each of which is supposed to contain the *guning* (spirit) of some animal, bird, fish, reptile, tuber, and so on. These sites are called *bud-bud* at Forest River, and *wulwiny* among the Lunga. By rubbing one of these or striking it with bushes and uttering a spell, the *guning* will go forth and cause the species with which it is associated to multiply."

The increase of a given species may be brought about merely by calling the appropriate name, as occurs in parts of the Kimberleys, and also in the Kimberleys, it can be caused by retouching the cave wall paintings of the animal. Another method is for men to drop blood from their arms onto a relevant site. Sometimes they try to produce an increase of a particular species by acting out aspects of its behaviour, or attempting to attract them. Some examples are provided by Elkin (1933: 73; 1954). One example comes from the Ungarinjin where "the increase of the various valuable animal and plant species and the maintenance of the operation of the various natural phenomena like the sun, moon, stars, wind and rain, is assured" by 'retouching the paintings in the various Wondjina (creative ancestral beings) galleries'. Increase is ensured when the paintings in caves and rock shelters are retouched, or new ones added, in western Arnhem Land. Elkin also reports increase rituals where stones are arranged in particular way, the designs each being associated with different species. At Some places they anoint these stone arrangements with red ochre or blood, or they may simply be disturbed. An example is the *talu* (increase) for honey among the Karadjeri, which is based on a mythical event. The ritual consists of the main men participating going to Nangula, which is a hole, where they brush it clean, then allow blood from their arms and subincised penises to drip into it. Some of the blood and dust mixture is then placed into small holes in a stick. They each place a stick with the blood-dust mixture in their hair until they place the sticks in various trees. The bees are expected to make their nests in those trees (Elkin, 1933: 37).

According to Spencer & Gillen (1938: 167-211), the *intichiuma* of the Aranda and neighbouring tribes are probably the best known increase rituals. During these rituals the participants visit the witchetty grub totem drawings at Emily Gap near Alice Springs, and other sacred sites, where special rituals are carried out. In the case of the witchetty grub totem sacred stones are uncovered, one of which represents the grub's chrysalis stage and another egg of the beetle. The performers rub the stones on their bellies to indicate repletion. In another ritual, after clearing a small patch of ground, the men drip blood from their arm veins onto it, which dries to form a hard surface. The sacred design of the emu totem is outlined on this with white pipe clay, red and yellow ochre, and a mixture of charcoal and grease. These ground drawings are marked out with blood in the central west of the Northern Territory, then white and red feather down is used to decorate them. Strehlow, (1947: Plate 4) is an example of this. Men play the part of *inniakwa*, the emu ancestors, performing the ritual wearing of decorated *tjurunga* on their heads. The women can watch the proceedings from some distance, but run back to the camp when the men approach them. After the ceremony is completed they destroy the ground drawing. All local totemic groups have their own *intichiuma* ceremony, each differing in some way from the others. Blood is dripped onto a stone representing a mass of Hakea flowers in the Hakea Flower rite.

Among the Dieri, the *mindari*, that is associated with the *muramura* Warugadi, emu, there are 2 groups involved. These are *wimabaia,* 'song bird' and *wimabili,* 'song bag'. White pelican feathers are placed by the **wimabili** men on a large mud-flattened mound they have built, then black and red ochre dots are added. Four women from the 2 moieties are chosen who walk across the mound, which represents the body of the emu, during the afternoon ritual. After this all the men sing about the **muramura**, Emu, emerging from Lake Eyre to attend the *mindari*. At the conclusion of the singing, the ceremonial leader, a man from the emu cult totem, uses a club to break up the mound, the parts being said to look like newly hatched emu chicks, while asking the emus to breed. The ritual ensured there would be plenty of emus in season. When night falls, the women who walked over the mound bring water to the participants of the ritual, who are still on the ceremonial ground, which they take into their mouths then spurt it over boomerangs, which belong to the **muramura** Emu, covered with red and black dots on the ground in front of them. The 'watering the boomerangs' ritual is intended to make the emus breed and lay eggs. After giving the water to the men the women return to the bush where the men visit them to have sex that is said to represent emus being fertilised.

Another example of an increase ritual among the Dieri focuses on the *badi* grub, which is found in the *badara* box tree. The ritual is associated with the myth of Wariliwulu; the Bat Man. Feathers are wrapped around the end of a navel cord, enclosed by a knitted bag that represents the grub, which is then hung in a *badara* tree. For the following 2 weeks a Wariliwulu cult totem man goes to the tree, sitting under it and, 'singing the tree' to make it green, in the hope the grubs will come, as well as to make the grubs breed and be plentiful in the country around the tree. The grub spirits were said to come from a waterhole they called Muharibalgabal-gajagubandru, the home of the muramura Wariliwulu, who is also associated with the muramura Darana.

The rituals associated with increase range in complexity from the very simple, such as moving the sacred stone, or retouching a painting, to the much more elaborate, as with the ***intichiuma*** or the *mindari*. Mythological and totemic characters have connections with the increase rituals, and also with the ritual sites and objects. The aim of all the rites is to induce the mythological beings to use their powers to bring about the desired end result, increased number of animals or plants which increases the food supply. A special attitude towards the supernatural is required if the rites are to be successful in gaining an increase in the animals. To gain the desired results any ritual participant must have a special relationship with the totemic being, such as a cult totemite, in which context he is nearly always considered to be either a descendant or reincarnation of the spirit being. These beliefs are part of a coherent belief system, nearly all rituals and ceremonies are concerned with the relationship between the person and his environment that is established and defined, as well as maintained, by the performance.

Blood may be used in the ritual, though it can be replaced by red ochre, both symbolising life and animation. The blood or red ochre releases the spirits whose assistance is sought. Blood is usually significant in all types of ritual.

Sexual relations are symbolic of fertility in general, as well as with human fertility, and can take different forms around the continent. It is not always necessary to have actual sexual relations between men and women; it can instead take the form of simulated sex between male participants on the ceremonial ground. The inclusion of sexual relations, real or simulated, is much more common than is usually reported in the literature, according to the Berndts.

The increase ritual can be used to induce rain, not just the animals and plants required for food. On the North West coast it may be used to get calm weather, as rough weather interferes with some types of fishing. In Cape York Peninsula it was sometimes used for a purpose that most would find strange, to increase flies that could be expected to annoy strangers. Sometimes it was used to increase leeches. Some rituals were usually performed just before the normal breeding season of the target species, while others were performed on any suitable occasion. Whenever the rites occurred, they were used to facilitate the normal processes of nature, not to change them.

Ara, the red kangaroo

Among the Aranda people of central Australia Ara was a red kangaroo totemic spirit being from the Dreamtime. In the Dreamtime Ara made 2 journeys, one during the day and the other during the night. Along the track of the daytime journey he visited 14 totemic sites between Ajaii at the western edge of the MacDonnell Ranges and Krantji, the most sacred site connected with Ara, then continued on to Ara-perka at the eastern end of the ranges. The night time journey took him from there, underground across the desert, as he could not live there, to ara-ngurunja in the far north. The increase ceremonies of the red kangaroo were held at Krantji, as it is the most sacred site of Ara. During the rituals, the rocks, trees and sacred hollows were struck to dislodge grains, each of which would become a red kangaroo when the next rain came.

Aboriginal Fertility Cults

The ubar

In western Arnhem Land, the ubar gong could be heard clearly across the plains near the East Alligator River, it was said to be the Mother calling men to the sacred ground. The women dance in the main camp, each holding a cat's cradle, an endless piece of string like young girls use, calling 'Gaidbaa! Gaidbaa!' to the beat of the ubar, answering the beat of the ubar. As the ubar continues, its sound is joined by that of the didgeridoo, and then the singing begins. When the dancing starts it is with men dancing separately, their arms either outstretched or raised holding a spear or spear thrower in each hand, other men surrounding them chanting 'ja, ja ja!' reaching a climax, 'Jei, Jei, gogjei, gogjei!' Meanwhile, the women in the camp continue their chant. After a period of silence a whistling begins that heralds the dancers being led in one at a time. Each is led by a ceremonial headman, taken to his position where he moves his head from side to side as the headman bends over him uttering the sacred words of the ubar. The whistling is believed to be to summon the wet season, the Rainbow Snake, the harbinger of rain and rejuvenator of the earth. When the winds of the wet season start blowing, the whistling of the wind is believed to be the wind blowing past the raised horns of the Rainbow Snake, and he arches his body, ascending the sky.

The Rainbow Snake is the instrument through which nature is reborn, with the help of the Mother.

An unusual feature of the ubar that is not known from any other part of Aboriginal Australia is the inclusion of a clown, a jester, who moves about the ceremonial ground during the ritual and at some of the most serious parts of the Rainbow Snake ritual makes fun of the dancers, mimicking them, and even the ritual, laughing in the faces of the participants. He is the only one who carries on in this fashion; none of the others take any notice of him. Part of his role is to test the novices, who are required to prove that nothing can distract them from the serious business they are taking part in. They have to act as though he doesn't exist.

A feature of the ubar is that women with white hair, said to be 'almost ready to die' are allowed to watch the ceremony on the sacred ground, though take no part in it, but must be accompanied by a close male relative, such as a son, who introduces her to the ubar. The people said that because of her advanced age she would be unlikely to be harmed by the power of the ubar, and the accompanying sacred rites. Men are required to protect the younger women and children from the dangerous forces, that while basic to human life, are too strong for anyone other than initiated men to cope with directly, the men mediating between the forces and the women and children.

The Berndts reported that some women said that the ubar Mother and the Kunapipi Mother only dealt with men because they were jealous of the women, to the point at which she is almost as jealous as a co-wife, and also the way a mother may help and cherish her son more than her daughters and for longer, the daughters being expected to be independent at a younger age. The ubar woman is a Mother, is a rival, as well as being concerned for the welfare of her adherents. Men need to approach her carefully, using the appropriate rituals, and women need to be even more careful.

Djanggawul

The rituals of the Djanggawul have been discussed in Warner (1937/1958 and Berndt (1952a). The preparations for the Djanggawul rites include the erection of a shelter on the sacred ground and preparation of the *rangga* emblems by leaders of the *Dua* moiety and linguistic groups. Among these is the *Mawulan* pole, said to be the pole used by the Djanggawul Brother as a 'walking-stick'. Spring water gushed when he plunged it into the ground, as happened when he did the same thing with the *djenda* goanna tail. His Two Sisters did the same with their *ganinjari* 'yam' stick or walking-stick. When he used the *djuda*, trees sprouted from the ground. These were the basic *rangga* forms, but they have been elaborated into a number of other forms. Ochre was used to decorate the objects with patterns the Djanggawul gave to the people. Most also have string decorated with red parakeet feathers attached to them, to symbolise the sun's rays, the red sky at sunset, or the Sisters' blood. The *ngainmara* mat is symbolised by the shelter made of branches. The shelter, and the whole of the sacred ground it is built upon, represents a uterus. Symbolically, the initiates are children of the Djanggawul, or *rangga*. The preliminary dances symbolise the rise and fall of the surf, and the sound of the sea, that is said to refer to the original journey when the Djanggawul travelled from Bralgu to Port Bradshaw by canoe. Throughout the dances and the *Nara* rituals, as well as when they return to the main camp, the men call out invocations. The women's role in the ceremonies is to provide the food, which are traditionally cycad palm bread and some meat and vegetables.

After a short break, people from other groups who have been summoned by special 'signed' message sticks, feathered string or miniatures of sacred objects moulded from the wax of wild bees, come in. Some men gather on the sacred ground to make sacred emblems, while others collect other sacred emblems from their storage places in water or mud. These are described as rangga taken from the Sisters' *ngainmara*, that is, children from the Sisters' wombs. They are dried and repainted with designs from water marks their original counterparts acquired during their journey. The sea dance is repeated while this is proceeding. The songs are about water from the sacred 'wells' the Djanggawul made with their *rangga*. This represents coitus between the Brother and the Two Sisters, the water symbolising the semen that fertilises humans and the earth. It also represents the coming of the wet season rains, also seen as a period of fertilisation.

When the main rites begin, the first of them relate to totemic species. These rites don't usually involve *rangga*. Neophytes are instructed and there is a ritual shaving of their facial hair. Older men leave short beards or tufts that are said to represent the fringe on a conical mat, to which they attach red parakeet feathers, like the pendent strings on the emblems. Women, children and uninitiated boys gather in a clearing in the main camp and are covered with *ngainmara* mats. They symbolise unborn children of the Djanggawul. The men dance from the sacred ground and surround them, carrying spears, spear throwers and sticks. The men call invocations that are mostly the names of places where the Djanggawul Sisters gave birth to the first people. The men poke the mats and the women and children beneath them respond by wriggling. The invocations called by the men then relate to sexual intercourse and childbirth, etc., leading to the 'birth', symbolised by the women and children emerging from beneath the mats. They sit watching the men as more invocations are called, then the ritual is over. The accent is again on fertility. The symbolic birth represents the desired goal, the replenishment of humans and the natural species they depend upon.

After several weeks of rituals the men come to the camp one night carrying flaming torches, symbolising the fire the Djanggawul sisters believed had destroyed their sacred bags that contained the *rangga*, only realising later that they had been stolen. The women dancing around the tree represent the Sisters dancing around the sacred *djudaI??* of life-giving properties. The totemic dancing of the men at the tree represents the Brother and his companions dancing in their sacred shade, and this in turn refers to the first performance when the Sisters danced out of the sight of the men, as at that time they still had control of all the sacred emblems and rites.

Over the following few weeks the *ngainmara* ritual is repeated in the main camp, and there are more totemic dances in the sacred ground. Only the minor emblems are shown to the neophytes, who are painted with sacred patterns, as are corpses, for their symbolic death during the rituals. The next event is ritual bathing, in which men representing geese or diving ducks dance to the billabong or beach and plunge in, after which all the people, whatever age, follow them. They call invocations and when they leave the water the men dance various totemic fish. This symbolises the wetting of the *rangga* as they travelled from Bralgu. The people are also the *rangga* that are returned to a sacred water hole at the completion of the *nara*. There are also a number of other symbolic meanings. This is the end of the *nara* proper, though it could be followed by other rites. As part of their instruction, some are shown to the neophytes. At others, only fully initiated men could attend, who are familiar with all the phases of the *nara*. Following this there is sacramental eating of cycad bread on the sacred ground, during which invocations are called as the feathered string is removed from the emblems.

Symbolically, the central theme is the human sequence that culminates in childbirth, and the cycle of growth and renewal in the natural environment. New plants grow, new foliage sprouts, and all the natural species are reborn.

Wawalag sisters

The Wawalag mythology is believed to be mostly indigenous to north-eastern Arnhem Land. The Kunapipi mythology was brought to north-eastern Arnhem Land from the south; it was also accepted in western Arnhem Land, having much in common with the belief of that area, such as Waramurungundju, the creative mother, Ngaljod, the female rainbow and her male rainbow counterpart, as were many assumptions connected with the **ubar**. Whether the local social structure emphasised patrilineal descent, eastern Arnhem Land, or matrilineal descent, western Arnhem Land, it was able to easily slot into the local mythology, with a small amount of name interchanging and identity shifting. The Kunapipi is very flexible, allowing a variety of interpretations around a central theme, and even some interpretation within this central theme. Certain modifications were made to the Kunapipi as it passed from one area to another, with the addition of new songs or old songs being translated in different ways by people unfamiliar with the language the songs were in when they reached the new area. In this case they have been told the meaning of the songs, allowing them to make their own interpretation.

The Wawalag mythology underlies 3 main sequences of ritual, the *djunggawon*, relating mainly to circumcision, the *gunabibi* or Kunapipi, with the same emphasis as the *nara* of the Djanggawul, and the *ngurlmag*, the most important, similar to the *maraiin* of western Arnhem Land, that is mainly revelatory.

The *djunggawon rituals* are linked to the same myths as those of the Kunapipi, boys are said to be swallowed by the python, as the Wawalag Sisters were. This is an act of propitiation in some versions to protect the whole camp from being swallowed. Eventually the boys are vomited, as if they had been reborn after dying temporarily.

The Fertility Mother

The concept of a Fertility Mother is widespread throughout aboriginal Australia (Elkin, 1954; Stanner, 1959-61; Berndt, 1951a, 1952a). The Wawalag were sometimes associated with Kunapipi (Gunabibi), one name for a mythical woman responsible for creating human beings and instituting sacred rituals. She too is called the Mother, or old Woman. In some stories the Wawalag are identified with 2 of her daughters, called Mungamunga, and the Julunggul python with the python or Rainbow Snake belonging to the Kunapipi series. In some versions of the Wawalag Sister stories they are associated with the Djanggawul Sisters, who were regarded as creative beings.

Kunapipi (Gunabibi) is called Galwadi and Gadjeri, in the central west of the Northern Territory and in the area around the Daly River and Port Keats, among the Guirindji, Malngin, Njining and Djaru, Gugudja and Walmadjeri from the Victoria River district across to the eastern Kimberleys. (Meggitt, 1955, and 1962 for the Wailbri) (from Berndt & Berndt, 1964).

Djanggawul Sisters

Waramurungundju

Wawalag (Wagilag, Wauwalak) Sisters

Much of the area that stretches eastward between the East Alligator River and the coast on the Gulf of Carpentaria, is made up of very hilly country, with rocky hills, sandstone ridges, gorges and creeks. Many of these rock formations have been associated with various Dreamtime beings. The rainbow, Ngaljod, transformed many of these beings into the rocky formations by swallowing them and vomiting up their bones which became the formations that still house their spirits. The translation of the term used by the Aborigines is 'they came into dreaming' (Berndt & Berndt, 1964). The Gunwinggu use the term djang for this type of representation. A djang, is an object, creature or spirit, containing some power or essence that derived directly from the dreamtime.

Some djang sites were believed to be dangerous to certain people, such as women or children, or all but the very old, or were taboo. A few places are believed to be so dangerous that everyone avoided them. The Gunwinggu word for such sites was -djamun, set apart, and hedged with prohibitions, not for everyday use (Berndt & Berndt, 1964). The same word is used for the men's sacred dancing grounds, sacred sites and objects, and food that is to be consumed during rituals. Mostly, the djang were of lesser importance than the Dreamtime beings such as Ngaljod, and are associated with specific localities, and with a limited range of influence.

Some, such as Wuragag (Tor Rock), a prominent landmark, are more widely known than others. Even when people know the name of a particular place, unless it is directly related to a person or his/her relatives, they may not know the myths associated with that place, often not even the basic story.

Links

List one

1. Australian Aborigines of Indian Origin?
2. Humans in Australia as long as 78,000 years ago
3. The revolution that didn't arrive: A review of Pleistocene Sahul
4. The Pleistocene Peopling of Greater Australia: A Re-examination
5. Aboriginal inventions
6. Jared Diamond Talk
7. Oldest evidence for deep-sea fishing found
8. http://anthropology.si.edu/HumanOrigins/ha/weid.html
9. Not Out of Africa but regional continuity
10. http://www.canovan.com/HumanOrigin/kow/kowswamp.htm
11. Cohuna & District Historical Society
12. Cohuna map
13. The gracile male Skelton from Late Pleistocene King Island
14. 1994: A flawed Version : sex and robusticity on King Island
15. Pleistocene human remains from King Island, south eastern Australia
16. Kow Swamp
17. Kow Swamp Images
18. Redating Kow Swamp Remains
19. Kow Swamp
20. Last glacial maximum ages for robust humans at Kow Swamp, southern Australia
21. Mungo Man
22. Not Out of Africa but regional continuity
23. Mungo Man older than thought
24. Mungo Man-The Dating Method Stretches Back the Human History of Australia
25. A younger Mungo Man
26. New age for Mungo Man, new human history
27. Australia's oldest human remains-age of the Mungo 3 skeleton

28. Mungo 3 (WLH 3)
29. Mungo Over Millennia-the Willandra Landscape and its People Current Anthropology
30. http://www.modernhumanorigins.net/wlh50.htm
31. http://cat.inist.fr/?aModele=afficheN&cpsidt=1557539
32. WLH 50
33. Halfway Human
34. Human origins and antiquity in Australia: an historical perspective
35. Possible causes and significance of cranial robusticity among Pleistocene–Early Holocene Australians
36. The Middle Palaeolithic and late Pleistocene Tasmania hunting behaviour: a reconsideration of the attributes of modern human behaviour
37. http://books.google.com/books?id=zTgG82RLc6MC&printsec=frontcover
38. An Australasian test of the recent African origin theory using the WLH-50 calvarium
39. On the reliability of recent tests of the Out of Africa hypothesis for modern human origins
40. Australoid Race
41. http://books.google.com/books?id=zTgG82RLc6MC&printsec=frontcover
42. The Adventures of Archaeology Wordsmith
43. Heritage of the Birdsville and Strzelecki Tracks: Part of the Far North and Far West Regions (Region 13)
44. Desert Walker
45. Alacaluf People
46. The Enigma of the Natives of Tierra del Fuego
47. Alacaluf images
48. DISTRIBUTION AND ABUNDANCE OF DARWIN IMPACT GLASS
49. *The Archaeology and Socioeconomy of the Gunditjmara: A Landscape Analysis from South west Victoria, Australia*
50. Lake Condah revisited: Archaeological constructions of a cultural landscape
51. The Stony Rises Project

52. The Lake Condah Restoration Project - Biodiversity Assessments
53. Camperdown and District Historical Society
54. Mt Rous & District Historical Society
55. Our Precious Heritage
56. Speaking of the Otways
57. Bass Point Sites Data
58. (Case, 1988, 1989)
59. Birrigai Rock Shelter, Tidbinbilla: A human history from 21,000 years ago
60. Parks Conservation and Lands Systematic seasonal land use by late Pleistocene Tasmanian Aborigines Burrill
61. Accessible Sites
62. Pleistocene Human Occupation and Extinct Fauna in Cloggs Cave, Buchan, South-east Australia
63. 8523 (8522)-24 The Thrust Fault Area
64. Pleistocene Man at Cloggs Cave: His Toolkit and Environment
65. Cranebrook Terrace Revisited
66. Nimji, Garnawala 2, Gordolya and Jagoliya sites
67. http://epress.anu.edu.au/terra_australis/ta25/mobile_devices/ch05.html#d0e1390
68. The Australian Pleistocene Australian Aboriginal prehistoric sites
69. Aboriginal Sites of New South Wales
70. 35,000 year old stone axe found in Australia
71. Pleistocene occupation in the south-east Queensland coastal region
72. The Sea People: Late Holocene Maritime Specialisation in the Whitsunday Islands, Central Queensland
73. Willandra Footprints
74. An Australasian test of the recent African origin theory using the WLH-50 calvarium
75. Pleistocene human footprints from the Willandra Lakes, south eastern Australia
76. Further research of the Willandra Lakes fossil footprint site, south eastern Australia
77. Early Human Occupation at Devil's Lair, South western Australia 50,000 Years Ago *Quaternary Research*, Vol.55, Issue 1, January 2001, p 3-13.

78. The Tasmanians: Part 8b: Archaeology and the Oldest Tasmanians The Tasmanians: Part 8b: Archaeology and the Oldest Tasmanians
79. Surviving an ice age: the zooarchaeological record from south western Tasmania
80. http://www.samuseum.sa.gov.au/ngurunderi/ng9htm.htm
81. http://www.samuseum.sa.gov.au/ngurunderi/ng9htm.htm
82. Pamwak Rock shelter: A Pleistocene site on Manus Island, Papua New Guinea
83. Faunal Composition of Pamwak Site, Manus Island, PNG Pamwak Rock shelter: A Pleistocene site on Manus Island, Papua New Guinea
84. Faunal Composition of Pamwak Site, Manus Island, PNG Archaeology and Rock Art of the Dampier Archipelago
85. Murujuga (Burrup Peninsula)
86. Sydney Aboriginal Rock Engravings
87. Ngadjonji History of the Rainforest People
88. Aborigines may have farmed eels, built huts
89. Fish Traps and Drainage Systems
90. Secrets of the stones
91. Coutts, P. J. F. (Peter J. F), *Aboriginal Engineers of the Western Districts, Victoria,* Records of the Victorian Archaeological Survey; No.7
92. Brewarrina Fish traps
93. Australian Aboriginal Wisdom
94. List of Australian Aboriginal Tribes
95. AusAnthrop Australian Aboriginal tribal database
96. Bogong Moths - The Australian Museum
97. Aborigines may have farmed eels, built huts

List two

1. Fish Traps and Drainage Systems
2. Secrets of the stones
3. Coutts, P. J. F. (Peter J. F), *Aboriginal Engineers of the Western Districts, Victoria,* Records of the Victorian Archaeological Survey; No.7
4. Brewarrina Fish traps

5. The Archaeology and Socioeconomy of the Gunditjmara: A Landscape Analysis from South west Victoria, Australia
6. Gunditj Mirring Partnership project
7. Proceedings, American Philosophical Society (vol. 96, no. 1)
8. The Dieri
9. World of the First Australians - Magic and sorcery
10. Before Cook
11. The revolution that didn't arrive: A review of Pleistocene Sahul
12. Backed Artefacts in North west Queensland
13. Backed Blades in Northern Australia
14. Australian indigenous tools and technology
15. Aboriginal Carved Weapons and Utensils
16. Backed Artefacts in North west Queensland
17. Backed Blades in Northern Australia
18. Backed into a Corner
19. Backed Artefacts in North west Queensland
20. Backed Blades in Northern Australia
21. Australian indigenous tools and technology
22. Aboriginal Carved Weapons and Utensils
23. The revolution that didn't arrive: A review of Pleistocene Sahul
24. Puntutjarpa
25. The Dreaming Origins
26. Ngurunderi
27. http://www.samuseum.sa.gov.au/ngurunderi/ng9htm.htm
28. The origin of the Narran Lake
29. The Black Swans
30. Exchange routs near Lake Eyre
31. Open the Book - Sun Mother Wakes the World - Diane Wolkstein
32. Australian Aborigine Creation Myth
33. Lake Eacham - Wikipedia
34. Ngadjonji Today

Revisiting the Past: Changing Interpretations of Pleistocene settlement Subsistence and Demography in Northern Australia

Appendix List

Appendix A - Archaeological Sites
1. Acheron Cave - Palewardia Walana Lanala
2. Allen's Cave
3. Anbangbang1 see Timeline Ground-Edge Waisted Hatchets
4. Anbangbang1 see Timeline Ground-Edge Waisted Hatchets
5. Artilla – Mt Conner
6. Bass Point
7. Batari, Papua New Guinea
8. Beeton Shelter, Badger Island, Furneaux Islands, Tasmania
9. Beginner's Luck Cave
10. Bevilaqua Cliffs, Discovery Bay Area, south western South Australia
11. Birrigai Shelter
12. Bluff Point - Whalebone huts
13. Bone Cave, south western Tasmania
14. Bookartoo (Parachilna)
15. Box Gully Site, Lake Tyrell, western Victoria
16. Bridgewater South Cave, Discovery Bay area, south western South Australia
17. Briggs Squeeze
18. Bullawinne Site, Maxwell River Valley
19. Burkes Cave - Flaked Stone Assemblage Variation in Western New South Wales, Australia
20. Burrill Lake Rock Shelter
21. Campbell Ranges Sites
22. Cape du Couedic, Kangaroo Island, South Australia
23. Cape Marten, Discovery Bay Area, south western South Australia
24. Capertree III
25. Carlton Bluff, south western Bluff
26. Carpenter's Gap Rock Shelter 1, the Kimberley
27. Cave Bay Cave, Hunter Island, off north west tip of Tasmania

28. Central & Lower Darling River, western NSW
29. Cheetup Shelter, near Esperance
30. Cleland Hills Faces (art site)
31. Cloggs's Cave, southern highlands, Victoria
32. Cohuna
33. Colless Creek Rock Shelter
34. Coobool Creek Crania
35. Cooma, New South Wales
36. Coral Bay, central coast, Western Australia
37. Cossack Skull
38. Cossack Skull
39. Cranebrook Terrace
40. Cuddie Springs, near Carinda
41. Curracurrang Rock Shelter, south coast New South Wales
42. Cutta Cutta Cave, NT
43. David's Dune, Wallpolla Island, north western Victoria
44. Devil's Lair, south western Australia
45. Devon Down Rock Shelter
46. Durba Springs
47. Early Man Shelter
48. East Monbong, Discovery Bay Area,
49. Elvina Track Engraving Site
50. Fern Cave
51. Flinders Island Middens, off north west coast Tasmania
52. Goalu Open Midden, Mitchell Plateau, western Kimberley
53. Goorurarmum, Keep River Region, eastern Kimberley
54. Gorge Quarry
55. Granilpi, Keep River Region, eastern Kimberley
56. GRE8 Rock shelter, gulf country north west Queensland
57. Green Gully, near Keilor
58. Gum Tree Valley Top, Burrup Peninsula
59. Gum Tree Valley Top, Burrup Peninsula

60. Hallett Cove
61. Hayne's Cave, Montebello Islands, central coast, Western Australia
62. Idayu Open Midden, Mitchell Plateau, western Kimberley
63. Ingaladdi Rock Shelter
64. Jansz Cave
65. Jimeri I see Timeline Ground-Edge Waisted Hatchets
66. Jimeri II see Timeline Ground-Edge Waisted Hatchets
67. Jinmium Rock shelter, Northern Territory
68. Jiyer Cave
69. Juunkan-1
70. Juunkan-2
71. Kaalpi
72. Kakadu
73. **Kangaroo Island**
74. Karadoc Swamp see Timeline of Shell Middens
75. Karlie-ngoinpool Cave, Mt. Gambier Region
76. Karlinga, Keep River Region, eastern Kimberley
77. Keilor Skull
78. Kenniff Cave
79. King Island Skeleton
80. Kufu, Buka Island, northern Solomon Islands
81. King Island Skeleton
82. Kintore Cave, NT.
83. Koolan Shelter 2, the Kimberley
84. Koonalda Cave
85. Koongine Cave, South Australia
86. Kow Swamp
87. Kulpi Mara
88. Kutikina Cave, south western Tasmania
89. Kwerlpe Rock Shelter
90. Lachitu Shelter, north coast Papua New Guinea
91. Lake George
92. Lake Mungo 3, western NSW
93. Lake Nitchie Burial
94. Lake Tandou Skull

95. Lake Victoria burials
96. Lene Hare Cave, East Timor
97. Liang Lemdubu, Aru Islands
98. Liang Nebulei Lisa, Aru Islands
99. Little Swanport Midden
100. Liverpool Plains - mound springs
101. Lower Darling River, western New South Wales
102. M86.2, south west Tasmania
103. Mackay see Timeline Ground-Edge Waisted Hatchets
104. Mackintosh 90/1 Cave, south western Tasmania
105. Malangangerr, Arnhem Land
106. Malankunanja II – now called Majebebe, Arnhem Land
107. Mammoth Cave
108. Mandu Mandu Creek Rock shelter, Cape Range Peninsula
109. Maneena Langatick Tattania Emita site, Nelson River Valley
110. Mannalargenna Cave, Prime Seal Island, Furneaux Islands, Tasmania
111. Marnggala Cave
112. Matenbek, New Ireland, Papua New Guinea
113. Matenkupkum New Ireland, Papua New Guinea
114. Merbeen Common, Murray River, South Australia
115. Milly's Cave
116. Miriwun Shelter, east Kimberley
117. Monak, Murray River, southern Australia
118. Monte Bello islands
119. Mount Gambier Caves
120. East Mass ?
121. Mount Rowland, ochre mining
122. Mt Cameron West
123. Mt Newman Rock Shelter, Hamersley Plateau
124. Mt Newman Rock Shelter, Hamersley Plateau
125. Mulanda Bluff, central coast of western Australia
126. Mushroom Rock
127. Mussel Shelter

128. Nacurrie western NSW, see Timeline Burials
129. Nacurrie, SW NSW see Timeline Burials
130. Nanwoon Cave
131. Nara Inlet I, Hook Island, central Queensland
132. Native Well I and II
133. Nauwalabila
134. Nauwalabila 1, Arnhem Land
135. Nauwalabila 1, Arnhem Land
136. Nawamoyn, Arnhem Land
137. Nawarla Gabarnmang Rock Shelter
138. New Guinea 2 Cave, Snowy River Gorge, southern highlands, Victoria
139. Newman Shelter, Ethel Gorge
140. Ngarrbullgan Cave
141. Nimji - Ingalarri Rock shelter
142. Noala Cave, Monte Bello Islands, western Australia
143. Noble's Rock, Discovery Bay Area, south western South Australia
144. Noola Shelter
145. North east Cape Midden I
146. Nunamira Cave (Bluff Cave), south western Tasmania
147. Nurrabullgin Cave
148. OLH, Gulf country, north west Queensland
149. Olive Down Quarry
150. Orchestra Shell Cave
151. Palana Beach, Flinders Island, off north west coast of Tasmania
152. Pallawa Trounta, south west Tasmania
153. Panaramitee Site, near Olary, South Australia
154. Parmerpar Meethaner Cave
155. Perry Sandhills, Wentworth
156. Pilgonaman Creek Rock shelter, Cape Range, central coast Western Australia
157. Point Hibbs, south western coast Tasmania
158. Punipunil, Keep River Region, eastern Kimberley
159. Puntutjarpa Rock Shelter See Sand Ridge Deserts

160. Puritjarra Rock Shelter, near Cleland Hills See Sand Ridge Deserts
161. Riwi Cave, the Kimberley
162. Rock Shelter ORS 7
163. Rocky Cape North Cave, Rocky Cape, North west coast Tasmania
164. Rocky Cave South Cave, south western Tasmania
165. Roonka Flat
166. Sandy Creek Shelter I
167. Serpent's Glen Rock shelter
168. Seton Site, Kangaroo Island, South Australia
169. Silver Dollar Midden, Shark Bay, central coast western Australia
170. Skew Valley Middens, Burrup Peninsula, central coast Western Australia
171. Sleisbeck Cave
172. Snowy River Gorge
173. Spring Creek Site
174. Stud Creek Site
175. Sutton's Rocks, Discovery Bay Area, south western South Australia
176. Thegoa Lagoon, Wentworth
177. Titans Shelter
178. Tulki Well, central coast Western Australia
179. Vlaming Head Middene I & IIa
180. Wadjuru Rock Pool, central coast Western Australia
181. Walkunder Arch Cave
182. Wallen Wallen Creek
183. Wargata Mina Cave, Southern Forests, south west
184. Warragarra Shelter
185. Warroora, central coast of Western Australia
186. Warreen Cave, south west Tasmania
187. West Point Midden – Human Remains
188. Widgingarri 1 & 2, the Kimberley
189. Widgingarri 2
190. Wilgie Mia, Weld Range, northern WA
191. Willandra Footprints
192. Willandra Lakes Burials

193. Willandra Lakes Homid 50
194. Willandra Lakes Homids
195. Wundadjingangnari Midden, Mitchell Plateau, Western Kimberley
196. Wyrie Swamp, South Australia
197. Yarar Rock shelter, south of Port Keats
198. Yardie Creek Midden
199. Yardie Well Rock shelter, Cape Range, central coast Western Australia
200. Yiwarlarlay rock art site

Appendix B - Timelines
Timeline of Sites with Notational Pieces in Sahul (Greater Australia)

1. 20,850   Cave Bay Cave, Hunter Island, Tasmania Bowdler 1984
2. 20,000   Spring Creek, south western Victoria Vanderwal & Fullagar (1989); White & Flannery (1995)
3. 13,000   Devil's Lair, south western Dortch (1976); cf Bednarik (1998); Dortch (2004)
4. 20,000   Yardie Creek Midden, central Western Australia   Kendrick & Morse (1982); Bowdler (1990 a,b); Morse (1996)

1. A macropod femur between 15,400 +/- 330 and 20,850 +/- 290 and a broken swan tarsometatarsus 6,640 +/- 390 and 3,960 +/- 110
2. A *Diprotodon* incisor 19,800 +/- 390
3. A limestone plaque between 19,00 and 13,200 (original dates 11,960 +/- 140 and 12,050 +/- 140), another plaque from a layer dated to between 24,950-26,050 (25,500 +/- 275) years ago (originally 20,400 +/- 1000)
4. The midden is undated, but is in an area dating to the early to mid-Holocene.

See Package of cultural Innovations

Timeline of Sites Containing Beads and Pendants in Sahul (Greater Australia)

1. 42,000   Riwi Cave, the Kimberley
2. 39,500   Buang Merabak, New Ireland
3. 32,000   Mandu Mandu Creek Rock shelter, Cape Range Peninsula, North Western Australia.
4. 20,000   Devil's Lair, south west Western Australia.
5. 12,000   Kow Swamp, northern Victoria
6. 8,000   Lake Nitchie, western New South Wales
7. 8,000   Roonka, South Australia
8. 14,000   Allen's Cave, Nullarbor Plain, South Australia
9. 9,800   Liang Nabulei Lisa, Aru Islands
10. 8,000   Vlaming Head Middens I & IIa and North West Cape Midden I, Cape Range Peninsula, Western Australia
11. 7,000   Nawamoyn, Arnhem Land, Northern Territory.
12. 7,000   Cooma, New South Wales Southern Tablelands
13. 8,000   David's Dune, WallPolla Island, northern Victoria
14. 8,000   Matenbek, New Ireland.
15.   Carpenter's Gap Rock shelter 1, the Kimberley

1. Riwi Cave, the Kimberley. Fragments of shell (***Dentalium sp.***) with smoothed openings, possibly resulting from being worn on a string as beads of a necklace. On 1 fragment there was a residue thought to be ochre, another had a fibre suggesting it had been on a string dating to at least 29,550 +/- 290 BP (Wk-7896) to 40,700 +/- 16\260 **BP** ANUA-13006) (>40,000), and possibly 42,000 years ago. (Balme, 2000; Balme & Morse, 2006).
2. Buang Merabak, New Ireland. A perforated tiger shark tooth dating from 39,500-28,000 BP. (Leavesley, 2007).
3. Mandu Mandu Creek Rock shelter, Cape Range Peninsula, north western Australia. 22 shell beads (***Conus sp.***) in the basal occupation horizon dated to 32,000 BP, between 34,200 +/- 1050 BP (Wk 1513) and 30,000 +/- 800 BP (Wk 1576). The ***Conus*** shells were about 20 cm below a date of 22,100 +/- 500 BP (Wk 1575). Of the 3 cone shell fragments, 1 appeared to have been modified. Their estimated age is 21,000 BP. A scaphopod shell (Dentalliidae sp.) and a fragment of either pearl oyster or ***Nautilus*** shell were found in late Pleistocene deposits. From ethnography they have been known to be worn as ornaments such as pendants (Morse, 1993a,b).

4. Devil's Lair, south west Western Australia. 3 beads made from macropod long bones dating from 20,000-12,000 BP. The original date was 17,370 +/- 290 BP (SUA-1248). It has been redated to 19,160 +/- 380 BP (SUA-976) & 19,835 +/- 75 BP (AA 19691). A small, tapering bone splinter that had been perforated has been dated to 12,000 BP. It is believed it may be a pendant. Other short pieces of perforated bone with unrounded ends are thought to have possibly been bead blanks; an oblong bone, 19 mm long, covered with scratches, possibly to be an ornament covered with gum; what is thought may be a broken bead blank that had a bone sliver inserted, It has been suggested the sliver may have been used to clean out the marrow cavity, that dated to 12,000 BP; a naturally perforated marl object that is thought was possibly a pendant. (Dortch & Merrilees, 1973; Dortch, 1979, 1984; Dortch & Dortch, 1996; Bednarik, 1997, 1998; Dortch, 2004).
5. Kow Swamp, northern Victoria. In a burial dated to about 12,000 BP was found a headband made from kangaroo incisor teeth that had traces of resin still on them, indicating that they had been stuck together. Burials at the site dated from between 14,000 BP and 9,000 BP. 19,160 +/- 360 and 19,835 +/- 75 years ago. Dortch & Merrilees (1973); Dortch (1979, 1984); Dortch & Dortch (1996); Dortch (2004).The burials had been dated to between 14,000 BP and 9,000 years ago. (Flood (1995).
6. Lake Nitchie, western New South Wales. A necklace made from 178 Tasmanian devil's teeth was found in a burial that dated to 6,820 +/- 200 years ago. A hole had been ground and gouged out of each tooth so they could be threaded on a string. (Mackintosh, 1971; Flood, 1995).
7. Roonka, South Australia. In the Roonka cemetery site were elaborate burials that date from the early to late Holocene. Roonka Phase II dated to 8,000 - 4.000 years ago. 6,910 +/- 450 BP. A large fossil oyster shell with holes drilled close together, dated to 6,910 +/- 450 BP (ANU-1408), was recovered from Grave 89. 2 native cat (Dasyurid) mandibles were recovered from Grave 63 had what appear to be drilled attachment holes. Roonka Phase III dates from later than 4,000 BP. In grave 108 were a child and a man. The man had a double-stranded band of notched wallaby teeth around his forehead and a skin cloak that was fastened with bone pins and the paws of an animal pelt at the shoulder. He had a second band of wallaby incisors on his left shoulder. On

the child were a bird skull pendant and a reptile vertebrae necklace. The child's feet had been stained with ochre. (Pretty, 1997; Flood, 1995; Pate et al., 1995).

8. Allen's Cave, Nullarbor Plain, South Australia. It has been suggested that an abalone shell (***Haliotis lacgivata***) found in the deposit was transported to the site as an ornament, possibly a pendant. 13-14,000 BP (Cane, 2001).
9. Liang Nabulei Lisa, Aru Islands. In the terminal Pleistocene deposit was found a shell (***Terebra subulate***) pendant. It had a hole drilled opposite the opercular opening 9.630 +/- 60 BP (OZD697) and 9,750 +/- 60 BP (OZD698). (Bulbeck, 2006a; O'Connor et al., 2006a).
10. Vlaming Head Middens I & IIa and North West Cape Midden I, Cape Range Peninsula, Western Australia. 3 bailer pendant fragments have been found, of which 2 were drilled and the 3rd had all its edges smoothed by grinding. The earliest date obtained for other sites on the peninsula are 7,810 +/- 115 BP (SUA 1735), most <6,000 years old. (Przewodnik, 2003).
11. Nawamoyn, Arnhem Land. 3 shells were found with holes drilled in their bases, 1 was estuarine (***Geloina sp.***), the other 2 were marine (***Anadara sp.***). It is believed they may have been pendants. One of the ***Anadara*** shells had been covered with red ochre. The shell midden they were found in began accumulating around 7,110 +/- 130 BP (ANU-53). (Schrire, 1982).
12. Cooma, New South Wales Southern Tablelands. In a burial dated to about 7,000 BP, were found 327 pierced kangaroo and wallaby incisors that were scattered throughout the grave. They are believed to have been part of a necklace. The teeth had been pierced from both sides in the root area of the tooth. Some were polished, suggesting they had been rubbing together on a string. (Feary (1996).
13. David's Dune, WallPolla Island, northern Victoria. A necklace of pierced Tasmanian devil canine teeth was found in Burial 20 that has been suggested to be similar to a necklace found at Lake Nitchie. It has been dated to 7,140 +/- 200 BP (ANU-8647). Pardoe, 1995).
14. Matenbek, New Ireland. A small shell bead has been dated to about 8,000 BP. Shells and shell fragments have been found with holes drilled in them and with modified edges. It has been suggested that these may have been used for utilitarian purposes, such as the manufacture of fish hooks.

They date from the late Pleistocene and the earlier Holocene. (Smith & Allen, 1999).
15. Carpenter's Gap Rock shelter 1, the Kimberley. Shell *(Dentalium sp.)* beads found in Pleistocene deposits. (O'Connor, 1995).

See Package of cultural Innovations

Timeline of Burials from Sahul (Greater Australia) (Pardoe, 1995)

1. 40,000 Lake Mungo, western New South Wales
2. 18,000 Aru Islands.
3. 15,000 Lake Tandou, south west New South Wales.
4. 14,000 Kow Swamp, possibly to as early as 22,000 BP.
5. 14,000 Coobool Creek, south west New South Wales
6. 13,000 Keilor, Victoria.
7. 11,000 Nacurrie, south west New South Wales.
8. 10,000 Lake Victoria, south west New South Wales
9. 8,000 Roonka, near River Murray mouth, South Australia.
10. 7,000 Lake Nitchie, western New South Wales.
11. 6,500 Cossack, Western Australia.
12. 6,000 Mossgiel, western New South Wales.

1. Lake Mungo, in the Willandra Lakes Region. There were more than 130 burials in the Willandra Lakes Region, the majority of which date to more than 15,000-10,000 BP. It has been estimated that LM1 (WL1) and LM3 (WL3) date from 40,000 +/- 2,000 BP. LM1 (WL1) is among the oldest known cremations in the world. There are a number of dates associated with this burial, 16,940 +/- 635 BP (NZA-231), 19,030 +/- 1,410 BP (ANU-618A), 24,710 + 1,270/-1,100 BP (ANU-618B), 24,745 +/- 2,400 BP (NZA-246), 25,120 +/- 1,380 BP (NZA-230), 26,250 +/- 1,120 BP (ANU-375B). There was also an OSL date of 40,000 +/- 2,000 BP; LM3 (WL3) was an extended burial that has been dated by OSL to 40,000 +/- 2,000 years ago. The remains were covered with red ochre. The nearest known sources of ochre are in the **Manfred Ranges**. Dates of LM3 (WL3) include ESR 31,000 +/- 7,000 BP, ESR 30,000 +/- 2,000 BP and OSL 40,000 +/- 2,000 BP. Based on ESR and U-series dating the "best age estimate" is 62,000 +/- 6,000 BP. It is believed WLH 135 may be of a similar age to that of LM1

& LM3. (Bowler 1970, 1973,2003; Bowler & Thorne 1976; Caddie et al., 1987; Webb, 1989, Pardoe, 1993,1995; Bowler, 1998; Gillespie, 1998; Thorne et.al., 1999). Photos of Mungo 3 (WLH 3)

2. Aru Islands. An adult female skeleton was found in a grave that was partially sealed by a flat stone at Liang Lemdubu. Secondary burial had been carried out, the corpse being dismembered. It has been dated on stratigraphy to about 18,000 BP to 16,000 BP. AMS dating of the bone collagen gave a date of 3,180 BP (OSD577), which is regarded as a minimum age. ESR dating of tooth enamel gave a date of 15,800 +/- 1,800 BP (early uranium uptake) or 18,800 +/- 2,300 (linear uranium uptake). Fragmentary remains of an adult female and 2 young children were found at Liang Nabulei Lisa. Secondary burial is indicated by comingling of the remains and evidence of burning. The secondary burial is believed to probably be from the Early to Mid Holocene, but they may date to the Late Pleistocene, though it has been suggested they could be much younger. (Bulbeck, 2006a, b; O'Connor et al., 2006b).

3. Lake Tandou, south west New South Wales. A burial of an individual in the kneeling position. Shell from what is believed to be the same stratigraphic unit gave a date of 15,200 +/- 160 BP (LLO-416). Cremation was dated to 12,530 +1,630/-1,350 BP (ANU-705). (Freedman & Lofgren, 1983; Pardoe, 1988,19995)

4. Kow Swamp, possibly to as early as 22,000 BP. At least 40 individuals were buried with grave goods, some of which were mussel shells, stone artefacts, marsupial teeth and ochre; The Cohuna cranium came from the Kow Swamp site. It has been dated to between 14,000-9,000 BP, but it has been suggested it may be between 22,000 BP and 19,000 BP; KS1 has been dated to 10,070 +/- 250 BP (ANU-403b); KS5-13,000 +/- 280 BP (ANU-1236); KS9, 9,300 +/- 220 BP (ANU-619b); KS9, 9590 +/- 130 BP (ANU-532); KS14, 8,700 +/- 220 BP (ANU-1038); KS17, 11,350 +/- 160 BP (ANU-1235); The **Kow Sand** where KS9 was buried, gave OSL dates of 14,400 +/- 800 BP & 19,000 +/- 1,100 BP. The **Cohuna Silt**, containing the burials of KS1, KS5, KS14 & KS17 gave an OSL date of 21,600 +/- 1,300 BP. (Thorne & Macumber. 1972; Brown, 1987,1989; Pardoe, 1988,1995; Stone & Cupper, 2003).

5. Coobool Creek, south west New South Wales. 33 individuals have been found in these burials. CC65 U/Th of

14,300 +/- 1,000 BP (LLO-416). CC65 AMS gave a date of 7,200 +/- 60 BP (Beta-90029). (Brown, 1987, 1989; Pardoe, 1995).
6. Keilor, Victoria. Near the Maribyrnong River the cranium of an adult male and femur fragments were found in a sand deposit. Bone collagen from the associated femur fragments have been dated to 12,900 +/- 120 BP (NZ-1327) and 12,000 +/- 120 BP (NZ-1327). Some dates were obtained from a carbonate crust on the skull. They ranged from 5,200 +/- 200 BP (NZ-1320) to 6,800 +/- 100 BP (NZ-1321). The carbonate on the femur fragments gave a date of 6,790 +/- 50 BP (NZ-1326). (Oakley et al., 1975, Mackintosh & Larnach, 1976; Brown, 1987, 1989).
7. **Nacurrie**, south west New South Wales. 2 individuals were recovered from this site. A male has been dated to 11,440 +/-160 BP (NZA-1069). (Brown, 1987, 1989; Pardoe, 1995).
8. Lake Victoria, south west New South Wales. At this site there is a cemetery that has been estimated to contain about 10,000 burials that date sometime after 10,000 BP (Pardoe, 1995).
9. Roonka Flat, near River Murray mouth, South Australia. This site is believed to contain about 120-140 burials, some of them multiple, with grave goods such as ochre and personal ornaments, such as headbands of wallaby teeth. Dates were obtained on associated charcoal and cortical bone collagen range from 7,480 +/- 440 BP (ANU 1428) to 220 +/- 80 BP (ANU 3262). In the Roonka II Phase, that dates from 8,000 - 4,000 BP, 12 burials have been found, of which 6 were of the shaft type. In the Rooka III Phase, postdating 4,000 BP, there are more than 70 known burials, most of which are extended or contracted primary interments in shallow pits or shafts. Roonka Grave 7 has been dated to 7,480 +/- 400 BP (ANU 1428). Roonka Grave 89 dates to 6,910 +/- 450 BP (ANU-1408), and Roonka Grave 48 to 3,930 +/- 120 BP (ANU-407). (Pretty, 1977; Pardoe, 1988, 1995; Pate et a., 1998).
10. Lake Nitchie, western New South Wales. An adult male in a small pit, semi-recumbent position, that had been covered with red ochre and was wearing a necklace of 178 pierced Tasmanian devil teeth. The skull shows early evidence of tooth avulsion. Bone collagen dated to 6,820 +/- 200 BP (NZ). (Marshall, 1971; Oakley et a., 1975; brown, 1987, 1989; Pardoe, 1993,1995).

11. Cossack, Western Australia. An adult male burial that dates to 6,500 BP (Freedman & Lofgren, 1979; Pardoe, 1993).
12. **Mossgiel**, western New South Wales. An adult male, a bone carbonate date of 6,010 +/- 125 BP (NZ-814). (Oakley et a., 1975; Brown, 1987; Pardoe, 1993, 1995).

Timeline of Shell Middens of Sahul (Greater Australia) (Cane, 2001)

1. 40,000 Buang Marabak, New Ireland. Papua New Guinea.
2. 36,000 Willandra Lakes, western New South Wales. (Possibly 40,000).
3. 35,000 archaeological sites.
4. 34,000 Mandu Mandu Creek, central Western Australia.
5. 36,000 Lower Darling River System, western New South Wales. (Possibly 40,000).
6. 28,000 Kilu, Buka Island, Solomon Islands.
7. 27,220 Noala Cave, Montebello Islands, off the central coast, Western Australia.
8. 26,000 Karadoc Swamp, Murray River, southern Australia.
9. 26,000 Merbein Common, Murray River, southern Australia.
10. 26,000 Monak, Murray River, southern Australia.
11. 24,000 Koolan Shelter II, West Kimberley.
12. 22,000 Box Gully site, Lake Tyrrell, western Victoria.
13. 20,000 Matenkupkum, New Ireland. Papua New Guinea.
14. 20,000 Matenbek, New Ireland. Papua New Guinea.
15. 17,750 Liang Lemdubu, Aru Islands.
16. 16,249 GRE8 Rock shelter, Gulf Country, north west Queensland.
17. 14,000 Lachitu Shelter, northern coast of Papua New Guinea.
18. 13,130 Liang Nabulei Lisa, Aru Islands
19. 13,000 OLH, Gulf Country, west north west Queensland.
20. 12,000 Bridgewater South Cave, Discovery Bay Area, south western South Australia.
21. 10,490 Yardie Well Rock shelter, Cape Range, central coast of Western Australia.
22. 9,990 Pilgonaman Creek Rock shelter, Cape Range, central coast of Western Australia.
23. 8,700 Cape Marten, Discovery Bay Area, south western South Australia.

24. 8,700   Beeton Shelter, Badger Island, off the North West coast of Tasmania.
25. 8,700   Carlton Bluff, south western Tasmania.
26. 8,520   Wadjuru Rockpool, central coast of Western Australia.
27. 8,490   Noble's Rock, Discovery Bay Area, south western South Australia.
28. 8,250   Bevilaqua Cliffs, Discovery Bay Area, south western South Australia.
29. 8,240   Hayne's Cave, Montebello Islands, off the central coast, Western Australia.
30. 8,230   Sutton's Rocks, Discovery Bay Area, south western South Australia.
31. 8,150   Nara Inlet 1, Hook Island, central Queensland.
32. 8,120   Rocky Cape South, Rocky Cape, North West coast of Tasmania.
33. 8,000   Widgingarri shelters 1 & 2, west Kimberley, Western Australia.
34. 7,960   East Monbong, Discovery Bay Area, south western South Australia.
35. 7,810   Warroora Central coast of Western Australia.
36. 7,320   Cape du Couedic, Kangaroo Island, South Australia.
37. 7,210   Mulanda Bluff, central coast of Western Australia.
38. 7,150   Palana Beach, Flinders Island, off the north west coast of Tasmania.
39.   Devil's Lair, south western Australia, Pleistocene levels.
40. 7,000   Currarong Shelters, south coast New South Wales.
41. 7,000   Nawamoyn, Arnhem Land.
42. 7,000   Skew Valley Middens, Burrup Peninsula, central coast of Western Australia.
43. 6,640   Cave Bay Cave, off the north west coast of Tasmania.
44. 6,640   Silver Dollar Midden, central coast of Western Australia.
45. 6,270   Coral Bay, central coast of Western Australia.
46. 6,000   Malangangerr, Arnhem Land
47. 6,000   Malakunanja II, Arnhem Land.
48. 5,660   Tulki Well, central coast of Western Australia.
49. 5,540   Rocky Cape North, Rocky Cape, North West coast of Tasmania.
50. 5,300   Point Hibbs, south western coast of Tasmania.

51. 5,000 Flinders Island Middens, off the North West coast of Tasmania.

1. Buang Merabak, New Ireland. Papua New Guinea. 40,090 +/- 570 BP, (ANUA-15809), 39,090 +/- 550 BP (NUA-15808), 33,270 +/- 560 BP (ANUA-16.302), 32,440 +/- 570 BP (ANUA-16303). (Allen et al., 1989a; Gosden, 1993; Beaton, 1995; Leavesley et al., 2002).
2. Willandra Lakes, western New South Wales. Willandra Lakes System, from 36,000 BP, and possibly from 40,000 BP. (Balme & Hope, 1990; Hope, 1993; Johnston, 1993; Balme, 1995; Allen, 1998; Gillespie, 1998).
3. Lene Hare Cave, East Timor. The species represented throughout this shell midden are mostly of species found on a rocky platform. Between 34,850 +/- 630 BP, (ANU-11418) and 31,110 +/- 320 BP (ANU-11398). (O'Connor et al, 2002).
4. Mandu Mandu Creek, central Western Australia. Between 25,000 to 22,000 BP there is some evidence of marine exploitation, becoming well established after 5,500 BP. Dates have been obtained on marine shells, 34,200 +/- 1,050 BP (Wk 1513), 30,000 +/- 850 BP (Wk 1576), 25,200 /- 250 BP (SUA-2354), 22,100 +/- 500 BP (Wk 1575), 20,040 +/- 440 BP (SAU-2614), 5,490 +/- 80 BP (Wk 1511). (Morse, 1988, 1993a, b; cf. Beaton, 1995).
5. Lower Darling River System, western New South Wales. (Possibly 40,000). 27,000 BP (possibly 35,000 BP) to 5,000 BP. ((Balme & Hope, 1990; Hope, 1993; Johnston, 1993; Balme, 1995; Allen, 1998; Gillespie, 1998).
6. Kilu, Buka Island, Solomon Islands. Shell midden dated from 28,000-20,140 +/- 300 BP (Beta 26149), 23,200 +/- 290 BP (Beta-26150), 28740 +/- 280 BP (ANU-5990). (Wickler & Spriggs, 1988; Wickler, 2001).
7. Noala Cave, Montebello Islands, off the central coast, Western Australia. A valve of a ***Polymesoda coaxans*** shell has been dated to 27,220 +/- 640 BP (Wk 2905). At the time, prior to the inundation of the shelf by the rising sea, was about 8 km from the coast. There is evidence from the late Pleistocene and Early Holocene of marine exploitation, 8,730 +/- 80 BP (Wk-2912). (Veth, 1993, 1995).
8. Karadoc Swamp, Murray River, southern Australia. 26,000-20,000 BP. (Richards et al., 2007).
9. Merbein Common, Murray River, southern Australia. 26,000-20,000 BP. (Richards et al., 2007).

10. Monak, Murray River, southern Australia. 26,000-20,000 BP. (Richards et al., 2007).
11. Koolan Shelter II, West Kimberley. Some evidence of marine shellfish at 24,000 BP. From 10,850 +/- 160 BP (Wk-1099) marine exploitation was well established. O'Connor, 1999).
12. Box Gully site, Lake Tyrrell, western Victoria. Some freshwater mussel shells have been dated to 22,015 +/- 125 BP (Wk-166). (Richards et al., 2007).
13. Matenkupkum, New Ireland. Papua New Guinea. Shell midden from 33,000-21,000 BP. Marine exploitation became more intense from 10,000 BP. 33,300 +/- 950 BP (shell degraded)(ANU-5070), 32,700 +/- 1,550 BP (shell not degraded)(ANU-5070), 32,500 +/- 800 BP (ANU-5065), 31,350 +/- 550 BP (ANU-5469), 21,280 +/- 280 BP (ANU-5953), 10,890 +/- 90 BP (ANU-5467). (Allen et al., 1989a; Gosden, 1993; Beaton, 1995; Leavesley et al., 2002).
14. Matenbek, New Ireland. Papua New Guinea. Shell midden from 20,000-19,000 BP, 18,560 +/- 360 BP (Beta-29009), 19,540 +/- (Beta-29008), 29,430 +/- 180 BP (Beta-29007). (Allen et al., 1989a; Gosden, 1993; Beaton, 1995; Leavesley et al., 2002).
15. Liang Lemdubu, Aru Islands. Some marine/estuarine midden material dated to 17,750 +/- 450 BP (OZC776). *geloina coaxans Terebralia sp., Nerita sp., Ellobium sp.* were found in late Pleistocene levels. Evidence of focused exploitation is found from the late Holocene. (O'Connor, 2006a,b).
16. GRE8 Rock shelter, Gulf Country, north west Queensland. Shell middens containing *Alathyria cf. pertexta*, a freshwater species, dating to 16,249 +/- 120 BP (Wk-12229), 38,360 +/- 340 BP (Beta-18431), 37,110 +/- 2,945 BP (Wk-11429). (Slack et al., 2004).
17. Lachitu Shelter, northern coast of Papua New Guinea. Shell midden from 14,000-12,000 BP. 12,300 +/- 110 BP (ANU-7699), 13,570 +/- 200 BP (ANU-7700), 13,940 +/- 160 BP (ANU-7603). (Gorecki et al., 1991).
18. Liang Nabulei Lisa, Aru Islands. Some marine/estuarine midden material dated to 13,130 +/- 80 BP (OZF518). (O'Connor et al., 2006a,b).
19. OLH, Gulf Country, north west Queensland. 12,886 +/- 83 BP (Wk-1222), 13,061 +/- 81 BP (Wk-12226), 13,092 +/- 85 BP (Wk-11430). (Slack et al., 2004).

20. Bridgewater South Cave, Discovery Bay Area, south western South Australia. There is evidence of sporadic marine exploitation from about 12,000 BP. 11,390 +/- 310 BP (Beta-3923). (Lourandos, 1983; Frankel, 1986; Godfrey, 1989).
21. Yardie Well Rock shelter, Cape Range, central coast of Western Australia. Early shell remains and middens dated to 10,490 +/- 100 BP (R11879/2), 7,290 +/- 110 BP (Wk 1477). (Kendrick & Morse, 1982, 1983; Bowdler, 1990a, 1999; Lorblanchet, 1982; Bradshaw, 1995).
22. Pilgonaman Creek Rock shelter, Cape Range, central coast of Western Australia. Marine shell dated to 9,990 +/- 270 BP (Wk 1520), 10,150 +/- 66 BP (R16098/2), 17,410 +/- 66 BP (R11879/1), 31,770 +/- 390 BP (R16098/1). (Kendrick & Morse, 1982, 1983; Bowdler, 1990a, 1999; Lorblanchet, 1982; Bradshaw, 1995).
23. Cape Marten, Discovery Bay Area, south western South Australia. Middens dated to 8,700 +/- 120 BP (NZ 69). (Lourandos, 1983; Frankel, 1986; Godfrey, 1989).
24. Beeton Shelter, Badger Island, off the north west coast of Tasmania. Middens dated to 8,70 +/- 125 BP (ANU-8752), possibly to 21,890 BP. (Flood, 1995; Porch & Allen, 1995).
25. Carlton Bluff, south western Tasmania. A midden dated to 8,700 +/- 200 BP. (Porch & Allen, 1995).
26. Wadjuru Rockpool, central coast of Western Australia. From 8,520 BP. (Kendrick & Morse, 1982, 1983; Bowdler, 1990a, 1999; Lorblanchet, 1982; Bradshaw, 1995).
27. Noble's Rock, Discovery Bay Area, south western South Australia. 8,490 +/- 70 BP (Wk-1262), 8,390 +/- 80 BP (Wk-605), 8,340 +/- 110 BP (Wk-410). (Lourandos, 1983; Frankel, 1986; Godfrey, 1989).
28. Bevilaqua Cliffs, Discovery Bay Area, south western South Australia. 8,250 +/- 60 BP (GaK 397). Bevilaqua Cliffs, Discovery Bay Area, south western South Australia.
29. Hayne's Cave, Montebello Islands, off the central coast, Western Australia. During the Early Holocene was found of marine and terrestrial exploitation between 8,240 +/- 90 BP (Wk-2911) and 7,460 +/- 70 BP (Wk-2914). At the time, the sea is believed to have been about 4 km from the sites on Monet Bello, apparently being abandoned about 7,500 BP, probably as a result of rising sea levels. (Veth, 1993, 1995).
30. Sutton's Rocks, Discovery Bay Area, south western South Australia. Midden dating to 8,230 +/- 60 BP (Wk-1263). (Lourandos, 1983; Frankel, 1986; Godfrey, 1989).

31. Nara Inlet 1, Hook Island, central Queensland. There is evidence of marine exploitation from at least 8,150 +/- 80 BP (Beta 27835), becoming more intensive after about 3,000 BP, between 3,990 +/- 60 BP (Beta 31742) and 2,090 +/- 50 BP (Beta 28,188). (Barker, 1989, 1991; cf Beaton, 1995).
32. Rocky Cape South, Rocky Cape, north west coast of Tasmania. A midden dating to between 8,120 +/- 165 BP (GXO-266) to 3,700 BP. (White & O'Connell, 1982; Bowdler, 1984; Flood, 1995).
33. Widgingarri shelters 1 & 2, west Kimberley, Western Australia. A marine shell has been dated to 7,780 +/- 390 BP (Wk-1101). After 4,660 +/- 60 BP (Wk-1398). (O'Connor, 1999).
34. East Monbong, Discovery Bay Area, south western South Australia. 7,960 +/- 90 BP (Wk-1105). (Lourandos, 1983; Frankel, 1986; Godfrey, 1989).
35. Warroora Midden. Central coast of Western Australia. Gastropod shells, a number of other molluscs, crabs, sea urchins and fish, 7,360 +/- 115 BP (Kendrick & Morse, 1982,1983; Bowdler, 1990a,1999; Lorblanchet, 1982; Bradshaw, 1995).
36. Cape du Couedic, Kangaroo Island, South Australia. Shellfish of mostly rocky shore species, limpets & periwinkles, 7,320 +/- 100 BP (Draper, 1987).
37. Mulanda Bluff Midden, central coast of Western Australia. 7,210 BP. (Kendrick & Morse, 1982, 1983; Bowdler, 1990a, 1999; Lorblanchet, 1982; Bradshaw, 1995).
38. Palana Beach Midden, Flinders Island, off the north west coast of Tasmania. The earliest shell midden dated to 7,150 +/- 135 BP (SUA-641). (Orchiston & Glenie, 1978; Porch & Allen 1995).
39. Devil's Lair, south western Australia, Pleistocene levels. Isolated shells of estuarine bivalves and shells marine species have been recovered from Pleistocene levels. The site was about 10-30 km from the sea at the time. (Dortch et al., 1984).
40. Currarong Shelters, south coast New South Wales. There is evidence of marine exploitation by 5,540 +/- 90 BP (SUA-224), possibly as early as 7,000 BP. (Lampert, 1971; White & O'Connell, 1982).
41. Nawamoyn Midden, Arnhem Land. Estuarine and marine shells beginning 7,110 +/- 130 BP (Schrire, 1982, cf. Beaton, 1985).

42. Skew Valley Middens, Burrup Peninsula, central coast of Western Australia. 7,000-2,200 BP. (Kendrick & Morse, 1982,1983; Bowdler, 1990a,1999; Lorblanchet, 1982; Bradshaw, 1995).
43. Cave Bay Cave, off the north west coast of Tasmania. Midden deposits begin at 6,640 +/- 100 BP (ANU-1797), 3,960 +/- 110 BP (ANU-1614). A later shell midden dated to 2,580 +/- 70 BP (ANU-1362) continuing in use until 990 +/- 90 BP (ANU-1616). (Bowdler, 1984).
44. Silver Dollar Midden, central coast of Western Australia. Fish and marine shellfish, mostly *Terebralia sp.*, 6,640 +/- 260 BP (ANU-7457), 6,950 +/- 70 BP (ANU-7456), 7,290 +/- 140 BP (Wk 2436), 7,360 +/- 190 BP (Wk 2435). (Kendrick & Morse, 1982,1983; Bowdler, 1990a,1999; Lorblanchet, 1982; Bradshaw, 1995).
45. Coral Bay Midden, central coast of Western Australia. 6,270 BP. (Kendrick & Morse, 1982,1983; Bowdler, 1990a,1999; Lorblanchet, 1982; Bradshaw, 1995).
46. Malangangerr, Arnhem Land. Shells of estuarine and marine shell species, from 5,980 +/- 140 BP (GaK-627) to 370 +/- 80 BP (GaK-626). (Schrire, 1982; cf, Beaton, 1985).
47. Malakunanja II, Arnhem Land. Estuarine shell species from 6,360 +/- 100 BP (SUA-264). (Jones & Negerevich, 1985).
48. Tulki Well Midden, central coast of Western Australia. Nearly all turban shell (*Turbo sp.*), 5,660 +/- 115 BP (AR-1245). (Kendrick & Morse, 1982,1983; Bowdler, 1990a,1999; Lorblanchet, 1982; Bradshaw, 1995).
49. Rocky Cape North, Rocky Cape, north west coast of Tasmania. This midden was used from 5,425 +/- 135 BP (V-89) to at least 450 BP. (White & O'Connell, 1982; Bowdler, 1984; Flood, 1995).
50. Point Hibbs Midden, south western coast of Tasmania. 5,300 BP. (Porch & Allen, 1995).
51. Flinders Island Middens, off the north west coast of Tasmania. 5 shell middens from 7,000 BP to 5,000 BP. (Porch & Allen, 1995).

Timeline of Bone & Wooden Tools in Sahul (Greater Australia)

1. 29,000 Bone Cave, south western Tasmania.
2. 26,000 Devil's Lair south western Australia
3. 22,750 Cave Bay Cave, south western Tasmania.
4. 22,000 Warreen Cave, south western Tasmania.
5. 21,000 New Guinea II, southern highlands, Victoria.

6. 20,000   Kutikina Cave, south western Tasmania.
7. 18,000   Clogg's Cave, southern highlands, Victoria.
8. 18,000   Liang Lemdubu, Aru Islands.
9. 17,000   Batari, Papua New Guinea.
10. 13,000   Liang Bebulei Lisa, Aru Islands.
11. 11,000   Seton, Kangaroo Island, South Australia.
12. 10,200   Wyrie Swamp, South Australia.
13. 10,000   Koongine Cave, South Australia.
14. 8,000   Rocky Cape South Cave, south western Tasmania.
15. 7,000   Nawamoyn, Arnhem Land, Northern Territory.
16. 7,000   Malangangerr, Arnhem Land, Northern Territory
17. 4,000   Roonka, South Australia.
18.   Widgingarri Shelters 1 & 2, west Kimberley, Western Australia.

1. Bone Cave, south western Tasmania. In this deposit 13 bone tools were found in layers that ranged from 29,000 BP to 14,000 BP, 13,700 +/- 860 BP (Beta-26509); 29,000 +/- 520 BP (Beta-29987). (Bowdler et al., 1977,1984; White & O'Connell, 1982; Ranson et al., 1983; Allen et al., 1989b; Webb & Allen, 1990b; Flood, 1995; Holdaway & Porch, 1996).
2. Devil's Lair south western Australia. 13 bone points were found, most dating to more than 26,000 BP, most to less than 20,000 BP. One bone point, made from a whole macropod fibula, was 149.42 mm long. It was found directly associated with charcoal that was originally dated to 19,250 +/- 900 BP (ANU-1361). It has since been redated to 24,930 +/- 335 BP. A number of other bi-points, 22 mm long, made from macropod bone segments, have been found. A 14 mm-long object, made from the proximal end of a bird fibula, that is thought to have been an awl, had a highly polished, pointed distal end. (Dortch & Merrilees, 1973; Dortch, 1984, 2004)
3. Cave Bay Cave, south western Tasmania. Bone artefacts, including bone points and a spatulate bone tool form, have been found in levels that date from 22,750 +/- 420 BP (ANU-1498) and 20,850 +/- 290 BP (ANU-1612). In a level dated 19,520 +/- 300 BP (ANU-1774), a bone tool with a spatulate end was found. A ground bone point, about 90 mm long, made from macropod fibula was associated with charcoal that dated to 18,550 +/- 600 BP (ANU-1361). 4 bone points were found in the shell midden deposits in layers that dated from 6,640 +/- 100 BP (ANU-1797) and 3,960 +/- 110 BP (ANU-1614). (Bowdler et al., 1977,1984; White &

O'Connell, 1982; Ranson et al., 1983; Allen et al., 1989b; Webb & Allen, 1990b; Flood, 1995; Holdaway & Porch, 1996).

4. Warreen Cave, south western Tasmania. Between 22,000 BP and 18,000 BP, 6 bone tools were found, 17,880 +/- 135 BP (Beta-42066), 21,980 +/- 310 BO (Beta-26960). (Bowdler et al., 1977,1984; White & O'Connell, 1982; Ranson et al., 1983; Allen et al., 1989b; Webb & Allen, 1990b; Flood, 1995; Holdaway & Porch, 1996).

5. New Guinea II, southern highlands, Victoria. 4 bone points made from macropod fibula were found that dated to between 21,000 +/- 800 BP (SUA-2222) and 4,660 +/- 110 BP (SUA-2217). (Ossa et al., 1995).

6. Kutikina Cave, south western Tasmania. A stout bone unipoint that dated to between 20,000 BP & 15,000 BP.

7. Clogg's Cave, southern highlands, Victoria. A bone point was recovered from a layer between level that dated to 17,720 +/- 840 BP (ANU-1044) and 13,690 +/- 350 BP (ANU-1182). Late Pleistocene levels have produced "burnishing pebbles", stones that were used to treat animal skins to make them soft and pliable. (Flood, 1980).

8. Liang Lemdubu, Aru Islands. 3 bone points were found in levels dating to between 18,000 BP & 9,000 BP. Between a level dating to between 16,570 +/- 510 BP (OZD460) and 9,250 +/- 60 BP (OZF357), 1 bone point was found. 2 bone points were found from dates around 16,770 +/- 110 BP (AA-32848), 16,850 +/- 120 BP (OZF248), 17,750 +/- 450 BP (OZC776), 13,330 +/- 300 BP (OZC777). (O'Connor et al., 2006a,b); Pasveer, 2006).

9. Batari, Papua New Guinea. Ground bone from this deposit has been dated to 16,850 +/- 700 BP (ANU-40). It has been suggested that the early date may not relate to early occupation of the site. A bipoint, as well as other small bone points, are from unstratified deposits or from deposits that date to <8,230 +/- 190 BP. (ANU-38a). There was also a complete, unstratified bone unipoint. (White, 1972; Davidson & Noble, 1992).

10. Liang Bebulei Lisa, Aru Islands. 11 bone tools, mostly unipoints and spatulate, from levels dating between 13,000 BP to 9,000 BP. 8,420 +/- 50 BP (OZF030), 9,320 +/- 60 BP (OZD696), 9,630 +/- 60 BP (OZD697), 9,750 +/- 60 BP (OZD698), 9,870 +/- 70 BP (OZD699), 9,450 +/- 60 BP (OZD700), 9,850 +/- 60 BP (OZD702). (O'Connor et al., 2006a, b); Pasveer, 2006).

11. Seton, Kangaroo Island, South Australia. In deposits dated to 10,940 +/- 60 BP (ANU-925), 2 bone points were found that had use-wear. (Lampert, 2001).
12. Wyrie Swamp, South Australia. In levels dating from between 10,200 BP and 8,000 BP were found 25 wooden artefacts made from sheoak (*Casuarina stricta*). There were boomerangs, digging sticks, spears with simple sharpened points and spears with barbed points. 10,200 +/- 159 BP (ANU-1292), 8,990 +/- 120 BP (ANU-1293) (Luebbers, 1975).
13. Koongine Cave, South Australia. A bone point was found that is believed to date from between 10,000 BP & 9,000 BP. 9,240 +/- 100 BP (Beta-15996), 9,710 +/- 180 BP (Beta -14861) (Frankel, 1986).
14. Rocky Cape South Cave, south western Tasmania. 37 bone points were recovered from the caves at Rocky Cape, dating from between 8,000 BP and 3,500 BP, mostly from 8,000 BP to 5,000 BP.
15. Nawamoyn Arnhem Land, Northern Territory. A variety of bone points were found throughout the midden deposits that had accumulated from 7,110 +/- 130 BP (ANU-53). No bone points were found in the sand layers below the midden. (Schrire, 1982).
16. Malangangerr, Arnhem Land, Northern Territory. A variety of bone points were found throughout the midden deposits that had accumulated from 7,110 +/- 130 BP (ANU-53). No bone points were found in the sand layers below the midden. (Schrire, 1982).
17. Roonka, South Australia. At this site bone points were recovered from elaborate burials. Among the items found was a 29 cm long bone implement that is believed to have possibly been a "pointed bone dagger". It was found in Grave 106 that has been dated to between 8,000 & 4,000 BP. In Grave 108 were found many bone pins used for fastening animal skin cloaks. This grave was later than 4,000 BP. (Pretty, 1977, Flood, 1995; Pate et al., 1998).
18. Widgingarri Shelters 1 & 2, west Kimberley, Western Australia. In this deposit were ground bone points and bone "indenters", and the appearance of bone points with pressure flaking. It is thought the bone points may be pressure flakers. (O'Connor, 1996, 1999).

Timeline of Ground-edge & Waisted Hatchets of Sahul (Greater Australia)

1. 40,000 Huon Peninsula: Bobongarra, Papua New Guinea.
2. 32,000 Sandy Creek 1, southeast Cape York, Queensland.
3. 28,000 Widgingarri 1 & 2, the Kimberley, Western Australia.
4. 26,000 Kosipe, Papua New Guinea.
5. 25,000 Nombe, Papua New Guinea.
6. 23,000 Malangangerr, Arnhem Land, Northern Territory.
7. 21,450 Nawamoyn, Arnhem Land, Northern Territory.
8. 20,000 Kuk, Papua New Guinea.
9. 19,975 Nauwalabila 1, Arnhem Land, Northern Territory.
10. 17,900 Miriwun, southeast Cape York, Queensland.
11. 12,100 Yuku, Papua New Guinea.
12. 11,000 Pamwak Rock shelter, Manus Island, Admiralty Islands.
13. 10,790 Jimeri I, Arnhem Land, Northern Territory.
14. 6,870 Mushroom Rock, southeast Cape York, Queensland.
15. 6,650 Jimeri II, Arnhem Land, Northern Territory.
16. 5,770 Anbangbang1, Arnhem Land, Northern Territory.
17. Kangaroo Island sites, South Australia.
18. **Mackay**, central Queensland.
19. Early Man Rock shelter, southeast Cape York Peninsula, Queensland.

1. Papua New Guinea sites. In excavations dating from possibly more than 40,000 BP, more than 100 waisted hatchets were found
2. Sandy Creek 1, southeast Cape York Sites, Queensland. Edge-ground waisted, and grooved pink quartz hatchet was found on bedrock that had been dated by stratigraphic methods to about 31,000 +700/-600 BP. There was also a flake with a ground surface that came from the upper, Holocene levels.
3. Widgingarri 1 & 2, the Kimberley, Western Australia. In levels dated to 28,060 +/- 600 BP (R11795) there were flakes of volcanic stone, that are believed may have detached from the working edge of ground stone hatchets. Artefacts of ground stone were also found in layers of Holocene origin.

4. Kosipe, Papua New Guinea. 20 ground-edge hatchets, the earliest of which has been dated to possibly more than 26,000 BP. 26,870 +/- 590 BP 26,450 +/- 880 BP. (Bulmer, 1977; White & O'Connell, 1982; Groube et al., 1986; Golson, 2001; Allen & O'Connell, 2004,2004).
5. Nombe, Papua New Guinea. 2 waisted and stemmed hatchets dating from possibly 25,000 BP.
6. Malangangerr, Arnhem Land, Northern Territory. In this deposit there were 5 edge-ground hatchets, 1 of which was described as waisted, in the lower sand deposits that have been dated from between 22,900 +/- 1,000 BP (ANU-77b) and 18,400 +/- 400 BP (ANU-19). A large flake, that it is believed may have been an incomplete edge-ground hatchet. A ground green schist "rod" was found that is believed to possibly have been part of a larger ground tool. It was in the lower sand deposit. A ground sandstone "rod" was found in the lower unit of the midden that dated from 5,980 +/- 140 BP (GaK-627) (Schrire, 1982).
7. Nawamoyn, Arnhem Land, Northern Territory. From the Holocene and Pleistocene, there were 9 ground-edge hatchets, and a rock with small depressions ground into its surface. There were also 22 pebbles that had evidence of being used for pounding, some the above dating to at least 21,450 +/- 380 BP (ANU-51). Some dated to more than 7,110 +/- 130 (ANU-53). (Schrire, 1982).
8. Kuk, Papua New Guinea. A waisted hatchet dating to about 20,000 BP.
9. Nauwalabila 1, Arnhem Land, Northern Territory. Pieces of exotic dolerite that have the general shape indicating they were probably hatchets or hatchet blanks, but weathering was too advanced to make their identification certain, and to determine if they originally had ground edges. They are believed to date from about 25,000-30,000 BP, being older than 19,975 +/- 365 BP (SUA-237). There were also small flakes, thought to possibly from the cutting edge of edge-ground hatchets. The oldest of these flake being found in levels dating from between 19,975 +/- 365 (SUA 237) and 13,195 +/- 175 BP (SUA 236). (Johnson, 1985b).
10. Miriwun, southeast Cape York, Queensland. A ground-edge hatchet was found that dated from 1,675 +/- 185 BP (SUA-142). A single flake was found that it is believed may have come from the cutting edge of a ground stone hatchet dated to between 17,980 +1,370/-1,170 BP (ANU-1008). (Dortch, 1977).

11. Yuku, Papua New Guinea sites. About 18 waisted hatchets in the upper levels, and 2 in earlier levels that are believed could be more than 12,100 +/- 350 (GX-3212B).
12. Pamwak Rock shelter, Manus Island, Admiralty Islands. In this deposit were found 5 edge-ground stone hatchets/adzes, 16 edge-ground *Tridacna* shell artefacts. Dates ranged from 12,400 +/- 80 BP (ANU-6980) to 11,730 +/- 280 BP (ANU-7124).
13. Jimeri I, Arnhem Land, Northern Territory. 2 small edge-ground hatchets made from porphyritic dolerite that dated to 3,820 +/- 100 BP (ANU-52) and up to possibly 10,790 +/- 100 BP (GaK-632). (Schrire, 1982).
14. Mushroom Rock, southeast Cape York, Queensland. The base of the deposits, well below a dated later of 6,870 +/- 150 BP, believed to possibly of late Pleistocene age, have produced fragments of edge-ground hatchets.
15. Jimeri II, Arnhem Land, Northern Territory. 11 small edge-ground porphyritic dolerite hatchets, together with possible waist flakes believed to have resulted from the making and/or use of stone implements that dated from between 6.650 +/- 500 BP (ANU-18) and 4,779 +/- 150 BP (ANU-50). (Schrire, 1982).
16. Anbangbang1, Arnhem Land, Northern Territory. A ground hatchet from levels earlier than 5,770 +/- 100 BP. (ANU-3206). (Jones & Johnson, 1985a).
17. Kangaroo Island sites, South Australia. Waisted hatchets that are believed to be of late Pleistocene to early Holocene age. (Lampert, 1981; Golson, 2001).
18. Mackay, central Queensland. Waisted hatchets were found on the surface (Groube, 1986).
19. Early Man Rock shelter, southeast Cape York Peninsula, Queensland. Flakes with grinding marks, which are believed to be from edge-ground hatchets, possibly of terminal Pleistocene age.

Appendix C - Some journal articles on Aboriginal Australia

Aboriginal Population Reconstructions - 5000 BP-first contact

According to Chris Johnson (Source 1) a rough estimate has put the Aboriginal population of Australia at about 1 million at the time Europeans arrived in Australia, and possibly about 250,000 at 10,000

BP. The reason for a growth of population is debated; one assumption being that the environment was improving. Johnson thinks this is unlikely. He says that any climatic change would most likely be in the opposite direction, towards a harsher climate, with less rainfall and more droughts, and generally more difficult for humans to flourish.

He suggests any population growth must have been intrinsic to what people were doing, such as reorganising their societies and some land management practices. Prehistoric population trends have been reconstructed by the use of radiocarbon dating of the evidence found at occupation sites, the assumption being that the population size could be estimated by the amount of evidence at the sites. Evidence lost from the older sites would cause the population at younger sites to be overrepresented, leading to uncertainty of the actual population growth, as opposed to the apparent growth. A model was designed by Johnson and Barry Brook to show how frequently occupation sites were abandoned, and how soon evidence was lost from such abandoned sites, the model showing apparent population increases through time. They concluded that this was not the cause of observed population increases in Australia, after running data through various simulations.

According to Johnson, actual population growth more appropriately explains the observed increase, the increase being slow at 10,000-5,000 BP and accelerating in the last 5000 years to first contact.

Johnson said "Our results imply that Aboriginal societies and cultures were dynamic and changing before the arrival of Europeans."

See Stone Tools, possible influence on population estimates from archaeological sites.

See Aboriginal Occupation of Greater Australia

Appendix D - Collapse of Prehistoric Aboriginal Society in North Western Australia triggered by an ENSO Mega-Drought

One of the largest collections of rock art in the world is present in the Kimberley region, Western Australia, which is characterised by 2 distinct art forms; the anthropomorphic figures of the Gwion

Gwion, or Bradshaw, paintings, that are fine-featured, and the Wandjina figures that are characterised by broad brush strokes. An age of at least 17,000 BP has been confirmed for the Gwion Gwion paintings by the most recent dates obtained by luminescence dating of mud wasp nests that were present on top of the Gwion Gwion paintings, with the most recent dates for these paintings being 7,000-5,000 BP, from near the mid-Holocene. It has been found by radiocarbon dating that there was a hiatus of at least 1,200 years following the latest of the Gwion Gwion until the earliest known appearance of the Wandjina rock art. In this paper the authors[1] show that in the mid-Holocene an ENSO event triggered a collapse of the Australian summer monsoon which led to a mega-drought that lasted for about 1,500 years and it was this long period of continuous drought that triggered the society responsible for the Gwion Gwion rock art to collapse. The authors suggest the severity of the drought, which was enhanced by positive feedbacks resulting from changes in the conditions of the land surface and an increase of atmospheric aerosol loading, which led to a weakening or complete loss of monsoon rains. According to the authors this confirms that a catastrophic upheaval occurred in Aboriginal societies, caused by rapid natural variability of the climate, and they also suggest these heavy rains of the wet season could possibly fail again if there is significant change to the ENSO.

Conclusion

According to the authors[1] they have shown the first evidence of significant rapid change in the monsoon over north western Australia that occurred during the Middle to Late Holocene. The Southern Hemisphere subtropical ridge was allowed to extend further to the north as the changes to the monsoon were linked to enhanced ENSO and associated breakdown of positive moisture-advection onto the Kimberley region. Prolonged aridity coeval with major change in rock art that resulted from the failure of the monsoon was confirmed by palynological and sedimentological evidence from the Black Springs site. The authors therefore concluded that a change in artists of the Kimberley rock art was the result of change of the north west Australian monsoon that was forced by ENSO.

See Holocene Changes in Australian-Indonesian Monsoon Rainfall - Stalagmite Evidence from Trace element & Stable Isotope Ratios.

Appendix E - Australian Aboriginals' Adaptation to their Environment – Temperature-Responsive of Thyroxine

Thyroxine-binding globulin (TBG) carries and stores thyroxine, the hormone that regulates mammalian metabolism, in the blood. In this paper the authors demonstrate that thyroxine is released from TBG by a temperature-sensitive mechanism, and they also demonstrate how this will provide a homeostatic thyroxine concentration adjustment that matches metabolic needs, as in the case of small animals when hypothermia causes torpor. In conditions such as infections in humans an accelerated release of thyroxine is triggered which results in a 23 % increase in thyroxine concentration at 39°C. In an environmental adaptation in Aboriginal Australians the *in vivo* relevance of this fever response is affirmed. The study found how 2 mutations incorporated in the TBG interact in such a way that the surge in thyroxine release will be halved, and therefore the metabolic rate boost that would otherwise occur at body temperatures exceeding 37°C is prevented. Insights are opened into physiological changes that accompany body temperature variations, as is notable in fevers by the overall findings.

Appendix F - Tulas - Are They Linked to ENSO in Australia? (Veth, Hiscock & Williams, 2011)

The tula is an endemic hafted tool used to work hardwoods by Aboriginal people throughout central and western Australia, totalling about 2/3 of the continent. Tulas also had other functions such as butchery and plant processing. Tulas appear to have spread rapidly across their range and to date no antecedent tool of this form is known of in Australia. According to the authors[1] tulas first appear in the archaeological record at the same time as the onset of the ENSO climatic conditions.

In this paper Veth, Hiscock & Williams (2011) propose that the appearance of this new, specialised tool at about 3,700 BP was likely to be a response to intensification of the ENSO, though the data is not yet sufficient to establish unequivocally a causal link between this tool and the ENSO intensification. As a result of this intensification aridity and climatic variability increased and lasted for nearly 2,000 years. The authors[1] propose the appearance of the tula was an element of the toolkit they adopted as part of their minimisation of risk, and was a part of the wider social and economic strategy adopted to cope with the increasingly difficult climatic uncertainty. This possibility has implications for the innovation process diversity operating in Australia in the Holocene. According to the authors[1] their discussion in this paper is a platform for future studies which they believe are necessary.

It has been noted that tulas used by Australian Aboriginal people were of a unique nature (Holdaway & Stern, 2004, 253-256). These distinctive tools that were used across much of the arid zone of Australia were comprised of a discoidal flake that had been retouched and hafted on the ends of wooden shafts. They were seen to be used for scraping wood, incising and adzing in the historical period. It is a composite tool which often has the stone implement fixed to a wooden shaft that was constructed by regular and distinctive production technology and they have been seen to be an endemic adaptation, adopted by Aboriginal people throughout 2/3 of the Australian continent, its use being geographically focused on central and Western Australia. Tulas are a technologically distinct form of tool which is useful in analysis and Veth, Hiscock & Williams (2011) have suggested that they may have had emic significance to the Aboriginal people who use them. Veth, Hiscock & Williams suggest they had adaptive significance, regardless of the perceptions of the knappers of these tools. The properties of tulas compared with those of unmodified stones varies between stratified sites that have been dated (e.g. data in Gould, 1977 vs Smith, 2006), and within palimpsest open sites (Veth, 1993), there is no suggestion of an emergence, and subsequent proliferation phase, at an earlier time, as there are for other tools such as backed artefacts. The authors[1] suggest that relatively high levels of residential mobility are indicated by a number of factors, such as the often 'exotic' provenance of tulas, the high numbers and ubiquity of tulas that are found in many sites in the arid zone. The careful, repeated production and selection of robust flakes that were *broad* platform and deeply convex, that were required for these tools, that were high-impact hafted tools, is unique, though the method of resharpening the tula flakes was not necessarily different from that used for retouching 'scrapers' that were in use prior to the appearance of tulas in the archaeological record, and there are no known antecedents of the tula (Hiscock & Veth, 1991).

Veth, Hiscock & Williams say their primary aim in this paper is to review the evidence of the appearance of the tula and using this evidence to discuss plausible innovation processes in the Holocene in Australia. Studies have shown that tulas began appearing in archaeological sites dated to 4,000-3,000 BP (Hiscock & Veth, 1991), though it was previously believed that tulas had been in use throughout the Holocene (e.g. Gould, 1977). Models of innovation of other tools used in Aboriginal Australia have been discussed extensively (e.g. Attenbrow, 2008, 2009), questions of the adaptive context in which tulas appeared and use of tulas over wide areas of Australia have not been addressed specifically. Veth, Hiscock & Williams suggest that the process of the emergence of the tula may have differed from that of other standardised stone tool types, though the adaptive context for the appearance and spread of the tula is similar to that of other standardised stone tools from the mid to Late Holocene. A study of the existing models of technological change in Australia clarifies the nature of these differences.

Percussion or a combination of percussion and pressure is used to produce bifacial points with strait or convex convergent retouched margins, which are mostly restricted to the north-west region of mainland Australia. Backed artefacts, found across much of southern and eastern Australia, have a margin that is retouched steeply, often with a bipolar technique, and in appearance it is similar to microliths from the Old World. Evidence has been found indicating that there is a long history of these implements in Australia dating back to the early Holocene, at least, and possibly as far as the terminal Pleistocene, which largely resolved the uncertainty of their chronology. For a number of millennia they were produced at low rates, the production rate increasing in the Late Holocene (e.g. Clarkson, 2007; Hiscock, 1993, 1994, 2002, 2006; Hiscock & Attenbrow, 1998, 2004; Slack et al., 2004). Proliferation events, the name used for periods in which implements were produced at much higher rates, one of which occurred between 4,000 and 2,000 BP for bifacial points in north west Australia and for backed artefacts in eastern Australia (Hiscock, 2006). Veth, Hiscock & Williams suggest proliferation events represent an adaptive response, and as they occur long after the invention and use of the tools, they involved the emphasising of a tool form that was pre-existing to new adaptive contexts (Hiscock, 2002; Hiscock & O'Connor, 2006).

It has been difficult to define the use of these tools and the circumstance that led to their regular production 4,000 to 2,000 BP has been achieved only for backed artefacts in eastern Australia. It has been found that backed artefacts were not often used for projectile armatures (points or barbs) as had been the initial belief, rather, combined residue and use-wear studies have shown they were used in a wide range of craft-related processing activities, such as wood-working, skin-working, plant-working and feather-working, and many specimens show evidence of multiple and different uses (Robertson et *al.*, 2009). It has been suggested (Attenbrow et al., 2009), based on the lack of any evidence that indicates any shift over time in the uses and tasks of backed artefacts, that backed artefacts were especially prolific in the period 4,000-2,000 BP because the tools in which they were hafted had multiple uses. The authors[1] suggest this evidence is consistent with a proposal that foragers in Australia emphasised composite tools that contained backed artefacts because of their readiness and multifunctionality, as they used them for nearly all tasks (Hiscock, 1994, 2002, 2006, 2008). It has been proposed (Hiscock, 2002, 2006) that tools that were standardised, ready and multifunctional, that had backed artefacts attached, were emphasised at the time of the proliferation event as a result of the increased level of environmental variability associated with ENSO conditions that were intensified at this time, and as there was a need for mobile hunter-gathering at these times. Such tools reduced the risks associated with foraging, in the context of increased resource variability, by providing tools that were reliable and easily repaired, and that increased resource acquisition and manipulation on most occasions. The conclusion that they had long use lives is consistent with observations that production rates of backed artefacts increased during the period 4,000-2,0000 BP, and more extensive maintenance was carried out of other retouched flakes (Hiscock, 2008; Hiscock & Attenbrow, 2005). According to Veth, Hiscock & Williams a similar proposal has been put forward for the articulation of northern bifacial point proliferation as the climatic variability increased with ENSO intensification (Hiscock, 2002, 2006), though the nature of tool use has been studied less for points.

An image of technological change during the Holocene has been provided by these inferences, the high production rate of some tools representing an adaptive response to greater variability of the climate, at least a significant factor, which involves an emphasis on tool forms that were pre-existing, as a solution to economic contests that were new. According to Veth, Hiscock & Williams they argue in this paper that the tula, the 3rd tool type to be widely distributed, appears over a time span that they describe as 'archaeologically instantaneous', correlating with the intensification of the ENSO that occurred between 4,000 and 2,000 BP.

Australian tula

According to Veth, Hiscock & Williams a common description for tulas is as semi-discoidal retouched flakes with a pronounced ventral bulb and a convex cutting edge when seen in plan view (Hiscock & Veth, 1991; Holdaway & Stern, 2004: 253-256; Spencer & Gillen, 1904). These stone tools were historically observed to be hafted at the end of wooden shafts and spear throwers, primarily by using ***Triodia***-based resin (Sheridan, 1979). Central and western Australia is the centre of focus of the geographic distribution of tulas, though examples of tulas or tula-like objects have been found along the eastern seaboard central regions (McNiven, 1993; Hiscock & Attenbrow, 2005).

Veth, Hiscock & Williams suggest composite tools that contained tulas probably had a variety of functions, one of which, that has been discussed, being as an adze for use with woods that were very dense, such as mulga, ***Acacia aneura***. Tulas could be used to scrape, grave, saw and chisel, and their construction often made them suitable for adzing hard timber (e.g. Sheridan, 1979). The authors[1] suggest when tulas were being used for wood-working scraping was likely to have been the dominant use over adzing, and they were probably used for a range of other tasks such as butchery, vegetable processing, and possibly others (after Gould, 1977). They also suggest that as a category tulas are multifunctional, though in other contexts were mainly used for wood-working. The distal working edge of the tula became blunt over a short time when it was being used for work on hardwoods that would require the distal edge to be sharpened by frequent retouching to extend its working life, Veth, Hiscock & Williams suggesting that this retouching would allow the tula to be used for more than an hour (Hayden, 1977). As the distal margin is being constantly retouched the cutting edge would gradually migrate towards the proximal end of the tula and in the process changing the plan shape of the retouched edge that changes from convex to straight and ultimately to concave (e.g. Cooper, 1954; Gould, 1977; Hiscock & Veth, 1991). The changes have been used as an exemplar of morphological changes accompanying maintenance of the edge (e.g. Dibble, 1995), the changes having been documented in assemblages that have been excavated (e.g. Hiscock, 1988). The tula 'slug' is either discarded or recycled as the tool becomes less firmly fixed to the resin haft, and becomes less able to be retouched and is of less use for heavy scraping or adzing. The ease with which it can be resharpened, and the likelihood of its being discarded, is affected by the steepness and character of the step terminations on the retouched edge. Tulas have been found in different stages of maintenance and use in archaeological sites, and tulas that have been completed that have remained unused have occasionally been found in archaeological sites (Veth, 1993), and caches of unused tulas have been found on rare occasions (Hiscock, 1988). At many sites slug stage specimens that have been used and retouched are frequently found. Known archaeological instances of tula and tula slug specimens in archaeological sites in Australia have been used to construct a chronology of this tool type.

Tula Technology - Chronology

As a result of sampling and taphonomic issues (Gorecki et *al*., 1997; Hiscock, 2001; Hiscock & Attenbrow, 1998) the construction of reliable chronologies for implements in Australia during the Holocene has been difficult. Veth, Hiscock & Williams suggest it may be difficult to be sure whether a few, or possibly no implements were made in a particular time period when the rate of implement manufacture was low, or archaeological assemblages are small, the probability of finding the rarer implements, such as tulas, is also low, in such circumstances large volume excavations and large assemblages are valuable. Another problem for determining the chronology of tools is the occurrence in some sites in which sediment accumulates rapidly, as these are often the most resilient sites in which vertical displacement of artefacts occurs after deposition. Another possible problem is the accuracy of the identification of an artefact as a tula, and in some cases this requires re-examination by an expert. Veth, Hiscock & Williams suggest these points must be remembered when reading the following account of the chronology of tulas.

The basis of the inference of a 10,000 BP Early Holocene age for tulas is the tool found at Puntutjarpa (Gould, 1977). The Puntutjarpa Rock Shelter is located near the Warburton Ranges in Western Australia that was excavated in the 1960s[2]. The claim of the age made by Gould is based on small flakes that had been retouched dorsally, believed by Gould to be small tulas that he called micro-adzes. The only artefacts recovered from the lower levels, dated to the Early Holocene, at this site were the 'micro-adzes', and the proposal that this tool category dated to the lower Holocene is dependent upon the correct identification of these tools as tulas. The 'micro-adzes' have been demonstrated to be technologically and functionally different from the tula, lacking small platforms, convex ventral surface and slug stage of reduction (Hiscock & Veth, 1991). It has been found that definite tulas and tula slugs, that had proportionally large platforms, are only present in the upper levels of the deposit, that probably dates to the middle or late Holocene (Hiscock, 2008: 213-214). Any further statement of age of tulas at this site has been made difficult by the imprecision of the dating of this site, Veth, Hiscock & Williams suggesting it is more profitable to look at other sequences and regions.

Tulas are known only from the most recent deposits at archaeological sites in Australia, suggesting an age of first appearance of no earlier than the late Holocene, in spite of extensive excavations being carried out at many archaeological sites in the arid zone, many of which have been dated to more than 30,000 BP (Gould, 1977; Hiscock, 2008; McNiven, 1993; Smith, 2006; Veth, 1993, 2005).

In the Cleland Hills, the deposits at Puritjarra Rock Shelter, the first appearance of tulas is at about 3,500 BP (Smith, 2006: 378). According to Veth, Hiscock & Williams, of the 34 tulas recovered all except 2 were distinctive slugs and 88 % had been made from chert and chalcedony, and both materials hold their edge well (Smith, 2006: 393-395). Sites such as the Devon Downs Rock Shelter on the Lower Murray, 3,500 BP; the Kwerlpe Rock shelter, Northern Territory, 3,635 BP (Gould, 1978; Smith, 1988); and the Mt Newman Rock Shelter on the Hamersley Plateau (Marwick, 2009), were other sites that contained tulas with early dates. These tulas were recovered from sites across much of arid and central Australia with consistent ages of about 3,700-3,500 BP.

Evidence of younger dates for the initial appearance of tulas comes from the east coast of Australia, though it is difficult to interpret this evidence. The maximum age that has been found in the north east is at Platypus Rock shelter, less than 2,700 BP, and Brooyar Rock shelter, also less than 2,700 BP; Broadbeach Aboriginal Burial Ground, about 1,300 BP; Gatton Rock shelter, about 1,000 BP (McNiven, 1993). At Capertee 3 Rock shelter, on the central part of the eastern seaboard, a tula has been found that dates to the last 1,700 years (Hiscock & Attenbrow, 2005:110). The maximum age of tulas found along the east coast is uncertain as the number found in the east coast sites is small, indicating that to date there are no known tulas dating to earlier than the Late Holocene.

It has been revealed by this review by Veth, Hiscock & Williams that there is a consistent chronological pattern, in spite of the current state of uncertainty, that the earliest tulas date to 3,700-3,500 BP across much of arid and central Australia, and in eastern Australia, from about 2,700-1,500 BP. Veth, Hiscock & Williams suggest this antiquity is consistent with the changes that occurred in the climate between 3,700-2,000 BP.

Implications for arid Australia of the ENSO intensification
Tulas - ENSO and technological change

Tulas suddenly appeared and proliferated between 4,000-2,000 BP in the archaeological records in central and Western Australia, coinciding with the intensification of the ENSO, which also occurred between 4,000 and 2,000 BP. According to Veth, Hiscock & Williams the chronological coincidence between the appearance of tulas and the ENSO intensification raises questions regarding the causes and processes of technological change. Veth, Hiscock & Williams propose that the appearance and dispersal of tulas that occurred over much of the continent between 4,000 and 2,000 BP has a connection with functional and economical changes that affected desert societies at this time that was triggered by an increase in aridity generally, as well as greater climatic variability. They pose the questions below that may advance this proposition by further research.

It has been concluded by a number of archaeological studies that forager settlement patterns were changed after 4,000 BP with residential mobility of groups increasing (Smith, 1988; Thorley, 1998; Veth, 1993). Veth, Hiscock & Williams suggest the increased mobility at this time may have been the result of reduced carrying capacity, greater patchiness of resources, and lower predictability, all resulting from intensification of the ENSO. Tulas are an example of curated tool (see Sheridan, 1979) and typically curated toolkits are associated with an increase of mobility. Alterations to toolkits would be expected to result in the context of increased residential mobility, and resources that are less reliable. It has been suggested that the tula, as a curated tool that has multiple purposes, was part of a technology developed for a risk minimising strategy linked to increased environmental stochasticity (Hiscock, 1994, 2006).

One of the technological and economic responses that could be predicted by modelling of risk response (Hiscock, 2008:159-161) Veth, 2005) is precisely the adoption by arid zone foragers of stone tools such as tulas. Technological shifts and innovations as part of a new behavioural suite that has incorporated new ways of using landscapes, and presumably conceptualising them, were included in prehistoric responses to foraging risk in Australia. Veth, Hiscock & Williams suggest there was probably a broad base for the responses to heightened risk that was present in the late Holocene, that included the technological evolution, as well as changes in the sizes of groups, their residential mobility, the area of their territory, their trade and exchange relations, and between the social and political dynamics within and between groups of hunter-gatherers.

Tulas represent a process of technological innovation that is different from that of other forms of implement that were abundant during the Holocene, especially backed artefacts and bifacial points. Veth, Hiscock & Williams say that tulas appear to have had no precursors in Australian archaeological assemblages prior to their appearance at about 3,700 BP, so they don't represent an emphasis on, or elaboration of, any forms that were pre-existing, that appear to underpin the backed artefact and point proliferations. Tulas therefore appear to have been a novel invention that represented a response to changed conditions of foraging in which the production and maintenance of wooden implements that were 'energy-extractive', and were of technological and evolutionary significance.

Conclusion

The first appearance in the archaeological record of the tula in the Late Holocene, based on current evidence, that can be dated to between 3,700-2,000 BP, as indicated by its sudden appearance in great numbers in a wide range of sites across central and western Australia. It is unquestionable that these timeframes coincide with the extreme ENSO conditions that were characterised by aridification across vast areas and the increased variability of climate across Australia.

Tulas appeared 'suddenly' in archaeological terms, and as there is no known evidence of precursors, Veth, Hiscock & Williams suggest the making of tulas may have been a strategic innovation in order to deal with changes in altered social and economic circumstances, a likely triggering possibly being intensification of ENSO conditions, that would have had their most extreme impact in central Australia. Veth, Hiscock & Williams postulate that, in the context of Australian environments in the Late Holocene, the toolkits assembled to assist foragers in the new, more difficult conditions, probably contained tools that were easily repaired and deployed for many tasks, some of which may have been unforeseen. Tulas are versatile stone tools that were used to make and repair a wide range of energy extractive wooden implements such as spears, spear-throwers, wooden bowls and digging sticks, and they remained serviceable for extended periods. Among people who are highly mobile nomadic foragers, for whom territoriality and residential mobility is at a premium, such wooden implements were very useful (Hiscock, 2008, 159; Yu, 2006).

Veth, Hiscock & Williams argue that the closeness of ENSO shifts of climate and the appearance in the archaeological record of tulas suggests a link that may hint at the process of innovation. Veth, Hiscock & Williams suggest that the evolutionary process applying to the class of tools called tulas is determined by the reason for the innovation of this tool compared to the evolution of other tools in the Holocene of Australia. If they were developed as a response to the onset of a climate change it would suggest their evolutionary process differed from that of other examples of technological change that occurred in the Holocene of Australia, such as backed artefacts and bifacial points, which display a proliferation of a pre-existing element of the tool-kit. According to Veth, Hiscock & Williams this is at the core of assumptions which are the basis of selectional approaches in Archaeology. According to the authors[1] these 'posit essentially that proliferation (or reward) of 'fit' behaviours and pre-existing technologies will occur, even if these are not known to be advantageous to the people at the time' (Veth, Hiscock & Williams). A selection process and its associated assumptions are not confirmed to by the sudden appearance of tulas in the archaeological record. The invention of an entirely new tool led to the appearance of tulas in the archaeological record, rather than the expected selection and proliferation of an extant tool.

Veth, Hiscock & Williams suggest the implications of these conclusions need to be addressed in future research. According to the authors[1] a number of questions have been raised but not answered by this study. One question is the reason different mechanisms of change occurred for different classes of tool? Do the differences inferred between selectionist (bifacial points, backed artefacts) and non-selectionist (tula) processes indicate differences in the nature of social and physical contexts or in contingent qualities of different groups or technologies? Another question arising from this study was the reason for the spread across the arid zone of tula use, as well as beyond the arid zone. The reason for the chronological difference between the earliest known tulas in arid central Australia and eastern Australia is not known. A question asked by Veth, Hiscock & Williams is whether this should be interpreted as indicating the speed of dispersal of the innovation, and should the similarity of the ages of the earliest known tulas found across central Australia be interpreted as evidence of rapid transmission by cultural means of the innovation. It is also not known if dispersion of tulas was because of its economic or social benefits, or was it associated with a dispersal of the population? Veth, Hiscock & Williams also ask if the function of the tula can be refined to provide insight into organic tool production, and such information could clarify the context of tula dispersal and innovation? They also raise the question of what the foraging risk could have been in the Late Holocene as to why it would trigger this kind of technological change.

It has been argued in the past that there may have been a significant effect on the Aboriginal populations in the arid zone that was caused by the ENSO. A time series analysis was carried out on a large database from radiocarbon dates sourced from the archaeological records of the Australian drylands. In the study it was postulated that changes in the sum probability curves in the arid interior, Pilbara region and the Murchison region were related to ENSO shifts. The relationship between ENSO and the Australian drylands was investigated when a study was subsequently carried out (Williams et al., 2008). It has been argued, using a similar 'dates as data approach' (Williams et al., 2008) that ENSO initiation in the Late Holocene resulted in a series of changes in the distribution of populations of Aboriginal people between 3,700-2,000 BP, including responses that were inferred as regional abandonment and a population that declined.

Appendix G - Desert mammals and Fire

In the 1930s and 1940s over much of inland Australia's arid zone the Aborigines were moved to mission stations and settlements to make way for agriculture on their former hunting grounds. Not long after the removal wildfires began to occur after good wet seasons. In the dry season following the wet seasons of 1973/1974 vast tracts of country were burnt out. Fires in the summer of 1974/1975 burnt out 120 million Ha.

At the time the Aborigines were moved from the land there were a number of desert mammals known to be common. By the time the first detailed scientific study of them was carried out in the 1970s many had disappeared completely. They had flourished during many thousands of years of hunting by the Aborigines and the regular burning, also for thousands of years, but very soon after the regular burning was replaced by less frequent wildfires they had gone. Some of those that have gone extinct are Pig-footed Bandicoot (***Chaeropus ecaudatus***), Desert Bandicoot (***Perameles eremiana***), Lesser Bilby (***Macrotis leucura***), Gould's Mouse (***Pseudomys gouldii***), Alice Springs Mouse (***Pseudomys fieldi***), Short-tailed Hopping-mouse (***Notomys amplus***), Long-tailed Hopping-mouse (***Notomys longicaudatus***), Greater Stick-nest Rat (***Leporillus conditor***), Central Rock-rat (***Zyzomys pedunculatus***), and Desert Rat-kangaroo (***Caloprymnus campestris***).

Some that are endangered are Western-barred Bandicoot (***Parameles bougainville***), Golden Bandicoot (***Isoodon auratus***), Sandhill Dunnart (***Sminthopsis psammophila***), Long-tailed Dunnart (***Sminthopsis longicaudata***), Kowari (***Dasyuroides byrnei***), Bilby (***Macrotis lagotis***), Numbat (***Myrmecobius fasciatus***), Western Quoll (***Dasyurus geoffroii***), Red-tailed Phascogale (***Phascogale calura***), Pebble-mound Mouse (***Pseudomys chapmani***), Desert Mouse (***Pseudomys desertor***), Dusky-hopping Mouse (***Notomys amplus***), Lesser Stick-nest Rat (***Leporillus apicalis***).

Appendix - H[26] Australian-Indian Phylogenetic Link Reconstruction

Studies based on morphology, archaeology and genetics have suggested that there was an early dispersal of behaviourally and biologically modern humans from their place of origin in Africa that occurred by at least 45 Ka by way of southern Asia. Non-overlapping distributions of haplogroups within pan Eurasian M and N macro haplogroups are shown by mtDNA lineages that have been sampled so far from South Asia, eastern Asia and Australasia. Also, support from archaeology remains ambiguous.

In the study carried out by Kumar et *al.* involving the complete sequencing of 966 mitochondrial genomes from 26 relic tribes in India 7 genomes have been identified which share 2 synonymous polymorphisms with the M42 haplogroups which is specific to Australian Aborigines.

Direct genetic evidence of an early colonisation of Australia through south Asia which followed the "southern route" has therefore been provided by the results of this study which show a shared mtDNA lineage between Indians and Australian Aborigines.

Most of the DNA and archaeological evidence agree with the proposition that a small group, maybe as little as 150-200 people, left Africa to colonise what is now the occupied world. There has been, however, disagreement over which route(s) they took and the time at which this spread of anatomically modern humans from Africa occurred. It is suggested by recent genetic studies, especially those that were based on mtDNA that a single "southern Route" of dispersal of modern humans extended from the Horn of Africa [north east Africa] into Arabia and southern Asia across the mouth of the Red Sea at some time before 50 Ka (Forster & Matsumura, 2005; Kivisild et al., 2006; Mellars, 2006; Metspalu et al., 2004; Oppenheimer, 2003; Quintana-Murci et al., 2004; Torroni et al., 2006). Modern human populations colonised Australia by at least 45 ka, which according to Kumar et *al.* is best represented by the anatomically modern skull at Lake Mungo 3 in New South Wales (Foster & Matsumura, 2005, Bowler et al., 2003; Field & Lahr, 2006; Macaulay et al., 2005; Mulvaney & Kamminga, 1999; O'Connell & Allen, 2004; Stringer, 2000; Stringer, 2002; Sun & Kong, 2006; Thangaraj et al., 2006), after having rapidly expanding along the coastlines of southern Asia, southeast Asia and Indonesia. Observations based on morphology have also suggested an early phylogenetic link between Indians and Australian Aborigines (Huxley, 2006). The documentation of individual steps in the process of colonisation based on genetics and archaeological evidence has been the major challenge to this scenario. A non-overlapping distribution of haplogroups within macro haplogroups M and N and its subclade R (Macaulay et *al.*, 2005) has been shown by mtDNA lineages that have been sampled to date from south Asia, eastern Asia and Australasia. At the moment the archaeological maps for both Arabia and India are mostly blank for the critical period from about 50 to about 60 ka (James & Petraglia, 2005; Petraglia & Alsharekh, 2003). Wherever there are hints of early human occupation that are available from the Patne site in western India, (Sali, 1989) Jwalapuram, southern India and Batadombalena in Sri Lanka (Deraniagala, Kennedy, 1989) they suggest closer affinities to Middle Stone Age traditions in Africa, (Mellars, 2006; Petraglia et *al*, 2007), while in the east of the Indian subcontinent, especially the areas of Australia and New Guinea that have been well explored, similarly "advanced" technologies in the area to the east of the Indian subcontinent have not been found (Mellars, 2006; Bowler et *al*., 2003; Mulvaney & Kamminga, 1999).

Results, Discussion

The Australians and New Guineans are indicated by the complete mtDNA sequencing to belong to the out-of-Africa founder types M and N, and therefore are descendants of the same African emigrants at about 50-about 70 ka as all other Eurasians (Hudjashov et al., 2007). In the context of the Eurasian phylogeny (Ingman et al., 20002; Ingman & Gyllensten, 2003; Thangaraj, 2005; Kong et *al*., 2003; Palanichamy et *al*., 2004; Kong et al., 2006; Kivisild et al., 2002; Tanaka et al., 2004; Kivisild et al., 2003; Hurles et al., 2005; Forster, 2004), however, shared branches that are more recent than the founding types M, N and R have not been reported so far, with the exception of a shared variant at nucleotide position 8793 between haplogroup M42, which is Australian specific, and haplogroup M10, which is specific for East/Southeast Asians (Hudjashov et al., 2007).

The complete mtDNA sequencing carried out by Kumar et *al*. of 966 individuals from 26 populations of central Dravidian and Austro-Asiatic tribes who they found shared 2 basal synonymous mtDNA polymorphisms G8251A and A9156T with the M42 haplogroup, which is specific to Australian Aborigines. Kumar et *al*. say the phylogenetic reconstruction of 7 Indian, in this study, and 6 Australian Aboriginal mtDNA sequences from a previously published source (Kivisild et al., 2006; Ingman et al, 2000; van Holst Pellekaan et al., 2006) was found to differ from previous reports (Hudjashov et al., 2007; van Holst Pellekaan et al., 2006) in the placement of G8251A polymorphism. Together with A9256T this polymorphism is present in all of the 7 Indian samples used in this study, as well as 1 previously reported Indian sample (i.e. PU202) that was based on RFLP (Passarino et al., 1996; Quintana-Murci et al., 1999; Barnabas, Shouche & Suresh, 2005) and in 4 out of 6 Australian sequences that were used in this reconstruction. The lack of G8251A in a sublineage of Australian Aborigines consisting of 2 genomes is an indication of a back mutation event, though G8251A and A9156T are both considered to be ancestral to M42. The present phylogenetic reconstruction of the haplogroup M42 seems, according to Kumar et *al.*, to be parsimonious and more stable than the previously suggested M10 and M42 link through 8793 polymorphism (Hudjashov et al., 2007), being based on the combination of 2 synonymous polymorphisms and the replication of a number of samples from India, 7 in this study and 1 previously reported (Passarino et al., 1996).

It is estimated that the coalescence time of the average sequence divergence of 55.2 ± 10.8 ka of the Indian and Australian M42 coding-region sequences from the root is consistent with the first evidence of the occupation by humans is provided by 11 silcrete flakes with platforms that are plain and relatively thick that were recovered from beneath the lowest gravels in the barrier sands of the Mungo B trench, (Shawcross, 1998) which is bracketed by ages of 50.1 ± 2.4 ka and 45.7 ± 2.3 ka (Bowler et al., 2003). There is also apparent agreement with the similar or slightly earlier ages for the initial arrival of humans in northern and Western Australia (Roberts, Jones & Smith, 1990; Roberts et al., 1994; Turney et al., 2001). It appears that at Mungo B trench the underlying deposits, which have been dated to 52.4 ± 3.1 ka, are culturally sterile (Bowler et al., 2003) which suggests that the colonisation of continental Australia took place from south Asia at some time after 50 ka.

Direct genetic evidence of the shared lineage provides evidence of the ancient link between India and Australia that has been long suggested (Huxley, **1870**; Redd & Stoneking, 1999; Redd, 2002). Though the deep divergence (55.2 ± 10.8 ky) of the branches from India and Australia within M42, together with the evidence of the earliest population expansion, which was also the most pronounced, outside Africa in Southern Asia, which has been estimated to have occurred at about 52 ka by use of Bayesian Skyline analysis (Atkinson, Gray & Drummond, 2008), followed by high mtDNA diversity in Indian populations (Kivisild et al., 2006; Metspalu et al., 2004; Macaulay et al., 2005; Sun et al., 2006; Thangaraj et al., 2005; Kivisild et al., 2004).

It is strongly suggested, however, that Australia, and possibly as well as East/Southeast Eurasia and Papua New Guinea (Hudjashov et al., 2007), was possibly populated from southern Asia, plausibly slightly prior to or in the beginning of the expansion of population that resulted in a large number of mtDNA lineages within macro haplogroups 'M' in India.

Conclusion

The results of this study have shown there is a shared mtDNA linkage between Indians and Australian Aborigines, and this provides direct genetic evidence that modern humans populated Australia after passing through south Asia following the "Southern Route" on their way from Africa. An early colonisation of Australia, at about 60 to 50 ka, which is quite in agreement with the archaeological evidence, is suggested by the divergence of the Indian and Australian M42 coding region sequences.

Appendix I[4] - Mungo and Willandra Lakes –Archaeology, Past and Future

In this paper Allen & Holdaway have reviewed archaeological research in the Willandra Lakes area carried out over the past 40 years and found a number of methodical and conceptual problems. Among these is the use of ethnographic models of Aboriginal behaviour to organise the data obtained by archaeology. In such models spatial relationships were privileged more than temporal relationships and minimised the extent of archaeological changes that occurred over time. Allen & Holdaway say Bowler's correlations of archaeological and hydrographic changes that have occurred since the Late Pleistocene have the best match of research to date of the limited archaeological data that is available. When the archaeology of Pleistocene age from Willandra Lakes is compared with that of the same age from Tasmania, time averages records that are amenable to analysis of patterns and mobility and material use are revealed, though not of sites that are functionally defined nor of assemblages of artefacts that are typologically defined. Large samples of stone artefacts that have been recovered from wide areas, together with a strategy of dating of land units based on radiocarbon and optical dates can be used to study the periodicity and intensity of human occupation of the Willandra Lakes. The reconsideration of the relationships between behaviour, function, space and time, as well as a reformulation of much of existing knowledge of the archaeology of Australia during the Pleistocene is required by such a strategy.

Conclusion

Allen & Holdaway say that when the manner in which ethnographic models and settlement pattern archaeology interact are considered in a detailed manner serious deficiencies in these approaches are revealed when they are applied to the Pleistocene archaeology of the Willandra Lakes. Allen & Holdaway also say that Bowler's exploration of the relationship between sedimentary strata, human occupation and changes in lake conditions that span the period from 50 ka to 15 Ka his alternative is the most successful to date. Bowler's methodology, without being reduced to determinism, at least provided a framework for the partial judgement of impacts of climate and environmental changes in the lake system on the subsistence patterns of Aboriginals. Going from observations of the presence or absence of archaeological materials in specific strata to a fuller assessment of human utilisation patterns requires a more specifically archaeological agenda. This approach will require a reconsideration of fundamental relationships that involve function, behaviour, space and time, based on the experience of Allen & Holdaway studying the Holocene archaeological record. Possibly the most critical for our constituency, which increasingly includes Aboriginal readers; it requires the development of innovative narrative structures relating more closely to the nature of the archaeological record.

Appendix J[3] - Spear Technologies
Innovation and change in Northern Australian Aboriginal Spear Technologies – Reed Spears[3]

Reed spears differed from the majority of spears used by Aboriginal people in Australia, being light weight that made optimal use of spearthrower technology. Small projectile points that were pressure flaked stone projectile points were mounted on reed spears in the Kimberleys. Small projectile points have been found in the archaeological record of the Kimberleys and western Arnhem Land. According to Allen & Akerman there is no record of how reed spears were mounted outside the Kimberleys. In this paper Allen & Akerman review the evidence for reed spears and small projectile points throughout the Northern Territory and North Western Australia, arriving at the conclusion that they represent associated technologies for which the primary role was feuding and conflict.

Allen & Akerman suggest the shift from hand thrown to spearthrower-thrown projectiles must be seen as a significant change in the technology of Aboriginals in Australia, which is believed to have taken place in the mid-Holocene. The rock art of northern Australia provides the most compelling evidence for this, with spearthrowers appearing late in the rock art style sequence (Brandl, 1973; Lewis, 1988; Walsh & Morwood, 1999). There are 2 lines of supportive evidence that the spearthrower was developed in the mid-Holocene, one being the presence of small stone projectile points, that are assumed to indicate spearthrower use, first appearing in the archaeological record about 5,000 BP (Allen, 1996), and ethnographic collections that demonstrate that multiple forms of spears and spearthrowers were used for hunting, fighting and symbolic markers of males throughout Australia (Allen, 1996: 148-9; Cundy, 1989; Davidson, 1934, 1936).

In the rock art of northern Australia the earliest known spears that have been recorded are 1-piece spears, either plain or with barbs that have been carved into the solid wood, most probably hardwood (Chaloupka, 1993: 146; Davidson 1934: 53; Walsh & Morwood, 1999). Allen & Akerman suggest that the move from this base to the wide diversity of spear and spearthrower forms that were present in the 19th and early 20th century required a considerable degree of innovation since that time of the earliest rock art that depicted spears:

the development of hardwood heads on hardwood shafts; the adoption of new types of shaft – softwood, bamboo and reeds; new methods of attaching spear heads to spear shafts, splicing and joining; multiple forms of mastics and glues; the use of bindings of string, sinew and cane, and heads of diverse types of wood, stone, bone, and post-contact, iron heads (Allen, 2011).

Spears that had a high mass which travelled at low velocity and were hand-thrown were used in Australia. In many parts of Australia hand-thrown spears continued to be used, though a number of them had specialised functions, e.g. 1-piece fishing spears that were used in the Cooper Basin (Davidson, 1934: 48). Also, the spearthrower, or any form of composite spears, was absent from Tasmania and on Bathurst and Melville Islands, which Allen & Akerman suggest indicates that Aboriginal societies did not require the spearthrowers or composite spears, surviving quite well without them, which suggests that projectile technologies had a wide margin of effectiveness.

The hallmark of an older, high mass, low velocity, spear technology is apparent in many of the spears used by Aboriginals, which has been adjusted to accommodate spearthrower technology (Allen, 2011; Cundy, 1998). According to Allen & Akerman it is suggested by this that the introduction of the spearthrower did not involve the wholesale replacement of the older hand-thrown forms of spear. The known evidence supports the case that the hand-thrown spears were modified to fit them for use with a spearthrower. Something that didn't change following the introduction of the spearthrower was the requirement for the highly developed stalking skills and an excellent knowledge of the behaviour of the animals they hunted, and this applied whether the spears were hand-thrown or by the use of a spearthrower. The advantage of the spearthrower when used for hunting was its speed and accuracy over the distance of its optimal use of about 10 m. When the spearthrower was used in set duels the use of a spearthrower increased the range of the projectile used.

The generalised spears for hunting and fighting are heavier and more robust than might be considered to be optimal for use with spearthrower technology, with the result that they did not make full use of the potential of the spearthrower (Cundy, 1998: 108). Allen & Akerman suggest it might be thought that there would be considerable selective pressure on the technology of the spear, as they were central to the survival of Aboriginal communities and individuals. What is clear from an examination of the spears used in eastern Arnhem Land, however, is that optimality was not determined by technical or aerodynamic efficiency on their own. Other factors that were considered included, ease of manufacture, materials availability and variable skill levels, where the mass of the heavier spears probably remained a factor in bringing down game (Allen, 2011). Most spear assemblages from northern Australia display a combination of generalised spear forms which could be used for multiple purposes, such as hunting and fighting, or forms that were more specialised, such as fishing or as harpoons. Australian spears, for the most part, do not seriate, as a result of the additive rather than their replacement quality. Allen suggests the exception seems to be the use of small stone spearheads, the pressure-flaked points replacing percussion-flaked points over time.

Reed spears and their spearthrower represent forms that were developed to make use of the spearthrower technology. It had been noted (D.S. Davidson) that the use of light-weight reed spears "… presuppose[d] the presence of the spearthrower" and that these spears required the acceptance and applications of new principles in the construction of spears, which is not the case for 1-piece and composite spears made of heavier materials (1934: 156; see also Cundy, 1989: 119). When light ***Phragmites*** sp. reeds were used as shafts of spears, they were part of a technology that was of low-mass, and high-velocity. In north western Western Australia reed spears were the predominant form of spear, where they were mounted with small pressure-flaked stone Kimberley points that were set in gum (Akerman, 1978).

Allen & Akerman says reed shafts should not be confused with spears that used indigenous bamboo (***Bambusa arnhemica***). It has been noted (Franklin, 2008) that ***Bambusa arnhemica*** is restricted to western Arnhem Land. The only bamboo spears in the Kimberleys have been obtained by trade. The heaviest spears in the Thompson collection from eastern Arnhem Land are bamboo spears with stone or metal heads, and the bamboo shafts are strong enough to carry either stone or metal heads (Allen, 2011: 77). When observers use terms such as bamboo, reed or cane interchangeably causes confusion, even in cases where the meaning is made clear in the context that ***Phragmites*** reed spears are being referred to.

In western Arnhem Land the rock art depicts spearthrowers as being generally associated with all types of composite spears; wood, bamboo or reed shafts and wood, bone or stone heads. As with reed spears, small projectile points are most suited to technology of low mass, their presence presupposing use with a spearthrower, even if stone points were used for other purposes (Davisson, 1934: 136; Luebbers, 1978). In archaeological deposits points occur across the northern region from the Kimberley to Western Arnhem Land, where reed spears were manufactured and used (Smith & Cundy, 1985: 34).

There are no known ethnographic examples of small percussion-flaked projectile points that have been hafted outside the Kimberleys, which leads to the conclusion that they ceased to be used as projectile points in Arnhem land at some time in the recent past (Akerman & Bindon, 1995: 91; Hiscock, 1999: 98). Also, it appears they dropped out of the record from the Kimberleys at about the same time (Maloney et *al*., 2014). In the region of the Victoria River the position is not as clear, where percussion-flaked points continue to be recovered from archaeological sites dating to throughout the past 1,000 years (Clarkson, 2006: 139-49).

It is claimed here that small stone projectile points associated with reed spears that is observed in the Kimberleys might also be extended to Arnhem Land, where there is no direct evidence of their association. A review of the evidence for reed spears has enabled Allen & Akerman to consider the factors that led to their development and to explore any potential connections between reed spears and small leaf-shaped stone projectile points, which were percussion flaked, in the archaeological sites of western Arnhem Land (Allen & Barton, `989; Hiscock, 2011; Jones & Johnson, 1985 Kamminga & Allen, 1973; Schrire, 1982). The fact that a specialist spearthrower, the goose-necked spearthrower, was developed in western Arnhem Land especially for use with reed spears has furthered this interest (Cundy, 1989: 116-20).

In spite of this the evidence for reed spears has not been reviewed in any detail. Allen & Akerman say it is the aim of this paper to review the current evidence for reed spears, and then use this evidence to suggest ways in which material culture and technology studies might contribute to understanding the archaeological past, in particular in regard to small stone projectile points. Reed spears from 2 areas of northern Australia, the northern part of the Northern Territory and the Kimberley region of Western Australia, have been concentrated on in this study.

Discussion

There are a number of elements of art, language and material culture that are shared between the Kimberleys and the northern part of the Northern Territory. Included among these changes in material culture, it is documented in sequences of art periods (Lewis, 1988; Walsh & Morwood, 1999) and also that non-Parma-Nyungan languages are spoken across this area (Evans, 1988). Ecological similarities exist in that ***Phragmites*** reeds (***Phragmites karka***) occur in moth regions (Akerman et *al.*, 2002: 20-21).

Small stone projectiles are found in archaeological deposits throughout the northern region, from the Kimberleys to western Arnhem Land. Percussion flaked points are the earliest points; they exhibit similar chronologies and similar patterns of archaeological expression. Across the wider region percussion-flaked points appear almost simultaneously, showing an efflorescence between about 1,500 and 3,000 years BP, then virtually disappeared from the record in the Kimberleys and western Arnhem Land at least 1,000 years ago, and were replaced in the Kimberleys only in the past 1,000 years by Kimberley points that were pressure flaked (Maloney et *al.*, 2014).

The situation has been described for the Kimberleys (Love, 2009: 93), the men spent much of the day, when they were not out hunting or at ceremonies, making stone spear heads and spears, which conforms to the archaeological evidence of point manufacture at western Arnhem Land sites (Allen, 1996: 149). Bone artefacts have been recorded in the Kimberleys for the final preparation of stone points, such as pointed and spatulate bone tools, as well as being common in middens in western Arnhem Land where they were in association with stone points (Akerman & Bindon, 1995: 95; Allen & Barton, 1989; Schrire, 1982).

It is suggested by ethnographic, traditional and rock art evidence that stone points that were percussion-flaked were found in association with a spear assemblage that included multiple composite spear forms, including reed spears, in Arnhem Land and the Kimberleys.

Manufacture/use/discard rates for percussion-flaked points in Arnhem Land and the Kimberleys appear to have peaked about 1,500-3,000 years ago. Reed spears appear to have been manufactured after this time, though 1,000 years ago the percussion-faked stone points had been dispensed with, Allen & Akerman suggesting it was possibly because of loss of belief in their mystical efficacy.

Trends in the Kimberleys and western Arnhem Land diverge after about 1,000 years ago. The manufacture of reed spears continued alongside a wider range of spear types and the development of specialised spearthrowers, goose-necked and sabre spearthrowers (Akerman, 1996). Heavy spears using stone, and more recently metal blades, were developed (Allen, 1997, 2011). Reed spears with pressure-flaked stone projectile points replaced all other forms of spear, with the exception of 1-piece fishing spears, in the north and central Kimberleys, becoming the predominant spear that was used for both hunting and fighting, where pressure-flaked stone points retained the mystical and symbolic powers that have been observed (Taçon, 1991).

In western Arnhem Land the multiple spear and spearthrower forms, cylindrical, notched lathe, goose-necked and sabre spearthrowers used represent an impressive, complex assemblage of projectiles, which indicates trade, historical influences and innovations. An ecologically diverse, rich environment is encompassed by the Kimberleys and coastal western Arnhem Land, where the populations of Aboriginal people were high, with multiple small local groups all of whom vigorously defended their territories, sacred property and their families (e.g. Warner, 1937: 155-90). Allen & Akerman suggest these circumstances are likely to foster innovations in spear and spearthrowers that were specialised for fighting. It has been documented that in this area rock art demonstrates that there is a long history of fighting, scenes of fighting being depicted throughout the sequence of its art styles. According to Allen & Akerman the balance of the technical, ethnographic and archaeological evidence that has been presented here suggest the association of reed spears and small percussion-flaked projectile points are part of a specialised technology to deal with conflict.

Allen & Akerman say the changes in Aboriginal projectile technologies that have been discussed in this paper were cumulative and directional, in terms of increased complexity of spear and spearthrower form. In the Kimberleys and Arnhem Land the complexity and innovation of projectile technology emerged as a result of the particular ecological and social conditions experienced by the Aboriginal hunter-gatherers. As material culture, reed spears and small projectile points are intertwined, it sheds light on the meaning of small projectile points in the archaeological record. Such meaning is clearly complex, involving technological, social and ecological relationships. Allen & Akerman say the study presented in this paper demonstrates how knowledge of Aboriginal material culture adds to the understanding of the archaeological and rock-art record in new and valuable ways.

Appendix K[42] Stone Tool Manufacturing Methods Flexibility on the Georgina River, Camooweal, Queensland[38]

Ethnographic observation has well-documented the highly flexible approach to stone technology that was often characterised by a high level of flexibility. According to Moore it appears that in the Australian context the function of a stone was related only loosely to its form. It has, nevertheless, been recognised in many ethnographic studies that artefact manufacture was "aimed at" the production of specific forms (Horne & Aiston, 1924: 92). In this study Moore has examined the rigidity in the manufacture of artefacts by an archaeological analysis of a large stone assemblage from Camooweal, North West Queensland, Australia. The reduction sequence followed to make the assemblage was modelled and the rigidity of the various trajectories that comprised the reduction sequence was used to assess the degree to which blanks for "aimed at" forms crossed between trajectories. The technological analysis indicated that blank production for "aimed at" forms was actually relatively rigid, though it is indicated by the ethnographic literature that various categories of artefact tended to be used in an ad hoc fashion. Moore suggests this is at odds with the sweeping generalisations concerning the flexibility of Aboriginal lithic technology.

According to Moore the "flexibility" of a lithic technology can be seen as the degree to which a stone might be used for multiple purposes. Moore says flexibility is a continuum that has a hypothetic "inflexible" structure at one end of the continuum, which is a reflection of the manufacture of a specific type of stone for a specific use, and at the other end a "hyper-flexible" structure, which is a reflection of the use of any stone for multiple tasks. Historical changes in the perspective of Australian scholars of the Aboriginal toolkit tacks a shift along this continuum. In the early years of Australian archaeology the models used by archaeologists were borrowed from paradigms of the Old World and applied assuming a degree of inflexibility of stone technology, i.e. artefact types that were archaeologically defined were believed to be a reflection of specific functions or cultural groupings (Veth et *al.*, 1998). In more recent decades the paradigm has shifted towards a consensus that stone tools were used by Aborigines in a manner that was highly flexible and tool form and function were rarely linked in any systematic way (Hiscock, 1998).

Enhanced appreciation of the ethnographic literature is the main reason for this intellectual shift. The observations of Daisy Bates of the use of stone tools among Aborigines in the 1920s is an example, inspiring her to rail against the assumptions of Australian antiquarians. When she was confronted by the claim that specific function is a reflection of specific types of artefact, she noted "no stone – except the initiation flint – can be said to be made for a definite purpose…[they] use their little knives and flakes for *any* purpose" Bates, 1922 in Wright, 1977: 2; emphasis in original).

A similar observation was made by George Aiston:

"In describing these tools it must always be remembered that the casual nature of the black does not allow him to keep any tool for the one purpose. He is just as likely to use his best stone knife to scrape a weapon as he is to use any flake he may pick up. At the same time he may get an affection for a certain tool and only keep it for the purpose for which it was most suitable… This casualness is what makes it so hard to say specifically that a tool is used for any one purpose… (Horne & Aiston, 1924: 91-92).

Though Aiston concludes "… but in describing them I have carefully asked [the Aborigines] until I could arrive at what was aimed at in each particular tool, and so have classed them" (Horne & Aiston, 1924: 91-92). A similar track was taken by other researchers, using observation and questioning what a stone tool was "aimed at", while discovering, often unexpectedly, that the tasks to which the tools were applied epitomised "casualness and opportunism" (Gould et al., 1971: 154). Therefore, Aboriginal people sometimes used large bladed "fighting knives" as adzes in woodworking (Cane, 1992: 25), "points" to engrave wooden tools (Davidson, 1935: 162; Kamminga, 1985), "woodworking adzes" as a tool to butcher animals (Thompson, 1964: 418) and throwing weapons (Davidson, 1935: 160), and axes as knapping hammers (Smythe, 1878: 379). Aboriginals have also been observed scavenging byproducts of "aimed at" tool manufacture for use in various tasks. An example is Horne & Aiston (1924: 87, 101) commenting that flakes produced in the manufacture of "ideal stones" were scavenged for use as "casual tools". Flakes that were struck during manufacture of axe blanks have been described (Basedow, 1625: 363-4) that were used as-is or retouched into scrapers, and flakes that were apparently struck in retouching a scraper were mounted as barbs on the heads of wooden spears (367). Percussion flakes struck in the manufacture of Kimberley points have been observed (Elkin, 1948: 11) being used for "cutting flesh," and it was implied by Tindale (1985: 9) that pressure flakes were used in ceremonies associated with initiation. It has been noted (Roth, 1904: 16) that the detritus from the manufacture of large blades might be retouched into scrapers, and it was indicated (Binford, 1989: 181-2) that sometimes large blades might be reduced as cores to produce small unmodified cutting tools. In some parts of Australia "hyperflexibility" is suggested by the manufacture of complex wooden implements by the use of stone pieces that are minimally modified or even unmodified (Mountford, 1941; Thomson, 1964: 412-4; Hayden, 1979; see also Gould et al., 1971: 163, Gould, 1978: 819). Sometimes even hafted stone tools that had been carefully crafted consisted of stones that were naturally occurring with little or no modification were used (e.g. Tindale, 1965: 133, 135, 160; Mountford, 1965: 316).

Moore suggests there is a tension in Australian lithic studies as a result of an apparent contradiction in these observations. It is clearly indicated in ethnographic studies that the functions of stone tools were unstructured and highly flexible, though it appears from archaeological analysis (e.g. Akerman, 1976; Akerman et al., 2002: 18-20; Hiscock, 1993; Moore, 2003a, b) and ethnographic evidence (Roth, 1904; Spencer & Gillen, 1904; Elkin, 1948, Baines, 1966), that the sequences of certain stone reduction were quite structured, or, in a phrase from Aiston, were "aimed at" specific artefact forms. Therefore, as a result of the overwhelming evidence supporting the unstructured tool use by Australian Aboriginals, Moore poses the question just how structured were the approaches to the manufacture of tools among Aboriginals? Exploring the source of blanks for the manufacture of "aimed at" retouched forms through sequence modelling is a way of examining this question. A reduction sequence model is a way to describe the manipulations used by a stone knapper to a block of stone. The presentation of the model can be in the form of a flow chart in which technological choices are shown as pathways or "trajectories". Flake blanks to be used in the manufacture of "aimed at" forms derive from the culmination of the technological steps within a single reduction trajectory in a rigid, inflexible structure. In this case technological structure consists of a set of distinct trajectories that involve a minimum movement of flake blanks laterally between them, these lateral movements being referred to in this paper as "crossovers". When a technological structure is flexible flake blanks for "aimed at" forms are derived from any number of trajectories that are highly interconnected.

In this study Moore examined the structural rigidity of the lithic technology that is reflected in large surface assemblage recovered on the upper Georgina River, North West Queensland. Moore summarised previous studies into this assemblage and described unpublished elements of the technology. To provide a reduction sequence model of the lithic technology on the Georgina River various technological reconstructions have been drawn together. It is suggested by the results that a relatively rigid structure was used in the manufacture of stone artefacts. The reduction sequence models for the upper Georgina River, the Hunter Valley, New South Wales, and Tasmania (Moore, 2000a, b) were compared and the implications for Australian lithic studies are discussed in this paper.

Conclusion

In this study the flexibility of lithic technology was examined from the standpoint of the production of blanks for "aimed at" forms. According to Moore there is a high degree of technological rigidity at Camooweal which Moore says is a bit surprising as the general characterisation of Aboriginal technology as casual, opportunistic, and ad hoc (e.g. Gould et *al.*, 1971). According to Moore in the upper Georgina River region this characterisation applies to the function of artefacts rather than to their manufacture. That the waste flakes produced in the different trajectories were sometimes used for multiple functions that involved the processing of both animal and plant materials is indicated by residue analysis that is ongoing (T. Loy pers. comm. to Moore, 2001; Loy & Nugent, 2002), which accords with the ethnographic observations discussed earlier. It has been suggested by residue analysis that incorporating a more realistic portrayal of use would involve the overlying of an intricate web of arrows linking the flakes produced at various stages of "aimed at" artefact manufacture, as well as the forms that are "aimed at", with many functions. Moore says this would reflect the high degree of functional flexibility that is apparently inherent in the upper Georgina River lithic technology.

Moore asks the questions, "Why were 'aimed at' forms produced in the first place?" The functions for these "aimed at" stone artefacts are indicated by ethnographic accounts to have had many functions, and these functions were also accomplished by ad hoc flakes, as well as non-stone elements of the material culture. E.g.., hardwoods were worked successfully with unmodified or minimally modified stones, tula adzes or hafted axes (Mountford, 1941); Thomson, 1964: 412-4; Hayden, 1979); wood, bone or teeth were used to tip spears instead of stone (Davidson, 1934; Kamminga, 1985:8); Digging sticks and large blades were used to dig and process yams instead of bifaces (O'Connell, 1974); see discussion in Moore, 2003c); and small flakes and blades were used for ceremonial fighting, instead of large leilira blades, which were ostensibly made for the purpose (Aiston, 1928: 129; Horne & Aiston, 1924: 96-7; see discussion i9n Moore, 2003a). White concluded that "... the majority of stone tool forms were not necessary, in a utilitarian sense, at all" (1977: 26), resonates, according to Moore, in this context.

It has been suggested by several authors that the link between technological and social domains of human existence is a defining characteristic in the emergence of modern human behaviour about 40,000 years ago in Eurasia (Kuhn & Stiner, 1998; Mithen, 1996a, b). According to this view, at the start of the Upper Palaeolithic, the explosion the forms of stone artefacts exploded, which reflects an expansion and embedding of stone technology from the economic domain into the social and symbolic realms of culture. There is a large amount of ethnographic evidence from Australia that indicates stone artefacts did in fact perform social and symbolic roles; therefore it is conceivable that the discordance that has been discussed here between the ad hoc function and rigid technological structure is related to the phenomenon. Since it possible that Australia was colonised by 50,000 BP, the study of Australasian stone artefact assemblages offers an important source of data, which is largely untapped, on the emergence and spread of modern human behaviour (Foley & Lahr, 1977). Moore suggests that an understanding of technological structure behind stone artefact assemblages is an important prerequisite for tapping this potential.

Appendix L - Point Technology in the Kimberley – New Data[39]

More robust data for point technology have been obtained from Bunuba Country, southern Kimberley, than have been available previously. At 3 sites in the southern Kimberley direct percussion points have been recovered associated with radiocarbon dates of 5,000 calBP, though the earliest pressure-flaked points have consistently been associated with dates within the past 1,000 years. It is therefore suggested that the earliest known direct percussion points predates the earliest known pressure points by 4,000 years in this region.

In museum holdings and displays direct percussion and pressure-flaked points from the Kimberley region are abundant, though they are mostly from surface collections in shelters and open sites, and they are poorly documented, though they are from well dated contexts. It is indicated by previous research that the earliest production of direct percussion points predates the earliest known production of pressure-flaked points (Dortch, 1977; Harrison, 2004; O'Connor, 1999); though the determination of the relationship between these classes of artefacts and their temporal separation has been made difficult by contexts that are poorly dated and the confusion over nomenclature. It is necessary to understand the temporal framework for production if an examination of these implications of these changes in terms of the technological restructuring are to be attempted. In this paper Maloney et al. review previous studies that relate to the chronology of the production of stone points in the broader region of the Kimberley, and then use the data from their new excavations in the southern Kimberley to describe the points and dating contexts

Point technology in the Kimberley has previously been described as being a range of *ad hoc* classifications. The term "Kimberley Point" has, e.g., been used to describe any artefact that has been retouched on an elongated flake which has converging margins, irrespective of retouch attributes (.g. Veitch, 1996: 70-2, 74, 76, 77, 79; see Veitch, 1999: 356). The term "Kimberley Point" to produce pressure-flaked points that display "denticulate" or "serrated" margins, however, has been used by Akerman & Bindon (1995). Alternatively, these authors have distinguished a Kimberley Dentate point (Akerman & Bindon, 1995: 93-4), where the notches that separate the teeth are wider than the teeth. In this paper Maloney et al. follow Harrison (2004: 2) by recognising a class of points that have been retouched by direct percussion, which are distinct from those that are produced by pressure-flaking, to avoid the confusion that can arise from the application of different typologies.

Discussion and conclusion

In 3 sites that have been excavated in the southern Kimberley there are 3 examples of direct percussion points that have been dated to earlier than 5,000 calBP and 4 pressure-flaked points that have been dated to the past 1,000 years. In the review of the literature by Maloney et al. it has been demonstrated that direct percussion points that have been recovered from excavated sites throughout the Kimberley consistently predate pressure-flaked points by more than 4,000 years. Points as old as those from the southern Kimberley have been reported from stratified sites in the Northern Territory (see Jones & Johnson, 1985: 206), though direct percussion points occur at a significantly earlier time in the southern and western Kimberley than in the north and east of the Kimberley.

At this stage of research knowing whether regional variation in the timing of the first appearance of point technology is difficult or if this appearance is an artefact of sampling, or is a result of differences in the spread and the uptake of new technologies. It has been argued (Hiscock, 1993: 177) that the size of a sample must be investigated to determine the relationship between vertical movement, dates and occurrences that are isolated occurrences of rare types of technology, such as points. It was stressed further by Hiscock that in any investigation into the earliest observations of new technologies analyses of sample size need to be carried out, arguing that the recovery of a rare type in a deposit reflects only the first known instance of discard within the boundaries of the area being discarded (Hiscock, 1993: 175). The appearance of bipolar backed artefacts in Australia in the Early Holocene has been claimed (Hiscock & Attenbrow, 1998: 170), based on 2 artefacts that have been dated by association (see also Hiscock & Attenbrow, 2004). Hiscock & Attenbrow (2004) argue there is no *a priori* reason for the uptake of new technology being uniform over time and space, and the possibility that new technology may spread and proliferation resulting in a widespread signature in the archaeological record thousands of years after its inception. In this sense, Maloney et *al.* suggest it is not unlikely the temporal patterning of pressure flaking across the Kimberley, as presented in this paper, is the proliferation of this new technology and earlier evidence of this technology could possibly still be recovered with a larger sample size.

Maloney et *al.* believe that though it is unlikely, it is also possible that artefacts that are associated with older dates have been subjected to vertical movement downwards in the deposits in the shelter. The direct dating of mastics or binders on the artefacts themselves will be the ultimate test of these alternatives. Those in the southern sites of the Kimberley that are discussed in this paper have been examined, but there is no remaining mastic. In other regions of the Kimberley future excavations are required to refine the dating and gain a better understanding of regional variability in the production of points.

The degree of similarity of the underlining causes of morphological variation in point technologies throughout the Holocene will, according to Maloney et *al.*, remain a question for Australian archaeology. An example of a question to be answered that is given by Maloney et *al.* is the degree of ecological, environmental or population change that has driven the development of, and the changes to point technology, in the Kimberley.

According to Maloney et *al.* it appears there has been a major change in the lithic production in the Kimberley within the past 1,000 years. The introduction of pressure flaking occurred earlier in the southern Kimberley than in the Northern Territory, where the technology was still being taken up as late as the 1930s. It appears that pressure flaking moves from the south to the north, on the basis of archaeological accounts and on accounts from ethnography. There are, however, parallels between the Kimberley and the Northern Territory, both being regions where there is evidence for the adoption of new types of projectiles about 1,000 BP. During this time different technologies were being adopted in Wardaman country in the Northern Territory, such as the increased production of large hafted blades which occurred during the past 1,000 years (see Clarkson. 2007: 104; Davidson, 1935: 68-70). Maloney et *al.* say that though they have dealt with the chronology in this paper, it should be a priority of future investigation to investigate these changes in association with evidence from archaeology and the environment for economic and social change.

Appendix M[20] - The Eve theory

Based on mitochondrial DNA analysis, Wilson, Stoneking and Cann (3) have concluded that all living humans have descended from a single common mother in South Africa about 200,000 years ago, the female descendants of all other mothers from that time either failing to reproduce at some point in their female line or having no daughters at some point in their line of descent. As mitochondria are passed only in the ovum (not in the sperm), they can be inherited only from the mother. Recombination doesn't occur in mt DNA, or is at least very rare, allowing the tracking of the descendants.

According to Burenhult (3), the results are consistent with archaeological evidence from Klasies River Mouth Cave. The interpretation of further DNA evidence indicates that as modern humans spread from Africa across the other continents they didn't interbreed much with the earlier archaic populations. The remains from Mt Carmel in Israel has been suggested as evidence of the movement from Africa prior to 100,000 years ago.

Australia has been suggested as a test case for the Out of Africa theory, as the time of entry of modern humans is known to be about 60,000 BP and the oldest skeletal material known, Mungo Man (WLH-3), is either 42,000 or 60,000 years old, depending on whose dates you accept, and modern humans are the only hominids to have entered Greater Australia (or Sahul), the continuous landmass of the Australian continent at the time of low sea level, that included New Guinea and the continental shelf. There are no other issues to consider, such as whether the first Australians interbred with Neanderthals or any other archaic humans. The variation in skulls from the Pleistocene, none of which look African, makes it difficult for some, e.g., Thorne, to accept that all of them descended from a purely African line that left Africa 10,000 years or less before they arrived in Australia, according to the recent replacement theory that suggests a small group left Africa about 70,000 years ago. See Australoids

1. Josephine Flood, Archaeology of the Dreamtime, J. B. Publishing
2. Phillip J. Habgood & Natalie R. Franklin, *The revolution that didn't arrive: A review of Pleistocene Sahul*, Journal of Human Evolution, 55, 2008
3. Goran Burenhult (general editor), **Peoples of the Past**, the Illustrated History of Human Kind, Vol 1, Fog City Press, 200

Links

1. New fossil study rejects "Eve theory" and supports a diverse ancestry of modern humans
2. Mitochondrial Eve
3. The Eve Controversy

Appendix N [66] Earliest Hominin Occupation in Sulawesi, Indonesia

Sulawesi is the largest island in Wallacea, the large zone of oceanic islands that separates continental Asia from Sahul, the combined landmass of Australia, including Tasmania, and New Guinea in the Pleistocene at times of low sea levels during glacial periods. An unknown hominin lineage had colonised Flores by 1 million years ago, which is immediately to the south (Brumm et *al.*, 2010), and by about 50,000 BP modern humans had crossed to Sahul (Clarkson et al., 2015; O'Connor, 2015). Van den Bergh et *al.* suggest that Sulawesi was probably pivotal in these dispersals, on the basis of ocean currents, position and biogeographical context (Morwood & Van Oosterzee, 2007). It is indicated by rock art in the limestone karst region of Maros, south west Sulawesi, where speleothems have been dated by uranium series, revealed that humans were present on the island at least 40,000 BP (Aubert et al., 2014). In this paper van den Bergh et *al.* report new excavations at Talepu in the Walanae Basin to the north east of Maros, where stone artefacts have been found *in situ* that are associated with fossil remains of megafauna (**Bulbalus** sp., **Stegodon** and **Celebochoerus**) were recovered from stratified deposits that had accumulated from prior to 200,000 BP to about 100,000 BP. Sulawesi is suggested by these findings to have hosted a long-established population of archaic hominins, as did Flores, though their ancestral origins and taxonomic status has remained elusive.

The discovery in the late 1940s in Walanae Basin, south Sulawesi of 'Palaeolithic' stone artefacts associated with fossil fauna dating to the Pleistocene (Van Heekeren, 1949) led to a considerable amount of speculation about the time depth of human occupation of the island (Bartstra, Keates, Basoeki & Kallupa, 1991; Van Heekeren, 1972). The lithic assemblages that were comprised of cores, choppers and flakes, the 'Cabenge Industry', and derived from surface collections that were not dated from along the eastern side of the Walanae River (Van Heekeren, 1949; Bartstra, Keates, Basoeki & Kallupa, 1991; Van Heekeren, 1972), which follows the Walanae Depression, an elongated basin that is fault-bounded and trends north-south. Van den Bergh et *al.* recovered from the same unstratified contexts (Hooijer, 1948; Hooijer, 1974) the fossils of several extinct species, such as 2 pygmy proboscideans, a giant tortoise, and a large endemic suid, **Celebochoerus**, as well as in excavations at various sites (van den Bergh, 1999). The stratigraphic context and the time range of the 'Cabenge Industry' was still unresolved because *in situ* stone artefacts were still lacking (van den Bergh, 1999), in spite of protracted investigations.

Surveys were conducted in the Cabenge area between 2007 and 2012 to clarify these issues which led to the discovery of 4 new sites that contained *in situ* stone artefacts in their stratigraphic context. Deep-trench excavations were undertaken at Talepu, one of the sites that were newly discovered. This site is located 3 km to the southeast of Cabenge and 13 km downstream from the point at which the Walanae River leaves the valley that confines it and enters a widening floodplain that is subsiding actively towards the north. East-west compression and wrench faulting along the Walanae fault zone resulted in uplift of the Sengkang anticline and the southern part of the Walanae Depression (Grainge & Davies, 1983; Sukamto, 1975). The folded sedimentary sequences from the Pliocene-Pleistocene of the Walanae Formation are now exposed in the uplifted areas (van den Bergh, 1999). Accumulations of fluvio-lacustrine sediments, dating to the Pleistocene to recent times, were facilitated in the northern part of the Walanae Depression by compressional down-folding. The Talepu site (4° 22' 6.5" S, 119° 59' 7" E) is situated near the hinge line between the southern part of the Walanae Depression, which is uplifted, and the northern part, which is subsiding.

The excavations were focused on the northernmost hill of an elongated ridge near the village of Talepu that was about 600 m to the west of the Walanae River. The summit of Talepu Hill is 32 m above sea level and 18 m above the adjacent floodplain of the Walanae River. There are deposits exposed along this ridge comprised of a sequence of sub-horizontal fluvio-lacustrine layers of sand and silt, which coarsens upwards, which is overlain by alluvial cobble gravels. At Talepu 2 deep excavations were carried out, trenches T2 and T4, which provided a combined length of 18.7 m long stratigraphic section that exposed 5 main sedimentary units: in descending order of depth, units A-E.

The first evidence of *in situ* stone artefacts to be found in Walanae Basin in stratified and dated contexts were revealed by these excavations. Van den Bergh et *al.* recovered 270 stone artefacts from between the surface and a depth of 4.2 m, which were associated with the high-energy fluvial gravel deposits of unit A by the T2 excavation. Most are therefore water-rolled to various degrees, though 21 % are still in relatively fresh condition. Silicified limestone cobbles that are coarse- to medium grained that have a diameter of up to 130 mm, are the main source of raw material. Most are flakes of medium- to large size, with cores that comprise 13 % of the assemblage. Hard hammer blows to one face (42 %) were used to reduce cores or bifacially (58 %) from striking platforms that were unprepared. Reduction of cores was not intensive, though 7 cobbles were rotated and multiplatform cores that were formed by subsequent reduction. Flakes that were struck from the cobbles were then reduced to 1 face (60 %) or bifacially (40 %). There is little evidence that the stoneworkers were constructing tools of a specific form; rather sharp-edged flakes were produced by stone flaking for use or a source for additional flakes, though there is patterning in the flaking techniques.

From T4 the topsoil and colluvium to a depth of 120 cm contained 41 artefacts. There were, however, 4 silicified limestone artefacts *in situ* in older strata that were exposed within the silt of subunit E_2, that provide the earliest stratigraphic evidence at Talepu of human activity. 2 unmodified flakes, at 2.2-2.4 m depth, were recovered and there are 2 that are angular scatter fragments at a depth of 3.0-3.1 m, which van den Bergh et *al.* suggest are probably the results of percussion flaking. The scatter fragments are made from distinctive mottled silicified limestone which appears to have been removed from the same core. There is no evidence on the artefacts of them undergoing transport by water, unit E not yielding any clasts that are indicative of high-energy water flow.

There was only 1 fossil that was identified from T2: a lower molar fragment of a bovid that was recovered from a depth of 4 m that is just above the size range of the lowland anoa, ***Bubalus depressicornis***, which is extant. 8 ***Celebochoerus*** dental elements, e.g., a lower canine and 3 fragments of bone that were not identifiable, were recovered from the silty interval of subunit E_2

between 3.1 and 4.0 m below the surface and just beneath the deepest stone artefacts. Van den Bergh et *al.* suggest at least some of these fossil remains can be ascribed to a single individual. A fragment of a milk molar from a ***Stegodon*** was recovered from a depth of 1.9-2.0 m and a dermal scute from a crocodile was recovered from a depth of 3.9-4.0 m.

Teeth and bones that had been recovered from subunit E2 were dated by uranium series by the laser ablation inductively coupled plasma mass spectroscopy (LA-ICP-MS) methods (Grün et al., 2014), to constrain the age of the deposits at Talepu. Sequential laser spot analyses were carried out on cross-sections of 8 fossils of ***Celebochoerus*** that had been recovered from a depth of between 0.2-0.5 m below the deepest known stone artefacts in the same silty unit. For each sample data sets were combined and a single age estimate was calculated by use of the diffusion-absorption-decay model (Sambridge, Grün & Eggins, 2012). There were infinite error bounds for most of the age results, so minimum ages were all that was possible (Grün et al., 2014). The fossil samples are indicated by the combined uranium-series results to be older than 200,000 BP. Silty layers of units A, C and E have normal magnetic polarities at all levels sampled based on palaeomagnetic samples. Taken together with the results of uranium series analysis the fossils therefore have an age of more than 200 ka and less than 780 ka.

In order to constrain the age of artefacts van den Bergh et *al.* used a multi-elevated-temperature post-infrared infrared stimulated luminescence (MET-pIRIR) dating procedure (Li & Li, 2011; Li, Jacobs Roberts & Li, 2014) was applied to feldspar grains that were rich in potassium that had been extracted from 5 sediment samples that spanned the entire sequence. The ages in stratigraphic order obtained for the 4 samples from T2 that were analysed are 103 ± 9 ka at a depth of 3 m to 156 ± 19 ka at 10 m depth. The Talepu cultural sequence ends at about 100 ka, or possibly earlier, as suggested by these results. Sediments dating to 156 ± 19 ka were deposited near the top of unit D, which lies above the sedimentary layer unit E from which the deepest artefacts were recovered, more than 3 m below. The oldest evidence for stone artefacts from Talepu that is securely dated therefore has an age of 194 to 118 ka at the 95 % confidence interval (2σ), though it is clear that the site was occupied earlier given the recovery of artefacts from the greater stratigraphic depths. In the lower trench, T4, a sample recovered from a depth of 8 m was found to have a minimum age of about 195 ka. This estimate of age is stratigraphically consistent with the MET-pIRIR ages for the T2 and with the minimum uranium ages of about 200 ka for the T4 fossil remains from subunit E_2.

It is suggested by the results of the Talepu excavation that it is now possible to conclude that the initial occupation of Sulawesi occurred at least 118 ka. As earlier assumptions had Sulawesi being only colonised by *H. sapiens*, which are believed at present to have arrived in the region by about 50,000 BP, the identity of these earlier inhabitants is of great interest. In island Southeast Asia the earliest skeletal remains of *H. sapiens* are from about 45,000 BP (Barker et al., 2007; Grün et al., 2005), though in the Levant (Grün et al., 2005) the earliest modern skeletal human remains have been recovered that date to about 120 ka, and possibly a similar time in Southeast Asia (Westaway, 2007). It appears possible, though controversial, that soon after *H. sapiens* evolved in Africa they spread to Sunda, the easternmost tip of continental Asia and by about 120 ka they crossed to Wallacea. However, by 1 million years ago early hominins had already reached Flores, which is far smaller and more remote than Sulawesi, van den Bergh et *al.* suggesting that they possibly arrived on Flores on debris from a tsunami (Morwood & Van Oosterzee, 2007). Therefore it is conceivable that the first humans on Sulawesi could possibly have arrived in a similar manner at around the same time or earlier or later.

The findings from Talepu attest to the presence on Sulawesi of early tool makers by the Middle Pleistocene, though a definitive answer as to which species of hominin was the first to arrive is precluded by the lack of human fossils dating to the Pleistocene. Van den Bergh et *al.* say there are at least 3 candidates in the region of potential island colonisers: the known and inferred distributions of *H. floresiensis* on Flores, about 190 ka or earlier (Brumm et *a;*., 2010), on the southern margin of Sunda (Java of the present), *H. erectus*, about 1.5 million years ago to about 140 ka (Zaim et al., 2011; Indriati et al., 2011), and 'Denisovans', who are suggested by van den Bergh et *al.* to have possibly extended into Wallacea (Cooper &

Stringer, 2013). When the currents of the Indonesian through-flow that are predominantly southerly flowing (Sprintall, 2014), van den Bergh et *al.* speculate that Borneo to the west, which was part of mainland Asia at times of low sea level is the most likely point of origin for the colonisers of Sulawesi, and to the north the Philippines, the northern extremity of Wallacea, with the implication that there may be records of archaic hominins on other islands in the region that are still to be discovered.

Van den Bergh, G. D., B. Li, A. Brumm, R. Grün, D. Yurnaldi, M. W. Moore, I. Kurniawan, R. Setiawan, F. Aziz, R. G. Roberts, Suyono, M. Storey, E. Setiabudi and M. J. Morwood (2016). "Earliest hominin occupation of Sulawesi, Indonesia." Nature **529** (7585): 208-211.

Appendix O[21] - Aboriginal Engravings analysis of the Kybra Site in Western Australia

In this paper Franklin presents the results of an analysis of Aboriginal rock engravings at the Kybra Site in the far south western corner of Western Australia that is known of a group of rock engravings called the Panaramitee, which are comprised of engravings that are predominantly animal tracks, in particular bird tracks, which have been engraved on flat tabular limestone pavements. The Panaramitee tradition, seen in engraving sites that are distributed widely across the Australian continent, has been represented as being homogeneous at a continental level. This study, which was based on a multivariate investigation using correspondence analysis and cluster analysis, compared the Kybra Site with other engraving sites in Western Australia and elsewhere. The study was aimed at determining whether the Kybra Site showed similarities with other Panaramitee engraving sites, and whether an explanatory framework, that is known as the Discontinuous Dreaming Network Model, could account for any similarities or differences that are identified. Franklin has shown by this study that the sites in Western Australia differ more from each other than from other sites in eastern Australia, and have shown similarities with engravings in Cape York Peninsula, the Carpentaria region and central western Queensland. According to Franklin this finding fits well with the tenets of the Discontinuous Dreaming Network Model, which holds that across vast distances of Australia similarities between engraving sites reflect the widespread links that were forged by Dreaming tracks as suggested by the trade and other social networks that sometimes spanned the continent. The engravings from the Kybra Site were found to group with sites from Cape York Peninsula and central western Queensland, both on the other side of the continent.

When rock art sites around the world are studied a major problem has been the measurement and explanation of paintings and engravings that are sometimes found at considerable distance from each other. The questions asked are what is the significance of the variation that is detected, and the method of comparing different sites? Multivariate analysis can then explore the significance of any variability that is detected.

The Discontinuous Dreaming Network Model was proposed (Franklin, 2004) to explain the widespread similarities that had been noted across the continent of a group of rock engravings termed the "Panaramitee style" (Maynard, 1979), and was supported by multivariate analysis (Franklin, 2004). The Panaramitee style, which was named after the type-site in South Australia, consists of pecked engravings of the tracks of macropods and birds, human footprints, circles, dots, crescents, spirals, radiate designs, together a small proportion of figurative motifs other than tracks. It was claimed that this style was homogeneous at a continental level in terms of technique, forms and proportions of motifs (Maynard, 1979). It was suggested by the Discontinuous Dreaming Network Model that similarities between engraving sites spread over vast distances of Australia was a reflection of the widespread links that had been forged by Dreaming tracks and suggested by trade and other social networks that sometimes spanned the continent. In Aboriginal cosmology and land occupation Dreaming tracks have been regarded as being particularly significant (e.g. Chatwin, 1987; David, 2002; Elkin, 1934; Gunn, 1997, 2003; Layton, 1992; Morphy, 1983; Moyle, 1983; Munn, 1973; Spencer & Gillen, 1938; Strehlow, 1978; Sutton, 1988, 1990). Dreaming tracks are reflections of the activities of the Dreamtime ancestors during the creative era as they emerged from the earth, to travel across the country along lengthy tracks, or circled within regions that were defined more narrowly. Considerable distances were sometimes covered across the continent by Dreaming tracks (e.g. Sutton, 1990), often extending across the boundaries of different groups, which facilitated meetings between local groups, and for travelling groups for gift exchange and for rituals that were associated with the relevant track. According to Franklin it is well documented (e.g. Ross, 1997), that similar motifs were used at sites across vast areas and suggested that a means for negotiating rights and obligations of travellers along the tracks are shared understanding of motif forms. A shared knowledge that assured travellers of their right to cross the country of a group and which established an affilial relationship between the occupants of a country and the travellers is provided by the repetition of motifs between regions. Therefore it is not surprising that frequently Dreaming tracks correlated with the trade routes that have been documented recently (Ross, 1997), which suggests that both the Dreaming tracks and Trade routes often were a means for the meeting of people across the landscape, as well as for the diffusion across vast areas of similar motifs.

In symbolic systems use of nonfigurative motifs, such as are found in the Panaramitee, also helps to explain the persistence of the overall pattern of the similarity between the engraving sites that have been identified in the multivariate analyses possibly over a prolonged time period based on chronological evidence that is available (e.g. minimum age of 13,000 BP for buried engravings at the Early Man site, the Laura region, Rosenfeld, 1981a) and the continued use of motifs of the Panaramitee style in recent Aboriginal artistic systems (e.g. Anderson & Dussart, 1988). It is suggested to be possible that the meanings of motifs might have changed over time, while the motif morphology remained unchanged, as the potential for nonfigurative motifs that have a range of different discontinuous meanings, i.e., a single motif may have a range of different meanings (Munn, 1966). The extreme simplicity of the Panaramitee motifs allows for this possibility. Rock engravings in the far south western corner of Western Australia were reported, the Kybra Site, (Clarke, J., 1983) (Department of Indigenous Affairs, Site No. S1786; Clarke, 1983; Fig. 1). In this part of Australia rock art sites are relatively sparse (Dortch, 1976, 1980; Hallam, 1971, 1972; Merrilees et *al*., 1973; Morse, 1984; Serventy, 1952; Webb & Gunn, 2004), and Kybra is one of the few rock engraving sites that are currently known. In this part of the continent there are few references to the forms of artistic expression that have been recorded from the time of European contact (Caroline Bird, pers. comm.). Even so, it appears there was a substantial body of mythology (Berndt, 1973; Hallam, 1972, 1974a, b, 1979), and ochre was traded into the south west, that possibly came from as far away as Wilgie Mia in the Murchison district (McCarthy, 1939; Meagher and Ride, 1979). Franklin suggested cultural expression classes other than art must have been used to maintain boundaries, as there are a large number of Aboriginal groups that are attested to in this area, which is resource rich, west of the limit of circumcision (Anderson, 1984; Berndt, 1973; Tindale, 1974).

A series of flat tabular limestone pavements in a cleared and fenced paddock on private land that is 3 km from the Southern Ocean was used for the engravings. The pavements extended over an area of 75 m north to south and about 25 m east to west including about 25 limestone blocks. More than 100 engravings, mostly of bird and macropod tracks, though also a star motif, single meandering lines, that are believed to possibly be a snake or lizard tracks, and outlines that are of several boomerang shapes, have been found. The engravings of animal tracks were usually somewhat larger than life-size. Engravings of large bird tracks, that are presumably the prints of emus, were the most common motifs. The next most numerous are tracks of smaller birds, possibly bustards, and unidentified wading types. A number of macropod track engravings have also been found, including both hind and fore prints (Clarke, 1983; Fig. 1).

As well as engravings at Yalgoo (Edah Station) that is 420 km north of Perth, and Yeelirrie, which is 680 km north east of Perth, it was noted (Clarke, 1983) that the Kybra Site appeared to extend the range of known engravings of the Panaramitee style (Maynard, 1979).

In this paper the Kybra Site is re-examined by Franklin in a broader context. It provides, in particular, a detailed comparison of the site with Panaramitee engravings from other sites spread across the continent that was undertaken by Clarke in 1983. This paper addressed the following questions:

- Are there similarities at Kybra with other Panaramitee style engraving sites?
- Can the Discontinuous Dreaming Network Model be used in an explanation of any similarities or differences that are identified between the Kybra sites and other Panaramitee sites that are located in other parts of the continent?

Conclusion

A comparison of a series of rock engravings from the Kybra Site in far south western.

Australia that was described originally (Clarke, 1983) with other sites where Panaramitee tradition engravings have been found in Western Australia as well as in other parts of the continent (see also Franklin, 2004, 2007) has been presented in this paper. A larger sample of sites was used in this study than was available to Clarke. It was similarly found that rock engravings at Edah Station were similar to those from the Carpentaria Region, which are also a considerable distance from the Kybra Site. Therefore these sites were found to be more different from each other than they are from sites that are great distances from them. Both of these findings were argued to be consistent with the tenets of the Discontinuous Dreaming Network Model (Franklin, 2004, 2007).

Franklin anticipates that the pattern of engraved motifs present at the Kybra Site will be confirmed by further detailed studies, where excavations are planned (R. G. Gunn, pers. comm.) which are expected to uncover more engravings and possibly settle any inter-recorder discrepancies there may be in the numbers of motifs that resulted from increased cover by grass over time.

Appendix P[30] - Sahul - Explanations for patterning in the "Package of Traits" of Modern Human Behaviour

The archaeological evidence that has been recovered from Sahul that dates to the Late Pleistocene has provided a test for the debate concerning the package of modern human behaviour. It was revealed by a detailed review of the archaeological record from the Late Pleistocene in Sahul (Franklin & Habgood, 2007; Habgood & Franklin, 2008) found patterning, both geographical and chronological, for the appearance of the individual traits, 4 broad Phases and 7 'Zones of Innovation'. In this study Habgood & Franklin considered the potential causes of this patterning, including taphonomy and the function of the artefacts, concluding that it reflects differences in material culture and cultural differences.

Taphonomy

The issues of taphonomy and archaeological sampling have been considered previously (Franklin & Habgood, 2007: 9-10; Habgood & Franklin, 2008:211-212). Habgood & Franklin held the view that the presence or absence of components of the "package" did not entirely result from taphonomic processes or linked directly to the excavation size, amount of recovered artefacts, and/or the intensity of the usage of the site, though they acknowledged that taphonomy and archaeological sampling can and do have an impact on the archaeological record that is preserved and/or recovered (e.g. archaeological material is generally preserved better in limestone caves than in sandstone shelters. Therefore, Habgood & Franklin concluded that patterning was evident in the archaeological record from Sahul in the Late Pleistocene, and that the presence or absence of a material culture item **was** the result of the cultural preferences of the Indigenous inhabitants of the site/region/continent, though multiple factors would impact on the assemblages present at the site.

How both small and extensive excavations, though only limited assemblages, have produced unique finds has previously been detailed by Habgood & Franklin, while sites containing large assemblages have produced few if any of the traits of the "package". In this paper they discuss this in more detail and provide additional examples.

Devil's Lair is a large limestone cave in South Western Australia where extensive excavations has been undertaken (Dortch, 1984). This site produced 13 bone points and 3 bone beads, both of which were made from long bones of macropods, that were possibly limestone and bone pendants, a notational piece and ochre (Dortch, 1984; Table 1b, Figure 2). This site has only limited archaeological assemblages, though unique finds were recovered from it. Though this site is closer to the coast, 50 km at the height of the LGM, than other sites with such finds, such as those in the Kimberley, no shell beads were identified.

The Kimberley sites in North Western Australia of Riwi Cave, Carpenter's Gap and Widgingarri Shelter 1 display patterns that are contrasting. At the Riwi Cave site, a limestone shelter, 10 **Dentalium** shell beads were recovered that date to 30,000-40,000 BP, from levels containing little shell material that has been preserved (Balme, 2000; Balme & Morse, 2006; Table 1a, Fig. 2). These marine shells had been transported more than 300 km to this site. Carpenter's Gap is a limestone shelter that is 100 km from the coast at present which has also produced **Dentalium** shell beads, but little other shell material (Balme & Morse, 2006; O'Connor 1995: 59), in spite of "exceptional preservation conditions" (O'Connor, 1995: 59). Widgingarri Shelter 1, as with Riwi and Carpenter's Gap, has very little shell dating to the Pleistocene, though it still has evidence for long-distance contact with the coast in the form of a ground sea urchin artefact in a level that dates to about 18,000 BP (O'Connor, 1999). It has no shell beads. Also, there are no bone points or bone beads at Widgingarri Shelter 1, though macropod bone is commonly found in the deposit in levels dating to the Pleistocene. There are macropod bones at all 4 sites, but no bone points or bone beads, and no pendants of bone or limestone have been identified. Contact with the coast has also been demonstrated in all 4 sites, though shell beads have been identified only at Riwi and Carpenter's Gap.

At the Mandu Mandu Creek site, a limestone rock shelter in central western Australia, extensive excavations have recovered 22 cone shell (**Conus sp.**) beads from levels that have been dated 32,000 BP (Morse, 1993a, b; Table 1a, Fig. 2). At this coastal site there were also negligible amounts of shell material recovered from deposits dating to the Late Pleistocene (Morse, 1993a: Fig. 2). No bone beads of bone points were recovered, though faunal material is present.

According to Habgood & Franklin Tasmanian sites dating to the Late Pleistocene provide an interesting contrast to those in Western Australia. Limestone cave sites in the Tasmanian south west have yielded very rich archaeological assemblages dating to the Late Pleistocene (Table 1b, Fig. 2). 37,000 stone artefacts and more than 250,000 fragments of animal bone were recovered from a volume of less than 1 m^3 of deposit, as well as a single bone point (Ranson et al., 1983). No bone beads were found. Bone Cave has similarly produced extensive faunal material and 13 bone points (Webb & Allen, 1990), but no beads.

Mannalargenna, a limestone Cave on Prime Seal Island in Bass Strait, which is currently off the northern coast of Tasmania (Brown, 1993), was situated on a hill on the Bassian Plain that joined the mainland to Tasmania at the time of peak occupation. There is an extensive archaeological assemblage in Mannalargenna Cave that was recovered from levels dating to 15,000-20,000 BP, which included stone and fossil-shell artefacts, faunal material, fragments of emu egg shell, pieces of red ochre and a bone spatula (Brown, 1993). There were no bone beads or shell beads that have been identified at the site, despite the preservation of some otherwise fragile items, such as the Emu egg shell.

Evidence has been found of exploitation of marine resources during the Late Pleistocene on Islands off the north east and north west coasts of Sahul, including Buang Merabak, Matenkupkum and Matenbek, New Ireland and Lene Hara Cave, East Timor (Habgood & Franklin, 2008: Table 8 and references therein). A perforated tooth from a tiger shark, ***Galeocerdo Cuvier***, has been recovered from Buang Merabak, New Ireland, in levels that have been dated to between 39,500-28,000 BP (Leavesley, 2007), though no marine shell beads have been identified at any of these sites.

Early Man Site is a sandstone Shelter on Cape York Peninsula. Faunal material, stone artefacts and ochre have been recovered from this site in levels dating to the Late Pleistocene, as well as rock engravings that date to at least 13,200 BP (Rosenfeld, 1981: Table 1, Fig. 2). No bone points or bone beads were recovered from the Pleistocene levels of this site. Nurrabullgin (Ngarrabulgan) Cave is another sandstone shelter in North Queensland which has also failed to yield bone points or bone beads, in spite of extensive amounts of bone being recovered from the Pleistocene levels (David, 1993: Table 2). Fern Cave, another limestone cave on Cape York Peninsula, has also produced stone artefacts, faunal material and ochre from the Late Pleistocene levels, but again, no bone points or bone beads (David, 1991).

It is demonstrated by these examples that the presence or absence of elements of the "package", specifically shell beads, bone beads and bone tools, is not linked directly to taphonomic processes or archaeological sampling in that:

- Shell beads have been found at sites that have little shell preserved, while sites that contain lots of shell do not contain shell beads;
- A site with a limited archaeological sample has contained bone beads, though not from sites with extensive faunal samples; and
- Sites in southern Australia have generally produced bone tools, though not sites in northern Australia, which have preserved macropod sites;
- Also, there are limited distributions of grindstones and hatchets, even though stone artefacts are found at sites throughout Sahul (Habgood & Franklin)

The patterning evident for the "package" must therefore reflect material culture differences and cultural preferences.

The distribution of some elements of the "package" has been found to possibly be related to the function of the artefacts (see Habgood & Franklin, 2008 and references therein. For example:

- Bone points: The majority of sites that have bone points from the Late Pleistocene are in southern Sahul, where, as the climate is cooler, they may have been used for skin working and cloak making.
- Grindstones: The multifunctional grinding tools from northern and south eastern Australia were used in the grinding of ochre, the processing and leaching of toxic plants and for the grinding of seeds.

- Hatchets: According to Habgood & Franklin edge-ground and waisted hatchets from northern Sahul may have been used for a range of adzing and axing activities, which included ringbarking and the clearing of trees, wood work, manufacturing watercraft and/or chopping holes in trees when hunting possums and collecting honey.

The incorporation of these activities and artefacts into adaptive strategies and material culture of different groups, is therefore be a reflection of chronological and geographical patterning.

Social and Symbolic

Population growth, population pressure, demographic expansion and increasing inter-population contact outside Sahul, have been suggested as possible reasons for the appearance of the "package", and/or behavioural traits needed in order to access limited resources (McBrearty & Brook, 2000; Kuhn et al., 2001; Shennan, 2001; Henshilwood & Marean, 2003).

With increasing aridity leading up to the Last Glacial Maximum (LGM) bounding and emblemic behaviour becomes evident, as throughout the continent groups aggregated in refuge areas (aggregation locales), with the result that regionally-based population pressure and/or the reaching of regional population thresholds at different times in different regions. During the LGM this process would have been especially evident. Bounding and emblemic behaviour is archaeologically apparent in the increasing level of regionality of rock art, the appearance of cemeteries and during the Late Pleistocene, the use of personal ornaments.

Therefore, there is both chronological and geographical patterning to the occurrence of symbolic behaviour after the initial colonisation of Sahul that can be explained within a demographic, social and symbolic framework. Habgood & Franklin disagree with the proposed explanation that is based a continent-wide increase in population and the reaching of a continental population threshold, suggesting that the chronological and geographical pattern they identified is not consistent with such a proposed explanation. At different times and in different regions the "driving forces" for the pattern may have been population pressure that was regionally-based and/or the reaching of regional population thresholds at different times in different regions.

Water is a crucial determinant of subsistence and settlement by Aboriginal people as Australia is an arid country, the result of which would have been varied population numbers at the regional level based on the availability of resources (Hiscock, 2008; Lourandos, 1997; Mulvaney & Kamminga, 1999). The availability and distribution of water, faunal species and resource plants within the landscape are impacted directly by changes of climatic and ecology. Population density/pressure would have been affected by changes in the availability of resources, which may be the trigger for population density/pressure thresholds at different times in different regions, as well as the appearance of "symbolic behaviour".

It is difficult to establish the size of the population and demographic changes for Sahul, though it is suggested by the number of sites and the intensity of usage of sites (rates of discard and sedimentation) that there were population densities that were relatively low throughout the Late Pleistocene. Models have been proposed that are based on the Late Pleistocene, mid-Holocene or bidirectional population growth before and after the LGM (see Hiscock, 2008). Habgood & Franklin agree with Hiscock (2008: 243) that fluctuations in population would have been complex in character, based regionally, of varying magnitude and on different scales. The demographic history in the Late Pleistocene would have involved the growth of population, expansion, replacement, contraction, and different degrees of population stress and pressure.

Leading up to the LGM increasing aridity would have significantly impacted the availability of resources and therefore the patterns of Aboriginal settlement, as well as the population numbers during the Late Pleistocene. It has been observed "timing and magnitude of climate change are unlikely to have been in parallel throughout the Late Pleistocene and the Holocene in both northern and southern Australia" (Veth, 1993: 7). It was detailed, e.g., (O'Connor et al., 1993) how during the LGM, the conditions in north western Australia would have been drier and colder, though in south western Australia conditions would have been wetter and colder. It was also demonstrated that discard rates/occupation intensity/population varied between the 2 areas at this time, decreasing in North Western Australia and increasing in the south west.

Much of Sahul was affected by increasing aridity during the LGM, which resulted in some sites and regions being abandoned, especially in areas that were more arid, while in other areas and/or sites there was a period of increased population intensity as people moved to refuge areas that had networks of permanent water sources and reliable resources (Hiscock, 2008; O'Connor et *al.*, 1993; Veth, 1993). Habgood & Franklin suggest this demographic process would have resulted in what was referred to as a "process of population compression" (Witter, 2007: 21). Habgood & Franklin suggest that similar processes occurred in order to manage increasing population pressure that would have been a response to increasing aridity, population compression and intensive utilisation and control of resources, with changes that resulted in symbolic and other behaviour as manifested in the appearance of art, personal ornament and cemeteries.

Therefore, do the broad phases that were identified by Habgood & Franklin relate to periods of climatic and ecological change that would have resulted in increasing population pressure from reduced resources and/or population compression? The phases identified by Habgood and Franklin are:

1. Phase 1: From about 40,000 BP.
2. Phase 2: From about 32,000 BP.
3. Phase 3: From about 20,000 BP
4. Phase 4: From about 5,000 BP.

Conclusion

In this paper Habgood & Franklin have argued for the establishment of regional symbolic activity dating from early in the process of colonisation of Sahul. They contend that the patterns they have identified in the "package" of modern human behaviour in Sahul during the Late Pleistocene most probably result from increasing momentum from social trends that were already well established and their consequent greater visibility in the archaeological record in more recent times.

Significant climatic, ecological and demographic change would have been experienced throughout the Late Pleistocene and continuing into the Holocene, the result of which would have been increasing population pressure from reduced resources and population compression. Habgood & Franklin say these changes are fundamental to an understanding of the appearance of symbolic behaviour and social organisation within Sahul.

The terms bonding and bounding behaviour were used in order to reflect the archaeological pattern that has been identified by Habgood & Franklin in the "package" of traits. Bonding behaviour is reflected in Similarities in art across large areas of the continent, and in the movement of materials over long distances, which included ochre and marine shells, following the initial colonisation of Sahul and movement throughout the continent. The sociological solutions that were adopted by the Aboriginal people in order to manage irregular aridity, population compression and intensive utilisation and control of resources in Sahul, led to these linkages becoming integral components of this sociological solution (see also Witter, 2007).

As aridity was increasing in Sahul leading up to the LGM bounding and emblemic behaviour becomes evident, groups throughout the continent aggregated in refuge areas (aggregation locales), which resulted in regionally-based population pressure and/or the reaching regional population thresholds at different times in different regions. During the LGM this process would have been especially evident. Bounding and emblemic behaviour is archaeologically apparent in the increasing extent of rock art, the appearance of cemeteries, and personal ornament use during the Late Pleistocene and Early Holocene.

Therefore, there is chronological and geographical patterning to the occurrence of symbolic behaviour which followed the initial colonisation of Sahul that is possibly explained within a demographic, social and symbolic framework.

Bindjarran Rock shelter, Manilikarr Country – the archaeology

Evidence of the settlement of humans on the floodplain of the East Alligator River from the terminal Pleistocene to the 20th century has been found by archaeological excavations at Bindjarran rock shelter in the Kakadu national Park, Northern Territory. In this paper Shine et *al.* summarise the archaeological excavation, ethnographic and rock art research from the site, with their work focussed on distributions of stone artefacts that have been dated. At Bindjarran Rock shelter the findings conform to the findings from archaeological excavations that have previously been carried out at other sites in the region, as well as contributing to a greater understanding of Aboriginal society in the region during the Big Swamp phase, Freshwater phase and over the last 600 years.

Bindjarran is the name of a small sandstone outlier located in a portion of Manilikarr Country, within Kakadu National Park (KNP), about 2.2 km south of the East Alligator River and 2.7 km south-south west of the Ubirr rock art complex. There are 2 rock shelters 30 m apart which are connected by a shallow overhang in the Bindjarran outlier which has a diameter of about 60 m in diameter: Bindjarran Rock shelter is about 26 x 5 x 3.5 m and the Nabarebarde Rock shelter is about 10 x 3.5 x 2 m. Both rock shelters were formed by disintegration or undercutting of the eastern face of the sandstone outlier. Apart from about 3 m between the 2 shelters, rock art extends in a continuous band along the face. The site complex is completed by a 3rd rock art gallery on the southern face.

Shine et *al.* say the name Bindjarran is derived from the Kunwinjku name for the eel-tail catfish, (***Neosilurus*** sp.), a fish that has distinctive barbells of 'whiskers' (Taçon, 1989). Nabarebarde is the Kunwinjku name for the bony brim or herring (***Nematolosa erebi***). These species are reflected in the images of the rock art throughout the site complex.

The results of the excavation, oral history and rock art suggest that occupation at Bindjarran began by at least 13,140-12,771 BP in the Late Pleistocene and was still being used in the 20th century. Based on an increase in lithics and burning activity the use of the site appears to have increased from about 8,014-7,858 BP to 7,164-6,936 cal. BP, after the end of a series of roof falls. Following a cessation of alluviation some time earlier than 6,956-6,670 cal. BP there was more intense use of the site in the mid-Holocene.

According to Shine et *al.*, a regional environmental change, the 'Big Swamp' phase, was broadly contemporaneous with increased use of Bindjarran during the mid-Holocene. The 'Big Swamp' phase was characterised by emerging mangrove/swamp environments across the lowlands of western Arnhem Land that occurred between 8,000-6,000 BP (e.g. Allen, 1987,1979; Brockwell et *al.*, 2009; Hope et *al.*, 1985; Woodroffe et *al.*, 1988). It has been documented previously at rock shelters close to mangroves that there was more intensive occupation during this period than has been previously documented, which include Nawamoyn at 8,182-7,679 cal. BP (ANU-53), Malangangerr at 7,231-6,490 cal. BP (GaK-627), Malakunanja at 7,463-7,013 cal. BP (SUA-251) and Malakunanja II at 7,678-6,664 cal. BP (SUA-264) (Allen & Barton, 1989; Kamminga &Allen, 19973; Schrire, 1982). In the mid-Holocene increased intensity of human activity at Bindjarran appears to be a localised expression of a regional trend in which rock shelters were occupied more intensively to enable foraging in mangrove areas that were being newly established.

At Bindjarran a second period of increased site use, as indicated by an increased rate of discard of stone artefacts and macrocharcoal, began sometime between 5,265-4,865 and 2,918-2,762 cal. BP, peaking at about 1,270-1,075 cal. BP. At Bindjarran peak activity, at about 1,200 BP, is broadly contemporaneous with the Freshwater phase, a time when the current hydrological environment is believed to have been established.

According to Shine et *al.* considerable variation is likely to have occurred (e.g. Allen, 1987, 1989; Allen & Barton, 1989; Jones, 1985) as different landforms and parts of the adjusted landscape variability to the new freshwater conditions (e.g. Clark & Guppy, 1988; Hiscock, 1997, 1999), though there was a general increase in both quantity and extent of site use on the freshwater flood plain as has been observed from at least 2,000 BP (Hiscock, 1999; Jones, 1985; Meehan et *al.*, 1985).

At Bindjarran the final period of peak intensity of occupation post-dates 622-510 cal. BP. After this date the highest level of flaking activity occurs, peaking in the protohistoric period. Shine et *al.* suggest this period of site use probably incorporates the use of Bindjarran that was ethnohistorically recorded, e.g., as a water buffalo hunting camp, when several of the rock art images, which include Yellow Charlie, were painted

The archaeological findings are supported by the rock art at Bindjarran and the rock art is consistent with the periods that are described. Throughout the site complex the earliest layers of rock art that are observed are representative of the Estuarine Period, 8,000-1,500 BP, as defined (Chaloupka, 1993). Included in this stylistic phase is imagery described as 'Naturalistic', such as species of estuarine fish, crocodiles, and different types of spear throwers, as well as 'Intellectual Realism', which is evidenced by complex x-ray and beeswax designs (Chaloupka, 1993). There is also other imagery present from the 'Freshwater Phase' of Chaloupka, from 1,500 BP, which includes magpie geese and complex spear throwers, as well as the 'Contact Period', from 300 BP, as evidenced by contact imagery.

Shine, Denis; Marshal, Melissa; Wright, Duncan; Denham, Tim; Hiscock, Peter; Jacobsen, Geraldine and Stephens, Sean-Paul. The archaeology of Bindjarran rock shelter in Manilikarr Country, Kakadu National Park, Northern Territory [online]. Australian Archaeology, No. 80, Jun 2015: 104-111. Availability: <http://search.informit.com.au/documentSummary;dn=237574513957781;res=IELHSS>
ISSN: 0312-2417

Birriwilk Rock shelter, Manilikarr Country, South west Arnhem Land, Northern Territory, a Mid- Late Holocene Site

The Birriwilk Rock shelter is comprised of an elevated terrace about 13 by 7 m, between a significant upward slope to the north-north east and a downward slope to the south-south west. A cliff overhang on the eastern side which formed by block disintegration or undercutting of the cliff face, partially encloses the site. According to Shine et *al.* this overhang is deceptively deep, between 3 and 5 m, though the site feels 'unroofed' as the result of its height of about 20 m of cliff face above. Panoramic views to the south over Birriwilk Lagoon, towards the Njanjmah rock art site, and west to the East Alligator River, is provided by the site. The billabong was only about 40 m south of the site during excavation in the mid- to late dry season, and the terrain falls sharply to the south towards the lagoon, at a rate of about 8 m per 20 m.

As well as rock art, some surface ochre and occasional grinding hollows were found that provide clear evidence of usage in the past. Apart from 2 minor 'hollows' that were potentially made by macropodoid marsupials or feral pigs (***Sus scrofa***); it is common to find pig 'wallows' on the adjacent valley floor. Dense vegetation covered the immediate vicinity of the site, with paperbarks, ***Melaleuca*** spp., and eucalypts, mainly ***Eucalyptus miniata***. These did not extend onto the rock shelter floor.

Evidence for settlement in the mid- Late Holocene settlement, including a major period of site use during the last millennium, has been revealed by recent excavations at the Birriwilk Rock shelter in Mikinj Valley, south west Arnhem Land. The site is important to the traditional owners, and there is a rich oral tradition associated with 'Birriwilk', an important ancestor of the Urningangk tribe, the image of Birriwilk being depicted in rock art at the site. According to oral traditions the Birriwilk site is linked with an adjacent lagoon, as well as a number of other rock art sites and features in the landscape, which includes the renowned Ubirr complex. Significant places to the Nayinggul family, traditional owners for the Manilikarr estate, include the Birriwilk site and its vicinity. Key archaeological findings at Birriwilk using stone artefact frequencies and faunal remains as proxies of occupation from about 5,000 BP are summarised in this post-fieldwork report. Within the last 700 years the most intense occupation occurred, a period which is characterised by foraging and hunting in adjacent wetland habitats, technological emphasis changing to bifacial point manufacture, increased rates of artefact discard and an increase in the grinding of ochre. There is little evidence of use of the site over the last 200 years, though it is indicated by oral histories that it was regularly visited until the mid-20th century. This site is still an important story site at the present.

Archaeological excavations were undertaken at Birriwilk, a rock shelter in Manilikarr country, in the East Alligator Region of south west Arnhem Land, Northern Territory, during September and October 2011. The excavations are part of a doctoral research program by the lead author that are community-led. The Nayinggul family were consulted in site selection, as they wished to gain a better understanding of the settlement history of Birriwilk, as they regard the rock shelter to be one of the most significant sites within their country. Excavation results are summarised in this short report, settlement history being interpreted through dated distributions of faunal remains and stone artefacts, augmented by analyses of burning patterns and worked ochre distribution. A future publication will assess the significance of the occupational sequence of the site, rock art and oral histories for the interpreting of spatio-temporal aspects of the Birriwilk story.

Manilikarr Country

This is a clan territory encompassing both side of the East Alligator River and is located to the south of Kunbarlanja (Oenpelli). It is primarily within west Arnhem Land, which was declared an Aboriginal reserve in 1931, though it extends into Kakadu National Park (KNP) of the present. Until 2011 the clan area was named after the senior traditional owner who was recently deceased, referred to in this publication by his skin name Nakodjok. The archaeological investigations at Birriwilk, as well as at 2 other rock shelters, Ingaanjalwurr and Bindjarran, and several members of his family participated in the excavations. Urningangk was the traditional language of Manilikarr Country, which was restricted to an area directly south of Kunbarlanja centred on Mikinj Valley (Birch, 2006). Nakodjok is said to be the last 'hearer' of this language, which has been displaced by Kunwinggu.

Prior to this research excavations had not been carried out in Manilikarr country since the 1960s (Schrire, 1982; White, 1967a, 1967b, 1971; White & Peterson, 1969), though there are several other rock shelters that have been excavated more recently in close proximity to the estate (e.g. Allen & Barton, 1989; Jones, 1985; Kamminga & Allen, 1973). A number of surveys of rock art have also been carried out in Manilikarr country (e.g. Brandl, 1968; Edwards, 1979; Gunn, 1992; Jelínek, 1976, 1978, 1979; Mountford, 1956; Taçon, 1989) and ethnographic information has been documented for the estate (e.g. Berndt, 1962; Chaloupka et al., 1985; Mountford, 1956). Oral histories were obtained and a partial record was produced of the rock art at Birriwilk in 1991 (Gunn, 1992). The significance of the site lies in the importance it has for the traditional owners and it association with the Rainbow Serpent, as well as potentially with creation stories for the East Alligator River.

Conclusion

It is indicated by excavations at Birriwilk that there were 2 principal phases of human settlement: from 4,500 BP ephemeral visitations and from 750-50 BP there was sustained settlement. Minor deposition of stone artefacts, worked ochre, calcined bone and evidence of increased burning are included in the earliest phase. Activity at this site in the Middle Holocene appears to have been minor, when considered in terms of its overall distribution of cultural materials, as well as evidence of burning, with the main period of site use beginning in the last millennium.

At Birriwilk the main occupation dates from about 750-50 BP. Site usage is suggested by the stone artefacts and faunal remains to have been most intensive from 750 BP to approximately 250-200 BP. Hunting and foraging was focussed on adjacent wetland habitats, as indicated by analysis of the faunal materials from this period. Birriwilk is distinguished from other sites that were investigated previously by this activity, and suggests the occupants of Birriwilk placed greater emphasis on freshwater resources. In the mythologies of Birriwilk the connection between the site and the freshwater environment continues to be recorded, which are still significant at the present; the adjacent lagoon is also regarded as a djang site. From 750 BP occupation was accompanied by the adoption of quartzite points as the preferred raw material and emphasis was placed on manufacturing bifacial quartzite points. More than half of the worked fragments of ochre were also recovered from these levels, which suggests that much of the rock art dates to about 750-200 BP, though such fragments were distributed throughout the site. Shine et al. suggest this age is consistent with ages that had previously been conjectured for the rock art at the site based on the prominence of freshwater species (Gunn, 1992).

The use of the rock shelter for activities related to subsistence appears to have declined after 250-200 BP. Limited amounts of stone artefacts and faunal material and large quantities of charcoal (suggestive of extensive burning) that date to 250-150 BP have been recovered suggesting continued accumulation. In the recent past (XUs 5-6) there was a further decrease in cultural materials, though worked ochre and 'European' finds from the uppermost excavation levels of the site still indicated that the site was being used. Nakodjok recalled rock art events and camping at the rock shelter, though archaeological evidence indicates recent occupation of the site was much less sustained than in the earlier period. At Birriwilk the occupation decrease was potentially the result of changing settlement patterns that were linked to the foundation of Kunbarlanja cattle station in 1909-10, which was followed by the development of the Kunbarlanja Anglican mission and town. An alternative suggestion is that at Birriwilk reduced activity in the usage of the site may reflect a shift in the usage of the site to a purely ritual focus, as opposed to a camp site that was used while hunting and fishing.

The results of the excavation at Birriwilk are consistent with many floodplain sites in the region (e.g. Brockwell, 1989; Hiscock, 1999; Jones, 1985). It is believed these sites expanded across the floodplains as the freshwater environment became stabilised in the last 1,500 years (e.g. Allen, 1987, 1989; Allen & Barton, 1989; Brockwell, 2011; Jones, 1985). Birriwilk is linked to the adjacent freshwater lagoon by the archaeological evidence, rock art and oral traditions which indicate the primary occupation period was short-lived, over a period of 500-700 years. Shine et *al*. suggest this raises the intriguing possibility that the Birriwilk story may have developed in this period as the changed freshwater landscape was reinterpreted. As outlined here, the history of settlement will be examined further in future publications to assess the antiquity of the Birriwilk story and help to clarify the changing character of the connection of the people to the landscapes of Western Arnhem Land during the later Holocene.

Shine, D., D. Wright, T. Denham, K. Aplin, P. Hiscock, K. Parker and R. Walton (2013). "Birriwilk rock shelter: A mid- to late Holocene site in Manilikarr Country, south west Arnhem Land, Northern Territory." Australian Archaeology **76**(1): 69-78.

Keep River Region. North Western Australia, Comparison of Histories Inside and Outside Rock shelters

In this paper comparisons are made between the archaeological evidence of Aboriginal occupation between inside rock shelters and the sand sheets outside these shelters, focusing on 2 locations in the Keep River region, north western Australia. It was revealed by radiocarbon and luminescence dating that sequences inside rock shelters are generally younger (<10,000 BP) than outside the same rock shelters (<18,000 BP). It was also found that differences in the chronology of occupation and artefact assemblages inside and outside rock shelters result from depositional and postdepositional processes, as well as shifts in function. Ward et *al.* suggest that the late build up of sediments within rock shelters, increased accumulation of artefacts, and reduced postdepositional disturbance in some settings may be accounted for by an increase in the regional rate of sedimentation from 10 cm/1,000 years to 20 cm/1,000 years in the Holocene. In the Late Holocene it is indicated by a change in hunting technology and greater rock art production that there was more intense use of the rock shelters. It is indicated by these results that some cultural interpretations might be flawed unless archaeological evidence from rock shelters and open-site excavations is integrated.

Rock shelters provide a fundamental source of archaeological evidence in many places in the world as they act to contain debris of occupation in a relatively limited area. It is often a problem to date the human use or occupation of such sites as a result of the complexity of the sedimentation (Farrand, 2001), including potential disturbance by humans (Stockton, 1973; Hughes & Lampert, 1973; Hughes & Lampert, 1977; Villa & Courtin, 1983; Theunissen et *al.*, 1998: Walthall, 1998).

In Australia archaeological studies commonly focus of rock shelters, even though it has been inferred from ethnographic and archaeological data that open camp sites were occupied much more frequently than rock shelters (Smith & Sharp, 1993; Lourandos & David, 1998). The archaeological perspective that Aboriginal people to have lived under shelter in open sites has been suggested (Attenbrow, 2002, p. 105; 2004), arguing that around the coast in the Sydney Sandstone country they commonly lived in caves and rock shelters. With the exception of any differences in the use of the site, the preservation of cultural material inside and outside the rock shelters are not likely to be similar because they each have a distinct suite of sedimentary processes that control the nature of preservation (Farrand, 2001; Ward & Larcombe, 2003). Also, it is clear there has been a bias favouring the dating of archaeological deposits from rock shelters rather than from open deposits, as well as inadequate sampling of open site occupation that at present constrains the interpretations of the history of settlement in Australian archaeology (Ulm, 2004; Ward, 2004). There have not been many comparative studies of cultural deposits or sedimentary processes inside and well outside the dripline of rock shelters (e.g., Morwood, 1981; Jones & Johnson, 1985; Morwood et al., 1995; Boer-Mah, 2002) with the result that understanding of site formation and settlement history remains incomplete. There is a general assumption that in rock shelters and caves conditions prevail that favour preservation and recovery of intact archaeological deposits than in open sites (Walthall, 1998; Ulm, 2004). Devil's Lair, a limestone cave in south western Australia, has provided a history of about 19,000 years (Dortch, 1986), compared with a deep sequence inside the cave that is now believed to span at least 43,000 years (Turney et al., 2001). It has been suggested that whether depositional sequences are longer inside or outside of cave or rock shelters may depend of cultural, sedimentological, and postdepositional processes (Farrand, 2001; Attenbrow, 2002, 2004; Ward, 2004; Ward et al., in press).

This case study of the Keep River's lower catchment, northern Australia questions that rock shelters necessarily provide better conditions for preservation of longer human occupation records than in open sandy environments. It has been indicated by previous research in the Keep River region that there are major discrepancies between apparent age of some rock shelters and adjacent sand sheet deposits (cf. Fullagar et al., 1996; Roberts et al., 1998, 1999; Galbraith et al., 1999), and between subsurface archaeological sequences and the painted and engraved rock art (Watchman, 1999; Taçon et al., 2003). These discrepencies highlight the need to identify the spatial and temporal scales of deposition in rock shelters and adjacent sand sheets, as well as to determine how rock art sequences are linked, if at all, with subsurface archaeological remains. In this paper Ward et al. have focussed on 2 site complexes that are archaeologically rich, Karlinga and Goorurarmum, comparing the records of deposition and disturbance inside of the rock shelter with the sand plain outside. In order to assess the implications for interpreting long-term changes in site function and the history of settlement Ward et *al*. attempted to distinguish cultural, sedimentological, and postdepositional processes.

Conclusions

A new framework within which the archaeological record can be interpreted has been provided by dating of sand sheet sediments and rock shelter sediments, though there are some discrepancies between TL, OSL and radiocarbon age determinations for the Keep River region. A record from the Late Pleistocene with a relatively abundant assemblage of artefacts, has been preserved in thick sand sheet deposits, whereas a Holocene record has been preserved in the rock shelter deposits, in which artefact assemblages are more abundant and varied only in the last millennium.

The presence in the sand sheets immediately outside the rock shelters dating to as early as about 20,000 BP indicates that rock shelters may have been used much longer than has been revealed by luminescence or radiocarbon dating of the shelter deposits themselves. There is an absence of deposits from the Late Pleistocene in the rock shelter sites in this region of the Keep River, which Ward et *al*. suggest may reflect sparse cultural deposition, though it may also reflect a geomorphological limitation for the accumulation of sediment.

From this study the overarching implication is that patterns and cultural interpretations may be fundamentally flawed if they are constructed predominantly by basing them on rock shelter deposits in similar sandy environments. Also, the environmental and climatic limitations imposed on archaeological reconstructions in northern Australia mean that multidisciplinary studies of rock shelters, sand sheets, as well as other types of open sites, are fundamental to understanding cultural change.

Ward, I. A. K., R. L. K. Fullagar, T. Boer-Mah, L. M. Head, P. S. C. Taçon and K. Mulvaney (2006). "Comparison of sedimentation and occupation histories inside and outside rock shelters, Keep-River region, north western Australia." Geoarchaeology **21**(1): 1-27.

References

1. Allen, H. ed., 2010, *Australia: William Blandowski's Illustrated Encyclopaedia of Aboriginal Australia*, Aboriginal Studies Press.
2. Jim Allen, in Murray, Tim, 1998, *Archaeology of Aboriginal Australia*, Allen & Unwin.
3. Allen, H. and K. Akerman (2015). "Innovation and change in northern Australian Aboriginal spear technologies: the case for reed spears." Archaeology in Oceania **50**: 83-93.
4. Allen, H. and S. Holdaway (2009). "The archaeology of Mungo and the Willandra Lakes: looking back, looking forward." Archaeology in Oceania **44**(2): 96-106.
5. Attenbrow, Val, Gail Robertson, and Peter Hiscock. "The Changing Abundance of Backed Artefacts in South-Eastern Australia: A Response to Holocene Climate Change?" Journal of Archaeological Science 36, no. 12 (12// 2009): 2765-70.
6. Jane Balme & Sue O'Connor in Dennell, Robin & Porr, Martin, eds., 2014, *Southeast Asia, Australia, and the Search for Human Origins*, Cambridge University Press.
7. Berndt, R.M. & C.H., 1964, *The world of the First Australians*, Ure Smith, Sydney
8. Berndt, R.M, 1952a, *Djanggawul*, Routledge & Kegan Paul, London
9. Bird, R. Bliege, D. W. Bird, B. F. Codding, C. H. Parker, and J. H. Jones. "The "Fire Stick Farming" Hypothesis: Australian Aboriginal Foraging Strategies, Biodiversity, and Anthropogenic Fire Mosaics." Proceedings of the National Academy of Sciences of the United States of America 105, no. 39 (2008): 14796-801.
10. Brown, Peter. "Pleistocene Homogeneity and Holocene Size Reduction: The Australian Human Skeletal Evidence." *Archaeology in Oceania* 22, no. 2 (1987): 41-67.
11. Clarkson, C., M. Smith, B. Marwick, R. Fullagar, L. A. Wallis, P. Faulkner, T. Manne, E. Hayes, R. G. Roberts, Z. Jacobs, X. Carah, K. M. Lowe, J. Matthews and S. A. Florin (2015). "The archaeology, chronology and stratigraphy of Madjedbebe (Malakunanja II): A site in northern Australia with early occupation." Journal of Human Evolution **83**(0): 46-64.
12. Cosgrove, Allen & Marshall in Murray, Tim, 1998, *Archaeology of Aboriginal Australia*, Allen & Unwin.

13. Curnoe D, Xueping J, Herries AIR, Kanning B, Taçon PSC, et al. (2012) Human Remains from the Pleistocene-Holocene Transition of South west China, Suggest a Complex Evolutionary History for East Asians. PLoS ONE 7(3): e31918. doi:10.1371/journal.pone.0031918, Editor: David Caramelli, University of Florence, Italy
14. David, Bruno et *al.*, March 1997, New optical and radiocarbon dates from Ngarrabullgan Cave, a Pleistocene archaeological site in Australia: implications for the comparability of time clocks and for the human colonization of Australia, *Antiquity*, Vol.71, No.271, pp. 183-188
15. Lopes dos Santos, Raquel A., Patrick De Deckker, Ellen C. Hopmans, John W. Magee, Anchelique Mets, Jaap S. Sinninghe Damste, and Stefan Schouten. "Abrupt Vegetation Change after the Late Quaternary Megafaunal Extinction in South eastern Australia." Nature Geosci 6, no. 8 (08//print 2013): 627-31.
16. Cane, Scott, 2013, *First Footprints: The epic story of the first Australians*, Allen & Unwin
17. Cooper, A., and C. B. Stringer. "*Did the Denisovans Cross Wallace's Line?*" Science 342, no. 6156 (October 18, 2013): 321-23.
18. Richard Cosgrove, Jim Allen & Brendan Marshall in Murray, Tim, 1998, *Archaeology of Aboriginal Australia*, Allen & Unwin.
19. David, Bruno, Jean-Michel Geneste, Ray L. Whear, Jean-Jacques Delannoy, Margaret Katherine, R. G. Gunn, Christopher Clarkson, *et al.* "Nawarla Gabarnmang, a 45,180±910 Cal Bp Site in Jawoyn Country, South west Arnhem Land Plateau." *Australian Archaeology*, no. 73 (2011): 73-77.
20. Flood, Josephine, 2004, *Archaeology of the Dreamtime*, J. B. Publishing
21. Franklin, Natalie R., 2007, Aboriginal engravings in the south west of Western Australia: analysis of the Kybra Site, *Records of the Western Australian Museum*, **24**: 65-79.
22. Fullagar, R., E. Hayes, B. Stephenson, J. Field, C. Matheson, N. Stern and K. Fitzsimmons (2015). "Evidence for Pleistocene seed grinding at Lake Mungo, south-eastern Australia." Archaeology in Oceania **50**: 3-19.
23. Fullagar, R. L. K., D. M. Price and L. M. Head (1996). "Early human occupation of northern Australia: archaeology and thermoluminescence dating of Jinmium rock-shelter, Northern Territory." Antiquity **70**(270): 751-773.

24. Gammage, Bill, 2011, *The Biggest Estate on Earth: How Aborigines Made Australia*, Allen & Unwin
25. Gough, Myles, Prehistoric Aboriginal Populations were growing, *Cosmos Magazine Online*, 11 May 2011
26. Brian Hayden in Murray, Tim, ed., 1998, *Archaeology of Aboriginal Australia*, Allen & Unwin
27. Helen Grasswill & Reg Morrison, *Australia, a Timeless Grandeur*, Lansdowne, 1981
28. Hiscock, P., S. O'Connor, J. Balme and T. Maloney (2016). "World's earliest ground-edge axe production coincides with human colonisation of Australia." Australian Archaeology **82**(1): 2-11
29. Habgood, Phillip J. & Franklin, Natalie R. *The revolution that didn't arrive: A review of Pleistocene Sahul*, Journal of Human Evolution, 55, 2008
30. Habgood, P. J. H. and N. R. Franklin2 (2010). "Explanations for patterning in the "package of traits" of modern human behaviour within Sahul " 30. From ttps://journals.lib.washington.edu/index.php/BIPPA/article/view/12027.
31. Chris Hunt and Graeme Barker in Dennell, Robin & Porr, Martin, eds., 2014, *Southeast Asia, Australia, and the Search for Human Origins*, Cambridge University Press.
32. Isaacs, Jennifer, 2005, *Australia Dreaming: 40,000 years of Aboriginal History*, New Holland Publishers.
33. Johnson, Christopher N. & Brook, Barry W,. Reconstructing the dynamics of ancient human populations from radiocarbon dates: 10 000 years of population growth in Australia, *Proceedings of the Royal Society B*, 11 May 2011.

34. Kumar, S., R. Ravuri, P. Koneru, B. Urade, B. Sarkar, A. Chandrasekar and V. Rao (2009). "Reconstructing Indian-Australian phylogenetic link." BMC Evolutionary Biology **9**(1): 1-5
35. Fullagar, R., E. Hayes, B. Stephenson, J. Field, C. Matheson, N. Stern and K. Fitzsimmons (2015). "Evidence for Pleistocene seed grinding at Lake Mungo, south-eastern Australia." Archaeology in Oceania **50**: 3-19.
36. Lamb, Lara. "Investigating Changing Stone Technologies, Site Use and Occupational Intensities at Fern Cave, North Queensland." *Australian Archaeology*, no. 42 (1996): 1-7.
37. Lee, Sharon & Gilchrist, Alyssa, *Aboriginal stone structures in south western Victoria - Report to Aboriginal Affairs Victoria*.

38. Lowe, K. M., L. A. Wallis, C. Pardoe, B. Marwick, C. Clarkson, T. Manne, M. A. Smith and R. Fullagar (2014). "Ground-penetrating radar and burial practices in western Arnhem Land, Australia." Archaeology in Oceania 49(3): 148-157.
39. Maloney, T., S. O'Connor and J. Balme (2014). "New dates for point technology in the Kimberley." Archaeology in Oceania 49(3): 137-147.
40. McGowan, Hamish, Samuel Marx, Patrick Moss, and Andrew Hammond. "Evidence of Enso Mega-Drought Triggered Collapse of Prehistory Aboriginal Society in North west Australia." Geophysical Research Letters 39, no. 22 (2012): L22702.
41. Memmott, Paul, 2007, *Gunyah, Goondie + Wurley: The Aboriginal Architecture of Australia*, University of Queensland Press
42. Moore, M. W. (2003). "Flexibility of Stone Tool Manufacturing Methods on the Georgina River, Camooweal, Queensland." Archaeology in Oceania 38(1): 23-36.
43. Charles P. Mountford, *Ayer's Rock, Its People, Their Beliefs and their Art*, Angus & Robertson, 1966
44. Mulvaney, Ken. "*Iconic Imagery: Pleistocene Rock Art Development across Northern Australia*." Quaternary International 285, no. 0 (2/8/ 2013): 99-110.
45. O'Connell, J.F., Allen, J. & Hawkes, K., March 2008, Pleistocene and the origins of seafaring
46. Olley, Jon M., Richard G. Roberts, Hiroyuki Yoshida, and James M. Bowler. "Single-Grain Optical Dating of Grave-Infill Associated with Human Burials at Lake Mungo, Australia." Quaternary Science Reviews 25, no. 19–20 (10// 2006): 2469-74.
47. Oppenheimer, S. (2009). "The great arc of dispersal of modern humans: Africa to Australia." *Quaternary International* 202(1–2): 2-13.
48. Oppenheimer, Stephen, in Dennell, Robin & Porr, Martin, eds., 2014, *Southeast Asia, Australia, and the Search for Human Origins*, Cambridge University Press.
49. Puntutjarpa - Research Data
50. Pugach, I., F. Delfin, E. Gunnarsdóttir, M. Kayser and M. Stoneking (2013). "Genome-wide data substantiate Holocene gene flow from India to Australia." Proceedings of the National Academy of Sciences 110(5): 1803-1808

51. Qi, Xiaoqiang, Wee Lee Chan, Randy J. Read, Aiwu Zhou, and Robin W. Carrell. "Temperature-Responsive Release of Thyroxine and Its Environmental Adaptation in Australians." Proceedings of the Royal Society B: Biological Sciences 281, no. 1779 (March 22, 2014).
52. Rampino, Michael R. *"Possible Relationships between Changes in Global Ice Volume, Geomagnetic Excursions, and the Eccentricity of the Earth's Orbit."* Geology 7, no. 12 (December 1, 1979): 584-87.
53. Reed, A. W., 1965, *Myths & Legends of Australia*, A.H. & A.W. Reed, Sydney, Wellington, Auckland
54. Reich, D., N. Patterson, M. Kircher, F. Delfin, Madhusudan R. Nandineni, I. Pugach, Albert M.-S. Ko, Y.-C. Ko, Timothy A. Jinam, Maude E. Phipps, N. Saitou, A. Wollstein, M. Kayser, S. Pääbo and M. Stoneking "Denisova Admixture and the First Modern Human Dispersals into Southeast Asia and Oceania." The American Journal of Human Genetics **89**(4): 516-528.
55. Richter, Daniel. "Advantages and Limitations of Thermoluminescence Dating of Heated Flint from Paleolithic Sites." Geoarchaeology 22, no. 6 (2007): 671-83.
56. Shephard, Mark, 1992, *The Simpson Desert: Natural History and Human Endeavour*, Reed
57. Shine, Denis; Marshal, Melissa; Wright, Duncan; Denham, Tim; Hiscock, Peter; Jacobsen, Geraldine and Stephens, Sean-Paul. The archaeology of Bindjarran rock shelter in Manilikarr Country, Kakadu National Park, Northern Territory [online]. Australian Archaeology, No. 80, Jun 2015: 104-111. Availability: <http://search.informit.com.au/documentSummary;dn=237574513957781;res=IELHSS> ISSN: 0312-2417
58. Justin Shiner, Simon Holdaway, Harry Allen and Patricia Fanning, June 2007, Burkes Cave and flaked stone assemblage variability in western New South Wales, Australia, Australian Archaeology, Vol. 64, pp. 35-45, article
59. Shine, D., D. Wright, T. Denham, K. Aplin, P. Hiscock, K. Parker and R. Walton (2013). "Birriwilk rock shelter: A mid- to late Holocene site in Manilikarr Country, south west Arnhem Land, Northern Territory." Australian Archaeology **76**(1): 69-78.
60. Aaron Smith, November 2010, Australian Geographic
61. M.A. Smith in Murray, Tim, 1998, *Archaeology of Aboriginal Australia*, Allen & Unwin.

62. Stone, Tim, and Matthew L. Cupper. "Last Glacial Maximum Ages for Robust Humans at Kow Swamp, Southern Australia." Journal of Human Evolution 45, no. 2 (8// 2003): 99-111.
63. Edited by Nigel E. Stork & Stephen M. Turton, *Living in a Dynamic Tropical Forest Landscape*, Blackwell Publishing, 1988
64. The Tasmanians: Part 8b: Archaeology and the Oldest Tasmanians
65. Thorley, Peter, Patrick Faulkner, and Mike Smith. "New Radiocarbon Dates for Kulpi Mara Rock shelter, Central Australia." Australian Archaeology, no. 72 (2011): 47-49.
66. Twidale, C.R. & Campbell, E.M., 2005, *Australian Landforms: Understanding a Low, Flat, Arid, and Old Landscape*, Rosenberg Publishing Pty Ltd
67. Penny Van Oosterzee, *The Centre - The Natural history of Australia's Desert Regions*, Reed Australia, 1993
68. van den Bergh, G. D., B. Li, A. Brumm, R. Grün, D. Yurnaldi, M. W. Moore, I. Kurniawan, R. Setiawan, F. Aziz, R. G. Roberts, Suyono, M. Storey, E. Setiabudi and M. J. Morwood (2016). "Earliest hominin occupation of Sulawesi, Indonesia." Nature **529**(7585): 208-211.
69. Veth, Peter, Hiscock, Peter & Williams, Allan, 2011, Are tulas and ENSO linked in Australia, *Australian Archaeology*, No. 72, June.
70. Ward, I. (2004). "Comparative Records of Occupation in the Keep River Region of the Eastern Kimberley, North western Australia." Australian Archaeology(59): 1-9.
71. Ward, I. A. K., R. L. K. Fullagar, T. Boer-Mah, L. M. Head, P. S. C. Taçon and K. Mulvaney (2006). "Comparison of sedimentation and occupation histories inside and outside rock shelters, Keep-River region, north western Australia." Geoarchaeology **21**(1): 1-27.
72. Warner, W.L., 1937/58, *A Black Civilisation*, Harper, New York
73. Webb, J.A. & Domanski, M, The Relationship Between Lithology, Flaking Properties & Artefact Manufacture for Australian Silcretes, *Archaeometry*, Oxford University, *Archaeometry*, 50, 4 (2008) 555-575
74. Webb, Eric K, (1997), *Windows on Meteorology, Australian Perspective*, CSIRO Publishing
75. White, Mary E., 2000, *Running Down, Water in a Changing Land*, Kangaroo Press,

76. Zazula, Grant D., 2000/2001, *The Peopling of Greater Australia: A Re-examination*, Nexus, Vol.14: 109-123

www.ingramcontent.com/pod-product-compliance
Lightning Source LLC
Chambersburg PA
CBHW071732150426
43191CB00010B/1541